Second Edition

Government Budgeting:
Theory, Process, and Politics

see

Second Edition

Government Budgeting: Theory, Process, and Politics

Albert C. Hyde

University of Pittsburgh

Harcourt Brace College Publishers

Fort Worth   Philadelphia   San Diego
New York   Orlando   Austin   San Antonio
Toronto   Montreal   London   Sydney   Tokyo

About the Author

Albert C. Hyde is an Associate Professor at the Graduate School of Public and International Affairs, University of Pittsburgh, and former Director of the Public Management and Policy program. He was also Director of the Public Administration program at San Francisco State University and has taught at the University of Colorado at Denver, University of Houston-Clear Lake, and Indiana University-Purdue University at Indianapolis. As a practitioner, he served as a Foreign Service Officer with the U.S. Department of State and was a senior associate with the New York State Legislative Commission on Expenditure Review. Dr. Hyde received his M.P.A. and Ph.D. degrees from the State University of New York at Albany.

Portions of this work were printed in previous editions.

Printed in the United States of America

ISBN 0-534-15258-9

7 8 9 0 1 2 3 4 5 6 016 9 8 7 6 5 4 3 2 1

Library of Congress Cataloging-in-Publication Data

Government budgeting : theory, process, and politics / [edited by] Albert C. Hyde. — 2nd ed.
  p.   cm.
  ISBN 0-534-15258-9
  1. Budget—United States. 2. Program budgeting—United States. 3. Zero-base budgeting—United States. 4. Budget.
I. Hyde, Albert
C., [date].
HJ2051.G68   1991
350.72′2′0973—dc20

91-8103
CIP

Sponsoring Editor: *Cynthia C. Stormer*
Editorial Associate: *Cathleen S. Collins*
Production Editor: *Ben Greensfelder*
Manuscript Editor: *Barbara Kimmel*
Permissions Editor: *Mary Kay Hancharick*
Interior Design: *Katherine Minerva*
Cover Design: *Roger Knox*
Art Coordinator: *Cloyce J. Wall*
Interior Illustration: *Kristen Y. Calcagno*
Typesetting: *Execustaff*
Printing and Binding: *Arcata Graphics/Fairfield*
Cover Printing: *Phoenix Color Corporation*

Preface

The title *Government Budgeting: Theory, Process, and Politics,* seems to imply that there exists a theory of governmental budgeting separate from the mechanics of the budgetary process, and, in turn, somehow separate from the politics of budgeting. Budgeting events in the 1980s leave little doubt that in reality the elements are so thoroughly fused that it is all but impossible to delineate theory, process, or politics from the whole that is government budgeting. How much budgeting has actually changed since the mid 1970s may be subject to debate, but no one seriously doubts the fact that budgeting and resource environments for all governments are dramatically different.

Yet there are historical threads that demonstrate how remarkably close to its roots public sector budgeting remains. Following an opening section devoted to the development of budget reform and budget theory, this edition is organized into three major sections, loosely organized around William Willoughby's three threads of budgetary reform noted in the selection from his work appearing as reading 2 in this text.

Section II (the thread of legislative-executive relations) examines governmental relations in budgeting: from legislative and executive interaction; to the roles of courts; to budgeting relationships among federal, state, and local governments.

Section III (the thread of popular control and democracy) introduces budgeting's new political–economic environment, focusing on various political control and economic management issues ranging from line-item vetoes and revenue limitation movements to deficits and taxes.

Section IV (the thread of management efficiency) reviews budgeting's management dimension with the traditional coverage of budgeting systems such as performance, PPBS, and ZBB, but adds special emphasis to financial management concepts and their central importance in budgeting.

Whereas this book develops various budgeting concepts historically, it is not a history of budgeting. Rather, it is intended as a source book that presents the practitioner and student with a collection of articles and viewpoints from a diverse array of experts, budget theorists, and researchers. The introductory sections, by design, have been kept brief and limited to providing historical context or background.

A significant omission from the first edition of this book is the comparative section. In its place is a section on the new political–economic environment. Discussion of the problems of budgeting in other countries is still an important topic; but the amount of material available in this area is now quite extensive and to integrate these dimensions into the full scope of budgetary theory, processes, and politics would require another volume. In placing emphasis on economic dimensions, this edition recognizes the significance of new fiscal realities and deficits, which so profoundly influence government budgeting decisions.

Acknowledgments

The advice and persistent encouragement of my long-time collaborator (and coeditor of the first edition of *Government Budgeting*), Jay Shafritz, was instrumental in pushing this second edition to publication. Jim Schloetter, my graduate assistant at San Francisco State University, was invaluable in assembling and tracking down articles for the collection. Sheila Kelly, my administrative assistant at the University of Pittsburgh, handled many of the permissions details in her usual superb professional fashion. Additionally, there are a number of colleagues who provided various thoughtful insights over the course of many conversations during this project. My thanks especially to Ray Pomerleau, Mike Graham, David Tabb, and Phil Siegelman at San Francisco State; Harvey White, Olivia Hidalgo-Hardemann, Mike Gold, Christine Altenberger, Don Goldstein, and Marshall Singer at GSPIA, University of Pittsburgh;

and in Washington, Tom Novotny of *The Bureaucrat,* Jackie Werth of GAO, and Katherine Naff of MSPB. The following reviewers gave valuable feedback on the manuscript: Stanley Botner, University of Missouri-Columbia (emeritus); George Guess, Georgia State University; Donald F. Kettl, University of Wisconsin-Madison; John Mikesell, Indiana University Bloomington; Fred Thompson, Willamette University; and John Wanat, University of Illinois at Chicago. Finally there is a considerable intellectual debt to David and Mary Novick who many years ago spent considerable time teaching someone—who was convinced he knew budgeting—what budgeting was really all about.

Albert C. Hyde

Contents

III
Budgeting, Economics, and Popular Control: An Instrument of Democracy
213

IV
Budgeting Systems and Management: An Instrument for Securing Administrative Efficiency and Economy
323

Second Edition

Government Budgeting: Theory, Process, and Politics

I

The Development of Budgeting and Budget Theory: The Threads of Budget Reform

Budgets are not merely affairs of arithmetic, but in a thousand ways go to the root of prosperity for individuals, the relation of classes, and the strength of kingdoms.

Gladstone

The Dimensions of Budgeting

Budgeting is, and always has been, the single most important decision-making process in governmental organizations. The budget itself is also a government's most important reference document. In their increasingly voluminous and complex formats, budgets simultaneously record policy decision outcomes; cite policy priorities and program goals and objectives; delineate a government's total service effort; and measure its performance, impact, and overall effectiveness.

A public budget has four basic dimensions. First, it is a political instrument that allocates scarce public resources among the social and economic needs of a jurisdiction. Second, a budget is a managerial and/or administrative instrument. It specifies the ways and means of providing public programs and services and establishes the costs and/or criteria by which its activities are evaluated for their efficiency and effectiveness. It is the budgeting process that ensures that all the programs and activities of a jurisdiction will be reviewed or evaluated at least once during each year (or cycle). Third, a budget is an economic instrument that can direct a nation's, state's, and even municipality's economic growth and development. At the national, state, and regional levels, government budgets are the primary instruments for evaluating redistribution of income, stimulating economic growth and development, promoting full employment, combating inflation, and maintaining economic stability. Fourth, a budget is an accounting instrument (now termed *financial management instrument*) that holds government officials responsible for both the expenditures and revenues of the programs over which they exercise control.

Over the past decade, it has been more and more apparent that the interconnections of these dimensions is the vital issue. For example, the very premise of the accounting dimension means that budgets are to hold governments accountable in the aggregate. After all, the basic concept of a budget implies that there is a ceiling or a spending limitation, which literally requires governments to live within their means. Yet the ever pervasive federal budget deficit is now viewed as the nation's number one political and economic problem. How is it, one might ask, that the very instrument designed to ensure balanced spending and funding decisions is viewed as the major obstacle in maintaining that balance?

Certainly it is not for lack of effort. Since the late 1970s, Congress and five presidents have waged veritable budget warfare over controlling spending and changing taxes through the federal budget process. Still, the country is mired in deficit. As late as this summer of 1990, the president and Congress were deadlocked in ''budget summits'' over new taxes and spending cuts, while federal employees were receiving furlough notices. As the military cold war comes to an end, it may well be replaced with a new form of economic and political warfare over budgets.

The reality is that budgeting links control to political and economic choice, or as Joseph White and Aaron Wildavsky make clear in their recent study, *The Deficit and the Public Interest* (Berkeley: University of California Press, 1989):

> Budgeting involves meeting obligations, keeping promises. It involves choices about values, about which purposes are of highest priority. It involves questions of power: How are we governed, and by whom. Most of all, tax and spending decisions involve real people with real pain and real benefits. What happens to any of us—the fate of farmers, the poor, or General Dynamics—may have meaning to others. In the rhetoric of deficit reduction, these other matters are either disparaged as ''special interests'' or worse ignored. Persistent deficits are blamed on a lack of courage or good will. Wrong. Deficits persist because all choices are bad. Choices are hard because important values are helped or hurt by alternatives. (pp. xviii–xix)

From its beginnings, the theory of budgeting has recognized that shaping such choices is of central importance. This was to a great extent what budget reform in government was all about.

This section opens with two classic articles about the origins and objectives of modern budgeting. Frederick A. Cleveland reviews the guiding forces behind the executive budget concept and examines its objectives in his 1915 study, ''Evolution of the Budget Idea in the United States.'' William F. Willoughby looks more directly at the state and local experience in his 1918 *The Movement for Budgetary Reform in the States*. In the excerpt from Willoughby's work, one will find a prophetic recognition of the essence of budget reform. Willoughby saw three main threads to budget reform: (1) providing for and advancing popular control; (2) developing and enhancing legislative and executive cooperation; and (3) ensuring and improving administrative and managerial efficiency. Just as a rope is woven out of strands, these threads must be intertwined if budgeting is to be an effective exercise in the process of governance. These threads have a special significance for this work: the three major sections of the book are organized and dedicated to Willoughby's three movements.

A Brief History of Budget Reform

The development of the executive budget itself was considered the first step of budget reform. It is important to keep in mind that government budgets as we know them today are relatively new phenomena. Prior to this century, they were little more than compilations of piecemeal appropriations reports passed by a legislature. The Budget and Accounting Act that began the establishment of today's federal budgeting mechanisms was not passed until 1921. Earlier budgeting efforts at the state and local levels go back to experiments and developments in New York City and other localities in the early 1900s. Until that time there was little perceived need for sophisticated budgeting mechanisms because government expenditures were relatively insignificant. Federal ''budgeting''—if it can even be called that—was primarily an exercise in getting rid of ''surplus funds'' accumulated by tariff revenues or for finding ways to fund major land purchases or wars.

In retrospect, the nation's first great public financial administrator, Alexander Hamilton, may have succeeded too well in putting the new republic on a solid financial footing. However, there were instances throughout the nineteenth century, such as the financial panic of 1837 and Abraham Lincoln's efforts to finance the Civil War, that generated some concern that there might be a need for a budgeting system. Later political and social forces, such as the progressive reform movement, the scientific management movement, and the emergence of more diverse and specialized government programs, provided impetus for more effective advocation of a budgeting system. The pioneering work done in some states and municipalities provided the federal government with further examples of the direction to go in budgeting. Indeed, the federal nature of the U.S. system of government has proven to be an essential factor in budgetary reform. Such reforms often emerge from "experiments" in state and local "laboratories," as with performance budgeting in New York City in the early 1900s, or zero-based budgeting in Georgia in the 1970s.

The thrust for reform came to a head in the report of the Taft Commission of 1912, which argued strenuously for a national budgeting system to serve the executive branch. Even in its infancy, a recurring theme of governmental budgeting was already apparent—the conflict between the legislative and executive branch as to who would control the budgeting process—and Congress quickly rejected the Taft Commission recommendations. After World War I, President Wilson rekindled the idea of an executive budget mechanism, but Congress proposed its own legislation, which Wilson promptly vetoed because of lack of executive control. Finally, in 1921, the Budget and Accounting Act was signed into law. It established a Bureau of the Budget (to be lodged in the Treasury Department), a formal budgeting mechanism to be controlled by the executive branch, and a General Accounting Office accountable to Congress.

It would be another eighteen years, however, before the Bureau of the Budget would become a direct staff branch of the Chief Executive. During this period, budgeting processes focused primarily on accountability and control, and the initial technology of budgeting was the line-item budget: a systematic, accounting-oriented method of recording public expenditures against various classification categories, such as salaries, travel, supplies, and equipment.

Against this backdrop, in 1940, V. O. Key, Jr. (who would later become one of the most influential U.S. political scientists) wrote a searching inquiry about the state of the art of budgeting, "The Lack of a Budgetary Theory." Greatly concerned about the overemphasis on mechanics, he posed what is still widely acknowledged as the central question of budgeting: "On what basis shall it be decided to allocate X dollars to activity A instead of activity B?" Key then went on to elaborate on what he felt were the major areas of inquiry that should be researched to develop a budgeting theory.

In the 1940s and 1950s, following the recommendations of the Brownlow Commission and later codified by the Hoover Commissions, performance budgeting emerged as the new and dominant budgeting system. Performance budgeting was above all a management-oriented system heavily focused on efficiency by relating costs to measured outputs. Its appearance during these two decades was well-timed to match immense increases in both the size and scope of governmental undertakings. The Second World War marked the advent of "Big Government" and an underlying confidence among public administrators that the new techniques and mechanics behind large scale public budgets were appropriately geared for the larger scaled, more efficiency-oriented structures that would surely characterize future administrative operations. Vision in the 1940s was blurred by the unprecedented scale of operations of the Second World War and the preceding economic war waged against the Depression.

Improved efficiency, however, was not an adequate response to Key's question of choice. Larger budgets, fueled by economic growth, made choices more important and increased concerns about how budgets should facilitate the idea of direct consideration of alternatives. First articulated by Verne B. Lewis in his 1952 article, "Toward a Theory of Budgeting," the idea of budget "alternatives" centered on the preparation of incremental budget submissions that would permit evaluation of various funding amounts in terms of levels or quantity of service. The administrative or managerial context of alternative budgeting provides a dual advantage. Budget submissions can be prepared in a manner that will facilitate comparison and demonstrate a range of choices for service and funding levels. At the same time, the final choice will provide a realistic contract; that is, specific, realistic expectations for the program manager. The implied rationale for this process was almost a restatement of V.O. Key's classic budgeting question: for X level of funding, Y level of service can be provided; for $X + (1/X)$ funding, $Y + (1/Y)$ services.

But the 1960s brought even more definitive responses. Aaron Wildavsky, then a professor at Oberlin College, countered that Key's question, as raised, was unanswerable. His 1961 article, "Political Implications of Budgetary Reform," paralleled the contentions Charles E. Lindblom made in his famous 1959 article in *Public Administration Review*, "The Science of Muddling Through." Budgeting, Wildavsky argued, was in reality a mode of incremental conflict resolution aimed principally at ordering whose preferences would prevail. The question of which criteria should determine what goes in the budget is synonymous with, and equally as unanswerable as, the question of what government ought to do in the first place. If an answer were possible, it would mean nothing less than a total resolution of conflict over government's role in society. Wildavsky's arguments in this early article were an important prelude to what would later be four editions of the classic *The Politics of the Budgetary Process*, and a completely revised edition in 1988 entitled *The New Politics of the Budgetary Process*. Section V presents Wildavsky's conclusion of how budget theory has changed, through the eyes of one of its foremost developers and critics.

Significantly, the 1960s marked a new era of increased government activity. Policy and programs were recast in bolder, more innovative terms with "social intervention" as the major premise. A new budgeting system emerged, called PPBS (Planning-Programming-Budget-Systems), emphasizing multiyear planning, policy analysis, and program objectives that focused on effectiveness. The system was widely heralded as a major breakthrough for public administration. Nicknamed the "pristine path to budget salvation" by its critics, PPBS dominated public sector budgeting like no other system had ever done before.

The case for depicting budgeting systems as an evolutionary process within management has been made best by Allen Schick in his 1966 article, "The Road to PPB: The Stages of Budget Reform" (later updated in his 1978 *Public Administration Review* article, "Road from ZBB"). His work is considered classic for its examination of the different orientations and purposes of budgeting and its presentation of budgetary change as an evolutionary process. The budgeting literature in particular has adopted his typology of budgetary reform, which consecutively illustrates shifts in budgetary emphasis from accounting-strict expenditure control (the line-item budget), to management-work efficiency (the performance budget), to planning-program effectiveness (PPBS). Schick traces the events leading up to each succeeding budgeting system, defines each system, and describes its implementation process, strengths, and weaknesses.

But by the 1970s, PPBS had failed. (If the minimum criteria for success is continuity, PPBS was discontinued in the federal government by the Nixon administration). Budget reform in the 1970s was beset by two more compelling developments: a new period of legislative–executive competition over who would control budgets and spending levels; and a new "era of resource scarcity," in which economic growth was no longer a constant, and unquestioning popular support for increased budgets and increased taxes was no longer valid. The other two threads of budget reform were now fully as important as the long dominant managerial thread.

Like most developments in budgeting, the vulnerability of public budgets to expenditure and revenue limitation initiatives (following the advent of Proposition 13 in California) was first felt at state and local levels. The resulting pressure on budgets was inescapable. Partly because of these new economic realities, budget reforms in the 1970s were marked by intense executive-legislative rivalry, which at the federal level produced a new budgeting law, *The Congressional Budget and Impoundment Act of 1974*. Rivalry may even be too mild a term. Alan Schick, in his influential account of the period (*Congress and Money*), calls the period leading up to the new act the "Seven Years' Budget War." Legislative Budgeting is covered in more depth in the following section, but at this juncture the reader needs to keep the new 1974 law in historical perspective.

There was one more major development within budget reform in the 1970s—the arrival of zero-based budgeting (ZBB) with the Carter administration. Launched with much fanfare in 1977, ZBB promised to counter the traditional incrementalism bias of budgets (i.e., that resource allocation decisions are made about the annual margins of budget change without altering the historical budget base) by using an elaborate system of decision units, packages of alternatives, and rank order of choices based on political relevance. Critics called it "decremental budgeting" in disguise and it was eventually overwhelmed by changing economic events. Ironically, a budget system purposefully designed to make ordered cuts in budgets in the event of necessary cutbacks was ignored when those circumstances prevailed. ZBB was rescinded in early 1981 by the Reagan administration and a new political–economic era ushered in.

Whither Budget Reform?

By 1980, budget reform stood at a crossroads. Clearly, the coming decade would be one of increasing complexity and difficulty. Outgoing GAO Comptroller General Elmer B. Staats made a speech that year that would be widely distributed, titled "The Continuing Need for Budget Reform." Staats reaffirmed the importance of positive movement for public sector budgeting to keep pace and provide leadership, but he provided several warnings about future problems. First of all, his concerns were federal credit activities and loan guarantees, their control difficulties, and potential impact on the budget. In the early 1990s, the nation faces a massive $500 billion estimated Savings and Loan bailout, which unfortunately underscored this early warning about the adequacy of budgetary information and the paucity of political will.

For budget reform, it was apparent that the eighties would be quite different, and that many of the budgeting rules would be changed. Naomi Caiden was one of the first to see the new directions and began a series of articles outlining the impacts and implications for budget theory and reform. Her 1983 article, "Guidelines to Federal Budget Reform," overviews the new political dimensions for budgeting change.

The 1980s may be remembered best as the decade when government budgeting was turned upside down. At the federal level; this was the era when a president called the whole budget process "Mickey Mouse," when the media labeled submitted budgets as "D.O.A." (dead on arrival because of their faulty and unrealistic economic assumptions), when "budget summits" were created, and when the first academic arguments were raised over whether or not the executive budget process itself had outlived its usefulness. Several articles in Section II will address many of these events.

For state and local governments, there were new strains of tax revolts and tax limitation propositions, and increasingly unpredictable cycles of good and bad times. California gave taxpayers a refund one year and sank into fiscal crises two years later. Massachusetts went from economic miracle to fiscal morass in the span of a presidential election year. City budgeting fortunes looked like roller coaster rides. Relations between governors and state legislatures and between mayors or city managers and city councils were no less acrimonious over budgeting. Budget disputes became newspaper headlines. Supportive relationships between federal and state and local governments also suffered during this decade, as several articles in Section III attest.

The 1980s have cast budgeting reform into limbo (Naomi Caiden once called it a black hole). Although there has been an incredible amount of activity in public budgeting, has there been any progress, much less any discernible direction? Irene Rubin poses the question another way in the concluding article to this historical section on budget reform, ''Budget Theory and Budget Practice: How Good the Fit'': to what extent has budget reform been responsible for limiting the potential impact of budgeting or for hindering the understanding of the complex phenomena that link budgeting processes and governance? She is unconvinced that budget reform as it has evolved has been all that useful, but remains hopeful that newer developments in the field of budgeting—particularly descriptive budget theory—will produce some meaningful change.

1

Evolution of the Budget Idea in the United States

Frederick A. Cleveland

Difficulty in tracing the evolution of the "budget idea" in the United States lies not so much in the historical material to be mastered as in decision as to what "idea" is to be discussed.

What Is the "Budget Idea"?

Most controversies grow out of the failure of parties contestant to make clear what they are talking about. Words in ordinary use make expression of thought difficult whenever exactness is required. It is for this reason that science has gone entirely outside the common language for its terms. The word "budget" is a term used in so many different ways that no one can write on any aspect of budgets or budget practice without risk of controversy about the facts until he has taken the trouble to tell what he conceives a budget to be. Writers, therefore, not infrequently begin with a definition. It is an interesting fact, however, that nearly all these definitions are so indefinite that the reader is still left in doubt.

Definition of Budget as Herein Used

In this essay the term "budget," is used to mean *a plan for financing an enterprise or government during a definite period, which is prepared and submitted by a responsible executive to a representative body (or other duly constituted agent) whose approval and authorization are necessary before the plan may be executed.*

In order that no room may be left for inference, each of these clauses may be enlarged on and the reason given for its use.

Source: The Annals of the American Academy of Political and Social Science (1915): 15–35.

1. The idea "budget" is classed as a "plan" instead of a "document" or a "statement" for the reason that it is in the nature of a definite proposal calling for approval or disapproval with such details and specifications attached as are thought to be useful to the approving body or agents in arriving at a decision.

2. It is differentiated from other plans by the phrase "for financing an enterprise or government during a definite period." This includes the first idea of Leroy-Beaulieu's definition. But if it stopped here it would be just as defective; anyone might make a plan for financing an enterprise or a government. For this reason it is further differentiated by the requirement that to be a budget it must be "prepared and submitted by a responsible executive."

3. One other essential is added, *viz.*, that it must be submitted to "a representative body (or other duly constituted agent) whose approval and authorization are necessary before the plan may be executed." Each of these qualifying phrases is so full of meaning and each so necessary to a budget practice that it is deserving of further comment.

The Budget as a Plan of Financing

The one thing that has been conspicuously lacking in our governmental business, federal, state and municipal, has been the element of careful, understandable, responsible planning. The lack of careful, understandable, responsible planning has been an incident of "invisible" or "irresponsible" government. Each year in every jurisdiction we have had "estimates" both of revenues and expenditures. But "estimates" in themselves do not constitute a budget. They only serve the purpose of laying the foundation for work plans and financial plans.

These estimates must be of two kinds, *viz:* (1) there must be estimates of needs, and (2) there must be estimates of the financial resources that may be availed of to meet needs. To be of value the estimates must be made by a great many persons. The estimate of needs must be made by persons who are familiar with the requirements of each kind of work to be done, or each service to be rendered—with the operating requirements, the maintenance requirements, the capital requirements. Then one or more persons must make up estimates of needs for certain things that are common to all services—those which are general, such as requirements for interest, sinking fund requirements, the requirements for payment of maturing obligations for which no sinking funds are provided, requirements for purchase of common lands and the conduct of common business transactions such as advertising, printing, etc. Then again, estimates of the financial resources which may be availed of to meet estimated financial needs, to be of the highest value, must be made up by a number of other persons who are familiar with present financial conditions; they must also be able to forecast probable revenues derivable under existing law; they must have knowledge of the present and probable future condition of appropriations and funds, having in mind present and proposed financial policies they must have the ability to forecast probable financial conditions of surplus and deficit at the beginning of the period to be financed and of probable surplus and deficit at the end.

Plan Must Be Made by a Responsible Executive

All these various estimates of expenditures, of revenues, and of financial condition must be brought together; they must be considered by someone who can think in terms of the institution as a whole; they must be brought to a conclusion; and conclusions must be stated as a definite proposal and a basis for action by some one person or agency that can be held to account. The only person who can be held to account is the one who is to execute the plan proposed. This executive therefore is the only one who can be made responsible for leadership.

The estimates and conclusions must be presented to the representatives of the people whose approval and action are required before spending officers are authorized to go ahead. They must be presented as a definite plan or prospectus which will show what is proposed to be undertaken. This plan must not only show what undertakings are proposed but what will be the probable cost on the one hand and how the cost is to be met. The financial plan must deal with great questions of public policy—must set forth how much is to be met by revenue, how much is to be met by borrowing, and how much, if any, is to be met from surplus. The plan must show what authorizations should be given to the executive to enable him to carry on the business efficiently and meet obligations as they mature. Not only is it necessary that the "estimates" be prepared by persons familiar with the facts, but it is quite as essential that the plan of work and of financing be proposed and submitted by the same person who is to be held accountable for directing the execution of the plan. This means the executive. To have a plan—in other words the "budget"—made by persons who have no responsibility for carrying on the business would be destructive of the very purpose of representative government.

The representative character of a government is to be found in its legislature and in its electorate. As has been pointed out, the constitutional or institutional purpose of a budget is to make the executive responsible and responsive to the people through their representatives and through the electorate. No plan or proposal can serve this purpose which comes from individual representatives any more than it could if it came from individual electors. In the first place it is incompatible that the proposer should also be the disposer of public funds. In the second place the proposal should not reflect the interests of a single individual or a single district—but the interests of the whole community of associated interests which are composed in the state or nation.

The one who submits the financial proposal should be responsible to all—he should be accountable for the management of the affairs of the whole government. Since the several parts of the government are interdependent, no legislative committee can prepare a budget unless the business of the government is to be managed by this committee as in a commission government, or in New York City where the executive power is in its Board of Estimate and Apportionment. But they must act together. Responsibility should be attached to some one man, or some group of persons acting as one man, who can be continued or retired as one man. It was for this reason that Great Britain did not succeed in establishing a true budget system till after 1800 when the principle of solidarity of responsibility was forced on the cabinet. Even then the budget could not be made effective until a means was provided for enforcing this responsibility through a truly representative parliament—until the reform acts of 1837 which made parliament in effect the people in session. In discussing the evolution of the budget idea in the United States, therefore, what is meant is the development of the idea of "a plan for financing the government during a definite period, which is prepared and submitted by a responsible executive to a representative body whose approval and authorization are necessary before the proposed plan may be executed.''

Budget Control by the Representative Body

As it is the institutional and constitutional purpose of the budget to serve as a means both of exercising control over what the government shall do and how it shall be financed and also for making the executive responsible and responsive to the people through their chosen representatives and through the electorate, the budget cannot be more than a proposal or request. Actual authorization must come from the representative or electorate body before a dollar can be raised or spent. Or if some latitude is given to the executive to spend without such action first obtained, the expenditures so made must come to representatives and the electorate for approval. A budget can have no force. A budget, as such, can convey no authority. It is only the "act" of appropriation, the revenue or the borrowing "measure" which gives authority to the executive. Therefore, the "act" and "enacted measure" must be clearly distinguished from the "plan" or "proposal" of the executive.

How Legislative Control May Be Made Effective

If the executive is to be held responsible for results, the legislature must do *three things: viz.:* (1) It must provide a means of enabling representatives to find out whether the executive has acted within his past authorizations and conducted the business efficiently; (2) it must provide a means of enabling representatives to inquire into the requests for future grants; (3) since the purpose of a representative system is to make the government responsible and responsive to the people, it must provide a means of reaching the people, of letting the people know what has been done and what is proposed and of getting controversies between a majority of representatives and the executive before the electorate for final decision. With provision made for these three things the representative system is adapted to the ends and purposes of a democracy; without provision for these

three things the representative system is not adapted to the ends and purposes of a democracy.

How Legislative Inquiry May Be Made Effective

The collateral means which have been found effective for keeping the executive within authorizations are the creation of an agency for independent audit and report on all transactions, the establishment of an independent judiciary for the settlement of legal controversies, and the authority of the legislature to make independent inquiries. But these are collateral means. The method which has been found to be most effective for enabling representatives to inquire into requests for future grants, and obtain exact information about what has been done as well as what is proposed, is to require the executive to appear personally before the representatives of the people at the time he makes his request for funds to answer questions and details.

How the Electorate May Be Reached

The method which has been found to be most effective for keeping the people in touch with public affairs and for having questions in issue settled by the electorate, is to make provision whereby each representative can openly question the executive and every item can be separately debated and voted on. And in case the executive is not supported to make further provision, the electorate may promptly retire either the executive or the opposing majority. What this means is, that a budget which is to serve its constitutional purpose must not only be an executive proposal submitted to a representative body, but it must be submitted under such rules of procedure that each representative may have a right to personally and publicly make inquiry of the executive concerning any matter or detail of the business in hand and also have the right openly and publicly to oppose any part of the plan which, in his opinion, is against the general welfare of the state. And the only procedure which has been found effective for doing this is to require that the estimates and the budget be considered and discussed in committee of the whole house with the executive present.

Furthermore, the financial plan which is to be considered as a budget must be laid before representatives of the people, in such a way that it will at all times be the measure of the responsible executive, and when approved or disapproved, the action taken must stand as the decision of sovereign power—must be the will of the people to support this responsible head of the government. The budget must be considered as the most important measure of any government.

Action on the Budget an Act of Popular Sovereignty

The passing of a budget, as the term budget is used in this discussion, is an attribute of sovereignty. When, as in a democracy, sovereignty is in the people, the authority given to the executive by the "acts" passed in response to executive request must come directly or indirectly from the people; therefore, the procedure to be effective must make the people an integral part of the action. This is what is meant by Leon Say in the statement that "Every member of the society or nation exercises a share of the prerogative of the budget which corresponds to the share of the sovereignty which is vested in him." It is on this idea of a budget that the theory that the "act" of appropriation and the revenue and borrowing "measures" are in the nature of contracts made between taxpayers on the one hand and the executive in power. But the "acts" or "measures" are quite a different thing from the plan or, as it is here called, the "budget" of the executive.[1]

The "budget idea" whose evolution in the United States is here traced bears little relation to the estimates presented by an irresponsible executive or to the devices by which financial legislation is passed in a scheme of invisible government, with no means provided for bringing executive and legislative action to the test of approval or disapproval by the electorate. Those methods, which do not make for responsible government, are not the subject of this essay. The view adopted is the only one that is compatible with the evolution of constitutional law where "control over the purse" has been effectively used to bring the institution and practices of a representative system into harmony with the ideals of democracy and popular sovereignty.

Taken as a whole it may be said that until within the last few years the "budget idea," as the term is here used, has had no evolution whatever in the United States. Our citizenship, our legislators, and our constitution makers have until recently been as innocent of such an idea as an unborn babe. True, President Wilson had written a masterly treatise calling attention to the *devolution* of our government—to the gross departure made from the ideals of the constitution as it was understood by the fathers—and in this pointed to the fact that the administration was gradually drifting over into the hands of some forty odd irresponsible congressional committees. True, President Lowell and other students of foreign government had also written volumes on the gradual development of the principle of executive responsibility under representative systems abroad, and pointed to the part that the "budget idea" had played in this development. But these writings were unnoticed, except in academic discussion. The "practical" man complacently turned a deaf ear, or, if he did not refuse to listen, patronizingly put an end to all suggestions and arguments with the bold assertion that the idea was "undemocratic" and "un-American." When a single Congress authorized a billion dollars of expenditures and the party in power was attacked for extravagance, the answer was that "this is a billion-dollar country." But increases in expenditures went on until within a few years we had a "two billion-dollar Congress." It was the uncontrolled and uncontrollable increase in the cost of government that finally jostled the public into an attitude of hostility to a system which was so fondly called the "American system." This growing hostility to doing business in the dark, to "boss rule," to "invisible government," became the soil in which the "budget idea" finally took root and grew. Questions raised by Mr. Tawney, as chairman of the committee on appropriations, with respect to the system of raising and spending money were not new. It was only the circumstance of the "two-billion-dollar Congress" that caused the public to be disturbed. The bold assertion of Senator Aldrich that if he could run the federal government as he would a private business he could save 300,000,000 a year did more to upset complacency and bring about a demand for change in the methods of doing business than all the treatises that had been written on defects in the organic law. But this dramatization of waste had a constructive value. It caused men to ask for a remedy. It caused people to read and reread what had been written by President Wilson in 1885; it caused editors and writers to consider the methods employed in other countries which had succeeded in making their governments responsible; it provided an occasion for editorial comment; it made an audience for Professor Ford's book,[2] which pointed to the fact that what had been so patronizingly characterized as un-American in methods of political control in England, continental Europe, Bermuda, Australia, and Japan were the methods used in the management of private business, and what had been so much lauded as the American system could be nothing else but wasteful and subversive of the very purposes of democracy.

Efforts Made to Apply the Budget Idea in the Federal Government

This brings us up to President Taft's administration. During President Roosevelt's two administrations, the ship of state had been rocked and tossed about by storms of abuse. In this both the President and Congress took an active part, but nothing towards constructive legislation was undertaken which had a distinct bearing on the methods of controlling the national finances. For a period of six months after March 4, 1909, these storms subsided only to break again with renewed force. But the storm center was not the cost of government; it was the tariff, "standpatism," "government for the privileged classes." From the viewpoint of those who were interested in the development of the "budget idea," this was unfortunate, for President Taft had seriously undertaken to use the great powers and the influence of his office to foster that idea.

The President's Inquiry into Methods of Doing Business

President Taft's answer to the demand for economy was to ask Congress in December, 1909, for an appropriation of $100,000 "to enable the President to inquire into the methods of transacting the public business . . . and to recommend to Congress such legislation as may be necessary to carry with effect changes found to be desirable that cannot be accomplished by executive action alone." As soon as this appropriation had been made available the President instructed his secretary, Mr. Charles D. Norton, to

make plans for the organization of the work. A preliminary inquiry was begun on September 27, 1910. The first task of Secretary Norton was to organize within each department a committee which would cooperate with the White House staff in developing a definite plan of work. Speaking on the magnitude and difficulty of the task, the President in his first report to Congress said:

I have been given this fund to enable me to take action and to make specific recommendations with respect to the details of transacting the business of an organization whose activities are almost as varied as those of the entire business world. The operations of the government affect the interest of every person living within the jurisdiction of the United States. Its organization embraces stations and centers of work located in every city and in many local subdivisions of the country. Its gross expenditures amount to nearly $1,000,000,000 annually. Including the personnel of the military and naval establishments, more than 400,000 persons are required to do the work imposed by law upon the executive branch of the government.

This vast organization has never been studied in detail as one piece of administrative mechanism. Never have the foundations been laid for a thorough consideration of the relations of all of its parts. No comprehensive effort has been made to list its multifarious activities or to group them in such a way as to present a clear picture of what the government is doing. Never has a complete description been given of the agencies through which these activities are performed. At no time has the attempt been made to study all of these activities and agencies with a view to the assignment of each activity to the agency best fitted for its performance, to the avoidance of duplication of plant and work, to the integration of all administrative agencies of the government, so far as may be practicable, into a unified organization for the most effective and economical dispatch of public business.

The Organization of the President's Commission on Economy and Efficiency

One of the conclusions reached as a result of the preliminary inquiry is the following:[3] "A very conspicuous cause of inefficiency and waste is an inadequate provision of the methods of getting before Congress a definite budget, *i.e.*, a concrete and well-considered program or prospectus of work to be financed."

The Need for a Budget One of the First Subjects of Inquiry

When the commission was organized sufficiently to permit a collective consideration of work to be done by it, a program of work was formulated which provided for five fairly distinct subjects to be handled, as follows: (1) The budget as an annual financial program; (2) The organization and activities of the government; (3) Problems of personnel; (4) Financial records and accounts; (5) Business practices and procedure.

In the preliminary inquiry one of the first steps taken had been to ask the several departmental committees cooperating with the President to reanalyze the estimates in such manner as to show the different kinds of things that were being purchased by the government and the amounts spent and estimated for each. As a result of this inquiry the President for the first time had brought before him a summary of such facts as the following: The amounts spent by each bureau, by each department, and the government as a whole analyzed to show what part was for such things as personal services; services other than personal; materials; supplies; equipment, etc. For the first time it became known that the government was spending nearly $400,000,000 for salaries and wages (the digest of appropriations made it appear that only $189,000,000 was for this purpose); that the government was spending $12,500,000 for the transportation of persons; that it was spending $78,000,000 for the transportation of things; that it was spending $8,000,000 for subsistence of persons and, in addition, was spending $18,500,000 for provisions, and $5,500,000 for wearing apparel, etc.

Among the first things undertaken by the commission after its organization was to continue the analytical work with a view of preparing a report on the need for an annual budget. In July, 1911, forms were drafted. These were discussed with department heads, and on August 1 were submitted to the President for his approval. On August 7 the President sent these forms to the departments and requested that they reclassify the data which was being obtained for the purposes

of official estimates then in preparation. The forms asked for information on three subjects: (1) Expenditures for fiscal year ending June 30, 1911; (2) Appropriations for the fiscal year ending June 30, 1912; (3) Estimates for appropriations for the fiscal year ending June 30, 1913. A different form was prepared for reporting on each of these subjects and a fourth form for a recapitulation. Each of these forms was so drawn as to provide for showing the amounts expended, appropriated or estimated: (1) By each organization unit; (2) For each class of work to be done; (3) By character of expenditure, such as current expenses, capital outlays, fixed charges, etc; and, (4) By the amount which had been expended, appropriated or estimated under each act or class of acts of appropriation—whether by annual appropriation, permanent legislation, etc. The heads of departments were asked to have these returns in by November 1, but it was not until after the first of the next year that they were made available to the President. This was due to the fact that the forms required by Congress were along entirely different lines, and it was necessary for the heads of departments to have the official estimates in the hands of the treasury and before Congress on a prescribed date.

The report of the commission on "the Need for a National Budget" was sent by the President to Congress with his approval on June 27, 1912.[4]

The President Urges Congress to Accept the "Budget Idea"

In his letter of transmission President Taft pointed to the fact that the Executive is charged by the Constitution with the duty of publishing "a regular statement of receipts and expenditures" and "that he is also enjoined from time to time to give Congress information on the state of the union and to recommend for consideration such measures as may be deemed expedient." With these constitutional prescriptions President Taft held that the President had the power to prepare and submit to Congress each year "a definite, well-considered budget with a message calling attention to subjects of immediate importance." The President stated, however, in his message that he did not assume to exercise this power except in cooperation with Congress; and he urged the necessity of repealing certain laws which were in conflict with the proposed practice.

The purposes of sending the report to Congress as described by the President were:

To suggest a method whereby the President, as the constitutional head of the administration, and Congress may consider and act on a definite business and financial program;

To have the expenditures, appropriations and estimates so classified and summarized that their broad significance may be readily understood;

To provide each member of Congress, as well as each citizen who is interested, with such data concerning each subject of interest as may be considered in relation to questions of public policy;

To have these general summaries supported by such detailed information as is necessary to consider the economy and efficiency with which business has been transacted;

In short, to suggest a plan whereby the President and Congress may cooperate, the one in laying before Congress and the country a clearly expressed administrative program to be acted on—the other in laying before the President a definite enactment for his judgment.

This was the first time that any responsible officer of the national government had advocated the "budget idea." This report not only contained a descriptive and critical report on the past practices of the national government with constructive recommendations, but supported these recommendations with an appendix of forms and a digest of the practices of thirty-eight other countries, in most of which the "budget idea" had already been incorporated and made a part of the public law.

Immediately following the submission of this report to Congress (July 10), President Taft issued an order to the heads of departments to depute some officer with the duty to see that estimates of summaries for the next fiscal year would be prepared in accordance with the recommendations contained in his message of June 27, and in a letter directed the secretary and treasurer

to print and send without delay to Congress the forms of estimates required by it; also to have sent to him (the President) the information asked for. . . . This will be made the subject of review and revision and a summary statement in the form of a budget with documents will be sent to Congress by a special message as the proposal of the administration.

Report and Recommendations Pigeon-Holed

At the time that this order was issued, Congress had not yet passed all of the annual appropriation bills—some of the bills as passed having been vetoed by the President. When on August 24 the sundry civil bill became law it contained one clause modifying the form of the estimates to incorporate some of the suggestions of the commission, and another clause requiring the heads of departments to submit the estimates in the form and at the time required by law to be submitted and at no other time and in no other form. Following this, when it came to the attention of President Taft that heads of departments expressed some doubt as to what were their duties in the matter, on September 9 the President sent a letter to each member of the cabinet, in which each was instructed to follow the orders both of the President and of Congress. With both houses of the legislature organized against the executive and making demands on the departments for information, the retiring chief executive had difficulty in obtaining the information desired. About February 1, however, all the data had been brought together and, on February 26, President Taft submitted to Congress a budget with a message, which was referred to the committee on appropriations and ordered to be printed with accompanying papers.[5] And there it lay without consideration, action or report.

Acceptance of "Idea" by the Public

The budget proposals of President Taft, however, were not pigeon-holed by the public. They were taken up by the press throughout the country. Almost unanimously they had the support of public opinion. This opinion was further registered in a referendum which was taken on the subject by the Chamber of Commerce of the United States. Furthermore, many leading men, and even some of the members of Congress who, at the time expressed themselves as being opposed to an executive budget, from time to time since then have come out strongly for the "budget idea." One of those who has been emphatic in his opinion, is Congressman John J. Fitzgerald, chairman of the appropriation committee, who at the time the budget was referred to his committee opposed the act as executive interference. But

Mr. Fitzgerald, speaking before the committee on state finances at the constitutional convention at Albany, June 26, 1915, said:

> We ought to have some way in the system of our government to fix direct responsibility, and you cannot fix responsibility if the power is too greatly scattered. . . . I would put it with the Executive. I would make him responsible at the outset. . . . Some persons object that we should not deprive the representatives of the people of the right to loosen up the purse strings, but the universal condition of this country today is not that we must safeguard the rights of the people to get money for things. The whole curse of our condition is that everybody is doing his utmost to get it and succeeds; and the evil to be corrected is the evil of excessive expenditure. . . . Now if there were some way by which that could be stopped. . . . it would do what is done in the governments where they had a responsible government with the budget system. If my constitutents were keenly interested in some matter that required an expenditure of public money, I would be compelled to present the matter to the department that had charge of it. They would make their investigations. They would determine whether it was one of those things that should be included, and they would have to take responsibility for requesting it.

Outlook for a Federal Budget

With President Wilson's long standing advocacy of a budget system, with Secretary McAdoo's reported determination to work for the introduction of a budget procedure; with the chairman of the appropriation committee outspoken in his belief as quoted above, it is confidently expected that something may be done in the next Congress to adapt the laws of the federal government and the procedure of Congress to a practical relation whereby the country may have the benefit of executive leadership and the voting of money may rest on a plane of openhanded dealing.

The Budget Idea in State Government

The provisions in the state constitutions as they were originally drawn having to do with the relations of the executive to the legislative branch follow very closely those of the federal constitution. At present, however, they differ very materially, due to the fact that the federal constitution, with few exceptions, is as it was originally drawn while the state constitutions have been frequently changed. With the federal government there has been a gradual departure in practice from the spirit and expression of the constitution as drawn. This was pointed out very clearly by President Wilson in his treatise on congressional government. In the state, the changed attitude of the people toward the government is found in the gradual decimation of executive power on the one hand and the increasing number of limitations placed on the legislature on the other.

Requirements of State Constitutions

It is of interest to note the duties that are imposed by state constitutions on the governor having to do with matters of money raising and accountability for expenditure. In every state in the union some such provision as this is made: That the governor shall "from time to time" or "at every session" or "at every regular session" give the legislature information on the condition of the state and make recommendations. In four states—Colorado, Idaho, Illinois and Kansas—it is required that he shall "recommend measures." As a matter of practice, however, these requirements have been construed in the same manner as the similar provision in the federal constitution. The governor has not been assumed to have any standing whatever before the legislature until a bill is passed. He has not been assumed to have any right personally to introduce any bill or to appear for or explain or defend any measure openly. Nine of the constitutions[6] "require that the governor shall present at the commencement of each regular session estimates of the amount of money to be raised by taxation for all purposes. These provisions, however, have not been so construed as to lay upon the governor the requirement of preparing and submitting a "budget," nor has any procedure been developed that is based on such an assumption. As a matter of fact, the constitutional provisions have been either perfunctorily complied with by subordinates or have been dead letters, as is pointed out in the report of the Committee on Efficiency and Economy of the state of Illinois.[7] Although the governor was specifically directed by the constitution to lay before the legislature the estimates of money required, the committee states that so far as they could ascertain no attention whatever had been paid to it. This, however, has only to do with the amount of money required to be raised by taxation; it does not lay upon the governor the duty of submitting estimates of proposed expenditure.

In the constitution of Maryland it is made the duty of the controller to prepare and submit estimates of revenues and expenditures. Other constitutions require that one or more other state officers shall prepare such estimates. In states where no constitutional requirement has been laid on the governor, or state officers, statutes have been passed providing that certain officers individually or acting as a board *ex-officio* shall prepare and submit estimates.

Boards of Control

The futility of efforts to establish a budget procedure without some means whereby the executive may be responsible for its proposal and in which the executive will be required to explain and defend the financial measure of the administration is shown by the experience in each of the forty-nine instances where it has been tried. In 1912 Wisconsin undertook to provide a means whereby a budget might be developed as a joint measure of the legislature and of the administration. It was in support of this idea that the report written by Dr. Lowrie was submitted through the State Board of Public Affairs. While this may be a desirable adaptation, as long as we are to assume that the governor is not to be a chief executive and that the government is to be divided up into various small jurisdictions over which there is no control other than that of the legislature, it is not a method which is consistent with the "budget idea."

New York undertook to interject into its budget procedure a means of central control by the same method.[8] The purpose of this board was to make a budget as the term was understood by the legislators. The board was made up of the governor, lieutenant governor, the president *pro tempore* of the senate, the chairman of the finance committee of the senate, the speaker of the assembly, the chairman of the ways and means committee of the assembly, the comptroller, the attorney general, the commissioner of efficiency and economy—and four members *ex-officio* of the legislative branch and five members *ex-officio* of the executive and administrative

branches. The first year that the estimates came before this board it was unable to come to any conclusion and made no report except such as was submitted through two officers of the board upon each of whom was laid the responsibility independently for submitting estimates with reports thereon.[9]

The unsatisfactory operation of the laws governing the administration of various states, within the last few years, has been the subject of much popular unrest. In recognition of this dissatisfaction several states have appointed commissions or committees of inquiry for the purpose of ascertaining wherein the methods of conducting business may be changed with a view to increasing efficiency and economy. In 1912, Massachusetts and New Jersey each appointed such a commission. In 1913, New York, Pennsylvania, Minnesota, Iowa, Illinois and California appointed commissions or committees with instructions to report. Most of these commissions have pointed to the irresponsive character of our state governments; all of them have made recommendations.

Under the federal constitution the President is made responsible to the electorate for the executive departments. It was the opinion of President Taft, set forth in a special message to Congress, that the President had the power, under the federal constitution, to prepare and submit a budget, although, without constitutional change or legislation, his proposals might receive no consideration. In the states, however, the executive branch has been so far carved up into independent jurisdictions that the governor could not obtain the information or cooperation required to make an executive budget effective. The only remedy is constitutional revision, which looks toward executive reorganization as well as a definite prescription for a budget.

New York, through its constitutional convention —the one which has just adjourned—is the first state that has ever undertaken to frame the financial measures of its constitution around the "budget idea." The extent to which the convention succeeded in injecting this idea into the constitution will appear from a reading of the draft which in November will be submitted to the electorate for their approval.

Budget Ideas Applied to Municipalities

The political consciousness of the duties of citizenship was first awakened in the government of our municipalities. There, attention was first given to matters of electoral reform and charter reorganization. Later, through the organization of independent civic agencies with staff equipment to inquire into matters of public business, attention became centered on methods and results. Among the first conditions which came to attention, after these agencies of citizenship began to direct their attention to details, was the fact that the accounts did not provide the information needed to show what the government was doing, how it was doing it, what results were being obtained and what was the cost of results— whether good, bad or indifferent. Furthermore, it was found that responsibility for these conditions could not be located. The whole administration had been carved up into little jurisdictions and the business put into pigeon-holes and pockets in each of which some officer or subordinate came to have what was regarded as a proprietary interest or right to control. As a means of breaking down these many petty jurisdictions and requiring information on standard lines to come to a central office where it could be summarized and coordinated, the cities were led to adopt the same general method that had been employed in the national government—namely, that of sub-dividing appropriation accounts to such an extent as to force administrative agencies to account in detail to the legislative committee charged with the consideration of the appropriation bill. This detailed subdivision of appropriation accounts has come to be called a "segregated budget"—an evident misnomer. What the cities did which developed a new appropriation procedure from the viewpoint of enforcing accounting requirements was to confuse the "act of appropriation" with a "budget." Since these legislative committees had no means of limiting administrative action in any other way, they substituted a highly detailed appropriation for control through a responsible executive by use of a "budget" under general law requiring detailed accounts to be prepared and submitted in support of the requests of a chief executive. This was only one more step in the direction of government by limitations instead of a step in the direction of responsible government with powers and a means of enforcing accountabilities.

But in another respect this experience has been misleading. The "budget idea" as it is here used assumes a responsible executive—in other words, such an idea cannot obtain in any jurisdiction, municipal, state or national unless there is some one who is responsible for executing the plans—for doing the things for which appropriations and revenue grants are requested. Where no such provision was made to definitize and locate responsibility and where no means was provided for enforcing efficiency and economy in administration what was called the "segregated budget" gained advocates through preventing officers from doing harm. The cities which have adopted this means have been able to exercise control but they have not been able to establish responsibility—in fact, the method is one which stands in the way of enforcing responsibility for that discretion in management which will make for efficiency.

Municipalities that have been attempting to make budgets have suffered as much from charter provisions, passed on the theory that the purpose of a charter was to keep officers from doing harm, as have the states in their constitutions. For example, the city of Philadelphia, which has done much toward working out the forms and procedures of budget control, has not been able to make this effective because, although it has a highly centralized executive organization, the mayor is not made the responsible leader before councils in securing measures for better administration—the comptroller is the only one who by charter is permitted to submit to the board of aldermen the estimates and no one is required to assume responsibility for a definite financial plan or proposal for the next fiscal period. The finance committee on councils stands in the same relation to the administration in this respect as does the committee on appropriations of the national government. It is not until the finance committee has completed its work that there is anything officially before councils for consideration.

The charter of the city of New York constitutes a board of eight members as the chief executive of the city, made up of the mayor, the president of the board of aldermen, the comptroller, and the five borough presidents. In this there is no provision for the principle of solidarity of responsibility. Although the constitution requires that this board prepare and submit each year to the board of aldermen a budget, it has never done so in the sense in which the term "budget" is here used. What it has done is to prepare and submit each year in November an appropriation bill which when enacted by the board of aldermen determines expenditures for another year. Following the budget principle the board of aldermen is not permitted to make any change except to reduce and in this respect the charter has gone farther than in some other cities. It is some months later that the revenue proposals come before the city authorities. In any event the board of estimate and apportionment of the city of New York never has prepared and submitted to the board of aldermen a financial plan which will bring before the city a prospectus of what is proposed nor a statement of affairs which will enable citizens or the board of aldermen to know what is the financial condition at the time that a vote is asked for.

Conclusion

In conclusion it may be said that the "budget idea" is just beginning to take hold of the American mind; that for a period of one hundred and twenty-five years American political institutions have been drifting steadily away from conditions which made the successful operation of a budget principle possible—away from responsible government; that the condition which is making possible the introduction of this idea into our political system has been a reaction against the results of irresponsible government, the political boss, log-rolling methods, pork barrel legislation; that the "budget idea" has finally come to be thought of as a constitutional principle—one which has been used effectively for the purpose of developing representative government and keeping it in harmony with the highest ideals of democracy.

While this idea has but recently been made a part of American political thinking it is one that is becoming rapidly absorbed and made a part of our political philosophy. More than any other principle of control, it is commanding the confidence and respect of those persons in the nation whose influence is being felt in legislatures and constitutional conventions, and other assemblies charged with the responsibility of redrafting our public law.

Notes

1. There are two special treatises on what the authors have chosen to call budgets in this country, *viz.*: Eugene E. Agger's *The Budget in the American Commonwealth*, 1907; and S. Gale Lowrie's *The Budget*, 1912. Both of these proceed from the notion that the documents which have been developed in American practice to carry out the various constitutional inhibitions and the devices used to control expenditures are budgets. While these works are highly meritorious exposés of American methods, the practices described are so far afield from what is here described as the "budget idea" that the contrast should be noted. And this distinction should be drawn if we are to consider the merits and demerits of these two widely differing practices.

2. *The Cost of Our National Government,* by Henry Jones Ford, 1910.

3. *See* report on the preliminary inquiry under authority of the civil act of June 25, 1910, prior to the organization of the President's Commission on Economy and Efficiency, covering the period September 27, 1910 to March 8, 1911—circular No. 29 of the commission.

4. This was printed as house document No. 854 of the 62d Congress, second session (568 pages). The members of the commission who participated in the preparation and signed the report, besides the chairman, were: Frank J. Goodnow, for twenty-six years professor of administrative law in Columbia University, now President of Johns Hopkins University; William F. Willoughby, for more than twenty years connected with the government service in various capacities, now constitutional advisor to the Chinese Republic; Walter W. Warwick, for many years connected with the comptroller's office and auditing service of the federal government, now the comptroller of the treasury; and Merritt O. Chance, for twenty-six years connected with various departments of the government, now postmaster at Washington. From June, 1911, to January, 1912, Mr. Harvey S. Chase was also a member of the commission, but due to illness he was not able to be in Washington during the time that the budget report was being prepared and therefore did not share in authorship or join in signing the report. The subsequent use which Mr. Chase has made of the report, however, indicates that he is in general accord with the recommendations of the commission.

5. *Senate document 1113,* 62d Congress, 3d session.

6. Ala. V, 123; Colo. IV, 8; Ida. IVA; Ill. V, 77; Mo. V, 10; Mont. VII, 10; Nebr. V, 77; Tex. IV, 9; W. Va., VII, 6.

7. *See* report of the Economy and Efficiency Committee of Illinois, p. 22.

8. *See* laws 1913, ch. 281—An act to establish a state board of estimate.

9. The commissioner of efficiency and economy was required to make a careful study of each office, examine the accounts, prescribe the form of submitting departmental estimates and examine these statements, and make recommendations. The comptroller was also required by law to prepare and submit to the legislature estimates of revenues and expenditures. Both of these officers performed the duties required by law, but the "board of estimate" were unable to come to any conclusion. Both of these officers were also members of the board of estimate.

2

The Movement for Budgetary Reform in the States

William F. Willoughby

Introduction: Origin of Movement

Of few movements for political reform is it feasible to determine precisely the causes to which it owes its rise or to fix exactly the date of its origin. If one seeks for an explanation of the modern movement, now under full way, for the adoption by the several governing bodies of the United States of a budget as the central and controlling feature of their systems of financial administration, it must be found in a number of more or less distinct movements which have each found in this device an important means for achieving or promoting the object sought.

The budget as an instrument of democracy. Among these first place must be given to that effort continuously being put forth to devise means by which popular government, in the sense that the affairs of government shall be conducted in conformity with the popular will, may become a reality in fact as in name. It is hardly necessary to point out that the popular will cannot be intelligently formulated nor expressed unless the public has adequate means for knowing currently how governmental affairs have been conducted in the past, what are present conditions and what program for work in the future is under consideration. Of all means devised for meeting this requirement no single one approaches in completeness and effectiveness a budget if properly prepared. It at once serves to make known past operations, present conditions and future proposals, definitely locates responsibility and furnishes the means for control. Professor A. R. Hatton is thus justified when he says:

Source: William F. Willoughby, *The Movement for Budgetary Reform in the States* (New York: D. Appleton and Company for the Institute for Government Research, 1918), pp. 1–8.

Above and beyond its relation to economy and efficiency in public affairs it (the budget) may be made one of the most potent instruments of democracy. Given at least manhood suffrage, any government so organized as to produce and carry out a scientific budget system will be susceptible of extensive and intelligent popular control. On the contrary those governments, whatever their other virtues, which fail to provide adequate budget methods will neither reach the maximum of efficiency nor prove to be altogether responsible to the people.

A new spirit in American politics is manifesting itself in the powerful movement for the reform of governmental organization and procedure in the interest of popular control and efficiency. There are naturally many features in the program for the accomplishment of this twofold object. No single change would add so largely to both democracy and efficiency as the introduction of proper budget methods.[1]

The budget as an instrument for correlating legislative and executive action. Closely associated with this demand that more effective means be provided by which the popular will and the principle of popular control may be made effective is the feeling that the present working conditions of our legislative bodies and particularly their relations to the executive branch of government are far from satisfactory. The conviction has been growing that a mistake has been made in seeking to make of our legislatures boards of directors to concern themselves with the details of the activities, organization and methods of business of administrative services; that the true function of the legislature should be that of acting as an organ of public opinion in the larger sense and as the medium through which those concerned with the actual administration of affairs should be supervised, controlled, and held to a rigid accountability for the manner in which they discharge their duties.

This had led inevitably to the position that upon the executive should be placed the responsibility for the formulation of work programs and the decision, in the first instance at least, of the means to be employed in the putting of these programs into execution. This would appear to carry with it a great strengthening of the executive at the expense of the legislative branch of government. So it does in one sense. It is a canon of administrative science, however, that when discretionary powers and authority are increased a corresponding increase should be made in the means of controlling and supervising the manner in which these augmented powers are exercised. If legislatures are to surrender to the executive increased powers in respect to the conduct of administrative affairs, they must strengthen the means by which they may assure themselves that these powers are properly exercised. There are two methods by which superior direction, supervision and control may be exerted, by specification in advance, or, by the establishment of a proper accounting and reporting system, by establishing means through which full information may be currently available regarding the manner in which delegated authority is being exercised. Legislatures are being asked to give up the first method of control. If they do so, it is imperative that the conditions stated in the second alternative should be met.

It is at this point that the demand for the adoption of a budget finds its place as an integral part of the movement for the improvement of the working relations between the two branches of government. In the budget is to be found far the most effective means that has yet been devised whereby larger responsibility for the formulation and execution of financial and work programs may be conferred upon the executive and yet the latter be held to a more rigid accountability for the manner in which this responsibility is discharged. In a very true sense, therefore, the movement for the adoption of budgetary systems by our governing bodies is an integral and essential part of the whole greater movement for the accomplishment of governmental reforms generally.

The budget as an instrument for securing administrative efficiency and economy. Still another movement which has logically resulted in the demand for budgetary reforms is that for placing the purely technical methods of governmental organization and administration upon a more efficient and economical basis. The question has been raised as to whether there are any inherent reasons why government officers should not be held to the same standards of efficiency and honesty as are demanded in the business world. The demand that they should be has become more insistent as the tasks imposed upon governments have become more numerous and complex and, in many cases, more nearly similar to the character of the tasks which private corporations are called upon to perform. In the business world it is recognized that no undertaking of magnitude, certainly none performed under a corporate form of organization, can be efficiently administered which does not have a system of accounts and reports that will permit the directing body, the board of directors, and the stockholders, to secure a clear picture of past operations, present conditions and future programs of activities. In all proposals looking to the reform of methods of business of governmental bodies, chief attention has consequently been placed upon the demand for the improvement of the methods by which their financial affairs are conducted. It is inconsistent to the last degree that governments should insist that corporations controlled by them should have systems of accounting and reporting corresponding to the most approved principles of modern accountancy while not providing for equally efficient systems for the management of their own financial affairs. The demand for improved methods of public administration has thus inevitably centered primarily upon the demand for improved methods of financial administration and, in order that this may be secured, upon the specific demand for the adoption of a budgetary system as the central feature of such improved system.

Use of budget first demanded as a feature of municipal reform. Turning now to a history of the movement itself, the point of departure must be found in the great movement which has been so much in evidence during the present generation, for the improvement of methods of municipal administration. After repeated disappointments persons interested in municipal reform came to an appreciation that permanent reform was not to be accomplished by the putting in the field of citizens' tickets and the ousting of officials who subordinated the public good to private gain. More and more it was borne in upon them that if lasting improvements were to be effected, the system of municipal government itself and methods of administration had to be changed, that there must be established principles of administration and means of direction, supervision and control that would automatically, as it were, result in better administration or at least make it possible for all interested parties to determine, without the necessity for special investigations, whether affairs were being efficiently and economically administered or the reverse. It was found, in a word, that the problem had to be attacked from the technical as well as the moral standpoint.

This change in the method of approach found expression not only in the altered character of the work attempted by such organizations as the National Municipal League, but in the appreciation that a thorough study of the technical problems of municipal administration with a view to the formulation of concrete measures of reform could only be successfully undertaken by permanent organization specially established and with a technically competent staff to undertake this work. Appreciation of this led to the creation by public spirited individuals of the large number of bureaus of municipal research which have contributed so powerfully during recent years to the improvement of methods of municipal administration in the United States. This is not the place to attempt any general characterization of the work of these bodies. It is only necessary for us to say that these bureaus have almost without exception concentrated a large part of their attention upon problems of financial administration and that all, likewise without exception, have bent their energies towards the securing by the cities with whose operations they concerned themselves of a budgetary system. This action was in large measure predicated upon the proposition that a municipality partakes in large measure of the characteristics of an ordinary business corporation and should be operated as such. This has meant that there should be employed by it the methods and agencies which have been found indispensable to the efficient operation of large business corporations. This view accepted, the demand at once arose that the expenditures of the city should be brought into direct relation to its possible or actual revenues and be based upon estimates and recommendations emanating from the spending departments. The advantage was at once seen of having the estimates and recommendations thus made by the several administrative services submitted to some central executive organ vested with authority to revise and reduce them when necessary and to bring them into due relation and proportion to one another. This was seen to be essential since spending departments are concerned primarily each in its own activities and are, therefore, interested in getting the largest possible allotment of funds from the general treasury. If the latter is to be protected and the relative as well as the absolute utility of different classes of work is to be determined some organ must exist within the administration which is not itself a spending department but has the special function of balancing demands of spending departments and of protecting the general treasury from the demands being made upon it beyond its resources.

This fundamental feature was appreciated by municipal reformers prior to the establishment of bureaus of municipal research. Thus the National Municipal League as early as 1899 included in its draft of a model municipal corporation act a section providing that:

> It shall be the duty of the Mayor from time to time to make such recommendations to the Council as he may deem to be for the welfare of the city and on the —— day of —— in each year to submit to the Council the annual budget of current expenses of the city, any item in which may be reduced or omitted by the Council; but the Council shall not increase any item in nor the total of said budget.

The course of budgetary reform in municipalities was also materially promoted by the Bureau of the Census through the continuous pressure which it exerted upon municipalities to improve their methods of accounting and reporting and especially through the standard classification of municipal expenditures which it worked out in connection with experts representing the accounting profession and the National Municipal League. In later years the development of the commission and city manager types of municipal government, and the policy adopted by a number of the leading cities in their recent charter revisions to provide for boards of estimates among whose functions the most important duty was that of passing upon and revising estimates as originally framed by the spending departments, have likewise contributed powerfully to the promotion of budgetary reform. These all represent the definite adoption of the most fundamental principle of a budget that there should be a central budget framing organ to stand between the estimating departments and the fund-granting authority. In few, if any, cases, however, has the principle been adopted of vesting final authority in respect to the framing of a budget in the chief executive officer.

After all is said, however, to the bureaus of municipal research and allied organizations established by boards of trade and other citizen agencies belongs the chief credit for the persistent demand that a budget be made the foundation stone of the system of financial administration of all municipalities. Not only have they urged this without ceasing but they have done a large amount of work in the way of working out and installing systems of financial administration in various cities resting on this basis.

Movement for budgetary reform carried over to the states.   It was inevitable that the movement for budgetary reform in municipalities, once fairly under way, should be carried over to efforts looking to the improvement of state governments. Every reason dictating the necessity for this reform in the case of municipalities existed with increased force in the case of these governments. Here the conditions to be met, however, were much more difficult than those obtaining in the case of municipal governments. Broadly speaking, the administrative branch of municipal governments corresponds to the integrated type of organization, with the mayor at the head as administrator in chief. It has been pointed out in our consideration of the nature and functions of a budget[2] how essential is this form of organization to the proper operation of a budgetary system. It is

unfortunate, both from the standpoint of budgetary reform and that of good administration generally, that this condition obtains in but few, if any, of the states. As is well known, in most if not all of the states the administrative branch consists of a large number of practically independent services. Only in small degree has the governor any positive powers of direction or any adequate power to control. The line of authority runs direct in each case to the legislature; and the authority of this body is often limited by the fact that the heads of these services owe their election to office, not to it, but to the people. It results from this that in the case of most, if not all, of the states the problem of the introduction of a thoroughly efficient budgetary system involves that of fundamentally recasting their systems of government.

Notes

1. Foreword to Public Budgets, *Annals of the American Academy of Political and Social Science,* November, 1915.
2. *The Problem of a National Budget,* pp. 1–29.

3

The Lack of a Budgetary Theory

V. O. Key, Jr.

On the most significant aspect of public budgeting, *i.e.*, the allocation of expenditures among different purposes so as to achieve the greatest return, American budgetary literature is singularly arid. Toilers in the budgetary field have busied themselves primarily with the organization and procedure for budget preparation, the forms for the submission of requests for funds, the form of the budget document itself, and like questions.[1] That these things have deserved the consideration given them cannot be denied when the unbelievable resistance to the adoption of the most rudimentary essentials of budgeting is recalled and their unsatisfactory condition in many jurisdictions even now is observed. Nevertheless, the absorption of energies in the establishment of the mechanical foundations for budgeting has diverted attention from the basic budgeting problem (on the expenditure side), namely: On what basis shall it be decided to allocate *x* dollars to activity A instead of activity B?

Writers on budgeting say little or nothing about the purely economic aspects of public expenditure. "Economics," says Professor Robbins, "is the science which studies human behavior as a relationship between ends and scarce means which have alternative uses."[2] Whether budgetary behavior is economic or political is open to fruitless debate; nevertheless, the point of view and the mode of thought of the economic theorist are relevant, both in the study of and action concerning public expenditure. The budget-maker never has enough revenue to meet the request of all spending agencies, and he must decide (subject, of course, to subsequent legislative action) how scarce means shall be allocated to alternative uses. The completed budgetary document (although the budget-maker may be quite unaware of it) represents a judgment upon how scarce means should be allocated to bring the maximum return in social utility.[3]

Source: American Political Science Review, 34 (December 1940): 1137–1140. Reprinted by permission.

In their discussions of the review of estimates, budget authorities rarely go beyond the question of how to judge the estimates for particular functions, i.e., ends; and the approach to the review of the estimate of the individual agency is generally directed toward the efficiency with which the particular end is to be achieved.[4] Even in this sort of review, budget-makers have developed few standards of evaluation, acting, rather, on the basis of their impressionistic judgment, of a rudimentary cost accounting, or perhaps, of the findings of administrative surveys. For decisions on the requests of individual agencies, the techniques have by no means reached perfection.[5] It is sometimes possible to compute with fair accuracy whether the increased efficiency from new public works, such as a particular highway project, will warrant the capital outlay. Or, given the desirability of a particular objective, it may be feasible to evaluate fairly precisely alternative means for achieving that end. Whether a particular agency is utilizing, and plans to utilize, its resources with the maximum efficiency is of great importance, but this approach leaves untouched a more fundamental problem. If it is assumed that an agency is operating at maximum efficiency, the question remains whether the function is worth carrying out at all, or whether it should be carried out on a reduced or enlarged scale, with resulting transfers of funds to or from other activities of greater or lesser social utility.

Nor is there found in the works of the public finance experts much enlightenment on the question herein considered. They generally dispose of the subject of expenditures with a few perfunctory chapters and hurry on to the core of their interest— taxation and other sources of revenue. On the expenditure side, they differentiate, not very plausibly, between productive and unproductive expenditure; they consider the classification of public expenditures; they demonstrate that public expenditures have been increasing; and they discuss the determination of the optimum aggregate of public expenditure; but they do not generally come to grips with the question of the allocation of public revenues among different objects of expenditure.[6] The issue is recognized, as when Pigou says: "As regards the distribution, as distinct from the aggregate cost, of optional government expenditure, it is clear that, just as an individual will get more satisfaction out of his income by maintaining a certain balance between different sorts of expenditure, so also will a community through its government. The principle of balance in both cases is provided by the postulate that resources should be so distributed among different uses that the marginal return of satisfaction is the same for all of them. . . . Expenditure should be distributed between battleships and poor relief in such wise that the last shilling devoted to each of them yields the same real return. We have here, so far as theory goes, a test by means of which the distribution of expenditure along different lines can be settled.''[7] But Pigou dismisses the subject with a paragraph, and the discussion by others is not voluminous.[8]

The only American writer on public finance who has given extended attention to the problem of the distribution of expenditures is Mabel Walker. In her *Municipal Expenditures,* she reviews the theories of public expenditure and devises a method for ascertaining the tendencies in distribution of expenditures on the assumption that the way would be pointed to ''a norm of expenditures consistent with the state of progress at present achieved by society.'' While her method would be inapplicable to the federal budget,[9] and would probably be of less relevance in the analysis of state than of municipal expenditures, her study deserves reflective perusal by municipal budget officers and students of the problem.[10]

Literature skirting the edges of the problem is found in the writings of those economists who have concerned themselves with the economic problems of the socialist state. In recent years, a new critique of socialism has appeared.[11] This attack, in the words of one who attempts to refute it, is '' . . . more subtle and technical than the previous ones, based on the supposed inability of a socialist community to solve purely economic problems. . . . What is asserted is that, even with highly developed technique, adequate incentives to activity, and rational control of population, the economic directors of a socialist commonwealth would be unable to balance against each other the worthwhileness of different lines of production or the relative advantages of different ways of producing the same goods.''[12] Those who believe this problem not insoluble in a socialist economy set out to answer the question: ''What is the proper method of determining just what commodities shall be produced from the economic resources at the disposal of a given community?''[13] One would anticipate from those seeking to answer this question some light on the problems of the

budget-maker in a capitalist state. But they are concerned only with the pricing of state-produced goods for sale to individuals in a socialist economy. Professor Dickinson, for example, excludes from his discussion goods and services provided in a socialist economy ''free of charge to all members of society, as the result of a decision, based on other grounds than market demands, made by some authoritative economic organ of the community.''[14] That exclusion removes from consideration the point at issue. Nevertheless, the critics of socialist theory do at least raise essentially the same problem as that posed in the present discussion; and their comment is suggestive.

Various studies of the economics of public works touch the periphery of the problem concerning the allocation of public expenditures. The principal inquiries have been prosecuted under the auspices of the National Resources Planning Board and its predecessor organizations. These reports, however, are concerned in the main with the question of how much in the aggregate should be spent, and when, in order to function as the most effective absorber of the shocks incidental to cyclical fluctuations. Two studies, by Arthur D. Gayer and John M. Clark, deal with public works outlays as stabilizers of the economic order and with related matters.[15] These works suggest factors relevant in the determination of the total amount of the capital budget; but in them the problem of selection among alternative public works projects is not tackled. In another study, the latter issue is approached by Russell V. Black from a rich background of city planning experience, and he formulates a suggestive but tentative set of criteria for the selection and programming of public works projects.[16]

Planning agencies and professional planners have been more interested in the abstract problem of ascertaining the relative utility of public outlays than has any other group. The issue is stated theoretically in a recent report: ''The problem is essentially one of the development of criteria for selecting the objects of public expenditure. As a larger and larger proportion of the national income is spent for public purposes, the sphere of the price system with its freedom of choice of objects of expenditure is more and more restricted. Concurrently, the necessity for developing methods by which public officals may select objects of expenditure which will bring the greatest utility or return and most accurately achieve social aspirations becomes more pressing. In a sense, this constitutes the central problem of the productive state. If planning is to be 'over-all' planning, it must devise techniques for the balancing of values within a framework that gives due regard both to the diverse interests of the present and to the interests of the future.''[17] Planning agencies have not succeeded in formulating any convincing principles, either descriptive or normative, concerning the allocation of public funds, but they have, within limited spheres, created governmental machinery facilitating the consideration of related alternative expenditures. The most impressive example is the Water Resources Committee (of the National Resources Planning Board) and its subsidiary drainage-basin committees.[18] Through this machinery, it is possible to consider alternatives in objectives and sequences of expenditure—questions that would not arise concretely without such machinery. Perhaps the approach toward the practical working out of the issue lies in the canalizing of decisions through the governmental machinery so as to place alternatives in juxtaposition and compel consideration of relative values. This is the effect of many existing institutional arrangements; but the issue is rarely so stated, and the structure of government, particularly the federal-state division, frequently prevents the weighing of alternatives.

It may be argued that for the best performance of individual public functions a high degree of stability in the amount of funds available year after year is desirable, and that the notion that there is, or needs to be, mobility of resources as among functions is erroneous. Considerable weight is undoubtedly to be attached to this view. Yet over periods of a few years important shifts occur in relative financial emphasis on different functions of government. Even in minor adjustments, the small change up or down at the margin may be of considerable significance. Like an individual consumer, the state may have certain minimum expenditures generally agreed upon, but care in weighing the relative utility of alternative expenditures becomes more essential as the point of marginal utility is approached. Moreover, within the public economy, frictions (principally institutional in character) exist to obstruct and delay adjustments in the allocation of resources in keeping with changing wants probably to a greater extent than in the private economy.

Efforts to ascertain more precisely the relative "values" of public services may be thought fruitless because of the influence of pressure groups in the determination of the allocation of funds. Each spending agency has its clientele, which it marshals for battle before budgetary and appropriating agencies.[19] And there are those who might contend that the pattern of expenditures resultant from the interplay of these forces constitutes a maximization of return from public expenditure, since it presumably reflects the social consensus on the relative values of different services. If this be true, the more efficient utilization of resources would be promoted by the devising of means more accurately to measure the political strength of interests competing for appropriations. That the appropriation bill expresses a social consensus sounds akin to the mystic doctrine of the "general will." Constantly, choices have to be made between the demands of different groups; and it is probably true that factors other than estimates of the relative political strength of contending groups frequently enter into the decisions. The pressure theory suggests the potential development in budget bureaus and related agencies of a strong bureaucracy strategically situated, and with a vested interest in the general welfare, in contrast with the particularistic drives of the spending agencies.

It is not to be concluded that by excogitation a set of principles may be formulated on the basis of which the harassed budget official may devise an automatic technique for the allocation of financial resources. Yet the problem needs study in several directions. Further examination from the viewpoints of economic theory and political philosophy could produce valuable results. The doctrine of marginal utility, developed most finely in the analysis of the market economy, has a ring of unreality when applied to public expenditures. The most advantageous utilization of public funds[20] resolves itself into a matter of value preferences between ends lacking a common denominator. As such, the question is a problem in political philosophy; keen analyses in these terms would be of the utmost importance in creating an awareness of the problems of the budgetary implementation of programs of political action of whatever shade. The discussion also suggests the desirability of careful and comprehensive analyses of the budgetary process. In detail, what forces go into the making of state budgets? What factors govern decisions of budgetary officials? Precisely what is the role of the legislature? On the federal level, the field for inquiry is broader, including not only the central budgetary agency, but departmental budget offices as well. Studies of congressional appropriating processes are especially needed.[21] For the working budget official, the implications of the discussion rest primarily in a point of view in the consideration of estimates in terms of alternatives—decisions which are always made, but not always consciously. For the personnel policy of budget agencies, the question occurs whether almost sole reliance on persons trained primarily in accounting and fiscal procedure is wise. The thousands of little decisions made in budgetary agencies grow by accretion into formidable budgetary documents which from their sheer mass are apt often to overwhelm those with the power of final decision. We need to look carefully at the training and working assumptions of these officials, to the end that the budget may most truly reflect the public interest.[22]

Notes

1. See A. E. Buck, *Public Budgeting* (New York, 1929); J. Wilner Sundelson, *Budgetary Methods in National and State Governments* (New York State Tax Commission, Special Report No. 14, 1938); *ibid.*, "Budgetary Principles," *Political Science Quarterly*, Vol. 50, pp. 236–263 (1935).

2. Lionel Robbins, *An Essay on the Nature and Significance of Economic Science* (2nd ed., London, 1935), p. 16.

3. If the old saying that the state fixes its expenditures and then raises sufficient revenues to meet them were literally true, the budget officer would not be faced by a problem of scarcity. However, there is almost invariably a problem of scarcity in the public economy —to which all budget officers, besieged by spending departments, will testify.

4. See Buck, *op. cit.*, Chap. 11.

5. The development of standards for the evaluation of the efficiency of performance of particular functions—entirely apart from the value of the functions—is as yet in a primitive stage. Such standards, for budgetary purposes at least, require cost accounting, which implies a unit of measurement. A standard of comparison is also implied, such as the performance of the same agency during prior fiscal periods, or the performance of other agencies under like conditions. In the absence of even crude measurement devices, budgetary and appropriating authorities are frequently thrown back upon the alternative of passing on individual items—three clerks, two messengers, seven stenographers, etc.—a practice which often causes exasperation among operating officials. Although our knowledge of budgetary behavior is slight, the surmise is probably correct that questions of the efficiency of

operation in achieving a particular end are generally hopelessly intermingled with the determination of the relative value of different ends. Operating officials often shy away from experimentation with devices of measurement, but it may be suggested that measures of the efficiency of performance should tend to divert the attention of budgetary and appropriating officials from concern with internal details to the pivotal question of the relative value of services.

6. See, for example, H. L. Lutz, *Public Finance*.

7. *A Study in Public Finance* (London, 1928), p. 50. See also E. R. A. Seligman, "The Social Theory of Fiscal Science." *Political Science Quarterly*, Vol. 41, pp. 193–218, 354–383 (1926), and Gerhard Colm, "Theory of Public Expenditures," *Annals of the American Academy of Political and Social Science*, Vol. 183, pp. 1–11 (1930).

8. For a review of the literature, see Mabel L. Walker, *Municipal Expenditures* (Baltimore, 1930), Chap. 3.

9. In this connection, see C. H. Wooddy, *The Growth of the Federal Government, 1915–1932* (New York, 1934).

10. In the field of state finance, a valuable study has been made by I. M. Labovitz in *Public Policy and State Finance in Illinois* (Social Science Research Committee, University of Chicago. Publication pending).

11. See F. A. von Hayek (ed.), *Collectivist Economic Planning* (London, 1935).

12. H. D. Dickinson, "Price Formation in a Socialist Community," *Economic Journal*, Vol. 43, pp. 237–250. See also, E. F. M. Durbin, "Economic Calculus in a Planned Economy," *Economic Journal*, Vol. 46, pp. 676–690 (1936), and A. R. Sweezy, "The Economist in a Socialist Economy," in *Explorations in Economics; Notes and Essays Contributed in Honor of F. W. Taussig* (1936), pp. 422–433.

13. F. M. Taylor, "The Guidance of Production in a Socialist State," *American Economic Review*, Vol. 19, pp. 1–8 (1929).

14. *Op. cit.*, p. 238. Of Soviet Russia, Brown and Hinrichs say: "In a planned economy, operating if necessary under pressure to accomplish a predetermined production, the decision with regard to major prices is essentially a political one." "The Planned Economy of Soviet Russia," *Political Science Quarterly*, Vol. 46, pp. 362–402 (1931).

15. J. M. Clark, *Economics of Planning Public Works* (Washington, Government Printing Office, 1935); A. D. Gayer, *Public Works in Prosperity and Depression* (New York, National Bureau of Economic Research, 1935). See also the essay by Simeon E. Leland In National Resources Committee, *Public Works Planning* (Washington, Government Printing Office, 1936).

16. *Criteria and Planning for Public Works* (Washington, National Resources Board, mimeographed, 1934). See especially pp. 165–168.

17. National Resources Committee, *The Future of State Planning* (Washington, Government Printing Office, 1938), p. 19. Mr. J. Reeve has called my attention to the fact that the problem of allocation of public expenditures has come to be more difficult also because of the increasingly large number of alternative purposes of expenditure.

18. For an approach to the work of the Water Committee in terms somewhat similar to those of this paper, see National Resources Committee, *Progress Report*, December, 1938, pp. 29–36. For an example of the work, see National Resources Committee, *Drainage Basin Problems and Programs, 1937 Revision* (Washington, Government Printing Office, 1938).

19. See E. B. Logan, "Group Pressures and State Finance," *Annals of the American Academy of Political and Social Science*, Vol. 179, pp. 131–135 (1935), and Dayton David McKean, *Pressures on the Legislature of New Jersey* (New York, 1938), Chap. 5.

20. This matter is really another facet of the problem of the determination of the "public interest" with which E. P. Herring grapples in *Public Administration and the Public Interest*.

21. For such studies, useful methodological ideas might be gleaned from Professor Schattschneider's *Politics, Pressures, and the Tariff*.

22. Helpful comments by I. M. Labovitz and Homer Jones on a preliminary draft of this paper are hereby acknowledged.

4

Toward a Theory of Budgeting

Verne B. Lewis

The $64.00 question on the expenditure side of public budgeting is: On what basis shall it be decided to allocate X dollars to Activity A instead of allocating them to Activity B, or instead of allowing the taxpayer to use the money for his individual purposes? Over a decade ago V. O. Key called attention to the lack of a budgetary theory which would assist in arriving at an answer to this question.[1] Pointing out that budgeting is essentially a form of applied economics, since it requires the allocation of scarce resources among competing demands, Professor Key urged that this question be explored from the point of view of economic theory.

The purpose of this article is to analyze three propositions that are derived from economic theory[2] and appear to be applicable to public budgeting and to be appropriate building blocks for construction of an economic theory of budgeting. In brief, the three principles are:

1. Since resources are scarce in relation to demands, the basic economic test which must be applied is that the return from every expenditure must be worth its cost in terms of sacrificed alternatives. Budget analysis, therefore, is basically a comparison of the relative merits of alternative uses of funds.

2. Incremental analysis (that is, analysis of the additional values to be derived from an additional expenditure) is necessary because of the phenomenon of diminishing utility. Analysis of the increments is necessary and useful only at or near the margin; this is the point of balance at which an additional expenditure for any purpose would yield the same return.

3. Comparison of relative merits can be made only in terms of relative effectiveness in achieving a common objective.

Source: Reprinted with permission from *Public Administration Review* 12, no. 1 (Winter 1952): 43–54. © 1952 by The American Society for Public Administration (ASPA), 1120 G Street NW, Suite 500, Washington D.C. 20005.

Part I of this article will be devoted to consideration of these principles. In Part II a proposal, which will be called the alternative budget procedure, will be outlined and analyzed in terms of the three principles. Primary emphasis throughout will be placed on the applicability of concepts developed by the economists to methods of analyzing budget estimates. The discussion is pointed specifically at problems of the federal government; the general ideas, however, should be equally applicable to state and local governmental units.

I

Relative Value

Budget decisions must be made on the basis of relative values. There is no absolute standard of value. It is not enough to say that an expenditure for a particular purpose is desirable or worthwhile. The results must be worth their cost. The results must be more valuable than they would be if the money were used for any other purpose.

Comparison of relative values to be obtained from alternative uses of funds is necessary because our resources are inadequate to do all the things we consider desirable and necessary. In fact, public budgeting is necessary only because our desires exceed our means. The desires of human beings are virtually unlimited. Although the supply of resources has been greatly expanded in recent decades, the supply is still short in relation to demands. It would be nice if we had enough to go around, but we do not. Some demands can be met only in part, some not at all.

Scarcity of resources in relation to demands confronts us at every level of public budgeting. Public services consume scarce materials and manpower which have alternative uses. If used for governmental activities, they cannot be used for private purposes. If used for Activity A of the government, they cannot be used for Activity B. Expressed in terms of money, the problem of scarcity arises in connection with appropriations. As individual taxpayers, we put pressures on Congress to hold down federal taxes so that a larger proportion of our already inadequate personal incomes will be available to satisfy our individual desires. In view of these pressures, Congress usually appropriates less than is requested by the President and interest groups. The President in turn usually requests the Congress to appropriate less than the total of the estimates submitted to him by agency heads. Rarely does an agency have sufficient funds to do all the things it would like to do or that it is requested to do by citizen groups.

Confronted with limited resources, congressmen and administrative officials must make choices. The available money will buy this *or* that, but not *both*. On what basis should the choice be made?

The economists, who specialize in problems of scarcity, have a general answer to this question. It is found in the doctrine of marginal utility. This doctrine, as applied to public budgeting, has been formulated by Professor Pigou as follows:

> As regards the distribution, as distinct from the aggregate cost, of optional government expenditure, it is clear that, just as an individual will get more satisfaction out of his income by maintaining a certain balance between different sorts of expenditure, so also will a community through its government. The principle of balance in both cases is provided by the postulate that resources should be so distributed among different uses that the marginal return of satisfaction is the same for all of them. . . . Expenditure should be distributed between battleships and poor relief in such wise that the last shilling devoted to each of them yields the same real return. We have here, so far as theory goes, a test by means of which the distribution of expenditure along different lines can be settled.[3]

Other aspects of the marginal utility concept will be considered in later sections; here we want to note that this concept poses the problem in terms of relative values rather than absolutes. To determine the distribution of funds between battleships and poor relief we must weigh the relative value of the results to be obtained from these alternative uses. Is it worth while to spend an additional $1,000,000 for battleships? We can answer "yes" only if we think we would get more valuable results than would be obtained by using that $1,000,000 for poor relief.

When the economists approach the problem in terms of costs rather than results they arrive at the same conclusion. Fundamentally, as the economists indicate in their "opportunity" or "displacement" concept of costs, "the cost of a thing is simply the amount of other things which has to be given up for its sake."[4] If Robinson Crusoe finds he has time to build a house *or* catch some fish, but not *both,* the cost of the house is the fish he does not catch or vice versa. The cost of anything is therefore the result that would have been realized had the resources been used for an alternative purpose.

Of what significance from the point of view of budget analysis are these concepts of relative value and displacement costs? They indicate that the basic objective of budget analysis is the comparison of the relative value of results to be obtained from alternative uses of funds. If an analyst is convinced after reading the usual argument supporting a budget request that the activity in question is desirable and necessary, his task has just begun. To be justifiable in terms of making the most advantageous use of resources, the returns from an expenditure for any activity must be more desirable and more necessary for any alternative use of the funds. On the other hand, a budget request for an activity cannot legitimately be turned down soley on the basis that the activity costs too much. Costs and results must be considered together. The costs must be judged in relation to the results and the results must be worth their costs in terms of alternative results that are foregone or displaced.

Incremental Analysis

If the basic guide for budget analysis is that results must be worth their costs, budget analysis must include a comparison of relative values. How can such a comparison of values be made?

The marginal utility concept suggests a way of approaching the problem. The method, briefly, is to divide available resources into increments and consider which of the alternative uses of each increment would yield the greatest return. Analysis of increments is necessary because of the phenomenon of diminishing utility. This means, roughly, that as we acquire more and more units of anything, the additional units have less and less use value. If enough units are acquired, an added unit may be of no value at all and may even be objectionable. To illustrate, four tires on a car are essential, a fifth tire is less essential but is handy to have, whereas a sixth tire just gets in the way. Although a sixth tire will cost as much as any of the first five, it has considerably less use value. In deciding how many tires to buy, we must therefore consider the use value to be derived from each *additional* tire.

Because of the phenomenon of diminishing utility, there is no point in trying to determine the *total* or *average* benefits to be obtained from total expenditures for a particular commodity or function. We must analyze the benefits by increments. If one million bazookas make a valuable contribution toward winning a war, we cannot assume that the contribution would be doubled if we had two million. Perhaps there are not enough soldiers to use that many. No matter how valuable bazookas might be in winning a war, a point would be reached sometime on the diminishing scale of utility where additional expenditures for bazookas would be completely wasted. Since we do not have enough resources to do all the things we would like to do, we certainly should not produce anything that will not or cannot be used.

But we cannot assume that we would make the best use of resources even if we produced no more bazookas than could be used. Perhaps the manpower and materials consumed in producing the last thousand bazookas would serve a more valuable purpose if they were used for producing additional hand grenades or some other item. This reasoning leads us back to the basic criterion for deciding how much should be spent for each activity. We should allocate enough money for bazookas so that the last dollar spent for bazookas will serve as valuable a purpose as the last dollar for hand grenades or any other purpose. If more than this amount is spent for bazookas, we sacrifice a more valuable alternative use. Thus, as is suggested by the marginal utility theory, maximum returns can be obtained only if expenditures are distributed among different purposes in such a way that the last dollar spent for each yields the same real return.

The marginal utility concept also indicates that a comparison of incremental values is meaningful and necessary only at or near the margins. When analyzing the value of the returns by increments of expenditure near the margins we would ask: How much will be sacrificed if proposed expenditures for Function A are reduced by $1,000? Can efficiency be increased so that output will not have to be reduced? What would be the consequences of lowering standards of quality? Of reducing quantities? Of postponing some portion of the work?

When these issues are explored, the payoff question can be tackled. Would the sacrifices be greater or less if the $1,000 cut is applied to Function B rather than to Function A? This question brings up the most difficult and most critical problem. How can the values of unlike functions be compared? How can the value of an atom bomb and cancer research be compared? Or public roads and public schools?

So far we have not indicated how this question can be answered. We have only narrowed the field by indicating that the value of functions must be compared by increments rather than in total and that the value of increments need only be compared near the marginal point of balance. Incremental analysis at the margins is just a tool, though a useful one, we believe. It does not supply the answers, but it helps to focus attention on the real points at issue.

Relative Effectiveness

The relative value of different things cannot be compared unless they have a common denominator. The common aspect of an atom bomb and cancer research, of public roads and public schools, is the broad purpose each is designed to serve. These items, as well as all other public and private activities, are undertaken to serve human needs and desires. We can only compare their values by evaluating their relative effectiveness in serving a common objective.

To revert to a previously used example, we do not make bazookas just for the sake of making bazookas. We make them because they help win wars. Although bazookas, hand grenades, and K-rations are unlike things, they serve a common military purpose. The relative values of these items can be weighed in terms of their relative effectiveness in fighting a war. We do not fight wars for their own sake either. They are fought for a larger purpose of national security. Economic aid to foreign countries also serves this purpose. Since they share a common objective, the relative value of military activities and economic aid can also be compared in terms of their effectiveness in achieving this objective.

Let us take a different type of case which is less general and more tangible than national security. Purchasing officers and engineers perform quite different functions. Yet, if they are working in an organization which does construction work, for example, they share the common objective of that organization. Operating within a ceiling on total expenditures, the head of the agency might be faced with this question: Would a part of the money allocated to the procurement section yield greater returns if transferred to the engineering section? This question involves value comparisons of unlike things, whether for a private firm or for a government agency. Moreover, the firm or the agency usually cannot express the contributions of procurement officers and engineers in terms of precise numbers. Nevertheless, reasonable men who are reasonably well informed arrive at substantially the same answer to such questions, provided the basic objective has been decided in advance. If the objective is to build a structure according to prescribed specifications in X months and at not to exceed Y dollars, this objective provides a common basis for evaluation. The answer will depend on forecasts of facts and will also be influenced by relative need. For example, if design is on schedule but construction is being delayed because purchase orders are not being issued on schedule, additions to the procurement staff would probably yield greater returns than additions to the design staff. On the other hand, if design is behind schedule and, as a consequence, the procurement staff has no material requisitions to process, more design engineers would yield the greater return.

Evaluation in terms of relative effectiveness in achieving a common objective is, therefore, a second fundamental method of budget analysis.[5]

Evaluation in terms of common purposes is another way of saying that alternative means can be evaluated in terms of the end they are designed to achieve. That end can be considered, in turn, as a means of achieving a broader end. This process requires, of course, that the ultimate ends be somehow established. How can these fundamental decisions be made? In a democracy we are not so much concerned with how they are made as by whom they are made. The ideal of democracy is that the desires of the people, no matter how they are arrived at or how unwise they may be, should control the actions of the government. The representatives of the people in Congress make the fundamental decisions as to the ultimate aims of governmental services. These decisions, in the form of laws and appropriation acts, provide the basis for economic calculation by administrative agencies in the same way as consumer action in the marketplace provides the basis for decisions in the private economy.

We now have some basic elements of an economic theory of budgeting. The economic aim of budgeting is to achieve the best use of our resources. To meet this test, the benefits derived from any expenditure must be worth their cost in terms of sacrificed or displaced alternatives. As a first step in applying that test, we can use incremental analysis at the margins as a means of concentrating attention at the areas where comparison of values

is necessary and meaningful. These values can be compared by determining their relative effectiveness in achieving a common purpose. Analysis in terms of common purposes requires a set of basic premises which are found in the ultimate ends or purposes established by Congress, acting for the people. This means that Congress is charged by the people with the basic responsibility for deciding what constitutes the "best use of resources," so far as the federal government is concerned.

Practical Limitations

Although the propositions outlined above concerning relative value, incremental analysis, and relative effectiveness constitute, in a sense, a formula for budget analysis which appears to be theoretically sound, the formula is not always easy to apply. Precise numbers to use in the equations are frequently unavailable. Although the formula will work in a theoretically valid manner, even if one has to guess the numbers to put into the equation, the practical usefulness of the answers will depend upon the accuracy of the numbers.

One area where firm numbers are hard to get involves forecasts of future needs and conditions. As we have noted, value is a function of need and need changes from time to time. In comparing the relative value of guns and butter, for example, we will strike a balance between them at different points at different times depending upon whether we are engaged in a hot war, a cold war, or no war at all. The balance between public health and police will be struck at one point if communicable diseases are rampant at a time when the traffic accident rate is low. The balance will be struck at a different point if the state of public health is good but the accident rate is alarming.

Budgetary decisions have to be based not only on relative needs as they are today but also on forecasts of what the needs will be tomorrow, next year, or in the next decade. The point is illustrated most dramatically by the decision made by the federal government during World War II to try to develop an atomic bomb. At the time, no one knew whether a bomb could be made, or if it could be made in time to help win the war. Hence, the government in deciding to divert tremendous quantities of scarce resources to this purpose had to take a calculated risk. Its decision was based not on firm facts but on forecasts and hopes as to the values to be realized.

There are probably as many budget arguments over forecasts of needs as there are over the relative merits of the expenditures which are proposed to meet those needs.

Not only must budget decisions be based, in some cases, on sheer guesses as to future needs and future accomplishments, but often the nature of governmental activities is such that accomplishments in relation to costs cannot be precisely measured even after the fact. How can one tell, for example, how much fire damage was prevented for each $1,000 spent by the fire department for fire prevention.

Perhaps it was the frequent difficulty in obtaining precise numbers that led Professor Key to question the applicability of the marginal utility theory to public budgeting. He concluded:

> The doctrine of marginal utility, developed most finely in the analysis of the market economy, has a ring of unreality when applied to public expenditures. The most advantageous utilization of public funds resolves itself into a matter of value preferences between ends lacking a common denominator. As such, the question is a problem of political philosophy.[6]

Whether firm numbers are available or not, judgments and decisions have to be made. The lack of precise numbers does not invalidate the basic principles or methods of calculation which we have outlined. The methods have to be judged on the basis of whether or not they lead to proper conclusions *if* it is assumed that the numbers used in the equations are the right ones. Obtaining the right numbers, though a fundamental and difficult problem, is separate and distinct from the problem of developing methods of calculation.

On the other hand, Professor Key may have been questioning the basic principle. It is perfectly true, as Key points out, that budgeting involves questions of value preferences which must be based on philosophy rather than science or logic. We agree that it is a problem for philosophers, but not exclusively, since the methods of the economists can also be applied. The problem of value has long been one of the central topics on the agenda of the economists. They do not approach the problem from the point of view of trying to develop an absolute standard of value or from the point of view of trying to prescribe which ends, goals, or objectives men should strive for. Rather they concentrate on methods

to be used to achieve the most valuable use of scarce resources as judged by whatever standard of value men embrace. While the philosopher helps us to decide which goals we should strive for, the economist helps us achieve those goals most efficiently. Thus, I believe, the economists' approach to the problem of value as expressed in the marginal utility theory can be accepted as a useful approach to public budgeting.

The views outlined in this article concerning the applicability of the methods of the economists to public budgeting run sharply counter to the views of some economists. Ludwig von Mises, for example, contends, in his book, *Bureaucracy*,[7] that there is no method of economic calculation which can be applied to government. It can be shown, I think, that the problem in government, so far as it exists, arises out of the lack of firm numbers rather than out of the lack of a method.

Dr. Mises' central argument is that bureaucrats have no means of calculating the relative usefulness of governmental activities because these activities have no price in the marketplace. Therefore, he contends, government agencies have no criterion of value to apply. In private business, he points out (p.26), "the ultimate basis of economic calculation is the valuation of all consumers' goods on the part of all the people" in the marketplace. Further, "economic calculation makes it possible for business to adjust production to the demands of the consumers" (p.27). On the other hand, he argues, "if a public enterprise is to be operated without regard to profits, the behavior of the public no longer provides a criterion of its usefulness" (p.61). Therefore, he concludes, "the problem of bureaucratic management is precisely the absence of such a method of calculation" (p.49).

We can agree with the part of his argument that says market prices provide a criterion of value which serves as a basis for economic calculation in private business; but we cannot agree that government agencies are completely lacking in such a criterion. As has been noted, appropriations, like market prices, indicate in quantitative terms how much the representatives of the people are willing to pay for goods and services rendered by the government. In appropriating funds, congressmen express their attitudes concerning the usefulness of governmental activities as definitely as individuals do when they buy bread at the corner bakery. Congressmen, in effect, are serving as purchasing agents for the American people.

What function does the market price criterion serve in determining whether an activity is worth its cost? One function is to provide the numbers necessary for determining how the cost of doing a particular job can be reduced to a minimum. Nothing, of course, is worth its cost if the same result can somehow be achieved at a lower cost. Market prices are as useful in government as they are in business in this regard. In constructing a road, a building, or a dam—even in running an office—the government has to pay market prices for the raw material and manpower it uses just as a private businessman does. If the guide to economic calculations is the market price, the government engineer has numbers to put into his equations just as his engineering brother in private industry has. Market prices provide the data he needs to calculate which combination of available materials, men, and machines will be least costly.

After all corners have been cut and the cost of doing a job has been reduced to the minimum, we face a broader question. Is the job worth doing? Dr. Mises undoubtedly would answer that a job is worth doing in private business if it yields a profit. In attempting to calculate whether a given activity will yield a profit, a businessman, however, faces some of the problems faced by government. He has to forecast market conditions. The numbers he forecasts may or may not be right. Likewise, a businessman cannot always determine even after the fact whether an individual activity has been profitable or not. No method has yet been found, for example, of measuring precisely how much of a company's profit or loss results from such activities as advertising, research and employee welfare programs. Moreover, a businessman, if he wants to maximize profits, cannot engage in an activity just because it is profitable. It must be more profitable than alternative activities open to him. Thus, he is faced with the same problem of relative value as is the government official. Suppose it costs $1.00 a pound to recover scrap materials in a private factory and that the scrap can be sold on the market for $1.10 a pound, thereby yielding a profit of 10 percent. Does it automatically follow that the scrap should be recovered? Not at all, since the firm might make a profit of 20 percent if the men and materials were used instead for making new products.

The method of calculation by a government agency for a similar situation would be exactly the same. In fact, if government appropriations specified precisely the quantities, quality, standards, and maximum permissible unit prices for each government service, the problem of economic calculation would not only be exactly the same but the answer could be expressed in terms of a profit equivalent. If the agency could produce at a lower unit cost than specified by Congress, the funds saved would be comparable to profit and would be returned to the Treasury as a dividend to the taxpayers.

In many cases, however, government services are of such a nature that Congress cannot enact precise specifications. For example, the production of plutonium by the Atomic Energy Commission has not yet reached the stage where such specifications can be written. Congress, in effect, tells the commission to produce as much plutonium as it can, according to specifications deemed most suitable by the commission, with a total expenditure not to exceed X million dollars. The commission then has no basis for knowing exactly what dollar value is placed on a pound of plutonium by the Congress. Nevertheless, the commission is not without means of making economic decisions. The problem might be to decide whether it is worth spending Y dollars to recover scrap plutonium which accumulates during the manufacturing process. The decision can be made on the basis of comparison of alternative means of accomplishing a common objective. This objective is to produce the maximum amount of usable plutonium during a specified period within the limits of available funds and other resources. In the light of this objective the commission can afford to spend as much per pound for recovery as it has to spend to produce a pound of new plutonium. If it spent either more or less than this amount, the total usable quantity of plutonium produced during a period would be less than the potential maximum. Faced with this kind of problem, a private business would calculate in precisely the same way. The common objective of new production and recovery operations might be expressed in terms of dollars of profit rather than pounds of product, but the answer would be the same.

When the problem facing the government involves activities such as education, foreign relations, and public recreation where the goals are less tangible, where the results are less subject to measurement, and where the amount of results arising from an increment of expenditures is more difficult to determine, the numbers used in the equations will be less firm. Even so, we conclude, Dr. Mises' arguments notwithstanding, that the differences between business and government in economic calculation lie not so much in the methods of calculation as in the availability of precise numbers with which to calculate.

II

In the foregoing analysis of economic ideas in relation to public budgeting, we have stressed the importance of looking upon budgeting as a problem of relative values and have examined the applicability of two methods—incremental analysis and evaluation of relative effectiveness—in achieving a common objective to budget analysis.

On the administrative implications of these ideas, Professor Key has said, "Perhaps the approach toward the practical working out of the issue lies in canalizing of decisions through the governmental machinery so as to place alternatives in juxtaposition and compel consideration of relative values."[8]

The budget machinery of the federal government does accomplish this purpose. The federal budget forces a simultaneous, or nearly simultaneous, consideration of all the competing claims by the President and the Congress. Moreover, at each level in the administrative hierarchy, the budget forces consideration of the relative merits of competing claims within each jurisdiction.[9]

Budget estimates and justifications are rarely prepared in a manner, however, which makes it easy to compare relative merits. We shall, therefore, now outline a budget system designed to facilitate such comparisons and to apply other ideas derived from the preceding economic analysis. After outlining this system, we shall compare it with other budget methods now being used.

The system to be described will be called the alternative budget system. Under this procedure, each administrative official who prepares a budget estimate, either as a basis for an appropriation request or an allotment request after the appropriation is made, would be required to prepare a basic budget estimate supplemented by skeleton plans for alternative amounts. If the amount of the basic estimate equals 100, the alternatives might represent, respectively, 80, 90, 110, and 120 percent of that amount. The number of alternatives might vary with the situation. Ordinarily, three alternatives would seem to

secure a sufficient range of possibilities. In the interest of providing a safety valve, each subordinate might be permitted to prepare one or more additional alternative budgets totaling more than the top figure prescribed by his superior. In order to focus attention on problems near the margins, the amounts of the alternative budgets should range from a little less than the lowest amount that is likely to be approved to a little more than the recommended amount. Increments of 10 percent might be appropriate in some cases; larger or smaller increments might be required in others.

The establishment of the alternative levels would have to start with the President. He would select alternative levels of overall governmental expenditure, and he would establish corresponding alternative levels for each department or agency. The head of each department or agency would, in turn, establish alternative levels for each of his subordinates which would be consistent with the prescribed departmental levels.

In preparing the alternative budgets, the subordinate official would first indicate, as he does under present procedures, the nature, quantity, and quality of services his agency could render the taxpayers if the amount of the basic budget were approved. In addition, he would indicate the recommended revisions in the plan of service for each of the alternative amounts and the benefits or sacrifices which would result.

At each superior level the responsible official would review the alternative proposals submitted by his several subordinates and select from them the features that would be, in his opinion, the most advantageous to the taxpayers for each alternative amount set for him by the next highest organization level. Finally, the President would submit alternative budgets to the Congress. At this level the alternatives would reflect the major issues involved in determining the work program for the entire government.

The advantages of the alternative budget procedure will be brought out by comparing it with other budget methods and techniques now in use. For convenience, the other techniques will be labeled (a) open-end budgeting, (b) fixed-ceiling budgeting, (c) work measurement and unit costing, (d) increase-decrease analysis, (e) priority listings and (f) item-by-item control. These methods are not mutually exclusive; some of them could very well be incorporated as features of the alternative budget plan. Some are used primarily in budget estimating, others in budget control.

Open-End Budgeting

Some agencies of the federal government (and in some years the Bureau of the Budget) permit subordinate officials to submit a single budget estimate for whatever amount the subordinate decides to recommend. This method has been used not only for preparing requests for appropriations but also for submission of allotment requests to agency heads after the appropriations have been made. This single estimate represents, by and large, the official's judgment as to optimum program for his agency for the ensuing year, tempered perhaps by his judgment as to what the traffic will bear in view of the general political and economic climate existing at the time. No restrictions are placed on him; the sky is the limit so far as the amount he can request is concerned. For this reason, we have selected the short title "open-end budgeting" as being descriptive of this method.

In justification for such a budget estimate, the official, in effect, says, "I think it is desirable (or important, or essential) that the taxpayers be given the services outlined in this budget. Such a program will cost X dollars. Any reductions in the amount requested will deprive the public of exceedingly valuable services." While such general statements are, of course, backed up by more or less specific facts and figures, the information provided leaves many gaps from the point of view of what the superior official needs in order to weigh the importance of each dollar requested by one subordinate against each dollar requested by other subordinates.

Statements which merely prove that a program is desirable do not fulfill the needs of a superior who is faced with the necessity of reducing the total amount requested by the subordinates, not because he thinks the requests are for undesirable or unnecessary purposes, but simply because the pattern is too big for the cloth. The subordinate's budget estimates and justifications, submitted to him under the open-end procedure, are deficient because they do not indicate specifically how plans would be changed if a smaller amount were available or specifically the subordinate's judgment as to the consequences of such a change in plans. Almost the entire burden, then, of ascertaining where the reductions can be made with the least harmful consequences is placed on the superior official, who naturally is less well informed on the details than are his subordinates.

In what way would the assistance rendered by the subordinate to his superior be enhanced if the alternative budget method were used? Under any circumstances the contribution of a subordinate official is limited by the fact that he is concerned with a segment rather than with the whole. His advice as to how much should be appropriated for his particular sphere of activities obviously cannot be accepted without careful scrutiny. He lacks information about other activities which would be necessary to make a comparison of relative importance. Even if he had complete information, he would be quite unique if he did not place a higher valuation on his own activities than others do. This generalization is borne out by the fact that the aggregate of requests from subordinate officials is invariably more than the public, acting through Congress, is willing to devote to public services.

The subordinate administrative official can be expected, however, to make substantial contribution in advising the Congress and the President on the relative merits of competing demands within his own jurisdiction, even though he cannot be expected to weigh those demands against demands in other jurisdictions. The subordinate official can perform an indispensable service by comparing the relative effectiveness of each activity in achieving the goals of his agency and by indicating how he thinks any specified amount of money can best be distributed among the programs of his agency. His service in this respect is valuable not only because considerable technical knowledge and experience usually is required as a basis for arriving at such judgments, but also because the pressure of time may force the President and the Congress to rely greatly on his judgment.

This phase of the contribution of the subordinate official to budget-making is comparable to services I can get from an architect if I should decide to build a house. The architect's advice as to whether I should spend eight, twelve, or sixteen thousand dollars for a house is not very helpful. On the other hand, the architect can be very helpful in advising me as to how I can get the most of what I want in a house for any given sum I choose to spend.

Another way in which a subordinate can be of service is in advising his superiors on probable gains or losses from appropriating more or less for his portion of the government's work. This kind of contribution is comparable to the assistance an architect can render by analyzing the additional features in a house which can be obtained for each increment of cost, and by indicating the features that would have to be sacrificed if costs were reduced by specified amounts.

Alternative budgets prepared by subordinates would take advantage of both of these types of assistance. The subordinate would indicate his judgment as to the best way of using several alternative amounts and in addition he would analyze the benefits to be gained by each increment of funds.

Fixed-Ceiling Budgeting

If the open-ended procedure is one extreme, the fixed-ceiling method represents the opposite pole. Under this plan, a fixed ceiling is established in advance which the subordinate's budget estimate cannot exceed. Such a ceiling creates for the subordinate a situation similar to that facing the President if he should decide to recommend a balanced budget. Then the amount of anticipated revenues constitutes the ceiling on the amount of expenditures he can recommend.

Whatever the merits, or lack thereof, of allowing revenues to determine the total amount to be spent by the government, working to a set ceiling does have the advantage of forcing consideration, at the presidential level, of relative merits to a greater extent than is likely to prevail under open-end budgeting. In open-end budgeting, it is easy to keep adding items that appear to be desirable and thereby pass the buck to the next level of review in the event the total cost of the "desirable" items exceeds an acceptable figure. But prescribing a single fixed ceiling in advance for subordinate levels of the executive branch involves the danger of judging a case before the evidence is heard. The basic reason for requiring estimates from subordinate officials is that higher officials do not have enough detailed information, time, or specialized skill to prepare the plans themselves. How can these officials judge the merits of the experts' plans before they are submitted? In setting the ceiling figures in advance, how can one be sure that the ceiling for one function is not set too high and the ceiling for another too low?

The alternative budget plan, like the fixed-ceiling practice, forces consideration of relative merits within a given amount at each organization level, but the final decision as to amount does not have to be made by the superior until the evidence is in.

Work Load Measurement and Unit Costing

Increasing emphasis has been placed in recent years on work load measurement and unit costing for budgetary purposes. The ultimate goal is to devise units of work and to determine unit costs wherever possible so that budget requests can be stated in this fashion: "It costs X dollars to perform each unit of this type of work. If you want us to perform 100 units, the cost will be 100 times X dollars. If you want only fifty units the cost will be fifty times X dollars."

This approach is useful for budgeting in many situations. It supplies some of the numbers needed for the economic calculation discussed in Part I. Precise, quantitative measures, if pertinent and feasible, are better than vague generalities. Some budget questions cannot be answered, however, in terms of work load and unit cost data. These data will show how many units are being done, but not how many should be done. They show what unit costs are, but not what they should be. They may or may not give an indication of the quality of the work, but they leave unanswered the question of the proper quality standards.

A further limitation on use of work load measurement is that the end product of many agencies is not measurable by any means yet devised. In other cases, the amount of work performed is not a measure of its significance or value. Some work is standby in character. Some facilities, for example, are maintained to meet emergencies if and when they arise. In such cases the less work there is to be done the better. Much of the work of military agencies and fire fighters is of this type. In other cases, too, the amount of work performed is inadequate as an index of results. This is true with respect to many research projects and enforcement activities. In the case of research, it is the final result that counts, not the amount of work required to achieve the result. In enforcement work, the number of infractions dealt with is not an adequate measure since the ideal would be to have no infractions at all.

Lacking an adequate way of measuring or even identifying the end product in precise terms, it is still possible in many cases to develop significant measures of work load of subsidiary activities that contribute to the end product. Examples are number of letters typed, miles patrolled, or purchase orders processed. Detailed data of this type are useful in budgeting but their use is largely confined to the lower organization levels. The sheer mass of such data precludes their extensive use at higher levels.

The alternative budget proposal would permit use of work load and unit cost data to the extent feasible in each case. Under each alternative total figure, the number of units of work that could be performed, the quality standards, and unit costs could be shown. Thus the benefits to be derived from work load measurement would be fully utilized under the alternative budget procedure. In addition, the judgment of subordinates would be obtained on questions which cannot be answered by work load data alone. Such questions involve, for example, the gains or losses of performing alternative amounts of work, the achievement of alternative quality standards, and the effects of spending more or less per unit of work.

Increase-Decrease Analysis

A common technique in the federal government is to require in budget estimates identification of the items representing increases and decreases as compared with the prior year's budget. Special explanations are required for the increases. Budget reviewers are frequently criticized for concentrating on the increases and giving too little attention to items in the base amount. This criticism is justified in part because the amount appropriated last year is not necessarily appropriate for this year and the activities carried on last year are not necessarily appropriate for this year. However, the sheer mass of work involved in reviewing budget estimates precludes examination of every detail every year. Even if it were possible, it would not be necessary, for conditions do not change so fast that every issue has to be rehashed every year.

The basic fault of the increase-decrease method is the fact that is does not require comparison of the relative values of the old and the new. While the proposed increase may be for an eminently desirable purpose, it does not necessarily follow that the appropriation of the agency should be increased. Perhaps other programs of the agency should be cut back enough, or more, to make room for the new. The alternative budget approach has all the advantages of the increase-decrease method without having this basic fault. It would require agencies to weigh the relative merits of all proposals, whether old or new, and thus would reflect the agency's evaluation of the importance of the proposed additions to the spending program in relation to the items composing the base.

Priority Listings

Subordinates are required, in some cases, to indicate priorities of items included in their budget estimates or allotment requests to assist reviewers in determining where cutbacks should be made. Budgets for construction of physical facilities, for example, might contain a listing in priority order of the facilities proposed. The assumption underlying this method is that a budget reduction would be met by eliminating enough projects at the lower end of the list to bring the estimated down to the desired level. When that is the case priority listings are useful. Elimination of the lowest priority items, however, is only one of several means of reducing estimates. Some of the other types of adjustments are as follows: cheaper materials may be used in some or all of the facilities; the size, strength, or durability of the facilities may be decreased; or certain features may be eliminated or postponed until a later date. All of these types of adjustments can be reflected in alternative budgets since they all affect dollar requirements. The priority approach reflects only the one kind of adjustment.

Item-by-Item Control

Approval of individual items of expenditure by higher authority is a common budgetary control technique. Equipment purchases, additions to staff, travel, expensive types of communications as well as entire projects, are frequently subjected to this type of control. An actual case will illustrate the problems involved. During World War II, the Secretary of the Navy was concerned about the expansion of the physical plant of the Navy in the continental United States. In an effort to assure that no facilities would be built unless vitally needed for war purposes and that costs and use of scarce materials would be minimized, the Secretary of the Navy required that all proposed construction projects should be subject to his approval. Prior to this approval they had to be screened at several different levels in the Navy Department. The projects were reviewed by officials in the sponsoring bureau, by the Bureau of Yards and Docks (to insure conformity to wartime engineering standards), by the Chief of Naval Operations (to determine their military necessity), and by a special committee in the Secretary's office composed mainly of civilian businessmen (to determine their overall justification). Even with this series of reviews, the Secretary apparently was not convinced that outlays for facilities were being held down as much as they should be. The process was something less than satisfactory to subordinate officials, too, but for different reasons. They complained of the delays involved in getting a decision and of the amount of time and effort required to justify and rejustify each proposal at the several screening points.

The root of the difficulty, if the thesis of this article is sound, is that controls of individual items do not require or facilitate systematic consideration of relative desirability. Item-by-item control poses the problem at each level of review in these terms: Is the proposal desirable, or essential, or justified? A more pertinent question is: Is the proposal more essential than any alternative use of the funds?

The alternative budget procedure could be applied to this situation in the following manner: bureau chiefs, as well as officials at lower levels, if desired, would be asked to prepare alternative programs for construction of facilities for the period in question. The bureau chiefs in presenting these alternatives would, in effect, tell the Chief of Naval Operations and the Secretary, "If only X dollars are available, I recommend using the money this way . . . ; if two X dollars are available, I think the money should be used this way. . . . The advantages and disadvantages of each plan are as follows: . . . " Having an opportunity to see the picture as a whole, having before him alternatives from which to choose, and having the judgment of his subordinates as to gains and losses resulting from each alternative, the Secretary, it would seem, would be able to make his decision fairly readily and with assurance. It is unlikely that he would have to spend as much time reviewing details as is necessary under the item-by-item approach. He would be in a better position to exercise his responsibilities while the subordinates would be freed from the delays, burdens, and irritation invariably involved in piece-by-piece screening processes.

In addition to the specific points discussed above, the alternative budget plan appears to have certain general advantages. It would, we believe, make budgeting a little more palatable to the technically minded operating official who must prepare and justify budgets. His role will be less that of a special pleader for *the* plan he thinks should be accepted and more that of an expert adviser. He will be less like an architect who tries to sell a client on a single plan costing a certain sum and more like an architect advising the client on the relative merits of several house plans and suggesting how the client can get the most for his money regardless of the amount he decides to spend.

Budget analysts under this plan would have a frame of reference which would enable them to operate more effectively. At present, much of their effort is directed toward determining desirability or necessity and not enough attention is given to issues of relative desirability. Under the plan suggested here, the primary job of the budget analyst would be to assist his superior in weighing the relative value of alternative uses of each increment of funds as a step in developing the alternatives to be submitted to the next higher level in the organization. Another aspect of his work would be to explore some of the many possible variations and combinations of features that could not be reflected in the limited number of alternatives formally submitted by the lower officials. Moreover, the analyst would have to check for accuracy, objectivity, and general adequacy the subordinate official's statements of the advantages and disadvantages of the alternatives submitted.

Another significant advantage of the alternative budget proposal is that it would make budgeting somewhat less authoritarian. It would make the budget recommendations of administrative officials less final without weakening in any way their usefulness.

At present, an item screened out of a budget by any administrative official even though it is of major importance is not considered at later stages unless it is brought to the attention of higher executive officials or the Congress by some method which is prohibited by the prevailing rules. To put it mildly, quite definite steps are taken to discourage late consideration. A bureau chief, for example, would be considered out of bounds if he appealed to the President for consideration of an item screened out of his budget by his departmental head. Any administrative officer is prohibited from recommending congressional consideration of any alternatives to the single proposal contained in the President's budget unless specifically requested to do so by a member of Congress. Publication of requests submitted by the departments to the President is also banned.

It is not at all unlikely that superior administrative officials or the Congress would want to adopt some of these screened-out items if they had an opportunity to consider them. Since Congress, in our form of government, is largely responsible for deciding what shall or shall not be done by the executive agencies, the wisdom of such strict censoring of proposals submitted for consideration by Congress seems questionable. Since the President's budget estimates are only recommendations, there would seem to be no disadvantage in his outlining the major alternatives from which he made his selection. In this way the views of subordinates who may have an honest difference of opinion with the President could be submitted to Congress for consideration openly and without subterfuge. After considering the evidence pertaining to each alternative, Congress could then take its choice. Since the making of such choices is involved in exercising congressional control over the purse strings—a control which historically and currently is a basic cornerstone of democratic government—the provision of information which will assist Congress in evaluating the major alternative courses is of vital importance.[10]

In general, the alternative budget plan is designed to emphasize throughout the budget process the economic ideas discussed in Part I of this article. Its purpose is to pose budget questions at every level in terms of relative value. It also is designed to make maximum use of the expert knowledge and judgment of officials at the lower organization levels by having them analyze, incrementally, the estimates of their agencies and evaluate the relative effectiveness of their several activities in achieving the goals of their organizations.

In proposing this system, I am not particularly concerned with detailed mechanics. There are undoubtedly other ways of accomplishing substantially the same results as this plan is designed to achieve. More important than the precise mechanics is the way of looking at budget problems, the approach to budget analysis and control which this plan reflects.

How practical is the alternative budget plan? How well will it work in practice? The answers to these questions depend in large measure on the relationships between superior and subordinate and between the administration and the Congress. Neither this system nor any other can work satisfactorily if the relations are strained, if the reviewer lacks confidence in the integrity or judgment of the official who is submitting the estimate, or if those who prepare the estimates are not sincerely interested in providing information which the reviewers need to form an intelligent judgment on the merits of the issues.

Perhaps undue faith in the rationality of man underlies the approach to budgeting outlined in this article. In real life, budget decisions are undoubtedly influenced to a greater or lesser extent by such noneconomic and non-rational factors as pride and prejudice, provincialism and politics. These aspects deserve consideration, but they lie beyond the scope of this article. My primary purpose herein has been to stimulate further consideration of the economic aspects of budgeting.[11]

Notes

1. V. O. Key, Jr., "The Lack of a Budgetary Theory," *American Political Science Review,* 34 (December, 1940), 1137–1144.
2. Ideas derived from Herbert A. Simon's works concerning the applicability of economic concepts to administration have been particularly useful for this purpose. See his *Administrative Behavior* (New York: Macmillan, 1947).
3. As quoted by Key, *op. cit.,* p. 1139.
4. L. M. Fraser, *Economic Thought and Language* (A. and C. Black Ltd., 1937), p. 103.
5. This method, as it applies to public administration in general, has been extensively analyzed by Herbert A. Simon under the heading of the "criterion of efficiency," *op. cit.,* pp. 172–197.
6. Key, *op. cit.,* p. 1143.
7. Ludwig von Mises, *Bureaucracy* (New Haven: Yale University Press, 1944), p. 47.
8. *Op. cit.,* p. 1142.
9. See also, Simon, *op. cit.,* p. 214.
10. Simon also has recommended submission of alternative budget plans to legislatures for substantially the same reason. *Op. cit.,* p. 195.
11. Note on relation to a performance budget. A performance budget, as proposed by the Hoover Commission, would give primary emphasis to the result or end product to be obtained with the money spent by the government. The commission wisely criticized budget presentations that deal only with the ingredients that are required to produce the end product. Certainly first attention should be given to what is to be accomplished rather than to the people who have to be employed, or the materials which have to be bought, in order to accomplish the basic purpose. Emphasizing performance or end results does not require us to ignore the ingredients or the means to the ends. It should not lead to that result. Important budget issues often involve only the means. While there may be agreement about purpose, the methods may be in dispute. For example, a conservation agency may be responsible for inducing producer-conservation of some natural resource. Should the objective be accomplished by an educational program, by regulatory action, or by subsidy? The alternative budget plan is flexible enough to be adapted to the situation. Alternative purposes as well as alternative methods could and should be reflected in the alternative budget estimates. Whether greater emphasis would be placed on purposes than on methods would depend upon the nature of the problem.

5

Political Implications of Budgetary Reform

Aaron Wildavsky

A large part of the literature on budgeting in the United States is concerned with reform. The goals of the proposed reforms are couched in similar language—economy, efficiency, improvement, or just better budgeting. The President, the Congress and its committees, administrative agencies, even the interested citizenry are all to gain by some change in the way the budget is formulated, presented, or evaluated. There is little or no realization among the reformers, however, that any effective change in budgetary relationships must necessarily alter the outcomes of the budgetary process. Otherwise why bother? Far from being a neutral matter of "better budgeting," proposed reforms inevitably contain important implications for the political system, that is for the "who gets what" of governmental decisions. What are some of the major political implications of budgetary reform and where should we look to increase our knowledge about how the budget is made? We begin with the noblest vision of reform: the development of a normative theory of budgeting that would provide the basis for allocating funds among competing activities.

A Normative Theory of Budgeting?

In 1940, in what is still the best discussion of the subject, V. O. Key lamented "The Lack of a Budgetary Theory." He called for a theory which would help answer the basic question of budgeting on the expenditure side: "On what basis shall it be decided to allocate X dollars to Activity A instead of Activity B?"[1] Although several attempts have been made to meet this challenge,[2] not one has come close to succeeding. No progress has been made for the excellent reason that the task, as posed, is

Source: Reprinted with permission from *Public Administration Review* 21 (Autumn 1961): 183–190. © 1961 by The American Society for Public Administration (ASPA), 1120 G Street NW, Suite 500, Washington D.C. 20005. All rights reserved.

impossible to fulfill.[3] The search for an unrealizable goal indicates serious weaknesses in prevailing conceptions of the budget.

If a normative theory of budgeting is to be more than an academic exercise, it must actually guide the making of governmental decisions. The items of expenditures which are passed by Congress, enacted into law, and spent must in large measure conform to the theory if it is to have any practical effect. This is tantamount to prescribing that virtually all the activities of government be carried on according to the theory. For whatever the government does must be paid for from public funds; it is difficult to think of any policy which can be carried out without money.

The budget is the life-blood of the government, the financial reflection of what the government does or intends to do. A theory which contains criteria for determining what ought to be in the budget is nothing less than a theory stating what the government ought to do. If we substitute the words "what the government ought to do" for the words "ought to be in the budget," it becomes clear that a normative theory of budgeting would be a comprehensive and specific political theory detailing what the government's activities ought to be at a particular time. A normative theory of budgeting, therefore, is utopian in the fullest sense of that word; its accomplishment and acceptance would mean the end of conflict over the government's role in society.

By suppressing dissent, totalitarian regimes enforce their normative theory of budgeting on others. Presumably, we reject this solution to the problem of conflict in society and insist on democratic procedures. How then arrive at a theory of budgeting which is something more than one man's preferences?

The crucial aspect of budgeting is whose preferences are to prevail in disputes about which activities are to be carried on and to what degree, in the light of limited resources. The problem is not only "how shall budgetary benefits be maximized?" as if it made no difference who received them, but also "who shall receive budgetary benefits and how much?" One may purport to solve the problem of budgeting by proposing a normative theory (or a welfare function or a hierarchy of values) which specifies a method for maximizing returns for budgetary expenditures. In the absence of ability to impose a set of preferred policies on others, however, this solution breaks down. It amounts to no more than saying that if you can persuade others to agree with you, than you will have achieved agreement. Or it begs the question of what kind of policies will be fed into the scheme by assuming that these are agreed upon. Yet we hardly need argue that a state of universal agreement has not yet arisen.

Another way of avoiding the problem of budgeting is to treat society as a single organism with a consistent set of desires and a life of its own, much as a single consumer might be assumed to have a stable demand and indifference schedule. Instead of revenue being raised and the budget being spent by and for many individuals who may have their own preferences and feelings, as is surely the case, these processes are treated, in effect, as if a single individual were the only one concerned. This approach avoids the central problems of social conflict, of somehow aggregating different preferences so that a decision may emerge. How can we compare the worth of expenditures for irrigation to certain farmers with the worth of widening a highway to motorists and the desirability of aiding old people to pay medical bills as against the degree of safety provided by an expanded defense program?

The process we have developed for dealing with interpersonal comparisons in Government is not economic but political. Conflicts are resolved (under agreed upon rules) by translating different preferences through the political system into units called votes or into types of authority like a veto power. There need not be (and there is not) full agreement on goals or the preferential weights to be accorded to different goals. Congressmen directly threaten, compromise, and trade favors in regard to policies in which values are implicitly weighted, and then agree to register the results according to the rules for tallying votes.

The burden of calculation is enormously reduced for three primary reasons: first, only the small number of alternatives which are politically feasible at any one time are considered; second, these policies in a democracy typically differ only in small increments from previous policies on which there is a store of relevant information; and, third, each participant may ordinarily assume that he need consider only his preferences and those of his powerful opponents since the American political system works to assure that every significant interest has representation at some key point. Since only a relatively few interest groups contend on any given issue and no single item is considered in conjunction with all others (because budgets are made in bits and pieces), a huge and confusing array of interests are not activated all at once.

In the American context, a typical result is that bargaining takes place among many dispersed centers of influence and that favors are swapped as in the case of log-rolling public works appropriations. Since there is no one group of men who can necessarily impose their preferences upon others within the American political system, special coalitions are formed to support or oppose specific policies. Support is sought in this system of fragmented power at numerous centers of influence—Congressional committees, the Congressional leadership, the President, the Budget Bureau, interdepartmental committees, departments, bureaus, private groups, and so on. Nowhere does a single authority have power to determine what is going to be in the budget.

The Politics in Budget Reform

The seeming irrationalities[4] of a political system which does not provide for even formal consideration of the budget as a whole (except by the President who cannot control the final result) has led to many attacks and proposals for reform. The tradition of reform in America is a noble one, not easily to be denied. But in this case it is doomed to failure because it is aimed at the wrong target. If the present budgetary process is rightly or wrongly deemed unsatisfactory, then one must alter in some respect the political system of which the budget is but an expression. It makes no sense to speak as if one could make drastic changes in budgeting without also altering the distribution of influence. But this task is inevitably so formidable (though the reformers are not directly conscious of it) that most adversaries prefer to speak of changing the budgetary process, as if by some subtle alchemy the irrefractible political element could be transformed into a more malleable substance.

The reader who objects to being taken thus far only to be told the obvious truth that the budget is inextricably linked to the political system would have a just complaint if the implications of this remark were truly recognized in the literature on budgeting. But this is not so. One implication is that by far the most significant way of influencing the budget is to introduce basic political changes (or to wait for secular changes like the growing industrialization of the South). Provide the President with more powers enabling him to control the votes of his party in Congress; enable a small group of Congressmen to command a majority of votes on all occasions so that they can push their program through. Then you will have exerted a profound influence on the content of the budget.

A second implication is that no significant change can be made in the budgetary process without affecting the political process. There would be no point in tinkering with the budgetary machinery if, at the end, the pattern of budgetary decisions was precisely the same as before. On the contrary, reform has little justification unless it results in different kinds of decisions and, when and if this has been accomplished, the play of political forces has necessarily been altered. Enabling some political forces to gain at the expense of others requires the explicit introduction and defense of value premises which are ordinarily missing from proposals for budgetary reform.

Since the budget represents conflicts over whose preferences shall prevail, the third implication is that one cannot speak of "better budgeting" without considering who benefits and who loses or demonstrating that no one loses. Just as the supposedly objective criterion of "efficiency" has been shown to have normative implications,[5] so a "better budget" may well be a cloak for hidden policy preferences. To propose that the President be given an item veto, for example, means an attempt to increase the influence of the particular interests which gain superior access to the Chief Executive rather than, say, to the Congress. Only if one eliminates the element of conflict over expenditures, can it be assumed that a reform which enables an official to do a better job from his point of view is simply "good" without considering the policy implications for others.

Arthur Smithies may stand as a typical proponent of a typical reform. Identifying rationality with a comprehensive overview of the budget by a single person or group, Smithies despairs of the fragmented approach taken by Congress and proposes a remedy. He suggests that a Joint (Congressional) Budget Policy committee be formed and empowered to consider all proposals for revenue and expenditure in a single package and that their decisions be made binding by a concurrent resolution. And he presents his reform as a moderate proposal to improve the rationality of the budget process.[6] If the proposed Joint Committee were unable to secure the passage

of its recommendations, as would surely be the case, it would have gone to enormous trouble without accomplishing anything but a public revelation of futility. The impotence of the Joint Committee on the Legislative Budget,[7] the breakdown of the single Congressional attempt to develop a comprehensive legislative budget,[8] and the failure of Congressional attempts to control the Council of Economic Advisers[9] and the Budget Bureau,[10] all stem from the same cause. There is no cohesive group in Congress capable of using these devices to affect decision making by imposing its preferences on a majority of Congressmen. Smithies' budgetary reform presupposes a completely different political system from the one which exists in the United States. To be sure, there is a name for a committee which imposes its will on the legislature and tolerates no rival committees—it is called a Cabinet on the British model. In the guise of a procedural change in the preparation of the budget by Congress, Smithies is actually proposing a revolutionary move which would mean the virtual introduction of the British Parliamentary system if it were successful.

Smithies (pp. 188–225) suggests that his proposals would be helpful to the President. But the membership of the Joint Committee would be made up largely of conservatives from safe districts who are not dependent on the President, who come from a different constituency than he does, but with whom he must deal in order to get any money for his programs. Should the Joint Committee ever be able to command a two-thirds vote of the Congress, it could virtually ignore the President in matters of domestic policy and run the executive branch so that it is accountable only to them.

I do not mean to disparage in any way the important problem of efficiency, of finding ways to maximize budgetary benefits given a specified distribution of shares. In principle, there seems to be no reason why policy machinery could not be so arranged as to alter the ratio of inputs to outputs without changing the distribution of shares. One can imagine situations in which everyone benefits or where the losses suffered in one respect are made up by greater gains elsewhere. There may be cases where such losses as do exist are not felt by the participants and they may be happy to make changes which increase their felt benefits. The inevitable lack of full information and the disinclination of participants to utilize their political resources to the fullest extent undoubtedly leave broad areas of inertia and inattention open for change. Thus, the "slack" in the system may leave considerable room for ingenuity and innovation in such areas as benefit cost analysis and the comparability and interrelatedness of public works without running into outstanding political difficulties or involving large changes in the system. Most practical budgeting may take place in a twilight zone between politics and efficiency. Without presenting a final opinion on this matter, it does seem to me that the problem of distributing shares has either been neglected entirely or has been confused with the problem of efficiency to the detriment of both concerns. The statements in this paper should be understood to refer only to the question of determining shares in the budget.

What Do We Know About Budgeting?

The overriding concern of the literature on budgeting with normative theory and reform has tended to obscure the fact that we know very little about it. Aside from the now classical articles on Congressional oversight of administration by Arthur MacMahon,[11] an excellent study of internal budgetary procedures in the Army by Frederick C. Mosher,[12] and an interesting case history by Kathryn S. Arnow,[13] there is virtually nothing of substance about how or why budgetary decisions are actually made. Of course, the general literature on decision making in national government provides some valuable propositions, but it is not keyed-in to the budgetary process. Yet the opportunities for developing and testing important propositions about budgetary decisions are extraordinarily good and I would like to suggest a few of the many possible approaches here.

How do various agencies decide how much to ask for? Most agencies cannot simply ask for everything they would like to have. If they continually ask for much more than they can get, their opinions are automatically discounted and they risk a loss of confidence by the Budget Bureau and Appropriations subcommittees which damages the prospects of their highest priority items. The agencies cannot even ask for all that they are authorized to spend because their authorizations commonly run way ahead of any realistic expectation of achievement. At the same time, they do not wish to sell themselves short. The result is that the men who make this choice (an official title is no certain guide to whom they are) seek signals from the environment—supporting interests, their own personnel, current events, last year's actions, attitudes of Congressmen, and so on—to arrive at a composite estimate of "what will go." A combination of interviews, case studies, and direct observation should enable the researcher to determine what these signals are, to construct propositions accounting for the agencies' budgetary position, and to generally recreate the environment out of which these choices come.

Once having decided what they would like to get, how do agencies go about trying to achieve their objectives? Today, we do not even have a preliminary list of the most common strategies used by participants in trying to influence budgetary outcomes. Again, the techniques listed above should bring the necessary data to light.

Perhaps a few examples will demonstrate the importance of understanding budgetary strategies. There are times when an agency wishes to cut its own budget because it has lost faith in a program, for internal disciplinary reasons, or because it would like to use the money elsewhere. If the agency is particularly well endowed with effective clientele groups, however, it may not only fail in this purpose but may actually see the appropriation increased as this threat mobilizes the affected interests. One budget officer informed me that he tried to convince the Budget Bureau to undertake two projects which the agency did not want but which several influential Congressmen felt strongly about. Otherwise, the official argued, the Congressmen would secure their desires by offering additional projects to their colleagues. The Budget Bureau turned him down and the result was nine unwanted projects instead of two.

The appearance of a budget may take on considerable importance, a circumstance which is often neglected by proponents of program budgeting. Suppose that an agency has strong clientele backing for individual projects. It is likely to gain by presenting them separately so that any cut may be readily identified and support easily mobilized. Lumping a large number of items together may facilitate cuts on an across-the-board basis. Items lacking support, on the other hand, may do better by being placed in large categories so that it is more difficult to single them out for deeper slashes.

We might also inquire (through questionnaires, interviews, direct observation, documentary research) about the participants' perceptions of their roles and the reciprocal expectations they have about the behavior of others. In speaking to officials concerned with budgeting I was impressed with how often the behavior they described was predicated on a belief about what others would do, how they would react in turn, how a third participant would react to this result and so on. Budgetary items are commonly adjusted on the basis of mutual expectations or on a single participant's notion of the role he is expected to play. I strongly suspect, on the basis of some interviewing, that if we studied conceptions of role prevalent on the House Appropriations Committee, their transmittal to new members and staff, and the consequent resistance of members to seeing party as relevant to choice, we would understand a great deal more about the characteristic behavior of many members as budget cutters.

My interviews suggest that the administrator's perception of Congressional knowledge and motivation helps determine the kind of relationships he seeks to establish. The administrator who feels that the members of his appropriations subcommittees are not too well informed on specifics and that they evaluate the agency's program on the basis of feedback from constituents, stresses the role of supporting interests in maintaining good relations with Congressmen. He may not feel the need to be too careful with his estimates. The administrator who believes that the Congressmen are well informed and fairly autonomous is likely to stress personal relationships and demonstrations of good work as well as clientele support. Priority in research should be given to study of these perceptions and the ways in which they determine behavior.

Another approach would be to locate and segregate classes of administrative officials who are found by observation to have or not to have the confidence of the appropriations committees and to seek to explain the differences. For if there is any one thing which participants in budgeting are likely to stress, it is the importance of maintaining relations of confidence and they are highly conscious of what this requires. Since it appears from preliminary investigation that the difference is not accounted for by the popularity of the agency or its programs, it is possible that applications of some gross psychological and skill categories would reveal interesting results.

Many participants in budgeting (in the agencies, Congress, the Budget Bureau) speak of somehow having arrived at a total figure which represents an agency's or an activity's "fair share" of the budget. The fact that a fair share concept exists may go a long way toward explaining the degree of informal coordination that exists among the participants in budgeting. Investigation of how these figures are arrived at and communicated would help us understand how notions of limits (ceilings and floors) enter into budgetary decisions. A minimum effort in this direction would require the compilation of appropriations histories of various agencies and programs rather than just individual case histories which concentrate on some specific event or moment in time. Investigation of the Tennessee Valley Authority's experience in securing electric power appropriations, over a twenty-five-year period, for example, reveals patterns and presents explanatory possibilities which would not otherwise be available.[14]

By its very nature the budgetary process presents excellent opportunities for the use of quantitative data although these must be used with great caution and with special attention to their theoretical relevance. Richard Fenno has collected figures on thirty-seven bureaus dealing with domestic policies from 1947 to 1958 from their initial estimates to decisions by the Budget Bureau, appropriations committees in both houses, conference committees, and floor action. Using these figures he expects to go beyond the usual facile generalizations that the House cuts and the Senate raises bureau estimates, to the much more interesting question of determining the conditions under which the patterns that do exist actually obtain.[15] Although such data do not by any means tell the whole story, they can be used to check generalizations about patterns of floor action or conference committee action which would not otherwise be possible.

After giving the matter considerable thought, I have decided that it would not be fruitful to devise a measure which would ostensibly give an objective rank ordering of bureaus and departments according to their degree of success in securing appropriations. The first measure which might be used would be to compare an agency's initial requests with its actual appropriations. The difficulty here is that agency estimates are not merely a measure of their desire but also include a guess as to what they can reasonably expect to get. The agency which succeeds in getting most of what it desires, therefore, may be the one which is best at figuring out what it is likely to get. A better measure, perhaps, would be an agency's record in securing appropriations calculated as percentages above or below previous years' appropriations. But this standard also leads to serious problems. There are fortuitous events—Sputnik, a drought, advances in scientific knowledge—which are beyond the control of an agency but which may have a vital bearing on its success in getting appropriations. Indeed, some "affluent agencies" like the National Institutes of Health may find that there is little they can do to stop vast amounts of money from coming in; they may not even be able to cut their own budgets when they want to do so. Furthermore, agencies generally carry on a wide variety of programs and the total figures may hide the fact that some are doing very well and others quite poorly. Thus it would be necessary to validate the measure by an intensive study of each agency's appropriations history and this would appear to make the original computation unnecessary.

The purpose of this suggested research, much of which the author intends to pursue, is to formulate empirically valid propositions which will be useful in constructing theories (general explanations) accounting for the operation and outcomes of the budgetary process. A theory of influence would describe the power relationships among the participants, explain why some are more successful than others in achieving their budgetary goals, state the conditions under which various strategies are or are not efficacious, and in this way account for the pattern of budgetary decisions.

With such a theory, it would become possible to specify the advantages which some participants gain under the existing system, to predict the consequences of contemplated changes on the distribution of influence, and to anticipate sources of opposition. Possibly, those desiring change might then suggest a strategy to overcome the expected resistance. But they would not, in their scholarly role, accuse their opponents of irrationality in not wishing to have their throats cut.

It would also be desirable to construct a theory of budgetary calculation by specifying the series of related factors (including influence relationships) which affect the choice of competing alternatives by the decision makers. This kind of theory would describe how problems arise, how they are broken down, how information is fed into the system, and how the participants are related to one another, and how

a semblance of coordination is achieved. The kinds of calculations which actually guide the making of decisions would be emphasized. One would like to know, for example, whether long-range planning really exists or is merely engaged in for form's sake while decisions are really based on short-run indices like reactions to last year's appropriation requests. If changes in procedure lead to different kinds of calculations, one would like to be able to predict what the impact on decisions was likely to be.

The Goals of Knowledge and Reform

Concentration on developing at least the rudiments of a descriptive theory is not meant to discourage concern with normative theory and reform. On the contrary, it is worthwhile studying budgeting from both standpoints. Surely, it is not asking too much to suggest that a lot of reform be preceded by a little knowledge. The point is that until we develop more adequate descriptive theory about budgeting, until we know something about the "existential situation" in which the participants find themselves under our political system, proposals for major reform must be based on woefully inadequate understanding. A proposal which alters established relationships, which does not permit an agency to show certain programs in the most favorable light, which does not tell influential Congressmen what they want to know, which changes prevailing expectations about the behavior of key participants, or which leads to different calculations of an agency's fair share, would have many consequences no one is even able to guess at today. Of course, small, incremental changes proceeding in a pragmatic fashion of trial and error could proceed as before without benefit of theory; but this is not the kind of change with which the literature on budgeting is generally concerned.

Perhaps the "study of budgeting" is just another expression for the "study of politics"; yet one cannot study everything at once, and the vantage point offered by concentration on budgetary decisions offers a useful and much neglected perspective from which to analyze the making of policy. The opportunities for comparison are ample, the outcomes are specific and quantifiable, and a dynamic quality is assured by virtue of the comparative ease with which one can study the development of budgetary items over a period of years.

Notes

1. V. O. Key, Jr., "The Lack of a Budgetary Theory," 34 *American Political Science Review* 1137–1144 (December 1940).
2. Verne B. Lewis, "Toward a Theory of Budgeting," 12 *Public Administration Review* 42–54 (Winter 1952); "Symposium on Budgetary Theory," 10 *Public Administration Review* 20–31 (Spring 1954); Arthur Smithies, *The Budgetary Process in the United States* (McGraw-Hill, 1955).
3. Key, in fact, shies away from the implications of his question and indicates keen awareness of the political problems involved. But the question has been posed by subsequent authors largely in the terms in which he framed it.
4. See Charles E. Lindblom, "The Science of 'Muddling' Through," 19 *Public Administration Review* 79–88 (Spring 1959), for a description and criticism of the comprehensive method. See also his "Decision-Making in Taxation and Expenditure" in National Bureau of Economic Research, *Public Finances: Needs, Sources, and Utilization* (Princeton University Press, 1961), pp. 295–327, and his "Policy Analysis," 48 *American Economic Review* 298–312 (June 1958).
5. Dwight Waldo, *The Administrative State* (Ronald Press, 1948); Herbert A. Simon, "The Criterion of Efficiency," in *Administrative Behavior;* 2nd ed. (Macmillan, 1957), pp. 172–197.
6. Smithies, *op. cit.,* pp. 192–193ff.
7. Avery Leiserson, "Coordination of the Federal Budgetary and Appropriations Procedures Under the Legislative Reorganization Act of 1946," 1 *National Tax Journal* 118–126 (June 1948).
8. Robert Ash Wallace, "Congressional Control of the Budget," 3 *Midwest Journal of Political Science* 160–162 (May 1959); Dalmas H. Nelson, "The Omnibus Appropriations Act of 1950," 15 *Journal of Politics* 274–288 (May 1953); Representative John Phillips, "The Hadacol of the Budget Makers," 4 *National Tax Journal* 255–268 (September 1951).
9. Roy Blough, "The Role of the Economist in Federal Policy-Making," 51 *University of Illinois Bulletin* (November 1953); Lester Seligman, "Presidential Leadership: The Inner Circle and Institutionalization," 18 *Journal of Politics* 410–426 (August 1956); Edwin G. Nourse, *Economics in the Public Service: Administrative Aspects of the Employment Act* (Harcourt Brace, 1953); Ronald C. Hood, "Reorganizing the Council of Economic Advisors." 69 *Political Science Quarterly* 413–437 (September 1954).
10. Fritz Morstein Marx, "The Bureau of the Budget: Its Evolution and Present Role II," 39 *American Political Science Review* 363–398 (October 1945); Richard Neustadt, "The Presidency and Legislation: The Growth of Central Clearance," 48 *Ibid.* 631–671 (September 1954); Seligman, *op. cit.*
11. Arthur McMahon, "Congressional Oversight of Administration," 58 *Political Science Quarterly* 161–190, 380–414 (June, September 1943).
12. Frederick C. Mosher, *Program Budgeting:* Theory and Practice, with Particular Reference to the U.S. Department of the Army (Public Administrative Service, 1954).
13. *The Department of Commerce Field Offices,* Inter-University Case Series No. 21 (University of Alabama Press, 1954).
14. See Aaron B. Wildavsky, "TVA and Power Politics," 55 *American Political Science Review* 576–590 (September 1961).
15. From a research proposal kindly lent me by Richard Fenno. See also his excellent paper, "The House Appropriations Committee as a Political System: The Problem of Integration," delivered at the 1961 meeting of the American Political Science Association.

6

The Road to PPB: The Stages of Budget Reform

Allen Schick

Among the new men in the nascent PPB staffs and the fellow travellers who have joined the bandwagon, the mood is of "a revoluntionary development in the history of government management." There is excited talk about the differences between what has been and what will be; of the benefits that will accrue from an explicit and "hard" appraisal of objectives and alternatives; of the merits of multiyear budget forecasts and plans; of the great divergence between the skills and role of the analyst and the job of the examiner; of the realignments in government structure that might result from changes in the budget process.

This is not the only version, however. The closer one gets to the nerve centers of budget life—the Divisions in the Bureau of the Budget and the budget offices in the departments and agencies—the more one is likely to hear that "there's nothing very new in PPB; it's hardly different from what we've been doing until now." Some old-timers interpret PPB as a revival of the performance budgeting venture of the early 1950's. Others belittle the claim that—before PPB—decisions on how much to spend for personnel or supplies were made without real consideration of the purposes for which these inputs were to be invested. They point to previous changes that have been in line with PPB, albeit without PPB's distinctive package of techniques and nomenclature. Such things as the waning role of the "green sheets" in the central budget process, the redesign of the appropriation structure and the development of activity classifications, refinements in work measurement, productivity analysis, and other types of output measurement, and the utilization of the Spring Preview for a broad look at programs and major issues.

Source: Reprinted with permission from *Public Administration Review* 26 (December 1966): 243–258. © 1966 by The American Society for Public Administration (ASPA), 1120 G Street NW, Washington, D.C. 20005. All rights reserved.

Between the uncertain protests of the traditional budgeteer and the uncertain expectations of the *avant garde,* there is a third version. The PPB system that is being developed portends a radical change in the central function of budgeting, but it is anchored to half a century of tradition and evolution. The budget system of the future will be a product of past and emerging developments; that is, it will embrace both the budgetary functions introduced during earlier stages of reform as well as the planning function which is highlighted by PPB. PPB is the first budget system *designed* to accommodate the multiple functions of budgeting.

The Functions of Budgeting

Budgeting always has been conceived as a process for systematically relating the expenditure of funds to the accomplishment of planned objectives. In this important sense, there is a bit of PPB in every budget system. Even in the initial stirrings of budget reform more than 50 years ago, there were cogent statements on the need for a budget system to plan the objectives and activities of government and to furnish reliable data on what was to be accomplished with public funds. In 1907, for example, the New York Bureau of Municipal Research published a sample "program memorandum" that contained some 125 pages of functional accounts and data for the New York City Health Department.[1]

However, this orientation was not *explicitly* reflected in the budget systems—national, state, or local—that were introduced during the first decades of this century, nor is it *explicitly* reflected in the budget systems that exist today. The plain fact is that planning is not the only function that must be served by a budget system. The *management* of ongoing activities and the *control* of spending are two functions which, in the past, have been given priority over the planning function. Robert Anthony identifies three distinct administrative processes, strategic planning, management control, and operational control.

Strategic planning is the process of deciding on objectives of the organization, on changes in these objectives, on the resources used to attain these objectives, and on the policies that are to govern the acquisition, use, and disposition of these resources. *Management control* is the process by which managers assure that resources are obtained and used

Table 1
Some basic differences between budget orientations

Characteristic	Control	Management	Planning
Personnel Skill	Accounting	Administration	Economics
Information Focus	Objects	Activities	Purposes
Key Budget Stage (central)	Execution	Preparation	Pre-preparation
Breadth of Measurement	Discrete	Discrete/activities	Comprehension
Role of Budget Agency	Fiduciary	Efficiency	Policy
Decisional-Flow	Upward-aggregative	Upward-aggregative	Downward-disaggregative
Type of Choice	Incremental	Incremental	Teletic
Control Responsibility	Central	Operating	Operating
Management Responsibility	Dispersed	Central	Supervisory
Planning Responsibility	Dispersed	Dispersed	Central
Budget-Appropriations Classifications	Same	Same	Different
Appropriations-Organizational Link	Direct	Direct	Crosswalk

effectively and efficiently in the accomplishment of the organization's objectives.

Operational control is the process of assuring that specific tasks are carried out effectively and efficiently.[2]

Every budget system, even rudimentary ones, comprises planning, management, and control processes. Operationally, these processes often are indivisible, but for analytic purposes they are distinguished here. In the context of budgeting, *planning* involves the determination of objectives, the evaluation of alternative courses of action, and the authorization of select programs. Planning is linked most closely to budget preparation, but it would be a mistake to disregard the management and control elements in budget preparation or the possibilities for planning during other phases of the budget year. Clearly, one of the major aims of PPB is to convert the annual routine of preparing a budget into a conscious appraisal and formulation of future goals and policies. Management involves the programming of approved goals into specific projects and activities, the design of organizational units to carry out approved programs, and the staffing of these units and the procurement of necessary resources. The management process is spread over the entire budget cycle; ideally, it is the link between goals made and activities undertaken. *Control* refers to the process of binding operating officials to the policies and plans set by their superiors. Control is predominant during the execution and audit stages,

although the form of budget estimates and appropriations often is determined by control considerations. The assorted controls and reporting procedures that are associated with budget execution—position controls, restrictions on transfers, requisition procedures, and travel regulations, to mention the more prominent ones—have the purpose of securing compliance with policies made by central authorities.

Very rarely are planning, management, and control given equal attention in the operation of budget systems. As a practical matter, planning, management, and control have tended to be competing processes in budgeting with no neat division of functions among the various participants. Because time is scarce, central authorities must be selective in the things they do. Although this scarcity counsels the devolution of control responsibilities to operating levels, the lack of reliable and relied-on internal control systems has loaded central authorities with control functions at the expense of the planning function. Moreover, these processes often require different skills and generate different ways of handling the budget mission, so that one type of perspective tends to predominate over the others. Thus, in the staffing of the budget offices, there has been a shift from accountants to administrators as budgeting has moved from a control to a management posture. The initial experience with PPB suggests that the next transition might be from administrators to economists as budgeting takes on more of the planning function.

Most important, perhaps, are the differential informational requirements of planning, control, and management processes. Informational needs differ in terms of time spans, levels of aggregation, linkages with organizational and operating units, and input-output foci. The apparent solution is to design a system that serves the multiple needs of budgeting. Historically, however, there has been a strong tendency to homogenize informational structures and to rely on a single classification scheme to serve all budgetary purposes. For the most part, the informational system has been structured to meet the purposes of control. As a result, the type of multiple-purpose budget system envisioned by PPB has been avoided.

An examination of budget systems should reveal whether greater emphasis is placed at the *central levels* on planning, management, or control. A *planning orientation* focuses on the broadest range of issues: What are the long-range goals and policies of the government and how are these related to particular expenditure choices? What criteria should be used in appraising the requests of the agencies? Which programs should be initiated or terminated, and which expanded or curtailed? A *management orientation* deals with less fundamental issues: What is the best way to organize for the accomplishment of a prescribed task? Which of several staffing alternatives achieves the most effective relationship between the central and field offices? Of the various grants and projects proposed, which should be approved? A *control orientation* deals with a relatively narrow range of concerns: How can agencies be held to the expenditure ceilings established by the legislature and chief executive? What reporting procedures should be used to enforce propriety in expenditures? What limits should be placed on agency spending for personnel and equipment?

It should be clear that every budget system contains planning, management, and control features. A control orientation means the subordination, not the absence, of planning and management functions. In the matter of orientations, we are dealing with relative emphases, not with pure dichotomies. The germane issue is the balance among these vital functions at the central level. Viewed centrally, what weight does each have in the design and operation of the budget system?

The Stages of Budget Reform

The framework outlined above suggests a useful approach to the study of budget reform. Every reform alters the planning-management-control balance, sometimes inadvertently, usually deliberately. Accordingly, it is possible to identify three successive stages of reform. In the first stage, dating roughly from 1920 to 1935, the dominant emphasis was on developing an adequate system of expenditure control. Although planning and management considerations were not altogether absent (and indeed occupied a prominent role in the debates leading to the Budget and Accounting Act of 1921), they were pushed to the side by what was regarded as the first priority, a reliable system of expenditure accounts. The second stage came into the open during the New Deal and reached its zenith more than a decade later in the movement for performance budgeting. The management orientation, paramount during this period, made its mark in the reform of the appropriation structure, development of management improvement and work measurement programs, and the focusing of budget preparation on the work and activities of the agencies. The third stage, the full emergence of which must await the institutionalization of PPB, can be traced to earlier efforts to link planning and budgeting as well as to the analytic criteria of welfare economics, but its recent development is a product of modern informational and decisional technologies such as those pioneered in the Department of Defense.

PPB is predicated on the primacy of the planning function; yet it strives for a multipurpose budget system that gives adequate and necessary attention to the control and management areas. Even in embryonic stage, PPB envisions the development of crosswalk grids for the conversion of data from a planning to a management and control framework, and back again. PPB treats the three basic functions as compatible and complementary elements of a budget system, though not as coequal aspects of central budgeting. In ideal form, PPB would centralize the planning function and delegate *primary* managerial and control responsibilities to the supervisory and operating levels respectively.

In the modern genesis of budgeting, efforts to improve planning, management, and control made common cause under the popular banner of the executive-budget concept. In the goals and lexicon of the first reformers, budgeting meant executive budgeting. The two were inseparable. There was virtually no dissent from Cleveland's dictum that "to be a budget it must be prepared and submitted by a responsible executive. . . . ''[3] Whether from the standpoint of planning, management or control, the executive was deemed in the best position to prepare and execute the budget. As Cleveland argued in 1915, only the executive ''could think in terms of the institution as a whole,'' and, therefore, he ''is the only one who can be made responsible for leadership.''[4]

The executive budget idea also took root in the administrative integration movement, and here was allied with such reforms as functional consolidation of agencies, elimination of independent boards and commissions, the short ballot, and strengthening the chief executive's appointive and removal powers. The chief executive often was likened to the general manager of a corporation, the Budget Bureau serving as his general staff.

Finally, the executive budget was intended to strengthen honesty and efficiency by restricting the discretion of administrators in this role. It was associated with such innovations as centralized purchasing and competitive bidding, civil service reform, uniform accounting procedures, and expenditure audits.

The Control Orientation

In the drive for executive budgeting the various goals converged. There was a radical parting of the ways, however, in the conversion of the budget idea into an operational reality. Hard choices had to be made in the design of expenditure accounts and in the orientation of the budget office. On both counts, the control orientation was predominant.

In varying degrees of itemization, the expenditure classifications established during the first wave of reform were based on objects-of-expenditure, with detailed tabulations of the myriad items required to operate an administrative unit—personnel, fuel, rent, office supplies, and other inputs. On these ''line-itemizations'' were built technical routines for the compilation and review of estimates and the disbursement of funds. The leaders in the movement for executive budgeting, however, envisioned a system of functional classifications focusing on the work to be accomplished. They regarded objects-of-expenditure as subsidiary data to be included for informational purposes. Their preference for functional accounts derived from their conception of the budget as a planning instrument, their disdain for objects from the contemporary division between politics and

administration.[5] The Taft Commission vigorously opposed object-of-expenditure appropriations and recommended that expenditures be classified by class of work, organizational unit, character of expense, and method of financing. In its model budget, the Commission included several functional classifications.[6]

In the establishment of a budget system for New York City by the Bureau of Municipal Research, there was an historic confrontation between diverse conceptions of budgeting.

In evolving suitable techniques, the Bureau soon faced a conflict between functional and object budgeting. Unlike almost all other budget systems which began on a control footing with object classifications, the Bureau turned to control (and the itemization of objects) only after trial-and-error experimentation with program methods.

When confronted with an urgent need for effective control over administration, the Bureau was compelled to conclude that this need was more critical than the need for a planning-functional emphasis. ''Budget reform,'' Charles Beard once wrote, ''bears the imprint of the age in which it originated.''[7] In an age when personnel and purchasing controls were unreliable, the first consideration was how to prevent administrative improprieties.

> In the opinion of those who were in charge of the development of a budget procedure, the most important service to be rendered was the establishing of central controls so that responsibility could be located and enforced through elected executives. . . . The view was, therefore, accepted, that questions of administration and niceties of adjustment must be left in abeyance until central control has been effectively established and the basis has been laid for careful scrutiny of departmental contracts and purchases as well as departmental work.[8]

Functional accounts had been designed to facilitate rational program decisions, not to deter officials from misfeasance. ''The classification by 'functions' affords no protection; it only operates as a restriction on the use which may be made of the services.''[9] The detailed itemization of objects was regarded as desirable not only ''because it provides for the utilization of all the machinery of control which has been provided, but it also admits to a much higher degree of perfection than it has at present attained.''[10]

With the introduction of object accounts, New York City had a three-fold classification of expenditures: (1) by organizational units; (2) by functions; and (3) by objects. In a sense, the Bureau of Municipal Research was striving to develop a budget system that would serve the multiple purposes of budgeting simultaneously. To the Bureau, the inclusion of more varied and detailed data in the budget was a salutory trend; all purposes would be served and the public would have a more complete picture of government spending. Thus the Bureau "urged from the beginning a classification of costs in as many different ways as there are stories to be told."[11] But the Bureau did not anticipate the practical difficulties which would ensue from the multiple classification scheme. In the 1913 appropriations act

> there were 3992 distinct items of appropriation. . . . Each constituted a distinct appropriation, besides which there was a further itemization of positions and salaries of personnel that multiplied this number several times, each of which operated as limitations on administrative discretion.[12]

This predicament confronted the Bureau with a direct choice between the itemization of objects and a functional classification. As a solution, the Bureau recommended retention of object accounts and the total "defunctionalization" of the budget; in other words, it gave priority to the objects and the control orientation they manifested. Once installed, object controls rapidly gained stature as an indispensable deterrent to administrative misbehavior. Amelioration of the adverse effects of multiple classifications was to be accomplished in a different manner, one which would strengthen the planning and management processes. The Bureau postulated a fundamental distinction between the purposes of budgets and appropriations, and between the types of classification suitable for each.

> An act of appropriation has a single purpose—that of putting a limitation on the amount of obligations which may be incurred and the amount of vouchers which may be drawn to pay for personal services, supplies, etc. The only significant classification of appropriation items, therefore, is according to persons to whom drawing accounts are given and the classes of things to be bought.[13]

Appropriations, in sum, were to be used as statutory controls on spending. In its "Next Steps"

proposals, the Bureau recommended that appropriations retain exactly the same itemization so far as specifications of positions and compensations are concerned and, therefore, the same protection."[14]

Budgets, on the other hand, were regarded as instruments of planning and publicity. They should include "all the details of the work plans and specifications of cost of work."[15] In addition to the regular object and organization classifications, the budget would report the "total cost incurred, classified by *functions*—for determining questions of policy having to do with service rendered as well as to be rendered, and laying a foundation for appraisal of results."[16] The Bureau also recommended a new instrument, a *work program*, which would furnish "a detailed schedule or analysis of each function, activity, or process within each organization unit. This analysis would give the total cost and the unit cost wherever standards were established."[17]

Truly a far-sighted conception of budgeting! There would be three documents for the three basic functions of budgeting. Although the Bureau did not use the analytic framework suggested above, it seems that the appropriations were intended for control purposes, the budget for planning purposes, and the work program for management purposes. Each of the three documents would have its specialized information scheme, but jointly they would comprise a multipurpose budget system not very different from PPB, even though the language of crosswalking or systems analysis was not used.

Yet the plan failed, for in the end the Bureau was left with object accounts pegged to a control orientation. The Bureau's distinction between budgets and appropriations was not well understood, and the work-program idea was rejected by New York City on the ground that adequate accounting backup was lacking. The Bureau had failed to recognize that the conceptual distinction between budgets and appropriations tends to break down under the stress of informational demands. If the legislature appropriates by objects, the budget very likely will be classified by objects. Conversely, if there are no functional accounts, the prospects for including such data in the budget are diminished substantially. As has almost always been the case, the budget came to mirror the appropriations act; in each, objects were paramount. It remains to be seen whether PPB will be able to break this interlocking informational pattern.

By the early 1920's the basic functions of planning and management were overlooked by those who carried the gospel of budget reform across the nation. First generation budget workers concentrated on perfecting and spreading the widely approved object-of-expenditure approach, and budget writers settled into a nearly complete preoccupation with forms and with factual descriptions of actual and recommended procedures. Although ideas about the use of the budget for planning and management purposes were retained in Buck's catalogs of "approved" practices,[18] they did not have sufficient priority to challenge tradition.

From the start, Federal budgeting was placed on a control, object-of-expenditure footing, the full flavor of which can be perceived in reading Charles G. Dawes' documentary on *The First Year of the Budget of The United States.* According to Dawes,

> the Bureau of the Budget is concerned only with the humbler and routine business of Government. Unlike cabinet officers, it is concerned with no question of policy, save that of economy and efficiency.[19]

This distinction fitted neatly with object classifications that provided a firm accounting base for the routine conduct of government business, but no information on policy implications of public expenditures. Furthermore, in its first decade, the Bureau's tiny staff (40 or fewer) had to coordinate a multitude of well-advertised economy drives which shaped the job of the examiner as being that of reviewing itemized estimates to pare them down. Although Section 209 of the Budget and Accounting Act had authorized the Bureau to study and recommend improvements in the organization and administrative practices of Federal agencies, the Bureau was overwhelmingly preoccupied with the business of control.

The Management Orientation

Although no single action represents the shift from a control to a management orientation, the turning point in this evolution probably came with the New Deal's broadening perspective of government responsibilities.

During the 1920's and 1930's, occasional voices urged a return to the conceptions of budgeting advocated by the early reformers. In a notable 1924

article, Lent D. Upson argued vigorously that "budget procedure had stopped halfway in its development," and he proposed six modifications in the form of the budget, the net effect being a shift in emphasis from accounting control to functional accounting.[20] A similar position was taken a decade later by Wylie Kilpatrick who insisted that "the one fundamental basis of expenditure is functional, an accounting of payments for the services performed by government."[21]

Meanwhile, gradual changes were preparing the way for a reorientation of budgeting to a management mission. Many of the administrative abuses that had given rise to object controls were curbed by statutes and regulations and by a general upgrading of the public service. Reliable accounting systems were installed and personnel and purchasing reforms introduced, thereby freeing budgeting from some of its watchdog chores. The rapid growth of government activities and expenditures made it more difficult and costly for central officials to keep track of the myriad objects in the budget. With expansion, the bits and pieces into which the objects were itemized became less and less significant, while the aggregate of activities performed became more significant. With expansion, there was heightened need for central management of the incohesive sprawl of administrative agencies.

The climb in activities and expenditures also signaled radical changes in the role of the budget system. As long as government was considered a "necessary evil," and there was little recognition of the social value of public expenditures, the main function of budgeting was to keep spending in check. Because the outputs were deemed to be of limited and fixed value, it made sense to use the budget for central control over inputs. However, as the work and accomplishments of public agencies came to be regarded as benefits, the task of budgeting was redefined as the effective marshalling of fiscal and organizational resources for the attainment of benefits. This new posture focused attention on the problems of managing large programs and organizations, and on the opportunities for using the budget to extend executive hegemony over the dispersed administrative structure.

All these factors converged in the New Deal years. Federal expenditures rose rapidly from $4.2 billion in 1932 to $10 billion in 1940. Keynesian economics (the full budgetary implications of which are emerging only now in PPB) stressed the relationship between public spending and the condition of the economy. The President's Committee on Administrative Management (1937) castigated the routinized, control-minded approach of the Bureau of the Budget and urged that budgeting be used to coordinate Federal activities under presidential leadership. With its transfer in 1939 from the Treasury to the newly-created Executive Office of the President, the Bureau was on its way to becoming the leading management arm of the Federal Government. The Bureau's own staff was increased tenfold; it developed the administrative management and statistical coordination functions that it still possesses; and it installed apportionment procedures for budget execution. More and more, the Bureau was staffed from the ranks of public administration rather than from accounting, and it was during the Directorship of Harold D. Smith (1939–46) that the Bureau substantially embraced the management orientation.[22] Executive Order 8248 placed the President's imprimatur on the management philosophy. It directed the Bureau:

> to keep the President informed of the progress of activities by agencies of the Government with respect to work proposed, work actually initiated, and work completed, together with the relative timing of work between the several agencies of the Government; all to the end that the work programs of the several agencies of the executive branch of the Government may be coordinated and that the monies appropriated by the Congress may be expended in the most economical manner possible to prevent overlapping and duplication of effort.

Accompanying the growing management use of the budget process for the appraisal and improvement of administrative performance and the scientific management movement with its historical linkage to public administration were far more relevant applications of managerial cost accounting to governmental operations. Government agencies sought to devise performance standards and the rudimentary techniques of work measurement were introduced in several agencies including the Forest Service, the Census Bureau, and the Bureau of Reclamation.[23] Various professional associations developed grading systems to assess administrative performance as well as the need for public services.

These crude and unscientific methods were the forerunners of more sophisticated and objective techniques. At the apogee of these efforts, Clarence Ridley and Herbert Simon published *Measuring Municipal Activities: A Survey of Suggested Criteria for Appraising Administration,* in which they identified five kinds of measurement—(1) needs, (2) results, (3) costs, (4) effort, and (5) performance—and surveyed the obstacles to the measurement of needs and results. The latter three categories they combined into a measure of administrative efficiency. This study provides an excellent inventory of the state of the technology prior to the breakthough made by cost-benefit and systems analysis.

At the close of World War II, the management orientation was entrenched in all but one aspect of Federal budgeting—the classification of expenditures. Except for isolated cases (such as TVA's activity accounts and the project structure in the Department of Agriculture), the traditional object accounts were retained though the control function had receded in importance. In 1949 the Hoover Commission called for alterations in budget classifications consonant with the management orientation. It recommended "that the whole budgetary concept of the Federal Government should be refashioned by the adoption of a budget based upon functions, activities, and projects."[24] To create a sense of novelty, the Commission gave a new label—performance budgeting—to what had long been known as functional or activity budgeting. Because its task force had used still another term—program budgeting—there were two new terms to denote the budget innovations of that period. Among writers there was no uniformity in usage, some preferring the "program budgeting" label, others "performance budgeting," to describe the same things. The level of confusion has been increased recently by the association of the term "program budgeting" (also the title of the Rand publication edited by David Novick) with the PPB movement.

Although a variety of factors and expectations influenced the Hoover Commission, and the Commission's proposals have been interpreted in many ways, including some that closely approximate the PPB concept, for purposes of clarity, and in accord with the control-management-planning framework, performance budgeting *as it was generally understood and applied* must be distinguished from the emergent PPB idea. The term "performance budgeting" is hereafter used in reference to reforms set in motion by the Hoover Commission and the term "program budgeting" is used in conjunction with PPB.

Performance budgeting is management-oriented; its principal thrust is to help administrators to assess the work-efficiency of operating units by (1) casting budget categories in functional terms, and (2) providing work-cost measurements to facilitate the efficient performance of prescribed activities. Generally, its method is particularistic, the reduction of work-cost data unto discrete, measurable units. Program budgeting (PPB) is planning-oriented; its main goal is to rationalize policy making by providing (1) data on the costs and benefits of alternative ways of attaining proposed public objectives, and (2) output measurements to facilitate the effective attainment of chosen objectives. As a policy device, program budgeting departs from simple engineering models of efficiency in which the objective is fixed and the quantity of inputs and outputs is adjusted to an optimal relationship. In PPB, the objective itself is variable; analysis may lead to a new statement of objectives. In order to enable budget makers to evaluate the costs and benefits of alternative expenditure options, program budgeting focuses on expenditure aggregates; the details come into play only as they contribute to an analysis of the total (the system) or of marginal trade-offs among competing proposals. Thus, in this macroanalytic approach, the accent is on comprehensiveness and on grouping data into categories that allow comparisons among alternative expenditure mixes.

Performance budgeting derived its ethos and much of its technique from cost accounting and scientific management; program budgeting has drawn its core ideas from economics and systems analysis. In the performance budgeting literature, budgeting is described as a "tool of management" and the budget as a "work program." In PPB, budgeting is an allocative process among competing claims, and the budget is a statement of policy. Chronologically, there was a gap of several years between the bloom of performance budgeting and the first articulated conceptions of program budgeting. In the aftermath of the first Hoover report, and especially during the early 1950's, there was a plethora of writings on the administrative advantages of the performance budget. Substantial interest in program budgeting did not emerge until the mid-1950's when a number of economists (including Smithies, Novick, and

McKean) began to urge reform of the Federal budget system. What the economists had in mind was not the same thing as the Hoover Commission.

In line with its management perspective, the Commission averred that "the all-important thing in budgeting is the work of service to be accomplished, and what that work or service will cost."[25] Mosher followed this view closely in writing that "the central idea of the performance budget . . . is that the budget process be focused upon programs and functions—that is, accomplishments to be achieved, work to be done."[26] But from the planning perspective, the all-important thing surely is not the work or service to be accomplished but the objectives or purposes to be fulfilled by the investment of public funds. Whereas in performance budgeting, work and activities are treated virtually as ends in themselves, in program budgeting work and services are regarded as intermediate aspects, the process of converting resources into outputs. Thus, in a 1954 Rand paper, Novick defined a program as "the sum of the steps or interdependent activities which enter into the attainment of a specified objective. The program, therefore, is the end objective and is developed or budgeted in terms of all the elements necessary to its execution."[27] Novick goes on to add, "this is not the sense in which the government budget now uses the term."

Because the evaluation of performance and the evaluation of program are distinct budget functions, they call for different methods of classification which serves as an intermediate layer between objects and organizations. The activities relate to the functions and work of a distinct operating unit; hence their classification ordinarily conforms to organizational lines. This is the type of classification most useful for an administrator who has to schedule the procurement and utilization of resources for the production of goods and services. Activity classifications gather under a single rubric all the expenditure data needed by a manager to run his unit. The evaluation of programs, however, requires an end-product classification that is oriented to the mission and purposes of government. This type of classification may not be very useful for the manager, but it is of great value to the budget maker who has to decide how to allocate scarce funds among competing claims. Some of the difference between end-product and activity classifications can be gleaned by comparing the Coast Guard's existing activity schedule with the proposed program structure on the last page of Bulletin 66-3. The activity structure which was developed under the aegis of performance budgeting is geared to the operating responsibilities of the Coast Guard: Vessel Operations, Aviation Operations, Repair and Supply Facilities, and others. The proposed program structure is hinged to the large purposes sought through Coast Guard operations: Search and Rescue, Aids to Navigation, Law Enforcement, and so on.

It would be a mistake to assume that performance techniques presuppose program budgeting or that it is not possible to collect performance data without program classifications. Nevertheless, the view has gained hold that a program budget is "a transitional type of budget between the orthodox (traditional) character and object budget on the one hand and performance budget on the other."[28] Kammerer and Shadoan stress a similar connection. The former writes that "a *performance* budget carries the program budget one step further: into *unit costs.*"[29] Shadoan "envisions "performance budgeting" as an extension of . . . the program budget concept to which the element of unit work measurement has been added."[30] These writers ignore the divergent functions served by performance and program budgets. It is possible to devise and apply performance techniques without relating them to, or having the use of, larger program aggregates. A cost accountant or work measurement specialist can measure the cost or effort required to perform a repetitive task without probing into the purpose of the work or its relationship to the mission of the organization. Work measurement—"a method of establishing an equitable relationship between the volume of work performed and manpower utilized"—[31] is only distantly and indirectly related to the process of determining governmental policy at the higher levels. Program classifications are vitally linked to the making and implementation of policy through the allocation of public resources. As a general rule, performance budgeting is concerned with the *process of work* (what methods should be used) while program budgeting is concerned with the *purpose of work* (what activities should be authorized).

Perhaps the most reliable way to describe this difference is to show what was tried and accomplished under performance budgeting. First of all, performance budgeting led to the introduction of activity classifications, the management-orientation of which

has already been discussed. Second, narrative descriptions of program and performance were added to the budget document. These statements give the budget-reader a general picture of the work that will be done by the organizational unit requesting funds. But unlike the analytic documents currently being developed under PPB, the narratives have a descriptive and justificatory function; they do not provide an objective basis for evaluating the cost-utility of an expenditure. Indeed, there hardly is any evidence that the narratives have been used for decision making; rather they seem best suited for giving the uninformed outsider some glimpses of what is going on inside.

Third, performance budgeting spawned a multitude of work-cost measurement explorations. Most used, but least useful, were the detailed work-load statistics assembled by administrators to justify their requests for additional funds. On a higher level of sophistication were attempts to apply the techniques of scientific management and cost accounting to the development of work and productivity standards. In these efforts, the Bureau of the Budget had a long involvement, beginning with the issuance of the trilogy of work measurement handbooks in 1950 and reaching its highest development in the productivity-measurement studies that were published in 1964. All these applications were at a level of detail useful for managers with operating or supervisory responsibilities, but of scant usefulness for top-level officials who have to determine organizational objectives and goals. Does it really help top officials if they know that it cost $0.07 to wash a pound of laundry or that the average postal employee processes 289 items of mail per hour? These are the main fruits of performance measurements, and they have an important place in the management of an organization. They are of great value to the operating official who has the limited function of getting a job done, but they would put a crushing burden on the policy maker whose function is to map the future course of action.

Finally, the management viewpoint led to significant departures from PPB's principle that the expenditure accounts should show total systems cost. The 1949 National Security Act (possibly the first concrete result of the Hoover report) directed the segregation of capital and operating costs in the defense budget. New York State's performance—budgeting experiment for TB hospitals separated expenditures into cost centers (a concept derived from managerial cost accounting) and within each center into fixed and variable costs. In most manpower and work measurements, labor has been isolated from other inputs. Most important, in many states and localities (and implicitly in Federal budgeting) the cost of continuing existing programs has been separated from the cost of new or expanded programs. This separation is useful for managers who build up a budget in terms of increments and decrements from the base, but it is a violation of program budgeting's working assumption that all claims must be pitted against one another in the competition for funds. Likewise, the forms of separation previously mentioned make sense from the standpoint of the manager, but impair the planner's capability to compare expenditure alternatives.

The Planning Orientation

The foregoing has revealed some of the factors leading to the emergence of the planning orientation. Three important developments influenced the evolution from a management to a planning orientation.

1. Economic analysis—macro and micro—has had an increasing part in the shaping of fiscal and budgetary policy.
2. The development of new informational and decisional technologies has enlarged the applicability of objective analysis to policy making. And,
3. There has been a gradual convergence of planning and budgetary processes.

Keynesian economics with its macroanalytic focus on the impact of governmental action on the private sector had its genesis in the underemployment economy of the Great Depression. In calling attention to the opportunities for attaining full employment by means of fiscal policy, the Keynesians set into motion a major restatement of the central budget function. From the utilization of fiscal policy to achieve economic objectives, it was but a few steps to the utilization of the budget process to achieve fiscal objectives. Nevertheless, between the emergence and the victory of the new economics, there was a lapse of a full generation, a delay due primarily to the entrenched balanced-budget ideology. But the full realization of the budget's economic potential was stymied on the revenue side by static tax policies and on the expenditure side by status spending policies.

If the recent tax policy of the Federal Government is evidence that the new economics has come of age, it also offers evidence of the long-standing failure of public officials to use the taxing power as a variable constraint on the economy. Previously, during normal times, the tax structure was accepted as given, and the task of fiscal analysis was to forecast future tax yields so as to ascertain how much would be available for expenditure. The new approach treats taxes as variable, to be altered periodically in accord with national policy and economic conditions. Changes in tax rates are not to be determined (as they still are in virtually all States and localities) by how much is needed to cover expenditures but by the projected impact of alternative tax structures on the economy.

It is more than coincidental that the advent of PPB has followed on the heels of the explicit utilization of tax policy to guide the economy. In macroeconomics, taxes and expenditures are mirror images of one another; a tax cut and an expenditure increase have comparable impacts. Hence, the hinging of tax policy to economic considerations inevitably led to the similar treatment of expenditures. But there were (and remain) a number of obstacles to the utilization of the budget as a fiscal tool. For one thing, the conversion of the budget process to an economic orientation probably was slowed by the Full Employment Act of 1946 which established the Council of Economic Advisers and transferred the Budget Bureau's fiscal analysis function to the Council. The institutional separation between the CEA and the BOB and between fiscal policy and budget making was not compensated by cooperative work relationships. Economic analysis had only slight impact on expenditure policy. It offered a few guidelines (for example, that spending should be increased during recessions) and a few ideas (such as a shelf of public works projects), but it did not feed into the regular channels of budgeting. The business of preparing the budget was foremost a matter of responding to agency spending pressures, not of responding to economic conditions.

Moreover, expenditures (like taxes) have been treated virtually as givens, to be determined by the unconstrained claims of the spending units. In the absence of central policy instructions, the agencies have been allowed to vent their demands without prior restraints by central authorities and without an operational set of planning guidelines. By the time the Bureau gets into the act, it is faced with the over-riding task of bringing estimates into line with pro-jected resources. In other words, the Bureau has had a budget-cutting function, to reduce claims to an acceptable level. The President's role has been similarly restricted. He is the *gatekeeper* of Federal budgeting. He directs the pact of spending increases by deciding which of the various expansions pro-posed by the agencies shall be included in the budget. But, as the gatekeeper, the President rarely has been able to look back at the items that have previously passed through the gate; his attention is riveted to those programs that are departures from the established base. In their limited roles, neither the Bureau nor the President has been able to inject fiscal and policy objectives into the forefront of budget preparation.

It will not be easy to wean budgeting from its utilization as an administrative procedure for financ-ing ongoing programs to a decisional process for determining the range and direction of public objec-tives and the government's involvement in the economy. In the transition to a planning emphasis, an important step was the 1963 hearings of the Joint Economic Committee on *The Federal Budget as an Economic Document*. These hearings and the pur-suant report of the JEC explored the latent policy opportunities in budget making. Another develop-ment was the expanded time horizons manifested by the multiyear expenditure projections introduced in the early 1960's. Something of a breakthrough was achieved via the revelation that the existing tax struc-ture would yield cumulatively larger increments of uncommitted funds—estimated as much as $50 billion by 1970—which could be applied to a number of alternative uses. How much of the funds should be "returned" to the private sector through tax reductions and how much through expenditure in-creases? How much should go to the States and localities under a broadened system of Federal grants? How much should be allocated to the rebuilding of cities, to the improvement of educa-tion, or to the eradication of racial injustices? The traditional budget system lacked the analytic tools to cope with these questions, though decisions ultimately would be made one way or another. The expansion of the time horizon from the single year to a multiyear frame enhances the opportunity for planning and analysis to have an impact on future

expenditure decisions. With a one-year perspective, almost all options have been foreclosed by previous commitments; analysis is effective only for the increments provided by self-generating revenue increases or to the extent that it is feasible to con-vert funds from one use to another. With a longer time span, however, many more options are open, and economic analysis can have a prominent part in determining which course of action to pursue.

So much for the macroeconomic trends in budget reform. On the microeconomic side, PPB traces its lineage to the attempts of welfare economists to con-struct a science of finance predicated on the princi-ple of marginal utility. Such a science, it was hoped, would furnish objective criteria for determining the optimal allocation of public funds among competing uses. By appraising the marginal costs and benefits of alternatives (poor relief versus battleships in Pigou's classic example), it would be possible to determine which combination of expenditures afforded maximum utility. The quest for a welfare function provided the conceptual underpinning for a 1940 article on "The Lack of a Budgetary Theory" in which V. O. Key noted the absence of a theory which would determine whether "to allocate x dollars to activity A instead of activity B."[32] In terms of its direct contribution to budgetary practice, welfare economics has been a failure. It has not been possible to distill the conflicts and complexities of political life into a welfare criterion or homo-geneous distribution formula. But stripped of its normative and formal overtones, its principles have been applied to budgeting by economists such as Arthur Smithies. Smithies has formulated a budget rule that "expenditure proposals should be consid-ered in the light of the objectives they are intended to further, and in general final expenditure decisions should not be made until all claims on the budget can be considered."[33] PPB is the application of this rule to budget practice. By structuring expendi-tures so as to juxtapose substitutive elements within program categories, and by analyzing the costs and benefits of the various substitutes, PPB has opened the door to the use of marginal analysis in budgeting.

Actually, the door was opened somewhat by the development of new decisional and information technologies, the second item on the list of influences in the evolution of the planning orientation. With-out the availability of the decisional-informational capability provided by cost-benefit and systems analysis, it is doubtful that PPB would be part of the budgetary apparatus today. The new technologies make it possible to cope with the enormous informational and analytic burdens imposed by PPB. As aids to calculation, they furnish a methodology for the analysis of alternatives, thereby expanding the range of decision-making in budgeting.

Operations research, the oldest of these technologies, grew out of complex World War II conditions that required the optimal coordination of manpower, material, and equipment to achieve defense objectives. Operations research is most applicable to those repetitive operations where the opportunity for quantification is highest. Another technology, cost-benefit analysis, was intensively adapted during the 1950's to large-scale water resource investments, and subsequently to many other governmental functions. Systems analysis is the most global of these technologies. It involves the skillful analysis of the major factors that go into the attainment of an interconnected set of objectives. Systems analysis has been applied in DOD to the choice of weapons systems, the location of military bases, and the determination of sealift-airlift requirements. Although the extension of these technologies across-the-board to government was urged repeatedly by members of the Rand Corporation during the 1950's, it was DOD's experience that set the stage for the current ferment. It cannot be doubted that the coming of PPB has been pushed ahead several years or more by the "success story" in DOD.

The third stream of influence in the transformation of the budget function has been a closing of the gap between planning and budgeting. Institutionally and operationally, planning and budgeting have run along separate tracks. The national government has been reluctant to embrace central planning of any sort because of identification with socialist management of the economy. The closest thing we have had to a central planning agency was the National Resources Planning Board in 1939–1943 period. Currently, the National Security Council and the Council of Economic Advisors have planning responsibilities in the defense and fiscal areas. As far as the Bureau of the Budget is concerned, it has eschewed the planning units: in the States, because limitations on debt financing have encouraged the separation of the capital and operating budgets; in the cities, because the professional autonomy and

land-use preoccupations of the planners have set them apart from the budgeteers.

In all governments, the appropriations cycle, rather than the anticipation of future objectives, tends to dictate the pace and posture of budgeting. Into the repetitive, one-year span of the budget is wedged all financial decisions, including those that have multiyear implications. As a result, planning, if it is done at all, "occurs independently of budgeting and with little relation to it."[34] Budgeting and planning, moreover, invite disparate perspectives: the one is conservative and negativistic; the other, innovative and expansionist. As Mosher has noted, "budgeting and planning are apposit, if not opposite. In extreme form, the one means saving; the other, spending."[35]

Nevertheless, there has been some *rapprochement* of planning and budgeting. One factor is the long lead-time in the development and procurement of hardware and capital investments. The multiyear projections inaugurated several years ago were a partial response to this problem. Another factor has been the diversity of government agencies involved in related functions. This has given rise to various *ad hoc* coordinating devices, but it also has pointed to the need for permanent machinery to integrate dispersed activities. Still another factor has been the sheer growth of Federal activities and expenditures and the need for a rational system of allocation. The operational code of planners contains three tenets relevant to these budgetary needs: (1) planning is future-oriented; it connects present decisions to the attainment of a desired future state of affairs; (2) planning, ideally, encompasses all resources involved in the attainment of future objectives. It strives for comprehensiveness. The *master plan* is the one that brings within its scope all relevant factors; (3) planning is means-ends oriented. The allocation of resources is strictly dictated by the ends that are to be accomplished. All this is to say that planning is an economizing process, though planners are more oriented to the future than economists. It is not surprising that planners have found the traditional budget system deficient,[36] nor is it surprising that the major reforms entailed by PPB emphasize the planning function.

Having outlined the several trends in the emerging transition to a planning orientation, it remains to mention several qualifications. First, the planning emphasis is not predominant in Federal budgeting at this time. Although PPB asserts the paramountcy of planning, PPB itself is not yet a truly operational part of the budget machinery. We are now at the dawn of a new era in budgeting; high noon is still a long way off. Second, this transition has not been preceded by a reorientation of the Bureau of the Budget. Unlike the earlier change-over from control to management in which the alteration of budgetary technique *followed* the revision of the Bureau's role, the conversion from management to planning is taking a different course—first, the installation of new techniques; afterwards, a reformulation of the Bureau's mission. Whether this sequence will hinder reform efforts is a matter that cannot be predicted, but it should be noted that in the present instance the Bureau cannot convert to a new mission by bringing in a wholly new staff, as was the case in the late 1930's and early 1940's.

What Difference Does it Make?

The starting point for the author was distinguishing the old from the new in budgeting. The interpretation has been framed in analytic terms, and budgeting has been viewed historically in three stages corresponding to the three basic functions of budgeting. In this analysis an attempt has been made to identify the difference between the existing and the emerging as a difference between management and planning orientations.

In an operational sense, however, what difference does it make whether the central budget process is oriented toward planning rather than management? Does the change merely mean a new way of making decisions, or does it mean different decisions as well? These are not easy questions to answer, particularly since the budget system of the future will be a compound of all three functions. The case for PPB rests on the assumption that the form in which information is classified and used governs the actions of budget makers, and, conversely, that alterations in form will produce desired changes in behavior. Take away the assumption that behavior follows form, and the movement for PPB is reduced to a trivial manipulation of techniques—form for form's sake without any significant bearing on the conduct of budgetary affairs.

Yet this assumed connection between roles and information is a relatively uncharted facet of the PPB literature. The behavioral side of the equation has been neglected. PPB implies that each participant will behave as a sort of Budgetary Man, a counterpart of the classical Economic Man and Simon's Administrative Man.[37] Budgetary Man, whatever his station or role in the budget process, is assumed to be guided by an unwavering commitment to the rule of efficiency; in every instance he chooses that alternative that optimizes the allocation of public resources.

PPB probably takes an overly mechanistic view of the impact of form on behavior and underestimates the strategic and volitional aspects of budget making in the political arena, data are used to influence the "who gets what" in budgets and appropriations. If information influences behavior, the reverse also is true. Indeed, data are more tractable than roles; participants are more likely to seek and use data which suit their preferences than to alter their behavior automatically in response to formal changes.

All this constrains, rather than negates, the impact of budget form. The advocates of PPB, probably in awareness of the above limitations, have imported into budgeting men with professional commitments to the types of analysis and norms required by the new techniques, men with a background in economics and systems analysis, rather than with general administrative training.

PPB aspires to create a different environment for choice. Traditionally, budgeting has defined its mission in terms of identifying the existing base and proposed departures from it—"This is where we are; where do we go from here?" PPB defines its mission in terms of budgetary objectives and purposes—"Where do we want to go? What do we do to get there?" The environment of choice under traditional circumstances is *incremental*; in PPB it is *teletic*. Presumably, these different processes will lead to different budgetary outcomes.

A budgeting process which accepts the base and examines only the increments will produce decisions to transfer the present into the future with a few small variations. The curve of government activities will be continuous, with few zigzags or breaks. A budget-making process which begins with objectives will require the base to compete on an equal footing with new proposals. The decisions will be more radical than those made under incremental conditions. This does not mean that each year's budget will lack continuity with the past. There are sunk costs that have to be reckoned, and the benefits of radical changes will have to outweigh the cost of terminating prior commitments. Furthermore, the extended time span of PPB will mean that big investment decisions will be made for a number of years, with each year being a partial installment of the plan. Most important, the political manifestations of sunk costs—vested interests—will bias decisions away from radical departures. The conservatism of the political system, therefore, will tend to minimize the decisional differences between traditional and PPB approaches. However, the very availability of analytic data will cause a shift in the balance of economic and political forces that go into the making of a budget.

Teletic and incremental conditions of choice lead to still another distinction. In budgeting, which is committed to the established base, the flow of budgetary decisions is upward and aggregative. Traditionally, the first step in budgeting, in anticipation of the call for estimates, is for each department to issue its own call to prepare and to submit a set of estimates. This call reaches to the lowest level capable of assembling its own estimates. Lowest level estimates form the building blocks for the next level where they are aggregated and reviewed and transmitted upward until the highest level is reached and the totality constitutes a department-wide budget. Since budgeting is tied to a base, the building-up-from-below approach is sensible; each building block estimates the cost of what it is already doing plus the cost of the increments it wants. (The building blocks, then, are decisional elements, not simply informational elements as is often assumed.)

PPB reverses the informational and decisional flow. Before the call for estimates is issued, top policy has to be made, and this policy constrains the estimates prepared below. For each lower level, the relevant policy instructions are issued by the superior level prior to the preparation of estimates. Accordingly, the critical decisional process—that of deciding on purposes and plans—has a downward and disaggregative flow.

If the making of policy is to be antecedent to the costing of estimates, there will have to be a shift in the distribution of budget responsibilities. The main energies of the Bureau of the Budget are now devoted to budget preparation; under PPB these energies will be centered on what we may term *prepreparation*—the stage of budget making that deals with policy and is prior to the preparation of the budget. One of the steps marking the advent of the planning orientation was the inauguration of the Spring Preview several years ago for the purpose of affording an advance look at departmental programs.

If budget-making is to be oriented to the planning function, there probably will be a centralization of policy-making, both within and among departments. The DOD experience offers some precedent for predicting that greater budgetary authority will be vested in department heads than heretofore, but there is no firm basis for predicting the degree of centralization that may derive from the relatedness of objectives pursued by many departments. It is possible that the mantle of central budgetary policy will be assumed by the Bureau, indeed, this is the expectation in many agencies. On the other hand, the Bureau gives little indication at this time that it is willing or prepared to take this comprehensive role.

Conclusion

The various differences between the budgetary orientations are charted in [Table 1]. All the differences may be summed up in the statement that the ethos of budgeting will shift from justification to analysis. To far greater extent than heretofore, budget decisions will be influenced by explicit statements of objectives and by a formal weighing of the costs and benefits of alternatives.

Notes

1. New York Bureau of Municipal Research, *Making a Municipal Budget* (New York: 1907), pp. 9–10.
2. Robert N. Anthony, *Planning and Control Systems: A Framework for Analysis* (Boston: 1965), pp. 16–18.
3. Frederick A. Cleveland, "Evolution of the Budget Idea in the United States," *Annals of the American Academy of Political and Social Science,* LXII (1915), 16.
4. *Ibid.,* p. 17.
5. See Frank J. Goodnow, "The Limit of Budgetary Control," *Proceedings of the American Political Science Association* (Baltimore: 1913), p. 72; also William F. Willoughby, "Allotment of Funds by Executive Officials, An Essential Feature of Any Correct Budgetary System," *ibid.,* pp. 78–87.
6. U.S., President's Commission on Economy and Efficiency, *The Need for a National Budget* (Washington: 1912), pp. 210–213.
7. Charles A. Beard, "Prefatory Note," *ibid.,* p. vii.

8. New York Bureau of Municipal Research, "Some Results and Limitations of Central Financial Control in New York City," *Municipal Research,* LXXXI (1917), 10.

9. "Next Steps . . . ," *op. cit.,* p. 39.

10. "Next Steps . . . ," *op. cit.,* p. 39.

11. "Some Results and Limitations . . . ," *op. cit.,* p. 9.

12. "Next Steps . . . ," *op. cit.,* p. 35.

13. *Ibid.,* p. 7.

14. "Next Steps . . . ," p. 39.

15. "Some Results and Limitations . . . ," *op. cit.,* p. 7.

16. *Ibid.,* p. 9.

17. "Next Steps . . . ," *op. cit.,* p. 30.

18. See A. E. Buck, *Public Budgeting* (New York: 1929), pp. 181–188.

19. Charles G. Dawes, *The First Year of the Budget of the United States* (New York: 1923), preface, p. ii.

20. Lent D. Upson, "Half-time Budget Methods," *The Annals of the American Academy of Political and Social Science,* CXIII (1924), 72.

21. Wylie Kilpatrick, "Classification and Measurement of Public Expenditure," *The Annals of the American Academy of Political and Social Science,* CXXXIII (1936), 20.

22. See Harold D. Smith, *The Management of Your Government* (New York: 1945).

23. Public Administration Service, *The Work Unit in Federal Administration* (Chicago: 1937).

24. U.S. Commission on Organization of the Executive Branch of the Government, *Budgeting and Accounting* (Washington: 1949), 8.

25. *Ibid.*

26. Frederick C. Mosher, *Program Budgeting: Theory and Practice* (Chicago: 1954), p. 79.

27. David Novick, *Which Program Do We Mean in "Program Budgeting?"* (Santa Monica: 1954), p. 17.

28. Lennex L. Meak and Kathryn W. Killian, *A Manual of Techniques for the Preparation, Consideration, Adoption, and Administration of Operating Budgets* (Chicago: 1963), p. 11.

29. Gladys M. Kammerer, *Program Budgeting: An Aid to Understanding* (Gainesville: 1959), p. 6.

30. Arlene Theuer Shadean, *Preparation, Review, and Execution of the State Operating Budget* (Lexington: 1963), p. 13.

31. U.S. Bureau of the Budget, *A Work Measurement System* (Washington: 1950), p. 2.

32. V. O. Key, "The Lack of a Budgetary Theory," *The American Political Science Review,* XXXIV (1940), 1138.

33. Arthur Smithies, *The Budgetary Process in the United States* (New York: 1955), p. 16.

34. Mosher, *op. cit.,* p. 47–48.

35. *Ibid.,* p. 48.

36. See Edward C. Banfield, "Congress and the Budget: A Planner's Criticism," *The American Political Science Review,* XLIII (1949), 1217–1227.

37. Herbert A. Simon, *Administrative Behavior* (New York: 1957).

7
The Continuing Need for Budget Reform

Elmer B. Staats

I chose to entitle my remarks today "The *Continuing Need* for Budget Reform" to underscore my conviction that we can never be satisfied for long with existing budget concepts and practices. One thing clearly stands out over the last several decades, that is, the budget system's constantly changing nature needs periodic reexamination and renewal. We last looked at basic budget concepts in the mid-1960s, and then, in the 1970s, we dealt with basic institutional relationships through the Congressional Budget and Impoundment Control Act and its implementation. Such continued change makes budgeting a challenging and at times frustrating activity, as you well know.

In response to the periodic need to appraise the operations of the federal government, including budget concepts and procedures, there have been several high-level studies. Prominent early examples include the work of the Brownlow committee in the late 1930s, and the first and second Hoover commissions of the 1940s and 1950s. Each of these early efforts led to certain reforms and an improved coherence and analytical content in the budget, along with the establishment of a new consensus on the approach to budgeting. However, in each case, the post-reform period soon witnessed the emergence of new budgeting issues, as well as the reemergence of old issues, and the renewed research for solutions.

I think that this kind of cycle—namely, the development of consensus around a set of reformed budget concepts and practices, followed by the gradual erosion of the consensus—is inevitable. This is because budgeting lies at the heart of our political process and is subjected to the pressures of the

Source: This is the text of an address given November 21, 1980, by Mr. Staats—who at the time was comptroller general of the United States—to the Fall Symposium of the American Association for Budget and Program Analysis, held at The George Washington University, Washington, D.C.

political arena and requirements of a changing society. We all must be alert to this natural evolution of budget systems, and periodically undertake the reexaminations and reforms needed to restore the budget's overall consistency, analytical adequacy, and its acceptance by the government's decision makers and the public at large.

The same is true today following recent major reforms that established the conceptual and institutional bases of current budgeting practices. It has been five years since the Congress began operating under the 1974 Congressional Budget and Impoundment Control Act, and 13 years since the underlying unified budget concept and other budget principles were set forth by the President's Commission on Budget Concepts in 1967. I believe that much of today's conceptual and institutional budgeting framework laid out for us in 1967 and 1974 is serving us well. No one seriously questions the value of a unified budget or the congressional actions to systematize the legislative budget-setting procedures.

However, there have been several developments in the wake of these changes that have placed strains on the capacity of existing budget concepts and procedures to serve the budget information and control needs of the Congress, the executive branch, and the public. The current strains and problems, which I will shortly discuss, present a two-pronged challenge to us. We must not only study them and devise a variety of individual solutions to the problems, but we must also be careful to adopt measures that, taken together, do not further complicate the budget process. *Indeed, in my opinion, the overall need is in the opposite direction: to find ways of simplifying and streamlining our set of budget concepts and procedures.*

But first, what are the recent developments that are creating strains for today's budget system?

For one thing, there has been an increase in the variety and complexity of federal programs. The federal budget has grown to the point where there are now about 1,300 appropriation accounts and 2,000 "programs." But more importantly, this growth has been accompanied by an increase in the range and complexity of federal programs as new socio-economic problems have evoked new kinds of federal responses. The dramatic increase in federal loans and loan guarantees is a notable example. Total federal direct loans outstanding have more than *tripled* since the time of the president's budget commission, going from about $47 billion in fiscal year

1967 to about $176 billion estimated for 1981. Guaranteed loans outstanding have more than *doubled* over the same period, increasing from about $100 billion to an estimated $253 billion. The $1.5 billion Chrysler loan guarantee program is, of course, a well-known recent case. I also should mention the recently enacted legislation establishing the United States Synthetic Fuels Corporation, authorizing $20 billion for Phase I loan guarantees and other activities, plus an additional $68 billion for Phase II guarantees and other forms of assistance.

The growth of federal credit activities has created certain budget information and control problems that need attention. Should the budget totals include budget authority for the estimated future expenses to the government of current credit aids, for example, the estimated future interest subsidy expenses on direct loans, or default expenses on guaranteed loans? If so, how should these expenses be measured and controlled? The methodological problems are particularly acute on the Chrysler-type guarantees where there may be relatively little basis for estimating the ultimate expenses to be borne by the government.

The current administration took a step toward more systematic control over federal credit activities when it included a "credit budget" package in the 1981 budget, entailing proposed appropriation act dollar limitations on aggregate and individual direct loans and loan guarantees. The Congress, for its part, has responded by including limits on total direct loans and loan guarantees in its First Concurrent Resolution on the Budget for Fiscal Year 1981.

Comprehensive controls over credit activities have long been needed, and the current credit budget approach is a step in the right direction. However, I think that we need to study further the possible implications of budget concepts embodied in the proposed credit budget. The creation of a credit budget outside of the regular budget authority and outlay totals lessens comparability among credit and noncredit programs, and adds to the confusion about the meaning of the budget's totals. It does not simplify and streamline the budget. We need to consider such alternatives as recording limitations on direct lending as budget authority amounts, and including such amounts in the regular totals of the budget. This would be a simpler and more direct way of controlling loan levels. It must be recognized, however, that this latter approach would increase the budget's totals—by $15 billion according to one estimate.

Another problem is the reemergence of budget coverage and organization issues, perennial issues addressed in one form or another by the previous major budget reform studies. The 1967 commission viewed as its most important recommendation the adoption of a unified budget under which all federally owned activities would be included. Since 1967, however, legislation has been enacted removing certain federal programs from the budget's totals, or establishing new organizations as off-budget entities. The off-budget activities today include those of the Rural Electrification Administration, the Federal Financing Bank, and others.

The dollar totals of these off-budget organizations are significant. The off-budget treatment of these activities could reduce reported budget outlay totals for fiscal year 1981 by about $18 billion. This certainly lessens the meaningfulness of the budget's totals including the reported budget deficit, and is contrary to sound budget policy. I should add that this off-budget matter is frequently discussed in the press, and undoubtedly feeds public wariness and skepticism concerning governmental institutions.

Of particular concern is the Federal Financing Bank's role in converting on-budget federal loan guarantees into off-budget federal direct loans. Such FFB direct loans could total about $11 billion in 1981. This raises a most serious budget control question, and reinforces the need to work to reestablish unified budget concepts and controls.

We may expect additional strains on the unified budget approach from the increasing number of proposals for special "budgets," namely, proposals for capital, regulatory, paperwork, and tax expenditure budgets. The deteriorating or outmoded nature of much of the nation's physical infrastructure heightens the need for adequate budget action on capital needs. The costs to society of the growing number of federal regulations and reporting requirements have brought about proposals or initial steps for regulatory and paperwork budgets, in order to disclose the estimated costs and permit actions to limit them. Similarly, "tax expenditures," which are special tax preferences granted through legislative actions, are seen by many as appropriate for budget recognition and control.

It would be advisable to study the possible consequences of these and any other special budgets on the unity of the budget. I think it is imperative to avoid actions that could fragment or unnecessarily complicate the budget and lessen overall understanding of the budget. This could easily happen if special budgets are used for control purposes, and not simply the reporting of information as part of the budget process. Before establishing special budgets as additional vehicles for exercising budget control over Federal activities, we should consider options within the existing unified budget. We need to study ways of revising the existing structure of budget functions, accounts, etc., to provide much of the information disclosure and opportunities for budget control envisaged in some of the special budget proposals.

This takes us to a related problem we're facing today: the proliferation of budget-related categories. The budget's amounts now are categorized not only by the object class categories of travel, personnel compensation, and so forth, but also by assorted programmatic, functional, and zero-base budgeting categories. There also are proposals for new "mission" budget structures. Furthermore, the categories used by authorizing committees, which are often different from the other categories, are becoming increasingly relevant as the Congress moves toward more specific and timed authorizations.

These numerous and often dissimilar categories complicate budget reporting and actions, and make it difficult to oversee or evaluate program and budget execution. Agency accountability can be seriously weakened. In our recent work at GAO we came across a case in one agency where officials operated under authorizing legislation that used one set of program categories, but initially developed their budget in a different, cross-cutting set of ZBB categories that tie to their long-range plans. Then, in a complicated crosswalk exercise, officials restructured the material for their final budget submission. Finally, the congressional appropriations committees acted on budget account subcategories that differed from those used in the budget.

This case illustrates a basic need: We should study ways of achieving greater simplicity and uniformity among the categories that are used in related authorization, budget, and appropriations actions. This not only would facilitate congressional understanding and review of agency programs, and increase agency accountability for meeting legislated or self-imposed goals and objectives, but it also would streamline the overall process by reducing the workload involved in crosswalking and reformatting budget material into assorted categories for various users.

This matter will assume even greater significance if the Congress adopts some form of oversight reform and establishes a schedule for reviewing and reauthorizing programs. This could be effected by general oversight reform legislation or internal congressional rule changes. In either event, it would be desirable to have standard program entities to be used as the basic reporting and accountable entities in both congressional authorizing and appropriations actions, as well as in executive branch budget actions. As more committees regularly undertake actions that directly bear upon the budget—and this seems to be the trend —it becomes increasingly important to streamline the processes and minimize the use of competing categories for information reporting and control purposes.

Strengthening the links between authorizing legislation and appropriations categories also will facilitate a clearer budget focus on what the federal government perceives the policy needs to be, and how it is allocating resources for them. This means that we should increasingly attempt to use authorizing legislation statements of needs, missions, and program objectives as the categories of appropriations actions. This would require some revisions of agency budget categories to bring together activities that address common agency needs and missions. GAO's recent work in developing a possible mission budget structure for the Department of Agriculture illustrates the kind of reordering that may be required.

There also are new budget measurement issues that need to be addressed. The 1967 commission recognized the importance of realism, comparability, and consistency in measuring budgetary resources and spending levels. It is clear from work in this area, however, that significant problems exist today. Furthermore, these technical problems can be expected to grow as the variety and complexity of programs continues to increase. I will briefly describe six measurement areas we believe deserve special attention:

• First, we need to examine *estimating* policies and methods in order to correct the overoptimistic bias that lessens the realism of budget authority, obligations, and outlay projections. Our projections too often give the appearance that the government can accomplish things faster and at less cost than is reasonable to expect. Matters deserving further study in this regard include policy and technical impediments to making projections represent "best estimates'' rather than optimistic ''targets.'' For example, what steps can be taken to get more realistic inflation factors built into our projections? We also should examine options for providing fuller budget disclosure on the legislative, economic, and other assumptions underlying projections, and for disclosing the ranges from which the ''best estimates'' were selected. Such information would give the public as well as congressional users of the budget, a greater appreciation for the nature of the budget figures.

• Second, another matter deserving attention is the continuing use of *offsetting business-type revenue* to reduce reported budget totals. For example, the offsetting practice reduced estimated on-budget and off-budget outlays for fiscal year 1981 by about $102 billion. We in GAO believe that this practice significantly understates outlay totals, and we favor the reporting of amounts on a gross basis. Also, I think this would be a step toward simplifying budget totals.

• Third, a related problem is the continued practice of treating sales of *certificates of beneficial ownership* as ''asset'' sales rather than borrowings. This practice, opposed by the 1967 Commission but sanctioned by statute today for some programs, further inflates offsetting receipts and stands in the way of a full disclosure of agency borrowing activities.

• Fourth, concerning agency borrowings, we find significant inconsistencies in agency practices of recording *budget authority for their borrowings.* In some cases, the recordings represent authorized net borrowing; in other cases the recordings are for authorized gross borrowing. To a certain extent this varying practice reflects differing statutory provisions governing agency borrowings. However, administrative action is possible to bring about more uniform treatment, as evidenced by some recent steps taken by the Office of Management and Budget in this regard.

Related to agency borrowings is the question of the proper budget treatment of the retirement of government-guaranteed debt. Our recent work on the retirement of Amtrak's debt showed the need for further study and the development of government-wide standards to insure that the budget treatment of such retirements fully disclose key aspects of the transaction and be subject to the congressional budget process.

• Fifth, there also are other unresolved issues pertaining to the *budget authority concept* and its application. It is, of course, most important to have meaningful, consistent, and well understood budget

authority recordings given the fact that budget authority is the key financial resource amount controlled by the Congress and executive branch in their annual budget-setting actions. Unfortunately, there is confusion about budget authority given the maze of varying applications.

For example, there is no general agreement on which *multiyear programs should be ''fully funded''* in their first year. I believe that the full funding approach, which OMB now prescribes for several programs, can facilitate more equitable comparisons of programs and the ''up front'' disclosure of total costs, and have therefore taken steps in GAO to develop criteria for the application of full funding. It is clear, however, that more work is needed to identify the programs where full funding should be applied.

Another confusing budget authority matter is the fact that budget authority recordings do not always *represent total new obligational authority even in one year programs.* There are many programs, including public enterprise revolving fund and emergency programs, where current conventions result in budget authority recordings that express far less than estimated or actual new obligational authority. In public enterprise revolving funds, for example, the recordings do not encompass the obligational authority that is generated by program business-type collections. I think that such varying practices among budget accounts lessen the meaningfulness of the budget authority concept, and add to the general confusion about the budget. This is another area where streamlining and simplification of budget practices is needed.

• Sixth, we need to look again at the concepts used to express dollar levels of programs activity. Both the Second Hoover Commission and the later Commission on Budget Concepts endorsed *cost-based budgeting and the reporting of receipts and expenditures on an accrual basis.* We have had only partial implementation of these recommendations, with attendant confusion and uncertainty. For example, although Federal agencies have taken significant strides to adopt modern accrual accounting systems, and the President's *Budget Appendix* now reports ''costs'' for many activities, budget decisions and controls continue to be on ''obligations'' rather than costs.

Expanding the use of costs and accrued expenditures in the budget process would require, among other things, rethinking the existing statutory definition of budget authority, which now defines budget authority as authority to enter obligations. It is most unlikely that we could move fully to cost-based budgeting and the reporting of expenditures on an accrual basis in the budget as long as the budget process continues to operate under statutory provisions that make budget authority for *obligations* the focus of the budget decisions and control. However, we can and are requiring agency accounting systems to produce cost data for internal operations and decision making when it is required by law or necessary for good management.

Over the past several years, the Department of Treasury and GAO with the help of other agencies have been experimenting with full accrual concepts in developing consolidated financial statements of the federal government. This effort is aimed at improving governmental accounting and financial reporting. One major inaccuracy noted is in the reporting of federal assets. For instance, it was recognized that earned but unpaid federal income taxes receivable should be included in financial reports since accrued but unpaid obligations are reported. As of September 30, 1978, accrued corporate taxes were estimated to be $7.7 billion. Methodologies have also recently been developed for estimating accrued federal individual income taxes and excise taxes to be included in federal consolidated statements.

Even more significant, dollar-wise, is the absence of reported values for public domain lands. It is roughly estimated that the fair market value of the approximately 1 billion acres of federally owned land would exceed $200 billion. Also, permanent improvements such as reforestation and monumentation are excluded from land values. Moreover, the outer continental shelf and proven reserves of inland oil, gas and mineral deposits are not reported.

In addition to studying these problems, the Department of Treasury and GAO are experimenting with measuring assets at their current values (current exchange prices) in consolidated report. Current values are helpful in assessing the financial viability of the federal government and are also helpful in assessing future resource needs of the federal agencies.

Moving beyond measurement problems, I would like to discuss another major development that is placing strains on existing budget procedures: the *growth in the "relatively uncontrollable" portion of the budget.* One of the most important changes over the past ten to fifteen years has been the increase in the part of the budget that cannot be significantly controlled in the annual appropriations process without prior changes in the authorizing legislation. OMB figures indicate that the relatively uncontrollable part of budget outlays grew from about 59 percent in fiscal year 1967 to about 77 percent estimated for 1981. This growth largely reflects the growth of federal entitlement programs and long-term demographic trends. About 50 percent of the proposed 1981 budget was for judicially enforceable entitlement payments.

I should add that the portion of the budget that is, from a practical point of view, relatively uncontrollable in any one year is probably even higher than the 77 percent. There are, for example, numerous operations and maintenance programs for public works, defense facilities, etc., that cannot be drastically reduced without unacceptable consequences. In this regard, we probably should consider additional or alternative classifications of programs to better bring out the gradations of programs between the strictly controllable and uncontrollable.

The growth in uncontrollables, and prospects for their continued growth, points to a critical need for the Congress and the executive branch to take budget actions with a *longer time horizon in mind*. In this manner, budget outcomes and priorities will increasingly reflect conscious choices made in a "strategic planning" type of process rather than being accepted as simple uncontrollable factors. Consideration should be given to enhancing multiyear planning and budget actions, and the organizational and procedural changes that may be required. The recent steps by OMB and the Budget Committees to include multiyear-planning amounts in the budget documents and resolutions is a big step forward, though it is too early to say how effective this will be in determining future budget decisions.

Furthermore, as uncontrollables grow, the budget arena will have to be systematically and formally expanded to include authorizing committees and their actions. Already, these committees are playing crucial roles in the congressional budget process. Existing budget documents and processes need to be examined to see whether they are adequate for addressing budget issues that are increasingly a matter for authorizing committee concern. For example, should budget schedules and narratives be revised to provide more explicitly information on the amounts that are contingent upon new authorizing legislation? Is there a need to organize the budget to better match the statement of goals in authorizing legislation?

This need will be magnified further if the Congress implements a schedule of oversight review and reauthorizations. In short, we should ask ourselves whether the budget processes that were largely put in place in a simpler era when most of the budget was controllable through the appropriations process, are suitable in today's more complicated and broadly participative environment.

Budget cycle timing and workload pressure are also mounting and require thorough study. In my opinion, a principal objective of any streamlining of the budget process should be to reduce unnecessary timing and workload pressures, thereby permitting more orderly action on the budget as well as more focused and sustained analysis of important policy and related budget issues. This better analysis should have as its objective revised and clearer statements of objectives and an improvement in the accountability of officials for their actions.

The Congress and the executive branch have placed themselves under additional budget scheduling and workload demands in recent years. The Congress for its part, through the landmark 1974 Congressional Budget and Impoundment Control Act, increased the number of congressional participants in budgeting, and established several new scheduling and reporting requirements. The 1974 act was a major step forward in developing a systematic, overall budget process, but it is uncertain even today, six years later, how many of the new procedures will evolve and take effect. The Congress' efforts to effect "reconciliation" through the First Concurrent Budget Resolution for 1981 certainly show that the process is still undergoing important improvements with many uncertainties remaining. I think that in the near future we can expect continued and perhaps even more sharp testings of the congressional budget process as demands for increases in "real dollar" defense spending compete with other demands for increased spending, for a balanced budget, and for a tax reduction. In such an environment, it will be vitally important for the Congress to enhance its capability for setting budget priorities and authorizing and appropriating funds in a systematic and timely manner.

I should add that congressional budget-related workload also is increasing due to the use of more detailed and short-term timed authorizations and appropriations.

On the executive branch side, the installation of ZBB procedures has significantly increased paperwork, increased the amount of time spent on the mechanics of budget formulation, and reduced the time available for agency analysis and monitoring of budget execution. I've already mentioned the problem of agencies increasingly having to develop budget information in a number of dissimilar categories for various users, which adds to workload.

The combined effect of these mounting pressures is probably a reduction in the time available for needed in-depth studies and analyses. Serious attention should be given to finding ways to reduce unnecessary workload so that better budget planning, policy analysis, monitoring, and evaluation may take place, and in a more coordinated and intensive way.

Modifying ZBB procedures to restrict comprehensive ZBB treatment to selected programs in accordance with some schedule—perhaps to coincide with a congressional oversight review and reauthorization agenda—would be one way of streamlining the process. Also, the Congress should consider moving from annual authorizations and funding actions to biennial or even less frequent actions in order to streamline the process and permit time to be devoted to the critical issues. Certainly a move in this direction would be warranted for many well-functioning, routine programs about which there is very little controversy. It strikes me as a misallocation of time and energy to devote as much work on these programs each year as on certain large and changing programs requiring thorough study and justification.

We need to be careful about spreading ourselves too thinly—a real danger at this time when we must deal with an increasing number of complex programs, "budget actors," and deadlines. Already, the task of putting a budget together is too frequently just a mechanical exercise divorced from planning, evaluation, and other management processes. One goal of streamlining the process should be to "close the loop" and reintegrate budget formulations and execution with these other important management and legislative processes.

Continued efforts also are needed to improve budget execution in order to assure that funds are used in an orderly and planned manner during the fiscal year. For instance, strengthening the apportionment process and better monitoring of spending patterns would be helpful in minimizing excessive year-end spending; but, at the same time, closer executive branch controls over spending could raise new impoundment and deferral questions. We therefore should consider whether the impoundment and deferral reporting requirements of the 1974 budget legislation create disincentives to curtailing wasteful spending. If so, we should devise new procedures that eliminate these disincentives while safeguarding essential congressional control over spending levels.

Finally, we should examine whether the kinds of information considered in budgeting and reported in the relevant documents are the kinds that will be needed by decision makers in the decade of the 1980s and beyond. For example, we probably should develop more information and analyses of global and national conditions, long-term trends, and alternatives, and relate these to the specific national needs and missions of the federal budget. I am thinking here of the kind of trend information contained in the recently released report of the Task Force on Global Resources and the Environment. This type of forward-looking information, along with strengthened special analyses of cross-cutting policies—for instance, research and development—would do much to strengthen the analytical content of the budget.

I have covered in this discussion many topics directly related to the budget. I should add that improving our system of budgeting is only one way, albeit a critical one, of increasing the overall effectiveness of the government. There are a number of other important administrative and organizational questions that our society and government need to consider to help us chart a course for sound governance over the next several decades. For this reason,

I support Chairman Bolling's proposal in H.R. 6380 for the establishment of another Hoover-type commission. However, as I have stated to Chairman Bolling and Chairman Brooks, I believe that there also is a need for a separate commission to study the kinds of budget matters I have discussed with you today. I think that special treatment of these matters is called for because of several factors: the highly technical nature of the subject area, the significant budget watershed we are now passing through, and the fact that much has already been done to identify the issues that need to be addressed.

I should add that it is important that we move ahead on certain needed budget reforms without waiting for action by a study commission. Some needed changes such as action by the Congress to return the ''off-budget'' federally owned entities to the budget should be undertaken as soon as possible. Also, the Congress should act now to improve congressional controls over federal credit programs, and require that agency sales of certificates of beneficial ownership be treated as borrowings rather than ''sales of assets.'' There may be other areas as well where immediate action should be taken.

We now have a project underway at GAO concerning outstanding budget issues, and we are identifying issues that can be acted upon now along with those requiring further study by a commission or some study group.

Whatever the outcome of these budget matters, I am sure that the next few years will be challenging and exciting ones for those of us concerned with the budget process. I wish this association and its members well in these coming years, and have enjoyed this chance to speak to you this morning about a subject that is of such importance to us all. Thank you.

8
Guidelines to Federal Budget Reform

Naomi Caiden
California State College, San Bernardino

Public budget systems are excellent barometers of the prevailing political environment. Where participants are in agreement on major issues, where resources are available to accommodate most goals, and where it is possible to look ahead with reasonable certainty and confidence, budget processes tend to be stable and routine. Budget reform may appear as a matter for technicians trying to make improvements to a generally satisfactory situation. But where there are irreconcilable differences about the goals of public policy and role of government, where lack of resources forces decisions to the detriment of certain groups, and where uncertainties obscure the way ahead, budget reform may be highly controversial, bringing into question the appropriateness and viability of the budget process itself.

For several years the capacity of the federal budget process to perform the functions expected of it has been a source of disquiet. Critics have pointed to ''uncontrollability'' of the majority of federal expenditures, confusing budget numbers which appear to move of their own volition, and important areas of federal financial activity omitted from the budget altogether. Each year the budget process is marked by complexity, confrontations, delays, and threats of breakdown. Budget deficits of a size once unimaginable have become routine.

These stresses have elicited a renewed interest in federal budget reform. Previously, reforms had generally concentrated on two areas. The first emphasized changes in budgetary classification and techniques to increase the analytical content of executive budgeting methods and bring about greater efficiency, effectiveness, and foresight in governmental programs.[1] The second focused on the congressional budget process, culminating in the Congressional Budget and Impoundment Act of 1974, designed to provide Congress with budget capacity commensurate with that of the executive branch in place of its previous somewhat haphazard and decentralized procedures.[2]

These approaches to reform left their mark on budget theory and practice, but neither has been entirely successful. Their deficiencies have been manifest less in the formal abandonment of sophisticated budget techniques or the prevailing debate over the effectiveness of the Congressional Budget Act than in the emergence of unanticipated areas of concern, to whose resolution neither approach appears entirely appropriate. Increasing federal responsibilities, particularly in the areas of social security and economic well-being, have brought about long-term commitments to future expenditures which are relatively difficult to alter. The linkage of the federal budget with the fortunes of a fluctuating economy has made short-term predictions hazardous and subject to frequent revision. Difficulties in control also arise because vast sums nominally within the control of the federal government are actually managed by others. In a fast-moving world, where public resources seem increasingly limited, accommodation to changing policy priorities amid political dissension has inevitably placed strain on the budget.

Frustration at the breakdown of familiar processes and the faltering of accepted institutions has sparked a variety of new reform proposals. Approached singly, each on its merits, these measures present a bewildering jumble of specific remedies for specific ills. Taken together, they constitute an identifiable reform movement incorporating a vision of an entirely different kind of budget process: a more responsive, credible, influential, consistent, and integrated budget. Specifically, reformers seek to improve budget capacity by lengthening the time frame of financial decision making, allowing greater flexibility to adjust to changing conditions, providing more relevant and inclusive information and analysis, improving control, and integrating budget policy.

The goals of reform appear irreproachable, but the very gap between vision and reality betrays obstacles to implementation which go beyond mere selection of instruments to serve agreed-upon ends. The concept of budget capacity encompasses a number of budget characteristics—flexibility, planning, control, responsiveness—which cannot easily be accommodated simultaneously and have serious political and institutional ramifications.

Source: Public Budgeting & Finance, 3, 4 (Winter 1983): 4–22. Reprinted by permission.

Reform objectives therefore constitute less an identifiable blueprint than an agenda for choice. What characteristics should be emphasized in the budget process at any specific time? The nature of federal expenditures suggests a more selective approach to budget reform, with decision categories and time cycles established according to perceptions of need, but the exact nature of any future budget process would depend on choices regarding relative values such as protection of commitments against flexibility, stability against change, policy directives against detailed control. Budget reform thus implies budget design and the probable transformation of familiar frameworks.

In the light of the changed nature of federal government functions and advances in sophisticated information handling, budget reform may seem well overdue. In fact, several changes have been made in recent years which point in the direction of future practices. But in stating the case for reform, it is also important not to overstate it. Budget reform is not a panacea for those budgeting problems which stem from fundamental differences in political outlook, inconsistent revenue and expenditure policies, and the results of pressure group politics. Budget reform cannot substitute for viable policy making, the careful building of agreement on legitimate objectives, or the dynamics of the political system. Nor is budget reform a category that can be defined a priori: rather it, too, is shaped by political choices and the development of consensus on what the ground rules of financial decision making should be. The proposals currently under discussion are therefore only a first step in the process of determining a framework for decision making which satisfies the needs of those who must work through it.[3]

The Need for Reform

Successful reform requires realistic analysis of failings. In what areas is the federal budget deficient? Why have budget processes not lived up to expectations?

Since debate on federal budgetary shortcomings has been extensive, only a brief summary is presented here. The main complaint seems to be that accountability in the federal budget system is denied by "uncontrollability" of the majority of federal expenditures, instability of budget numbers, fragmentation of accounts, and repetitiveness of procedures.

"Uncontrollability"

Over three quarters of expenditures in the federal budget are classified as "relatively uncontrollable," that is, mandated by legislation.[4] They include interest payments, multiyear contracts, and entitlements to individuals. The amount of entitlements varies each year according to the number of persons eligible to receive them and, because many are indexed, with the rate of inflation. Many of these long-term commitments have been placed outside the normal appropriations process to stabilize and protect them.

The recent change in budget procedures, which placed the reconciliation process at the beginning of the budget cycle, has had the effect of reincorporating entitlements within the annual budget debate. Reconciliation, used in conjunction with the first concurrent budget resolution, enables Congress to instruct its committees to achieve a stipulated level of savings by making legislative changes.[5] But bringing entitlements into the annual budget cycle does not really solve the problem of coping with long-term commitments: it short-circuits accepted legislative processes and debate, increases uncertainties among those dependent on the federal government, fails to stem federal deficits, and may raise the degree of budgetary conflict beyond a tolerable level. Some acceptable means of balancing continuity against adaptation to changing circumstances and of relating long-term commitments to short-term exigencies has yet to be devised.

Instability

Because so much of the budget is taken up by open-ended commitments and automatically indexed payments, it is highly vulnerable to economic fluctuations. Budget numbers are volatile, subject to re-estimation as assessments of conditions change, and open to disagreement depending on competing economic assumptions. Budgets are determined less by deliberate decision than by economic conditions. There are also difficulties in understanding the impact of budgetary decisions, since the multiple steps of the budget process provide a number of possible starting points for calculation, many of which may be estimates rather than firm quantities. As the budget process proceeds, the budget itself seems more and more opaque, problematic, and open to political manipulation.

Fragmentation

The federal budget extends over so many complex areas that adequate budget scrutiny of every program is virtually impossible. Many federal activities are carried out indirectly through contracts, state and local governments, or third-party reimbursements. Certain financial transactions are not even recorded in the budget. These include off-budget agencies of various kinds, loans and loan guarantees, and expenditures offset against revenues by agencies engaging in business-type activities. The budget also does not take account of tax expenditures, special exemptions from the tax code, or costs imposed on the private sector through regulation, although these have important economic repercussions. Fragmentation impairs budgetary effectiveness both through direct loss of budgetary control and by the distortion of the information on which decision making is based. It may be argued that the federal budget has not kept up with the developing role of the federal government as a directing rather than an implementing organization, doing less and influencing more.[6]

Repetitiveness

The passage of the budget through Congress has evolved into a highly complex and repetitive process. The Congressional Budget Act of 1974 superimposed a measure of integration upon the previous practice of dealing with appropriations without any notion of the budget as a whole. The act added two concurrent budget resolutions, budget committees, and a timetable, but because the first budget resolution's totals were not binding, members of Congress could vote for constraints on the budget as a whole while simultaneously voting for appropriations inconsistent with them.[7] The transfer of reconciliation to the beginning of the process, allowing Congress to instruct committees to achieve savings and enforcing a single vote on the consolidated cuts, together with later change which made the first resolution binding, prevented whipsawing between votes for totals and appropriations. But reconciliation added one more step to a process already burdened with resolutions, authorizations, and appropriations, all dealing with the same subject matter. As stress on the budget has grown, extra votes have been needed on continuing resolutions, increases in the debt limit, and supplementary appropriations. Under the strain the budget process seems increasingly vulnerable to breakdown and prolonged delays, and its complexity augments rather than eases budgetary conflicts.

The criticisms of the budget process indicate a widely perceived gap between budget tasks and budget capacity. Despite significant changes, budget methods still appear unable to answer the demands made upon them. From this imbalance between performance and expectations has emerged a variety of suggestions for improvement.

Toward Budget Reform

It is not easy to summarize recent proposals for federal budget reform because they generally address specific deficiencies rather than the concept of the budget process as a whole. Since suggestions overlap and recur at different times, with or without modification, a comprehensive listing is well-nigh impossible. In some cases a single proposal attempts to deal with a number of goals, so that exclusive categorization is also difficult. But the majority of the proposals cluster around four main themes: time frame, volatility, program control, and integration.

Time Frame

Lip service long paid to the need to extend the annual time frame of the federal budget has found more concrete form in bills for a biennial budget, directed primarily at relieving the workload of Congress by allowing more time for decision making and oversight. Because decisions would have to be made only once every two years, time would be available for better evaluation of the merits and costs of federal programs and agencies and for long-range planning, while the two-year funding pattern would provide greater stability for recipients of federal monies.[8] The budget process would be strengthened and streamlined by ensuring a clearer distinction among its various elements, so that congressional control and public accountability would be improved. The idea of a biennial budget, however, raises a number of questions. How might elements of the budget process be allocated over two years? How ought the budget cycle to be aligned with the political cycle? How would a biennial budget maintain control of programs and agencies? The four major biennial budget bills presented to Congress during 1983 resolve these problems in different ways.[9]

Table 1
Allocation of the budget process over two years in major biennial budget bills presented in 1983

	Year 1	Year 2
Roth Bill S.20	Budget process, including concurrent resolution but open to change by two-thirds of congressional membership, and an omnibus appropriations bill.	Oversight. President and CBO report to Budget Committees, January 15 and July 15.
Cochran Bill S.922	Budget process, including concurrent resolution but for first-year budget authority only.	Presidential revisions. Budget authority for second year.
Ford Bill S.12	First concurrent resolution. Authorizations.	Presidential revisions. Appropriations. Second concurrent resolution. Reconciliation.
Panetta Bill H.R. 750	Oversight. Committees report authorizations. Budget Committees report concurrent resolution.	Presidential revisions. Completion of authorizations and appropriations. Completion of concurrent resolution. Reconciliation.

The allocation of the congressional budget process over a two-year period is summarized in Table 1. The Roth bill (S.20) reserves the first year for the budget process, (extending it by changing the beginning of the fiscal year from October to January), leaving the second year for oversight. The Cochran bill (S.922) places the general framework of the budget process within the first year, but maintains separate budget authority for each of the two years, so that every year it would still be necessary to pass separate authorizations and appropriations for the following year. The Ford bill (S.12) splits the process fairly evenly, requiring the first concurrent resolution and authorizations in the first year and appropriations, second concurrent resolution, and reconciliation in the second. The Panetta bill (H.R. 750) uses the first year for oversight and preliminary committee reports only, leaving the second year for definitive budget decisions on authorizations, appropriations, a concurrent resolution, and reconciliation.

In a biennial budget process, it is important that budget and political cycles are aligned so that neither incoming executive nor legislature is confronted with a two-year period in which it cannot influence events. The Ford and Panetta bills would begin the fiscal period in October of even-numbered years; the Cochran bill would start it in October of odd-numbered years. The Roth bill, by alternating budget process and oversight years, enables the two-year fiscal period to begin at the end of the first year of a presidential term (see Table 2).

Advocates of a biennial budget assert that it would bring greater control of programs and agencies because it would allow more time specifically for their oversight. The Roth bill allows the entire second year for oversight. The Panetta bill makes detailed provisions for committees to conduct oversight so that their reports might feed into the budget process. But a biennial budget would also allow (except for the Cochran bill) agencies and others to enjoy funding for two years, which may be unacceptable in the light of a congressional trend toward more one-year program authorizations.[10]

Perhaps the most difficult problem relates to the question of revision during the two-year process. The Roth bill provides for reports from the president and the Congressional Budget Office (CBO) during the second year and reconciliation at any time during the process, while the other bills allow for presidential revisions at the beginning of the second year. But the bills do not make clear the permissible limits of these revisions or whether Congress may debate them. If modifications are too great, they may destroy the work done in the first year and reopen the entire budget. The Panetta and Ford bills to some degree mitigate the problem by providing for

Table 2
S. 20 (Roth Bill): The biennial budget and political cycles for three budgets (I, II, III)

Year of presidential term	Year of congressional term	Budget in process	Budget in effect
1	1	Budget II	Budget I: 2nd year
2	2	Oversight	Budget II: 1st year
3	1	Budget III	Budget II: 2nd year
4	2	Oversight	Budget III: 1st year

definitive decision making late in the process, with completion of a single or second concurrent resolution right at the end, but this reserving of options may be gained at the price of coherent guidelines for the process as a whole. On the other hand, the Roth and Cochran bills, which plan a single concurrent resolution at the beginning of the process, run the risk that later revisions may destroy the resolution or that it may be outdistanced by later events. Biennial budgeting, however, faces in slightly more acute form the same problem that afflicts annual budgeting—keeping the budget up to date in a volatile environment.

Volatility

Volatility of budget numbers occurs because changes in the economy impinge automatically on the volume of revenues and expenditures, particularly indexed entitlements and debt payments. Budgeting in conditions of economic uncertainty is less a matter of the advance stipulation of quantities than making assumptions about key economic indicators and the effects of their expected behavior on the budget. There are, therefore, a number of proposals which seek to gain greater stability and clarity in federal budgeting by gaining agreement, objectivity, and flexibility in the use of assumptions.

In a proposal put forward by Rudolph Penner, all parties would agree in December on a common set of economic forecasts and projections to be used throughout the first budget resolution and might also project the implications of different sets of assumptions on policy decisions. The assumptions might be updated for the administration's July budget revisions and the second budget resolution. Agreement on assumptions might enable budget participants to distinguish more clearly between issues of policy and issues arising from different assumptions.

A bill sponsored by Representative Richard Gephardt also aims to fix a common set of budget assumptions. It would establish a Board of Revenue Estimators consisting of chairman of the Board of Governors of the Federal Reserve System, the director of the Office of Management and Budget (OMB), and the director of CBO. This board would determine revenue estimates to be used in the budget resolutions over a three-year period.

A third proposal by Representative Robert Michel (H.R. 6400) suggests that the figures for outlays, revenues, and deficits or surpluses in the budget resolutions be replaced by ranges of numbers. These ranges would remain in effect for sixty days, after which the budget committees would review them and, if the economy had drastically changed, might recommend revisions.[11] Even if agreement were possible on assumptions, however, it is doubtful whether that alone would solve the problem of volatility. As long as the economy is subject to very sharp short-run cyclical effects generated by exogenous forces, no procedure that would simply unify or lead to agreement on budget assumptions will be satisfactory. Budget stability seems impossible in the face of economic instability and means have still to be devised for budget processes to meet this challenge.

Program Control

Recent reform proposals to improve program control and accountability have taken two main forms: those directed at more detailed and systematic oversight of programs, and those concerned with budget coverage and inclusiveness.

During the late 1970s concern with the difficulties of gaining adequate evaluation of programs led to a number of bills advocating "sunset" procedures. These bills provided that unless programs were reauthorized by a specific date, they would automatically terminate. More recently similar proposals have emphasized a systematic and efficient oversight review process by congressional committees. For example, during 1981 a wide variety of bills called for periodic review and reauthorization every four

(S. 581), five (H.R. 1130, H.R. 2547), six (H.R. 331), or ten (H.R. 2) years. A schedule would be set up for oversight reviews by Congress (H.R. 434, H.R. 58, H.R. 1130), or the committees themselves (H.Res. 100), or by the comptroller general (H.R. 2547). Alternatively, oversight plans would be included in authorizing legislation (S. 581). The committees would report on their findings to Congress (H.R. 2, H.R. 58). There were also several proposals for a program inventory (H.R. 2, H.R. 58, H.R. 434, H.R. 1130). Agencies would be required to report to the committees (H.R. 2, H.R. 58) and to carry out their own evaluations (H.R. 434). Other proposals suggested a one-year pilot testing of all new programs (S. 149) and a special period set aside for oversight (H.Res. 218).

Greater information and control have been sought by proposals reforming the structure of the budget. At its simplest level, this approach calls for incorporating all off-budget expenditures into the unified budget, accurate reporting of gross expenditures, and consistency in recording complex transactions such as those of revolving funds or certificates of beneficial ownership.

More complex proposals have addressed the diversity of federal expenditures through measures to set up special categories of decision making both within and outside the budget. For example, a bill to establish a capital budget (H.R. 6591, 1982) aimed to provide better information on public capital infrastructure, identify deficiencies, rank expenditures, and improve oversight. It stressed the need for a comprehensive approach and consistent policy making in the planning and implementation of capital investment.

Several bills have gained considerable support for a separate credit budget.[12] For example, one such bill (H.R. 2372, 1981) sought greater efficiency in the allocation of loans and loan guarantees, coordination of credit policy with fiscal policy, monitoring the economic effects of credit activities, and maintaining control over them. Twice a year the secretary of the Treasury in consultation with the Council of Economic Advisors would report on federal credit activities, the condition of the economy and credit market, and federal fiscal and monetary policy. The views and estimates by the various committees submitted to the Budget Committees would include information on credit, and the Banking Committees of each house would also make reports. Appropriate levels for credit programs

would be included in the budget resolutions and be subject to budget processes in the same way as direct expenditures.

Similar proposals have been framed relating to tax expenditures, aiming to establish a process in which claims for tax benefits might be weighed against budgetary considerations, and tax expenditures would be decided in the context of overall budget policy.[13] A bill for this purpose (H.R. 4882, 1981) would set ceilings on the overall level of revenue losses from tax expenditures each year, in the hope of moving toward tax reform and lower taxes. Another bill (S. 193, 1981) would establish a ceiling on revenue losses from tax expenditures at 30 percent of the level of net revenues and require authorizing legislation for new tax expenditures. A similar proposal (S. 582, 1981) would limit authorizations of new tax expenditures to ten years and require reconsideration of existing tax expenditures by 1992.

Integration

The movement toward budget integration, the orderly development of the budget in which detailed decisions take place within the framework of determined aggregates, found expression in the Congressional Budget Act of 1974. In 1980 a further step was taken to gain enforcement for budget totals by transferring the reconciliation procedure to the beginning of the process. In 1982 the first budget resolution was made binding by providing that if the second resolution were not passed by the stipulated date, the totals of the first resolution would be enforced.

The flexibility of the congressional budget process, which may be altered without formal amendment, means that reforms may come quickly and also often informally. There are several proposals to gain greater integration in the process. The majority center upon the first concurrent resolution: suggestions have been made for an extraordinary majority to increase first resolution ceilings or pass a resolution after the second resolution (S. 148, S. 938); to eliminate the second resolution altogether (S. 20); to expand budget resolution targets to include total entitlement levels; and even to eliminate the first resolution and require Budget Committee plans only.[14] Other proposals center on appropriations, suggesting an omnibus appropriations bill (S. 1683, S. 2471, 96th Congress) or holding the enrollment of appropriations bills until all had passed. Reconciliation has also attracted attention with recommendations including returning it to the end of the process,[15] allowing it any time (S. 20), and reserving it for selective use on matters not addressed in the annual process.[16]

This listing of reform proposals is by no means complete. There are a wide variety of others varying from ''fail-safe'' funding to cover periods when Congress is unable to agree on a continuing resolution to maintain interim operations in the absence of appropriations, to allowing a presidential line-item veto of appropriations. What this brief survey has sought to do is to sketch the main lines of development in current thinking about budget reform. How many of the suggestions will actually find acceptance is open to conjecture. But suppose they were implemented—what kind of budget process would then emerge?

The Vision of Budget Reform

Despite the current ferment of suggestions on the improvement of the federal budget process, the goals of reform have rarely been spelled out. Proposals have usually been designed to remedy specific perceived defects, with little thought about what a reformed budget process would look like. Obviously, the proposals described here spring from different sources. Nevertheless, it is possible to distill from them a generalized picture of a reformed budget system, a kind of vision of budget reform which would probably satisfy most of the reformers, though they would differ on details.

A Foresighted Budget

A favorite theme for many years has been the need for long-term budget planning. Budget horizons should be extended beyond an annual perspective because the implications of many decisions stretch well beyond a single year.[17] Annual budgeting impedes policy planning. Most federal spending is long-term in nature, reflected in the predominance of ''uncontrollables'' in the budget: if these long-term, open-ended commitments are to be brought under control, some form of multiyear budgeting is essential. A longer time perspective would also provide a measure of stability and assurance for those dependent on federal grants to maintain continuing projects and activities, reducing the uncertainties of annual funding.[18]

A Responsive Budget

The budget must be able to respond to changing conditions during the period of the budget cycle, if necessary changing policy direction and adjusting programs. The budget is seen as a means of making adaptations in policy, both in details and in the aggregate.[19] It is necessary to preserve flexibility so that budget decisions may be made in the light of the most recent assessments of economic conditions.[20] The budget should be responsive to the budgetary preferences of the voting public, and provide a means for effective choice.[21]

A Credible Budget

One of the major functions of a budget is to act as an information system, providing data and analyses upon which viable policies may be built. It is therefore essential that budget numbers be clear and consistent. Budget estimates should be as accurate as possible and variances should be systematically analyzed.[22] Budget information should be readily attainable and understandable. It should be accurate, categorized in forms useful for decision making, and based upon realistic, objective, and open assumptions so that it is not manipulated for political purposes.[23] In view of fast-changing conditions, budget figures should be kept up to date through an effective scorekeeping and monitoring system.[24] They should also include accurate projections of likely outcomes of budgetary decisions.[25] It is assumed that the budget would be comprehensive and cover all federal government expenditures.

An Influential Budget

The budget is not an end in itself, but an instrument of control. All federal expenditures should be subject to its influence. The budget should be backed by an effective financial management system which would ensure that expenditures were made in accordance with budgetary stipulations. The budget system would include machinery for the evaluation of programs to assess their accomplishments in meeting their goals.[26] It would provide timely analyses so that budget priorities could be set in accordance with relevant information.[27] The budget would be a means of relating resources and programs to assure efficiency and effectiveness.[28]

A Consistent Budget

The budget is seen as a policy-making instrument through which consistent choices might be made.[29]

The budget should be "an orderly system for developing tax and spending policies and for making choices between various national priorities."[30] It should establish and control fiscal policy with regard to the overall economic picture and broad choices on national priorities.[31] It should be a means for conducting a rational fiscal policy.[32] It should be a tool for examining federal policies on the allocation of resources within the economy.[33]

An Integrated Budget

The budget process is seen as a logical framework, in which initial decisions are carried through in later ones.[34] Decisions made on aggregates should act as binding constraints on detailed spending choices.[35] In this way arguments of overriding national concern may be weighed against specific program issues.[36] Budget procedures should provide for the establishment of overall budget priorities and the subsequent imposition of fiscal discipline on appropriations.[37] Once the framework of limits on spending and taxes has been set, differences should be decided within those limits.

Because there has been relatively little disagreement on these goals, budget reform may appear as a simple matter of assessing the adequacy of proposals to meet them. But experience suggests that budget reform has been a remarkably difficult undertaking and that reformers have been frustrated as much by their assumptions about its nature as by the means through which they have attempted to achieve their goals.[38] If, then, current reform proposals are to become a reality, their assumptions require careful consideration. In particular, those relating to optimality, neutrality, and permanence of traditional frameworks are open to serious question.

Optimality

Reformers typically advocate multiyear budgeting and the use of the budget as a planning tool, but they also acknowledge a need for adjustment to short-term assessments of economic conditions. The compatibility of long-term commitments and short-term flexibility is problematical. Decisions for the future that are constantly revised are quickly perceived as worthless, but advance decisions rigidly adhered to may turn out to be irrelevant or prevent realistic policy making. The dilemma of budgetary planning in unstable times affects not only long-term decisions over a number of years, but even decisions for a single year where initial figures require repeated revision. Similarly, the goals of program control and policy direction coexist uneasily. Whereas in a small and simple budget system both general direction and detailed oversight may be easily accommodated, in large and diverse systems the sheer weight of detailed decision making may drive out consideration of policy direction. Conversely, concentration on policy choices may curtail the possibility of detailed intervention in program control.

These potential inconsistencies among goals suggest that optimality in budget reform may be illusory.[39] Rather than expecting the achievement of the entire vision, it is necessary to choose among the goals and determine which may have to be sacrificed or gained by other means. In other words, budget reform might be envisaged not as a single end state to be accomplished once and for all but as a series of unstable and dynamic tradeoffs, shifting according to the requirements of the time. Moreover, these tradeoffs go beyond abstract theoretical argument to concrete issues of institutional power.

Neutrality

The neutral face of budget reform terms such as "budgetary effectiveness" or "budgetary capacity" conceals their highly charged political nature. Budget integration, for example, involves increased centralization, binding agreements made at high levels, and greater power for the leadership. Against these might be placed an entirely different set of values—the characteristics of an open system, decentralized decision making, representativeness, and ready access to budget action. To the extent that these values are favored and that participants are unwilling to give up power in favor of stronger policy-making capacity, budget reforms toward greater integration, consistency, and direction in the budget process will be unacceptable. In other words, many of the goals of budget reform involve choices among values and, therefore, demand sacrifices of values.

The values involved in budget reforms extend beyond process issues to the substantive outcomes of budgetary decision making. Budget processes affect resource allocations. Changes in procedures potentially shift power among participants, raise or lower revenues and expenditures, facilitate or impede specific policies, alter the balance between legislature and executive. Institutional arrangements may determine whether it is easier to augment or cut a budget.

Budget reforms will, therefore, inevitably be judged not by their theoretical benefits or rationality, but by their impacts on the power struggle and their probable effects on budget allocations. Budget reform is thus political and often suspected of cloaking hidden purposes unconnected with overt goals.

Budget processes also reflect the prevailing political climate. The goals of budget reform stress cohesive policy making, long-term decision making, clear information and analysis, and deliberate choices between competing claims. These goals may conflict with characteristics of the political system, which, it has been contended, emphasizes diffused and incremental decision making, preservation of options, blurring of issues, and avoidance of conflict. If this were true, budget reforms, even if enacted, might be undermined by unsympathetic political norms.

Agreement on neutral goals need not, therefore, translate into support for specific proposals or guarantee that enacted reforms would gain expected results. Successful reform would require agreement among all parties and assurances against loss of present power or compensation for potential losses. For this reason, historically, budget reforms have usually added to rather than changed existing institutions. But there may come a point where familiar frameworks can no longer accommodate the demands placed upon them and may hinder rather than facilitate reform.

Permanence of Traditional Frameworks

Even as reformers attack the inadequacies of budget processes, they appear to assume that their aims can be accomplished within traditional budgeting frameworks. For the most part, they assume that the annual unified budget is a reasonably sound institution requiring only certain adaptations to fulfill its objectives. This assumption may be unwarranted.[40]

According to traditional budget theory, a single finite time cycle for decisions and comprehensive uniform treatment of all financial transactions are sufficient to ensure attainment of budgetary objectives. Where conditions are stable, conflict is contained, and expenditures are directly under bureaucratic control, this kind of decision making may be appropriate. But where instability is so great the budget does not last a year, where contention is so fierce that the budget cannot be made in a single year, and where the majority of expenditures are beyond immediate bureaucratic control, traditional budget systems no longer attain budget goals. The concept of annual budgeting distorts under pressure to adapt to an environment for which it was never designed.

The framework of the annual unified budget, already under strain, would have further difficulty in accommodating the objectives of reform. These objectives emphasize major policy determinations, but budget theory demands comprehensive decisions on all programs.

Even at present it is difficult to compress all decisions within the budget cycle, while reform would require an even greater workload (as the proposal for a biennial budget recognizes). The reform vision requires policy making on a number of areas of financial decision making whose varied time spans do not fit easily within a uniform funding cycle. The rapid outdating of budget estimates suggests that decision making in annual increments is no longer a realistic means of control. If the vision of budget reform were to be implemented, it would imply far-reaching changes in fundamental budget concepts.

The apparent imbalance between decision-making needs and decision-making capacity indicates reforms are in order. But the assumptions of the prevailing vision of budget reform may no longer be tenable. Budget reform seems less an optimal end state than an agenda for choice, less a neutral objective than a series of political negotiations, less an adjustment within an institutional framework than a transformation of that framework itself. If budget reform is to be more than a vision, it will be necessary for reformers to confront the implications of this change in orientation.

New Directions in Federal Budget Reform

If budget reform is really an agenda for choice, which goals should be preferred? If it implies continuing transformation of budget processes, what considerations should govern their design? What kinds of decision making should the federal budget process serve in the last quarter of the twentieth century?

Answers to these questions deserve much fuller discussion than is possible within the brief confines of this article. The purpose of this section is not to establish a definitive blueprint for federal budget reform, to sift through existing proposals, or to substitute others for them. Rather it is to set out some general considerations regarding the direction of budget reform which might act as a starting point for further discussion.

It would seem that for some time to come the federal government will be held responsible for guidance of the economy through fiscal and monetary policies. The majority of its expenditures will continue to consist of large programs: four items—defense, social security, debt service, and medicare—make up over 90 percent of the budget, and other large entitlement programs account for much of the rest. Much of the budget will involve long-term commitments, highly sensitive to changes in economic indicators, and controllable primarily through indexing and eligibility policies. Many programs will continue to be administered indirectly through state and local governments, quasi-autonomous governmental authorities, and private or not-for-profit organizations.

Such a pattern of finances suggests a budget process which is policy-oriented and capable of answering major questions about the direction of the finances, the impact of social and economic trends on the budget, and the effectiveness of federal programs. What are the implications of current budget policies for the future? What would be the impact of changes in federal policy on significant budget indicators, now and later? How should growing commitments be paid for or, alternatively, how may they be reduced? How are different areas of federal policy affected by proposals for increases or reductions in funding? How are we doing? What should we be looking at?

If these perceptions are correct, then a more selective focus on the budget would seem indicated. Policy concerns would generate budget categories, whose exact nature would depend on consensus regarding their usefulness. They might cut across program categories, budgeting for such items as capital expenditures, research and development, or credit financing. They might also aggregate expenditures, both comprehensively and by groups (similar to the Canadian "envelope" concept). These budget categories would not be purely informational but would drive the budget to channel funds and set constraints as appropriate.

A selective focus would also extend to budget time cycles, which might vary as appropriate: it is not necessary to decide everything every year.[41] In any

case, much of the budget is really funded continuously and automatically, representing stable commitments by the federal government to individuals. These entitlements might well be recognized for what they are and abstracted from annual decision making altogether, subject to periodic debate to ensure adaptations to demographic, economic, and social trends by means of changing formulas for indexing and eligibility.

These facets of a more differentiated budget process interlock with one another, since the separation of different policy areas and functions allows for different time cycles. Decision-making needs might be met more effectively by reducing the annual workload, focusing attention on crucial policy-making areas, cutting down the level of conflict and repetitiveness, providing more stable funding, and recognizing different requirements for different parts of the budget. But these things could not be achieved without costs. They involve tradeoffs in favor of centralization, integration, and leadership against decentralization, access, and representation; in favor of executive against congressional administration of details; in favor of the primacy of broad policy direction against program by program control; in favor of stability of funding and protection of commitments against capacity to respond to immediate circumstances. It is necessary to weigh the values that might be sacrificed and devise appropriate means for preserving or compensating for them.

A major issue is flexibility. Federal decision makers require flexibility to implement macroeconomic policies and avoid large unplanned deficits resulting from short-term economic fluctuations. Flexibility, in the sense of capacity to revise initial estimates and take action to cope with the effects of unforeseen expenditure growth and diminished revenues, may be achieved either by raising taxes, cutting expenditures, or tolerating large deficits. If, as seems likely, federal budget makers will continue to live with uncertainty and revenue constraints, they will be forced to devise means to gain flexibility without destroying carefully constructed budget frameworks. Presently, the protection of long-term commitments restricts options and increases pressures on the unprotected areas of the budget. One option is, therefore, to abstract certain entitlements from the budget and establish them as self-sustaining systems with their own sources of funding which could be increased as required, with provisions for limited borrowing or access to other revenues in specified circumstances. Remaining expenditures and revenues could be monitored closely and provision made for interventions at specified intervals to defer or rescind expenditures, raise (or lower) taxes, or change monetary policy. The destabilizing effects of rapid changes in decisions might be mitigated by the use of a contingency fund, "trigger" taxes, or alternative budgets set in advance. But it should be clear that reforms relating to flexibility would involve choices regarding tolerance of deficits, acceptability of tax increases, and the degree of uncertainty which should be borne by recipients of entitlements, beneficiaries of other programs, public employees, and taxpayers.

Emphasis on broad policy considerations and extended budget cycles would also imply less detailed control through the budget process. In any case the annual budget has not by all accounts served this function satisfactorily, particularly where administration is by third parties. It would seem better to ensure control of programs through stronger accounting, financial management, and audit systems. Congressional oversight could be conducted separately or according to schedules related to more flexible budget cycles. Annual appropriations are also not a very effective way of controlling agency policies, and other means of intervention need to be devised, balancing administrative discretion against legislative control.

Few social institutions are entirely impervious to their environment and fail to make some adaptation to prevailing circumstances. The federal budget is no exception. Increasingly it represents a continuous flow of revenues and expenditures with periodic initiatives to modify them. Reform proposals recognize the need to routinize these interventions through such measures as oversight schedules, separate budgets, cross-cutting categories, biennial frameworks, and revisions of assumptions. Decisions are being made within the bounds of more general frameworks and multiyear projections are a vital part of debate. At least one area—social security—has been explicitly recognized as an issue apart from the annual budget to be decided by different means. Repeated recourse to funding adjustments throughout the year and continuing resolutions underline the continuity of federal spending, while recent executive initiatives for fail-safe measures to ward off possible funding gaps and "trigger" taxes are also responses to the impossibility of exact prediction in

contemporary budgeting. Many appropriations are long-term in nature, and agencies have considerable flexibility in programming of funds.[42]

As time goes on, more developments of this kind may be expected, but neither the pace nor direction of budget reform is pre-ordained. It is not possible to paint the picture of the budget of the future in more than general terms, because the path of reform depends at each point on the options chosen, each of which has profound political and institutional ramifications. Nor may it be assumed that budget reform is the solution to budget problems. It cannot substitute for consistent policy making, clear thinking, or recognition of the future consequences of present actions. It cannot promise balanced budgets in times of slowing economic growth, confidence in the public sector, lower taxes, or greater predictability in human events. It cannot promise to solve the intrinsic budget problem of reconciling resources and claims, or to harmonize "the legislative imperative for fragmentation with the drive for integrated budget outcomes."[43] Budget processes are shaped as much by their environment as they shape them. But it is hoped that budget reforms might focus debate on relevant categories of decision, provide realistic forums for debate, enable the use of reliable and accurate data and analysis, and help enable agreement rather than hinder it.

Notes

1. See Allen Schick, "The Road to PPB: The Stages of Budget Reform,"*Public Administration Review* 26 (December 1966), pp. 243–258.
2. See Allen Schick, *Congress and Money: Budgeting, Spending, and Taxing* (Washington, D.C.: The Urban Institute, 1980).
3. Reform of processes is not the only response to federal budget problems. An alternative approach is to advocate a radical reduction in federal government activities, particularly through constitutional limitation of federal expenditures and a balanced budget. An automatic external mechanism would impose positive changes in budgetary behavior and bring the budget under control. The constraints of budget balance and expenditure limitation would of themselves endow budget processes with the capacity to resolve budget problems. Although the simplicity of this solution appears tempting, consensus on radical reduction of federal activities is far from complete, and external ceilings on expenditures and revenues might increase

rather than alleviate the strains on the budget process. Even if a constitutional amendment were passed, further reforms of budget structure and processes would probably still be demanded. For this reason, constitutional limitation of federal expenditures and a balanced budget lies outside the scope of this article. See Aaron Wildavsky, *How to Limit Government Spending* (Berkeley: University of California Press, 1980) and Senate Committee on the Judiciary, *Balanced Budget: Tax Limitation Constitutional Amendment,* July 10, 1981.

4. Allen Schick, *Congressional Control of Expenditures,* House Committee on the Budget, January 1977; Joseph A. Pechman and Robert W. Hartman, "The 1980 Budget and the Budget Outlook," in Joseph A. Pechman (ed.), *Setting National Priorities: The 1980 Budget* (Washington, D.C.: The Brookings Institution, 1979), p. 54; and U.S. Comptroller General, *Federal Budget Concepts and Procedures Can Be Further Strengthened* (Washington, D.C.: General Accounting Office, March 3, 1981), (PAD-81-36), p. 17.

5. See Allen Schick, *Reconciliation and the Congressional Budget Process* (Washington, D.C.: American Enterprise Institute, 1981).

6. Frederick Mosher, "The Changing Responsibilities and Tactics of the Federal Government," *Public Administration Review* 40 (November-December 1980), p. 547.

7. See House Committee on the Budget, First Concurrent Resolution—Fiscal Year 1982, Supplemental Views of Hon. David R. Obey and Hon. Richard A. Gephardt, April 16, 1981, pp. 327–332.

8. Testimony of Charles A. Bowsher, comptroller general, on S. 2629, The Budget Reform Act of 1982, Senate Committee on Governmental Affairs, August 19, 1982, p. 3.

9. Budget Reform Act of 1983 (S.20, Roth), Budget Procedures Improvement Act of 1983 (S. 12, Ford), Two Year Budgetary Planning Act of 1983 (S. 922, Cochran), and Biennial Budgeting Act of 1983 (H.R. 750, Panetta). The majority of these bills had been presented in similar form in previous years. Discussion here is limited to the bills under consideration in 1983.

10. Louis Fisher, "Annual Authorizations: Durable Roadblocks to Biennial Budgeting," Public Budgeting & Finance 3 (Spring 1983), pp. 23–40.

11. Testimony of Charles A. Bowsher, comptroller general, on improvements to the Congressional Budget and Impoundment Control Act of 1974, House Committee on Rules, Task Force on the Budget Process, September 29, 1982, pp. 29–31.

12. See statement by Alice M. Rivlin, director, Congressional Budget Office, House Committee on the Budget, Task Force on Enforcement, Credit and Multiyear Budgeting, October 28, 1981; and statement by Alice

M. Rivlin, Senate Committee on the Budget, Task Force on Credit, December 10,1981.

13. See Statements on Proposed Control of Tax Expenditures by Harry Havens, assistant comptroller general, Allen Schick, and Alice M. Rivlin, Committee on Rules, December 9, 1981.

14. Obey and Gephardt, pp. 330–332.

15. Statement of Jamie L. Whitten, chairman, House Appropriations Committee, Senate Committee on Governmental Affairs, October 6, 1981, p. 4.

16. Statement of David A. Stockman, director, Office of Management and Budget, Senate Committee on Governmental Affairs, hearings on oversight of the Congressional Budget and Impoundment Control Act, October 6, 1981, p. 7.

17. Statement of Pete V. Domenici, Senate Committee on Governmental Affairs, hearings on oversight of the Congressional Budget and Impoundment Control Act, October 6, 1981, p. 8; and Alice M. Rivlin, "Congress and the Budget Process," *Challenge* (March-April 1981), p. 37.

18. Richard A. Snelling, paper for symposium on "The Congressional Budget Act and Process—How Can They Be Improved?" convened by the Committee for a Responsible Federal Budget and the Joint Educational Consortium (Arkadelphia, Arkansas, January 12, 1982), p. 3; and Bowsher, testimony on improvements to the Congressional Budget and Impoundment Control Act, pp. 2, 40, and 51.

19. Stockman, p. 7; Statement of Alice M. Rivlin, Senate Committee on Governmental Affairs, October 29, 1981, pp. 4–5.

20. Statement of Mark Hatfield, chairman, Senate Appropriations Committee, Senate Committee on Governmental Affairs, hearings on oversight of the Congressional Budget and Impoundment Control Act, October 6, 1981, p. 6.

21. Richard A. Musgrave, "Outline of Comments on the Need to Recognize the Interdependence of Expenditure and Revenue Budgeting" (paper presented at the symposium on "The Congressional Budget Act and Process—How Can They Be Improved?" January 12-13, 1982), p. 1.

22. Kenneth Hunter, "Monitoring and Reporting to the Congress and the Public on Governmental Performance" (paper delivered to the American Association for Budget and Program Analysis, Washington, D.C., April 17, 1980), p. 13.

23. Bowsher, testimony on improvements to the Congressional Budget and Impoundment Control Act, p. 28.

24. Stockman, p. 8.

25. Robert Giaimo and Henry Ballmon, convenor's paper presented to the svmposium on "The Congressional Budget Act and Process—How Can They Be Improved?" p. 5.

26. Hunter, p. 10.
27. Bowsher, testimony on improvements to the Congressional Budget and Impoundment Control Act, p. 14.
28. Stockman, p. 13.
29. Bowsher, testimony on the Budget Reform Act of 1982, p. 2.
30. George Gross, "The Congressional Budget Process: Review, Assessment and Suggestions for Change" (paper presented to the symposium on "The Congressional Budget Act and Process—How Can They Be Improved?"), p. 8.
31. Domenici, p. 11.
32. Musgrave, p. 3.
33. Rivlin, statement to the Senate Committee on Governmental Affairs, p. 7.
34. Ibid., p. 5.
35. Domenici, p. 10; and Giaimo and Bellmon, p. 5.
36. Stockman, p. 4.
37. Statement of Senator William V. Roth, Jr., Senate Committee on Governmental Affairs, hearings on oversight of the Congressional Budget and Impoundment Control Act, October 6, 1981, p. 2.
38. See Allen Schick, "A Death in the Bureaucracy: The Demise of Federal PPB," *Public Administration Review* 33 (March-April 1973), pp. 146–156.
39. Aaron Wildavsky, "A Budget for All Seasons? Why the Traditional Budget Lasts," *Public Administration Review* 38 (November-December 1978), p. 502; and Naomi Caiden, "Dilemmas of Budget Reform," in Gerald Caiden and Heinrich Siedentopf (eds.), *Strategies of Administrative Reform* (Lexington, Mass.: Lexington Books, 1982), pp. 102–103.
40. See Naomi Caiden, "The Myth of the Annual Budget," *Public Administration Review* 42 (November-December 1982), pp. 516–523.
41. Yehezkel Dror, "The Politics of Defense Allocations in Western Europe," *Public Budgeting & Finance* 3 (Spring 1983), p. 14.
42. See Bernard Pitsvada, "Flexibility in Federal Budget Execution," *Public Budgeting & Finance* 3 (Summer 1983), pp. 83–101.
43. Schick, *Congress and Money*, p. 7

9

Budget Theory and Budget Practice: How Good the Fit?

Irene S. Rubin
Northern Illinois University

Theory in budgeting, like much of public administration, has been of two kinds, descriptive and normative. Descriptive theory is based on close observation or participation in public sector activities. Theorists describe trends, sequences of events, and infer causes, paying attention to local variations as well as uniformities across cases. Normative theory—advice—may be based on a much narrower range of observations than descriptive theory and its proposed solutions may be based on values rather than observations. If the explanatory power of the descriptive theory is too weak, or if the advice of normative theory is not adopted by public officials or is adopted and abandoned because it does not work, the gap between theory and practice may become unacceptably wide.

An examination of the gap between budget theory and practice requires separate examination of the success over time of normative and descriptive budget theory. This article is therefore divided into two parts, one on normative theory and one on descriptive theory. In each part, the past, present, and likely future of the relationship between theory and practice is outlined. Where the analysis indicates deterioration of the relationship, suggestions are made on how the relationship might be improved.

The Content of Normative Budget Theory

Normative budget theory dates back at least to the turn of the century. Lively budgeting debates took up whole issues of journals in a variety of social

Source: Reprinted with permission from *Public Administration Review* (March/April 1990): 179–189. © 1990 by the American Society for Public Administration (ASPA), 1120 G Street NW, Suite 500, Washington, D.C. 20005. All rights reserved.

science disciplines. The practical advice reformers gave about accounting and budget exhibits was supported by a theory of government and the way budgeting relates to the state. Individual theorists differed on particulars, but the executive budget reform proposals[1] were generally based on a federalist model of government. Reformers looked longingly back at Hamilton's financial authority and across at the political systems of England, Switzerland and Germany.[2] They wanted a stronger, more independent executive, more like the Prime Minister in a parliamentary form of government, and less role for parties and party caucuses; generally they sought a smaller role for legislators. Their concern for the growth of government spending often led them to recommend that the legislature in general, and Congress in particular, give up the option of increasing executive-branch recommendations of the executive. These proposals led to debate on the role of the budget process in a democracy.[3]

While many reformers were concerned to limit the growth of government and the access of special interests, it mattered to them how it was to be done. They looked at the evolution of line-item controls that legislative bodies had devised to control machines, especially in New York City, and they argued that although effective in achieving their purpose, they hamstrung the executive and created less efficient government.[4] It was not only spending control the reformers were after, but efficient government. They specifically rejected line item budgets and detailed appropriations in favor of lump sum appropriations that allowed better management.

The program for achieving the reformers' goals included not only the expansion of the power of the executive to formulate policy and review proposals but also new budget formats to convey decision-making information about programs to the legislature and the public for their review. Public accountability was an important theme in this reform literature, and it could only be achieved by improving the quality of budget information and publicizing that information. The public as well as the legislature should understand what the government was doing and how much it was spending to achieve particular goals.

These reformers did not argue that new services should not be included in the budget, only that the cost for doing so should be the lowest possible commensurate with the quality of services demanded. They therefore advocated cost accounting (with its program budgeting implications) and detailed performance budgets based on unit costs. The assumption was that when such information was made public, there would be an outcry if one city's park services cost much more than another's.[5]

The budget reformers at the turn of the century also emphasized the role of planning in the budget. They argued that budgets must contain a work plan and provide funding for future as well as current needs. Some of the reformers went further and argued that budget planning was a way of finding and responding to unmet needs in the community. Otho Cartwright, for example, argued that he would go further than his fellow budget advocates in arguing for a state law that would provide the means to ask the public what its needs were. He argued that members of the public should be allowed to present their case to the proper government authority. He envisioned civic societies that would advocate particular policies, such as more industrial safeguards or better sanitation in the schoolhouses.[6]

While there was considerable variation in the scope of planning advocated by the early reformers, they agreed that planning was inherent in budgeting. Some of the reformers explicitly linked city planning and budgeting, arguing that poor planning for growth and inadequate sewers, streets, and tunnels cost more money in the end and were inefficient. They implied that a vision of the future city, which would bring order out of chaos, had to be linked to the budget and plans for capital and service spending.[7]

Budget planning meant at the least choosing particular target levels of service by activity and figuring out in advance what it would cost in personnel and supplies to accomplish those specific goals. The reformers rejected a model of budgeting that allowed the departments to ask for what they wanted instead of requesting what they needed to accomplish particular tasks. They were convinced that there was much waste in government and that expenditures could be cut back without losing much in the way of services. They did not think that changes could be implemented only at the margins. They told stories of cutting departmental budgets in half while improving services.[8]

Paralleling these early budget reformers were the public economists, who advocated some of the same kinds of reforms, but from a different theoretical perspective. While the budget reformers emphasized both the need to run government like a business and the constitutional basis for their reforms, the public economists based their arguments on what they perceived as rational choices and optimization of decision making. Both groups emphasized the need to get the most from each dollar, but the public economists were less concerned with cost accounting and management and more concerned with choices between options, laying out the options carefully, and choosing between them on carefully specified grounds.

Over the years, many specific budget reforms have been formulated and advocated, then adopted, rejected, or modified. Many of these reforms have the same goals or purposes as those of the reformers of the early 1900s. Program budgeting, for example, and its explanation of what government is trying to accomplish at what cost, addresses specific concerns raised by the early reformers; the linking of planning to programming in the Planning Programming Budgeting System (PPBS) was also foreshadowed many years earlier. Performance budgets, with their varied emphasis on measuring demands and workloads or efficiency and unit costs, also reflect earlier concerns. The idea of determining desired service levels, associating costs with each one, and budgeting for only desired levels of service is the heart of Zero-Based Budgeting (ZBB) and Target-Based Budgets, but it was also part of the early reformers' attempts to judge what was needed versus what was wanted and to get out of the budget waste that had accumulated over the years. Current models of budgeting for outcomes perfectly express the activist, efficiency, and accountability goals of the early reformers. Management by objectives links the specific annual goals of the city to work loads and the personnel evaluation system, an elaboration of the old reformers' goals.

Normative Theory and Practice

How successful has this normative theory and its specific offspring been? Evaluations of budget reforms, both specifically and generically, have often been negative. The reformers urged wide public participation in budgeting, with open hearings, advertisements, public presentation of budget exhibits, and budgets that were explanatory to the average person. Such participation was either short lived or did not materialize. Calls for a consolidated budget that explained to the public the range of programs and types of spending have dimmed in the face of continuing fragmentation, multiyear budgets, off-budget accounts, and different types of spending. Specific reforms, such as Management by Objectives (MBO), PPB, and ZBB have been evaluated and declared to be failures.[9]

More generically, the incrementalists argued that many reforms required comprehensive evaluation of programs and specific delineation of spending for specific purposes, which would have negative effects. A great number of programs could not be compared at one time, and the effects of making spending clearer would undoubtedly be more conflict. They disapproved of the idea of bringing the public more into the budgeting process for fear of increased and conflicting demands. They argued that budgeting should not be reformed.[10]

A review of the literature suggests that budgeters have underestimated the success of normative theory for a variety of reasons. One reason is that once a reform has been widely adopted, people tend to forget the role of normative theory in bringing the changes about. The federal government, most of the states, and nearly all cities with over 10,000 population have adopted the executive-budget model. Other kinds of recommendations, such as keeping enterprise funds separate, setting rates for public enterprises so as not to make a profit, and using the modified accrual basis of accounting have become accepted budgetary practices. The distinction between the detailed budget presentation of the President to Congress and the lump sum appropriation of Congress in its approved budget was suggested by the budget reformers, and it has been the dominant pattern in the federal government for many years. The idea that budgets should be tools for public accountability, and therefore should be easy to read, has been widely accepted and often inventively implemented.[11]

Even more recent and controversial recommendations for budget reform like zero-based budgeting, program budgeting, management by objectives, and performance budgeting have been far more successful than many people in public administration have thought. Some studies suggested that many budget reforms were fads that had few or no lasting effects; in some cases they changed the budget formats but not the decision making.[12]

Some of the most discouraging of the evaluations have been at the federal level. But there is only one federal government, it is highly complex and unusual, and it is not typical of the states or local governments or of public budgeting in general. Historically, state and local governments have often innovated first successfully and then the innovation has spread to the federal government. That such innovation should be judged essentially by what happens in the federal government seems unjustifiable. Budget innovations have been much more widely adopted and implemented at state and local levels, especially in the past decade.

Other reasons that success with normative budgeting has been underestimated are that evaluators looked too quickly to find consequences and tried to find the innovation in the exact form in which it was introduced. "The absorptive character of government, gradually adapting and incrementally augmenting its activities, suggests that change may more easily be measured on a time scale congenial to a forester or a geologist than to a Congress or a White House in a hurry."[13] Many of the innovations were clumsy when introduced, so that public administrators adopted and then adapted them, piecing together parts of reforms that suited their environments. Consequently, if one looked right away for the impacts of a specific budget innovation, one was likely to see fumbling implementation or even evasion of key provisions, but if one looked a decade or more later, one was likely to see a blending of pieces of different reforms that were functioning well in some places.

The reforms were often oversold, leading to the inevitable claim that they could not deliver. "In order for major reform legislation to become law, exaggerated claims are made for its future performance."[14] If one claims that a budget reform will reduce the federal deficit and the federal deficit remains, the reform appears to have failed, even if a variety of more modest improvements were made. Evaluations that examine the evolution of goals over time and evaluate outcomes on a scale of achievement have found budget innovations moderately successful.[15]

Normative Theory and Practice on the State and Local Levels

At the municipal level in the United States, many proposed budget reforms have been adopted in whole or in part and have been adapted to the needs and capacities of the local communities. Sometimes it has taken cities many years to implement the changes because they did not have the necessary information base, accounting system, or staff time. Sometimes the reform has been interrupted or delayed, or even lost, but budget changes can occur gradually. The direction of the change is obvious when looked at over the period of a decade or more.

One study of a national sample of cities compared a 1976 International City Management Association survey with a study using the same survey instrument in 1982 and 1983. Over that time period, the change in reported budget sophistication was dramatic. The use of program, zero-base, or target budgeting had increased from 50 percent to 77 percent of the sample; the use of MBO increased from 41 percent to 59 percent; and performance monitoring was up from 28 percent to 68 percent. About two thirds of the sample reported they used program budgeting, while a third reported using either ZBB or Target-Based Budgeting, which is a form of ZBB. The number of cities reporting that they had tried and dropped these innovations was not negligible, but it was still quite low. Reports of effectiveness varied by specific technique, but the ones which reported the most widespread adoption, such as program budgeting, were considered effective by about 44 percent of the respondents. Only performance measurement among the widely adopted tools got generally low ratings for effectiveness.[16]

A more recent study looked at the same budget practices in 1987 and found little additional use of these techniques but considerable stability in the numbers of users. The authors concluded that these tools "have become staples rather than fads in public management."[17] All of these studies do not include very small cities and so exaggerate somewhat the overall rate of usage. Still for cities with over 25,000 in population, the use of these tools remains high and constant.

Cross-sectional studies on self-reported data are useful, especially when done at intervals with the same instrument, but they leave one wondering what those who reported them meant by ZBB or MBO. Did it mean that the city went through all the information gathering and analysis implied in the process or that a vague statement of goals was added to the budget before each program? Nor is it clear from these studies if cities are gradually adding to existing reforms in a logical way so that one builds on the next or if they are modifying existing practices to be less threatening or more effective. To answer some of these questions, a mini-panel study was designed, looking at the budgets of 15 cities across the country over approximately 10 years, from about 1977 to about 1987. The smallest of the cities was about 40,000 population.[18]

Briefly, the results confirm the cross-sectional data. In 1977 nine cities out of the fifteen had relatively straightforward line-item budgets; ten years later, only five cities had straight line-item budgets. There was increasing use of some form of performance measures, although the definition and measures of performance were not stable either across departments or across time. The use of ZBB or Target-Based Budgeting was low but stable: two out of the fifteen used zero-based or target-based budgeting at the beginning and at the end of the period. The most dramatic change was in MBO. In 1977 none of the cities used this technique as part of the budget format, but by 1987, four of the fifteen were using it. From the budgets themselves it appears that some of the cities were using the formats more seriously as part of their decision-making process than others. And some cities included a variety of formats not specifically named.

To get a sense of smaller cities and the most recent data, 12 municipal budgets from suburban Dupage County, Illinois were examined. Sizes ranged from 6,700 to 90,000 population. One had no real budget (which is legal under Illinois law), six had straight line-item budgets, the others had some combination of program budgets with goals and objectives statements, or program budgets with MBO and performance measures. Cities of 14,000 and smaller population were much more likely to have straight line-item budgets. This is not really surprising, as their municipal operations are likely to be much simpler, and staff and council are much more likely to know each other and the programs intimately without the help of management controls and informative budgets.

It is clear from reading these budgets that in most cases the budget process itself has changed, not only the format. For example, in Hanover Park, a village of about 32,000 population, the President and the Board of Trustees first set forth their goals for the year, and then the departments' objectives are set and supporting goals are established. The process lasts over six months. In the budgets, the departments and boards list their previous year's objectives, which ones they obtained on time and which ones are still ongoing, and then describe their objectives for the next budget year. In Bensenville, population about 16,000, the budget introduction lists the goals and objectives for the city for the upcoming year: these include both potential service expansions and possible mergers and reorganizations of service delivery. The year's tasks include an evaluation of a neighborhood survey of citizen satisfaction with services and redesign of the city's handling of complaints. Each department lists concrete and extensive objectives and goals in the budget.

The most dramatic of the budgets from Dupage County is that of Downers Grove, population about 43,000. That budget combines program budgeting, line-item controls, and an MBO system. The system was developed over more than a decade. It has been combined with a five-year financial plan to create what the manager calls "results budgeting." The five-year plan is an integrated long-range operating budget and capital improvement plan. It describes where the city is headed and what the financial requirements will be. Portions of the plan appear in the annual budget. The City Manager, Kurt Bressner, argues, "The importance of integrating the MBO system into the budget cannot be overstated. Through this step, the desired results are directly linked to the resources necessary to achieve them."[19] This is exactly what the budget reformers of the early 1900s were trying to achieve. Many cities have pieces of this integrated system, and they seem to be moving in this direction, even though they do not have it all assembled yet.

This is not to say that no simple line-item budgets exist out there. Commission cities, of which only a few remain in the whole country, tend to budget in a line-item and highly decentralized fashion, but as an outdated and largely abandoned reform, commission cities are not typical of future trends. Small cities, counties, and some rural cities still budget with simple line items with no explanation, but they probably do not need much more sophistication.

The response of state governments has been similar to that of the cities. More than half the states make use of program budgets, performance reporting and monitoring, program analysis, program evaluation, and forward year projections of revenue and expenditure. Seventy-four percent of the states report using program budgeting; 38 percent of the users report that it is highly effective, and 62 percent report that it is somewhat effective. ZBB is used by fewer states, 20 as opposed to 37 that use program budgeting, but the proportion of those reporting

effectiveness is about the same. Performance monitoring is fairly widespread, but a lower percentage of states that report such monitoring consider it highly successful. Nevertheless, a high proportion consider it somewhat effective. Most of these budget innovations have been hybridized and adapted, using parts of some and parts of other reforms.[20]

What is equally interesting are the reforms that now seem to represent the state of the art. Increasingly, planning is merging with budgeting. The result is multiyear budgeting, which is not just a projection of budget numbers but a corporate plan which includes statements of policy, underlying assumptions, and goals for the community.[21] In drawing up the plans, consideration is given to unmet needs, changes in the community, anticipated growth, and changing technology. Perhaps more common in rapidly growing and changing communities, these plans are the local adaptations of PPBS, home grown, to fit the local need. Even when no corporate long-term plan exists, there is often a capital long-term plan with the explicit goal of creating a preapproved list of priorities in which the first year of the plan pops out as a section of the next year's budget.[22]

The recent integration of MBO with the budget implies that goal setting, personnel evaluation, work loads, and budget are being integrated in some budgets. The program manager in essence promises to do so much work and gets so much budget to do it. When integrated with the budget, this work load data gives the citizen a good look at exactly what his or her money is doing. MBO has the advantage of linking the budget with the personnel evaluation system, and hence it is more than a plan or report.

What budget reform has not yet generally achieved at the local level is good cost accounting and good performance budgeting. Cost accounting has sometimes become political. When a particular service is sorted out for a cost analysis, council members may view the service as too expensive and try to use cost accounting to make it politically vulnerable. Or a manager may try to make a program look less expensive through cost accounting to defend it from its detractors. Cost accounting does not have the appearance of a neutral skill that can help save money. With respect to performance measures, departments have resisted what appears to them to be unfair evaluations. The department heads often fear, with some justification, that low efficiency ratings will be blamed on them and the council will take away resources from them in a misguided effort to increase efficiency. Since departments seldom have complete control over what are viewed as departmental outcomes—such as dollar losses for fires—department heads fear that they will be blamed for such things as a rash of arson fires, regardless of the quality of their work. Nevertheless, some elements of performance budgeting have crept into municipal budgets, even if they are not yet working to everyone's satisfaction.

In short, contemporary budgeting at the state and local levels reflects many of the practices recommended by budget theory, and it continues to evolve. Public administration has clearly been successful in proposing reforms that are attractive to practitioners when those reforms have appeared to have the capacity to solve budgetary problems. The reforms have not always worked to everyone's satisfaction, but the relation between normative budget theory and budget practice has been close, especially at state and local levels.

Normative Theory and Practice at the Federal Level

In recent years the record at the federal level has not been as strong. Budget reformers had a major hand in designing the executive budget process in 1921, and reform ideas were evident in the redesign of congressional budgeting in 1974. But reform ideas played little role in the 1985 deficit reduction act known as Gramm-Rudman-Hollings.

The 1974 reform emphasized the role of professional budget staff to enable Congress to have sufficient information to make budget decisions. It also emphasized the importance of having overall budget targets and ways of setting and enforcing budget priorities. These were two persistent themes in the reform literature.

By contrast, the Gramm-Rudman-Hollings deficit reduction act set up a variety of across-the-board cuts—with many of the most popular entitlement programs exempted—that would automatically be invoked if the normal budget process could not achieve a specified target for deficit reduction. Where previous budget reforms had tried to include entitlement programs to bring them into budget scrutiny and to make them part of budget tradeoffs, Gramm-Rudman-Hollings exempted them; where previous budget reforms had striven to make thoughtful comparisons among competing programs, Gramm-Rudman-Hollings cut across the board.

The Gramm-Rudman-Hollings deficit reduction law was often referred to as a bad idea whose time had come.[23] The reported intent of the law was to make the mandatory cuts so distasteful to both Democrats and Republicans that they would join together to make a proper budget that would reduce the deficit below the trigger level for the automatic cuts. Instead, the law has worked to enhance the incentives to make deficits look smaller than they are (to get below the trigger level) by using "smoke and mirrors." Senator James Exon has argued, "Rather than force action, the Gramm-Rudman process fakes action. . . . After two years of operation, Gramm-Rudman has not worked."[24]

It was not just Gramm-Rudman-Hollings that suggested that normative theory was not working at the federal level; many other budget reform proposals of the past few decades have not worked well at the federal level. Part of the reason seems to be the size and complexity of the federal government. Putting together a citywide list of priorities coming from a half dozen or even a dozen city departments is a massive task but not an impossible undertaking. Putting together a priority list of programs in one department of the complexity of the federal Health and Human Services without an agreed upon set of criteria for such a ranking may well be impossible or so difficult as to overwhelm any advantage the process might have produced.

Another problem has been that reform proposals have not kept up well with the increased complexity of the federal budget over the years. Parts of the federal budget receive continuing appropriations that are semi-permanent and do not go through annual budget review. Many capital projects such as weapons systems are authorized for expenditure over a period of years, and the matter of what part has been spent or remains to be spent clouds the logic of an annual comprehensive review. Reformers' programs have included consolidated annual budgets with explicit comparison between major categories of spending, but the reality of federal budgeting today is multiple budgets, and parts of the budget are multiyear.[25] More important, some compelling reasons exist for the increased complexity, and it is not likely to go away any time soon. The result is that many old reform proposals no longer make much sense.

Other reform proposals have been taken as far as they usefully can be taken. For years, the reform proposal for assuring balanced budgets was increasingly to strengthen the power of the chief executive over the budget. In the states, for example, the governors have been given stronger and stronger budget vetoes. But the reform has probably already gone too far, contributing to an atrophy of legislatures, and the trend for the past 10 to 20 years has been back in the other direction, to give legislatures more balanced responsibilities over budget matters.[26] It has become increasingly clear that legislatures are not necessarily more profligate than governors and that Congress is not historically more likely to spend than the President.[27] Some executives are more prone to spending, and some legislatures are more prone to spending. A reform that purports to control spending by giving the executive more and legislatures less spending power seems wrong-headed.[28]

Part of the problem of the recent failure of budget reform at the federal level has been the focus on trying to reduce the size of the deficit through reforming budget processes or legislating discipline. A budget reform can help carry out the goals of politicians once they have made up their minds, but it cannot make up their minds. Public administration may have been asking budget reform to do the impossible.

Some of the increasing complexity of the budget that has made federal reforms so difficult has affected state and local levels as well. Capital projects may sprawl across years. Budgets at all levels are likely to contain a variety of resources, including loan guarantees, loans and revolving funds, contracts, insurance, grants, subsidies, and direct service delivery. The problems of exaggerated executive budget power are more extreme at the state and local level than they are at the national level. As a result, many traditional bits of reform advice are becoming less relevant at all levels of government.

Improving the Relationship Between Normative Theory and Practice

How can the relationship of normative budget theory and practice be improved in the coming years? First, a better understanding is needed of what the budget process and format can and cannot do so that reform proposals will be realistic. Greater clarity is required about the difference between being idealistic,

asking for budgets to be completely transparent, for example, and suggesting budget reforms as solutions to broader problems that such reforms may influence only marginally. The former is an important part of public administration; the latter at best makes budget reform look impotent, and at worst, detracts attention from more likely solutions.

Second, reconsideration is needed to what accountability means and how to achieve it in budgets that allocate multiple resources on a multiple year basis. For example, what does "consolidated" mean in such a budget? One does not want to add tax expenditures to outlays—they are different kinds of numbers and they do not meaningfully add. One does not want to include the balances in trust funds to offset the deficit, as the United States government now does, when those funds can never be spent to reduce that deficit. So some parts of the budget should remain separate; full consolidation in the context of different types of expenditures and expenditure restrictions should not be a goal.

However, openness and clarity of presentation are more urgent in this context of multiyear and multisource budgets than they were when budgets were simpler. The completeness of the budget takes on increasing importance. Are the costs of tax breaks adequately represented? How are the costs of loans presented? Are various subsidies reported? How? What about the shifting of costs through regulation of the economy? How are unfunded liabilities being reported, where, and with what accuracy? In short, what is not in the budget that should be? This avenue of budget reform needs to be continued and applied more widely at state and local levels.

The appropriate level of budgetary secrecy must be reexamined. Openness of budget decision making to the public also opens the budget process to interest groups; is that an adequate argument for closing budget decisions? To what extent have procedures been created or endorsed to close deliberations to the public and press while still keeping them open to interest groups? One could argue, for example, that the federal black budget for security agencies is a secret only from the American public and not from foreign powers. Can budget processes be prescribed that buffer decision makers somewhat from interest groups and still keep them open and accountable to the public?

What level of secrecy is justified and at what potential and actual cost? The tendency has been to create budget systems that are closed on the executive side and open on the legislative side; as budget power has shifted overwhelmingly toward the executive branch, what has been the impact on public accountability and democratic government? Is the trend toward greater balance between the legislature and the executive gradually solving the problem of accountability, or is the legislature going to become more isolated or insulated as it regains more budget power?

Third, indicators are needed to give early warning when various processes or interests are getting out of balance, with potentially serious and unwanted consequences on the budget. Perhaps indicators need to flash a warning when the budget estimates have become too rosy. Governments need to avoid the extremes of centralization or decentralization, of executive or legislative dominance, of openness and secrecy. Perhaps a need exists to measure and monitor the swings, to give early warning of needed adjustments. It would also be useful to monitor the budget process itself for signs of excessive strain and potential future collapse. How much stress can the process take? How much delay is too much? What does failure of the budget process look like?

Fourth, balance needs to be struck between precontrols and postcontrols in budget implementation. How effective have various measures to evaluate programs been with respect to the budget? Are program audits or even financial audits used in the preparation of new budgets? Is there a way to make such audits more useful, more accessible to more people? Varied controls are at governments' disposal now, but how many are too many? Budget practice is alert to the possibility of giving agencies too much autonomy, but how should governments guard against the inefficiencies of giving them too little? This was a problem that bothered the early reformers, but normative budgeting has not yet worked out a good set of answers.

If ways can be recommended to improve accountability in complex budgets, the link between taxpayers and public decision makers can be strengthened. If ways can be recommended to public officials to explain what they are doing and how well they are doing it, perhaps the anti-government flavor of tax revolts can be moderated. The match between theory and practice may also be improved if budgeters learn to give conditional rather than absolute advice. It is necessary to learn when particular reforms are likely to work and when they have outlived their usefulness. If reform can be reconceptualized, reaching for a new set of ideals beyond reducing the deficit and even beyond traditional goals of increased efficiency and fiscal control, budgeters will have a better chance of affecting the future of budget practice.

The Historical Linkage Between Descriptive Theory and Practice

If, in normative theory, budgeters were more successful than they knew, in descriptive theory, scholarly evaluation may have been overly optimistic. Incrementalism, which was intended not only as a normative theory but also as a descriptive theory, was dominant and in many ways inadequate. It prevented many budgeters from seeing the changing budget reality in front of them and theorizing about it. As a result, theory and practice grew unacceptably far apart.

At the national level, Aaron Wildavsky's well known study, *The Politics of the Budgetary Process,* emphasized the role of agencies in the budget process, assumed their desire for growth, and discussed their strategies in dealing with the congressional review process, especially the appropriations committees. That book came out in 1964 and was updated at intervals until 1984. The author gave up the framework and wrote a new book, *The New Politics of the Budgetary Process,* published in 1988. Two years after Wildavsky's 1964 book, Richard Fenno's blockbuster, *The Power of the Purse: Appropriations Politics in Congress,* was published. This book is still treated as a classic, and together they framed the incrementalist assumptions about budgeting at the national level. They emphasized the centrality of a legislatively dominated budget, the importance of agencies in the process, the decentralization of the process, and the lack of comparison between alternatives for spending. The incrementalist model argued that no major changes in budgets from year to year and hence that few choices of policy consequence were being made in the context of the budget.

These assumptions may have seemed more descriptive in the 1960s than later, but even then they left major elements out of the picture. The entitlement programs had been created during the Great Depression of the 1930s, the U.S. Office of Management and Budget (OMB) had become an office in the Executive Office of the President in 1939; and Presidents had certainly taken on policy roles in budget formation from time to time. But the incrementalist model left out these features, and others did not fill in the blanks for years.

At the state level, Thomas Anton wrote a detailed case study of budgeting in Illinois,[29] published in 1966, describing the role of all the major budget actors and concluding that no one, not even the governor, had much policy input. He described the budget process as relatively unchanging, despite the recent evolution of budgeting before the period of his study. Budgeting continued to change dramatically after his study. By 1970, the governor had a centralized office of budgeting, which became a major tool in imposing the governor's priorities on the budget, and the revised state constitution gave the governor a reduction veto, increasing his power over the budget enormously. But Anton never revised the study, and no one else wrote as comprehensive a study of state budget politics in Illinois. The 1960s and 1970s were periods of major change and reform in state budgeting, but the incrementalists seemed to ignore most of it.[30]

At the local level, Arnold Meltsner did one of the Oakland, California, studies on the politics of local revenue, published in 1971.[31] This study described Oakland as having little autonomy over taxes and being constrained by public opposition to taxes that resulted in fragmented revenues and low property taxes. He described the citizens as being generally uninterested in government, and he concluded that budgeting presented few policy issues for public reaction. Though he undoubtedly captured some element of revenue processes common at the local level, he missed many of them and perhaps inadvertently suggested that what he said about Oakland was typical of other cities across time.

These studies were followed for many years with quantitative studies of budgetary outcomes that seemed to reaffirm that budgets changed little and did not involve policy choices. These models focused attention on the difference between last year's budget and this year's and the size of the increment for different departments or programs. They made assumptions about the definition of the base budget, because the theory divided all budgets into unquestioned bases and sometimes superficially examined increments. Zero-based budgets and in fact any kind of budget tradeoffs were explicitly rejected by the incremental modelers. Even those who wished to disprove the incrementalists' assumptions and conclusions followed the incrementalists' hypotheses in order to disprove them.

Though there have always been a few dissenters, incrementalist theory dominated budgeting literature for close to two decades, and it focused attention away from phenomena that did not fit the theory. Only when something dramatic happened, such as a constitutional crisis or a major reform, did attention shift to describing what had happened.

For example, incrementalism postulates a decentralized budget process, which focused attention away from the actual level of centralization and coordination of the budget process. Congressional budget reforms in 1974 eventually forced attention to the issue, but those focusing on it had to work outside the theory of incrementalism. It was not until 1980 that Allen Schick's (nonincrementalist) comprehensive description of the causes and functioning of the 1974 Budget and Impoundment Control Act was published.[32] That study brought home a fact that should have been obvious much sooner, that the level of centralization of budget processes varies, and that theory needs to describe and explain that variation.

Due to the incrementalist model, budgeters did not focus for many years on the role of the budget office as a policy formulator. Incrementalism argued that budgeting does not really deal with policy, that policy is dealt with somewhere else. The changing role of OMB at the national level ultimately forced attention on the issue, but theory did not direct attention there.[33]

Incrementalism assumes that moderate revenue growth will create a positive increment to be distributed among the departments and agencies. It did not deal with the possibility of frozen or declining revenues. The deep recession of 1974–1975, Proposition 13 in California, and expansion of the tax limitation movement in the later 1970s culminated in major federal cuts of the early 1980s under President Reagan, giving budgeters pause. These environmental changes brought about startlingly obvious changes in budgeting. A large number of studies were done documenting and trying to explain what was happening outside the context of incrementalist theory. By the early 1980s, budgeters were beginning to theorize about what it all meant.[34] One conclusion was that budgeting was both top down and bottom up, and the balance changed over time in response to environmental changes. More broadly, it meant both that the level of resource availability affected budgeting and that budget behavior was conditional and not absolute.[35] It also meant the budget base was not inviolable and that cuts were often not across the board.[36]

The budget reforms of 1974 in Congress were precipitated in part by a constitutional crisis about who had control over spending, Congress or the President. This issue focused attention on the historical evolution of the location and balance of budget power.[37] Debate about the success of the 1974 congressional budget reform helped to focus attention on the issue of what such budgetary changes were accomplishing, and hence focused attention on previous historical reforms, their circumstances, and their outcomes.[38] When this focus was blended with the realization that budgeting varied in the degree of top-down emphasis and also varied with resource levels, the outcome was the beginning of a reformulated budget theory that emphasized historical conditions and developments over time.[39] Incrementalism had been static, arguing that changes in budgeting were few. The theory examined changes from one year to the next, downplaying major historical changes. That mold has now been broken, and budgeting has a much more self-conscious concern with change.

Similarly, incrementalist theory directed attention away from issues of budget tradeoffs for many years. When the issue was finally addressed, it tended to be at least initially by nonbudgeters, many of whom were outside public administration completely. This literature was primarily quantitative, often comparative, and generally at the national level. Many authors tried to prove statistically that tradeoffs had to occur in the budget process. Even at the local level, where the level of discretion in spending is often small, budget tradeoffs occur over time.[40]

At the local level, the lack of adequate descriptive theory has been acute. The most important omission has been the neglect of the linkage between municipal policy making and budgetary decisions. Incrementalism blocked the view for many years by asserting that policy issues were not dealt with in the budget process. Recent observation suggests otherwise.

Most major policy issues decided at city hall involve budgetary decisions, and most are made in the context of budgetary decision making. Will businesses be subsidized at the expense of homeowners, or will single-family homeowners be subsidized at the expense of apartment buildings? Will the poor or the "well to do" bear the greater burden of taxation? What range of services will the city provide, and to whom? What work will be done on what projects, and how much money will be allocated to the capital as opposed to the operating budget? How will the city deal with requests for grants, loans, or subsidies from social service providers, builders, or merchants? These issues routinely come up in the budget process. They do not always come up directly in the hearings between the departments and the budget office, however, which may have misled incrementalists into thinking that such decisions were not part of the budget process.

Policy decisions of varying scope occur with some regularity. For example, for the last few years cities have been wrestling with how to cope with the loss of General Revenue Sharing. In De Kalb, Illinois, the resulting debate forced a confrontation between social services and so-called basic services. The city decided to increase taxes to replace the lost revenues. The tax increase that was decided on was regressive and grouped earmarked capital funding with social services as the beneficiaries of the tax.[41] It is difficult to imagine a more far-reaching discussion on the priorities of the city and on definitions of need, equity, and balance between group interests. Two years later, De Kalb's city council was struggling with a choice of making appropriations for economic development (expansion) or absorbing the costs of drainage problems for existing homeowners, a problem that was being exaggerated by economic development at the city's margins. Again, this is a common policy issue raised in the context of the budget, requiring resolution in the budget through choice of projects and funding alternatives.

Other policy-laden decisions occur at intervals or at periods of city growth or decline. The time span of the observer has to be long enough to see these events, or the observer has to be lucky enough to come across them. Cities, for example, examine their revenues at intervals. They tend to set up commissions to explore a variety of options and to make recommendations. When the city goes for a new tax or a tax increase, it is a time of public accounting, a time when the city has to demonstrate that it is well run and that it is doing what the citizens want it to do. This is a decidedly nonincremental part of municipal decision making, and it has been undertheorized.

A second issue that has been relatively ignored because of the incrementalists' focus on departmental autonomy and legislative budgets is the amount of centralized executive review of the budget proposal, the amount of policy input from the executive and the legislature in the formation of the proposal, and the level and timing of the involvement of the council in decision making. In many cities, perhaps half, the budget process begins with a meeting between the executive and the council to discuss budget priorities. These priorities are then reflected in the budget that the executive proposes. Such a model implies that the departments are given guidance on what to emphasize in their proposals, and that the departments follow such guidance. This is not the only model of the budget process, but it is an important one, and, with its emphasis on central control and cooperation between the legislature and the executive, it is outside the realm of much budget theory. It happens, but what does it mean?

Municipal budgeting looks incremental only in the sense that revenues tend to increase slowly, and most changes occur at the margins. This is not a very significant discovery, since it would not be reasonable to expect that cities would terminate their fire departments and instead, double their police departments. Reorganizations—shifting and merging functions, emphasizing some tasks at the expense of others—occur with considerable frequency but are not easily detected in an incremental analysis of budget totals. Detection requires a perspective that goes inside the departments. In short, many nonincremental decisions are part of the municipal budget process and have been relatively unexplored.

The history of the relationship between descriptive theory and practice in budgeting suggests a worsening of the relationship from the middle 1960s until the early 1980s, followed by a rapid improvement. Continued accumulation of good descriptive studies is needed to encourage budgeters to theorize about trends and causation. More descriptive theory is needed. Openness and variety should be the guiding principles: explore everything that might be relevant. Explore the relationship between budgeting and society and the link between budget processes and democracy. Look at trends over time; try to link changing environmental conditions, budget processes, and budget outcomes. Budget theory has been too restrictive about what is important for far too long. Budgeting is complex, and no simple theory will ever be adequate to describe it.

Summary and Conclusion

The relationship between budget theory and practice has been different, depending on whether one was looking at normative or descriptive theory. On the normative side, budget theory has generally been more successful than imagined; that is, it has set attractive goals that have often been a guide for behavior. On the side of descriptive or even predictive theory, budget theory has been much weaker, often unable to see the phenomena in plain view or theorize about their meaning.

Projecting to the near future, successes in normative theory may be limited unless budget theory can formulate some recommendations that address the complexity of modern multifunction, multisource, multiyear budgets. By contrast, descriptive research has improved enormously in recent years, and the near future for descriptive theory looks bright.

Budgeters have regained the ability to see what is in front of them, and they are beginning to recapture the ability to theorize from what in fact is there. The field is poised for a mushrooming of descriptive theory over the next few years. The match between descriptive theory and practice will almost certainly improve over the next decade. Unfortunately, recent proposals for reform have often been attempts to curb the deficit or curb the level of national spending. The result has been a series of unrelated, and sometimes worn-out proposals, many of which have little potential for success. But perhaps the growth in descriptive theory will suggest some useful reforms.

Notes

1. For a definition and well-known exposition of the arguments for an executive budget, see Frederick A. Cleveland, "The Evolution of the Budget Idea in the United States," American Academy of Political and Social Sciences, *The Annals,* vol. 62 (November 1915), pp. 15–35.
2. For the theoretical underpinnings of this reform, see particularly Henry Ford Jones, "Budget Making and the Work of Government," American Academy of Political and Social Science, *The Annals,* vol. 62 (November 1915), pp. 1–14.
3. One elegant version of this argument appears in Edward A. Fitzpatrick's *Budget Making in a Democracy* (New York: MacMillan, 1918). He opens his book with a quote from Gladstone, "Budgets are not merely affairs of

arithmetic, but in a thousand ways go to the root of prosperity of individuals, the relation of classes and the strength of kingdoms'' (p. vii).

4. The argument that New York City had overdone budget controls through excessively detailed line items is made by Henry Bruére, "The Budget as an Administrative Program," *The Annals*, vol. 62 (November 1915), pp. 176–191. Fitzpatrick emphasizes this failure in drawing up his proposals for a more reformed and effective legislature and better information in the budget format for legislators to review. See Fitzpatrick, chs. 5 and 6.

5. See, for example, Paul T. Beisser, "Unit Costs in Recreational Facilities," *The Annals*, vol. 62 (November 1915), pp. 140–147.

6. Otho Grandford Cartwright, "County Budgets and Their Construction," *The Annals*, vol. 62 (November 1915), pp. 229–230.

7. See, for example, J. Harold Braddock, "Some Suggestions for Preparing a Budget Exhibit," *The Annals*, vol. 62 (November 1915), p. 157. He waxes rhapsodic on the relationship between city planning and budgeting. "It means that the great distributive function of our economic life is to be articulated with the other great function, production, in agreement with the dominant principle of the day—efficiency."

8. For one such example, see Tilden Abramson, "The Preparation of Estimates and the Formulation of the Budget—The New York City Method," *The Annals*, vol. 62 (November 1915), p. 261.

9. Allen Schick, "A Death in the Bureaucracy: The Demise of Federal PPB," *Public Administration Review*, vol. 33 (March/April 1973), pp. 146–156, and Richard Rose, "Implementation and Evaporation: The Record of MBO," *Public Administration Review*, vol. 37 (January/February 1977), pp. 64–71. For a negative pronouncement on ZBB, see Allen Schick, "The Road from ZBB," *Public Administration Review*, vol. 38 (March/April 1978), pp. 177–180.

10. Arnold Meltsner and Aaron Wildavsky, "Leave City Budgeting Alone! A Survey, Case Study, and Recommendations for Reform," in John P. Crecine, ed., *Financing the Metropolis: Public Policy in Urban Economics*, vol. 4, Urban Affairs Annual Reviews, (Newbury Park, CA: Sage, 1970), pp. 311–358.

11. For example, Elgin, Illinois, lists each year all the interfund transfers, where they came from, where they went to, and for what reason. (This is an innovation I would recommend for many other cities.) Budget issues are described for each program before the numbers are presented. The Town of Windsor, Connecticut, has a budget that reports demand data, such as the number of fire incidents per year over a five-year period and the reported crime rate over a decade. This data outlines the basis on which a budget

is formulated. Windsor's extremely clear program layout describes the functions of each program, describes any changes, and discusses key issues. Program narratives tell the reader what specific issues the program is dealing with each year and why.

12. Thomas Lauth in his article, "Zero-Based Budgeting in Georgia: The Myth and the Reality," *Public Administration Review*, vol. 38 (September/October 1978), pp. 420–430, argues that those who expected Zero-Based Budgeting to eliminate programs were disappointed, that budgeting remained incremental, and that ZBB took place in that context. Allen Schick makes a similar point for the federal level in "The Road from ZBB," *Public Administration Review*, vol. 38 (March/April 1978), pp. 177–180.

13. Rose, *op cit., supra*, p. 64.

14. Howard Shuman, *Politics and the Budget* (Englewood Cliffs, NJ: Prentice Hall, 1984), p. 276.

15. See, for example, David Sallack and David Allen, "From Impact to Output: Pennsylvania's Planning-Programming-Budgeting System in Transition," *Public Budgeting and Finance*, vol. 7 (Spring 1987), pp. 38–50. Another example of this type of analysis is in Shuman, *Politics and the Budget*, chapter 10. Rudolph Penner and Alan Abramson, *Broken Purse Strings: Congressional Budgeting, 1974–88* (Washington: The Urban Institute, 1988), evaluate the 1974 Budget Impoundment and Control Act of 1974 over a 14-year period, with careful evaluation of what the original goals of the Act were for those who designed it, rather than some of the claims later made for it. They argue, as others have argued, that the reform was neutral in terms of aims to increase or decrease spending, and hence the law cannot reasonably be judged on failure to curtail spending. They claim some successes and some failures of the reform over time.

16. Theodore Poister and Robert P. McGowan, "The Use of Management Tools in Municipal Government: A National Survey," *Public Administration Review*, vol. 44 (May/June 1984), pp. 215–223.

17. Theodore Poister and Gregory Streib, "Management Tools in Municipal Government: Trends over the Past Decade," *Public Administration Review*, vol. 49 (May/June 1989), p. 242.

18. The cities are New York City; Pittsburgh, Pennsylvania; Baltimore, Maryland; San Antonio, Texas; Durham, North Carolina; Cambridge, Massachusetts; Tucson, Arizona; Wichita, Kansas; South Bend, Indiana; Amarillo, Texas; Baton Rouge, Louisiana; Victoria, Texas; Oklahoma City, Oklahoma; Spokane, Washington; and Grand Forks, North Dakota. These cities were chosen on three criteria, range of size, distribution across the country, and the availability of sample budgets ten years apart. There may have been some bias in the sample, as cities with better

budgets may have been more eager to send a sample to an archive.

19. The quotation is from Downers Grove's 1989-1990 budget introduction.

20. Stanley Botner, "The Use of Budgeting/Management Tools by State Governments," *Public Administration Review,* vol. 45 (September/October 1985), pp. 616–620.

21. Sixty percent of respondents in the 1987 Georgia State Survey said they had used strategic planning. Seventy percent reported using some form of financial trend monitoring, and 68 percent reported using multiyear revenue and expenditure forecasts. Poister and Streib, *op. cit., supra,* p. 242.

22. The author served as consultant to such a planning process in 1988-1989 for the city of Warrenville, population about 9,000. A fictionalized version of the process is described in a teaching case written by this author, "Dollars, Decisions, and Development," in *Managing Local Government,* James Banovetz, ed., the International City Management Association, 1990.

23. Lance LeLoup, Barbara Luck Graham, and Stacey Barwick, "Deficit Politics and Constitutional Government: The Impact of Gramm-Rudman-Hollings," *Public Budgeting and Finance,* vol. 7 (Spring 1987), pp. 100–101.

24. This quote is from Penner and Abramson, *op. cit. supra,* p. 76; they cite their source as Hedrick Smith, *The Power Game: How Washington Works,* (New York: Random House, 1988), p. 667.

25. For a good discussion of the level of complexity in recent federal budgeting and its implications for public budgeters, see Naomi Caiden, "Shaping Things to Come: Super-Budgeters as Heroes (and Heroines) in the Late-Twentieth Century," in Irene Rubin, ed., *New Directions in Budget Theory* (Albany: SUNY Press, 1988), pp. 43–58.

26. For a discussion of this historical trend and specific examples, see Irene Rubin, *The Politics of Public Budgeting: Getting and Spending, Borrowing and Balancing* (Chatham, NJ: Chatham House, 1990).

27. For a good summary of the evidence with respect to the federal level, see Norman Ornstein, "The Politics of the Deficit," in Phillip Cagan, *Essays in Contemporary Economic Problems: The Economy in Deficit, 1985* (Washington: The American Enterprise Institute, 1985) pp. 311–334. R. Douglas Arnold has been instrumental in debunking the argument that the tendency of a Member of Congress to support pork projects has increased and is causing increases in federal spending. Such spending has decreased as a proportion of the budget in recent years. "The Local Roots of Domestic Policy," in Thomas Mann and Norman Ornstein, eds., *The New Congress* (Washington: The American Enterprise Institute, 1981), pp. 250–287. For a summary of the argument that governors may be expansionist or tightfisted, see Aaron Wildavsky, *Budgeting, A Comparative Theory of Budgetary Processes,* 2d. ed. (New Brunswick, NJ: Transaction Press, 1986), pp. 229–236.

28. Evidence from the states is not supportive of the argument that more and more powerful executives mean less expenditure per capita. States without line-item vetoes for the governors do not spend more per capita than states that have such enhanced executive budget powers. Benjamin Zycher, "An Item Veto Won't Work," *Wall Street Journal,* 24 October 1984. Line-item and reduction vetoes often do not reduce expenditures, but rather substitute the governor's proposals and wishes for those of the legislature. See, for example, Calvin Bellamy, "Item Veto: Dangerous Constitutional Tinkering," *Public Administration Review,* vol. 49 (January/February 1989), pp. 46–51. See also Glenn Abney and Thomas Lauth, "The Line-Item Veto in the States: Instrument for Fiscal Restraint or an Instrument for Partisanship," *Public Administration Review,* vol. 45 (May/June 1985), pp. 372–377.

29. Thomas Anton, *The Politics of State Expenditures in Illinois* (Urbana: University of Illinois Press, 1966).

30. S. Kenneth Howard is an exception to this generalization. He wrote about the budgetary changes in the states in the 1970s but remained pretty much in the incrementalist framework. See *Changing State Budgeting* (Lexington, KY: Council of State Governments, 1973).

31. Arnold Meltsner, *The Politics of City Revenue* (Berkeley: University of California Press, 1971).

32. Allen Schick, *Congress and Money: Budgeting, Spending and Taxing* (Washington: The Urban Institute Press, 1980).

33. One of the first pieces to call attention to the changing role of OMB from one of neutral competence to one of more political loyalty was Hugh Heclo's "OMB and the Presidency—the problem of neutral competence," *Public Interest,* vol. 38 (Winter 1975), pp. 80–98. Interest was stimulated in OMB by the role it played under President Nixon when he began to deal with the Watergate scandal and OMB took over micromanaging the agencies. Larry Berman's history of OMB, *The Office of Management and Budget and the Presidency, 1921–1979* (Princeton, NJ: Princeton University Press, 1979) was written in the same vein. But the majority of articles on the policy role of OMB were written in response to the dramatic increase in political role of the office under President Reagan and Budget Director David Stockman. See, for example, Chet Newland, "Executive Office Policy Apparatus: Enforcing the Reagan Agenda," in Lester Salamon and Michael S. Lund, eds., *The Reagan Presidency and the Governing of America* (Washington: The Urban Institute Press, 1984), pp. 135–180, and Bruce Johnson, "From Analyst to Negotiator: the OMB's

New Role," *Journal of Policy Analysis and Management,* vol. 3 (Summer 1984), pp. 501–515.

34. One landmark article was published in 1982 by Barry Bozeman and Jeffrey Straussman, "Shrinking Budgets and the Shrinkage of Budget Theory," *Public Administration Review,* vol. 42 (November/December 1982), pp. 509–515. Bozeman and Straussman contended that top-down budgeting had characterized the three previous administrations but that budgeters had not theorized about it, in part because incrementalism limited their view. While casting aside large chunks of the incrementalist model, Bozeman and Straussman added to budget theory several key themes, especially that budgeting has both top-down and bottom-up elements and that the emphasis on each changes with the environment.

35. See Allen Schick, "Budgetary Adaptations to Resource Scarcity," in Charles Levine and Irene Rubin, eds., *Fiscal Stress and Public Policy* (Newbury Park, CA: Sage, 1980), pp. 113–134.

36. The literature suggests that cuts often begin in places that are difficult to see, such as in delayed maintenance or delayed capital projects. Money is gathered up which is not yet spent so that new hires are delayed or the slots eliminated, and purchases not yet made are cancelled. The result of this kind of decision rule is anything but across the board; it impacts some agencies much more heavily than others. Sometimes what started out as an across-the-board cut affected only some agencies when others were able to mobilize political support to prevent cuts. For some examples and rudimentary theory for the local level, see Charles Levine, Irene Rubin, and George Wolohojian, *The Politics of Retrenchment* (Newbury Park, CA: Sage, 1981).

37. This literature grew up outside of the incrementalist model. See, for example, Louis Fisher, *Presidential Spending Power* (Princeton, NJ: Princeton University Press, 1975), and James Sundquist, *The Decline and Resurgence of Congress* (Washington: Brookings, 1981).

38. See, for example, the work of Charles Stewart on congressional budget reforms of the post-Civil War era and their consequences, *The Design of the Appropriation Process in the House of Representatives, 1865–1921* (Cambridge, England: Cambridge University Press, 1989).

39. Some excellent historical work on municipal budgeting and finance has been published recently. See, for example, Terrence McDonald, *The Parameters of Urban Fiscal Policy: Socioeconomic Change and Political Culture in San Francisco, 1860–1906* (Berkeley: University of California Press, 1986), and Terrence McDonald and Sally K. Ward, eds., *The Politics of Urban Fiscal Policy* (Newbury Park, CA: Sage, 1984). Budgeting during the Great Depression is still relatively unexplored, but one exciting exception is Jeff Mirel, "The Politics of Educational Retrenchment in Detroit, 1929–1935," *History of Education Quarterly,* vol. 24 (Fall 1984), pp. 323–358.

40. On tradeoffs in New York City's budgets, see Charles Brecher and Raymond Horton, "Community Power and Municipal Budgets," in Irene Rubin, ed., *New Directions in Budget Theory* (Albany: SUNY Press, 1988), pp. 148–164. Most of the literature that calls itself "tradeoffs" is in political science. See, for example, Bruce Russett, "Defense Expenditures and National Well-Being," *American Journal of Political Science,* vol. 76 (December 1982), pp. 767–777. In public administration, tradeoffs are considered in evaluations of ZBB and other budget processes that create explicit targets for spending for various parts of the budget.

41. This case is described in greater detail in Irene Rubin, *The Politics of Public Budgeting, supra,* ch. 1.

II

Budgeting and Intragovernmental Relations: An Instrument for Correlating Legislative and Executive Action

Budget laws or other legislative enactments cannot change human nature, and while compelling the letter of cooperation, cannot compel its spirit, which is, above all things, essential in business organization.

Charles G. Dawes, 1921
First Director of the U.S. Bureau of the Budget

Legislative Dimensions

First and foremost, budgeting is an intragovernmental process. The most obvious test of budgeting as an effective governmental process is legislative. Whatever the executive branch does in the budgeting process, it is in the end subjected to legislative review and approval. The extent to which this process represents a rubber-stamp ratification or a zealous, totally independent, and often contradictory restructuring of an entire budget submission depends on two considerations: first, the strength of the legislature; and second, the nature of the legislature's budgeting powers.

Over the years, much research has focused on the politics of the legislative process. That is, the strengths of the legislature vis à vis the executive, the bureaucracy, the public, the interest groups, the media, or any other viable group that seeks to influence or exert pressure on the legislature. Extensive consideration of the legislative budgetary process is more recent, in large measure in response first to the Congressional Budget and Impoundment Control Act of 1974, and second to the Balanced Budget and Emergency Deficit Control Act of 1985 (Gramm-Rudman-Hollings). But the research focus is still largely national. Little systematic attention is being given to legislatures at the state, county, municipal, and town levels, or even to parliaments and assemblies in developing countries or international organizations. Yet all of these legislatures approve budgets and they add or subtract from executive recommendations to suit their own wills.

Executive budgeting has basically dominated legislative budgeting. There are many reasons for this. Most important are the considerations of specialization, complex information and high technology, increasingly higher expenditure levels, program fragmentation, and superior bureaucratic expertise and information control that literally leave the legislature hopelessly outstaffed, outprocessed, and outcomputered in the annual budgeting review process. It doesn't seem realistic to expect legislatures to be able to confront and totally oversee budget submissions, nor, it is argued, would they be expected to do so since that role is being performed by the central budget office or budget officer. What is expected is a selective, sharply focused review with corresponding modifications of the most controversial or most expendable aspects of the budget. This legislatures do, with varying degrees of effectiveness.

Legislative budgeting as a process is generally concerned with authorizations, appropriations, and revenues. The U.S. Congress, for example, has numerous committees with responsibilities for designing and recommending bills that establish various public policies and programs. However, the lifeblood of any policy or program is public funding. With the exception of treaties and testimonials, legislation without the approval or appropriation of funds is of dubious value. When an authorization committee recommends a bill for a program, they include a price tag—what they authorize for supporting and establishing that program. Authorizations generally carry over certain periods of time from one to several years.

The decision to fund is usually separated from the decision to spend. Another legislative committee must decide exactly how much funding will be provided in any given fiscal year. This, usually called the "appropriation," is determined by an appropriations committee that has the primary responsibility for budgetary oversight. Generally, appropriations committees split up the executive budget submission into the respective areas of their subcommittees. They conduct hearings with the responsible program officials or budget officials as part of their review of the budget recommendations of the executive. Finally, there is still one more set of significant legislative participants; the revenue committees. These committees are responsible for tax and revenue acquisition decisions, or specifying the means by which the government will raise the revenues to fund its programs.

With three different legislative functions involved, the potential for conflict as opposed to cooperation is high. This is why the legislative budget process is so critical: it sets the framework for making budget decisions within very short periods of time. If the economy is growing, resources are available, and the public is generally willing to support higher taxes for increased levels of public services, then budget decision making is not terribly difficult. The tendency is for cities to calculate costs and set tax levels to provide the necessary funds. States project their revenues and count on economic growth to provide the necessary increases to cover higher budgets or float bond issues to establish new programs and capital projects. The Congress simply spends what is needed to cover the major programs, pass supplemental budgets, and raise debt ceilings, and it counts on the nation's leading international economic position and increasing levels of growth to make the whole system solvent. It sounds very simplistic and almost unreal, but the 1950s and 1960s were clearly periods of public sector expansion and positive budget growth.

But when economic circumstances are strained, the budget process may be hard pressed to provide a conducive framework to make "disciplined" decisions. Take the federal example. If the congressional budget process before 1974 seemed very decentralized, it was so by design. After all, budgeting was conducted in an environment that Alan Schick has called "Relaxed Scarcity." But when economic conditions changed and the executive branch threatened to and then impounded funds, blaming a "spendthrift Congress" for the nation's economic woes, the process had to change. As Dennis Ippolito explains in this section's first article, the lack of overall guidance and general expertise were major reasons for the reforms contained in the Congressional Budget and Impoundment Control Act of 1974. To provide guidance, new budget committees were created to oversee the process, guide the setting of targets, (budget resolutions) and direct the enforcement of spending limitations (budget reconciliation). To provide expertise, a new staff function, the Congressional Budget Office, was created to make revenue and expenditure forecasts, analyze major resource allocation decisions, and assess the economic and financial dimensions of the budget. Some context is needed to understand the path of congressional budget reform. For this section's purposes, Dennis Ippolito provides a comprehensive overview of the "new" process, rationale, and objectives of the mid-1970s in "The Power of the Purse: Congressional Participation."

The next two articles in this section provide some assessments of how well the new congressional budget process has worked. Both evaluations, "The First Decade of the Congressional Budget Act: Legislative Imitation and Adaptation in Budgeting" by Mark S. Kamlet and David C. Mowery, and "Ten Years of the Budget Act: Still Searching for Controls" by Louis Fisher, were written in 1985 and thus not tainted by the ensuing storm over the nation's first $200 billion deficits. A more personal (and critical) view of the budget process is provided by former Budget Director David Stockman in his article, "The Crises in Federal Budgeting." Stockman's perspectives are influenced principally by the budget deficit, and he holds the congressional budget process responsible.

Of course, 1985 was a crossroads year because of the passage of Gramm-Rudman-Hollings. It was the product of a very specific time frame. Congress had passed the 1974 budget process act after a long period of frustration and review of its "war" with the executive branch over control of the federal budget. However, the 1985 Budget and Emergency Deficit Control Act was created, as Stanley Collender states, with "a single purpose in mind: to reduce the deficit." In contrast to the extensive deliberation over the passage of the budget act in 1974, the 1985 deficit control act was passed within 90 days without even the benefit of hearings.

Questions of its constitutionality were immediately raised, however. This was certainly apparent when the U.S. Supreme Court struck down part of the provisions of Gramm-Rudman-Hollings in 1986. In 1983, in *INS* v. *Chadha,* the Supreme Court had set a precedent by striking down the legislative veto and serving notice that separation of powers would be interpreted much more strictly henceforth. This was the basis for a legal challenge to the 1985 deficit control act: it contained an automatic triggering mechanism to be carried out by the Comptroller General. Lance T. LeLoup, Barbara Luck Graham, and Stacy Barwick provide a superb overview of the original act, the court's intervention, the restructuring of Gramm-Rudman-Hollings, and a preliminary assessment of the law in "Deficit Politics and Constitutional Government: The Impact of Gramm-Rudman-Hollings."

The next major assessment of Gramm-Rudman-Hollings was played out in major newspapers throughout the country in 1990. The technical aspects and sequencing are well described in Appendix A. The Budget Director's message (contained in Appendix B) provides a superb executive interpretation of the budget and deficit problem and the consequences of a Gramm-Rudman-Hollings imposed solution. Problems with the deficit escalated so severely that in the early fall of 1990, federal employees were sent furlough notices for the coming fiscal year, which would have meant the largest mass furlough in federal experience. Everyone prepared for federal budget gridlock.

Events played out quite differently, however. A revolt by House Republicans sent the entire compromise budget-tax package—worked out in relative secrecy by the congressional leadership and the administration—to the showers. The president closed the government for one weekend while Congress prepared a series of continuing resolutions (temporary funding measures) which the President keep threatening to reject, but invariably did sign. Press coverage was monstrous and reporters wrote that the budget fiasco had done more to spark the anti-incumbency mode of the public than any other factor in recent history. Yet in the end a deficit deal was struck— The Budget Enforcement Act of 1990—that produced a $500 billion five-year plan of spending cuts and tax increases to reduce the deficit.

But hidden in two of its five subtitles were some interesting changes to the federal budget process, including some major revisions of Gramm-Rudman-Hollings. While analysis of the impact of these changes will surely dominate budgeting literature in 1991, the reader will have to be content with the Congressional Research Services' summary of the main provisions of the new Budget Enforcement Act (Appendix C). To be sure, this new act will provide the next test of legislative and executive cooperation as an objective of effective budgeting.

Legislative and Executive Powers in Budgeting

The federal experience in legislative and executive budgetary interaction (or better yet, inaction) is complex and fascinating, but it makes generalizations difficult. It must be remembered that the power of the appropriations process, or legislative budgeting, is strongly affected by the legal rules and procedures that have been established. Two generally accepted models represent the two extremes in legislative–executive budgeting relationships. In the *strong executive–weak legislative model,* the chief executive is allowed to have the more formidable budgeting powers, foremost among them being the line-item veto, which sets executive budget recommendations as a ceiling. The legislature can reduce a program's budget, which must be accepted by the executive. If the legislature attempts to increase the spending recommendations for a program, however, the executive may veto anything over the initial recommendation. This veto power can extend to each individual line item in the budget.

At the other end of the scale is the *strong legislature–weak executive model.* In the federal example the line-item veto is forbidden; at the state level the veto is limited (or provisions exist to override it). The model is characterized as one in which legislatures can virtually rewrite the entire budget to their own liking, submit it as one package incorporating all of a government's expenses, and present it to the chief executive on a take-it-or-leave-it basis.

Weak executive models often have another major characteristic: the extensive "earmarking" of revenues or maintaining high levels of "uncontrollable spending." *Earmarking* is the tying of tax revenues or user fees from specific sources to legislation that dictates that the funds must be used solely for certain programs, such as gas tax revenues for road repairs or alcoholic beverage taxes for mental-health institutions. *Uncontrollable spending* describes various programs in which the annual appropriations can't be changed easily, at least not without changing the substantive law behind the specific programs. Entitlement programs for social services and veterans are examples. The level of expenditures for each year can't be set in advance; instead they are tied to eligibility requirements and automatic cost adjustments (usually tied to cost-of-living increases). These types of uncontrollable spending (or "backdoor spending" as it is sometimes called) or the earmarking of taxes may result from conflicts within the legislative branch: disputes between authorization and appropriations committees or disputes between the legislative branch and the executive branch. In either case, the executive's control of the budget process is what is most severely affected. Still, a chief executive's control of information and the specialized expertise available can frequently offset the inherent executive handicap in the strong legislative model.

Obviously, adverse economic conditions have played a major role in plaguing the spirit of legislative and executive cooperation, which William Willoughby deemed a critical thread of budget reform. But the crisis states of the current federal budget (the most visible case) and many state and local governments require that the analysis stretch beyond fiscal stress. To this end, Section II focuses on two different viewpoints. Jeffrey D. Straussman asks that the intra-governmental framework itself be broadened in his article, "Courts and Public Purse Strings: Have Portraits of Budgeting Missed Something?" Specifically, government's third branch of government, the judiciary, has come to play an increasingly more important role in the budget process. Using state and local examples, Straussman explores this neglected structural dimension of the budgetary process.

Perhaps the most controversial article in this book is Bernard T. Pitsvada's provocative work, "The Executive Budget—An Idea Whose Time Has Passed." Pitsvada speaks the unspeakable. If it doesn't work, if the budgets that are submitted are D.O.A. (Dead on Arrival), then maybe the whole process, as developed over nearly seventy years since the Budget and Accounting Act of 1921, is unworkable and ought to be scrapped in favor of another model. In his case—using the states model in South Carolina and Mississippi—Pitsvada proposes a joint legislative-executive budget process. Whatever the initial response to his suggestions, as the frustrations mount over the federal, state, and local budget crises in the 1990s, change is clearly imperative.

Budgeting and Intergovernmental Relations

The other dimension so critical to understanding the new political–economic environment of budgeting is intergovernmental relations. Increasing attention has been given in the last two decades to the roles that the federal, state, and local governments play and how these roles are financed. Fiscal federalism is a complex subject that: (1) assesses the political–economic situation of governmental units; (2) analyzes the level of fiscal effort (i.e., the level of taxation the jurisdiction is willing to support) and the fiscal capacity of each government; and (3) evaluates the flow of revenues provided by each level of government to each other, via grants and payments.

All of these aspects are intertwined and difficult to sort out, especially on the fiscal side. The term *multi-pocket budgeting* is often ascribed to the resulting mix of fiscal transfers and outlays inherent in the intergovernmental framework. For example, the federal government provides funding to state governments, who in turn pass on certain levels of funding to local governments. In the case of some forms of local governmental assistance, the state governments make their own payments and provide their own levels of support for certain programs or activities.

Even the collection of taxes is affected, because some local governments "piggy-back" their collection of taxes on the state collection of revenues, as with sales taxes for example. All of this is justified, of course, because the federal government provides mandates for state and local governments, while state governments have a whole range of legal requirements for local governments. Whether the policy area is transportation, education, human services, or environment, federalism establishes a distinct intergovernmental mold to revenue and expenditure decisions.

The more difficult question to be addressed is, What of the future now that the federal government has made tremendous reductions in its level of fiscal support for state and local governments? Many will remember the Reagan administration's plans for a "New Federalism," in which the federal government would 'forego' fiscal responsibility for some of the bigger social programs in exchange for a myriad of smaller social programs. New Federalism was never accepted, but major cuts went into effect anyway. Richard P. Nathan and John R. Lago examine the major shift in federal and state governmental fiscal relations in their 1988 article entitled "Intergovernmental Relations in the Reagan Era."

A parallel perspective is provided by John Shannon and James Edwin Kee in their 1989 article, "The Rise of Competitive Federalism." They see a new type of federalism emerging out of the fiscal ashes of the 1980s and are quite optimistic about the resiliency of state and local fiscal ability. Of course, even this picture of intergovernmental fiscal and budgetary relations would be incomplete if it only mentioned governments. Over the past fifty years, governments—

especially at the state and local levels—have relied upon and contracted with non-profit organizations or third party government to operate public programs, especially those involving human services. In the early 1980s, the Urban Institute, under the leadership of Lester Salamon, began a major research study of the role of nonprofit organizations (i.e., third-party governments) in the fiscal system and what impact the Reagan administration's plans to cut domestic spending would have on their budgets. Their involvement in intergovernmental budgeting will be an important theme for budgeting in the 1990s.

10

The Power of the Purse: Congressional Participation

Dennis S. Ippolito

The power of the purse has traditionally been the basis of congressional authority, "underpinning all other legislative decisions and regulating the balance of influence between the legislative and executive branches of government."[1] But while the reach of the taxing and spending authority is substantial, Congress has been frustrated in recent decades by its inability to exercise this authority with maximum effectiveness. Since the early 1920s there have been several congressional attempts to organize, reorganize, and revise its budget process and procedures as well as those of the executive, with the latest and one of the most extensive efforts being the 1974 Congressional Budget and Impoundment Control Act. In this instance, as well as in the previous, unsuccessful attempts to establish legislative budgets, omnibus budgets, and budget ceilings in the post–World War II period, Congress has sought to achieve several objectives: (1) to provide comprehensiveness and coherence in budget decisions by relating spending decisions to revenue decisions; (2) to enforce congressional program preferences and priorities by relating spending decisions to each other within an overall spending limit; and (3) to limit executive influence and independence in budget decisions.

During the nineteenth century, there was no elaborate budget system in either the executive branch or Congress. Government spending and revenues were usually quite limited, and presidential participation in the budgetary process was minimal. Therefore, the major developments in the budgetary process were essentially limited to congressional decisions concerning the jurisdiction and influence of committees. In 1802, for example, the House vested jurisdiction over spending bills and

revenue bills in the Ways and Means Committee, and in 1816 the Senate created a Finance Committee with similar jurisdiction. It was not until 1865 that the House transferred jurisdiction over spending legislation to an Appropriations Committee, with a counterpart committee established in the Senate two years later. However, these committees did not retain exclusive control over spending legislation for very long. In the period 1877 to 1885, the House removed 8 of the 14 annual appropriations bills (accounting for approximately one-half of total spending) from its Appropriations Committee and transferred them to the legislative committees. This apparently reflected growing dissatisfaction with the independence and emphasis on economy displayed by the Appropriations Committee.[2] While these transfers allowed the legislative (or authorizing) committees greater influence over spending decisions affecting their programs, the result was a diffusion of responsibility for financial policy.

The increases in spending and the debt resulting from World War I led Congress once again to revise its spending procedures and also to establish a budgetary system for the executive. In 1920 the House returned exclusive spending controls to its Appropriations Committee, and in 1922 the Senate followed the House lead. Moreover, as part of the Budget and Accounting Act of 1921, Congress established the General Accounting Office (GAO) to strengthen its supervision of spending by executive agencies. But with the establishment and development of executive responsibility and influence in the budget process and with the dramatic spending increases that have occurred since the New Deal, Congress has been under continuing pressure to centralize its budget procedures in order to counter executive influence. Attempts to do so, however, have generally failed, in part because centralization has been resisted by the legislative committees. The difficulty of reconciling these internal and external pressures is enormous even under the best of circumstances, and Congress has not been blessed with favorable circumstances very often. There is a considerable body of opinion both in and out of Congress that the executive has been allowed to achieve unwarranted influence in a variety of policy areas since the New Deal period, and in this context the 1974 reform of the budgetary process can be viewed as part of a broader effort to redress an imbalance in executive and congressional relations.[3] Whether this

Source: From *The Budget and National Politics,* by Dennis S. Ippolito, pp. 81–108, 118–124. Copyright © 1978 by W. H. Freeman and Company. Reprinted with permission.

budget reform succeeds would appear to depend more on its internal suitability for Congress than its planned rationality in dealing with the President, but the outcome will undoubtedly affect the relative authority of Congress and the President over national policy.

Development and Exercise of Congressional Authority

The powers to tax, spend, and borrow are essential elements in financial control and in the determination of fiscal policy. Over the past several decades, the scope and impact of these powers have increased as federal budgets have grown and federal responsibility for economic management has become established. These changes have necessarily affected the standing committees with primary responsibilities for taxing and spending decisions—the House Ways and Means Committee, the Senate Finance Committee and the Appropriations Committees of the House and Senate.

Taxing Power

The constitutional basis for the power to tax and spend is found in Article I, Section 8, clause 1: "The Congress shall have power to lay and collect taxes, duties, imposts and excises, to pay the debts and provide for the common defense and general welfare of the United States." With the exception of the Supreme Court's 1895 decision invalidating the income tax[4]—which was superseded by the adoption of the Sixteenth Amendment in 1913—the power to tax has been liberally interpreted, and the "general welfare clause" has provided a broad authority for the exercise of the taxing power. Until the passage of the income tax amendment, federal revenues were drawn primarily from tariffs (duties on imported goods) and excises (taxes on the manufacture, transfer, or sale of domestic goods).[5] But it has been the taxes on individual and corporate incomes along with the payroll taxes established during the 1930s (to finance programs such as social security and unemployment compensation) that have provided a steadily expanding revenue base to finance federal activities. Thus, the importance of tax policy for revenue purposes, regulation, and economic stimulus or restraint has grown substantially during this century.

The Committee on Ways and Means. The Constitution specifies that revenue bills must originate in the House of Representatives. This means that the House must complete action on a tax bill before the Senate can begin its deliberation, and this initiative has traditionally been reflected in the power of the Ways and Means Committee. Prior to 1975, when it was affected by a series of personnel, party, and procedural changes, Ways and Means had long been acknowledged as one of the most powerful and prestigious committees in Congress.[6] While it retains considerable power because of its jurisdiction, its ability to adapt to these changes and maintain its effectiveness will substantially affect the power of the House to determine tax policies as well as the more general operations of the new congressional budget process.

Until the recent changes, Ways and Means was a relatively small, senior, and strongly led committee. Its jurisdiction was broad, covering trade, debt, customs and trade, social security, and general revenue-sharing legislation. Its 25 members were House veterans whose professional approach to legislation and restrained partisanship contributed to the Committee's high status and influence in the House.[7] The Committee worked closely with Treasury Department officials and staff and with the highly expert staff of the Joint Committee on Internal Revenue Taxation in drafting its complex and technical bills,[8] and its legislation was generally reported to the floor under a closed rule. This meant that the bill was not open to amendments from other House members, and as a result Ways and Means was usually successful in having its legislation accepted as written.[9]

The standing and influence of the Ways and Means Committee can be traced to a variety of factors, some peculiar to the Committee and others reflecting congressional or at least House characteristics. Its broad jurisdiction coupled with the extremely effective leadership of Wilbur Mills, who served as chairman from 1958 through 1974, was certainly important. Mills, for example, was considered to be "one of the most influential committee chairmen in recent years, if not in history."[10] In addition, the strong consensus within the Committee on maintaining its influence in the House and preserving its independence and that of the House in relationships with the President or the Senate contributed substantially to the decision-making autonomy of Ways and Means.[11] Indeed, the influence of the House on tax policy rested in large part on the power of Ways and Means. As John Manley concluded in his study of the Committee through the mid-1960s:

A study of the relationship between the Ways and Means Committee and the executive branch shows that the Committee and Congress generally are by no means subservient to executive branch policies. Ways and Means, particularly in the area of taxation, is an independent force in policy-making that is responsive to demands not aggregated by the Treasury Department, that is well-equipped to compete on equal terms with the expertise of the executive, and that stands as a formidable challenge to presidents and their programs.[12]

By 1976, however, it appeared that Ways and Means had lost much of its status and effectiveness. As one lobbyist commented, "Ways and Means has now become like any other committee."[13] Wilbur Mills had resigned his chairmanship in 1974 under pressures resulting from his highly publicized personal problems. The Committee had survived major challenges to its jurisdiction, but it was greatly increased in size—from 25 to 37 members—in 1975, with many of the new and liberal members disinclined to accept or support strong leadership within the Committee.[14] The Committee was forced to form subcommittees (under Mills, all business was considered by the full committee), and along with other House committees, to conduct most of its business in public rather than executive session. The Democrats on the Ways and Means Committee, who had previously served as the committee on committees for the House Democrats, lost their assignment function to the Democratic Steering and Policy Committee. Perhaps most important, the Democratic caucus took an aggressive stance toward Ways and Means. It effectively foreclosed the Committee's ability to get a closed rule by indirectly sponsoring floor amendments. Throughout 1975 the Ways and Means Committee found it difficult to develop legislation, to pass legislation on the House floor in recognizable form, and to present a united front in conference with the Senate Finance Committee.[15] While the Committee has since managed to overcome these problems to some extent, its members remain divided over whether its more "democratic" internal procedures

and the open floor procedures have adversely affected its legislative product and its effectiveness.[16]

The Finance Committee. The Senate counterpart of the Ways and Means Committee—the Committee on Finance—often exercises very liberally its power to propose amendments to House-passed revenue bills. Indeed, much of the Senate's participation on tax legislation involves the sponsorship of amendments reflecting the constituency interests or personal policy preferences of individual Senators.[17] The Committee has been characterized in the past as less cohesive, less specialized, and considerably less concerned with having its bills pass intact on the floor than Ways and Means has been.[18]

Senate rules do not allow the Finance Committee the floor protection once available to Ways and Means. Even when a tax bill emerges from the Finance Committee in much the same form as it passed the House, it may be substantially amended on the floor. While this does not always occur, there are some legendary examples. In 1966 the Foreign Investors Tax Act—originally fairly narrow legislation dealing with the balance of payments—was amended in the Finance Committee and on the Senate floor with provisions affecting the financing of presidential candidates, self-employed businessmen, mineral ore entrepreneurs, large investors, hearse owners, and an aluminum company.[19] Among the various "Christmas tree bills"—so named because of the special tax benefits for numerous groups— the 1966 bill remains a classic. In 1969 a House-passed measure on tax reform provisions emerged from the Finance Committee relatively intact only to be heavily amended on the floor. Provisions were included on medical deductions for the elderly, social security minimum benefits, tax credits for college expenses, and investment tax credits for small businesses and economically depressed areas (which included the entire state represented by the sponsoring Senator).[20] Several years later, a House bill on import duties was "revised" with Senate amendments involving charities, a life insurance company, state-run lotteries, flood disaster victims, family farming, low-income housing, and medical studies for servicemen.[21]

In the Senate, the Finance Committee has not performed the control function that traditionally characterized Ways and Means in the House. Rather, the Committee has allowed its members as well as other

Senators to pursue specific and particularistic benefits in dealing with tax legislation. Participation in determining tax legislation has been more widespread in the Senate than in the House. As a result, the Finance Committee's relations with its parent chamber have tended to be less adversarial than relations between the Ways and Means Committee and the House.

The conference. The difference between the House and Senate versions of a bill are resolved by a conference committee, with the conferees normally chosen from those committees that originally considered the bill. In the case of Ways and Means and Finance; the conference generally consists of ten conferees (three majority party members and two minority party members from each committee), with the chairman of Ways and Means presiding. As in all conferences, the House and Senate sides each vote as a unit with the majority vote controlling on each side.

In the past, the House conferees have been successful in removing many of the Senate amendments (as with many of the amendments noted above), but the Senate conferees have often won important disputes on tax, social security, and trade legislation.[22] It is not at all clear that either side has usually dominated, but it is apparent that considerable bargaining and compromise do occur between the Senate and House positions.[23] As during the committee stage, the conferees work with congressional staff and Treasury tax experts, and the result is usually a highly technical document. The conference report is then presented to each chamber and, if passed, goes to the President for his signature.

Over the past several years, the secrecy and discretion of conference committees have been curtailed. Unless a majority of either the House or Senate conferees vote publicly to close a session, conferences are now open. Also, the appointment of House conferees—formerly the prerogative of committee chairmen although formally exercised by the Speaker—has come under increasing scrutiny by the Democratic caucus. The desired result is conferees who will be responsive primarily to the House-passed bill rather than to the committee that first considered it. The effect of these changes on the revenue committees, particularly Ways and Means, is not altogether clear, but it is doubtful that such changes will enhance committee autonomy.

In the past, then, the Ways and Means Committee has not necessarily dominated the conference, but its general role in financial decision making has benefited greatly from its advantages of initiation and autonomy. With changes in the latter, the influence of Ways and Means in relation to both the Senate Finance Committee and the executive branch would appear to be diminished, and this loss of influence may be especially evident during the conference stage.

Relations with the executive. While the executive branch has generally taken the lead in proposing major changes (and has usually worked very closely with the revenue committees), Congress has occasionally initiated tax legislation. In 1969, for example, Congress initiated and developed a major revision of the tax code with minimal executive participation. Moreover, Congress has frequently revised or rejected executive proposals for changes in the tax codes. The context within which tax policy has been considered, however, has been considerably broadened since the early 1960s. Up until that time, consideration of tax legislation was governed primarily by revenue requirements. The Kennedy administration, however, adopted the argument of many professional economists in emphasizing the economic policy effects of tax increases and tax reductions. According to this view, the economy can be stimulated by tax cuts, while tax increases can be utilized when restraint is needed. While the 1964 tax cut was credited with assisting economic expansion, later attempts to use tax increases to reduce inflationary pressures were considerably less successful, particularly the delay in enacting a surtax to cover increasing war costs in 1967 and 1968. In 1975 and 1976, however, Congress again was receptive to temporary tax cuts.

One of the problems in the exercise of this type of policy is timing. Congress often does not or cannot act quickly enough to provide the stimulus or restraint at the "proper" time—that is, when the administration or economists think necessary. President Kennedy accordingly proposed in 1962 that Congress grant the President standby authority to adjust tax rates temporarily (and to initiate public works spending). This request was ignored by the revenue committees, as were similar administration requests in 1963 and 1964 and a 1966 recommendation by the Joint Economic Committee. Thus, while there has usually been executive-congressional cooperation with respect to the more technical aspects of tax legislation, Congress has guarded its authority with respect to tax policy.

Taxation and the budget. A major consideration in budget decision making is, of course, the availability of resources, resulting in a direct relationship between revenue decisions and spending decisions. This does not mean that actual or potential revenues represent an absolute constraint on spending, since the federal budget has run quite large deficits in recent years. It also does not mean that such an absolute constraint would necessarily be desirable. As has been noted, planned deficits and tax cuts have often been utilized to stimulate the economy. Inevitably, however, revenue decisions do serve to define in large part what the government will have available for financing its agencies and programs, thereby focusing attention on budget aggregates—revenue totals and spending totals. Just as those responsible for spending decisions cannot entirely ignore the limits on available revenues, those who are responsible for determining tax policy cannot escape the budgetary implications of their decisions. Since 1974 Congress has explicitly recognized this by adopting revenue and spending targets to guide the decisions of its revenue and spending committees.

Revenue decisions, then, are an integral part of the budgetary process. The revenue committees play a major role in effecting the fiscal policy choices made by Congress and providing the resources to implement congressional spending decisions. At the same time, however, the Ways and Means Committee and the Finance Committee must deal with tax policies in other contexts. For example, certain tax legislation—such as protective tariffs or certain excise taxes—has a regulatory rather than a revenue-raising purpose. Moreover, the methods and sources of raising revenues are intensely political issues in their own right. The House and Senate have frequently been in conflict with each other and with the executive branch not only over how much revenue should be raised but also over how a given revenue level should be derived. In 1975 and 1976, for example, the Ways and Means and Finance Committees differed sharply over tax code revisions despite the fact that they were attempting to effect similar total revenue levels. The concerns of the revenue committees, then, extend beyond the budgetary process, and many of their most important decisions may be made primarily in response to pressures or issues only indirectly related to the budget. Nevertheless, the revenue side of the budgetary process represents a major vehicle for implementing congressional priorities and fiscal policy choices.

Spending Power

Congressional spending decisions are made through a multistep process that has become increasingly complicated in recent years. As discussed in Chapter One, spending first requires an authorization. This means that a law must be passed establishing a program or agency, specifying the objectives or aims involved, and in most cases setting a maximum amount on the monies that can be used to finance the program or agency. Authorization bills are handled by the substantive legislative committees. For example, legislation authorizing the Department of Defense to initiate a weapons research and development program would be required in advance of the actual appropriation of funds for that purpose. This legislation would be handled by the House and Senate Armed Services Committees.

Subsequent to the passage of authorizing legislation, the appropriations stage is initiated to grant the actual monies that have been authorized (although the maximum amount authorized need not be appropriated). By tradition, and despite occasional Senate challenges, appropriations bills originate in the House.

House Appropriations Committee. Like the Ways and Means Committee, the House Committee on Appropriations has been generally recognized as extremely powerful and influential. Also as in the case of Ways and Means, there have been some recent challenges to its independence and authority. Appropriations is a large committee (55 members during the 95th Congress, comprising 37 Democrats and 18 Republicans), which operates through 13 subcommittees, each of which has in the past exercised substantial discretion within its jurisdiction (see below). Thus when the President's budget is received, the complex and detailed work of examining and deciding on appropriations requests is conducted within these House subcommittees.

Jurisdictions of House and Senate Appropriations Subcommittees 95th Congress (1977–1978)
Agriculture and Related Agencies
Defense

District of Columbia
Foreign Operations
Housing and Urban Development—Independent
   Agencies
Interior
Labor—Health, Education and Welfare
Legislative
Military Construction
Public Works
State, Justice, Commerce and Judiciary
Transportation
Treasury—Postal Service—General Government

In the past, the subcommittees have worked independently of each other, and the full committee has generally approved without major modification the appropriations bills and reports prepared by its subcommittees. At least a partial measure of committee influence is provided by its success rate on the House floor. A study of decisions from 1947 through 1962 found the House accepting Appropriations Committee money recommendations without change in approximately 90 percent of the cases.[24] Since the subcommittee leadership is responsible for managing its bill on the House floor, it is apparent that the reputation that the subcommittees have acquired for diligence, dedication, and expertise are an effective component of their influence in the House.[25]

One source of the Appropriations Committee's influence is the perception that its strength and unity help the House of Representatives to maintain its independence and power against the executive branch and to a lesser extent the Senate. The Committee has also benefited from its decision-making initiative, which allows it to set the "direction and magnitude of most congressional appropriations decisions. . . . It cherishes the appropriations function more dearly and defends it more strenuously than does any other group."[26]

In recent years, however, the Appropriations Committee has been challenged. Most important for both the Senate and House Committees are the series of budgetary process changes incorporated in PL 93-344, the 1974 Congressional Budget and Impoundment Control Act, and the developments in nonappropriations spending discussed later in this chapter. In addition, the House Appropriations Committee has been particularly affected by procedural changes, such as those requiring open committee and

subcommittee sessions (during the 1950s and 1960s the Committee usually conducted its important business in executive sessions), earlier circulation of committee reports and bills, and recorded votes in the Committee of the Whole. As part of their 1974–1975 internal reforms, House Democrats required that Appropriations subcommittee chairman nominations be submitted to the caucus for approval.[27] This was an attempt to increase responsiveness to the caucus and to decrease the control of the committee chairman, George Mahon of Texas. As the disputes over the relationship between the caucus and the standing committees multiplied during the first months of 1975, Mahon suggested that committee chairmen "ought to be responsive to the caucus on big issues. We ought to let legislation come out so it can be considered. But instructing committees on specifics is out of the question. That would destroy the committee system."[28]

Senate Appropriations Committee. The Senate and House Committees differ in several respects. The Senate members have additional committee assignments, sometimes serving on both the authorizing committee and the appropriations subcommittee for an agency or program.[29] Senate subcommittees generally do not engage in the lengthy or detailed work of the House subcommittees. Like other Senate committees, Appropriations is "permeable"—not exclusive in its membership, less autonomous in its procedures, closely interlocked with other committees, and more responsive to the policy preferences of nonmembers. The decision-making process on appropriations legislation is much less committee-dominated than it is in the House; as a consequence the independent influence of the Senate Appropriations Committee is considerably less than that of its House counterpart.[30]

Particularly important is the greater emphasis that the Senate Committee has placed on financing programs and projects as opposed to the House emphasis on economy. This reflects the broader "policy environment" in which the Senate subcommittees operate—a context in which the executive branch, colleagues on other committees, and various clientele groups come independently to them.[31] As Richard Fenno describes it:

> The Senate Committee prescribes for itself the tasks of an appellate court, which makes decisions

on the basis of agency appeals for the restoration of the incremental reductions made by the House Committee. This goal expectation—which contrasts with the House Committee's expectation of budget reduction—is primarily a result of the fixed appropriations sequence. . . . By prescribing an appeals court task for itself, the Senate Committee makes it very likely that it will, in fact, grant increases.[32]

Because the Senate Committee is usually able to accommodate this broader policy environment and to emphasize the need for financing programs that the Senate membership supports, its success on the floor has been impressive. In a study of 36 bureau appropriations recommendations covering a 15-year period, the Committee's recommendation was upheld in 88.5 percent of the cases (as compared to 89.9 percent for the House Appropriations Committee).[33] There are, as in the case of the House, relatively few successful amendments.

Conference. Differences between the House and Senate versions of an appropriations bill are usually substantial enough to require conference committee reconciliation. As with revenue bills, bargaining and compromise are characteristic of the process. The House's advantage stemming from decision-making initiative in the appropriations process is countered, at least partially, by the greater support that Senate conferees have within their chamber. The more widespread participation in appropriations decisions in the Senate means that the Senate bill is usually more representative of the policy preferences of the chamber than is the House bill. In addition, the Senate usually benefits from defending the higher appropriation:

The demands for increased appropriations become more concentrated and intense as appropriations decision-making moves from stage to stage and as the controversial increment of the budget progressively narrows. Individuals and groups have more time to mobilize, have more information, and have fewer issues to contest at each succeeding stage—from House to Senate, from Senate to conference. Conversely, economy sentiment (unless maintained by extraordinary external events) tends to take the form of evanescent moods, to become progressively weaker with the passage of time and with the intrusion of new legislative events.[34]

Thus, the House does not clearly dominate the conference stage,[35] although its influence in the entire appropriations process is more pervasive than that of the Senate.[36]

Limits on appropriations control. The Appropriations Committees have traditionally had to contend with executive pressures in the budget decision-making process, but since the early 1950s they have also been faced by challenges within Congress, particularly the use of annual authorizations and various forms of backdoor spending. The first of these, annual authorization, has been aimed at the House Appropriations Committee. It represents an attempt by the authorizing committees to maintain their influence over agencies and programs by requiring the same annual review as that provided by the appropriations process.

In part, the double review—first by the authorizing committee and then by the Appropriations Committee—provides the House with information and judgments from more than one source, lessening its dependence on the Appropriations Committee. In addition, the double review encourages the development of program and financial expertise among authorizing committee members. Two of the persistent complaints about Appropriations—its lack of communication with nonmembers and its excessive involvement in legislative matters (since it is difficult to distinguish in many cases where the line between financial and programmatic judgments should be drawn)[37]—have thus been manifested in the increasing emphasis on annual authorization. Since the authorizing and Appropriations committees in the Senate are more closely linked, these complaints have not been as widespread as in the House, but the House has managed to gain the Senate's acquiescence to annual authorizations in most instances.

The second challenge—backdoor spending—reflects some of the same authorizing committee versus Appropriations Committee antagonisms, except that here the authorizing committees attempt to establish exclusive or dominant control over spending decisions. Budget authority is usually in the form of appropriations, but the latter term has been broadened to include not only measures that pass through the Appropriations Committees but also other legislative actions that create obligations or make funds available for obligation or expenditure.[38]

The earliest examples of backdoor spending involved contract authorization and loan authority. Under the first, an authorizing committee sponsored legislation creating statutory authority for a department or agency to enter into contracts or obligations before specific appropriations were approved. Once contracts had been entered into or obligations incurred, appropriations were necessary to liquidate the obligations, but neither the Appropriations Committees nor Congress had much discretion about providing the necessary funds. With loan authority, certain agencies were allowed to borrow funds directly from the Treasury rather than having to go through the appropriations process. Here, too, the jurisdiction was with the authorizing committees.

Both these approaches thus allowed programs to circumvent effectively the Appropriations Committees and their increasing use by authorizing committees during the 1950s finally resulted in a legislative battle in the House. The House Appropriations Committee challenged both these practices and succeeded, during the early 1960s, in gaining the authority to review the granting of loan authority and to set annual maximum limits on contract authorizations.[39] This has cut down, although not eliminated, these forms of backdoor spending. In 1975, for example, approximately $11.5 billion in contract authorizations and $1.5 billion in loan authority were available without current action by Congress.[40]

At the same time, however, other forms of backdoor spending have emerged and become an extremely significant portion of annual spending. In recent years "mandatory entitlements" have become especially important. These are payments to persons or to state and local governments that the federal government is obligated to make when the legal requirements for receiving payment are fulfilled. The costs of such entitlements are determined by the pool of eligible recipients. As the size of this pool increases (or decreases), costs fluctuate and automatically affect spending. For example, the eligible pool of food stamp recipients grew substantially during the early 1970s—3.5 million persons were added between June 1974 and December 1974, bringing estimated participation to 17 million people. But because of the lack of clarity in the legislative and administrative guidelines, it was still unclear as to how many persons were actually eligible but not participating or participating but not actually eligible. Some studies estimated that the program's "target population" was between 27 and 39 million people with additional fluctuations possible if economic conditions changed.[41] Thus, for programs of this type, spending decisions are a product of eligibility requirements, economic conditions, and administrative efficiency rather than appropriations decisions made in advance of spending.

A related type of effect occurs when payments are tied to various indexes. For example, retirement benefits can be linked to changes in the cost of living. As the consumer price index changes, program costs automatically change. Here again, actual spending will result from economic conditions that are not always predictable in advance. The authorizing committees, by sponsoring legislation that establishes an automatic increase in payments or benefits under various programs can evade effective review by the Appropriations Committees for programs within their jurisdiction.

The result of these types of backdoor spending is that many budget decisions are made outside the regular, annual appropriations process. Spending control is therefore fragmented between the authorizing committees and the Appropriations Committees. The growing seriousness of this problem led Congress to set certain controls on backdoor spending as part of the broader revision of the budgetary process in 1974.

Controlling Spending— Attempted Reforms

Throughout its history, Congress has had considerable difficulty in designing budget procedures that could resolve the competing goals and claims of its standing committees. One persistent tension has been that between the authorizing committees, with their emphasis on support for programs within their respective jurisdictions, and the Appropriations Committees, with their relatively greater emphasis on economy and other financial considerations. When Congress has moved to centralize spending control in its Appropriations Committees, as it did after the Civil War and during the 1920s, the authorizing committees have inevitably challenged this centralization (as they successfully did between 1877 and 1885) or have developed backdoor spending methods to circumvent the appropriations process (as they have done for the past several decades). A second area of tension involves the relative influence of Congress and the President with respect to government spending. As discussed in Chapter Two, the executive budget process has become increasingly important and influential since its establishment in 1921, and this has presented a continuing challenge to Congress' budget capabilities. Prior to 1974, Congress was unable to resolve fully either of these tensions, much less to find a method of reconciling both satisfactorily.

Since the mid-1940s, Congress has made several attempts to revise and improve its budgetary process, with the most recent and elaborate revision being the 1974 Congressional Budget and Impoundment Control Act. Some perspective on this latest effort can be gained by surveying the fate of two earlier attempts.

Legislative budget. As part of the 1946 Legislative Reorganization Act, Congress established a legislative budget. Four committees (Ways and Means, Finance, and the Appropriations Committees) were to meet as the Joint Budget Committee at the beginning of each session and to prepare estimates of total receipts and expenditures. By February 15 their report, along with a concurrent resolution setting the maximum amount to be appropriated for the following fiscal year, was to be sent to the House and Senate for consideration. Further, the appropriations limit could not exceed estimated receipts unless the resolution specified a necessary increase in the public debt; if a surplus was estimated, a reduction in the debt was to be recommended.

Congress unsuccessfully attempted to develop a legislative budget in 1947, 1948, and 1949. Estimates on revenues and spending were inaccurate, spending ceilings were violated, and the Senate and House had continual disagreements.[42] One major problem was the February 15 deadline for reporting a spending ceiling. This did not allow the Committee adequate time to study the President's budget in detail or to specify where budget cuts were to be made. Since there was no provision for amending the ceiling, the procedure did not allow Congress to take into account changes in economic conditions or other circumstances as it made its spending decisions.[43] Moreover, the feasibility of operating such a large committee (the Joint Budget Committee had more than 100 members) as well as the perceived inadequacy of available staff presented serious problems, which were complicated by policy disagreements

between the congressional parties and by the hostility of the House Appropriations Committee.[44] In 1947 the Senate and House could not come to agreement on the size of the cut in the President's budget or on the disposal of the unspent funds, and no legislative budget was adopted. In 1948 both chambers agreed on a $2.5 billion cut in the executive budget, but there was no specification of what form this cut would take. Congress then violated the spending ceiling by appropriating $6 billion more than specified in the concurrent resolution. The following year Congress finally changed the date for adopting the concurrent resolution to May 1, but since most appropriations bills had been passed by that time, no legislative budget was adopted. By 1950 the concept had been effectively dropped.[45]

Omnibus Appropriations Bill. In 1950 Representative Clarence Cannon, chairman of the House Appropriations Committee, tried to establish a different type of expenditure control by combining all of the separate appropriations bills into one measure. The assumption was that acting on separate bills one by one made it quite difficult to control total outlays, but that a comprehensive consideration would allow for an effective check on total outlays. During its 1950 trial, the omnibus bill cut the President's budget requests significantly, although large supplemental appropriations were soon necessitated by the Korean war.[46] More important, the subcommittee chairmen of the House Appropriations Committee viewed the omnibus approach as a threat to the power and autonomy of their subcommittees. In 1951 the omnibus approach was abandoned, and Senate-sponsored attempts to revive the practice have not been supported by the House. Subsequently, additional revisions—such as separate budget sessions, expenditure ceilings, and Joint Budget Committees—have been proposed, but these have not been both acceptable and effective.

1974 Congressional Budget and Impoundment Control Act

Congress has, then, periodically if unsuccessfully attempted to revise and improve its budgetary organization and process. Both the legislative budget and omnibus appropriations bill experiments reflected a concern with controlling expenditures, which became pronounced once again with the expenditure increases of the early 1970s. In addition, however, Congress was faced in 1972 with a sharp executive challenge to its budget authority. When Congress did not agree to the Nixon administration's request for a $250 billion ceiling on fiscal 1973 expenditures, the President accelerated the use of impoundments to impose the ceiling.[47] This presidential challenge was perceived by some observers as extremely effective politically, since it played on the electorate's growing concern with federal spending. Louis Fisher, for example, suggested that congressional budgetary reform was necessary if Congress was to retain control over national policy making:

> Unless Congress can improve its budget capability it will remain a patsy, forever being bulldozed around by executive assaults and encroachments— no matter how factually unsound or spurious in design they are. Such capability is needed not merely to restore a balance between the two branches and to protect congressional spending prerogatives, but to raise the level of public debate and the quality of public policy.[48]

As part of its 1972 debt limit legislation, Congress therefore established a Joint Study Committee on Budget Control and directed it to provide recommendations for improving congressional control and coordination of budget outlays and receipts. The Committee's report was issued in April 1973; after significant modifications of its recommendations, budget reform legislation was signed into law July 12, 1974. Within a relatively short period, Congress had instituted the most substantial budget reform in over half a century, and the overwhelming support for this reform reflected widespread agreement about the severity of the problems that had developed under the old process.[49]

The Problems

During congressional consideration of budget reform legislation, attention focused on a series of major problems that characterized Congress' handling of the budget.[50]

1. The lack of coordination in the budget process made it difficult to relate taxing and spending actions to fiscal policy needs. Because taxing and spending measures were considered by numerous committees with no required coordination, congressional taxing and spending decisions were often unrelated to each other. This meant that Congress had no mechanism for setting fiscal policy and thus for challenging the executive's dominance over fiscal policy decisions. In addition, it meant that members of Congress were not forced to make conscious and explicit decisions about total spending and to relate them to available revenues.

2. The lack of coordination in the budget process had negative effects on Congress' ability to manage programs—many of the outlays in a given year were removed from the regular appropriations process or represented long-term commitments over which control was limited. The budget was increasingly inflexible and resistant to congressional policy preferences. Since Congress was unable to control substantial amounts of short-term spending, its ability to use the annual budget as a means for implementing its policy preferences was circumscribed.

3. The traditional budgetary process did not provide a mechanism through which Congress was forced to make necessary but difficult choices on priorities. Indeed, under the traditional process, appropriations bills were passed at different times, and Congress was able to avoid direct confrontations about competing priorities. Moreover, there was growing concern about the massive spending increases and deficits in previous years, indicating that Congress would inevitably be forced to consider spending decisions not only in relation to each other but also in relation to their cumulative impact on the budget.

4. There was no staff organization responsible to Congress to provide fiscal policy and program analysis. Congress was accordingly too reliant on information and analyses provided by the President and the Office of Management and Budget (OMB).

5. The timing of congressional budget actions was unsatisfactory—action on appropriations bills was seldom completed by the beginning of the fiscal year. One result was that many agencies operated with stopgap funding (continuing resolutions) for part or all of a fiscal year.

6. Executive claims of impoundment authority challenged Congress' appropriations powers and threatened its exercise of the power of the purse. The unprecedented use of impoundment by President Nixon and the expansive claims of federal authority that accompanied it could not be continually tolerated if Congress was to preserve its institutional integrity and authority.

The problems, then, were serious, since they ultimately affected Congress' capacity to make and control policy. At the same time, however, there were differing expectations about the effects of budget reform. Conservatives, for example, supported budget reform, since they viewed it as the means to limit the growth in federal spending and to eliminate budget deficits. Liberals, on the other hand, focused on those aspects of reform that would allow Congress to challenge the President on fiscal policy and to enforce its spending priorities and policy decisions. Thus, there were questions from the first about the survival of the new budgetary process, given these differing expectations and the partisan and ideological battles that would inevitably occur.[51]

Under PL 93-344, the Congressional Budget and Impoundment Control Act, Congress enacted a number of important procedural and organizational changes. New Budget Committees were created, and a congressional budgetary staff organization was established. The fiscal year was changed as was the fiscal year timetable for congressional consideration of the budget. Elaborate and complex procedures were adopted that governed executive and congressional budget participation. Major revisions were made to deal with backdoor spending and impoundment.

Budget Committees and Staffs

A standing Committee on the Budget has been established for each chamber, and these committees have broad jurisdiction over the congressional budget process. They are responsible for reporting to Congress each year at least two concurrent resolutions that allow Congress to set its fiscal policy choices and to adopt guidelines to be used in its actions on revenue, spending, and debt legislation. The Committees are also responsible for studying the budgetary effects of existing and proposed legislation and for overseeing the operations of the Congressional Budget Office (CBO). Each committee also has its own staff.

There are differences in the rules governing selection and tenure on the Budget Committees. As initially set up in 1975, the Senate Committee included 16 members selected by normal committee selection procedures—that is, by the Democratic and Republican conferences. There is no required rotation for Senate Budget Committee members, although they are restricted in the number of additional committee and subcommittee positions they can hold. Under new Senate rules adopted in

1977, each Senator can serve on two major committees and one minor committee. The Budget Committee was designated as a minor committee for the 95th Congress and as a major committee beginning in 1979. For members newly appointed to the Committee in 1977, however, the Committee was classified as a major committee. In addition, members of the Senate Budget Committee were allowed to serve on three subcommittees, as opposed to the limit of two applied to other minor committees. Membership on the Committee has been set at 16, with the party ratio for the 95th Congress being 10 Democrats and 6 Republicans. Senator Edmund Muskie (D-Maine) has served as the Committee's chairman since its establishment.

The House Committee is larger and has more elaborate rules governing its membership. Rules adopted in 1975 set total membership at 25, with 5 seats assigned to Ways and Means Committee members, 5 seats to Appropriations Committee members, and the remainder apportioned among the legislative committees and party leadership. Tenure on the panel is restricted, with each member limited to serving four years in any ten-year period. For the 95th Congress, the party ratio was set at 17 Democrats and 8 Republicans with Representative Robert Giaimo (D-Conn.) being selected as chairman.[52] He succeeded Brock Adams, who had been appointed as Secretary of Transportation by President Carter.

Congressional Budget Office. The CBO is a major innovation. It is an attempt to develop a professional budget staff in Congress that will combine certain functions performed by the OMB, the Council of Economic Advisers, and the Treasury Department in the executive budget process. The CBO is to provide the Budget Committees and Congress with a variety of budget and policy analysis information.[53] Certain CBO functions are prescribed by the 1974 act. These include: (1) preparation of an annual report on budget alternatives, including fiscal policy options, levels of tax expenditures, and budget priorities; (2) issuance of five-year budget projections; (3) estimates of costs, when possible, of bills reported by House and Senate committees; and (4) issuance of periodic "scorekeeping" reports—tracking the effect of specific congressional budgetary actions on the overall budget targets established by Congress. In addition, the CBO assists the Budget Committees and, to a lesser extent, other committees by preparing commissioned research reports on economic and budgetary issues. It has also developed data management systems to support the congressional budget process.

Timetable, Process, and Procedures

The revised budgetary process includes a new fiscal year timetable and a number of procedural requirements. The beginning of the fiscal year has been moved from July 1 to October 1 to provide an additional three months for congressional consideration of the budget. Moreover, since presidential budget estimates are now due approximately eleven months in advance of the beginning of a fiscal year, the budget sequence on the congressional side now covers almost one full year. Figure 1 lists the various

---

October–December: Congressional Budget Office submits five-year projection of current spending as soon as possible after October 1.

November 10: President submits current services budget.

December 31: Joint Economic Committee reports analysis of current services budget to budget committees.

Late January: President submits budget (fifteen days after Congress convenes).

Late January–March: Budget committees hold hearings and begin work on first budget resolution.

March 15: All legislative committees submit estimates and views to budget committees.

April 15: Budget committees report first resolution.

May 15: Committees must report authorization bills by this date.

May 15: Congress completes action on first resolution. Before adoption of the first resolution, neither house may consider new budget authority or spending authority bills, revenue changes, or debt limit changes.

May 15 through the 7th day after Labor Day: Congress completes action on all budget and spending authority bills.

- Before reporting first regular appropriations bill, the House Appropriations Committee, "to extent practicable," marks up all regular appropriations bills and submits a summary report to House, comparing proposed outlays and budget authority levels with first resolution targets.
- CBO issues periodic scorekeeping reports comparing congressional action with first resolution.
- Reports on new budget authority and tax expenditure bills must contain comparisons with first resolution, and five-year projections.
- "As possible," a CBO cost analysis and five-year projection will accompany all reported public bills, except appropriation bills.

August: Budget committees prepare second budget resolution and report.

September 15: Congress completes action on second resolution. Thereafter, neither house may consider any bill or amendment, or conference report, that results in an increase over outlay or budget authority figures, or a reduction in revenues, beyond the amounts in the second resolution.

September 25: Congress completes action on reconciliation bill or another resolution. Congress may not adjourn until it completes action on the second resolution and reconciliation measure, if any.

October 1: Fiscal year begins.

Figure 1

Congressional budget deadlines. *Source:* Congressional Quarterly Almanac, Vol. XXXI, 1975 *(Washington, D.C.: Congressional Quarterly, Inc., 1976), p. 918.*

deadlines involved in the development of the congressional budget.

1. The first step is submission of the current services budget by the President on November 10. This budget estimates the budget authority and outlays required to continue government policies and programs under existing legislation and current economic assumptions. It is intended to provide, therefore, an estimate of the spending levels required without program changes or new programs. The current services budget is reviewed by Congress' Joint Economic Committee, which is directed to assess its estimates and economic assumptions and to report these assessments to the Budget Committees.

2. Within 15 days after Congress convenes in January, the President submits his budget for the upcoming fiscal year. This contains the usual information and recommendations concerning economic assumptions, revenues and outlays, budget authority, and fiscal and program policy choices. There are additional requirements that it provide estimates of and recommendations for changes in tax expenditures and five-year estimates of federal spending under existing commitments.

3. By March 15 the Budget Committees are to receive reports on budget recommendations and proposals from other congressional committees. The CBO report on budget options and priorities is due April 1. On the basis of these reports, the President's budget proposals, and hearings or other sources of information, the Budget Committees are required to develop and report to Congress the first concurrent resolution on the budget.

4. April 15 is the deadline for reporting the first concurrent resolution. This resolution sets targets for expenditures and revenues to guide subsequent congressional budget decisions. The resolution specifies total outlays and revenues and the projected surplus or deficit. Within the outlays total, spending is broken down by the functional categories used in the President's budget.[54] Congress has until May 15 to debate this resolution and to adopt a final version.

5. May 15 is also the deadline for reporting most authorizing legislation that will be required for the upcoming fiscal year.[55] (Administration requests for authorizing legislation are due one year in advance of this date).

6. From May 15 through early September, the regular appropriations process proceeds with initial consideration by the House Appropriations subcommittees. However, spending decisions as well as tax proposals being considered by the revenue committees are to take into account the guidelines established in the first concurrent resolution. Each appropriation bill will go sequentially through the traditional route; after final House and Senate agreement, the individual bills can be sent separately to the President or all can be held until September.

7. After action has been completed on spending and revenue bills, but on or before September 15, Congress must adopt a second concurrent resolution. This second resolution will either affirm or revise the targets set in May for spending, revenues, and the debt limit. It will also review the spending and revenue decisions that Congress has taken in the interim (on appropriations, entitlements, tax legislation, and so forth). If ceilings have been exceeded, estimated revenues are insufficient, or the debt limit must be revised, the second resolution will direct those committees with the appropriate jurisdiction to make and report the necessary legislative changes. This could include revising appropriations or other spending legislation, raising or lowering revenues, adjusting the debt ceiling, or any combination of these. If the changes are confined to one committee in each chamber (for example, a tax bill revision by the Ways and Means and Finance Committees), then the changes are reported directly to the floor. If the necessary changes are more extensive, the Budget Committees are responsible for combining the changes in a reconciliation measure that is then reported to the House and Senate. This measure is to be adopted by September 25 and is then sent to the President. If Congress has withheld all appropriations and other budget-related bills, this measure then becomes the final budget legislation. If individual bills have been passed, this measure—if signed by the President—supersedes all previously passed legislation.

By October 1, then, the budgetary process is to be completed, although congressional delays or presidential vetoes could obviously carry the process past the deadline. Indeed, the specified deadlines can be waived by the House and Senate. Moreover, Congress can also pass additional budget resolutions and revise its earlier decisions once the fiscal year has begun.[56] Nevertheless, the process envisions an orderly congressional review of budget measures and provides for the comprehensive consideration of

Stage 1. **November 10–** **April 15**	Information gathering, analysis, preparation and submission of congressional budget by Congressional Budget Office and Budget Committees.
Stage 2. **April 15–** **May 15**	Debate and adoption of congressional budget by both houses; establishment of national spending priorities.
Stage 3. **May 15–** **Early September**	Enactment of spending bills.
Stage 4. **September 15–** **September 25**	Reassessment of spending, revenue, and debt requirements in second budget resolution; enactment of reconciliation bill.

Figure 2

Four stages of the budget process. *Source: House Committee on the Budget,*
Congressional Budget Reform, *93rd Congress, 2nd Session (Washington, D.C.:*
Government Printing Office, 1975), p. 16.

revenue and spending measures and fiscal policy choices in a four-stage process (see Figure 2).

This elaborate procedure has several objectives. First, Congress is able to make explicit decisions on fiscal policy by voting on budget aggregates—total spending and total revenues—and thus setting a budget deficit or surplus level that it believes appropriate. Second, the concurrent resolution that Congress adopts in the spring establishes expenditure and revenue targets to guide subsequent authorization, appropriation, and revenue decisions. If congressional spending or revenue decisions do not fall within these targets, the second concurrent resolution forces Congress to make the necessary adjustments in its budget totals. Third, since the concurrent resolutions include expenditures by functional categories, Congress must consider its spending decisions in relation to each other, which provides for congressional determination of priorities. And fourth, the new budgetary process is designed to insure passage of budget legislation before the beginning of the fiscal year to which it applies. If the deadlines are met, the funding for agencies and programs should be firmly established once the fiscal year begins. Moreover, since the beginning of the fiscal year has been advanced to October 1, Congress has almost eleven months—

beginning with submission of the current services budget—to work on its budget.

Budget Controls

In addition to changes in congressional organization and in the budget process, the 1974 law also contained provisions designed to strengthen congressional budgetary controls. These included new procedures for dealing with backdoor spending, estimating and reporting tax expenditures, and most important, establishing a congressional check on presidential impoundment.

Backdoor spending. With certain exceptions, new backdoor spending in the form of contract or borrowing authority and entitlements was made subject to increased control by the Appropriations Committees. Most new contract or borrowing authority, for example, was made dependent on prior appropriations. This changed new contract or borrowing authority into a standard authorization subject to the funding recommendation of the Appropriations Committees. In addition, the Appropriations Committees were given the authority to review new entitlement legislation, but only if the legislation provided budget authority in excess of the latest budget resolution allocation for that function. More important, spending for certain trust funds, such as social security, was exempted from review.

Tax expenditures. Provisions relating to tax expenditures dealt primarily with reporting. In the case of any committee reporting tax expenditure legislation, estimates must be prepared (in consultation with the CBO) that detail the effects of the proposed legislation on the existing level of tax expenditures and project the costs for a five-year period. Since the CBO is also required to furnish five-year projections for all existing tax expenditures, Congress can more adequately assess the short- and long-term revenue effects of new tax expenditure legislation.

Impoundment. Title X of the 1974 act established impoundment controls and represented a major check on executive spending discretion. This section established two categories of impoundments—deferrals and rescissions. If the President wishes to defer the actual spending of appropriated funds during a fiscal year, he must inform Congress by special message of the amount, time period, justifications, and estimated program effects of the proposed deferral. Either the Senate or the House can disapprove the deferral by adopting an impoundment resolution, in which case funds must be made available for obligation. If funds are to be rescinded permanently— that is, if budget authority is to be eliminated—the President must notify Congress by special message of the amount, justification, and estimated program impact of the rescission. Unless Congress adopts a rescission bill within 45 days of continuous session after receipt of this message, the President must release the funds proposed for rescission.

Policy Evaluations

Congress also recognized the necessity for program review and evaluation in budget decisions. It authorized committees to exercise their oversight responsibilities by contract or by requiring federal agencies to conduct evaluations. In addition, the GAO was directed to assist committees in their evaluations and in developing statements of legislative objectives or intent, and the GAO was authorized to establish an Office of Program Review and Evaluation. Finally, the Budget Committees were directed to study proposals for improving budget decision making, including time limitations for program authorizations,

pilot testing of programs, and other testing and evaluation techniques. The 1974 act did not provide a great deal of specificity relating to program evaluation and review, but it did signal a growing congressional awareness of the need to expand committee oversight and thereby to improve Congress' ability to evaluate its past budget decisions and make more informed future choices. . . .

Summary

Congress has traditionally found it difficult to exercise the power of the purse effectively. During the past several decades this difficulty has been magnified by the growing influence of the executive over budget decision making. Thus, many efforts at reforming the congressional budget system have been aimed at redressing a perceived imbalance in executive-congressional relations. The 1974 revision of the budget system is no exception.

A second source of difficulty, however, has been internal. What is meant by effective exercise of the power of the purse is not necessarily a matter of agreement between the House and Senate or among the appropriations, revenue, and authorizing committees in each chamber. Just as the power of the purse is a source of institutional power in executive-congressional clashes, pieces of that power are sources of individual and committee influence in Congress. Thus, a workable budget system in Congress must provide benefits for individual members as well as promote the collective benefit of a "more effective Congress."

The 1974 Congressional Budget and Impoundment Control Act is an unusually far-reaching attempt to resolve these difficulties, and it might be helpful to offer some tentative assessments of its effects. First, the new budget process provides Congress with the mechanism to act on fiscal policy and to challenge executive dominance in economic management. Second, Congress can use the budgetary process to make priority choices by considering spending decisions in relation to each other. The budget resolutions therefore also make it possible for Congress to specify how its priorities differ from those of the President. Third, Congress has developed budgetary staff and information resources that reduce considerably its reliance on the executive for budget data and analysis. Fourth, the impoundment control provisions of the 1974 legislation establish clear congressional checks on the President's discretionary spending authority. Thus, where the objectives of budget reform relate directly to congressional versus executive influence over budget decision making, Congress' institutional authority has been enhanced.

The accomplishment of other major objectives appears less certain. The provisions affecting backdoor spending and entitlements are relatively weak and do not place these and other forms of uncontrollable spending under strict, centralized control. There is also some question about Congress' willingness to use the budget system to curtail overall spending increases and deficits. This is especially true in the House, where pressures for increased spending pose a potential threat to the budget process. If President Carter does attempt to achieve a balanced budget by the end of his first term, congressional spending pressures can no longer be absorbed by planned deficits, and Congress will be faced with much more difficult either/or choices on policy than it has faced thus far. Based on its recent approach to budget decision making, the Senate appears more likely than the House to achieve the necessary fiscal discipline to make such decisions. The House has not been able to establish a clear role for its Budget Committee, nor has it really decided what its own role should now be in budget decision making. Thus, the potential for breakdown of the budget process in the House does exist, and it will tend to increase if either the President or Senate (or both) exerts serious pressure on the House to limit spending increases.

The budget process, then, still faces serious challenges in Congress. While Congress has been strengthened institutionally with respect to the President, it has also received increased responsibility. Congress has in effect stipulated that it has the discipline and judgment to deal with fiscal matters in a coherent and comprehensive fashion. The budget reform was in large part a response to presidential attacks that Congress was incapable or unwilling to act responsibly to control spending. Unless Congress shows that it is willing to contain the spending pressures of its members in exchange for its new influence over fiscal policy and program priorities, these criticisms will reemerge. Congress will thus run the risk of losing its new authority—and much of its power over spending—to a President whom the public regards as better able to guard the Treasury.

Notes

1. Richard F. Fenno, Jr., *The Power of the Purse: Appropriations Politics in Congress* (Boston: Little, Brown, 1966), p. xiii.

2. Ibid., pp. 43–44.

3. For a balanced discussion of these efforts and their possibilities for success, see Richard E. Neustadt, *Presidential Power: The Politics of Leadership with Reflections on Johnson and Nixon* (New York: Wiley, 1976), pp. 1–68. On the budget reforms, Neustadt (p. 66) states, "At least it can be said that in the budget process Congress has reached for a tool which—if it musters leadership to handle—does create a sort of parity with any President, across the board of governmental programs. . . . Of all details to watch with care in the years just ahead, none will convey more portents for the future than details of organization and procedure, whether strengthening or weakening, in the first few congressional budgets.

4. In *Pollock v. Farmer's Loan and Trust Co.*, 158 U.S. 601 (1895), the Court held that a 2 percent tax on incomes over $4000 was a "direct tax" that had to be apportioned among the states according to population (under Article I, Section 2, paragraph 3). This apportionment restriction was removed from income taxes by the Sixteenth Amendment.

5. During the first half of the nineteenth century, most federal receipts were generated by customs duties. After the Civil War, customs duties and excise taxes provided most federal revenue. Since the adoption of the income tax, however, the proportion of federal revenues generated by these sources has declined steadily. It should also be noted that beginning in the 1930s, Congress has delegated considerable authority over tariffs to the President.

6. See John F. Manley, *The Politics of Finance: The House Committee on Ways and Means* (Boston: Little, Brown, 1970).

7. Ibid. See also Richard F. Fenno, Jr., *Congressmen in Committees* (Boston: Little, Brown, 1973), especially chap. 3.

8. This joint committee was established in 1926. It includes ten members from the Ways and Means and Finance Committees. There are certain legal responsibilities that this committee has, but the most important aspect is its professional staff, which serves as the revenue staff of Congress and provides the necessary technical expertise in writing tax legislation.

9. From 1953 through 1964, the Committee won 94 percent of the roll calls on which its decisions were tested. As Fenno notes, "The Committee probably has the highest percentage of passed-and-unamended bills of all the committees in the Congress." *Congressmen in Committees*, p. 203. See also Manley, *Politics of Finance*, chap. 5.

10. Manley, *Politics of Finance,* p. 100.
11. Fenno, *Congressmen in Committees,* especially pp. 202–212.
12. Manley, *Politics of Finance,* p. 379.
13. "Ways and Means in 1975: No Longer Pre-Eminent," *Congressional Quarterly Weekly Report, 34,* no. 2 (January 10, 1976), 40.
14. The Ways and Means Committee did lose jurisdiction over revenue-sharing and export control legislation, but it retained control over tax, welfare, trade, Social Security, unemployment, and health legislation.
15. "Ways and Means in 1975," pp. 40–44.
16. The loss of the closed rule, or at least its diminished use, might prove to be a major blow against Ways and Means' ability "to put a damper on particularism in tax and tariff matters and to protect what members call the 'actuarial soundness' of the social security program." According to this interpretation, Ways and Means serves as a "control committee" for the House, insulating it from demands and pressures that members would otherwise find difficult to resist. In return for their contributions toward this institutional maintenance, members of the Committee are accorded prestige and influence in the House. David H. Mayhew, *Congress: The Electoral Connection* (New Haven, Conn.: Yale University Press, 1974), pp. 154–156.
17. Fenno, *Congressmen in Committees,* pp. 181–187.
18. Ibid. See also Manley, *Politics of Finance,* chap. 6.
19. *Congressional Quarterly's Guide to the Congress of the United States: Origins, History and Procedure* (Washington, D.C.: Congressional Quarterly, 1971), p. 182.
20. Ibid., p. 183.
21. *Congressional Quarterly Weekly Report, 32,* no. 36 (September 7, 1974), 2433.
22. See Manley, *Politics of Finance,* pp. 269–294.
23. Ibid. In 1975 the Senate did unusually well in conferences on tax and energy legislation, and the Senate Finance chairman, Russell Long, was able to dominate the bargaining. This perhaps reflected the weakened status of Ways and Means and the less forceful leadership style of Representative Al Ullman, the successor to Wilbur Mills as chairman of Ways and Means. *Congressional Quarterly Weekly Report, 34,* no. 2 (January 10, 1976), 40–44.
24. Fenno, *Power of the Purse,* p. 450.
25. Fenno, *Congressmen in Committees,* pp. 193–202.
26. Fenno, *Power of the Purse,* p. xv.
27. See Lawrence C. Dodd and Bruce I. Oppenheimer, "The House in Transition," in *Congress Reconsidered,* ed. Lawrence C. Dodd and Bruce I. Oppenheimer (New York: Praeger, 1977), pp. 21–53.
28. *Congressional Quarterly Weekly Report, 33,* no. 18 (May 3, 1975), 912.
29. This was limited by the 1977 Senate reorganization (S. Res. 4), passed February 4, 1977, which restricted each Senator to service on two major committees and one minor committee. The Appropriations Committee was established as a major committee under this plan, but it was exempted from the provision that each Senator could serve on no more than three subcommittees of a major committee. The reorganization plan's limits on the committee and subcommittee memberships for each Senator eliminated also the practice of having members of legislative committees sit as ex officio members of the counterpart Appropriations subcommittee. See *Congressional Quarterly Weekly Report, 35,* no. 7 (February 12, 1977), 279–285. Prior to this change, about one-half of the Senate participated directly in the work of the Appropriations Committee, since three ex officio members were allowed for eight legislative committees. See Fenno, *Congressmen in Committees,* p. 149.
30. Fenno, *Congressmen in Committees,* pp. 146–149.
31. Ibid., pp. 154–155.
32. Fenno, *Power of the Purse,* p. 562.
33. Ibid., p. 597. However, one study of the Senate Appropriations Committee suggests that the Committee does not fully utilize its potential effectiveness in the Senate or in Congress generally. See Stephen Horn, *Unused Power: The Work of the Senate Committee on Appropriations* (Washington, D.C.: Brookings Institution, 1970). Horn argues that for most Senators on the Committee, the power of the purse is attractive primarily for its utility in serving their states rather than for more generalized policy control.
34. Fenno, *Power of the Purse,* p. 666.
35. According to Horn, however, Senate success in conference is often exaggerated by focusing simply on the dollar amounts in the final bill as compared with the original House and Senate versions. *Unused Power,* p. 213.
36. Fenno, *Power of the Purse,* p. 663. He states that *"dominance in the conference committee must never be confused with dominance in the appropriations process as a whole."* (Italics in original.)
37. Ibid., pp. 33–39.
38. Louis Fisher, *Budget Concepts and Terminology: The Appropriations Phase* (Washington, D.C.: Congressional Research Service, November 21, 1974), p. 22.
39. *Congressional Quarterly's Guide to the Congress,* p. 188. However, these limits apply only to the amount of annual payments, not to the total payments made over the life of a contract, which may run 40 or 60 years. See Fisher, *Budget Concepts and Terminology,* p. 24.
40. Fisher, *Budget Concepts and Terminology,* p. 25.
41. Comptroller General of the United States, *Report to the Congress, Observations on the Food Stamp*

Program (Washington, D.C.: General Accounting Office, February 28, 1975), pp. 1–3.

42. Ralph K. Huitt, "Research Study Seven, Congressional Organization and Operations in the Field of Money and Credit," in Commission on Money and Credit, *Fiscal and Debt Management Policies* (Englewood Cliffs, N.J.: Prentice-Hall, 1963), p. 441.

43. See James P. Pfiffner, "Congressional Budget Reform, 1974: Initiative and Reaction" (paper presented at the 1975 annual meeting of the American Political Science Association, San Francisco, September 2–5, 1975), pp. 6–7.

44. On this last point, see Fenno, *Power of the Purse,* p. 122.

45. Pfiffner, "Congressional Budget Reform," pp. 7–8.

46. *Congressional Quarterly's Guide to the Congress,* p. 21.

47. The administration first requested that Congress allow it to cut spending in order to hold the ceiling. The House voted to allow this, but the Senate would not agree to do so without restrictions on the size of the cuts and the programs affected. The conference committee was unable to reach agreement, and the authority was subsequently withheld. Louis Fisher, "Congress, the Executive and the Budget," *Annals of the American Academy of Political and Social Sciences, 411* (January 1974), 104.

48. Ibid., p. 113.

49. The Congressional Budget and Impoundment Control Act passed the Senate by 75–0, and the House by 401–6.

50. For an informative discussion of these problems and the different ways in which they were perceived, see John W. Ellwood and James A. Thurber, "The New Congressional Budget Process: The Hows and Whys of House-Senate Differences," in *Congress Reconsidered,* ed. Lawrence C. Dodd and Bruce I. Oppenheimer (New York: Praeger, 1977), pp. 164–169.

51. Ibid.

52. In December 1976 the Democratic caucus changed the selection process for Budget Committee members. Previously the chairmen of the Ways and Means and Appropriations Committees had each nominated three members for designated seats on the Budget Committee (the other two designated seats for each committee were allocated to the Republican party). Under the revised rules, this responsibility was vested in the Democratic Steering and Policy Committee, which serves as the Democrats' committee on committees. This allowed the Budget Committee to be set up several weeks earlier than in the past. In addition, the Democratic Steering and Policy Committee does not nominate a chairman. Any member of the Budget Committee can seek it, with the choice being made by the Democratic caucus.

53. The CBO staff is under a director appointed for a four-year term by the Speaker of the House and president pro tem of the Senate upon recommendation of the Budget Committees. The first appointee was Alice M. Rivlin, an economist and senior fellow at the Brookings Institution, who had also served as an assistant secretary in the Department of Health, Education and Welfare during the Johnson administration. As originally set up, the CBO had budget analysis, tax policy analysis, and fiscal policy analysis sections, along with program divisions covering broad policy areas. As of early 1976, the program divisions included natural resources and commerce, human resources and community development, and national security and international affairs. In addition, a section was established on management programs.

54. These include categories such as national defense, international affairs, agriculture, and commerce and transportation. See Table 1.1 for presidential recommendations and congressional targets in these functional categories for the fiscal 1978 budget.

55. This deadline does not apply to social security and other entitlement programs.

56. It did so in the spring of 1977, when the new Carter administration requested an economic stimulus package with spending increases and tax reductions for the fiscal 1977 budget, which had gone into effect the previous October.

11

The First Decade of the Congressional Budget Act: Legislative Imitation and Adaptation in Budgeting

Mark S. Kamlet
David C. Mowery
Carnegie-Mellon University

Abstract

The influence of institutions on budgetary behavior at the federal level is the subject of this article, which examines the Congressional Budget Act of 1974. While its impact on budgetary priorities and growth seems modest at best, the Act has had a substantial impact on the process of budgetary decisionmaking, the nature of budgetary debate, and the budgetary strategies employed within Congress. These new and generally dysfunctional forms of congressional budgetary behavior are consequences of a budgetary reform that attempted to transfer many of the resource allocation procedures of the Executive branch to a legislative context. The transfer of many Executive branch budgetary procedures has led to the appearance within Congress of budgetary behavior previously confined largely to the Executive branch. The article also discusses attempts to render the congressional budget process more compatible with the legislative environment, analyzing the

Source: Policy Sciences (Amsterdam: Elsevier Science Publishers B.V., 1985), pp. 313–334. Reprinted by permission of Kluwer Academic Publishers.
Earlier versions of this article were delivered at the Workshop on Budgetary Control in the Public Sector, Brussels, Belgium, October 13–14, 1983, the meetings of the Association for Public Policy Analysis and Management, October, 1983, and the meetings of the American Political Science Association, September, 1983. Allen Schick, Robert X. Browning, Alex Hicks, Robert Strauss, John R. Hibbings, Evelyn Brodkin, and Rod Kiewiet provided helpful comments, and Pamela Reyner provided secretarial assistance. All remaining deficiencies are the responsibilities of the authors.

modifications in the original budget process that have been effected and proposed in recent years.

Introduction

The Congressional Budget Reform and Impoundment Control Act of 1974 instituted the first major procedural change in congressional budgeting in more than 20 years. Since 1974, this process has been further modified, and a number of proposals for additional changes recently have been advanced in the House of Representatives.[1] This article examines the principles underlying the original design and subsequent modifications of the Congressional Budget Act. We analyze the evolution of the congressional budget process during the previous decade and consider the importance of institutional design and decisionmaking processes for budgetary behavior and outcomes.

A key argument in our analysis, linking these two concerns, is that the original design of the congressional budget process transplanted many key budgetary procedures and policy variables from the Executive branch to Congress. However, the Executive and congressional policy arenas differ markedly in several dimensions that affect budgetary behavior. Major differences include the ability of the respective institutions to limit internal debate and dissent, the ability of each institution to restrict extraorganizational access to internal decisionmaking processes, the importance and existence of well-defined channels through which information and power flow, and the strength of authority relationships. Many of the problems of the reformed congressional budget process are due to these differences in institutional characteristics and political norms. Conversely, the modifications in the process made or proposed thus far intended to adapt it to the realities of a legislative setting.

The Congressional Budget Act (CBA) was designed in part to improve congressional coordination of fiscal and budgetary policy.[2] The budgetary process instituted by the CBA was grafted onto (significantly, it did not replace) an atomistic one, in which the aggregate implications of individual spending bills received little attention. An extensive literature has considered the impact of the CBA on budgetary outcomes. Although far from unanimous, these works generally conclude that the new congressional budget process has not succeeded in better coordinating fiscal and budgetary policy, holding down expenditures generally, or significantly altering congressional budgetary priorities.

Despite this minimal impact on budgetary outcomes, the Act has affected Congress during the past decade in ways extending well beyond the formal procedures of congressional budgetary decision-making. Both the nature of budgetary debate and the budgetary strategies employed within Congress have changed. The amount of time devoted to the budget, the fluidity of the budgetary base in budgetary debates, and the degree of politicization of economic and demographic assumptions, all have grown. The CBA also has increased the salience of outlays in congressional budgeting, leading to budget authority-outlays "side payments."[3]

The Act's modest impact on budgetary outcomes over the past decade and its simultaneous encouragement of new and generally dysfunctional forms of congressional budgetary behavior both stem from the attempt to transfer many of the resource allocation procedures of the Executive branch to a legislative setting. Indeed, as we discuss below, many of the "new rules" and other aspects of budgetary behavior cited by Schick (1983) and Caiden (1982, 1984) reflect the appearance within Congress of behavior long characteristic of the Executive branch. Such behavior typically is held in check within the Executive branch by limits on both the duration of debate and the range of issues subject to debate, as well as restrictions on access to the process. Lacking these institutional characteristics, budgeting in Congress has been greatly complicated by the appearance of Executive forms of budgetary strategy and behavior.

Relecting the incompatibility of Executive branch budgetary procedures with the legislative environment, the modifications the congressional budget process adopted since 1974 have sought to make the process more compatible with legislative realities. Central elements of these modifications are the elimination of the second budget resolution and the increased use of reconciliation instructions in the first budget resolution. Both of these procedural changes represent a substantial break with the original design and purpose of the CBA. Such modifications may enable Congress to control spending more smoothly and effectively, but they are likely to reduce the importance of fiscal policy within congressional budgetary decisionmaking. The more recent reforms

proposed by Representative David Obey and the task force chaired by Representative Anthony Beilenson, which are discussed below in greater detail, essentially codify and extend the general principles of congressional budgetary reform embodied in the *ad hoc* changes made thus far.

Immediately below, we discuss the extent to which the structure of the policy process developed in the Congressional Budget Act resembles that of the Executive branch. Section 3 [The Impact of the Congressional Budget on Outcomes] briefly summarizes the evidence concerning the impact of the CBA on budgetary outcomes, followed by a short description of strategic budgetary behavior within the Executive branch. We then consider the ways in which similar forms of strategic behavior have manifested themselves in the new congressional budget process. Section 5 [Recent and Proposed Modifications in the Congressional Budget Process] evaluates the procedural changes in the congressional budget process that have been adopted and those recently proposed. The conclusion discusses some general issues concerning the budgetary role of Congress within a system of shared powers.

Emulation of the Executive Branch in the Congressional Budget Act

The structure of the Executive branch budgetary process is both centralized and hierarchical. Reflecting the importance of the budgetary surplus or deficit for economic policy, Executive branch budgeting throughout the post war period has required the integration of budgetary and fiscal policy concerns.[4] This requirement has endowed total outlays and revenues with particular significance within the decisionmaking process. Prior to 1974, there existed no comparable procedure within Congress for the aggregation of spending allowances and the integration of budgetary and fiscal policy formulation. Instead, individual appropriations subcommittees' spending bills were reported and considered separately.

Congressional procedures and institutions similar to those within the Executive branch were established by the Budget Act, reflecting the desire of its authors to integrate congressional fiscal and budgetary policies more closely. What are the structural similarities and differences between the Executive budgetary process and the process installed by the

CBA? In both, a central budgetary authority exists. The House and Senate Budget Committees were established to perform a function analogous to that of the Office of Management and Budget (OMB) within the Executive Branch process. Like OMB, the budget committees were to set overall outlay targets for broad budget categories early in the annual congressional budget cycle, based on fiscal and budgetary policy priorities. Indeed, another indication of the structural similarities between the Executive budgetary process and that designed in the CBA is the fact that outlays, as well as budget authority assumed considerable importance in the new congressional budgetary process. While both of these quantities have always been important in the Executive budget process, prior to 1974 Congress was concerned primarily with budget authority. The CBA also established the Congressional Budget Office to provide expert analysis of budgetary and macroeconomic issues, a function carried out within the Executive branch by OMB, the Council of Economic Advisers, and the forecasting apparatus of the Treasury Department. As CBA's first Director noted, the organizational structure of this congressional staff agency was patterned on that of OMB.[5]

The temporal sequence of the Executive and congressional budget processes, and the roles of various actors in each, also were similar in the original process established by the CBA.[6] The authorization and appropriations committees provided information to the House and Senate Budget Committees for the formulation of the first budget resolution, in a process that resembled the agency request of the spring preview within the Executive branch. The spending targets in the tentative agency budget ceilings that appeared at the close of the Executive branch preview were analogous to those of the first congressional budget resolution, passed on May 15. Following passage of the first budget resolution, appropriations subcommittees were to employ these aggregate spending targets in formulating spending bills for specific agencies and programs.

Over the course of the summer, appropriations committee deliberations and agency budget development took place in Congress and the Executive branch, respectively, culminating in an autumn review period within each branch. In Congress, the spending recommendations of the appropriations apparatus were sent back to the Budget Committees, and reevaluated in the light of changing fiscal and budgetary policy goals in formulating a second budget resolution. An analogous activity in the Executive branch was the autumn budget review. Within Congress, the passage of the second budget resolution was followed (in the original design of the Budget Act) by reconciliation, in which appropriations were to be made compatible with the revised target totals; the Executive analogue is the annual "Director's Review." Indeed, the general reconciliation procedure was proposed by (among others) Charles Schultze, Director of the Bureau of the Budget in the Johnson Administration.[7]

Scholars and other authorities differ on the extent to which these structural and temporal similarities reflected a deliberate effort to replicate the structure of the Executive branch budget process within Congress. Fisher (1984) argued that

> The Budget Act assumed that Members of Congress would behave more responsibly by having to vote explicitly on budget aggregates, facing up to totals rather than deciding in "piecemeal" fashion the spending actions in separate appropriations and legislative bills. . . . The model of the Executive budget looked appealing (p. 180).

Schick (1980), on the other hand, suggested that the architects of the Budget Act consciously attempted to avoid complete duplication of the Executive process:

> While legislative norms propel Congress toward the fragmentation of power, budgeting invites the concentration of power. . . . The critical test for congressional budgeting is the extent to which it harmonizes the legislative imperative for fragmentation with the drive for integrated budget outcomes. . . . In fact, the Congressional Budget Act has expanded the budgetary roles of the tax, appropriations and authorization committees, but at the price of trying to compel them to function within the discipline of the new process. In this way, the 1974 Act tries to accommodate both the budget's need for fiscal cohesion and Congress's need for legislative collegiality and diffusion of power (pp. 6–7).

Both of these interpretations are partially correct. Indeed, many of the problems of the new congressional process reflect the awkward compromise between the hierarchical requirements of budgeting and the realities of legislative power that was embodied in the 1974 Act.

The bureaucratic structure of the Executive branch, which is both hierarchical and insulated to some extent from external (i.e., external to the Executive branch) political and other influences, simplifies the tasks of budgetary formulation. Reflecting the fact that power flows within well-defined channels, a "top-down" sequential approach to budgetary formulation is feasible within this environment.[8] A target for total outlays is determined first, based on fiscal policy concerns, and subsequently disaggregated across agencies and departments. The situation on Capitol Hill represents a sharp contrast to the bureaucratic environment. Far from being insulated, Congress offers numerous channels of entry for interest groups. The congressional policy process also is characterized by power relationships that are far less well-defined and hierarchical than those of the Executive, especially in the wake of the reforms of the committee structure of the mid-1970s.[9] Norms of decentralization and reciprocity are far more important within congressional decision processes than is true of the Executive branch.

The Budget Act did not alter these basic characteristics of the legislative environment. As such, critical enabling conditions associated with the Executive budgetary process were lacking. Achievement of the goal of greater integration of budgetary and fiscal policy development would have required a major increase in centralized power over budgetary issues within Congress. The CBA also did not increase or otherwise affect the insulation of the congressional budget process from external influences. While the CBA provided some enforcement mechanisms for the House and Senate Budget Committees, in the form of points of order that could be raised in floor consideration of appropriations bills that breached budget resolution ceilings for total spending, a majority of the full House or Senate was necessary for the operation of these mechanisms. Ultimately, the Budget Committees had to rely heavily on persuasion in enforcing their budgetary and fiscal priorities. The 1974 reform thus did not alter existing congressional resource allocation procedures, instead adding another layer of committees and processes. The relationship between the old and new congressional resource allocation processes has been complex and often uneasy.

The Impact of the Congressional Budget Act on Outcomes

What has been the impact of the new congressional process? There is little agreement on the criteria by which any such impact should be measured. Schick (1980) has suggested that the mere presence of a new budgetary process per se cannot be expected to change trends in budgetary growth or priorities within Congress; in his view, these respond to more fundamental political forces. For Schick, the appropriate criteria by which to judge the performance of the new budgetary process are procedural—have the provisions of the Act been followed?[10] Most other scholars have looked to changes in congressional budgetary behavior for evidence of the impact of the CBA. Such evidence has assumed qualitative and quantitative forms. Sundquist (1981) praised the newfound ability of Congress " . . . to adopt a considered fiscal policy responding to the political and economic circumstances of a particular period . . . ",[11] while LeLoup (1983) contended that "until 1981 the Budget committees acted primarily as 'adding machines' in aggregating the requests of the standing committees."[12] Fisher (1984) suggested that the Act actually had encouraged spending growth.

Most quantitative assessments of the impact of the CBA on aggregate budgetary outcomes have examined its impact on spending growth, budgetary priorities, and/or fiscal policy. In general, these studies suggest that the impact of the Act has been modest or nonexistent. Based on analyses of budgetary priorities and growth trends observable before and after 1974, LeLoup (1980), Ellwood (1983), and Kamlet and Mowery (1984) suggest that prior to 1981, the Act had little effect on spending growth or aggregate budgetary priorities. Ippolito (1981) adopted a middle position, arguing that the new process had "a very limited impact on budget policy".[13] Since 1981, of course, the congressional budget process has ratified a substantial shift in federal spending priorities. However, the congressional budgetary process in the watershed year of 1981 served as a vehicle for the Reagan Administration's radical revision of spending priorities, rather than a mechanism for the assertion of congressional spending autonomy. Moreover, the budget that was adopted in 1981 can scarcely be cited as a model of the integration of budgetary and fiscal policy.

The impact of the Congressional Budget Act on congressional budgetary priorities through most of the period of the Act's operation thus seems modest. Neither the degree of interdependence between defense and nondefense outlays, nor the responsiveness of outlays to revenues seem to have been enhanced by the procedures mandated by the Act.[14]

The possibility that the Budget Act worked to forestall even greater spending growth, however, off-setting the fiscal impact of the changes in the institutional (e.g., the weakening of the seniority system and reduction in closed committee sessions) and political environment of Congress, cannot be dismissed out of hand. While this question cannot be settled definitively, for present purposes the ambiguous nature of the Act's impact on outcomes is less important than the stronger evidence of significant changes in congressional budgetary behavior since 1974. These changes are considered in the next section.

The Impact of the Congressional Budget Act on the Process of Budgetary Decisionmaking

In establishing a budget process with a strong resemblance to that of the Executive branch, the CBA fostered the appearance within Congress of budgetary politics previously confined largely to the Executive branch. Moreover, these forms of budgetary behavior, which complicate but do not paralyze Executive branch budgeting, can have a major detrimental impact within the politically charged congressional environment. Issues that formerly were debated within the Executive bureaucracy, and presented to Congress as resolved, are now the focus of political debate and dispute in Congress. The range of issues subject to debate, the intensity of the debate, and the number of actors in congressional budgetary politics have expanded as a result of the CBA, hampering the ability of Congress to deal with budgetary issues and displacing other activities.

Strategic Behavior in the Executive Budgetary Process

In order to understand the nature and origins of the new forms of congressional budgetary behavior, it is necessary to consider the basis for strategic behavior within the Executive budgetary process. The strong link between budgetary and fiscal policy within the Executive branch is an important influence on such behavior.[15] One way in which this linkage affects behavior is by blurring the distinction within the Executive budgetary process between the budgetary "base" and "increment." In contrast to the predictions of incrementalist analyses of budgetary behavior, this distinction frequently is very imprecise.[16] Both the definition of the base and the assumptions used in it computation are the subjects of extensive negotiations between OMB and agencies within the Executive branch budgetary process, negotiations that concern both "controllable" and "uncontrollable" programs.

Another behavioral correlate of the fiscal-budgetary policy link within the Executive budgetary process is budget authority-outlays side payments. A side payment consists of the granting to agencies by OMB of increases in budget authority that are larger than the corresponding outlays increases. Side payments are a direct consequence of the dual role of the presidential budget as an instrument of both economic policy and public resource allocation. The presidential budget document consists of two budgets, one in terms of outlays, and one in terms of budget authority, for all line items. Whereas the key budgetary quantity for short-term fiscal policy is outlays, budget authority is the source of future outlays and as such is more important for long-term budgetary control and resource allocation. Faced with the simultaneous need to satisfy both agency desires for long-term budgetary growth and the requirements of the White House for a defensible short-term fiscal policy, OMB on occasion has resorted to budgetary side payments. Side payments were widespread under presidents (such as Kennedy) who placed great emphasis on fiscal policy, and have also been observed under Reagan.[17]

Strategic Behavior in the Congressional Budgetary Process

The importance of the budgetary base within the Executive branch process, the negotiations over its definition, the debate about the relevant economic and other assumptions employed in computing the base, and the differential treatment of outlays and budget authority, all stem from the complex relationship between budgetary and fiscal policy within the Executive branch. Inasmuch as the new congressional process was designed to strengthen such interdependence, similar strategic budgetary behavior should be discernible within Congress after the passage of the CBA.

Several important aspects of congressional budgetary behavior now resemble Executive branch behavior. The fluidity and political character of the budgetary base have increased markedly since 1974. Prior to the CBA, the definition of the budgetary base employed by the House and Senate Appropriations

Commitees was largely agreed upon by all actors.[18] However, agreement within Congress on the definition of the budgetary base no longer exists. Both the House and Senate Budget Committees frequently have employed a definition of the budgetary base that differs from the one utilized in the Appropriations Committees. This practice has created severe problems in the compatibility of budget resolutions and appropriations actions. Moreover, the House and Senate Budget Committees themselves frequently use different definitions of the budgetary base, with disastrous consequences for the conference committees charged with the development of a joint budget resolution. As Schick (1982) noted, these varied definitions of the budgetary base have developed for explicitly political reasons.[19]

The insertion of fiscal policy issues into congressional budgetary debates also has greatly increased the importance and accordingly, the political sensitivity, of assumptions concerning the economy and a wide range of other variables. The size of the budgetary base, however defined, is critically influenced by assumptions concerning inflation, the size of the target program population, and economic growth. In addition, outlays totals and deficit projections, formerly not subjects of congressional deliberations, are extremely sensitive to economic assumptions. Indeed, a measure of President Reagan's political strength in 1981 was his success in embedding his optimistic economic and budgetary assumptions in the "Gramm-Latta II" reconciliation package.[20]

The CBA greatly increased the significance of outlays within congressional budgeting by attempting to link fiscal and budgetary policymaking within Congress. Outlays, as well as budget authority, are now key quantities in House and Senate Budget Committee deliberations. However, the Budget Committees are alone among congressional committees in considering outlays, a fact that is indicative of the weakness of the links between the Budget Committees and budgetary activities in other committees. As Senate Budget Committee Chairman Domenici noted in 1982, the congressional appropriations apparatus remains unconcerned with outlays:

It is amazing. And this came to light most forcibly [sic] when we had that last continuing resolution battle with the Congress, House and Senate, that appropriators did not appropriate outlays. They appropriate budget authority. . . . We are even told frequently that they do not know what the outlays are. It does not even carry any weight in the debates (Domenici, 1982, p. 27).

The new salience of outlays has done more than simply complicate the relationships between the Budget and Appropriations Committees. Faced with the need to reconcile the demands of their constituents for the simultaneous achievement of a prudent fiscal policy and growth in domestic programs, congressional Budget Committee politicians have followed the example of their White House counterparts in pursuing budget authority-outlays side payments.[21] Such side payments have been apparent in the behavior of outlays and budget authority allowances in the second congressional resolutions for budget totals, defense spending, and selected controllable nondefense items during fiscal 1976–83, as well as defense spending in the fiscal 1985 and 1986 budget resolutions.[22] The result of such behavior, which holds down current-year outlays, is higher long-term growth in government spending. Congressional tradeoffs between budget authority and outlays thus have come to resemble those within the Executive as a result of the clash of budgetary and fiscal policy demands.

Schick (1983) and Caiden (1982, 1984) cite these congressional disputes over the budgetary base and economic assumptions as evidence of a new political context for budgeting in both the Executive and Congress. While we agree with these scholars on the appearance and character of these new forms of budgetary behavior in Congress, such behavior in fact is not unprecedented within the federal budgetary process. Kamlet and Mowery (1980), and Mowery, Kamlet and Crecine (1980) suggest that these budgetary disputes and strategies have pervaded the Executive branch throughout much of the postwar era. Such behavior within the Executive branch stemmed from the same underlying causes as does its more recent appearance within Congress—the linkage between the components and the total of government spending that arises from attempts to integrate budgetary and fiscal policy concerns and processes. Much of what Caiden, Schick, and Bozeman and Straussman (1982) cite as novel in fact simply may have become more visible in recent years, by virtue of its appearance within the congressional budgetary fishbowl.

The nonhierarchical and highly political atmosphere within Congress means that nonaccommodative behavior or debates over assumptions can impede the budgetary process to a much greater extent than is true of the Executive branch budgetary process.[23] Ellwood (1983), has compiled data suggesting that the new budget process occupies an increasing portion of the legislative calendar of Congress, while the number of appropriations bills passed after the beginning of the new fiscal year has grown.[24] One behavioral result of emulation of the Executive branch thus seems to be further overloading of a policy process that is already under severe strain.

Recent and Proposed Modifications in the Congressional Budget Process

The preceding analysis and critique of the original design of the Congressional Budget Act form the basis for a consideration of the ad hoc modifications in the CBA adopted thus far, as well as those recently proposed. Major changes adopted since 1974 include the dropping of the second budget resolution, and the use of reconciliation in the first resolution. These modifications were made under the elastic Section 310(b)(2) of the 1974 Act, which authorizes the Budget Committees to undertake "any other procedure which is considered appropriate to carry out the purposes of this Act."

The abandonment of the second budget resolution reflects the utility within Congress of procedures that limit, or at least prevent the reopening of, debate.[25] Rather than enhancing the flexibility of congressional decisions on budgetary matters as a means (among other things) of accommodating new economic realities in a second budget resolution, this change reduces procedural flexibility. The contrast between the roles of the second budget resolution and reconciliation in the original and revised congressional budget processes is striking. While the Executive budgetary process increasingly is centered around the late summer and fall, in order to retain fiscal policy flexibility, this change in the congressional process was intended to shift the bulk of congressional authorizations and budget committee activity toward the spring, so as to increase spending control. The reduced importance of the fiscal-budgetary policy linkage within Congress is due in part to the severe difficulties that have attended the previous decade's efforts to combine procedural flexibility and economic responsiveness with the task of

budgeting.[26] In addition, as federal deficits have loomed larger in recent years, spending control has become more important than the formulation of countercyclical economic policy within the congressional budgetary process.

Reconciliation also has assumed a more permanent and prominent position within congressional budgeting. The increased use of reconciliation and its incorporation in the first budget resolution are of great significance for two reasons. One of the goals of the CBA was the enforcement of budgetary and fiscal policy discipline on the decisions of the authorization and appropriations committees within Congress. Reconciliation is a potentially powerful tool, exploited most thoroughly in 1981 by the Reagan White House, for the achievement of this goal. The shift in the timing of reconciliation from the second to the first budget resolution also bespeaks an important change in the purpose of reconciliation. As Schick (1981b) notes, reconciliation originally was intended to control appropriations actions of the *current* congressional session, and thus was to be invoked in the second budget resolution, after the passage of major appropriations bills. However, reconciliation now is targeted mainly on *previous* congressional sessions' authorizations of entitlements, and therefore is part of the first (and only) budget resolution. Rather than trying to reduce appropriations for future spending, the new reconciliation process fixes entitlement spending targets. Instead of perpetuating the uneasy duplication of budgetary oversight by the budget and appropriations committees, reconciliation now is employed to reduce spending on entitlement programs that was determined in prior authorizations. The reconciliation procedure that has emerged in the past four years allows budget committee oversight of entitlements to complement appropriations committee oversight of discretionary spending.[27]

The proposals for reform in the congressional budget process that have been advanced in the past several years attempt to codify and delimit many of the ad hoc procedural changes adopted since 1974. In so doing, these proposals extend the general principles of the modifications made thus far in the congressional budgetary process. Two major reform proposals have originated in the House of Representatives, the locus of much of the more vociferous dissatisfaction with the CBA. Representative David Obey, a former member of the House Budget

Committee and a member of the House Appropriations Committee, has proposed a revised budget process, employing a single comprehensive budget resolution, that would incorporate targets for total spending, appropriations bills, and revenue recommendations.[28] An alternative bill (H.R. 5247) has been proposed by a task force organized by the House leadership, drawing on members of the House Rules, Budget and Appropriations Committees, and chaired by Representative Anthony Beilenson. Both reform proposals seem likely to strengthen spending control, even as they weaken the linkage between budgetary and fiscal policy that characterizes Executive branch budgeting.

The two reform proposals have a number of features in common. The central importance of spending control, rather than the development of countercyclical fiscal policy, is reflected in both proposals' elimination of the second budget resolution. Each proposal also expands the coverage of the budget resolution to incorporate off-budget credit activities and tax expenditures, as well as strengthening controls on entitlement spending. Both the Obey and task force proposals specify procedures for the definition of the budgetary base and the formulation of economic assumptions that are agreed upon by all participants in the budgetary process. The Obey bill stipulates that a definition of the "budgetary baseline" is to be included in the revised Budget Act, and states that the Congressional Budget Office will be the source of all cost estimates for revenue and spending measures reported by House and Senate Committees and conference committees. Both proposals also advocate the formation of a bipartisan "user's group" within each chamber of Congress, composed of Congressmen and Senators, to advise the leadership and Rules Committees on scorekeeping procedures and assumptions. The elevation of scorekeeping and economic assumptions to the status of issues resolved by Senators and Congressmen, rather than by anonymous economists, bureaucrats, and staff, indicates the dramatic increase in the political sensitivity of these assumptions that has occurred since 1974.[29]

Conflicts between committees over the definition of the budgetary base, as well as problems in the enforcement of budget resolutions, also are addressed by the Obey and task force proposals. Both proposals specify that the Budget Committees will develop "discretionary" spending targets for the appropriations committees. In other words, the ability of a committee to obtain budgetary increases by underestimating "mandatory" expenditure levels, a subterfuge long employed within the Executive budgetary process, is to be prohibited by central directive. Both proposals also strengthen enforcement mechanisms in other ways. The budget resolutions specified in both reform proposals are more detailed than those currently employed, which specify mandatory targets only for total spending and revenues.[30] Moreover, the Obey proposal's inclusion of all appropriations and revenues actions in its budget resolution confers considerable powers of specific enforcement on the drafters of such a resolution. The Beilenson task force proposal strengthens enforcement by making the failure of appropriations committee bills to adhere to the budget resolution's targets for individual spending categories a cause for a point of order.[31]

Inasmuch as much of the recent growth in federal spending has been concentrated in entitlement programs, both reform proposals include provisions designed to control entitlement spending. The task force bill in particular strengthens Budget Committee oversight of entitlement spending, providing for a separate category in the budget resolution devoted to entitlements. As was noted above, efforts to control entitlement spending in recent years have required the use of reconciliation instructions in the first budget resolution. Both the Obey and Beilenson task force proposals incorporate key components of the reconciliation procedures that have evolved over the past five years, and attempt to define the role and limits of these procedures.

The detail and coverage of reconciliation instructions in the first budget resolution are sensitive political issues, reflecting the fact that nearly all congressional actions have budgetary implications. A comprehensive set of reconciliation instructions, such as was passed in 1981, effectively allows a single bill to dictate the terms of legislation throughout Congress. Consistent annual resort to such sweeping reconciliation procedures is not sustainable, in view of the vast powers that this procedure concedes to the Budget Committees. Accordingly, both the Obey and Beilenson task force proposals attempt to define and delimit the scope of reconciliation, in particular working to restrict its coverage of legislation that authorizes appropriations. The Obey proposal prohibits reconciliation instructions within the budget resolution that cover authorizations for appropriations. The Beilenson task force originally opposed the extension of reconciliation to cover any authorizations for appropriations; however, the House Rules Committee approved an amendment to H.R. 5247 removing this prohibition,[32] while paradoxically continuing to express disapproval of the inclusion of authorizations for appropriations in reconciliation.[33] In opposing the use of reconciliation to affect legislation authorizing discretionary appropriation, both reform proposals seek to avoid the charge (heard frequently during 1981) that reconciliation places the Budget Committees in each chamber in a position to dictate the terms of substantive, as well as spending, legislation.

Both reform proposals restrict the scope of reconciliation somewhat by comparison with its application in 1981. Nonetheless, the relationship among the budget authorizations and appropriations committees within Congress that would result from the adoption of the Obey proposal differs greatly from that outlined in the Beilenson task force proposal. The Obey proposal's budget resolution incorporates and combines all of the appropriations and revenue actions reported by the finance and appropriations committees, thereby requiring a far-reaching transfer of power from the authorization and appropriations committees to the budget committees. By contrast, the Beilenson task force proposal would preserve (with slight modifications) and institutionalize the division of labor that has developed recently among these committees.

In strengthening the visibility and oversight of entitlements within the congressional budgetary process, the process outlined in the task force report provides an important complement to the oversight of authorizations for appropriations undertaken by the appropriations committees. Whereas entitlement spending previously operated largely outside of the oversight of any but the authorizing committees, these proposed changes greatly strengthen the powers of the budget committees to control entitlement spending, and do so (in contrast to reconciliation, 1981 style) without significantly impairing the powers of the appropriations committees. The proposal thus enhances the complementary oversight relationship between the budget and appropriations committees in each chamber that has developed during the past five years.

Both reform proposals also address the inability of Congress to pass appropriations bills prior to the start of the fiscal year, a chronic problem since the late 1960s. In recent years, the budget process has been blamed for the tardiness of appropriations bills, which cannot be considered until a budget resolution has been agreed to. The Obey proposal deals with the problem by combining appropriations bills with the budget resolution. The task force proposal addresses this problem as well, but merely recommends a new and tighter set of dates by which action on the budget resolution and authorizations must be completed. Neither proposal is likely to be effective in this regard, since neither one addresses the underlying cause of the problem. It is the intense political conflict over spending priorities, rather than imperfections in the calendar or other features of the process, that leads to budgetary gridlock and delays in appropriations bills. On the one hand, the revised calendar recommended by the Beilenson task force is no more likely to be observed than the existing calendar. The Obey proposal, on the other hand, provides even greater opportunities for intransigent individuals or groups to hold the entire budget process hostage, as Schick has noted.[34]

The procedure actually adopted in 1985 closely resembles the proposal made by Representative Jamie Whitten of Mississippi, Chairman of the House Appropriations Committee, in his testimony before the Beilenson task force.[35] Rather than waiting for the achievement of a House-Senate conference agreement on the budget resolution, appropriations bills have been called up in the House and voted on through the summer, based on the House budget resolution. This procedure has the considerable advantage of reducing the number of hostages to political conflict. Unfortunately, it also undercuts the power of the House Budget Committee.

A final major difference between the task force and Obey bills, and an area in which the task force bill represents a fundamental departure from the Executive model of budgeting, is in the treatment of outlays. The Obey bill largely preserves the current structure of the budget resolution, which includes both outlays and budget authority. The task force bill, however, would shift the focus of congressional budgeting authority, and thereby reduce the importance of fiscal policy considerations within the process. While the budget resolution designed by the task force bill includes revenues and total outlays, the task force report is adamant in disavowing the use of outlays spending targets:

H.R. 5247 does not require the allocation of outlays to committees for control purposes. The task force bases this recommendation on its conviction that budgetary controls can be successfully applied over the long run only when committees are held accountable for that over which they do exercise direct control. Allocating outlays may give the illusion of control, but in the long run the inability of committees to control these amounts causes confusion and ultimately breeds contempt for the entire control system (House Rules Committee, 1984b, p. 29).

This rejection of outlays targets symbolizes clearly the rejection by the task force of a budgetary process in which fiscal and budgetary policy are both controlled through the single instrument of the annual budget, as in the Executive branch. Instead, the Beilenson task force proposal outlines a system of resource allocation similar to the pre-1974 congressional mechanism, centered on the appropriations committees; the annual budgetary cycle is employed solely as an instrument for spending control. As a result, the task force bill may reduce the incidence of outlays-budget authority side payments within the congressional process. However, to the extent that the fiscal policy constraint (i.e., the size of the budget deficit) represents an effective incentive for spending control, the inability to decompose aggregate outlays into categorical targets ultimately may undermine budgetary control across the board.[36]

The procedures outlined in the task force proposal concede the primary role in discretionary spending control for fiscal policy to the Executive branch. Were H.R. 5247 to become law, congressional fiscal policy formulation would be confined largely to decisions on revenues. While under the terms of any conceivable reform, the President's budget would remain a key instrument of fiscal, as well as budgetary, policy; the congressional budget process proposed in H.R. 5247 focuses solely on budgetary policy. The Obey proposal, by contrast, retains the importance of outlays, as well as budget authority, and thus preserves a role for Congress in the use of spending targets as an instrument of fiscal policy.

Summary and Conclusions

As the magnitude and rate of growth of federal spending have increased in political saliency during the past decade, so too has the importance of congressional budgeting. As a result of the unprecedented pressures on federal budgeting, the process will continue to change, in an effort to match the functional requirements of this policy process with its institutional context and political sensitivity. In pursuing this goal, it is important to recognize that budgetary debates that are manageable in a bureaucratic context may mushroom in the more politicized legislative arena. One implication of this argument is that the budget is a very unwieldy congressional instrument for the conduct of discretionary fiscal policy. However, changes in the structure of the congressional budgetary process also reflect changes in the goals of congressional budgeting. The desire to combine budgetary and fiscal policy objectives in congressional budgeting that motivated many of the original provisions of the CBA now appears far less prominent than the goal of spending control.

Many of the problems that "comprehensive budgeting" proposals of any form have encountered within Congress (recall the fate of the budgetary reforms of 1948 and 1951)[37] stem from the nature of Congress as an institution and the place of Congress within a political system of shared powers. The organizational requirements of comprehensive budgeting and fiscal policy formulation are quite different from those of representation, accessibility, and pluralism that have historically (although not consistently) been characteristic of Congress. The U.S. Congress is not an institution whose sole mission is budgeting; as such, it is unrealistic to expect Congress to adhere to the same complex procedures as those employed in the Executive branch institutions whose primary responsibility is the preparation of the annual budget.

In view of the fact that Congress performs a vast range of functions beyond that of budgeting, the criteria by which to evaluate the performance of congressional budgeting are not obvious; neither are the normative principles on which further modifications should be based. One such criterion is the ability of the congressional budget process to achieve better integration of budgetary and fiscal policies. Our analysis and review of the literature on budgetary outcomes since 1974 suggest that the CBA has not succeeded in this area. In the nature of the case, of course, this evaluation cannot address the possibility that congressional spending behavior would have been far less restrained in the absence of the budget process.

In considering the impact of the CBA on congressional budgetary behavior, the problem of evaluative criteria may be less severe. Our analysis of behavior is less evaluative than descriptive in illustrating the extraordinary behavioral changes that have arisen within Congress since 1974, and pointing out the ways in which this behavior now resembles that of the Executive branch in a number of key areas. In considering normative principles for congressional budgetary reform, this analysis does, however, suggest a number of ways in which some of the new forms of congressional budgetary behavior might be controlled.

A process that is better adapted to the congressional environment must develop a more widely accepted set of definitions and measurement procedures for important budgetary variables, e.g., outlays and budget authority, economic projections, and budgetary assumptions. In this dimension, greater emulation of the Executive seems desirable. The apparatus established by the new congressional budgetary process for the oversight and control of spending also should complement, rather than duplicate, existing congressional systems for oversight and control of the individual components of public spending. A paradox of congressional budgeting is the fact that as long as the budgetary process is potentially capable of overriding all other policy processes on Capitol Hill, as in reconciliation 1981 style, the budgetary process will not be allowed much power (recall that the Executive, rather than Congress, was the leader in the 1981 reconciliation process).[38] As the limits of the budgetary process are codified and defined, however, the process itself can assume much more substantive power within a clearly demarcated area.

A final tradeoff that congressional budgetary reform inevitably must face is the degree to which budgetary and fiscal policy processes are combined within the congressional process. The procedural flexibility of the Executive process, which facilitates the joint development of budgetary and fiscal policy, does not conform easily to the requirements of Congress for control of the quantity and range of budgetary debate. The recent elimination of the second congressional budget resolution allows for more tractable budgetary debates, while simultaneously reducing the flexibility of Congress to respond to economic fluctuations. The Beilenson task force proposal goes still further in removing Congress from countercyclical spending policy, in its disavowal of outlays targets. Spending control, rather than fiscal policy flexibility, is the goal of this proposal. The Obey proposal preserves a significant congressional role in spending decisions in fiscal policy, albeit at the cost of considerable centralization and procedural complexity.

Future reforms of the congressional budget will be heavily influenced by the balance that is struck between centralization and representation, and by the role that Senators and Members wish to play in fiscal policy formulation. Nonetheless, a budget process that is capable of both controlling government spending and supporting countercyclical fiscal policy formulation may yet require stronger centralized authority than the Congress or the 1980s will allow.

Notes

1. See House Rules Committee (1984a, 1984b).
2. See Ippolito (1981), Fisher (1984), Havemann (1978), LeLoup (1980), Sundquist (1981), and Schick (1980, 1981a, b, 1983).
3. Kamlet and Mowery (1983).
4. See Mowery, Kamlet, and Crecine (1980) for additional discussion.
5. Rivlin (1983).
6. Obviously, these similar sequences take place in different calendar years for a given fiscal year's budget. Thus, the President's budget for fiscal year t is the outcome of an Executive branch planning process that consumes most of calendar $t - 2$, while the congressional deliberations on fiscal year t's budget occur during calendar year $t - 1$.
7. "Charles Schultze suggested that the first resolution be regarded as tentative and that Congress be allowed to appropriate without restriction. After appropriations and other budget-related legislation had been enacted, there would be a 'reconciliation process' at the end of the session, whereby the Budget Committees recommend revisions in earlier actions on individual appropriations, other spending authority and tax measures in the context of an overall integrated budget." (Schick, 1981b, p. 4, quoting House Rules Committee, *Hearings on Budget Control Act of 1973,* 1973, p. 318).
8. Surprisingly, Bozeman and Straussman (1982), Caiden (1983), Schick (1985) and Heclo (1985) cite "top-down" budgeting as a new feature of the Executive process, identified with Reagan and OMB Director Stockman. The reliance on "top-down" budgeting and aggregate targets is in fact far from new, and is amply documented in the archives of OMB and the

Eisenhower, Kennedy, Johnson, and Ford Presidential Libraries. See Crecine (1976), Mowery, Kamlet and Crecine (1980), or Kamlet and Mowery (1980), for further discussion. Among other things, this collision between "bottom-up" and "top-down" spending pressures supports strategic behavior with respect to the base.

9. See Huntington (1983), Dodd (1981), Ornstein, Peabody and Rohde (1981), Price (1981), and Dodd and Oppenheimer (1981) for additional discussion.

10. Elsewhere, Schick (1980, p. 576) has suggested that the Act's emphasis on spending totals has increased the awareness by Members of Congress of the financial implications of legislative actions. However, this argument is difficult to assess without detailed evidence—congressional budgetary outcomes provide little evidence of heightened financial consciousness among members and Senators since 1974.

11. Sundquist (1981), p. 231.

12. LeLoup (1983), p. 30.

13. Ippolito (1981), p. 243.

14. See Kamlet and Mowery (1984) for an analysis of the effect of the CBA on the extent of interdependence among the defense, nondefense, and revenue components of budgetary formulation within Congress. The analyses discussed above do not test for the impact of the congressional budget reform on allocations *within* either the defense or nondefense components of the budget. However, the design of the 1974 Act and its subsequent operation were not directed to these more detailed allocational issues.

15. See Mowery, Kamlet and Crecine (1980); Kamlet and Mowery (1983).

16. See Kamlet and Mowery (1980).

17. See Kamlet and Mowery (1983); Huntington (1983).

18. Indeed, incrementalist analyses of budgetary behavior (e.g., Wildavsky, 1964) were influenced heavily by observations of the Congressional budget process during the pre-1974 period.

19. "The current-policy approach was devised during the first years of the congressional budget process by the Senate Budget Committee in cooperation with the Congressional Budget Office. The Senate Budget Committee wanted a neutral baseline that would enable it to distinguish between discretionary changes made by Congress and 'automatic' changes resulting from past decisions, economic conditions, and other factors. Democratic members of the Budget Committee recognized another advantage in the current-policy baseline: It would be possible to 'cut' the budget while increasing expenditures. . . . After several years of use, the current-policy baseline came under severe attack from Republicans on the Senate Budget Committee who argued that it had an expansionary bias and provided by law. . . . Why did the Republicans on the Senate Budget Committee who, only a few years earlier, lambasted the current-policy concept as distorted and expansionary embrace this approach in 1981? And why were they joined by the Office of Management and Budget and others who previously were reluctant to use this baseline? The simple but sufficient answer is that Republicans in both the Executive and legislative branches wanted to magnify the apparent size of the savings. The Democrats made common cause with the Republicans on this procedural issue because they wanted the actual cuts to be lower than they appeared to be. The Republicans claimed more savings and the Democrats saved more programs, a happy combination for political institutions faced with difficult choices." (pp. 31–32).

20. The politicization of economic assumptions also is attributable to the increasing number of participants in the forecasting exercise, a group no longer restricted to the Executive branch "Troika." Forecasts now are developed, or purchased, independently by House and Senate Budget Committees, as well as the Congressional Budget Office.

21. In testimony before the House Budget Committee Task Force on the Budget Process, Schick (1979) noted that " . . . multiyear budgeting might provide a way out of some stalemates. Some members who are disappointed by what they regard as inadequate allocations for the programs they favor might be persuaded to vote for the budget resolutions in exchange for larger allocations in future bills. This tactic has been used by the Senate Budget Committee with some success, although the Senate Budget Committee has not faced the extensive political and ideological opposition which has plagued the budget process in the House." (p. 8).

22. The nondefense budget allowances are those for the functional categories of "transportation and commerce," "natural resources and environment," "community and regional development," "education," and "general government." In a majority of the second budget resolutions for fiscal 1976–1983, budget authority allowances for these nondefense activities were increased over the first resolution by a larger amount (relative to the president's budget) than outlays, which in one instance were cut. This gap between outlays and budget authority amounted to more than $20 billion for fiscal 1976–1983, and stood at more than $33 billion for fiscal 1976–1979 and 1983. Similarly, in the arduous negotiations over the budget resolution for both fiscal 1985 and 1986, defense outlays have been cut, while budget authority has been protected. Measures of the contribution of Executive branch side payments to budgetary growth may be found in Kamlet and Mowery (1983).

23. Evidence cited by Reischauer (1983) suggests that the congressional budget process has been associated with

a decline in accommodative behavior in congressional budgetary politics. Clearly, numerous factors are at work in this area, but the association between the new process and this more adversarial behavior is of interest.

24. Copeland (1984) also argues that budgetary matters are consuming a growing portion of floor debate and staff time in recent years.

25. Congressman Jack Brooks, chairman of the House Government Operations Committee, noted that "In budgetary, as in other matters, we must settle things as rapidly as possibly [sic], and seemingly endless and repeated debate over the same issues that were fought out in the spring should be eliminated if there is any feasible way to do it." (House Budget Committee, 1982, pp. 106–107.)

26. An analysis of the negotiations over the fiscal 1986 budget resolution, widely criticized for its employment of unrealistic and outdated economic assumptions, stated that "Economic assumptions made in January at the start of the budget process are outdated by events almost every year before Congress starts writing a budget, but the assumptions usually have not been revised. Members of Congress explain that revising them in the midst of the budget debate this year would have made it almost impossible for the House and Senate to reach the goal set in January of $50 billion in savings in 1986, and might have doomed the budget exercise altogether." (Feuerbringer, 1985, p. 8.)

27. This complementary oversight now appears to operate even prior to the passage of a House-Senate budget resolution. Prior to the final agreement between House and Senate negotiators on the fiscal 1986 budget resolution, appropriations bills were being passed in the House to hold spending to approximately the levels specified in the House budget resolution. One staff member observed that " . . . the authorizing process is being relegated to a role of little importance; the budget and appropriations processes are running together." (Richard P. Colon, quoted in Pear, 1985, p. 14.) Oversight of authorizations for entitlements through the reconciliation process assumes even greater importance in the Senate, where Rauch (1985) argues that recent budget resolutions have relied more heavily on entitlement reductions than is true of the House.

28. The budget resolution specified by the Obey scheme "would include all regular appropriations, all new entitlement and credit legislation, and all revenue measures that are expected to become effective in the coming fiscal year. The final title of the budget bill would be a budget plan setting appropriate levels of total outlays, budget authority, entitlement authority, credit authority, revenues and tax expenditures." (House Rules Committee, 1984b, p. 215.)

29. Further evidence of the salience of such assumptions, as well as the desire to reduce the proliferation of conflicting estimates and assumptions, is the proposal advanced by Representatives Frost, Gephardt, Hoyer, and Panetta for a public committee, comprising the Chairman of the Federal Reserve Board, and the Directors of OMB and the CBO, charged with developing revenue estimates that would be binding on both the Executive and Congress. See the testimony of Rep. Hoyer in House Rules Committee (1983), pp. 252–253.

30. Following 1980, delayed enrollment of appropriations bills, in which the "enrollment" into law of a spending bill after its passage that exceeded the mandated ceiling for a given category was delayed until a revised budget resolution was passed, was employed as a partial solution to this problem. However, delayed enrollment does not affect the floor consideration of a spending bill; as two experienced observers have noted: " . . . if a bill is once passed and the conference report agreed to, it is highly likely any subsequent budget will accommodate its cost—rather than requiring changes in it." Statement of Henry Bellmon and Robert Giaimo, House Budget Committee (1982), p. 82.

31. Interestingly, neither proposal recommends a shift from an annual to a biennial budget resolution, an omission that reflects the other political pressures operating within congressional budgetary processes. The biennial budget resolution, a proposal advanced by Rep. Panetta, represents a logical extension of a congressional retreat from the politically punishing pursuit of budgetary flexibility; comprehensive budget votes occur once in each Congress, rather than annually. However, the requirements of a biennial budget resolution for biennial authorizations are likely to conflict with the growing importance of annual congressional authorizations. Biennial budgeting, which promises to reduce the demands on Congress for votes on comprehensive, redistributive proposals, thus collides squarely with the strong political incentives, noted by Schick (1980, pp. 170-175) and Fiorina (1977) for the retention of annual authorizations.

32. This action was intended to extend reconciliation to cover "appropriated entitlements." Approximately 13% of total entitlement spending results from these bills, which, despite their name, are largely controlled by authorizations, rather than appropriations, committees: " . . . appropriated entitlements are only nominally under control of the appropriations process. The entitlement legislation creates an obligation to make payments so that even if sufficient budget authority is not provided in advance by an appropriation act, the people or governments eligible according to the law would have legal recourse for the benefits." (House Rules Committee, 1984b, p. 27.)

33. "While the Committee on Rules is convinced of the need to strike the prohibition against directives to change authorization levels, the Committee continues

to oppose the use of reconciliation to make changes in levels of authorizations for discretionary appropriations. That is, the Committee opposes the use of reconciliation to make policy changes that have no direct budget impact." (House Rules Committee, 1984b, p. 21).

34. See Schick's testimony in House Rules Committee (1984c).

35. See House Rules Committee (1983).

36. According to Schick (1980), pp. 332–333, however, such "top-down" spending discipline never operated within the post-1974 congressional process as a constraint on spending pressures.

37. See Burkhead (1947), Leiserson (1948), or Nelson (1953).

38. Ornstein (1985) notes that the Holman rule, adopted by the House in 1876, allowed the House Appropriations Committee to insert general legislation into appropriations bills in order to reduce expenditures. The result of this early form of reconciliation was " . . . reduced expenditures but also a tremendous expansion of the legislative power of the Appropriations Committee. With years of big surpluses, the political interests of individual members of Congress began to come to the fore, and resentment over both the tremendous power wielded by the Appropriations Committee and its pruning-knife attitude led in the 1870s and 1880s to a near revolt in the House. That revolt ultimately crippled the appropriations process and the Appropriations Committee, sending spending bills to a number of other committees more interested in logrolling than in spending restraint." (p. 314).

References

BOZEMAN, B., and STRAUSSMAN, J. (1982). "Shrinking budgets and the shrinkage of budget theory," *Public Administration Review* 42: 509–515.

BURKHEAD, J. (1947) "Budget classification and fiscal planning," *Public Administration Review* 7: 228–235.

CAIDEN, N. (1982) "The myth of the annual budget," *Public Administration Review* 42: 16–23.

CAIDEN, N. (1983). "Federal budget reform," *Public Budgeting and Finance* 3: 4–23.

CAIDEN, N. (1984). "The new rules of the Federal Budget game," *Public Administration Review* 44: 109–118.

COPELAND, G. W. (1984). "Changes in the House of Representatives after the passage of the Budget Act of 1974," in W. T. Wander, F. T. Hebert, and G. W. Copeland (eds.), *Congressional Budgeting: Politics, Process, and Power*. Baltimore: Johns Hopkins University Press.

CRECINE, J. P. (1976) "Making defense budgets," in Appendix IV, *Commission on the Organization of the Government for the Conduct of Foreign Policy*. Washington, DC: U.S. Government Printing Office.

DODD, L. C. (1977). "Congress and the quest for power," in L. C. Dodd and B. I. Oppenheimer (eds.), *Congress Reconsidered*, 1st ed. New York: Praeger.

DODD, L. C. (1981). "Congress, the Constitution, and the crisis of legislation," in L. C. Dodd and B. I. Oppenheimer (eds.), *Congress Reconsidered*, 2nd ed. Washington, DC: Congressional Quarterly Press.

DODD, L. C., and OPPENHEIMER, B. I. (1981). "The House in transition: Change and consolidation," in L. C. Dodd and B. I. Oppenheimer (eds.), *Congress Reconsidered*, 2nd ed. Washington, DC: Congressional Quarterly Press.

DOMENCI, SENATOR P. (1982). Comments in *Congressional Budget Office Oversight*. Hearings before the Senate Budget Committee. Washington DC: U.S. Government Printing Office.

ELLWOOD, J. W. (1983). "The great exception: The congressional budget process in an age of decentralization," in L. C. Dodd and B. I. Oppenheimer (eds.), *Congress Reconsidered*, 3rd ed. Washington, DC: Congressional Quarterly Press.

ELLWOOD, J. W. and THURBER, J. A. (1977). "The new congressional budget process: The hows and whys of House-Senate differences," in L. C. Dodd and B. I. Oppenheimer (eds.), *Congress Reconsidered*, 1st ed. New York: Praeger.

ELLWOOD, J. W. and THURBER, J. A. (1981). "The politics of the Congressional budget process re-examined," in L. C. Dodd and B. I. Oppenheimer (eds.), *Congress Reconsidered*, 2nd ed. Washington, DC: Congressional Quarterly Press.

FEUERBRINGER, J. (1985, August 3). "Deficit forecasts seen as off target," *New York Times*.

FIORINA, M. P. (1977). *Congress: Keystone of the Washington Establishment*. New Haven: Yale University Press.

FISCHER, G. W. and KAMLET, M. S. (1984) "Explaining presidential priorities: The competing aspiration levels model of macrobudgetary decision making," *American Political Science Review* 78: 356–371.

FISHER, L. (1982). "The Budget Act of 1974: Its impact on spending," paper delivered at the Conference on the Congressional Budget Process, Carl Albert Congressional Research and Studies Center, University of Oklahoma, February 12–13.

FISHER, L. (1984) "The Congressional Budget Act: A further loss of spending control," in W. T. Wander, F. T. Hebert, and G. W. Copeland (eds.), *Congressional Budgeting: Politics, Process, and Power*. Baltimore: Johns Hopkins University Press.

HARTMAN, R. W. (1982). "Making budget decisions," in J. Pechman (ed.), *Setting National Priorities: The 1983 Budget*. Washington DC: The Brookings Institution.

HAVEMANN, J. (1978). *Congress and the Budget.* Bloomington: Indiana University Press.

HECLO, H. (1985). "Executive budget making," in G. B. Mills and J. L. Palmer (eds.), *Federal Budget Policy in the 1980s.* Washington, DC: Urban Institute.

HUNTINGTON, S. P. (1983). "The defense policy of the Reagan Administration, 1981–1982," in F. Greenstein (ed.), *The Reagan Presidency: An Early Assessment.* Baltimore: Johns Hopkins University Press.

IPPOLITO, D. S. (1980). "Budget reform, impoundment, and supplemental appropriations," in K. A. Shepsle (ed.), *The Congressional Budget Process: Some Views from the Inside.* St. Louis: Center for the Study of American Business.

IPPOLITO, D. S. (1981). *Congressional Spending.* Ithaca: Cornell University Press.

IPPOLITO, D. S. (1982). "Budget reform and Congressional-Executive relations," paper delivered at the Conference on the Congressional Budget Process, Carl Albert Center for Congressional Research and Studies, University of Oklahoma, February 12–13.

KAMLET, M. S., and MOWERY, D. C. (1980). "The budgetary base in Federal resource allocation," *The American Journal of Political Science* 4: 804–821.

KAMLET, M. S., and MOWERY, D. C. (1983). "Budgetary side payments and government growth, 1953–1968," *American Journal of Political Science* 27: 636–664.

KAMLET, M. S., and MOWERY, D. C. (1984). "A comparative analysis of Congressional and Executive budgetary priorities," paper presented at the 1984 American Political Association Meetings, Washington, DC.

LEISERSON, A. (1948). "Coordination of Federal budgetary and appropriations procedures under the Legislative Reorganization Act of 1946," *National Tax Journal* 1: 118–126.

LELOUP, L. T. (1980). "The first half-decade: Evaluating congressional budget reforms," In K. A. Shepsle (ed.), *The Congressional Budget Process: Some Views from the Inside.* St. Louis: Center for the Study of American Business.

LELOUP, L. T. (1983). "Congress and the dilemma of economic policy," in A. Schick (ed.), *Making Economic Policy in Congress.* Washington, DC: American Enterprise Institute.

MCEVOY, J. (1980). "The politics of the budget process: A view from the Senate," in K. A. Shepsle (ed.), *The Congressional Budget Process: Some Views from the Inside.* St. Louis: Center for the Study of American Business.

MASTERS, N. (1980). "The politics of the budget process: A view from the House," in K. A. Shepsle (ed.), *The Congressional Budget Process: Some Views from the Inside.* St. Louis: Center for the Study of American Business.

MOWERY, D. C., KAMLET, M. S., and CRECINE, J. P. (1980). "Presidential management of budgetary and fiscal policymaking," *Political Science Quarterly* 95: 395–425.

MOWERY, D. C., and KAMLET, M. S. (1982). "Coming apart: Fiscal and budgetary policy processes in the Johnson Administration," *Journal of Public Budgeting and Finance* 2: 16–34.

NELSON, D. H. (1953). "The Omnibus Appropriations Act of 1950," *Journal of Politics* 15: 274–288.

ORNSTEIN, N. J. (1985). "The politics of the deficit," in P. Cagan (ed.), *Essays in Contemporary Economic Problems, 1985: The Economy in Deficit.* Washington, DC: American Enterprise Institute.

ORNSTEIN, N. J., PEABODY, R. L., and ROHDE, D. W. (1981). "The contemporary Senate: Into the 1980s," in L. C. Dodd and B. I. Oppenheimer (eds.), *Congress Reconsidered,* 2nd ed. Washington, DC: Congressional Quarterly Press.

PEABODY, R. L. (1981). "House party leadership in the 1970s," in L. C. Dodd and B. I. Oppenheimer (eds.), *Congress Reconsidered,* 2nd ed. Washington, DC: Congressional Quarterly Press.

PEAR, R. (1985, July 28). "Spending freeze favored in House despite deadlock," *New York Times.*

PRICE, D. E. (1981). "Congressional committees in the policy process," in L. C. Dodd and B. I. Oppenheimer (eds.), *Congress Reconsidered,* 2nd ed. Washington, DC: Congressional Quarterly Press.

RAUCH, J. (1985, July 6). "Stalemate threatening budget process as well as efforts to cut the deficit," *National Journal* 1556–1559.

REISCHAUER, R. D. (1983). "Mickey Mouse or Superman? The Congressional budget process during the Reagan Administration," working paper, Changing Domestic Priorities Program, The Urban Institute, Washington, DC.

RIVLIN, A. (1983). "Interview: Alice Rivlin on the Budget," *The Brookings Review* 2: 25–27.

SCHICK, A. (1979). Testimony in *Budget Act Review.* Hearings before the Task Force on the Budget Process, House Budget Committee, Washington, DC.

SCHICK, A. (1980). *Congress and Money.* Washington, DC: The Urban Institute.

SCHICK, A. (1981a). "The first five years of congressional budgeting," in R. Penner (ed.), *The Congressional Budget Process After Five Years.* Washington, DC: American Enterprise Institute.

SCHICK, A. (1981b). *Reconciliation and the Congressional Budget Process.* Washington, DC: American Enterprise Institute.

SCHICK, A. (1981c). "The three-ring budget process: The Appropriations, Tax and Budget Committees in Congress," in T. E. Mann and N. J. Ornstein (eds.), *The New Congress.* Washington, DC: American Enterprise Institute.

SCHICK, A. (1982). "How the budget was won and lost," in N. J. Ornstein (ed.), *President and Congress: Assessing*

Reagan's First Year. Washington, DC: American Enterprise Institute.

SCHICK, A. (1983). "The distributive Congress," in A. Schick (ed.), *Making Economic Policy in Congress.* Washington, DC: American Enterprise Institute.

SCHICK, A. (1985). "The budget as an instrument of Presidential policy," in L. M. Salamon and M. S. Lund (eds.), *The Reagan Presidency and the Governing of America.* Washington, DC: Urban Institute Press.

SHUMAVON, D. H. (1981). "Policy impact of the 1974 Congressional Budget Act," *Public Administration Review* 41: 339–348.

SUNDQUIST, J. L. (1981). *The Decline and Resurgence of Congress.* Washington, DC: Brookings Institution.

WILDAVSKY, A. (1964). *The Politics of the Budgetary Process.* Boston: Little Brown.

U.S. House of Representatives, Committee on the Budget (1980). *Budget Act Review Hearings,* 96th Congress, 1st Session. Washington, DC: U.S. Government Printing Office.

U.S. House of Representatives, Committee on the Budget (1982). *Hearings on Budget Process Review,* 97th Congress, 2nd Session. Washington, DC: U.S. Government Printing Office.

U.S. House of Representatives, Committee on Rules (1983). *Hearings on the Congressional Budget Process,* 97th Congress, 2nd Session. Washington, DC: U.S. Government Printing Office.

U.S. House of Representatives, Committee on Rules (1984a). *Report of the Task Force on the Budget Process.* Washington, DC: U.S. Government Printing Office.

U.S. House of Representatives, Committee on Rules (1984b). *Report on Congressional Budget Act Amendments of 1984 (H.R. 5247).* Washington, DC: U.S. Government Printing Office.

12

Ten Years of the Budget Act: Still Searching for Controls

Louis Fisher

The Budget Act of 1974 has led a charmed life. Rarely has a statute missed goals by such wide margins without being repealed or severely amended. Modifications have occurred in practice, of course, and yet the statute remains virtually untouched. Only in recent years has the Act encountered unfavorable reviews. For most of its existence it has been treated with respect, if not reverence.

It is this sacrosanct quality that makes analysis of the Budget Act so difficult. Even when members of Congress were appalled by the results of the budget process, most of them rallied to its defense. For much of the early years, "protect the process" functioned as an all-purpose talisman. Recent years have given rise to a different and wholly contradictory defense. If budget results are too dreadful for anyone to condone, we now learn that the results stem not from the process but rather from outside political pressures. In the language of a cliché now making the rounds: the process is not the problem: the problem is the problem.

This won't do. If the process is not the problem, why did we make such fundamental changes to the congressional budget process in 1974? No one at that time thought of explaining deficits and late appropriations by "outside forces." Such an excuse or rationalization would have been transparently lame. Congress selected a process that it thought could deal best with political forces, both internal and external.

It is not necessary, or possible, to place the "whole blame" on the Budget Act of 1974. Nor is it acceptable to absolve the Budget Act of all responsibility. The Budget Act made a difference. We can disagree on what those effects have been, but we should not now describe the Budget Act process as inconsequential. We cannot at the same time argue that the Budget Act is not responsible for deficits and late appropriations and then oppose repeal or modification because the Budget Act offers the last best hope for discipline and accountability.

We need to break with this decade-long defensiveness. We should be able to look at the original objectives of the Budget Act and determine the extent to which they have been satisfied. We should reexamine those objectives and make a judgment as to whether they make sense in terms of the institutional strengths and weaknesses of Congress. Perhaps the original objectives were misguided and yet the Budget Act, as it has evolved, offers significant benefits unforeseen by those who drafted and passed the Budget Act. If so, we should say that. But let's be candid about where we are and where we want to go.

The first part of this article reviews the general record of the Budget Act: its use as a macroeconomic tool and the growing complexity of budget resolutions. The second part identifies and evaluates nine objectives of the Budget Act.

Macroeconomic Policy

The history of the Budget Act divides into two broad periods. From 1975 to 1978 a fledgling process struggled for survival. To gain the votes necessary to pass a budget resolution, the newly created House and Senate Budget Committees played an essentially accommodating role among the established authorizing, tax, and appropriations committees of Congress. At the macro level, Congress used the process principally to stimulate the economy and reduce unemployment. It deliberately subordinated the goal of budgetary restraint to economic recovery. The record on deadlines looked promising. Congress generally adhered to the Budget Act's timetable for adopting budget resolutions and passing the regular appropriations bills.

The years since 1978 have witnessed mounting deficits, inflation, and high interest rates. Citizen groups across the country advocated curbs on public spending and supplied momentum for a constitutional amendment to balance the federal budget. Congress

Source: Public Budgeting & Finance (Autumn 1985): 3–28. Reprinted by permission.

Louis Fisher is with the Congressional Research Service, Library of Congress. The views expressed here are solely those of the author, although he would like to express his appreciation for helpful comments at the draft stage from Ron Boster, Sante J. Esposito, Robert A. Keith, and Allen Schick.

responded by adopting a number of procedures, including reconciliation, to constrain the growth of federal domestic programs. These techniques, combined with the application of budget resolutions to credit activities and to outyears, exacerbated relations between the legislative and executive branches and within Congress itself. Budget resolutions and appropriations bills were delayed, estimates for outlays and revenues became increasingly unrealistic, and members of Congress complained that the budget process had become so time-consuming and complex that it side-tracked other essential legislative duties.

Congress first attempted a "dry run" of the budget process in 1975 (for fiscal 1976). Both houses agreed that it was important to gain experience with the main features of the Budget Act, even though full implementation would not be required until fiscal 1977. After President Ford sent his fiscal 1976 budget to Congress, the two Budget Committees prepared a first budget resolution restricted to the five aggregates: revenues, budget authority, outlays, deficit, and public debt. The committee reports subdivided the aggregates for budget authority and outlays into 16 functional categories. The breakdowns by functional category would be placed in future budget resolutions.

Both Houses of Congress adopted budget resolutions designed to stimulate the economy—the House more so than the Senate. As part of a deliberate anti-recession strategy, Congress accepted the need for a deficit higher than recommended by Ford. The congressional priority favored economic recovery over budgetary restraint. The same legislative preference was applied the next year to Ford's budget for fiscal 1977 (Table 1).

Final figures for budget authority greatly exceeded the estimates in the first and second budget resolutions. Nevertheless, outlays fell short of congressional expectations. This discrepancy became known as "shortfalls" in spending. Congress at first welcomed the development, accepting the news about shortfalls as evidence that the Budget Act was contributing to budgetary discipline. But shortfalls had been a chronic problem for years, reflecting a systematic and persistent bias on the part of agencies to overestimate outlays. Late congressional action on supplemental appropriations bills also made it difficult for agencies to spend available budget authority. In some cases Congress was too optimistic about the ability of agencies to implement new federal programs and expand existing ones. Finally, Congress had an incentive under the Budget Act to overestimate outlays. A high figure provided a cushion against unanticipated expenses (supplying valuable "running room") and therefore lessened the need for a third budget resolution.[1]

Under the first two years of the Carter administration, Congress continued to use the Budget Act to stimulate the economy and combat unemployment. One of its first actions, in February 1977, was the adoption of a third budget resolution for fiscal 1977 to accommodate an economic stimulus bill. The purpose of the third resolution, said the House budget Committee, was "to arrest the sharp decline in economic activity since adoption of the second budget resolution in September [1976]."[2] Carter

Table 1
Congressional action on Ford's budgets ($ billions)

	President's Budget	First Budget Resolution	Second Budget Resolution	Actual
Fiscal 1976				
Budget Authority	$385.8	$395.8	$408.0	$415.3
Outlays	349.4	367.0	374.9	364.5
Receipts	297.5	298.2	300.8	298.1
Deficits	51.9	68.82	74.1	66.4
Fiscal 1977				
Budget Authority	$433.4	$454.2	$451.55	$465.2
Outlays	394.2	413.3	413.1	400.5
Receipts	351.3	362.5	362.5	355.6
Deficits	43.0	50.8	50.6	44.9

Table 2
Congressional action on Carter's budgets ($ billions)

	President's Budget	First Budget Resolution	Second Budget Resolution	Actual
Fiscal 1978				
Budget Authority	$507.3	$503.45	$500.1	$501.5
Outlays	459.4	460.9	458.2	448.4
Receipts	401.6	396.3	397.0	399.6
Deficits	57.75	64.65	61.25	48.8
Fiscal 1979				
Budget Authority	$568.2	$568.85	$555.65	$556.7
Outlays	500.2	498.8	487.5	491.0
Receipts	439.6	447.9	448.7	463.3
Deficits	60.6	50.9	38.8	27.7
Fiscal 1980				
Budget Authority	$615.5	$604.4	$638.0	$658.8
Outlays	531.6	532.0	547.6	576.7
Receipts	502.6	509.0	517.8	517.1
Deficits	29.0	23.0	29.8	59.6
Fiscal 1981				
Budget Authority	$696.1	$697.2	$694.6	$718.4
Outlays	615.8	613.6	632.4	657.2
Receipts	600.0	613.8	605.0	599.3
Deficits	15.8	(+)0.2	27.4	57.9

revised Ford's budget for fiscal 1978 to make room for the economic stimulus package. His revised budget added $6.2 billion in outlays and reduced receipts by $4.7 billion, increasing the size of the projected deficit from $57.2 billion to $68 billion. Congressional action on budget resolutions closely tracked the aggregates requested by Carter.

Carter's budget for fiscal 1979 was still basically expansionary. His message to Congress explained that his budget "provides for a continuing recovery of the nation's economy from the 1974–75 recession."[3] To provide stimulus, the budget called for an increase of $38 billion in outlays and a deficit of $61 billion. The high level of the deficit reflected his decision to reduce taxes by $25 billion "to help assure continued economic recovery and reduction in unemployment."[4]

The first budget resolution for fiscal 1979 gave Carter what he wanted in aggregates for budget authority and outlays. Because of a higher estimate for revenues by Congress, the deficit projected in the resolution was $10 billion lower than the president's budget. In the second budget resolution, Congress reduced the aggregates for budget authority, outlays, and deficit, while keeping revenue estimates at the same level (Table 2). The Budget Committees expressed concern about inflation, but predicted a range between 6 and 7 percent for fiscal years 1978 and 1979.[5] Inflation was much higher than 7 percent for fiscal 1979, pushing taxpayers into higher brackets. Ironically, this increased the amount of receipts and brought a reduction in the deficit.

Beginning with Carter's budget for fiscal 1980, both branches became more concerned about inflation and the need to restrain spending. Carter's budget message referred to fiscal constraint as "an imperative if we are to overcome the threat of accelerating inflation."[6] Whereas earlier reports from the House Budget Committee had placed the spotlight on unemployment and economic stimulation, the focus now fell on spending restraint, inflation control, and concern for a balanced budget. The Committee noted that the consumer price index had jumped to an annual rate of 8.8 percent from July to October 1978, requiring a switch from sustaining economic growth to restraining inflation.[7] The first budget resolution projected budget authority at $11 billion below Carter's budget, outlays at approximately the same level as Carter's, about $6 billion more in receipts, and therefore a deficit of $23 billion instead of Carter's $29 billion estimate.

Comments during floor debate on the first budget resolution reinforce the impression that 1979 was indeed a turning point for the budget process. Robert Giaimo, chairman of the House Budget Committee, described the resolution as putting "an end to the spending pattern of recent years, when program after program year after year was given a sizeable incremental funding increase, almost regardless of its effectiveness."[8] A year later he told his colleagues: "This budget marks a departure from past years. It is not a 'spending as usual' budget. It is not loaded with fiscal sweeteners to please this group or that group or this member or that member."[9]

Although the Budget Committees assumed the posture of fiscal restraint, Congress found it difficult to control spending or the size of the deficit in fiscal years 1980 and 1981. As a means of imposing discipline, the Senate Budget Committee proposed reconciliation in the second budget resolution for fiscal 1980, requiring seven committees to cut outlays and the budget deficit by $4 billion. The House resisted, producing a deadlock that delayed adoption of the second budget resolution until November 28, more than two months past the statutory deadline. The two houses eventually agreed to strike the reconciliation instructions.

Results for fiscal 1980 were disappointing. The budget deficit ended up not at the $23 billion anticipated by the first budget resolution, or the $29.8 billion in the second resolution, or the $46.95 billion in the revised second, but at $59.6 billion. Even for fiscal 1981, when Congress for the first time enacted a full-scale reconciliation bill, budget deficits could not be controlled. Carter initially recommended a deficit of $15.8 billion, revised that two months later to $16.5 billion, and Congress (largely on the basis of higher revenue estimates) adopted a first budget resolution that called for a surplus of $200 million. As the fiscal year unfolded, the surplus evaporated and was replaced by increasingly higher predictions of deficits. Despite a reconciliation effort that reduced the deficit by about $8 billion (through a mix of spending cuts and tax increases), the final deficit soared to $57.9 billion. Total revenues were not as high as expected, while outlays far outpaced the estimates in the budget resolutions (Table 2).

President Reagan reworked Carter's budget for fiscal 1982 by cutting domestic spending, increasing military spending, and reducing federal taxes. The estimate for outlays was cut by $44 billion, budget authority by $37.4 billion, and receipts by $54 billion. As a result, the projected deficit rose from $27.5 billion to $45 billion. Despite major retrenchments in the Reconciliation Act of 1981, which reduced fiscal 1982 outlays by $35.2 billion, the budget continued to grow. The first budget resolution, which basically endorsed the aggregates requested by Reagan, was so out of date by the summer of 1981 that Congress preferred to adopt a pro forma second budget resolution that simply reaffirmed the numbers in the first resolution.

The Budget Committees recognized that the numbers being reaffirmed were unrealistic. When the House Budget Committee began its markup on the second resolution, it estimated the deficit at $87.2 billion.[10] The outlook for fiscal 1982 continued to deteriorate. By the time the fiscal year was over, receipts were far lower than expected, outlays had climbed $33.1 billion above Reagan's budget, and the deficit reached $110.7 billion.

Budgetary miscalculations also marred the record for fiscal 1983. Reagan's budget continued his objective of restraining domestic spending, as did the two Budget Committees (although their figures for budget authority and outlays were somewhat higher). Because of section 7 in the first budget resolution, the identical figures for budget aggregates took effect on October 1 as the second resolution without any further action by Congress. The same procedure was adopted for fiscal 1984 and fiscal 1985, allowing language in the first budget resolution to automatically trigger the second resolution if Congress failed to act by October 1. In effect, Congress eliminated the second resolution.

The recession of 1981–82 cut deeply into revenues. Outlays increased because of costs associated with unemployment compensation and other recession-related programs. Despite the cutbacks achieved through another reconciliation effort, outlays were about $50 billion above the President's budget. Congress passed a special tax bill to bring in additional revenues. Even so, the combined effects of declining receipts and rising outlays more than doubled the deficit, pushing it from the $91.5 billion estimated in Reagan's fiscal 1983 budget to $195.4 billion (Table 3).

In submitting his fiscal 1984 budget, President Reagan confronted new power relationships on Capitol Hill. House Democrats had picked up 26 seats during the 1982 elections, while Republican

Table 3
Congressional action on Reagan's budgets ($ billions)

	President's Budget	First Budget Resolution	Second Budget Resolution	Actual
Fiscal 1982				
Budget Authority	$ 772.4	$ 770.9	$ 770.9	$ 779.9
Outlays	695.3	695.4	695.4	728.4
Receipts	650.8	657.8	657.8	617.8
Deficits	45.0	37.65	37.65	110.6
Fiscal 1983				
Budget Authority	$ 801.9	$ 822.4	$ 822.4	$ 866.7
Outlays	757.6	769.8	769.8	796.0
Receipts	666.1	665.9	665.9	600.6
Deficits	91.5	103.9	103.9	195.4
Fiscal 1984				
Budget Authority	$ 900.1	$ 919.5*	$ 919.5*	$ 949.8
Outlays	848.5	849.5*	849.5*	851.8
Receipts	659.7	679.6	679.6	666.5
Deficits	188.8	169.9	169.9	185.3
Fiscal 1985				
Budget Authority	$1,006.5	$1021.4	$1,021.4	$1,064.9 est.
Outlays	925.5	932.1	932.1	959.1 est.
Receipts	745.1	750.9	750.9	736.9 est.
Deficits	180.4	181.2	181.2	222.2 est.

* Excludes reserve fund amounts.

senators were hastily distancing themselves from the White House. Reagan's projected deficit of $188.8 billion triggered another attempt at reconciliation. Committees were directed to cut spending by $12.3 billion and to increase taxes by $73 billion over a three-year period. By the end of the year, however, the deficit reduction plan was derailed because of disagreements between the House and the Senate. Legislation was passed to cut outlays by $8.5 billion over the three-year period, but neither house approved tax increases to meet the reconciliation requirement.[11] The budget resolution anticipated a deficit of $169.9 billion for fiscal 1984; the actual deficit came to $185.3 billion.

Reagan's budget for fiscal 1985 produced a major stalemate. Both Houses of Congress regarded his deficit projections as unacceptable: a deficit of $180.4 billion for fiscal 1985, with higher levels after that. Although both houses fought for months over reductions in defense spending and enacted a deficit reduction act (producing a "downpayment" of about $150 billion over a three-year period), the budget resolution adopted on October 1, 1984 called for a deficit of $181.1 billion for fiscal 1985 followed by larger deficits in fiscal years 1986 and 1987.

Over the first six years of the Budget Act, Congress and the president were generally accurate in estimating receipts (even underestimating them in fiscal 1979 when inflation pushed taxpayers into higher brackets). The record since then has been one of massive overestimates. President Reagan overestimated receipts by $33 billion in fiscal 1982 and by $65.5 billion in fiscal 1983. Congress also overestimated receipts for those years. Outlays have generally exceeded the projections of Congress and the president. This pattern of overestimating receipts and underestimating outlays resulted in deficits far above presidential and congressional projections.

Growing Complexity of Budget Resolutions

The legislative history of the Budget Act suggests that budget resolutions were meant to be used for two purposes: debating macroeconomic policy and deciding broad issues of budgetary priorities. Congressman Richard Bolling, serving as House floor manager for the budget reform bill, said that the budget resolution "does not get into particular programs, agencies, appropriations, or projects. To do so would destroy the utility of the congressional budget process as an instrument for making national economic policy."[12]

Despite Bolling's admonition, budget resolutions became a means of voting (at least indirectly) on specific programs and activities. The preparation and review of budget resolutions opened the door to duplication of effort and to conflict among committees. Much of this was inevitable and predictable. Congressman George Mahon, who objected that the House Budget Committee had invaded the jurisdiction of his Appropriations Committee, admitted that it was "certainly appropriate for the [budget] committee to have an awareness of individual spending programs in order to arrive at its recommendations."[13]

The budget process presents many opportunities for the Budget Committees to consider program details. First, the authorization and appropriations committees supply program details in their March 15 reports to the Budget Committees. Second, testimony at Budget Committee hearings covers program details, even though the legislative history of the Budget Act suggests that the Budget Committee hearings should concern "economic conditions and national priorities at a high level of aggregation."[14] Third, votes within the Budget Committees on amendments to the proposed budget resolutions often focus on specific program interests. Fourth, the Budget Committee reports permit discussion of program details, as do amendments offered on the floor during action on budget resolutions. Fifth, although budget resolutions are restricted to aggregates and functional categories, every member of Congress has access to committee markup documents or computerized backup sheets to determine whether a particular program is covered by a budget resolution. Members are basically program oriented and want to know if a budget resolution allows room for projects and programs of interest.

With each passing year the debates on budget resolutions descended ever more deeply into program details. The number of floor amendments offered to budget resolutions increased each year. On the House side, the number of floor amendments submitted for the first budget resolution climbed from 6 in fiscal 1976, to 16 for each of the fiscal years 1977 and 1978, to 26 for fiscal 1979, and to 50 for fiscal 1980. The House responded by adopting restrictive rules to limit floor amendments. These rules, in turn, became increasingly complex as the House attempted to balance two conflicting needs. There was a need to expedite action on budget resolutions, but members also insisted on an opportunity to offer alternative packages. Both Houses of Congress spent increasing amounts of time debating budget resolutions.

Budget resolutions grew longer and more complex. At first restricted to aggregates and functional categories, they added sections on outyears, reconciliation, deferred enrollment, federal credit, and other objectives. Section 301(a) of the Budget Act permits the first budget resolution to include (in addition to aggregates and functional categories) "such other matters relating to the budget as may be appropriate to carry out the purposes of this Act." Section 301(b)(2) also allows the Budget Committees to place in the first budget resolution any procedure "which is considered appropriate to carry out the purposes of this Act."

Aggregates and Functional Categories

The first two budget resolutions, adopted for the "dry run" in fiscal 1976 and the transition quarter (July 1 to September 30, 1976), included only the five aggregates. The resolutions did not subdivide the aggregates into functional categories. For fiscal 1977, Congress implemented the Budget Act in full by providing in the budget resolutions a breakdown of budget authority and outlays into 17 functional categories.

Beginning in fiscal 1980, the first budget resolution added a multi-year perspective by adopting aggregates for fiscal years 1981 and 1982. The second budget resolution not only established aggregates for those years but provided functional subtotals as well. Budget resolutions now supply a detailed breakdown for four years: the current year, the upcoming year, and two years beyond that. Each functional category, for the four years, contains dollar amounts for new budget authority, outlays, and credit operations. The budget resolutions for fiscal 1977 ran about four to five pages. Contemporary resolutions are now ten times that long.

Reconciliation

The first budget resolution for fiscal 1980 asked committees to recommend savings and suggest ways to reduce unobligated and unexpended balances. It also identified the need to control off-budget spending. As part of a reconciliation effort, the Senate adopted instructions in the second budget resolution to direct seven committees to cut $3.6 billion in spending. The House refused to go along, arguing that its committees had already made substantial cuts to meet the targets of the first resolution and that it would be unreasonable to ask them to redo their work at such a late stage. As finally adopted, the second resolution merely reiterated the request for legislative savings.

This experience convinced both houses that reconciliation could not work as the Budget Act intended. Reconciliation was supposed to come in the fall, after action on the second budget resolution, and was actually used that way for the second resolution for fiscal 1976, which directed the tax committees to reduce revenues by $6.4 billion. However, the effort in fiscal 1980 to use reconciliation in the fall to cut spending was so unsuccessful that Congress conceded that full-scale reconciliation had to be timed for the first resolution in the spring.

Reconciliation instructions, itemizing for each committee the proposed reductions in budget authority and outlays, began with the first budget resolution for fiscal 1981. House and Senate committees were directed to cut spending and raise revenues. Some of the savings resulted from pushing spending from fiscal 1981 to the next year. To counter this kind of tactic in the future, the Budget Committees decided to require reconciliation savings over a multi-year period. For example, the first budget resolution for fiscal 1982 included reconciliation instructions for fiscal years 1982, 1983, and 1984. Similarly, the first budget resolution for fiscal year 1983 applied reconciliation to fiscal years 1983, 1984, and 1985.

Reconciliation instructions for fiscal 1984 reached out to fiscal years 1985 and 1986, but Congress became deadlocked over the amounts, particularly the requirement of $73 billion in revenues. The end of the year arrived without action by Congress to implement reconciliation, although legislation in April and July 1984 achieved some of the outlay savings.

Credit Budget

Congress initiated a "credit budget" in the first budget resolution for fiscal 1981. The credit budget included both the loans made directly by the federal government and the loans it guarantees. The first budget resolution established dollar limits for new direct loan obligations and for commitments on new primary loan guarantees. It also divided new direct loan obligations into two categories: off-budget and on-budget, placing dollar ceilings on each. The second budget resolution for that year established dollar levels for new direct loan obligations, new primary loan guarantee commitments, and a third element of the credit budget: new secondary loan guarantee commitments. New direct loan obligations were again divided into off-budget and on-budget components. For both the first and the second budget resolutions, the aggregates for the credit budget represented targets rather than binding ceilings.

In adopting a credit budget for fiscal 1982, Congress allocated the three basic aggregates of the credit budget among 19 functional categories. Limits (expressed as a sense-of-Congress resolution) were placed on the operation of the Federal Financing Bank and the off-budget and on-budget portions of new direct loan obligations. The second budget resolution for fiscal 1982 was passed in form identical to the first.

The credit totals for fiscal 1982, even though subdivided by functional category, were advisory rather than binding. For fiscal 1983 Congress attempted to impose mandatory limits on federal credit. It did this by incorporating in the front part of the first resolution (covering new budget authority and outlays for each functional category) specific dollar levels for three aspects of the credit budget: new direct loan obligations, new primary loan guarantee commitments, and new secondary loan guarantee commitments. On October 1, those figures were automatically adopted as part of the second budget resolution, and that practice has been followed for fiscal years 1984 and 1985. However, the procedure has yet to produce binding and enforceable ceilings on federal credit.

Off-Budget Spending

Closely associated with the credit budget are the efforts to control off-budget spending, most of which consists of lending programs. For example, off-budget outlays result from the transactions of the Federal Financing Bank and the Rural Electrification Administration, both of which have been excluded from the unified budget. The first budget resolution for fiscal 1980 recommended that "a way be found within the congressional budget process to relate accurately the estimates of off-budget federal entities and capital expenditures in the unified budget." The second resolution for that year reaffirmed the commitment to relate the outlays of off-budget federal agencies to the congressional budget. It estimated that off-budget outlays (and hence off-budget deficits) were about $16 billion for fiscal 1980.

In initiating a credit budget, the first budget resolution for fiscal 1981 divided the target ceiling for new direct loan obligations into its off-budget and on-budget components. After increasing the dollar amounts for each component, the second resolution reiterated the limits for off-budget and on-budget direct loan programs.

For fiscal 1982, the first budget resolution established the sense of Congress that the president and Congress, through the appropriations process, should limit the off-budget lending activity of the federal government to a level not to exceed $17.73 billion. In its second budget resolution for fiscal 1982, Congress reaffirmed the first resolution.

When Congress incorporated credit figures in the front part of the first budget resolution for fiscal 1983, it did not separate direct loan programs into off-budget and on-budget. It did state, later in the resolution, that it was the sense of Congress that budget resolutions should reflect "the full range of fiscal activities of the federal government" and that each resolution, beginning with the first resolution for fiscal 1984, "shall list, for each functional category, the off-budget activities associated with that category, as well as the new budget authority, outlays, new direct loan obligations, new primary loan guarantee commitments, and new secondary loan guarantee commitments associated with that category." On October 1 the first budget resolution for fiscal 1983 automatically became the second resolution for that year. That material was not included in the budget resolutions for fiscal 1984 and fiscal 1985.

Deferred Enrollment

Under section 301(b)(1) of the Budget Act, the first budget resolution may require that all or certain bills and resolutions providing new budget authority, or providing new spending authority described as entitlements, shall not be enrolled until the second budget resolution has been agreed to. Moreover, if reconciliation is required under the provisions of a second budget resolution, enrollment may be delayed until Congress has completed action on reconciliation.

In the spring resolution for fiscal 1981, Congress for the first time prohibited the enrollment of bills that exceeded the budget authority allowed by that resolution until Congress completed action on the fall resolution and any reconciliation required. Congress also delayed the enrollment of bills that would reduce federal revenues in fiscal 1981 by more than $100 million. Deferred enrollment was used again in the first budget resolution for fiscal 1982. In prohibiting the enrollment of bills that provided new budget authority or entitlements in excess of the budget resolution, Congress specifically selected as ceilings "the appropriate allocation or subdivision made pursuant to section 302" of the Budget Act. Enrollment of bills in excess of those ceilings could not occur until Congress completed action on the second budget resolution and any reconciliation required.

The House Budget Committee included deferred enrollment in the first budget resolution for fiscal 1983, tightening the process still further by selecting as ceilings "the allocations or subdivisions required by section 302(b) of the Budget Act." The effect was to adopt not merely the 302(a) allocations by committee but the 302(b) allocations by subcommittee. Congressman Jamie L. Whitten, the chairman of the House Appropriations Committee, successfully offered an amendment to delete the deferred enrollment procedure. He objected that it put another obstacle in the way of timely action on appropriations and placed unreasonable controls on discretionary spending while exerting little control over entitlement programs.[15]

A Scorecard for the Budget Act

How well has the Budget Act performed over the years? To what degree has it met its objectives? To some the answer is self-evident. The House Rules Committee noted in 1984: "Critics of the budget process often forget what fiscal decision-making was like prior to the adoption of the Congressional Budget Act."[16] The apparent message: "It's bad now but you should have seen it before." Clearly the contemporary record is bad; it is less clear that the record ten years ago was worse. That must be demonstrated by comparing the two periods. Nevertheless, there are those who question whether the Budget Act contains goals tangible enough to measure.[17] Such a position makes the Act virtually immune either to praise or criticism; it would be incapable of evaluation. However, the objectives of the Budget Act are sufficiently well-defined by the statutory language and its legislative history.

Restrain Spending

Several studies conclude that the Budget Act was meant to be neutral toward spending. They claim that the process could be used for higher or lower spending, bigger or smaller deficits.[18] It would seem difficult to argue that Congress overhauled its budget process, set up new committees, and created new institutions, such as the Congressional Budget Office, simply to make the process neutral toward spending. The overwhelming motivation was to restrain the growth of federal spending. The legislative record on spending had produced, by the campaign year 1972, an acrimonious battle between President Nixon and Congress. They found themselves locked in a collision course over a spending ceiling of $250 billion for fiscal 1973. In an unusual attack on the internal procedures of a co-equal branch, Nixon criticized the "hoary and traditional procedure of the Congress, which now permits action on the various spending programs as if they were unrelated and independent actions."[19] In a nationwide radio address he warned that "excessive spending by the Congress might cause a congressional tax increase in 1973."[20]

The premise of congressional irresponsibility led to the creation of the Joint Study Committee on Budget Control in October 1972. Given the political climate from 1972 to 1974, it is incongruous to characterize the Budget Act as neutral toward spending. There was a clear expectation that it would give Congress more effective ways to restrain spending. Congressman Robert Giaimo, testifying as the chairman of the House Budget Commitee, offered this perspective in 1978: "We don't need a Budget Act to enable us to spend more. We need a Budget Act in order to impose a discipline on ourselves, which was the very purpose of the Budget Act, to establish and change priorities, but within an overall discipline, within overall limitations."[21] Four years later, speaking now as a private citizen, he described the Budget Act of 1974 as "basically a contract whereby Congress agreed to curb its undisciplined spending habits and the president gave up his impoundment powers."[22]

This link between spending constraint and impoundment control is important to understand. The history of impoundment legislation reinforces the view that the Budget Act was meant to restrain federal spending. Each house had passed legislation in 1973 to limit the president's authority to impound funds. However, members were reluctant to present a bill to the president because such legislation had a "pro-spending" quality. The public would interpret the bill as another effort by Congress to spend more than the president wanted, offering further proof of uninhibited congressional spending. A statutory control on impoundment would be politically acceptable only if Congress attached it to a measure that promised greater congressional control and responsibility over spending. That union was achieved by making the Impoundment Control Act the final title of the Budget Act.

Has the Budget Act restrained spending? No one can predict what would have resulted without the Act, but a number of procedures associated with the Act have encouraged higher spending; the preferred status of entitlements (more on that later); the March 15 estimates that invite greater advocacy from congressional committees; the existence of the Budget Committees as another access point for members of Congress and lobbyists rebuffed by the authorization and appropriation committees; the use of "current services" and "current policy" to adjust the spending levels of every program for inflation (a giant hold-harmless procedure); and the adoption of generous aggregates in budget resolutions to serve not as ceilings on congressional spending but as floors. The process allows members of Congress to justify amendments to increase appropriations by arguing that the higher spending would still be within the totals sanctioned by the budget resolution. Instead of keeping within the president's aggregates, members can vote on bountiful ceilings in budget resolutions and then tell their constituents that they have "stayed within the budget." Which budget—the president's or Congress'—is never made clear.[23]

The growth of federal spending has not been slowed by the Budget Act. Taking the Office of Management and Budget's figures for budget outlays computed in constant fiscal 1972 prices, outlays climbed from $183 billion to $266.4 billion from fiscal 1966 through fiscal 1975, or an annual increase over that ten-year period of 4.2 percent. This period is distorted by the buildup in fiscal years 1967 and

Table 4
Budget outlays in constant fiscal 1972 prices

Fiscal Year	Outlays ($ billions)	Dollar Increase	Percent Increase
1960	143.3	—	—
1961	149.9	6.6	4.6
1962	162.4	12.5	8.3
1963	163.0	0.6	0.4
1964	170.4	6.6	4.0
1965	166.8	–3.6	–2.1
1966	183.0	16.2	9.7
1967	207.6	24.6	13.4
1968	224.7	17.1	8.2
1969	220.3	–4.4	–2.0
1970	220.3	—	0.0
1971	222.7	2.4	1.1
1972	230.7	8.0	3.6
1973	233.3	2.6	1.1
1974	238.0	4.7	2.0
1975	266.4	28.4	11.9
1976	279.5	13.1	4.9
TQ	69.9		
1977	286.3	6.8	2.4
1978	300.2	13.9	4.8
1979	304.4	4.2	1.4
1980	324.4	20.0	6.6
1981	337.1	12.7	3.9
1982	346.1	8.7	2.6
1983	360.1	14.0	4.0
1984	366.3	6.2	1.7
1985	397.0	30.7	8.4

Source: Office of Management and Budget, *Historical Tables: Budget of the United States Government, Fiscal Year 1986,* Table 6.1.

1968 to finance the Vietnam War, and the years immediately following that benefited from decreases in national defense spending (Table 4). It also includes the 11.9 percent increase for fiscal 1975, which reflected a dramatic rise in payments to individuals. Over the next decade, from fiscal 1976 through fiscal 1985, outlays rose from $279.5 billion to an estimated $397 billion, or an average annual increase of 4.2 percent.

Reduce Deficits

By curbing spending, Congress hoped to limit the size of federal deficits. The Joint Study Committee began its report by noting that the federal government had been in a deficit position 37 times in the 54 years since 1920. Of the 16 years of budget surplus, 10 occurred before 1931. In the 43 years since 1931, only six years yielded surpluses. Other than the World War II years, the largest deficits had appeared in recent years. Not only were deficits a fixture of contemporary budgets, they were growing larger. Deficits reached $23 billion for fiscal years 1971 and 1972 and $14.8 billion for fiscal 1973. For their time (though not for ours), the deficits were immense. The Committee concluded that the "constant continuation of deficits plus their increasing size illustrates the need for Congress to obtain better control over the budget."[24]

In the ten years from fiscal 1966 through fiscal 1975, deficits averaged $14.8 billion a year. For the

Table 5
Budget deficits

Fiscal Year	Deficit ($ billions)	Fiscal Year	Deficit ($ billions)
1960	+ 0.3	1975	45.1
1961	3.4	1976	66.4
1962	7.1	TQ	13.0
1963	4.8	1977	44.9
1964	5.9	1978	48.8
1965	1.6	1979	27.7
1966	3.8	1980	59.6
1967	8.7	1981	57.9
1968	25.2	1982	110.6
1969	+ 3.2	1983	195.4
1970	2.8	1984	185.3
1971	23.0	1985	222.2 est.
1972	23.4		
1973	14.8		
1974	4.7		

decade from fiscal 1976 through fiscal 1985, the average annual deficit increased to about $100 billion a year (Table 5). The future looks worse. The budget resolution adopted on October 1, 1984, called for deficits of $192.7 billion for fiscal 1986 and $207.6 billion for fiscal 1987, based on rather optimistic assumptions about economic growth. Any slowdown or downturn in the economy would push those figures much higher.

Voting on Aggregates

The Joint Study Committee concluded that "the failure to arrive at congressional budget decisions on an overall basis has been a contributory factor" in the continuation of deficits. No committee was responsible for deciding "whether or not total outlays are appropriate in view of the current situation. . . . As a result, each spending bill tends to be considered by Congress as a separate entity, and any assessment of relative priorities among spending programs for the most part is made solely within the context of the bill before Congress."[25]

The Budget Act supposedly supplied the antidote for the fragmented, splintered system that had operated up to 1974. "It is almost inconceivable," said the House Rules Committee a decade later, "that Congress would return to the old system of acting independently on each piece of budgetary legislation and then adding up the results and calling that a budget."[26] A study that same year claimed that prior to the Budget Act "Congress examined programs and considered appropriations individually, so that it had neither a coherent view of aggregate levels of federal spending nor a view of how individual programs fit into those aggregate spending levels."[27]

These descriptions of conditions before 1974 are overdrawn and incorrect. Such stereotypes are used to exaggerate the virtues of the new system over the old. In fact, the "old system" was not nearly so fragmented, incoherent, and irresponsible. The Joint Committee on Reduction of Federal Expenditures prepared "scorekeeping reports" and circulated them on a regular basis. These reports were printed in the *Congressional Record.* Members of Congress therefore knew, from month to month, how legislative actions compared to the president's budget. Through informal techniques, Congress managed to coordinate its actions and change the shape of the president's budget without exceeding its size. The results reveal a systematic pattern, not chaos. This is apparent by examining the five-year period immediately preceding the Budget Act. From fiscal 1969 through fiscal 1973, appropriations bills were $30.9 billion below the president's budgets. Over that same period, backdoors and mandatory entitlements exceeded the president's budgets by $30.5 billion.[28] Basically, Congress was cutting defense and foreign assistance while adding to such programs as Labor-HEW and environmental protection. The totals, however, remained within the ballpark of the president's budget. Congressional spending was not wildly out of control.

The Budget Act assumed that members of Congress would behave more responsibly if they voted explicitly on budget aggregates and faced up to totals, rather than deciding spending actions in "piecemeal" fashion on separate appropriations and legislative bills. Members presumably wanted to vote on budget totals and be responsible for them. However, the behavior of Congress has been increasingly one of irresponsibility. Congressman David Obey recently remarked:

> Under the existing conditions the only kind of budget resolution you can pass today is one that lies. We did it under Carter, we have done it under Reagan, and we are going to do it under every president for as long as any of us are here, unless we change the system, because you cannot get members under the existing system to face up to what the real numbers do. You always wind up having phony economic assumptions and all kinds of phony numbers on estimating.[29]

Members have discovered a number of ingenious methods to avoid a vote on aggregates, especially deficits. First they adopted a second resolution in 1981 that "reaffirmed" the totals in the first resolution, even when everyone knew that the earlier figures were wholly unrealistic. In a burst of euphemism, supporters of the Reagan administration quite charitably called the figures "noncurrent economic assumptions." A second step away from responsibility was the automatic device that triggered the second resolution in 1982, 1983, and 1984, thus dispensing with the need to vote on higher deficits. The aggregates in the spring resolution, no matter how unrealistic or discredited, become the fall resolution if Congress does not act by October 1 (Table 6). It is evident that Congress has no intention of debating and passing a second resolution that will reflect the conditions of the fall months. Still another step toward unaccountability was to tuck the higher deficits into a revised second resolution adopted the following spring. No separate vote or debate on the higher deficits is conducted because by that time Congress turns its attention toward the upcoming year.

In 1979 the House figured out a way to handle increases in the public debt limit without voting on them. Instead of taking a separate vote on a debt limit bill, the new procedure lifts the public debt limit from the first budget resolution and places it in a joint resolution, which is then "deemed" to have passed the House. The only House action is to incorporate by reference the debt limit in the budget resolution. This may seem an efficient system, since one vote serves two purposes, but the public debt limit rarely commands much attention or interest during debate on the budget resolution, and recent budget resolutions have been notoriously unrealistic about deficits.

Table 6
Dates for adopting budget resolutions

Fiscal Year	First Budget Resolution (May 15 Deadline)	Second Budget Resolution (September 15 Deadline)
1976	May 14	December 12
1977	May 13	September 16
1978	May 17	September 15
1979	May 17	September 23
1980	May 24	November 28
1981	June 12	November 20
1982	May 21	December 10*
1983	June 23	**
1984	June 23	**
1985	October 1	**

* The second resolution merely "reaffirmed" the figures in the first resolution.
** No second resolution was adopted for these years. The first resolution automatically became binding as the second resolution on October 1.

Another step away from accountability occurred in 1983 when the House Budget Committee advocated an "adjustment resolution" that would raise budget totals to take into account "technical and economic adjustments." This category included changes in economic assumptions and technical estimates, such as inflation and unemployment rates. The adjustment resolution would have been handled with fast-track procedures and limited time for floor debate. Fortunately, the Senate refused to go along, partly because the vagueness of "technical estimates" invited misuse and escapist budgeting. The availability of an adjustment resolution could serve as an incentive for adopting unrealistic and overly optimistic figures in the first resolution, with realism inserted at some later stage, where it would have less visibility and accountability.

Coordinate Appropriations and Revenues

Congress adopted two strategies in 1974 to control deficits: placing restraints on spending and consciously relating outlays to revenues. The Joint Study Committee condemned the failure to decide congressional budget decisions on an overall basis. To correct this deficiency, the Committee proposed that each house create a Budget Committee to review the budget on a comprehensive basis. The House committee would have 21 members, the Senate committee 15. In both cases, one-third of the members would be drawn from the Appropriations Committees, one-third from the tax committees, and one-third from the legislative committees.

In essence, the Joint Study Committee wanted the Budget Committees to play a coordinating role between the interests of the appropriations and tax panels. The Budget Act, however, followed a different course. Instead of the appropriations and tax committees having 14 of the 21 seats on the House Budget Committee, the number dropped to 10 out of 23. The allotment of 10 seats remained fixed as the Budget Committee grew to 25 members in 1975, 30 members in 1981, and 31 members in 1983. The two-thirds control therefore declined over the years to one-third. In the case of the Senate Budget Committee, the Budget Act did not provide specific quotas for the Appropriations and Finance Committees.

Allen Schick concluded that the "most far-reaching dilution of Budget Committee power came as a by-product of the shift from coordinative to representative committees." If the Joint Committee recommendations had prevailed, the Budget Committees "would have operated as agents of the revenue and Appropriations Committees, not as independent power centers," and their position would have been strengthened "by the status of these powerful committees."[30] A coordinative approach might have forced the two money committees to keep spending and revenues in better balance, avoiding the extraordinary deficits of the decade following 1974.

The Joint Study Committee also wanted a tax surcharge imposed if receipts plus the "appropriate deficit" (as specified in the concurrent resolutions) did not equal estimated expenditures in the final concurrent resolution. The surcharge would not have been triggered unless the discrepancy exceeded one percent.[31] This procedure was omitted from the Budget Act.

The years since 1974 have not been characterized by close coordination between appropriations and revenues. The Budget Committees never recruited a staff capable of dealing with the jurisdiction of the tax committees, which consists of far more than revenues. Because of such programs as Social Security, Medicare, as well as interest on the public debt, the tax committees are responsible for as much spending as the Appropriations Committees. As late as 1982, Congressman Leon Panetta could testify that Congress had created "almost a hemorrhage" on the revenue side by adopting various tax credits and deductions: "We are just now beginning to look at the whole picture, and the whole picture includes revenues. . . . "[32] During the Reagan years, reconciliation became the means of reaching the expenditures within the jurisdiction of the tax committees. Over half of the spending reductions in the reconciliation acts of 1981 and 1982 were within the jurisdiction of the House Ways and Means Committee and the Senate Finance Committee.[33]

Control Backdoors

The Joint Study Committee expressed alarm about the "splintering" of the appropriations process. Of the spending estimated for fiscal 1974, the Committee reported that only 44 percent was associated with items to be considered in appropriations bills.[34] Even some of that amount was pro forma, since entitlement legislation required the Appropriations Committees to provide whatever amounts were necessary to meet legal obligations. Another form of backdoor spending was contract authority, which allowed agencies to obligate funds prior to receiving appropriations. The Appropriations Committees must later provide funds to "liquidate" these obligations. Congress passed the Budget Act shortly after the Clean Water Act of 1972, which provided $18 billion in contract authority over a three-year period. The third backdoor was borrowing authority, allowing agencies to borrow from the Treasury Department or from the public without coming to Congress for appropriations.

The Budget Act of 1974 placed controls on new backdoors. New forms of contract or borrowing authority would function essentially as ordinary authorizations. Agencies could not enter into obligations without an appropriation. Title IV of the Budget Act therefore puts new contract and borrowing authority through the front door. However, Title IV does not apply to certain types of spending authority which were exempted, such as 90 percent self-financed trust funds or outlays of government corporations. Entitlements, then, were given preferred treatment, even though the drafters of the Budget Act recognized that entitlements represented the most explosive growth area of the federal budget.[35]

Although the Budget Act has helped curb new backdoors, the growth of entitlement spending continued to undermine the position of the Appropriations Committees. In 1970 the Appropriations Committees had responsibility for two-thirds of gross outlays; other committees had responsibility for only one-third. The responsibility is now almost evenly divided. If we take into account the entitlements that are subject to annual appropriations, an exercise that is purely ministerial and mechanical on the part of the Appropriations Committees, the other committees are now responsible for more than half of budget outlays. The bulk of this consists of Social Security, Medicare, and interest on the public debt, which are within the jurisdiction of the tax committees.[36]

Debate Budget Priorities

The Joint Study Committee anticipated that its proposals would lead to "an improved congressional system for determining relative funding priorities."[37] One of the five declared purposes of the Budget Act is "to establish national budget priorities." To permit decision and debate on priorities, Congress adopted the system of functional categories used for decades by the executive branch.

Functional categories represented a compromise between the extremes of budget aggregates (total outlays and total budget authority) and specific line items for programs and projects. With the Budget Act it was contemplated that Congress would consider the budget in terms of 16 broad categories, such as national defense, income security, health, and agriculture. The number of functional categories has fluctuated over the years.

The choice of functional categories was partly compelled by political and practical considerations. To allocate the budget by committee jurisdiction might have exacerbated conflicts among committees. Functional categories blurred the lines, requiring "cross-walking" to convert functional allocations to committee jurisdiction. But the choice of functional categories came at a cost. For example, the functional category "Commerce and Transportation" is too broad and diffuse to allow a member of Congress to know whether the amount is too large or too small. Even the subfunctions (water transportation, ground transportation, and air transportation) are too abstract to permit reasoned debate over budget priorities. Members of Congress and their constituents do not think in such terms. Instead, the debates are framed in terms of mass transportation versus private automobiles, the deregulation of air fares, the cost of seatbelts and air bags, and other specific policy questions.

Functional categories have not provided a happy medium by which members can alter budget priorities. "Transfer amendments" (proposing that funds be taken from one functional category and placed in another) are rarely successful. Members seem to follow the time-honored principle: never openly do harm. Under the old system, budget priorities could be altered indirectly by reporting an appropriations bill with less than the administration wanted, while adding more to a different appropriations bill. Members could trim the defense appropriations bill and add to the Labor-HEW appropriations bill without ever explicitly taking money from one department and giving it to another.

In short, it might have been easier to change budget priorities under the older fragmented, decentralized system than under the Budget Act of 1974. In 1980 Allen Schick estimated that Congress did more reordering of budgetary priorities "before it had a budget process than it has since."[38] More recently he remarked that "the more Congress is organized to make redistributive decisions, the less capable it is of doing so."[39]

Enact Appropriations on Time; Eliminate Continuing Resolutions

In reporting the Budget Act, the House Committee on Rules said that one of the "visible disabilities of the existing congressional budget process is the failure to complete action on appropriations bills prior to the start of the new fiscal year." The legislative schedule would be even more demanding because of action on budget resolutions. The Committee concluded that the fiscal year would have to be moved forward by three months—from July 1 to October 1—"to put an end to the continuing resolution practice."[40] The Budget Act included this change for the fiscal year.

Part of the delay in passing appropriations was related to the growth of annual authorizations. To accelerate action on appropriations, the Joint Study Committee recommended that authorization bills be enacted a year in advance of appropriations.[41] Authorizing committees found this proposal unacceptable. As a substitute procedure, the House Rules Committee established a deadline of March 31 for the enactment of authorizing legislation, reserving for itself the consideration of waivers for emergency authorizations. Authorizing committees regarded this requirement as wholly unrealistic. As modified by the Senate and the conference committee, Section 402(a) of the Budget Act adopted a deadline of May 15 for reporting authorization bills. The Act also required passage of all regular appropriations bills by early September.

The conferees on the Budget Act believed that "in the future it will be necessary to authorize programs a year or more in advance of the period for which appropriations are to be made." They expected Congress to develop a pattern of advance authorizations for programs that would be authorized on an annual or multi-year basis.[42] In recent years there has been a push for biennial budgeting—particularly for authorization bills. Nevertheless, there has been no uniform trend toward advance authorizations or two-year authorizations. In fact, most of the direction has been toward shorter cycles: converting programs authorized on a permanent basis to a two-year cycle or moving two-year authorizations to an annual review.[43]

For the first few years after the Budget Act, the record of action on appropriations bills looked promising. For fiscal years 1977 and 1978, most of the appropriations were passed by the House in June and enacted by October 1. The record slipped a bit in fiscal 1979 and has grown worse ever since.[44] Before the Budget Act it was highly unusual if all twelve months of a fiscal year went by without passing the regular appropriations bills. It is now a common occurrence.[45] From fiscal 1968 through fiscal 1975, only two appropriations bills were under a continuing resolution for an entire fiscal year. From fiscal 1976 through fiscal 1985, that figure jumped to 27.[46]

Congress has fallen into the habit of placing entire appropriations bills in a continuing resolution. For example, the giant continuing resolution (P.L. 98-473) passed at the end of the 98th Congress contains the full text of five regular appropriations bills: Interior, Military Construction, Foreign Assistance, Defense, and Transportation. This is a phenomenon that is entirely post-1974.

The timetable is now far behind what it was before 1974, even with the additional three months gained by changing the fiscal year. The Appropriations Committees used to blame late authorizations for their failure to pass appropriations on time. Now they have a multitude of new explanations: late action on budget resolutions, late action on 302(a) and 302(b) allocations, and the deferred enrollment process. Appropriations bills are also delayed because of the prospect of contentious legislative riders on such issues as abortion, school prayer, and school busing.

To eliminate some of these excuses, the House of Representatives could resolve the present conflict between the Budget Act and House Rule XXI. The Act merely requires that authorizations be reported by May 15. Under House rules, appropriations bills may not be reported unless authorizations have been enacted. It would be helpful to allow appropriations bills to come to the floor after a certain date, such as June 1, regardless of progress on authorization bills and budget resolutions. The Appropriations Committees can be expected to stay within the dollar amounts recommended by authorizing committees in the most recent phase of their deliberations: committee markup, the reported bill, the bill passed by the House, or the amount provided in a conference report. A June 1 go-ahead date would encourage authorizing committees to move more quickly.

Independent Institutional Expertise

The Joint Study Committee recommended that the Budget Committees be provided with a joint staff headed by a legislative budget director. The director and the staff would be "highly trained, professional and nonpartisan" to give Congress "its own center of congressional budgetary operations. . . . "[47] The Budget Act created staffs for each of the Budget Committees, established the Congressional Budget Office, and directed the General Accounting Office to redouble its efforts on program evaluation. These steps were meant to offset the technical advantage of the Office of Management and Budget and the agencies.

The process established by the Budget Act supplies more information and a better understanding of macroeconomic developments, but improvements in these areas do not automatically translate into more responsible or intelligent decisions on the budget. Information can clarify; it can also confuse. Congressman John Dingell offered this observation in 1984:

> What we have done over the past decade is to create a budget process that is so complex as to be incomprehensible to almost everyone. Most of the members do not understand it beyond a superficial level. The press does not understand it. The business community does not understand it. The financial community does not understand it. And most important of all, the public does not understand it.[48]

The power of the purse is not merely a means by which Congress controls the executive branch. It is also the way the public controls government. Any process that confuses legislators and the public, no matter how much it may delight the conceptual dreams of technicians, is too costly for a democracy. In a critique of the obfuscation practiced by the legal community, Justice Cardozo warned that "justice is not there unless there is also understanding."[49] Similarly, without comprehension no budget process is worth maintaining.

The Budget Act has encouraged multi-year budgeting, an approach that began decades ago. Congress enacted legislation in 1956 to require five-year estimates by the executive branch.[50] The Legislative Reorganization Act of 1970 also required five-year estimates.[51] Congress discovered in 1980 that a multi-year approach was needed for reconciliation to prevent committees from meeting their assigned cuts by pushing costs from the current year to the next year. However, information needed for a multi-year focus can also foster irresponsibility. Instead of confronting reality in the current year and making hard choices, Congress can salve its conscience by concocting rosy projections for the outyears. These figures give members momentary peace of mind but never materialize. They are figments in the purest sense. Outyear projections invite procrastination. The aggregates required for a balanced budget are never in the current year, or upcoming year, but always three to five years out.

Control Presidential Impoundment

The Nixon administration's attempt to withhold appropriated funds sparked a series of confrontations during the 92d and 93d Congresses.[52] Members of Congress protested that the administration was using impoundment to substitute its sense of budget priorities for those enacted and funded by Congress. The Impoundment Control Act of 1974 (Title X of the Budget Act) narrows the president's authority to accumulate budgetary reserves. The Act recognizes two types of impoundment: rescissions and deferrals. If the president wants to rescind (cancel) budget authority, he must obtain the support of both houses within 45 days of continuous session. If he wants to merely delay the obligation of budget authority, either house could disapprove at any time.

This latter control, the one-house legislative veto, is now invalid as a result of the Supreme Court's decision in *INS* v. *Chadha* (1983). But Congress had already begun to disapprove deferrals by placing language in the regular or supplemental appropriations bills. Since this type of disapproval is included in a bill sent to the president for his signature, it is permissible under the Court's test.

The effect of Title X has been to regularize the impoundment process, giving the administration a solid base of legal support while allowing Congress to overturn deferrals it disagrees with. Significantly, the rescission process puts the burden on the president to secure the support of both houses within a limited number of days. Otherwise, the congressional priorities are to be respected and carried out.

Suggestions have been made in recent years to change the burden of the rescission process by requiring Congress to enact a joint resolution of disapproval to prevent the president from rescinding funds. Of course the president could veto the joint resolution, placing on Congress the additional burden of mustering a two-thirds majority in each house for the override. Besides altering the balance between the branches, this reform would entail multiple votes and extraordinary majorities to restate a budgetary choice already expressed in a duly enacted statute. Congress might have to act four times: enacting an appropriation bill which the president then vetoes; overriding the veto; passing a joint resolution to disapprove a rescission; and voting to override this veto. Members of Congress have regarded this repetition of a congressional preference as demeaning to their institution.[53]

Conclusions

Some of the objectives in 1974 could have been achieved without creating a complex procedure dependent on the passage of budget resolutions. Title IV has been effective in restricting new backdoors. Title X has been helpful in resolving impoundment disputes between Congress and the president. The Congressional Budget Office has established itself as a valuable agency for estimating the cost of pending legislation, performing scorekeeping tasks, and making macroeconomic projections.

Authorization bills have been speeded up somewhat because of the May 15 deadline for reporting. Congress could accelerate action on appropriations bills by allowing them to be reported for floor action after June 1. This change would resolve the present inconsistency between the Budget Act and House Rule XXI. A June 1 green light would make it possible to complete action on appropriations bills before the start of the fiscal year. As matters now stand, the delays resulting from the adoption of budget resolutions and Section 302 allocations make it practically impossible for Congress to complete action on other than a handful of appropriations bills by October 1.

What purpose is served by passing budget resolutions? They appear to encourage spending, delay appropriations, confuse the members and the public, and invite escapist, irresponsible budgeting. It is time to rethink the rationale behind budget resolutions and determine whether the liabilities far exceed the benefits. The risks are high when an inherently decentralized Congress tries to imitate the president by producing a budget. As Mark Kamlet and David Mowery warn:

The organizational requirements of comprehensive budgeting and fiscal policy formulation are quite different from those of representation, accessibility, and pluralism that have historically (although not consistently) been characteristic of Congress. The U.S. Congress is not an institution whose sole mission is the preparation of the annual budget; as such, it is unrealistic to expect Congress to adhere to the same complex procedures as those employed in the executive branch institutions whose primary responsibility is the preparation of the annual budget.[54]

Without budget resolutions, committees would not have to spend time producing March 15 reports; there would be more floor time to act on authorizing, appropriations, and tax bills; members would not have a reason to offer amendments to bring appropriations up to the ceiling provided by a budget resolution; and the phrases "below budget" and "above budget" would once again have meaning. Congressional performance could be scored unambiguously against a single benchmark: the president's budget.

As matters stand now, there is chronic confusion about which budget is the budget: the president's, the first budget resolution, the second budget resolution, the second budget resolution revised, or a succession of reestimates, updates, and revised baselines. Dozens of legislators are able to put together their own "budgets," complete with aggregates and breakdowns for functional categories. Elimination of budget resolutions might reinvigorate the president's budget, which has become increasingly irresponsible since 1974. It may well be that the politics of congressional budgeting has undermined the central tenet of the Budget and Accounting Act of 1921: the president's responsibility to submit and stand behind an executive budget.

Some members continue to support budget resolutions, despite misgivings about their contents, because they fear that a failure on the part of Congress to pass a resolution would send a signal to the country that Congress was incapable of controlling the budget. These fears might be misplaced. There is little evidence that the public (or even the "attentive public" or the "opinion leaders") have much more than a vague notion about the mechanics of the Budget Act. But the public can comprehend the bottom line: deficits of enormous size. Using the Budget Act to reduce the deficit from $200 billion to $150 billion a year will not be enough to win public support or confidence.

Doing away with budget resolutions need not return us to the Dark Ages (or to the "Old System"). Budget Committees can continue to monitor backdoors, issue "early warning reports" to alert Congress to budgetary excesses, and propose improvements in the budget process. The Budget Committees can be reshaped to perform as explicit agents of the party leadership. They could be made responsible for coordinating the spending decisions of the authorizing committees (entitlements), for coordinating appropriations and revenues, and exploring action needed in such areas as permanent appropriations, tax expenditures, federal credit, and off-budget agencies. Without having to propose and pass budget resolutions, the Budget Committees might play a more important role in recommending fiscal policy and pursuing multi-year strategies.

Notes

1. Congressional Budget Office, "Estimates of Federal Budget Outlays," Staff Working Paper, February 1978. See also CBO's "Analysis of the Shortfall in Federal Budget Outlays for Fiscal Year 1978," Staff Working Paper, March 1979, and House Committee on the Budget, "Federal Budget Outlay Estimates: A Growing Problem," Committee Print, April 1979.
2. U.S., Congress, House, H. Rept. No. 12, 95th Cong., 1st sess., 1977, p. 4.
3. *The Budget of the United States Government, Fiscal Year 1979* (Washington, D.C.: Government Printing Office, 1979), p. 3.
4. Ibid., p. 4.
5. H. Rept. No. 1456, 95th Cong., 2d sess., 1978, p. 12; U.S., Congress, Senate, S. Rept. No. 1124, 95th Cong., 2d sess., 1978, p. 13.
6. *The Budget of the United States Government, Fiscal Year 1980* (Washington, D.C.: Government Printing Office, 1980), p. 3.
7. H. Rept. No. 95, 96th Cong., 1st sess., 1979, p. 21.
8. 125 *Congressional Record* 9028 (1979).
9. 126 *Congressional Record* 8809 (1980).
10. H. Rept. No. 369, 97th Cong., 1st sess., 1981, p. 6.
11. House Committee on the Budget. "A Review of the Reconciliation Process," Committee Print (October, 1984), pp. 40–45.
12. 120 *Congressional Record* 19673 (1974).
13. 121 *Congressional Record* 36155 (1975).
14. S. Rept. No. 579, 93d Cong., 1st sess., 1973, p. 19.
15. See Whitten's statement in "Congressional Budget Process," *Hearings* before the House Committee on Rules, 97th Cong., 2d sess., 1982, pp. 311–12.
16. H. Rept. No. 1152, pt. 1, 98th Cong., 2d sess., 1984, p. 5.
17. John W. Ellwood, "Budget Control in a Redistributive Environment," in *Making Economic Policy in Congress,* Allen Schick, ed. (Washington, D.C.: American Enterprise Institute, 1983), p. 73.
18. Allen Schick, *Congress and Money* (Washington, D.C.: The Urban Institute, 1980), pp. 72–74; John M. Palffy, "The Congressional Budget Process," in *Mandate for Leadership II* (Washington, D.C.: Heritage Foundation, 1984), p. 388.
19. *Public Papers of the Presidents of the United States. Richard Nixon, 1972* (Washington, D.C.: Government Printing Office, 1974), p. 742.
20. Ibid., p. 964.
21. U.S., Congress, Senate, "Can Congress Control the Power of the Purse?", *Hearings* before the Senate Committee on the Budget, 95th Cong., 2d sess., 1978, p. 13.
22. "Congress Must Get Serious," *The Washington Post* (June 4, 1982), p. A19.
23. For more on the incentives for higher spending provided by the Budget Act, see Louis Fisher, "The Budget Act of 1974: A Further Loss of Spending Control," in W. Thomas Wander et al., *Congressional Budgeting: Politics, Process and Power* (Baltimore, Md.: Johns Hopkins University Press, 1984), pp. 170–189.
24. H. Rept. No. 147, 93d Cong., 1st sess., 1973, p. 1.
25. Ibid.
26. H. Rept. No. 1152, pt. 1, 98th Cong., 2d sess., 1984, p. 5.
27. Charles S. Konigsberg, "Amending the Congressional Budget Act of 1974," *Journal of Legislation* 11 (Winter 1984), p. 94.
28. H. Rept. No. 147, 93d Cong., 1st sess., 1973, p. 30.
29. U.S., Congress, House, "Congressional Budget Process," pt. 1, *Hearings* before the House Committee on Rules, 97th Cong., 2d sess., 1982, p. 239.
30. Schick, *Congress and Money,* p. 84.
31. H. Rept. No. 147, 1973, p. 7.
32. "Congressional Budget Process," pt. 1, *Hearings* before the House Committee on Rules, p. 27.
33. Ibid., p. 345.
34. H. Rept. No. 147, 1973, p. 10.
35. Ibid., pp. 12–13.
36. Statistics are provided by James L. Blum, Assistant Director for Budget Analysis in the Congressional Budget Office, reprinted in "Issue Presentations Before the Rules Committee Task Force on the Budget Process," prepared by the House Committee on Rules, 98th Cong., 2d sess., 1984, pp. 25–26.
37. H. Rept. No. 147, 1973, p. 4.
38. Schick, *Congress and Money,* p. 332.

39. Allen Schick, ed., *Making Economic Policy in Congress* (Washington, D.C.: American Enterprise Institute, 1983), p. 4.

40. H. Rept. No. 658, 93d Cong., 1st sess., 1973, p. 31.

41. H. Rept., No. 147, 1973, p. 30.

42. H. Rept. No. 1101, 93d Cong., 2d sess., 1974, p. 56.

43. Louis Fisher, "Annual Authorizations: Durable Roadblocks to Biennial Budgeting," *Public Budgeting & Finance* 3 (Spring 1983), pp. 25–30.

44. See the author's chart reprinted in "Issue Presentations Before the Rules Committee Task Force on the Budget Process," p. 81.

45. Ibid., p. 83.

46. H. Rept. No. 1152, pt. 1, 98th Cong., 2d sess., 1984, p. 43.

47. H. Rept. No. 147, 1973, p. 3.

48. "Congressional Budget Process," *Hearings* before the House Committee on Rules, 1984, p. 161.

49. Anon Y. Mous, "The Speech of Judges: A Dissenting Opinion," *Virginia Law Review,* 29 (1943), p. 638.

50. 70 Stat. 652 (1956).

51. 84 Stat. 1140, 1169 (sec. 221), 1173-74 (sec. 252) (1970).

52. Louis Fisher, *Presidential Spending Power* (Princeton: University Press, 1975), pp. 175–201.

53. See remarks by Senator Sam Ervin, Jr., 119 *Congressional Record* 15236 (1973).

54. Mark S. Kamlet and David C. Mowery, "The First Decade of the Congressional Budget Act: Legislative Imitation and Adaptation in Budgeting," unpublished manuscript, January 1985, p. 18.

13

Deficit Politics and Constitutional Government: The Impact of Gramm-Rudman-Hollings

Lance T. LeLoup
Barbara Luck Graham
Stacey Barwick
University of Missouri at St. Louis

The 1985 Balanced Budget and Emergency Deficit Control Act, known as Gramm-Rudman-Hollings or simply as Gramm-Rudman, is one of the most controversial and misunderstood acts of Congress in recent years. It not only proposed fixed deficit targets and required mandatory budget cuts if targets were not met, but included the most far-reaching changes in congressional budget procedures since the passage of the Budget and Impoundment Control Act of 1974. It also raised serious constitutional issues of separation of powers and the relative roles of Congress and the president in guiding the fiscal affairs of the nation. Despite the fact that the law's rapid passage and tumultuous first year provide limited grounds for generalization, we believe that Gramm-Rudman is more than an isolated event. It can be understood more accurately as the most dramatic in a series of procedural adaptations by a frustrated Congress in response to increasing policy and political constraints.

In an article published in the Autumn 1986 volume of this journal, Harry Havens reviewed the origins of Gramm-Rudman, the deficit reduction machinery, and the actual sequester of $11.7 billion in early 1986.[1] In this article, we address an overlapping but essentially different set of issues: the relationship of the adoption of the law to recent political and fiscal trends, constitutional issues surrounding the role of Congress and the president, and the impact of the law on Congress itself. We review the emergence

Source: Public Budgeting & Finance (Spring 1987): 83–103. Reprinted by permission.

and the passage of the bill in 1985, mandatory deficit reduction and budget process changes, budget politics in 1986, and the effect of court decisions on Gramm-Rudman. We conclude by assessing the impact of Gramm-Rudman, considering both the short-term prospects for change as well as possible long-term consequences of the law. We begin by examining the changes in national budgeting over the past decades that created the context for such an experiment to be launched.

Increasing Constraints and Growing Instability in the Congressional Budget Process

For half a century the congressional appropriations process was a model of stability and predictability.[2] Since the late 1960s, however, congressional decisions on taxing and spending have been characterized by instability, adaptation, and experimentation. The Budget and Impoundment Control Act of 1974 was the major statutory change, but budgeting procedures have remained in flux in subsequent years. Gramm-Rudman is the most radical experiment. Congressional performance in budgeting over the past two decades can be explained on the basis of several theoretical factors: the behavioral motivations of members of Congress, perceptions of constitutional imbalance between legislative and executive branches, and fundamental changes in the structure of the budget itself. A full examination of these factors is beyond the scope of this study, but attention to some of the underlying forces is essential to understand deficit reduction efforts.

Gramm-Rudman-Hollings emerged as a result of increasing political and policy constraints that have destabilized the budget process, particularly in Congress. Policy constraints have increased the pressure on the legislature while narrowing members' discretion. The result has been procedural instability: changes in rules, timing, voting alignments, committee roles, leadership actions, and coalition building strategies. Ultimately, we believe, these political and policy constraints led a frustrated Congress to try a mandatory process in an attempt to check burgeoning budget deficits. Four constraints in particular served to reduce flexibility and help explain the volatility in congressional budgeting.

1. *Growing inflexibility caused by changes in budget composition.* Changes in the composition of the budget, the growth of entitlements and multiyear spending commitments have rendered the federal budget increasingly inflexible for decision makers.[3] These well-documented changes in the composition of the budget created both political and technical constraints. With outlays composed largely of social security, health entitlements, interest on the debt, and a growing defense share, the range of expenditures available for annual manipulation has been sharply reduced. The shrinkage in the 1980s of the so-called nondefense discretionary portion of the budget from 25 percent to around 17 percent has exacerbated the situation. Not only does a smaller component remain to be cut, but congressional resolve not to make further domestic spending cuts has hardened.

2. *The increasing vulnerability of budget totals to changes in aggregate economic performance.* National budgeting has increasingly become a multiyear process based on projections and estimates. Budget totals are increasingly vulnerable to changes in aggregate economic performance. For example, a decrease in annual GNP growth of one percent below the estimate can increase deficits by a total of $90 billion in five years. Estimation errors between projected and actual economic growth since 1976 have averaged 1.15 percent for OMB and .98 percent for CBO.[4] Difficult cuts achieved at high political costs can evaporate overnight when aggregate economic performance and the resulting budget baselines are reestimated.

3. *Historically large, chronic structural budget deficits.* The deficits themselves have become the dominant policy constraint. The five year revenue loss from the Economic Recovery Tax Act of 1981 (ERTA) of $635 billion was not compensated by expenditure reductions, leading to the chronic structural budget deficits that ensued. By late 1981 economic and budget projections revealed rapidly growing outyear deficits exacerbated by a recession. Table 1 compares deficit estimates in the presidential and congressional budgets with actual deficits. Congress and the president found themselves chasing a moving target as actual deficits consistently exceeded policy expectations. The growing deficits and decreasing flexibility in spending and revenue totals began a series of ad hoc budget process changes in the 1980s.

4. *Actions taken by the president to reduce congressional options.* The actions of the president in the 1980s increased policy inflexibility, further exacerbating procedural instability in congressional budgeting. While the proposals and the pronouncements of the president have long been recognized as a key determinant of congressional decision making,[5] the establishment of tight presidential parameters in concert with deficits, problematic economic projections, and growing outlay inflexibility created a uniquely restrictive setting for congressional budgeting in the 1980s. Instead of maintaining an active budgetary role throughout his presidency, after 1981 Ronald Reagan engaged in a series of changing political strategies, varying levels of White House participation in an attempt to achieve administration objectives.[6] Using the executive budget, the veto threat, and other actions, the president established additional constraints prior to congressional consideration, most notably a fixed rate of real growth for defense and a nonnegotiable stance on revenue increases. While the president, like the congress, is subject to the limitations imposed by structural deficits and mandatory spending, the Reagan administration was more concerned about long-term ideological goals than the deficits. Congress, more short-term oriented, struggled with its procedures and processes in an attempt to control the deficits.

In the face of these growing political and policy constraints, the congressional budget process showed the signs of strain. Because the budget process created by the 1974 Budget Act remained unpopular with many members of Congress, particularly key committee chairs, reformers were leary of formally revising the law. As a result, much of the procedural adaptation in the 1980s was informal but highly significant. Perhaps most important was the shift of reconciliation towards the beginning of the procedure and its institutionalization as a regular part of the budget process.[7] In addition, the second concurrent resolution which had proved to be ineffectual, was effectively dropped after 1982. Provisions were added to the first resolution specifying that it would become binding if no second resolution was passed.

While these two changes may arguably be seen as strengthening the process, many of the procedural developments clearly reflected an unraveling of the process.[8] Supplemental appropriations were

Table 1
Comparison of annual deficits ($ billions)

FY	President's Budget	Binding Congressional Budget Resolution	Actual
1986	180.00	171.90	220.70
1985	180.40	181.20	212.30
1984	188.80	169.90	185.30
1983	91.50	103.90	195.40
1982	45.00	37.65	110.60
1981	15.80	27.40	57.90
1980	29.00	29.80	59.60
1979	60.60	38.80	27.70
1978	57.75	61.25	48.80
1977	43.00	50.60	44.90
1976	51.90	74.10	66.50

Source: Congressional Research Service: Congressional Budget Office, 1986.

increasingly used to avoid discipline or replace cuts. Fewer appropriations bills were passed on time, leading some to conclude that the situation was worse than it had been before 1974. As a result, more spending bills, both authorizations and appropriations, were lumped together in huge omnibus packages. These massive spending bills not only invited nongermane amendments of every description, but were increasingly difficult to pass. Shutdown of the federal government often seemed to be the only way to break an impasse. Some authorization bills were never passed, leading to an increase in appropriations not authorized by law, a violation of House and Senate rules.[9] Finally, procedural controls and enforcement mechanisms seemed to weaken while waivers to the budget act increased.

Leaders in the House and Senate continued to complain about the constant budget and deficit crises while considering ways to improve congressional control. Numerous committees and task forces reviewed the budget process and recommended changes. Perhaps the most comprehensive review of the congressional budget process was conducted by Representative Anthony Beilenson (D-CA) whose House Rules Committee Task Force recommended a comprehensive revision.[10] Those recommendations, largely ignored in 1984, would prove important when Congress struggled with Gramm-Rudman-Hollings the next year.

Despite dissatisfaction with the budget process, Congress actually made substantial budget cuts in the 1980s. Although deficits remained in the $200 billion range, without several major budget-tightening measures passed in the 1980s, deficits would have been in the $300 billion range. These difficult and divisive decisions only heightened frustration. Greater attention to macrobudgeting, shifting strategies, and informal changes in the budget process had failed to dent the deficit problem. Late in the session in 1985 a group of Senators fixed upon an idea to force deficit reduction, finally making it the top priority of Congress.

Deficit Politics: Forging a Mandatory Solution

The Original Gramm-Rudman-Hollings Plan

When Senators Phil Gramm (R-TX), Warren Rudman (R-NH), and Ernest Hollings (D-SC) introduced their mandatory budget-balancing amendment to the debt ceiling extension (H.J.Res. 372) on 25 September 1985, they probably did not anticipate the degree to which the issue would dominate Congress for the rest of the year. As the deficit continued to grow and the budget stalemate of 1985 dragged into late summer, both Rudman and Gramm's staffs were working on extraordinary methods of forcing deficit reductions. Hollings had long advocated a budget "freeze" as a means to control the deficit. Coordinating their efforts, they fell in line behind Gramm's proposal for fixed deficit targets and a mandatory sequester—across-the-board cuts—if Congress failed to meet those targets on their own. Congress had five years to reduce the deficit to zero.

The philosophy of the mandatory approach, as explained by the sponsors, was not actually to resort to indiscriminate cuts. Rather, the process was to serve as a forcing mechanism, creating such an unattractive alternative that Congress would reach deficit targets on their own. In case they did not, the sponsors found the automatic cuts preferable to huge deficits.

The Gramm-Rudman-Hollings amendment had several other key provisions. It exempted social security from automatic cuts, but specified that half of the cuts would come from entitlements and other federal retirement programs. The other half would come from other programs including defense procurement. The amendment called for changing the congressional budget process, advancing the timetable, and attempting to increase enforcement mechanisms. Finally, the plan specified a process to trigger automatic cuts based on estimates made jointly by OMB and CBO.

Deficit reduction was an issue no one could be against. Although many senators were suspicious of such a mechanical approach, Senator Gramm had found a legislative vehicle—the debt ceiling extension—that had to pass the Senate. Several years earlier, the House had adopted a plan whereby the debt limit was extended automatically as part of the budget resolution. In the Senate, however, separate legislation was needed to enable the federal government to borrow to meet its obligations. The sponsors did not intend to allow a debt extension without their deficit reduction plan.

Despite the mixed reviews received by this plan, leaders quickly recognized its unstoppable political momentum. Democratic Senators Robert Byrd (D-WV), the minority leader, and Lawton Chiles (D-FL), the ranking minority member on the Budget Committee, offered an alternative that would reach the deficit targets by equal amounts of defense cuts, domestic cuts, and tax increases.[11] When this alternative failed to gain support, they worked with Majority Leader Robert Dole (R-KS) and Budget Committee Chair Peter Domenici (R-NM) to make the original amendment more palatable. In a comment to reporters he later regretted making, Senator Rudman called his bill, "a bad idea whose time has come." This seemed to sum up well the reaction of most senators who on October 9 approved it by a vote of 75–24.[12]

The House Response

Across the rotunda in the House of Representatives, the dominant reaction of majority Democrats was frustration and anger. Animosity towards Phil Gramm, who had helped orchestrate Reagan's 1981 budget plan before he switched parties, remained high. Many members felt that the plan allowed the president to avoid all responsibility for the deficits. Some felt their own Democratic leaders had failed to seize the initiative on deficits and had been left completely on the defensive. Serious opposition to the Gramm-Rudman-Hollings plan centered on several key elements:

The programs subject to automatic cuts. Opponents felt that the plan as passed by the Senate was unfair and unbalanced because cuts would fall disproportionately on domestic social programs. Few were anxious to throw social security into the pool of vulnerable programs, but felt that revenues and other exempt programs should be considered for reducing the deficit as well.

The impact on defense. The actual share of cuts to be levied on defense was in dispute. Members feared that cuts would be "irrational," shielding slow-spending weapons procurement while damaging fast-spending categories such as personnel, operations, and maintenance. If the president declared a national security emergency to avoid defense cuts, it was not clear whether the cuts would be made up on the domestic side.

The impact on the economy. The original amendment provided that in the case of a recession (negative or no real growth for four consecutive quarters), the automatic cuts would not take effect. Opponents, however, felt this exemption was inadequate and would eliminate the ability of the government to use discretionary fiscal policy to manage the economy.

The power of the president. Opponents feared that one result of the plan was a massive transfer of budgetary power from the Congress to the president. While proponents disputed this charge, it was uncertain in the original amendment exactly how much discretion the president would have.

The constitutionality of the plan. Members questioned if it was constitutional for one Congress to bind the hands of future Congresses—whether it was within the doctrine of separation of powers for the legislature to pass a law mandating that the executive make certain cuts. It was also not certain that if part of the law were determined to be unconstitutional, other parts would remain operative.

Despite the concerns, having extended the debt ceiling two months earlier, the House opted to move directly to conference with the Senate. House leaders agreed in principle with some form of automatic cuts; so it was clear from early October 1985 on that some sort of dramatic new process would be enacted. The first conference convened on October 16 amidst vast publicity and high levels of emotion. It was a strange reversal of the legislative process. Gramm-Rudman had never been subjected to legislative hearings or committee markup; the conference was the first opportunity to examine some of the details of the plan. House leaders appointed forty-eight conferees to negotiate with the nine Senate managers.

The speed with which Gramm-Rudman appeared on the political landscape not only caught the House unprepared, but the White House as well. The administration quickly endorsed the concept, but various officials expressed reservations. OMB Director James Miller raised several constitutional issues in his appearance before the committee while supporting the basic approach. Secretary of Defense Caspar Weinberger was less enthusiastic, indicating that he had grave doubts about the impact of Gramm-Rudman on national defense. "We can't have our defense and our security policy be a total prisoner of a rigid formula designed to reduce the budget."[13] Nonetheless, on the highly charged issue of the deficit, the administration was in no better position to oppose Gramm-Rudman than the House Democrats.

The conference committee was simply too large to resolve the divisive issues. As the negotiators remained in deadlock at the end of October, facing default by the government on November 1, each set of conferees reported separate versions back to their respective houses. The House passed its own version of a mandatory deficit reduction plan in a near party-line vote of 249–140.[14] Even liberal Democratic members who opposed the plan voted for it to prevent passage of the Senate version. The House version altered the deficit targets and allowed fewer cuts if real economic growth slipped below an annual rate of three percent. The Senate adopted a revised version of its own. Concerned over the constitutional role of CBO, the revised Senate plan introduced the Comptroller General of the GAO into the trigger process to certify the OMB/CBO figures and issue final sequester instructions to the president.

Although each body continued to insist on its own version, the partisan rhetoric obscured the fact that the House and Senate already were in agreement on the broad outlines and most of the details of mandatory deficit reduction. This was particularly true of the far-reaching changes in the congressional budget process which had been included in the legislation. Many of the recommendations of the Beilenson plan had been incorporated into both versions. With imminent threats of government default and headlines about draconian budget cuts, these important procedural developments were largely overlooked. Differences between the House and Senate remained on protection of medicare, the FY 86 deficit target, the technical question of whether deficit targets would be scored on budget authority or outlays, and the severability of any unconstitutional portion of the new process.

Compromise and Final Passage

As the next date for default, November 15, neared, and as President Reagan prepared to leave for Geneva to meet Soviet leader Mikhail Gorbachev, combatants on both sides agreed to yet another temporary extension of borrowing authority. The treasury calculated that the next default would occur on December 12. Following the early November votes, a second, smaller conference was appointed. Most of the real progress was made, however, by a select group of negotiators working behind closed doors. House Majority Whip Thomas Foley (D-WA), House Democratic Caucus Chair Richard Gephardt (D-MO), Senate Finance Chair Robert Packwood (R-OR), and Senate Budget Chair Domenici hammered out the key compromises. The break in the impasse came when Senate negotiators offered to split mandatory cuts equally between defense and domestic programs. House leaders accepted and in turn agreed to delay the FY 86 cuts until March and backed off on their insistence that if any part of the bill was found to be unconstitutional, the entire process would be negated. They also agreed to the role of GAO, which many believed would solve the constitutional separation of powers issue raised by the involvement of CBO. Although a few difficult issues remained, the deadlock had been broken.

House Democrats were reassured when conferees agreed that if defense cuts were blocked by the president for national security reasons, no cuts would be made in other programs. On December 11 both chambers approved the compromise plan. After a full day of floor debate, the Senate approved by a

61–31 margin.[15] While proponents continued to extoll the virtues of the plan, opponents like Senator Patrick Moynihan (D-NY) called the bill a "suicide pact." After Senate passage, the House approved by a 271–154 vote; 153 Republicans and 118 Democrats voted for the bill.[16] The next day, despite some apparent misgivings, President Reagan signed the bill, noting that it was "an important step toward putting our fiscal house in order." Just hours after the bill was signed into law, Representative Mike Synar (D-OK) filed suit in federal district court for the District of Columbia challenging the constitutionality of the law. He would later be joined in the suit by a dozen other members and a public employees union, and still later, found his challenge supported by the United States Justice Department.

The Balanced Budget and Emergency Deficit Control Act of 1985

Gramm-Rudman-Hollings,[17] as finally passed by Congress and signed by the president, retained the fundamental forcing mechanism devised by the sponsors. It set maximum deficit levels in both the executive and legislative budget of $171.9 billion in FY 86, $144 billion in FY 87, $108 billion in FY 88, $72 billion in FY 89, $36 billion in FY 90, and no deficit by FY 91. If the estimated deficit exceeded the targets by more than $10 billion, the mandatory sequester process would take effect. A special time-table and procedures were provided for FY 86 as well as a limit on the total amount that could be sequestered.

Revision of the Congressional Budget Process

Table 2 shows the revised budget and deficit reduction timetable that went into effect in 1986 for FY 87 and subsequent years. Advancing the time-table, moving reconciliation to the beginning of the process, dropping the second budget resolution, and strengthening enforcement procedures in both chambers were among the most important procedural changes. The changes promised to continue the uncertainty in the relative powers and responsibilities of the money committees in Congress.

Key dates from the submission of the president's budget to the passage of spending bills were advanced. Perhaps the most important changes were the April 15 date for passage of the first resolution, the June 15 date for reconciliation, and the June 30 date for appropriations bills. The May 15 deadline for reporting authorizations, long an irritant to the standing

Table 2

Revised budget and deficit reduction process under Gramm-Rudman-Hollings

Action	To Be Completed By
President submits budget	Monday after January 3
CBO report to Congress	February 15
Committees submit views and estimates to budget committees	February 25
Senate Budget Committee reports budget resolution	April 1
Congress passes budget resolution	April 15
House Appropriations Committee reports appropriations bills	June 10
Congress passes reconciliation bill	June 15
House passes all appropriations bills	June 30
Initial economic, revenue, outlay and deficit projections made by OMB and CBO	August 15
OMB and CBO report tentative contents of sequester order to GAO	August 20
GAO issues deficit and sequester report to the president	August 25
President issues sequester order	September 1
Fiscal year begins and sequester order takes effect	October 1
OMB and CBO issues revised projections based on subsequent congressional action	October 5
GAO issues revised sequester report to president	October 10
Final sequester order becomes effective	October 15
GAO issues compliance report on sequester order	November 15

Source: Balanced Budget and Emergency Deficit Control Act of 1985.

committees, was eliminated altogether. In an attempt to force themselves to meet the deadline, Congress adopted language that attempted to prevent adjournment for the Independence Day holiday if action on spending bills was not completed.

In addition to advancing the timetable, Congress attempted to strengthen enforcement of budget reduction requirements to facilitate the goal of deficit reduction. First, totals and subtotals in the budget resolution were made binding as opposed to targets under the old process. Second, committees are given ten days to publish their internal allocations of outlays, budget authority, entitlements, and credit among its subcommittees (Section 302(b)). Legislation emanating from committees that have not done so are made subject to a point of order on the floor. This requirement allows the Budget Committees and party leaders to more closely monitor compliance with overall totals. Third, no legislation providing new budget, entitlement, or credit authority may come to the floor until a budget resolution is passed. Exempt from this constraint are bills taking effect in the next fiscal year, and House appropriations bills after May 15. Fourth, no budget resolution is in order in either house of Congress if it would exceed the maximum allowable deficit. Fifth, legislation from any committee—even committees that have made their 302(b) allocations—may be subject to a point of order if it would cause the committee's allocation to be exceeded. In the House, budget, credit, and entitlement authority are covered. In the Senate, this is applied to budget authority and to estimated outlays. Finally, in the Senate, waivers of these restrictions can only be adopted with a three-fifths majority vote. In the House, waivers of conference reports, budget resolutions or reconciliation bills exceeding targets must also receive a three-fifths majority. All other provisions may be waived by a simple majority in the House.

With the exception of exempting social security and moving it "off-budget," Gramm-Rudman-Hollings moved to make the federal budget more comprehensive and realistic. Previously off-budget entities were moved on-budget; credit authority in the form of direct and guaranteed loans were made part of the president's budget. Social security, while excluded from overall totals, is included for purposes of calculating the deficit.

On the surface, the revisions of the budget process accomplished through the passage of the Gramm-Rudman plan appear to strengthen and further centralize congressional taxing and spending decisions. Both budget committees would appear to have increased their power relative to authorizing and appropriations committees. As experience with congressional budgeting in recent years has indicated, however, it takes more than legislation to change procedures and power bases in Congress. Spending committees found many ways to circumvent restrictions under the previous system. Actual enforcement continues to depend on the will of House and Senate to use the parliamentary procedures made available to them.

The Deficit Reduction Process

House Democrats had wanted to make cuts in the FY 86 budget immediately after adoption primarily for anticipated shock value. They finally conceded this point in conference, agreeing to postpone the first cuts to 1 March 1986, and capping the total reductions. As a result, Gramm-Rudman spelled out a separate process and timetable for FY 86 and one for subsequent years. Only 7/12s of the excess deficit could be sequestered up to the maximum of $11.7 billion dollars in 1986, because only 7 months of the fiscal year remained.

The act specifies how an excess deficit is determined and the procedures for reducing it. A joint OMB/CBO report is issued in August, estimating the deficit for the coming fiscal year based on assumptions specified in the law. The Comptroller General was required under the original law to review the data, assumptions, and methodologies of the report, making a final determination of the figures in the joint OMB/CBO report.

If an excess deficit is identified, the president is required by September 1 to issue a sequestration order. The law as enacted allowed the president no flexibility in determining cuts except for a limited number of defense accounts in 1986.[18] The deficit timetable provides a month that allows, but does not require, Congress to achieve the required reductions by some other means. OMB, CBO, and GAO revise their budget and deficit estimates based on any subsequent congressional action, and GAO issues the final report to the president by October 10. The president's final sequester order goes into effect by October 15. The Comptroller General reports to Congress on compliance with the order by mid-November.

Allocating and Calculating
the Reductions

Gramm-Rudman introduced the concept of "budgetary resources" to describe the budget, entitlement, and borrowing authority on which outlays are based. Since mandatory reductions are triggered by outlays, which are not directly controlled by Congress, the sequester order, must reduce budgetary resources to lower outlays by the requisite amount. Unobligated defense balances were made subject to sequestration.

As agreed in conference committee, half of the total reduction would come from defense, the rest from all other programs. Exempt programs include: interest; social security; railroad retirement; veterans' compensation and pensions; aid to families with dependent children (AFDC); supplemental security income (SSI); women, infants, children (WIC); child nutrition; food stamps; medicaid; and several other trust and claims payments and funds. Special rules for making reductions were written for unemployment, federal pay, student loans, child support enforcement, foster care and adoption assistance, and the Commodity Credit Corporation (CCC). Programs with automatic spending increases could be reduced only to the extent of reducing or abolishing the cost of living adjustments (COLAs). Percent limits on cuts were applied to health programs: medicare, veterans' medical care, community health, migrant health, and Indian health facilities and services. The controversial medicare cuts were limited to 1 percent in FY 86 and 2 percent in subsequent years.

Defense reductions are made by first calculating the savings achieved by abolishing military retirement COLAs which occur in the nondefense portion of the budget but are counted in the defense half of the cuts under Gramm-Rudman. The remaining cuts are made by computing a fixed percentage reduction in defense outlays from new budget authority and unobligated balances. Outlays from prior obligations, about 40 percent, are not subject to sequestration.

The Balanced Budget and Emergency Deficit Control Act of 1985 attempted to provide an alternative to budget stalemate. A speedier budget process with more enforcement muscle replaced the ten-year-old congressional budget process to help Congress reach its goal of a balanced budget. Yet the future of the plan very much depended on the courts, the economy, the president, and how Congress would adapt to the new requirements.

Implementing Gramm-Rudman-Hollings in 1986

As members returned to begin the second session of the 99th Congress, OMB, CBO, and GAO had already begun preparing estimates of the deficit reductions that would have to be made in the FY 86 budget. Committees geared up to attempt to meet the new deadlines in the revised congressional budget process. It was to be a session where Gramm-Rudman affected almost every operation of Congress.

Making Mandatory Reductions
for FY 86

Economic and budget projections in January of 1986 confirmed that the deficit that year would exceed $220 billion—far above the fixed target in Gramm-Rudman. CBO and OMB each reported their version of the cuts on January 15, filling an entire volume of the Federal Register.[19] GAO resolved the relatively minor differences between the two estimates. On February 5 the House rejected a Republican resolution to force Congress to come up with an alternative to avoid the mandatory cuts, insuring that the new deficit reduction process would go into effect.

Harry Havens has carefully documented how the fiscal 1986 cuts were calculated using the methods described in the previous section.[20] Details of that process and the actual cuts are not reported here, but several factors bear special attention. When exempt and partially exempt programs were removed from the calculations, only 20 percent of outlays were subjected to the across-the-board cuts. The cuts fell heavily on defense personnel, operations and maintenance, procurement and research accounts. On the domestic side, cuts fell on education, health, housing, natural resources, and the activities of independent agencies. The across-the-board cuts were 4.9 percent in defense accounts and 4.3 percent in domestic accounts. Potential mandatory cuts in the FY 87 budget would be even more severe. CBO estimated that under their February estimate for a deficit of $166.6 billion, cuts for FY 87 would be 6.2 percent for defense and 8.4 percent for domestic programs. If the economy performed worse than expected, however, the deficit could rise to $194 billion requiring cuts of 14.2 percent in defense and 20.9 percent in domestic spending.[21]

On February 7 a three-judge federal district court panel ruled the automatic trigger provision of the Gramm-Rudman-Hollings law unconstitutional because of the role of GAO. The lower court finding, however, cast further doubt among members about the viability of the process. Standing committees struggled to meet the new February 25 date for views and estimates to meet the earlier deadline for the budget resolution. And on 1 March 1986, cuts totaling $11.7 billion were ordered for the programs not exempted from the Gramm-Rudman scalpel.

Effects on the Congressional Budget Process

One of the first test votes on the enhanced enforcement capability under Gramm-Rudman came in March when the Senate voted 61–33 not to exempt additional loans for farmers from the Gramm-Rudman restrictions.[22] The Senate Budget Committee moved quickly under the new timetable, reporting a budget on March 19 that differed significantly from the president's. Its inclusion of significant new revenues evoked quick opposition from the White House. The Budget Committee's report was to be the last semblance of timeliness in what would become a year of missed deadlines. As April 15 passed, the new date for the concurrent resolution on the budget to be adopted, the Senate had taken no floor action. The House Budget Committee prepared its own version while waiting for the Senate to act. With bipartisan support, Senate leaders passed a $1 trillion budget on May 2, despite White House opposition. The Senate budget projected a deficit of $144 billion, the exact Gramm-Rudman target.

One of the key effects of Gramm-Rudman-Hollings became apparent during Senate consideration of the 1987 budget and the sweeping tax reform package. The new larger majorities required to waive provisions of the budget act combined with additional restrictions created the need for "offsets." This effectively meant that all amendments offered on the floor had to be "deficit neutral": increased spending had to be compensated by outlay reductions or revenue increases somewhere else. While not eliminating all amendments, this had a dramatic impact on Senate floor procedures, making it much more difficult to amend either the budget or the tax bill.

The House followed its own tradition of partisan budgets when it adopted a budget resolution specifying a deficit of $137 billion, savings were based on sharp cuts in defense and some modest revenue increases. While funding increased for selected social programs, President Reagan labeled the House version a "radical anti-defense budget."[23] Gramm-Rudman proved to be a mixed blessing for the president and a formidable weapon for House and Senate leaders. Because of the 50–50 split in mandatory defense and domestic spending, failure to reach an alternative package of cuts would result in even greater defense cuts. Senate leaders linked acceptance of some tax increases with continuation of the president's desired defense buildup. In conference, however, House Democratic negotiators refused to approve additional revenues without some sign of acceptance from the White House. The result was a deadlock that left the congressional budget process stalled.

Despite the breakdown of the revised timetable, Gramm-Rudman was having a significant effect on committees. The appropriations committees in particular found themselves under greater restrictions than in the past.[24] Under the 302(b) allocations, unlike past practice, the full appropriations committees could not adjust subtotals internally to keep within the overall cap. This increased conflict within subcommittees during markup. Scoring the deficit on outlays, not budget authority, had a noticeable effect on the appropriations committees. Senate appropriations are subject to a point of order if their bills exceed outlay allocations, and House leaders tried to enforce the same procedure. This hit defense appropriations particularly hard because of differences in the rate that programs convert budget authority into outlays. The revised budget process seemed to give the budget committees and party leaders greater control over the appropriations committees because of the specificity of the 302(b) allocations. It also precluded the president's using the sympathetic defense authorization and appropriations process to override cuts made by the budget committees.

With no budget resolution, the June 15 deadline for reconciliation was missed and it was obvious that no spending bills would be passed by June 30. The new prohibition against recessing for the Independence Day holiday in this case was quietly waived on June 19 by the Congress. House and

Senate conferees finally reached a compromise, and on June 26 enacted the budget resolution for FY 87. It envisioned a deficit of $142.6 billion based on outlays of $995 billion and revenues of $852 billion. Most of the budget savings came from defense, some $28 billion below the president's request. Congress had given in to the president on taxes but placed deficit reduction over defense. As members left Washington for the Fourth of July, spending bills, reconciliation, and extension of the debt ceiling all remained. Before they would return, the Supreme Court would settle some of the constitutional issues surrounding the controversial deficit reduction law.

Gramm-Rudman-Hollings and the Courts: The Constitutional Flaw

The deficit reduction plan raised constitutional questions from the start. The key question presented to the courts was whether certain provisions of the Gramm-Rudman-Hollings Act were constitutional under the principle of separation of powers. This doctrine, more accurately described as one of separated institutions sharing powers, creates indistinct boundary lines that permit each branch of government to participate to some degree in the principal activities of the others. In the 1970s, the Supreme Court adopted a more relaxed interpretation of the separation of powers principle.[25] However, in *INS* v. *Chadha* (1983), the Court employed a formalistic model of separation of powers in striking down the legislative veto. This strict interpretation was again utilized in the case of *Bowsher* v. *Synar* decided on 7 July 1986.[26] Despite some sweeping constitutional issues, the finding that Gramm-Rudman violated the Constitution was restricted to a narrow, technical question: whether Congress has chosen the wrong official to carry out the trigger function of the mandatory budget cuts.

Both Congress and the executive expressed doubts about the constitutionality of the automatic trigger mechanism.[27] Anticipating an immediate challenge to the act, a fallback procedure was added to take effect in the event that any of the reporting procedures described in the law were invalidated. The fallback procedure called for the report prepared by the directors of OMB and CBO to be submitted to the Temporary Joint Committee on Deficit Reduction instead of the Comptroller General. This committee, composed of the entire membership of the budget committees of both houses of Congress, must report a joint resolution in five days to both Houses. Congress then must "certify" the cuts by voting on the resolution under special rules. The resolution, if passed and signed by the president, serves as the basis for the presidential sequestration order.

The District Court Challenge: *Synar* v. *United States*[28]

A special three-judge district court panel was convened in early 1986 to consider three principal issues:[29] (1) whether the plaintiffs had standing to challenge Gramm-Rudman, (2) whether the Gramm-Rudman-Hollings Act violated the delegation doctrine, and (3) whether the role of the Comptroller General in the deficit reduction process violated the doctrine of separation of powers. In a unanimous *per curiam* decision the District Court held that the plaintiffs had standing to challenge certain provisions of the Gramm-Rudman-Hollings Act.[30] However, the court found that the section of the act that delegated the Comptroller General broad power in the deficit reduction process was unconstitutional because he can be removed by Congress. The court observed that the Comptroller General, while appointed by the president and confirmed by the Senate, is removable not only by impeachment but also by joint resolution of Congress for specified causes.[31] According to the court, the purpose of the removal provision was to make the Comptroller General, an officer of the legislative branch, subservient to Congress. Under separation of powers, the court concluded that Congress may not retain the power of removal of an officer performing executive functions. On this point, the court recognized that

> Once an officer is appointed, it is only the authority that can remove him, and not the authority that appointed him, that he must fear and, in the performance of his functions, obey. Giving such power over executive functions to Congress violates the fundamental principle expressed by Montesquieu upon which the theory of separated powers rests: "When the legislative and executive powers are united in the same person, or in the same body of magistrates, there can be no liberty; because apprehension may arise, lest the same monarch or senate should enact tyrannical laws, to execute them in a tyrannical manner."[32]

The plaintiffs also argued that the Gramm-Rudman-Hollings Act delegated broad, if not excessive powers to administrative officials in making economic calculations that determined the estimated deficit which required budget cuts in violation of Article I of the Constitution. The District Court ruled that it did not have to consider this question since the law was unconstitutional on other grounds. In *obiter dicta*[33] however, the court was not persuaded by the plaintiffs' argument on why Gramm-Rudman violated the delegation doctrine and concluded that the delegation made by the Act was constitutional. This was a defeat for Synar who argued that Congress had declined to make hard political choices by authorizing excessive power to administrative officials such as the directors of OMB and CBO to affect spending levels for a range of federal programs.

The Supreme Court Review:
Bowsher v. *Synar*

The District Court's ruling was automatically appealed under a provision in the law that granted expedited review to the Supreme Court. *Synar* v. *United States* provided much of the reasoning for the Supreme Court's final ruling in the case. In affirming the District Court decision, the Supreme Court in a 7–2 decision struck down the automatic trigger mechanism in Gramm-Rudman-Hollings, employing a strict interpretation of the separation of power doctrine. The majority opinion, written by Chief Justice Burger, concluded:

> Congress cannot reserve for itself the power of removal of an officer charged with the execution of the laws except by impeachment. To permit the execution of the laws to be vested in an officer answerable only to Congress would, in practical terms, reserve in Congress control over the execution of the laws. . . . The structure of the Constitution does not permit Congress to execute the laws; it follows that Congress cannot grant to an officer under its control what it does not possess.[34]

According to *INS* v. *Chadha* (1983)—the controlling precedent—the majority further stated that, "To permit an officer controlled by Congress to execute the laws would be, in essence, to permit a congressional veto. Congress could simply remove, or threaten to remove an officer for executing the laws in any fashion found to be unsatisfactory to Congress."[35] Based on their ruling in *Chadha*, the Court

found this kind of control over the execution of laws constitutionally impermissible. Bowsher, the Comptroller General, argued that rather than striking down the automatic cut mechanism, the appropriate remedy would be to nullify the 1921 statutory provisions that authorized Congress to remove the Comptroller General. The Court declined to take such a step, referring to the language of Gramm-Rudman-Hollings that creates fallback provisions that take effect if any of the procedures in the law are invalidated. Burger also argued that invalidating the removal provision would be contrary to congressional intent in the 1921 law that created the GAO.

In concurring in the Court's judgment, Justice Stevens, joined by Justice Marshall, disagreed with the majority's view on why the Constitution prohibits the Comptroller General from exercising his power under Gramm-Rudman. They argued that neither the removal power of Congress nor the Comptroller General performing executive functions is the real question.[36] They argued that the issue is a matter of delegating to an officer of Congress power to make national policy. Justice Stevens argued that "It is, in short, the Comptroller General's report that will have a profound, dramatic, and immediate impact on the government and on the nation at large."[37] When Congress legislates, it must follow the procedures set forth in Article I—enactment by both Houses and presentment to the president.

The separate dissenting opinions by Justices White and Blackmun expressed the view that the constitutional flaw in *Bowsher* did not justify the remedy it imposed. Justice White argued that the majority imposed an overly formalistic view of the separation of powers doctrine. He stated that the 1921 law for removal of the Comptroller General has never been used, is of minimal practical significance, and should be regarded as a triviality. He rejected the argument that the removal of the Comptroller General by Congress imposes subservience on the part of the Comptroller General since removal must take place by joint resolution and the president plays a substantial role. Justice Blackmun argued, as did Justice White, against invalidating one of the most important federal enactments of the past several decades in order to preserve a 65-year old removal of power that has never been exercised and appears to have been all but forgotten. Blackmun concluded that the 1921 law calling for the removal of the Comptroller General should have been struck down.

How would Congress respond? Would the Court's decision mark the end of Gramm-Rudman's only effective way of forcing action on the deficit? Would the backup procedure work or could the law be amended to make it constitutional?

Resolving the FY 87 Deficit and the Constitutional Flaw

As they had the year before, Senators Gramm, Rudman, and Hollings viewed the debt limitation as the key legislative vehicle for repairing their mandatory deficit reduction scheme. Their initial option for fixing the constitutional flaw was to eliminate the power of Congress to remove the Comptroller General. This option, however, quickly encountered opposition. Representative Jack Brooks (D-TX), Chair of the House Government Operations Committee that oversees the GAO, was against any such change.

Congress quickly disposed of another problem caused by the Supreme Court's decision, however. On July 17, both the House and Senate approved resolutions certifying the March 1 cuts in FY 86 spending that had been invalidated by the Court. The fallback procedure was employed with slight parliamentary modification to retain the resolution's privileged status in the Senate. Members seemed unwilling to reopen the question of cuts already made and approved by large majorities in both bodies.

By the time the Senate reported the debt ceiling extension, proponents had chosen a second method: empowering OMB to determine the scope and distribution of spending cuts to achieve the deficit targets. Under the revised process proposed by Senators Gramm, Rudman, and Hollings, GAO still played a role in formulating the estimates, but OMB would issue the final report to the president. OMB discretion would be limited by barring the agency from making changes between the preliminary reports except to reflect changes in laws approved by Congress or regulations. The date for the president's budget was moved back to February from the earlier date, and a provision was included to revert to the original process if the Comptroller General was made an executive branch official. "Gramm-Rudman II," as it was dubbed by some, also met with strong opposition in the House and only grudging acceptance by the White House because

of the limitations on OMB. Nonetheless, the amendment was adopted by the Senate on July 30 by a 63–36 vote. But the effort to fix the constitutional flaw bogged down as members prepared for an August 15 recess. House leaders wanted to rely on the backup procedure without any changes. Other members wanted to defer decisions until the August deficit reestimates were released. Despite the efforts of Gramm and his allies to prevent passage of any debt ceiling legislation, Congress agreed to a temporary extension without the Gramm-Rudman amendment.

The early August estimates by OMB and CBO confirmed what many had feared: the deficit for FY 86 and the projected deficit for FY 87 were much larger than expected. OMB's estimate of the FY 86 deficit had jumped $27 billion in six months. On August 20, CBO estimated the deficit for the coming fiscal year at $170.6 billion while OMB estimated it at $156.2 billion. Without the GAO to reconcile differences, the average was taken: $163.4 billion. The cuts outlined in the congressional budget would be insufficient to reach the deficit targets. The deficit target suddenly became $154 billion rather than $144 billion, taking advantage of the fact that sequestration would not be ordered unless Congress missed the deficit target by more than $10 billion. An additional $9.4 billion in cuts or revenue increases were needed to avoid a vote on mandatory cuts.

Most members agreed that despite the disappointing budget numbers, across-the-board cuts should be avoided for FY 87 at all costs. Still lacking appropriations bills and reconciliation, the congressional budget timetable was in shambles. As leaders focused on preparing an omnibus spending bill and making additional cuts to reach the $154 billion deficit target, the Gramm-Rudman amendments were again postponed. The package of additional cuts agreed to by both parties and the administration was a solution no one seemed to like but was considered better than all the alternatives. Relying primarily on revenues from the one-time sale of government assets such as Conrail, legislators proposed "golden gimmicks" worth around $13 billion using "smoke and mirrors."[38] As many had predicted early in the year, the critical FY 87 budget decisions were finally made in late night sessions in early October, after the fiscal year had begun. Another deadline was missed when the deficit reduction package was not enacted before October 1. As Congress struggled with continuing resolutions to keep the government running, a $576 billion omnibus spending bill, deficit reductions, debt extension, and the Gramm-Rudman-Hollings amendment, many noted that the congressional budget process looked pretty much the same in 1986 as it had in recent years.

Congress finally completed action on the budget with a deficit estimated at around $151 billion, below the target specified in Gramm-Rudman-Hollings. Despite attempts to block extension of the government's borrowing authority unless the bill contained their amendment to repair the deficit reduction process, Senators Gramm, Rudman, and Hollings were unsuccessful. Senate leaders, however, agreed to only a six month extension so that on May 15, 1987, proponents could once again attempt to remedy the constitutional flaw and make the process mandatory.

Gramm-Rudman-Hollings: An Assessment

The Balanced Budget and Emergency Deficit Control Act of 1985 was both hailed as the salvation of the republic and condemned as a testament to the failure of budgeting in a democracy. Obviously, it is neither as good as its proponents nor as bad as its opponents claimed. Just as no single factor can explain its adoption, no single judgment can accurately assess its effect after one year. Like other policies, it has elements of success and failure.

The case that Gramm-Rudman-Hollings was a failure is relatively easy to document. Virtually without exception, every date in its ambitious new timetable for congressional budgeting was missed and missed badly. The Supreme Court ruled that the crucial trigger mechanism designed to make cuts automatically was unconstitutional. Congress failed to repair the constitutional flaw. Gramm-Rudman proved no panacea to the legislative-executive deadlock that has characterized budgetary politics in the 1980s. Congress struggled with the same issues in the same climate of internal discontent over its budget procedures. Budget decisions in 1986 dramatized a basic flaw in the timetable: legislators are increasingly unlikely to make difficult choices on anything other than final budget baselines. Unless the basis of decision making can be made more certain, incentives to miss deadlines and delay the tough decisions until September or October will be compelling.

Beyond the prominent features of Gramm-Rudman's failures lies perhaps an even more serious indictment. Despite its claim to make Congress more attuned to deficit reduction as a long-term problem, it only emphasized Congress' short-term and short-sighted instincts as an institution. It did not eliminate expediency in budgeting; it exacerbated expediency. The $10 billion cushion allowed in the law to account for estimation error and economic changes was simply added to allow a larger deficit. The package of reductions adopted in October of 1986 to technically meet the target will significantly increase the deficit in outyears.[39] Advanced revenue collections and delayed outlays in FY 87 will have a similar effect on future deficits.

Many of the flaws of Gramm-Rudman-Hollings noted by critics at the outset remain. The process is an essentially irrational approach to budgeting. It has potentially damaging effects on both domestic and defense programs because of the way it cuts current year outlays. It threatens the health of the economy by eliminating the countercyclical potential of the budget, threatening to make cuts or raise revenues at precisely the wrong time. The recession escape clause would come into effect long after the crucial decision-making time had passed. Despite the Court decision, many broader questions of legislative-executive power remain unsettled. While provisions of the law may be within the letter of the Constitution, they seem to be counter to the spirit of the Constitution which gave Congress ultimate responsibility for decisions on taxing and spending.

Despite the negative case, Gramm-Rudman had some positive effects. Its goal of making federal deficits the top legislative priority was achieved; it simply could not legislate away the factors which had made deficits chronic in the first place. Gramm-Rudman permeated almost every facet of the second session of the 99th Congress. And despite the unenviable record detailed above, Gramm-Rudman communicated to the public congressional resolve to deal with deficits. Its failures, however, may make voters even more cynical.

Gramm-Rudman provided the initiative to reexamine and reform the congressional budget process. Despite the failure to meet the timetable, other changes served to centralize and strengthen macrobudgeting in Congress. The spending committees exhibited more discipline as a result of being subjected to greater accountability for budget totals.

The budget committees and party leaders were strengthened. Reconciliation, for all the controversy surrounding it, was acknowledged as a crucial element of congressional budgeting. Enforcement under new rules was enhanced, especially in the Senate. The provisions requiring offsets to preserve deficit neutrality had a profound effect on the legislative process in 1986. The results were evident in the sweeping tax reform that passed and in a reduction in the amendments to the omnibus spending bill. Despite all the criticism, budget growth between FY 86 and FY 87 was the lowest in decades. While not balancing the budget, many of these changes may have a long-term positive impact on the ability of Congress to make fiscal decisions.

Victory by the Democrats in the Senate in the 1986 election will only make the task of those seeking to restore the mandatory provisions of the law in 1987 more difficult. Recall, however, that Gramm-Rudman-Hollings garnered significant Democratic support in numerous Senate votes in 1985 and 1986. Economic forecasts may be a greater obstacle than Democratic control. Estimates in late 1986 suggest that the deficit will far exceed $151 billion in FY 87 and that cuts as high as $70 billion may have to be made to reach the target of $108 billion for FY 88. Such results would seriously threaten the Gramm-Rudman approach. Many economists predict disastrous results for the economy if such drastic cuts are made.

Congress has several options for dealing with Gramm-Rudman-Hollings, none very appealing. First, the mandatory process could be restored by fixing the constitutional flaw in the original version by methods already proposed or others. Second, Congress could try to meet the original deficit targets but simply rely on the backup method to certify cuts. Third, Congress could amend the law to add a more sophisticated economic escape clause, changing the deficit targets by formula based on aggregate economic performance. This is similar to an amendment proposed by Representative David Obey during consideration of the bill in 1985, but not adopted. Fourth, Congress could simply amend the targets, restating their commitment to a balanced budget but adopting a more gradual phaseout that recognizes economic reality. Finally, Congress could simply scrap Gramm-Rudman by ignoring it as they do other statutes such as the Humphrey-Hawkins Act of 1978. Despite their antipathy to Gramm-Rudman, Democratic members in particular are suspicious of this approach, and fear handing the Republicans a ready-made campaign issue for 1988.

Whatever course Congress chooses for the future, Gramm-Rudman is one more milestone in its struggle to exercise its constitutional power of the purse. Despite some positive effects, Gramm-Rudman reveals once more that choosing one problem to solve does not make related problems disappear. As long as Congress faces increased policy and political constraints, procedural instability and high levels of conflict will result. With budget totals that remain inflexible to manipulation but vulnerable to the economy, it will continue to be difficult to budget with certainty. While deficits remain high, Congress will continue to seek some method to deal with the budget that still accommodates their other policy and political objectives. Gramm-Rudman-Hollings is a fascinating example of that search.

Notes

This research was made possible in part through a grant from the Everett M. Dirksen Endowment for Legislative Research and a grant from the University of Missouri Weldon Spring Endowment. Their support and assistance is gratefully acknowledged.

1. Harry S. Havens, "Gramm-Rudman-Hollings: Origins and Implementation," *Public Budgeting and Finance* 6 (Autumn, 1986): 4–24.
2. Richard Fenno, *The Power of the Purse,* (Boston: Little Brown, 1965) and Aaron Wildavsky, *The Politics of the Budgetary Process* (Boston: Little Brown, 1964).
3. Lance T. LeLoup, *Budgetary Politics* (Brunswick, Ohio: Kings Court Inc., 1986), 33–37.
4. Louis Fisher, Congressional Research Service, *Statement Before House Committee on Government Operations,* (October 17, 1985), Table 1.
5. Wildavsky (1964).
6. Allen Schick, "The Budget as an Instrument of Presidential Policy," in Lester M. Salamon and Michael S. Lund (eds.), *The Reagan Presidency and the Governing of America* (Washington, D.C.: Urban Institute Press, 1985), 91–125.
7. Lance T. LeLoup, "After the Blitz: Reagan and the U.S. Congressional Budget Process," *Legislative Studies Quarterly* 7 (August 1982): 331–339; Allen Schick, *Reconciliation and the Congressional Budget* (Washington, D.C.: American Enterprise Institute, 1981).

8. Louis Fisher, "Ten Years of the Budget Act: Still Searching for Controls," *Public Budgeting and Finance* 5 (Autumn 1985): 3–28.

9. House Rule XXI, clause 2(a) and Senate Rule XVI.

10. U. S. House of Representatives, Committee on Rules, *Report on the Congressional Budget Act Amendments of 1984* (October 1984), 98th Cong., 2nd sess.

11. *Congressional Record*, October 5, 1985, S12730-12732.

12. *Congressional Record*, October 9, 1985, S12988.

13. *Congressional Quarterly Weekly Reports*, October 26, 1985, 2148.

14. *Congressional Record*, November 1, 1985, H9615.

15. *Congressional Record*, December 11, 1985, S17444.

16. *Congressional Record*, December 11, 1985, H11903.

17. This section is based on Public Law 99-177, The Balanced Budget and Emergency Deficit Control Act of 1985.

18. Allen Schick, "Explanation of the Balanced Budget and Emergency Deficit Control Act of 1985," prepared for Congressional Research Service (December 1985), 9–13.

19. *Federal Register*, vol. 51, no. 10, book 2, (January 15, 1986).

20. Havens (1986): 15–20.

21. Congressional Budget Office, *The Economic and Budget Outlook: Fiscal Years 1987–1991*, Report to the House and Senate Committees on the Budget, Part I (February 1986).

22. *Congressional Quarterly Weekly Reports*, March 15, 1986, 315.

23. *Congressional Quarterly Weekly Reports*, May 17, 1986, 1079–1081.

24. Stephen Gettinger, "Spending Panels Confront Life After Gramm-Rudman," *Congressional Quarterly Weekly Reports*, June 7, 1986, 1258–1261.

25. *United States* v. *Nixon* 418, S.Ct. 683 (1974), *Train* v. *City of New York* 420, S.Ct.35 (1975), and *Buckley* v. *Valeo* 424, S.Ct. 612 (1976).

26. *Charles A. Bowsher, Comptroller General of the United States* v. *Mike Synar, Member of Congress et al.*, 106 S.Ct. 3181 (1986).

27. For example, Trent Lott (D-MS) asked the American Law Division of the Congressional Research Service to prepare a constitutional analysis of the controversial provisions. The CRS responded by finding that Gramm-Rudman did not violate the Constitution on the four areas in question. See *Congressional Record*, October 24, 1985, E4793-4795.

28. Eleven members of Congress subsequently joined Synar's suit. This case was consolidated with *National Treasury Employees Union* v. *United States,* a virtually identical suit. In this case, the National Treasury Employees Union sued because Gramm-Rudman suspended a 3.1 percent cost of living increase its members were to have received in retirement benefits on January 1.

29. *Synar* v. *United States,* 626 F. Supp. 1374 (D.D.C. 1986).

30. The opinion was signed by all three judges, Scalia, Johnson, and Gasch, but the author of the opinion was not identified. It was widely speculated that Antonin Scalia, formerly of the U.S. Court of Appeals for the District of Columbia and currently Associate Justice of the Supreme Court, wrote the opinion. See *Wall Street Journal,* "Supreme Court Ruling Clouds the Outlook for Deficit Reduction," July 8, 1986, 27, col. 3; and Richard Cohen, "Judicial Whim," *National Journal,* July 26, 1986, 1863.

31. The causes for removal of the Comptroller General are impeachment or joint resolution of Congress after notice and an opportunity for a hearing only for: permanent disability, inefficiency, neglect of duty, malfeasance, or a felony or conduct involving moral turpitude (626 F. Supp. at 1391, 1986).

32. *Synar* v. *United States,* 626 F. Supp. at 1401–1402.

33. In this instance, the District Court provided its views on this question so that the Supreme Court, in case it decided to address this issue, would have the benefit of the lower court's views and would not result in delay if it were necessary to remand the case.

34. *Bowsher* v. *Synar* at 10 (slip opinion).

35. *Bowsher* v. *Synar* at 11 (slip opinion).

36. Justices Stevens and Marshall took a broader view of the separation of powers doctrine in *Bowsher.* They argued that the majority's question that the Comptroller General performs executive functions rests on an unsound premise based on distinct boundaries between the three branches of government. Their view is the functions performed by the Comptroller General are legislative.

37. *Bowsher* v. *Synar* at 19 (slip opinion).

38. *Congressional Quarterly Weekly Reports,* September 20, 1986, 2179.

39. Elizabeth Wehr, "Gramm-Rudman Both Disappoints and Succeeds," *Congressional Quarterly Weekly Reports,* November 15, 1986, 2879–2882.

14
The Crisis in Federal Budgeting

David Stockman

Looking at the large sweep of things, it would not be hard to deliver a damning indictment of the 1974 Budget Act after ten years, based on the apparent outcome. I would note, for instance, that in fiscal 1974, the last full fiscal year before passage of the act, the federal government had a $6.1 billion deficit, which was .4 of 1 percent of GNP.

After ten years, in fiscal 1985, we have about a $210 billion deficit, equal to about 5.5 percent of GNP, a ten-fold expansion of the deficit relative to the size of the economy. In the 186 years prior to the passage of the Budget Act, we managed to accumulate $544 billion in public debt. In the first ten years under the Budget Act, we added another $1.2 trillion. In 5 percent of the time we accumulated 70 percent of the national debt.

Even if one looks at the deficit in cyclical terms, the record is not favorable. In 1985, the third year of this economic expansion (generally the deficit diminishes as the economy recovers), the deficit will likely amount to 5.5 percent of GNP. As we reached the third year of expansion in the 1975–1976 cycle, the deficit was, by contrast, only 1.7 percent of GNP. In the cycle before that, it was less than 1 percent.

My conclusions about the Budget Act, however, are almost the reverse of what might be implied by these apparent outcomes. Specifically, I believe the fiscal situation has deteriorated radically since 1974 in spite of the Budget Act, not because of it.

The notion that we would be better off without the budget process—a view expressed in some quarters from time to time—amounts to superficial folly. Two questions that ought to be cleared up are: (1) Why are the outcomes so bad? and (2) Is it reasonable to believe that any mere institutional change in the federal government—a reformed

Source: Allen Schick, *A Decade of Congressional Budgeting* (Washington, D.C.: American Enterprise Institute for Public Policy Research, 1986), pp. 57–66. Reprinted by permission.

Budget Act or budget process—could have made a substantial difference in these outcomes?

My answer is that the current fiscal disorder results from powerful, long-term, macroeconomic policy and political trends that have thoroughly overwhelmed the budget process in the mechanical sense. Likewise, the correction of the current situation requires extraordinary measures of political will and consensus, which, by definition, must originate outside the budget process itself—through the elected leaders, the public, and perhaps even the catalytic force of economic crisis.

Tinkering with the Budget Act is not likely to change the fiscal problems that we are grappling with in any significant way. It is very easy to conclude that because the outcomes are so bad something must be fundamentally wrong with the process. We therefore spend a great deal of time figuring out how to rewire the process, restructure it, and change it. But unless we examine why we are in the situation today, which, from either the fiscal point of view, or from any point along the political spectrum is not desirable, we may be led astray trying to rewire the process in ways that would make politics an even more difficult problem.

The Sources of Budgetary Imbalance

The long-term sources of the budget problem are what, for lack of a better term, I would call a generational anomaly in the progress of fiscal events over a two-decade period. The politicians of the 1970s benefited from the favorable fiscal trends. They enjoyed the easy choices, mostly dispensing the favors of government rather than extracting its costs.

Their successors in the 1980s face hard labor in the political salt mines to confront the relentless imperative to take from the people rather than give. It is in this contrast between past fiscal largess and current fiscal stress that the problem lies, producing outcomes that we do not like.

In a basic sense, the national budget is an instrument of redistribution. Each year's set of choices is a mix of giving and taking. But the explicit content, the formulation of that mix, presents itself in varying proportions at different times.

In the 1970s, everything that could happen to make short-run fiscal choices easier did in fact happen—a kind of Murphy's law in reverse. In the

1980s, however, the laws of economics and the imperatives of national security have conspired to revive the old and familiar Murphy's law in acute and virulent form.

This can be readily seen by comparing the compositional profile of the budget in three benchmark years—1970, 1980, and 1985. In 1970, spending for defense and for what I call national interest programs (foreign aid, security assistance, Energy Department programs, and so forth) amounted to 9.3 percent of GNP or $245 billion in 1986 dollars.

By 1980, this claim for defense and national interest programs had shrunk in absolute terms to 210 billion constant dollars. But more important, in relative terms it dropped to only 5.7 percent of GNP. The main reasons for this decline are fairly obvious. The Vietnam demobilization dramatically reduced the operating force structure costs. A huge amount of new equipment purchased at the end of that period was available in inventory to be drawn on in part of the 1970s. The post-Vietnam policy of withdrawal had a severe chilling effect on both new defense and security assistance commitments.

The key point is that without raising taxes, this decrease in defense spending made available an enormous fiscal dividend for new domestic expenditures. The government's current purchasing power increased by nearly $200 billion (3.5 percent of GNP) as a result of the collapse of national interest and defense spending from over 9 percent of GNP to about 5.5 percent.

Budgeting became a pleasure—deciding which domestic constituencies and needs would receive the dividends. In hindsight, however, the rundown of national security spending went beyond the point of prudence and was not sustainable. After 1978 Carter and Congress attempted to raise national security spending significantly. Appropriations rose 28 percent from 1978 to 1980. By then inflation was rocketing upward; as a result, the gain was only 8.5 percent in real terms, far less than had been intended.

In the 1980s the attrition in defense had to be corrected, and it was. Despite the annual skirmishing over defense spending, the strong consensus was, for five straight years, to sustain rapid expansion of real budget resources. The 1985 appropriations for defense and national interest programs were $304 billion, 50 percent more in real terms than in 1980. They amounted to 7.5 percent of GNP, nearly 2 percentage points over the 1980 level.

This extra 2 percent became part of the fiscal burden of the 1980s, to be taken either from taxpayers or from newly entitled domestic constituencies that had benefited enormously from the vast runup of domestic expenditures in the 1970s.

A second dimension of this long-term fiscal reversal between the two decades was the big matter of servicing the national debt. For several decades prior to 1973, when the greatest sustained peacetime inflation in U.S. history commenced, the real Treasury bill rate averaged about 1.2 percent. Over the remainder of the 1970s the Treasury bill rate averaged a negative 1.7 percent and was nearly a negative 2 percent in 1980. These low and negative rates reduced the cost of financing the national debt. It was nice while it lasted, or, should I say, while the money lasted. But when the financial markets and the electorate demanded an end to inflation and cheap money in 1980, the game was over. Since then we have financed the debt at an average real rate of 4.3 percent, nearly six hundred basis points higher than the actual Treasury bill rate in real 1980 terms.

The combination of added debt generated by a deep and prolonged recession required to correct the inflation of the 1970s, and the persistence of inflationary expectations embodied in current interest rates, has ballooned the debt service claim on GNP from under 2 percent in 1980 to more than 3.5 percent in 1985. This has increased the excess fiscal burden of the 1980s by another 1.5 percent, adding to the difficulty of funding choices and to the imperative to take from rather than give to domestic constituencies and creating another road block to the quest for a budgetary consensus and solution.

The third favorable trend of the 1970s to be reversed was the galloping inflation that made it possible for Congress to dispense tax cuts several times after 1974, while at the same time permitting the real tax burdens to rise via "bracket creep." During the 1973–1976 period, for example, personal income taxes averaged about 8.3 percent of GNP. Despite subsequent tax deductions, mainly in 1978, personal taxes climbed to 9.5 percent of GNP by 1980. Overall, the federal tax burden rose from an average of 18.9 percent of GNP for the decade from 1968 to 1978 to nearly 21 percent of GNP in 1981, a gain above the trend of nearly 2 percentage points.

The high interest rates and the unvoted tax increases met a superior force in 1980 and 1981 in the overwhelming demand of the electorate for personal income tax cuts to compensate for the rapid increases that occurred in the late 1970s and for either de facto or explicit indexing to preserve real or effective tax rates in the future.

While partisan competition in response to this demand led to excessive tax cutting in 1981, two facts remain. First, perversely, the Budget Act, with its three-year disciplined framework focusing on the effects for the 1982–1984 fiscal years, led to a back-loading of the big tax giveaways into the outyears, 1985 and 1986, and beyond. Consequently, the 2 percent cut in the revenue share of GNP in 1982, the first year of the tax cut, ballooned to a 6 percent reduction in current law by 1988.

The backloading of revenue reduction gave the system time to correct the overshoot in several subsequent tax increase bills. As a result of these increases, current law revenues will be about $80 billion higher in 1986 than they would have been had nothing been done after 1981.

As a consequence, the revenue claims have been restored to the status quo of before 1981, about 19 percent of GNP. What has been accomplished with the big reduction in 1981 and the four subsequent increases since then? There has been a cut of the 1 to 2 percent bracket creep of the late 1970s, which disguised the true degree of the budget imbalance in the 1980 budget. This cut adds another 1 to 2 percent to the burden of explicit fiscal choice in the 1980s.

Finally, the federal government started the 1970s in a relatively good fiscal position with the deficit at .4 percent of GNP in 1969–1970. Despite the 1971 recession, the budget returned to about a 0.5 percent deficit by 1974. By present standards, therefore, there was some room for the total expenditure claim to rise without forcing requests for tax increases or raising the specter of severe economic harm from a rising, excessive trend in the level of deficit.

Over the course of the 1970s, this room for deficit expansion, at least in the short term, was narrowed. Spending rose from 20 percent of GNP at the beginning of the decade to 23 percent by 1980. At the end of the decade and the end of the business cycle, the deficit was nearly 3 percent of GNP, compared to the .5 percent it had been at the beginning. Moreover, the 3.5 percent of GNP no longer being spent on defense and national interest programs became available for domestic spending.

The defense and fiscal dividend and the increase in the size of the structural deficit opened the possibility for truly staggering increases in domestic spending over the decade, which in fact happened. In 1970 total domestic spending amounted to $250 billion in 1986 dollars, or 9.4 percent of GNP.

By 1980 it had rocketed to $540 billion in the same constant dollars, to 15.1 percent of GNP. In short, the budgeting game of the 1970s delivered a $300 billion jackpot (5.5 percent of GNP) of new domestic benefits to domestic constituencies without explicitly raising taxes or moving the budget into a clear and present danger zone of imbalance. Such were the temporary rewards of cheap money, the ability to draw on the defense inventory, and bracket creep.

Most of this domestic spending breakout cannot be charged to the Budget Act. The costly policy decisions and actions were taken prior to 1975, while the full bills did not become due until the late 1970s and 1980s. Social security, for example, grew from 2.6 percent of GNP in 1962 to 3.1 percent in 1970 and 4.5 percent in 1980. It was driven up mainly by demographic factors, rising lifetime earnings that affect current benefits, and by the big benefit increases enacted in 1972, before the act.

The Medicare and Medicaid claim on GNP doubled during the decade. It rose from less than 1 percent to nearly 2 percent—mainly because of the real cost trends in the medical sector, not new policy liberalizations after 1974.

Of the other big entitlement expansions—in nutrition, housing, SSI, student aid, and some others—most were initiated and enacted into law between 1970 and 1975, before the Budget Act was implemented, although they did not reach full cost and did not affect the fiscal envelope until the end of the decade.

In short, the Budget Act did not encourage profligacy in new spending initiatives. Indeed, hardly a single fiscally significant new program or liberalization has been enacted since 1975. Those that were enacted after 1975, such as the Middle Income Student Assistance Act, the Low Income Energy Assistance Program, and some others amount to about $5 billion a year in a $1 trillion budget—not very much.

The current malady stems from the larger trends I have described and the inability of our system to develop a coherent and durable political consensus about the inherent fiscal imperative of the 1980s—namely, the massive taking away of benefits from the electorate after a decade of fevered giving.

From the perspective of 1980, the GNP shares for the years ahead, would have appeared as follows. First, in 1980, because of bracket creep, we were living on borrowed revenues. Spending constituencies had already demonstrated that the stealthy hand of inflation would not be permitted to make budget life easier because the major cash programs were indexed in the early 1970s. It was only a matter of time before the taxpayers demanded and got equal treatment.

Second, we were living on cheap debt. The bond market revolted in January 1980, shutting off this option.

Third, we had reached the end of the string in drawing down the defense and national interest claims on GNP. Afghanistan and the aborted Iranian hostage rescue effort shocked the system into action and propelled defense onto an expansionary budget path.

Fourth, in hindsight, it seems rather certain that we were destined to absorb another round of major recession-induced increments to the national debt that have to be serviced in the future. There is little plausible basis for believing that the pervasive and virulent double-digit inflation of the late 1970s could have been purged from the economy without undergoing a period of output loss and adjustment.

Finally, the heavy hand of history presented one more burden: demographics, real wage gains, and the rising real costs of medical care would have caused social insurance—social security and Medicare, and related pension programs to rise under 1980 law from 7.2 percent of GNP to 8.2 percent by 1985—another full percentage point to be accommodated in the overall fiscal equation.

Therefore, taken all together, these factors mean that the attainment of practical fiscal equilibrium by 1985, defined here as a deficit of less than 1 percent of GNP, would have required the explicit extraction of about 6 percent of GNP either from the taxpayers in higher taxes or from 1980 domestic program beneficiaries.

To have to remove, from either spending constituencies or taxing constituencies, so large a magnitude of money would have been a truly traumatic, shocking task for the political system. After having given away 5 to 6 percent of GNP in the 1970s, the political system was not prepared or structured to cope with the imperative tasks of the 1980s.

Toward Fiscal Equilibrium

Some progress has been made. The 1985 social insurance cost, for instance, will be $21 billion lower than the 1980 law provided—a .6 percent GNP reduction in claims. Nevertheless, the GNP share of social insurance in 1985 is still greater than it was in 1980. So, therefore, social insurance has aggravated the budget problem; the changes in law have only modestly contributed to the solution. All other 1985 domestic spending is down $50 billion from the 1980 law, a reduction of more than 2 percentage points from the 1980 claim of 8 percent of GNP. Yet the dilemma remains.

If 6 percent of GNP had to be taken from taxpayers or spending beneficiaries in order to accommodate defense, debt service, and tax indexing and to achieve a tolerable 1 percent of GNP deficit, then only about 1.5 percent of that 6 percent gap has been closed.

A brief review of the House and Senate differences on the fiscal 1986 budget resolutions readily highlights the enduring political problems preventing that task from being accomplished. First, the defense issue has been settled. The low growth rates in the real budget authority for the next several years mean that defense and national interest programs will remain stable at the current level of 7.5 percent of GNP, 2 points above 1980. Therefore, closing the gap will require the extraction of 4.5 percent of GNP from one or more of three sources: social insurance beneficiaries, taxpayers, or the whole gamut of smaller domestic programs—from agriculture to veterans. Here the impediments to political consensus are obvious and awesome.

The Democratic leadership and the vast majority of the House as a whole will not change their position on social insurance. While moderate COLA (cost-of-living allowance) restraints and increased Medicare beneficiary charges could save up to 1 percent of GNP, the social security issue is just too politically intractable and is not likely to produce significant savings. The administration and conservative Republicans will not waver from their determination to limit taxes to 19 percent of GNP for several reasons: first, holding the line on taxes has become the central and paramount political pledge of this era. Second, twenty-five years of history shows that 19 percent of GNP revenues can suffice. Third, in correcting the overshoot from 1981 when tax claims dropped to 17.5 percent of GNP the public's perception is that we have already raised taxes massively.

A bipartisan majority in Congress, reflecting regional and constituency alliances, has blocked further significant retrenchment in the remainder of the domestic budget; they are unlikely to give ground, especially if the total deficit-reduction package is dramatically inadequate because social insurance and taxes are not in the mix.

In the final analysis, then, we will continue to incur outsized deficits because the fiscal imperatives of the 1980s demand huge extractions of benefits from domestic constituencies or of revenues from national taxpayers, a task that cannot be accomplished unless there is a strong and broad political consensus on the required actions. With the country divided between an antitax White House and a defend-the-inherited-spending House of Representatives, with the Senate itself divided in between, the prospect for the emergence of this consensus is dim indeed.

If the Budget Act had not been enacted, the situation would be much worse. Let me take one example: the overshoot, in terms of the outyears, of revenue reduction in 1981. In the summer of 1981, we were focusing on the three-year budget path. Under the economic assumptions used at the time by both the CBO and the OMB, our calculations about what was possible were not radically off track. But then Congress gave everybody what they wanted, with much of the revenue loss deferred to 1985 and 1986.

As we looked to 1983–1985, 1984–1986, and 1985–1987, the budget process gradually began to focus on the huge losses that loomed ahead and pushed Congress to enact some tax adjustments and spending cuts in 1982 and 1984.

An enormous gap between revenues and spending still exists, but the Budget Act can be credited with moving sentiments, viewpoints, and actions in Congress to deal with those problems.

Many improvements in the budget process could be suggested, among them a two-year budget resolution—there is no point in a yearly budget resolution, particularly because we work within a three-year time frame; a requirement for a joint rather than a concurrent resolution that would provide stronger institutional pressure for a consensus between the two branches of Congress and the administration; and perhaps a simpler functional structure with five or six categories in the budget rather than the twenty we have now.

Some of the proposed changes in the Budget Act are worth debating. But they are only marginally relevant to the political-fiscal dilemma that I have described. Frankly, other institutional mechanisms that we in the administration advocated are probably in the same category. A line item veto, for example, would be a wonderful tool for the director of the OMB. There are those on Capitol Hill who recognize this, and therefore its adoption is a long shot. But an item veto would not accomplish much in terms of fixing the fiscal problem. It would be largely an instrument of political control and discipline. There is not enough money in the appropriated budget, other than for defense, to make a large difference. We argue with Congress over $80 or $90 billion of nondefense appropriations, but those that are truly discretionary amount to only a few billion dollars a year—not enough to fix a $200 billion problem.

In tinkering with the budget process, it is necessary to recognize that the appropriated accounts are not really the problem. The problem is the automatic spending that makes up most of the domestic budget, and that takes an act of political will to change. The current law will remain in effect indefinitely unless a positive majority in both houses and a presidential signature change it.

Those are the problems with the budget. Careful examination of appropriated spending reveals that it is not quite as discretionary as it appears. Much of appropriated spending is a quasi-entitlement that would be only marginally affected during the year. Take, for example the $10 billion we spend on veterans' health care. What can the appropriations really do about that from year to year? Very little. The real issue is the entitlement for the veterans' health care. Who is eligible? Should health care services be supplied directly or through vouchers? These are the policy questions and choices that make a difference. Appropriated spending is not a strong issue either way, regardless of whose accounting you use.

A constitutional amendment requiring a balanced budget is not likely to be adopted or made effective until, one way or another, a good part of this problem has been solved. If we had had a balanced budget amendment in 1970, we could have locked in the favorable budget position of the early 1970s, and we probably would not be in the mess we are in today. But as for solving the enormous imbalance that has accumulated, I am not sure anybody has the complete answer.

Previously, the OMB had not—as an institution—been sufficiently involved in the congressional budget process. Under the Budget Act it has been necessary to change the style of the institution from producing one document a year which jumps out of a big computer into a big book, into an on-line policy process which is oriented to both executive and legislative action.

One of the great strengths of our governmental system is the division between the legislative and the executive branches. But this division makes it inherently difficult to formulate a national budget in today's world with today's commitments. The more that we can do informally to bridge the gap, the more likely the process will work just a little bit better. In a small way this is what we have done at the OMB—create informal mechanisms to help bridge the political gap in our system.

These processes or institutional fixes are no substitute, however, for political consensus on a monumental problem of governance: how to deal with the fiscal hangover of the 1980s. Whether one wants to criticize or reform the budget process, this overriding problem must be kept in mind. It is a problem of political consensus, not of the process alone. And finally, it is a problem of the political system.

15
Courts and Public Purse Strings: Have Portraits of Budgeting Missed Something?

Jeffrey D. Straussman
Syracuse University

Do judges make budget decisions? At one time the question would have seemed preposterous. No formal constitutional role exists for the courts in the budget process, nor do various portraits of budgeting include a place for the judicial branch. Yet, few would argue that disputes have come before the courts in which resolution has required forms of budgetary action. Consider two easily recognizable illustrations:

The federal courts have been particularly active in the area of prison reform—especially the issue of prison overcrowding. Arkansas was the first state to have its corrections system judged to be in violation of the Eighth Amendment prohibition against cruel and unusual punishment beginning with *Holt* v. *Sarver* in 1969. Since then 35 states have experienced similar litigation against their prison systems. Research has indicated that state spending for corrections has been affected by court decisions; capital expenditures have tended to increase in the years immediately following a court judgment, and corrections spending as a percentage of the total state budget has increased after a court order.[1]

This form of court involvement—usually referred to as "institutional reform litigation"—has also involved constitutional challenges to the conditions found in state psychiatric institutions and in facilities

for the mentally retarded. In 1972 litigation was initiated against the State of New York by the New York Association of Retarded Children, the American Civil Liberties Union, and parents of persons institutionalized in a state facility known as Willowbrook. The suit charged that the conditions in the facility were violations of constitutional rights. The litigation resulted in a consent decree which included a policy of "deinstitutionalization" of patients, improved staff-client ratios, and improved services to the newly deinstitutionalized population. The budgetary impact was extensive for the rest of the decade.[2]

Do judges know what they are doing—in a budgetary sense, that is? Cooper's case studies of *Bradley* v. *Milliken* (1971) and *United States* v. *City of Parma, Ohio* (1980), point out that judges are not oblivious to the budgetary dimensions of their remedial decrees. He notes that the judges in both cases urged the respective governments to seek federal funds as a way to soften the financial ramifications of their decisions.[3] Similarly, Judge Frank Johnson assumed that changes brought about in the psychiatric institutions in Alabama in the aftermath of the *Wyatt* decision would permit the state to qualify for medicare and medicaid funds—thereby easing the budgetary impact of his decree.[4] In general, judges have rejected the claim by defendant agencies that financial exigencies do not permit remedial action to correct constitutional violations. Therefore, if budgets reflect policy preferences, then it would seem important to determine how judges may influence budgetary decisions. How would a judicial presence challenge current assumptions about the nature of public budgeting?

Enter the Courts: A Challenge to Incrementalism?

While the budgeting literature is practically devoid of references to litigation and the courts, conventional notions of how the process operates provides "rules of thumb" from which judicial-administrative interactions may be anticipated. Consider a frequently observed behavioral pattern of agency budgeting—the principle that agencies adopt strategies aimed at budgetary expansion.

Budgeting has been described by a number of participants as a series of disaggregated decisions

Source: Reprinted with permission from *Public Administration Review* (July/August 1986): 345–351. © 1986 by the American Society for Public Administration (ASPA), 1120 G Street NW, Suite 500, Washington, D.C. 20005. All rights reserved.

The author acknowledges helpful comments on previous drafts from Jesse Burkhead, Phillip Cooper, Irene Rubin, Aaron Wildavsky, and anonymous referees. Financial support was received from the Center for Interdisciplinary Legal Studies, College of Law, Syracuse University.

that take place in a limited time frame with a few basic constraints. These include: the number of total players, formalized "rules," and fiscal constraints. By and large these constraints simplify an otherwise complicated process and provide budgeting with a degree of stability. Decisions are made by a set number of participants; the budget *cycle* is invariant over time. Strategy often centers around the effort to expand one's budget since expansion is equated with prestige and other perquisites of office. While other strategies (like the desire for budgetary stability) may sometimes compete with the goal of budget maximization, some research studies have shown that agency heads who pursue aggressive strategies have, on the whole, been successful.[5]

How might an administrator use the actual, or even better, the potential intervention of the courts to achieve budget expansion? Consider just one possibility drawn from Wildavsky's "crisis technique." As Wildavsky notes: "A number of agency officials are famous in budgetary circles for their ability to embellish or make use of crises. By publicizing a situation, dramatizing it effectively, and perhaps asking for emergency appropriations, an agency may maneuver itself into a position of responsibility for large new programs."[6] The threat of a lawsuit and subsequent judicial intervention in the budgetary process is one example of the kind of situation calling for the crisis technique.

An agency head may claim that prior funding has been inadequate. As a consequence, service levels are below what is considered "acceptable"—thereby providing the potential for litigation. Notice that the administrator need not admit failure. Rather, he or she simply argues that services are provided efficiently, but that the funding is inadequate. If the level of service is not raised (or services are not improved), the administrator suggests that the agency will most likely be sued. The crisis can be ameliorated (that is, the probability of a lawsuit may be lowered) if the appropriations for the agency are increased.

It is important to realize that the crisis could be either real or manufactured. The agency head may sincerely believe that, given the current funding, the probability of litigation is high. On the other hand, the agency head may exaggerate the situation. In either case, assume that the legislature has less than perfect information and therefore interprets the administrator's estimate of the probability of litigation as being reasonably accurate. Consider, now, how litigation *may* affect budgetary strategy.

When the administrator faces the legislative sponsors, an initial expectation by all involved is that the new budget level will be a fair share increase over last year's appropriation. This follows from incremental theory. Call this budget level F1. The threat of a successful lawsuit implies a higher *court mandated* budget. Call this level F3. Between these two levels is a budget level that the administrator may wish to obtain through the use of the crisis technique. This may be considered the "threat" level—F2. The three levels are obviously related in the following way: $F1 < F2 < F3$.

An important part of the administrator's strategy is specifying the likelihood of a successful suit. If the threat of a suit is to be effective in producing an appropriation above F1, the agency head would most likely tie agency performance to the budget level. The relationship need not be linear, nor need it be the same for all agencies that may be the target of litigation. Nevertheless, it is necessary that some claim be made that differential budget levels produce different performance levels. In this way the legislature is in a position to influence the agency's performance by its control of the purse strings. It then follows that the legislature may be able to affect the probability of a lawsuit by changing the agency's level of funding.

The administrator's strategy is clear—identify the existence of the threat of a suit and then try to convince the legislature to "buy" a reduction in the likelihood by identifying the probability at the F1 funding level and the expected reduction that an F2 level will produce. The administrator then asks for the F2 level.

The legislature does not, of course, automatically concede and give the agency head a higher (F2) budget. After all, the legislature, like the agency head, also has objectives that influence appropriations levels. Three are particularly relevant: (a) the legislature wants to control aggregate levels of spending and cannot, therefore, routinely grant all funding requests that are predicated on "crises," (b) the legislature may want to retain its power over budget making (rather than letting it slip into the hands of the courts), (c) the legislature has policy goals that may or may not be in agreement with the courts. These three objectives are not necessarily consistent with one another at a given point in time; their individual or joint impact on the legislature's likely response to the agency head's claims about the prospects of litigation are probably uncertain.

Essentially the legislature wants to know whether to provide an F2 budget, and if so, how large the F2 level should be. Obviously the legislature can choose to reject the administrator's threat. The legislature may do this because the lawmakers simply think that the administrator is wrong; they perceive no serious likelihood of a suit. If this happens, obviously the question of the size of F2 is irrelevant. If the legislature believes that the threat of a suit is credible, it need not accept the estimates provided by the agency head. Room still exists to negotiate over the size of F2 since the analytic question is the amount of reduction in the likelihood of a suit that different F2 levels will buy.

Does budgetary strategy and negotiation really unfold in this way when the threat of judicial intervention in agency operations is present? Diver, discussing institutional reform litigation, observed, "the lawsuit gives the operating manager unprecedented leverage to obtain additional resources. A judicial decree weakens the resistance he usually encounters in seeking funds."[7] The logic, of course, follows from the crisis technique; in addition, more general expectations of the "natural" inclination of administrators to expand budgets would certainly lead one to the strategic use of litigation outlined above. It is understandable, however, that few administrators would actually acknowledge that they in fact have adopted such a budgetary stance toward litigation—and only a smattering of anecdotal evidence even hints that the scenario outlined is plausible.[8]

From the standpoint of budgetary behavior, incrementalism is very much intact in this revised standard model. The courts may influence strategic behavior, but the process is largely unaltered. This is so because budgeting is still carried out largely by addition—adding modest amounts to the budgetary base of the agencies with little concern for the aggregate. While this portrait of the budget process has always received some criticism, it is nevertheless fair to say that, in the past, budgeting was usually described as a series of disjointed "bottom-up" decisions with little explicit attention to fiscal limits. In a positive sum budget atmosphere where all agencies *appear* to be winners, judicial intervention merely facilitates the strategic game for some of the players.

When increments are no longer guaranteed, the game is altered. Fiscal scarcity alters the game even without the intervention of the courts. In particular, the major features of incrementalism—

compartmentalized budgetary roles, negotiation strategies, marginal adjustments to a previous year's budgetary base, and stability—are jeopardized by a deteriorating fiscal climate. As the fiscal environment worsens, the ability to sustain incremental features of the process erodes. For example, marginal adjustments are no longer guaranteed, the value (or importance) of negotiation strategies becomes diminished since there is less to negotiate about, and perhaps most important, the budget process becomes less predictable.[9] Even a casual glance at the federal budget process over the past five years would provide several illustrations of these observations.

Courts are likely to aggravate the situation. Judges, after all, are not fiscal managers; unlike governors, the judiciary operates with no balanced budget constraint. In fact, judges have said that defendant agencies cannot offer lack of funds as a reason for failure to remedy constitutional violations. The involvement of the courts in developing policy in a deteriorating fiscal environment *could* be profound. After all, if fair share adjustments are no longer guaranteed, court-mandated spending puts judges in a budgetary Robin Hood position. When the court dictates budgetary winners by requiring injunctive relief for the plaintiffs, there *must* be budgetary losers (given the budget constraint imposed by fiscal austerity). Are all agencies that face the wrath of judges inevitable budgetary winners? The next section identifies three factors that are likely to determine the strategic position of the agency: the fiscal climate, the probability of litigation (or the passage of time since the initial litigation), and agency agreement with the policy intent of the judicial decision. Using these three factors, conditions are described which lead to budgetary environments that differ from patterns expected from incremental behavior.

Judicial-Budgetary Environments: Alternative Strategic Expectations

The previous section specified a revised model of budgetary incrementalism in an environment with some likelihood of litigation. The portrait of budgeting included a few restrictive assumptions. First, some probability of a lawsuit exists. Second, the administrator is willing to use that probability to try to extract a budget larger than the one otherwise anticipated by using the crisis technique. Third, the expected value of an expanded budget is greater than either the cost of being caught bluffing by the legislature or the budget office *or* the cost of a judicially imposed policy change which is unacceptable to the agency. This situation is a particular judicial-budgetary environment with the following characteristics:

- judicial activity was present or anticipated prior to the agency's use of the threat strategy;
- agency actually used the threat as part of the budget submission;
- agency is positive or at least neutral with respect to the likely policy outcome of litigation (assuming that the agency, as defendant, should lose the suit).

This portrait of the judicial-budgetary environment is similar to Diver's description of "litigation as a bargaining game."[10] The image of litigation as a bargaining game is useful because it shows how, under certain (restrictive) conditions, the budget process *could* be used as a vehicle for substantive policy changes pertaining to due process rights. The determining condition of this first environment is the willingness of the agency to use the threat of a lawsuit as a budget ploy.

Consider a *second* environment. Here, litigation has already developed to the point that a court has rendered a judgment against the defendant agency. *If* the agency is in agreement with the policy enunciated by the court, the policy has a high probability of being implemented because the court's objective —*compliance*—and the agency's objective—*budget expansion*—seem to be compatible. Frequently, a judge facilitates negotiations between the parties, often resulting in a consent decree where the judge authorizes the implementation of some variation of the plaintiff's demands.

The time frame is one to three years after a court decision has been reached in this second situation. The agency asks for increased budget levels to implement the court's decision. The agency is expected to be either in agreement or, at minimum, neutral with respect to the policy direction of the court's decisions. Also, the agency expects a net increase in the budget beyond any anticipated fair share so that compliance with the court order does not take budgetary resources away from other programs managed by the agency.

Prison conditions in Rhode Island in the late 1970s illustrate this second environment. In August 1977,

a district court judge found conditions in the state's maximum security facility to be in violation of the Eighth Amendment. After some initial resistance, the state began to implement the court's decision. Among the explanations offered for the state's compliance was the governor's general agreement with the policy implications of the court decision. Also, legislative resistance was softened by federal funds from the Law Enforcement Assistance Administration (LEAA) that would be used to defray some of the increased budgetary costs of compliance.

The *third* situation follows logically from the second. In many cases, a court decision, after a period of three or more years, has not been implemented to the satisfaction of the court. Accounts of well known institutional reform litigation cases such as *Holt* and *Willowbrook* have described this situation. The agency, as defendant, becomes embroiled in protracted litigation that takes place over several years. Sometimes the level of judicial involvement intensifies over the life of the litigation as the court searches for ways to enforce compliance. If the year that the decision was first announced is "*t*," what impact would judicial involvement have on the budgetary character of the agency in, say, *t*+3 (or more) years—assuming that the agency *still* accepts the policy implications of the court's actions? From the vantage point of budgetary strategy only, the agency is unlikely to be in an advantaged position. First, the agency can obviously no longer use the threat of judicial sanction as a ploy in budget formulation. Second, the passage of time provides the legislature and the budget office with the opportunity to assess the consequences of noncompliance. Third, factors not related directly to the litigation may impinge on implementation. These may include the intergovernmental dimension of the dispute and the budgetary options available to the state. In a nutshell, both compliance *and* budgetary expansion are now made more problematical.

Many institutional reform cases probably fall into this third environment. The following observation by M. Kay Harris and Dudley P. Spiller, Jr. concerning the problems implementing the *Holt* v. *Sarver* (1969) decision in Arkansas is instructive: "The massive changes ordered in *Holt* required expenditure of funds in excess of the amount then in the control of the defendants. Although the defendant correctional administrator was not explicitly required to raise or spend additional revenues, as a practical matter compliance required that additional revenues be raised and spent. . . . The administrator at the time the implementation process began, who had welcomed the litigation as tool to make needed reforms, was unable to persuade the legislature to appropriate required funds.''[11] A judicial-budgetary environment may offer options—as well as restrict options—for administrators and legislators. For example, in Alabama, Judge Johnson nudged the state toward a position of budgetary opportunity in *Wyatt* because improvements in mental health facilities would permit the state to become eligible for federal funding. However, when compliance requires large increases to an agency's operating budget (rather than expansion through capital spending), resistance is likely to be strong.

A *fourth* situation is one in which possible litigation is a threat to the agency. Unlike the first environment, the agency is *not* in agreement with the policy which the court would hand down in the event that the defendant agency lost the suit. Now, the administrator's self-interest principle—defined as budgetary maximization—is not self-evident. While the prospects for budget expansion still exist, nonbudgetary concerns of the agency, particularly judicial ''encroachments'' on executive terrain, may likely override the budget maximizing objective. An earlier study of administrative reactions to judicial decisions in California found that some prison officials resented what they felt was judicial interference in their administrative responsibilities.[12] While this does not completely obviate the feasibility of the crisis technique outlined in the first environment, it means that the costs associated with the unsuccessful use of the tactic are likely to be higher. Consequently, high risk administrators may still act *as if* the situation is like environment one, whereas risk averse managers may choose to marshall support against the court's involvement in the administration of their agencies even if some gains may be made from such judicial involvement.

Ohio's prison case, *Chapman* v. *Rhodes* (1977), illustrative of this fourth amendment. The director of Correction and Rehabilitation in Ohio at the time of *Rhodes* was opposed to the policy direction being taken by the federal courts in prison reform cases. The director believed that judges were not the allies of beleaguered corrections administrators in their struggles with the budget office or the legislature. On the contrary, the director generally

had difficulties trying to increase his operating budget while, at the same time, developing a capital budget construction program. He felt that judicial involvement would only exacerbate his negotiations with the legislature. From his point of view, *Rhodes* provided no budgetary bonanza.[13]

A *fifth* situation may arise one to three years after the onset of litigation. Unlike environment two, in this situation the defendant agency finds the court mandated policy objectionable. Notice that nonbudgetary considerations may override simple budget-maximizing objectives. What are some of the agency's likely responses? First, *delay* would probably be related to the severity of the policy objections *and* the extent of judicial involvement. Second, the degree of resistance may be influenced by alternative programmatic options that are available to the agency. And third, the agency's responses may be affected by the type of budgetary consequence that is likely to follow. For instance, if judicially mandated improvements to facilities can be funded by intergovernmental grants, resistance may be less than in a situation requiring funding through a redistribution of the agency's operating budget. Perhaps the cases that best reflect these general conditions are those involving school desegregation where delay became routine political responses to judicial decisions. Two insiders in the Boston school desegregation saga summarized their view of the fiscal ramifications of desegregation in the following way: ''It is avoidance, ineptitude, confusion and then conflict, that give rise to the costliness of desegregation in some cities.''[14] One need not reach the same harsh judgment to appreciate that both antipathy to the policy direction of the courts and the anticipated adverse effect on the fiscal environment have combined to produce delay and resistance in this environment.

A *sixth* environment follows logically from the one above. This is a situation three or more years after the onset of litigation. Like the previous environment, the agency is opposed to the policy direction of the court. The agency's resistance is expected to be high. Similarly, the legislature and/or executive tends to resist implementation *unless* the court's threat to take over political functions is considered highly credible.[15] In general, the larger the policy shift and the larger the reallocation of resources, the stronger the resistance will be. In this environment the prospects for successful judicial implementation are low.

Overcrowding conditions in local jails often reflect this environment. An Advisory Commission on Intergovernmental Relations study on jails included the observation, "In the race for local budgetary eminence, jails have long been functional losers."[16] Litigation has complicated the budgetary problem. While some local governments with inadequate jail facilities have responded by initiating capital budget projects, legislatures have been reluctant to put additional funds into existing structures while construction is planned or in progress. Judges have not turned a blind eye to the conditions in existing facilities merely because improvements are anticipated in the future. In this environment agency and/or legislative resistance is likely to be protracted as illustrated by the conflict between the courts and New York City and the State of New York concerning unconstitutional conditions of facilities located in the city.

When the Increment Is Mortgaged Through Judicial Involvement

Judicial intervention in the budget process *may* not necessarily alter budget routines. If it cannot be shown that budgetary *methods* have been visibly altered as a result of judicial involvements in taxing and spending decisions, it can at least be argued that the courts have, on occasion, become none-too-silent forces in the budget process. Since participation of the courts requires litigation, and since litigation must be initiated by plaintiffs seeking injunctive relief, it follows that judicial involvement in budgeting is difficult to predict. What consequence does this loss of predictability have?

From the vantage point of the principal actors in the budget process, the unanticipated involvement of the courts impinges on the ability of actors to calculate the likely results of their strategic behaviors—and the responses expected from others to their behaviors. Since judicial behavior is not random, at this level we could say that the involvement of the courts in the budget process increases complexity and uncertainty—and thereby makes calculations more difficult. Does this make incrementalism obsolete? Not necessarily. Increased complexity and uncertainty make calculation more difficult; however, this is not likely to affect the entire process. Rather, budgeting is made more

unpredictable for only those agencies influenced by litigation.

Can a budget process, then, be *partly* incremental? That depends where one looks. Surely agencies unaffected by litigation may utilize the standard model, except in conditions of budgeting stringency. But this pertains only to budget formulation up to the legislative phase of the budget cycle. A factual problem may exist. If fiscal conditions are deteriorating *and* courts are mandating improvements in one or more agencies, can it be assumed that incremental methods will remain unaffected in the review and appropriations phases of the cycle? Or can it be inferred that top-down influences will alter incremental methods? If so, with what results?

Answers depend on the aggregate size of the increment. This is, of course, a different use of the concept, one more conventional though analytically vacuous. This refers to the real year-to-year increases in a government's budget. A handy classification of different levels of fiscal scarcity has been suggested by Schick.[17] To use his terminology, under conditions of "chronic" scarcity (or worse), budget managers are inclined to try to dampen agency spending appetites since requests will necessarily exceed available resources. In such instances of fiscal stringency, Schick says that incremental methods and processes cannot prevail. The hard choices in a scarcity or cutback environment become aggravated by judicially mandated spending. The logic is simple enough; in this situation courts mortgage the modest budgetary increments. Both positive and normative consequences follow.

Positive consequences pertain to institutional regularities that are altered as a result of external conditions, such as the fiscal environment, that affect the budget process. Research on budget processes in environments of fiscal austerity has shown that basic patterns of strategy, negotiation, and accommodation are constrained by fiscal limits.[18] The impact of judicial intervention outlined here, however, is not a mere variation on the fiscal stress theme. Jurisdictions that can anticipate fiscal stringency fit Wildavsky's description of "poor and certain."[19] Poverty, in a budgetary context, is self-explanatory. Certainty refers to strategy and calculation. The process, in broad strokes, is essentially incremental. Judicial intervention in the process can alter these conditions.

Consider, first, the growth motive. Is it conceivable that agency heads could be in a position to resist budgetary expansion? Models of budgetary growth do not easily incorporate such a perverse possibility. But when resources are scarce, managers may not want to be responsible for expanded programs, facilities, or activities with which they are not in agreement—even if budgets grow. How might a manager actually *avoid* budget expansion when such expansion is predicated on judicial policy that is anathema to the manager? It depends on the implementation options available to the defendant agency. For example, injunctive relief to ameliorate prison overcrowding has been implemented in some states by moving prisoners out of state correctional facilities to county jails. While obviously a temporary approach, it has been used as a way to reduce overcrowding. Neither option neatly fits a model whereby the courts may be used as administrative leverage to pursue budgetary objectives.

The problem with the courts—from a budgetary perspective—is that they do not go away. This implies that short-term palliatives that produce incomplete implementation responses are unlikely to satisfy courts. Judges seem to have great staying power, as the history of institutional reform in Alabama prisons and psychiatric facilities under the watchful eyes of district court judge Frank Johnson demonstrates. When agencies welcome the courts, it is not difficult to interpret budgetary behavior; the "crisis technique" is relatively straightforward. But judicially mandated spending requires interpretation that does not easily come from basic models of what drives budgets—and how they are controlled.

From a political standpoint judges may be in positions to mortgage budgetary increments. The consequence is not trivial *if* a government in an austere fiscal climate finds that an agency is advantaged by judicial intervention. For instance, the budgetary climate in the City of New York has improved considerably since the financial crisis of 1975; nevertheless, spending control is still heavily emphasized. Yet, because of judicial decisions concerning prison overcrowding, the corrections department has found itself in a relatively favored position (compared to other city agencies). This is not due to budgetary skill on the part of the agency's managers; rather, the court has, in effect, mortgaged part of the modest budgetary increment. The same observation could be made about judicial involvement in the areas of the homeless and special education in which advocacy groups foster litigation. From a conceptual standpoint, the interaction between the fiscal climate and judicial intervention wrecks havoc with the traditional stability that once enhanced understanding of public budgetary processes.

A Return to V. O. Key's Basic Budgetary Question

Is this bad? It depends on what is expected from budgeting. This analysis supports V. O. Key's classic question concerning the basis for allocating budgetary resources among competing purposes.[20] Of course, Key posed the question in terms of a principle, or a set of principles, of nonmarket allocation. Such principles, to the extent that they exist, are found in the application of microeconomics to public budgeting. But few would argue that, for example, the Paretian principle helps much in analyzing government budgets. This is one reason why budget researchers continue to pursue Key's query about the basis for allocating to activity x versus activity y.

Economists may rail at the suggestion, but political scientists have done no worse—and perhaps they have done a bit better at answering the question. Pluralist roots of incremental budgetary theory have served fairly well in the past to explain—post-hoc, to be sure—why there have been budgetary winners and budgetary losers. As long as the notion is accepted that competing purposes within a constrained budget force choice, the analytic problem—whether from the vantage point of microeconomics or even pluralism—is established. The major difference is that the normative underpinnings of microeconomics are easier to detect; political scientists have always been a bit squeamish about revealing their value-based presuppositions—partly because nothing rivals, say, the efficiency argument in allocation decision.[21] But this may be pushed too far. After all, many reasons are offered for the general failure of budgetary reforms which attempt to make the process more "rational"—a code word for taking politics out of budgeting. One explanation is that the goal of making allocation decisions on the basis of efficiency sometimes conflicts with the norm of reciprocity.

Fiscal stringency does not automatically alter the normative dimensions of the allocation decision. However, most observers of budgeting would concede that zero-sum outcomes are more unpleasant than the "budgetary illusion" of positive sum (the term budgetary illusion is used since, even with real growth, some lose in terms of their *relative* share of the growth dividend). But even a casual glance at federal budgetary politics in FY1986 highlights the rudiments of pluralist budgetary politics—though they are somewhat constrained by top-down fiscal management decisions.

Little if any of this seems to fit budgetary situations which are impacted by court actions. Judges need not worry about either the analytics or the normative bases of allocation decisions. The protection of rights often seems divorced from fiscal limits and other organizational constraints. Advocates of due process protection could probably mount a strong argument that fiscal constraints *are* irrelevant. Logically, however, if a court mandates a change that must be funded within a budgetary constraint, the decision forces budgetary redistribution. Unlike redistribution that takes place, say, during the appropriations process—where claimants can attempt to exert their influence—those affected adversely by the budgetary fallout of the court's decision have no obvious place to turn.

The intervention of the courts in the budget process, then, requires taking Key's question to the high ground of political debate. Perhaps the search for budget theory has always been misplaced. Positive approaches to budgeting, after all, are really derived from propositions about individual and collective behavior that are said to be generalizable beyond the confines of public budgeting. Can budget theory be imagined without Simon and Lindblom?[22] When the spectre is raised of allocation decisions influenced by the courts, that likewise raises fundamental issues of constitutional and representative democracy—the degree to which decisions reflect constitutional fundamentals and/or electoral preferences—and discrepancies between them.

Notes

1. Linda Harriman and Jeffrey D. Straussman, "Do Judges Determine Budget Decisions? Federal Court Decisions in Prison Reform and State Spending for Corrections," *Public Administration Review*, vol. 43 (July/August 1983), pp. 343–351.
2. Robert Martiniano, "The Willowbrook Consent Decree: A Case Study of the Judicial Impact on Budgeting" (Rockefeller College of Public Affairs and Policy, New York Case Studies in Public Management, September 1984).
3. Phillip Cooper, "Between the Legal Rock and the Political Hard Place: Interactions of Federal District Court Judges and State and Local Officials" (presented at the Annual Meeting of the American Political Science Association, Chicago, September 1–4, 1983).
4. Phillip Cooper, "Pressure Point: A Comparative Case Analysis of Federal District Court Equitable Decrees" (Presented at the Annual Meeting of the Western Political Science Association, Sacramento, . April 12–14, 1984), p. 33.
5. See, for example, Lance T. LeLoup and William B. Moreland, "Agency Strategies and Executive Review: The Hidden Politics of Budgeting," *Public Administration Review*, vol. 38 (May/June 1978), pp. 232–239.
6. Aaron Wildavsky, *The Politics of the Budgetary Process*, fourth edition (Boston: Little, Brown and Company, 1984), p. 119.
7. Colin Diver, "The Judge as Political Broker: Superintending Structural Change in Public Institutions," *Virginia Law Review*, vol. 65 (February 1979), p. 85.
8. See, for example, Allen L. Ault, "Resource Utilization in Corrections," *Corrections Today*, vol. 42 (July/August 1980), p. 13.
9. For an extended argument see, Barry Bozeman and Jeffrey D. Straussman, "Shrinking Budgets and the Shrinkage of Budget Theory," *Public Administration Review*, vol. 42 (November/December 1982), pp. 509–515.
10. Diver, *op. cit.*, pp. 64–88.
11. M. Kay Harris and Dudley P. Spiller, Jr., *After Decision: Implementation of Judicial Decrees in Correctional Settings* (Washington: American Bar Association, November 1976), p. 13.
12. Note, "Judicial Intervention in Corrections: The California Experience—An Empirical Study," *UCLA Law Review*, vol. 20 (February 1973), pp. 452–580.
13. Phillip Cooper, *Hard Judicial Choices: Federal District Judges and State and Local Officials* (New York: Oxford University Press, forthcoming).
14. Robert A. Dentler and Marvin B. Scott, *Schools on Trial* (Cambridge: Abt Books, 1981), p. 216.
15. William A. Fletcher, "The Discretionary Constitution: Institutional Remedies and Judicial Legitimacy," *Yale Law Journal*, vol. 91 (March 1982), pp. 635–697.
16. Advisory Commission on Intergovernmental Relations, *Jails: Intergovernmental Dimensions of a Local Problem* (Washington: ACIR, 1984).
17. Allen Schick, "Budgetary Adaptations to Resource Scarcity," in Charles H. Levine and Irene Rubin (eds.), *Fiscal Stress and Public Policy* (Newbury Park: Sage, 1980), pp. 113–134. Also, Allen Schick, "Macro-Budgetary Adaptations to Fiscal Stress in

Industrialized Democracies,'' *Public Administration Review,* vol. 46 (March/April 1986), pages pending.

18. Naomi Caiden and Aaron Wildavsky, *Planning and Budgeting in Poor Countries* (New York: Wiley, 1975); see also, Jane Massey and Jeffrey D. Straussman, ''Budget Control Is Alive and Well: Case Study of a County Government,'' *Public Budgeting & Finance,* vol. 1 (Winter 1981), pp 3–11.

19. Aaron Wildavsky, *Budgeting* (Boston: Little, Brown and Company, 1975), pp. 114–116.

20. V. O. Key, ''The Lack of a Budgetary Theory,'' *American Political Science Review,* vol. 34 (December 1940), pp. 1137–1144.

21. See Richard R. Nelson, *The Moon and the Ghetto* (New York: Norton, 1977), pp. 41–47.

22. Herbert A. Simon, *Administrative Behavior,* 3d. ed. (New York: The Free Press, 1976); Charles E. Lindblom, ''The Science of 'Muddling Through,' '' *Public Administration Review,* vol. 19 (Spring 1959), pp. 79–88.

16

The Executive Budget—An Idea Whose Time Has Passed

Bernard T. Pitsvada
George Washington University

In recent years the most pervasive criticism of Congress from all parts of the political spectrum has been its perceived failure "to control spending." Periodically, presidents at odds with Congress over national priorities have also leveled this charge. However, the executive branch rarely enters into debates over which branch of government really speaks for the "people," that is, should legitimately set priorities. Instead, the attacks concentrate on how Congress does business. Criticism focuses on process rather than outcomes.

For example, the presidential budget message accompanying the Fiscal Year (FY) 1987 budget submission to Congress, stated, "The Congressional budget process is foundering; last year it fell apart time and time again. The budget resolution and appropriation bills were months late in passing. . . . "[1] To correct this problem, as though it were the heart of the differences between the president and Congress, President Reagan suggested several procedural reforms—the balanced budget Constitutional amendment, the line-item veto, and Presidential signature (approval) of congressional budget resolutions. Thus repairing the "process" fixes the "problem."

The FY 1988 budget message continued the debate. "The current budget process has failed to provide a disciplined and responsible mechanism for consideration of the Federal budget. Budget procedures are cumbersome, complex, and convoluted. They permit and encourage a process that results in evasion of our duty to the American people. . . . " After a brief summary of his objections, Reagan concluded "The words alone are obscure and confusing; the process behind it is chaotic. The process must be streamlined and made more accountable."[2]

Source: Public Budgeting & Finance (Spring 1988): 85–94. Reprinted by permission.

The "congressional budget process," the subject of so much criticism, is the set of procedures and actions initiated by the Budget and Impoundment Control Act of 1974 as amended by the Balanced Budget and Emergency Deficit Control Act of 1985 (otherwise known as Gramm-Rudman-Hollings). Currently these laws provide for Congress to pass, on a predetermined schedule, a budget resolution which sets targets and binding limits on federal spending by nineteen broad functional categories such as Income Security, Transportation, Agriculture and National Defense. This process did not replace previous procedures but simply added to them. Congress must still pass authorizing legislation and thirteen appropriation acts to implement the budget resolutions (unless Congress resorts to an omnibus appropriation as it did in 1986).

The current budget process is complex and cumbersome. Critics point out that the budget has become so consuming that there is time for little else on the congressional agenda. Despite all this effort Congress has been able to pass all the appropriation acts before the beginning of the fiscal year only once since the 1974 Act has been in place—and that law moved the beginning of the fiscal year from July 1 to October 1. Late appropriations and thus continuing resolutions have become the norm and not the exception.

It has also been charged that the congressional budget process has heightened conflict, both with the executive and within Congress itself. Debates and votes on the total size of the budget with its resulting deficits are more difficult politically than the piecemeal enactment of various parts of the budget as was the rule before the act was passed.

The "budget problem" is thus traced to complexity and conflict, allegedly a direct result of the congressional budget process. The solution usually offered is to amend the Congressional Budget Act. But conflict preceded the act as well as followed it and may be held to stem from difficulties in adapting to resource constraints prevalent in many Western industrialized countries, rather than specific procedures. Complexity may equally derive from political circumstances, a reaction to polarization and refusals to compromise. Overall, it is possible that current budgetary difficulties may rest in some other part of the process.

The Federal Executive Budget

It may be somewhat eccentric to suggest that perhaps it is not the congressional budget process that is at fault but rather that venerable tribute to orthodox public administration theory—the Budget and Accounting Act of 1921 that is the heart of the budgetary process problem. The 1921 act mandated the submission of an executive budget to Congress fifteen days after Congress convened each year. Gramm-Rudman-Hollings moved this submission date to the first Monday after January 3 regardless of when Congress convenes. An executive budget is a document estimating receipts and outlays submitted by the chief executive to the legislature covering all components of the executive branch. The proposal requests appropriations, indicates the executive's programs and priorities and acts as an executive management tool for execution and accountability. At the federal level the chief executive, the president, with the assistance of the Office of Management and Budget and the multitude of federal agencies, submits a consolidated unified budget request to Congress in a single, prescribed format.

While contemporary public administrators viewed the executive budget as a means of improving economy, efficiency and accountability by consolidating power and responsibility under the president, Congress originally hoped to use the new budget document and the process used to prepare it to reduce spending and make government more businesslike in its operations. The debates before passage of the 1921 act abound with observations such as those by Senator Swanson (D., Va):

> I believe it will coordinate the various departments of the Government and make them more economical and effective and save much duplication in work and much waste and extravagence of expenditure.[3]

and Senator Edge (R., N.J.):

> it will have a wonderful moral effect on the present state of mind of all the American people if we do adopt the budget plan of administering the Government, and through that action they recognize that their Congress is preparing to transform the Government of their country, their Government, into something resembling a business organization, with its consequent saving.[4]

The few voices that questioned such optimism were quickly quieted and the bill was enacted into law giving the president the major responsibility for budget preparation of a consolidated document on the grounds that "He is the only officer of the administrative branch who is interested in the Government as a whole rather than in one particular part. He is the only administrative officer who is elected by the people and thus can be held politically responsible for his actions."[5]

In reading the select committee report that recommended the 1921 law with 65 years of hindsight it is significant to note (1) in that era of limited government, Congress viewed the individual cabinet and bureau officers rather than Congress itself as the president's opposition regarding what should be included in the budget and (2) the extent to which Congress convinced itself that the power to prepare the executive budget did not enhance executive power at the expense of legislative power.[6] Time has demonstrated the extent of these two congressional miscalculations as agreement between the president and Congress on budgetary content has not always been present and executive power has grown in budgetary matters largely at the expense of Congress.

Assigning responsibility to the president to submit a comprehensive budget plan for the entire executive branch which Congress would debate and then enact resulted in delegating to the president the establishment of a baseline from which decisions were to be made. The assumption that the presidentially-prepared executive budget would be an adequate point of departure against which to base the congressional review of the budget has proved a workable premise for most of the period since 1921.[7] This has been the case because budgets were largely "controllable" and presidents and Congresses have generally seen eye to eye through hot wars, cold wars, limited wars, recessions and prosperity on the size and general direction of annual budgets. The disagreements on details were worked out through a series of incremental changes as described by Wildavsky and Fenno in their pioneer works.[8] "Incrementalism" was the general rule of the day. However, there have been two periods when differences over budget priorities between the president and Congress were major issues and resulted in public battles.

During the early to mid 1970s when Republican President Nixon lacked the votes in either house of the Democratically controlled Congress to impose his priorities on the budget, he resorted to the practice of impounding funds, i.e., declining to spend appropriated funds on the grounds of "fighting inflation" or "controlling spending." The fact that these attempts were focused on programs that President Nixon opposed was not lost on his critics. After resorting to case-by-case law suits by individual members of Congress to force the spending of impounded funds, Congress as a whole resorted to a more permanent solution. It passed a law, the Budget and Impoundment Control Act of 1974, to clarify the conditions under which presidents could delay or refuse to spend appropriated funds. Mr. Nixon's departure from the presidency shortly thereafter put the final touch to this budgetary battle. In this case amending procedures had a positive effect on defusing conflict.

The second major set of budgetary battles between the two branches began in 1981 with the election of Ronald Reagan to the presidency. Except for the successful resort to the device of reconciliation in that first year, budgetary impasse has been the name of the game despite the fact that the Senate was controlled by the president's party between 1981 and 1986. At the base of the current budgetary confrontation is the persistent congressional reaction to the president's budget submissions as being unrealistic and unpassable documents. The current jargon is that the budget is "dead on arrival" or even "dead before arrival" on Capitol Hill. This implies that the budget document is simply the first proposal on the table and that serious negotiations and major compromise must follow. The president for his part usually refuses to negotiate a compromise at first, and holds to his position that the submitted executive budget truly reflects "his" position. When compromise is reached it comes after long delays and bitter negotiations. The authors of the 1921 law have had their way in the name of strengthening the chief executive and executive accountability. But a question may be raised as to who is really "responsible" for a budget that is perceived to be unrealistic in the light of current political realities by those called upon to enact it? Is this what the framers of the 1921 law had in mind? I doubt it.

Why It Doesn't Work

One major reason for these apparent differing perceptions regarding its utility is that the executive budget today is a far different document than it was a half century ago. The composition of the budget has changed drastically since 1921. Most of the current budget is locked in by previous decisions. Debt servicing and rising levels of entitlements are not susceptible to short-run changes through the appropriations process (approximately 60 percent of outlays in FY 1986 were in this category). They are indeed "uncontrollable" in the short run, therefore, not susceptible to change from year to year. In addition, budgetary programs are intertwined with the overall performance of the economy. This necessitates preparing assumptions regarding economic growth, inflation, unemployment and interest rates upon which to base budgetary estimates. Outcomes in the economy however, are not under government control and these have a direct affect on government outlays. As a result outlays often differ significantly from what was proposed in the budget and thereby reduce the utility and credibility of the budget submission. Regardless of agreement or disagreement the executive budget today offers less discretion and less opportunity for control by the executive than it did in previous years. Defense now remains the only major area of budgetary discretion.

What appears to be in order is a budget document prepared by a process that more closely reflects the political and economic realities of the day. It would also help the budget to be enacted if it did not embody every political issue of the day. This tends to cause the process to break down simply because of overload. One possibility out of the current impasse is to formulate a budget that reflects a legislative-executive consensus before the budget is prepared and submitted. Such a budget would represent a significant departure from the executive budget we now have. The executive budget concept is so widely accepted in public administration as the conventional tool for budgetary submission that to question it appears out of the question. It is used throughout all levels of government in this country, including most large cities and virtually all states—but there are exceptions.

Throughout most of our history we have looked at the several states as a logical testing place for innovation and reform. States tried new devices for governing, and if they worked the case could be made for adoption by other states or the federal government. In this sense states have been viewed as laboratories for testing new ideas about governing or as one recent source labeled them as " . . . experimental stations for social policy. . . . "[9] This is true regarding procedural changes as well as substantive policy measures. As a case in point the executive budget concept itself was successfully tried at the state and local level before federal adoption of the idea in 1921. For a variety of reasons we have tended to neglect this source of innovation in recent years. Perhaps it would be worthwhile to examine how the states prepare their budgets to ascertain if there is something that works at that level which might be applicable to the federal level. Because a process or procedure is perceived "to work" at one level of government does not mean that it will necessarily be applicable to another level or in another setting. Nevertheless, despite differences in size, outlook and history, simply to ignore what the states are doing represents a degree of intellectual arrogance that we can ill afford.

The major fundamental differences in state budgeting when compared with federal budgetary practices have been discussed in the relevant literature. This list ordinarily includes capital budgeting, biennial budgets, line-item vetoes, balanced operating budgets, laws mandating budgetary equilibrium or growth limitations, differing fiscal years and restrictions on legislative changes to executive budgets. Of all these procedures biennial budgeting appears the most likely change that will be adopted at the federal level. In fact the Department of Defense submitted a biennial budget in FY 88–89. Beyond this usual litany, two states have what appear to be significantly different approaches to budget preparation—in effect departures from the traditional idea of an executive budget.[10]

Alternative State Models

The two states that depart the most from the executive budget concept are South Carolina and Mississippi—both states with relatively "weak" governors (structurally, not personally). In the 1940s, V. O. Key quoting state politicians referred to South Carolina government as "legislative government."[11] These states' budget practices demonstrate rather ingenious methods to defuse budgetary conflict before it begins.

South Carolina has a State Budget and Control Board (BCB) which is composed of individuals from the executive and legislative branches. The board consists of the governor as chairman and four other members, who are also elected officials. They are the state treasurer, the comptroller general, the chairman of the Senate Finance Committee and the chairman of the House Ways and Means Committee. The board also has an independent staff.

The BCB staff assists in the development of revenue estimates for the state thereby setting the parameters for the budget. Since the South Carolina constitution precludes deficit spending these estimates become a critical part of budget preparation. The BCB staff also provides guidelines for agency budget preparation including monetary ceilings. The agencies prepare the budget requests and submit them to the BCB and after the BCB deliberates and makes its decisions, the budgets are returned to agencies by the BCB staff for preparation of a line-item detail budget. The line-item budget is incorporated into a General Appropriation Bill to be reviewed by the legislature and passed. After this sequence of events the budget is reviewed by the legislature (first the House and then the Senate), enacted and signed by the governor into law. The governor does have an "item veto" which enables him to exercise a degree of final flexibility over the appropriations.

The South Carolina Supreme Court upheld the constitutionality of the BCB in 1977 (*State, ex rel. McLeod* v. *Edwards,* 269 S.C. 75 at 84).[12] Since the BCB includes two key members of the legislative branch, the legislature is likely to approve the budget. In addition, the high degree of legislative involvement in the administration of state programs which is typical in South Carolina is further increased by BCB direct participation in the earliest stages of budget development.

The state of Mississippi has another unique system. In Mississippi there is a Joint Legislative Budget Committee whose membership consists of the president pro tem of the state senate, the lieutenant governor, chairman of the Senate Appropriations Committee, one member of the Senate designated by the lieutenant governor, chairman of the House Ways and Means Committee, chairman of the House Appropriations Committee, the Speaker of the House and two additional House members appointed by the Speaker. Governed by this committee is a Legislative Budget Office (LBO) which is mandated to prepare a balanced budget every year. The LBO requires all state agencies to file budget requests in a form and level of detail mandated by the LBO. The LBO then can reduce or eliminate any item requested. The office is authorized to conduct hearings in order to determine valid agency requirements. Notice of such proposed hearings is given to the governor's budget officer who may attend to look out for the governor's interest. Since 1984 the governor has the legal responsibility to submit a balanced budget to the LBO. Any recommendations from the governor that would unbalance the budget must include recommended revenue sources.

Obviously what works in South Carolina and Mississippi will not necessarily work anywhere else. After all 48 states do use a system closer to the executive budget. Overall, it is very unlikely that either the South Carolina or Mississippi approach to budget preparation would ever be adopted *in toto* at the federal level. They are detailed here only to demonstrate the imaginative type of approach that is used and works elsewhere. The moral of the story is simply that government does not collapse where chief executives share budget preparation responsibilities with the legislature.

While the details and specifics of these two states differ, the basic idea underlying such techniques for preparing the state budget are the same. They are attempts to overcome the built-in problems inherent in the separation of powers. In effect they represent a melding of the budgetary powers of the legislature and executive in an attempt to improve performance. The literature of political science reform is filled with ideas about how to overcome deadlocks in policy that appear to result from the separation of powers. The usual preferred solutions would take our federal system several steps closer to parliamentary government. However, such changes would require amending the Constitution. For this very reason the proposals rarely are taken seriously.

In discussing state governments the most recent *Book of the States* observes, "Considerable executive-legislative stress still exists in the budget process and in determining the role each branch should play in the development and implementation of the budget."[13] The same holds true at the federal level to the detriment of our ability to govern ourselves. Gramm-Rudman can only be understood in this context. According to David Stockman, one of the chief actors in the budget breakdowns of the 1980s, Gramm-Rudman was a "two-by-four" approach Congress used to send the president a message about the budgetary imbalance (spending vs. revenues) after they were unable to communicate in a more

reasonable manner.[14] Budgeting by two-by-four is a questionable way to do business. It certainly does not represent the separation of powers in the best light.

Proposal: The Federal Joint Budgetary Council

What is worth thinking about is to consider some version of the South Carolina-Mississippi concept of a joint legislative-executive council to decide what should be included in the annual federal budget submission. For example, I propose a council consisting of representatives of the president, secretary of Treasury, Speaker of the House, president pro tem of the Senate and comptroller general be established as a starting point. OMB and the Congressional Budget Office could act as honest brokers to develop common economic assumptions, perform the necessary calculations and project appropriate estimates of budgetary proposals in support of the Joint Budgetary Council. The basic objective of this council, or any similarly composed group, would be to develop a budget proposal that was "alive on arrival" on Capitol Hill and could be used as a recognized baseline against which Congress could make incremental adjustments. To facilitate agreement, the council would have to adopt certain limiting ground rules regarding the extent to which new program initiatives or program terminations could be included in the annual budget submission. Fisher aptly points out that today "There is chronic confusion about which budget is the budget: the president's, the first budget resolution, the second budget resolution, the second budget resolution revised or a succession of reestimates, updates, and revised baselines."[15] Fine tuning of existing policies from an agreed upon baseline is probably all the budget cycle can realistically accommodate on an annual basis within legislatively mandated time tables and fiscal year constraints.

Congress as an entity of 535 individuals cannot build a budget from the ground. It needs a viable starting place for its review and neither the budget resolutions nor executive budget has been a definitive enough starting place in recent years. Incrementalism as a decision-making tool has both its critics and advocates. Nevertheless, the extent to which the basic economic assumptions and programs are agreed upon, the more readily can incremental adjustments be reached. In reality since so much of the budget is "uncontrollable" and related to price level adjustments, we have a variation of this at present.[16] Why not recognize and build on it? Under a Joint Budgetary Council approach the debate over whether something is included in the budget would precede budget submission. This should help eliminate the inclusion of "pie in the sky" proposals such as to eliminate the Departments of Energy and Education from the budget submissions. Legislation for such change should of necessity be considered separately and in its own schedule and not clutter up the budget timetable.

Whether or not we have a Department of Energy is a policy question more than it is a budgetary question, although it certainly has budgetary aspects. When we try to saddle the budget with all the controversial issues on the political agenda we overload the budgetary system and increase the likelihood of missed deadlines and continuing resolutions. In summary, major changes to programs should be submitted by the administration to be considered as normal aspects of the legislative process. The impact of such proposals would not be included in the budget submission. The budget submission should be limited to incremental adjustments to all ongoing programs within certain parameters (say ± 5 percent or ± 10 percent) agreed upon by a joint legislative-executive council. For those programs such as debt payments, unemployment compensation and social security payments, the joint OMB/CBO projections determine the budgeted amount. If the council could agree on larger changes to specific programs there would be nothing to preclude it in exceptional cases.

As a residual benefit of such a procedure, a joint legislative-executive budget should eliminate the necessity that Congress pass any budget resolutions to establish the parameters of a "congressional budget." The budget when submitted could move directly to the authorization/appropriation process. This act alone should free numerous legislative hours currently diverted to wrangling with the president over budget priorities. In addition the budget could probably be submitted to Congress two or three months later than is now required. This later submission date should enhance the accuracy of budgetary projections because of closer proximity to the beginning of the budgetary fiscal year.

This approach if implemented by law certainly would not cause any great additional difficulty if the legislative and executive branches were controlled by the same political party. Similar practice already occurs informally when both branches are in agreement. In cases where the two branches are not in agreement as they have not been since 1981, the question can be asked, "Could this way of doing business be any worse than what we now have?" Something needs to be done to restore amity and stability to the budget process because similar budgetary problems are likely to continue for the remainder of the century. The public's confidence needs to be restored. Closing down the government for eight hours does little in this direction. Political battles are part of a healthy, democratic system but political posturing should not bring the workings of government to a halt.

The issue might be raised as to whether or not such a joint legislative-executive council would run afoul of the separation of powers on Constitutional grounds. The answer is probably not although predicting Supreme Court decisions is a risky business especially when the Court tends to see the separation of powers as a rather mechanical process as described in the *Chadha* decision. As a country, we operated from 1787 to 1921 with an informal system that developed the so-called Book of Estimates based upon unwritten agreements and understandings between cabinet and bureau level officials and congressional committee chairmen. While few would advocate a return to this type of freelance, undisciplined approach the overriding principle remains— members of the executive branch and members of the legislative branch can work together to determine the direction of budget policy.

Conclusion

There is not necessarily superior wisdom, a higher sense of purpose nor greater concern with execution of the laws in the executive branch than in the legislative branch or vice versa. As Fisher has stated, "The record is inescapable: long before the New Deal period or even the Budget and Accounting Act of 1921, Congress decided that fiscal accountability and control could not be safeguarded by vesting those powers solely in the President and his assistants."[17] Some authors find the recent trend toward reducing the "integrity and responsibility" of the executive budget as properly disturbing.[18] Equally disturbing however is persistent budgetary impasse that portends possible long-run economic disaster for the country. Recent congressional hearings on reform of the budget process continue to focus on proposals such as multi-year budgeting, consolidating the authorizing and appropriating functions, better economic assumptions and projections and a modified line-item veto authority.[19] The question remains as to whether this type of minor adjustment is enough.

The bottom line to this entire matter is that the executive budget no longer provides the advantages that its sponsors assumed in 1921. In fact it offers several disadvantages its sponsors never dreamed. Presidents and Congresses often have differing views on national needs as embodied in budgetary programs and priorities. Both views are legitimate and must be resolved through the political process where political power counts more than questions of administrative efficiency. New procedures and processes are needed and these can be achieved simply by amending the Budget and Accounting Act of 1921 to call for a joint legislative-executive council budget to replace the executive budget. The executive budget was not found inscribed in stone on some sacred mountain and discovered by Warren G. Harding of all people. It is time to rethink the concept and seriously consider alternatives such as the one offered in this paper.

Notes

I would like to extend my thanks to Mr. William T. Putnam, former Executive Director of the State of South Carolina Budget & Control Board, who acquainted me with how that body operates and for having read an early version of this manuscript. The viewpoints and opinions expressed in this paper are mine and do not reflect the position of my employer.

1. *Budget of the United States, Fiscal Year 1987*, p. M-9.
2. *Budget of the United States, Fiscal Year 1988*, pp. M-12, M-13.
3. *U.S. Congressional Record*, 66th Congress, 2d Sess., (1920), Vol 59, Part 6, 6280.
4. Ibid, 6350.
5. U.S. Congress, House of Representatives, Select Committee of the Budget, *National Budget System* (Washington: Government Printing Office, 1921) p. 5, 67th Congress, 1st Sess., Report No. 14, 5.
6. Ibid, 4–7.

7. A highly perceptive article by Naomi Caiden, "Paradox, Ambiguity, and Enigma: The Strange Case of the Executive Budget and the United States Constitution," *Public Administration Review,* 47 (Jan./Feb. 1987):84–92, traces the evolution of the executive budget in this role and the reasons why it no longer fulfills its original purpose.
8. Aaron Wildavsky, *The Politics of the Budgetary Process* (Boston: Little, Brown and Company, 1964) and Richard Fenno, *The Power of the Purse* (Boston: Little, Brown and Company, 1966).
9. Robert B. Albretton and Ellen M. Dran, "Balanced Budgets and State Surpluses: The Politics of Budgeting in Illinois", *Public Administration Review,* 47 (Mar./Apr. 1987): 143.
10. *The Book of the States 1986–87 edition,* (Lexington, Kentucky: The Council of State Governments, 1986), 220–221. The chart dealing with State Budgetary practices indicates three states have budget making authority rest with other than the governor. Mississippi, South Carolina and Texas are the three states (pp. 220–221). However, in Texas the agency responsible for preparing the budget document is the Director of Management and Budget in the governor's office. In the other two states budget making authority and budget preparation exist outside the Governor's office (pp. 223–224).
11. V.O. Key, Jr., *Southern Politics* (New York: Vintage Books, 1949), 150.
12. Luther F. Carter and David S. Mann, eds. *Government in the Palmetto State* (Columbia, S.C., University of South Carolina Bureau of Governmental Research and Service, 1983), 142–146.
13. *The Book of the States,* 29.
14. David A. Stockman, *The Triumph of Politics* (New York: Avon Books, 1987), 457.
15. Louis Fisher, "Ten Years of the Budget Act: Still Searching for Controls", *Public Budgeting & Finance,* 5 (Autumn, 1985): 26.
16. Bernard T. Pitsvada and Frank D. Draper, "Making Sense of the Federal Budget the Old Fashioned Way— Incrementally," *Public Administration Review,* 44, (Sep./Oct. 1984): 401–406.
17. Louis Fisher, "The Administrative World of *Chadha* and *Bowsher*," *Public Administration Review,* 47 (May/June 1987): 215.
18. Louis Fisher, *Constitutional Conflicts between Congress and the President* (Princeton: Princeton University Press, 1985), 7.
19. U.S. Congress, House of Representatives, Committee on Government Operations, Subcommittee on Legislation and National Security, *Reform of the Federal Budget Process,* (Washington: Government Printing Office, 1987) 100th Congress, 1st. Sess.

17

Intergovernmental Relations in the Reagan Era

Richard P. Nathan
John R. Lago
Princeton University

In this article we examine the effect of the Reagan presidency on intergovernmental relations, focusing on federal fiscal flows. We begin our assessment with a summary of the recent history of federal aid to state and local governments going back to 1961. In the twenty-five year period, 1961–86, a number of important shifts occurred. Figure 1 compares federal aid to states and localities with state aid to local governments in constant dollars. In the early part of the period, which included Johnson's Great Society programs and the Nixon years, federal aid rose rapidly, but still remained below state aid to localities. This relationship shifted near the end of the Ford administration when Congress enacted stimulus spending programs in response to the 1973–75 recession and due to the rise in that period of unemployment compensation.

Federal spending reached its peak in 1978 under President Carter. Carter added to and expanded the stimulus grant programs started under Ford. By the end of fiscal 1978, Congress had appropriated more than $19 billion for antirecession revenue sharing grants, public works spending, and public service jobs. Typical of countercyclical federal aid programs, this boost came as the nation was coming out of the recession at the end of the Ford administration.

However, after the Carter stimulus, the picture changed markedly. Federal aid began to fall off at the end of the Carter period, an event we attribute to the shift in the country towards a more conservative mood, signalled by the adoption in June 1978 of Proposition 13 in California. Three months before the adoption of Proposition 13, President Carter on 27 March 1978 had submitted his trumpeted

Source: Public Budgeting & Finance (Autumn 1988): 15–29. Reprinted by permission.

"national urban policy" to Congress to target federal aid on cities. This program, in effect, would have made permanent many of the major components of his earlier antirecession stimulus package. But the new conservative mood of the country, manifest in pressure for public-sector retrenchment, seemed to cool President Carter's ardor. He pulled back from his own national urban policy initiative, and in the final two years of his presidency took steps to stem the rise in federal domestic spending.

The Reagan administration entered the scene in 1981 well disposed to continue this retrenchment movement. Striking while the iron was hot, Reagan's biggest cuts in federal aid came in 1981. The Omnibus Budget Reconciliation Act of that year cut federal grant outlays in fiscal 1982 by $6.6 billion compared to the previous year, a seven percent reduction in nominal terms (13 percent in real terms). The largest outlay reductions came in education, training, employment, and social services. Outlays in this functional area were cut by $4.9 billion, 23 percent compared to spending in fiscal 1981.

Then in 1981 there was another recession. Congress responded by enacting two antirecession stimulus measures, and federal aid outlays began to rise again, ultimately achieving levels in nominal terms above those in the Carter years. Although federal aid spending increased in real terms after 1982, it continued to remain below the funding levels for the last years of the Carter administration (see Table 1).

Figure 1 shows that not only did federal aid rise in real terms after 1982, but also state aid increased. In part in response to the Reagan administration's decentralization policies, the states began to do more. State aid to local governments, which had been relatively flat in real terms in the latter part of the 1970s and the early years of the 1980s, began to rise at a fast clip. In the three state fiscal years between 1983 and 1986, state aid to localities grew at a real annual rate of 5.6 percent.

Also notice in Figure 1 that once again (from 1981 on) state aid exceeded federal aid. A lot has happened in the twenty-five year period. The close reader of this history should also note that Table 1 shows another decline in federal aid outlays in both real and nominal terms under Reagan in 1987, which is attributable mainly to the demise of the local share of the revenue sharing program.

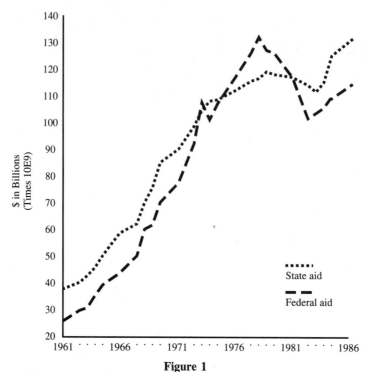

Figure 1
Federal and state aid outlays in constant (1986) dollars.
*Notes: State aid is shown for state fiscal year, which for most states begins
on July 1 and ends June 30. Federal aid is shown for the federal fiscal
year, which up until 1976 also began on July 1 and ended June 30.
Federal outlays after 1976 are for the federal budget period beginning
October 1 and ending September 30. Inflation adjustments based
on the Consumer Price Index.*
Sources: Office of Management and Budget, Historical Tables, Budget of
the United States Government Fiscal Year 1988, *and U.S. Census,*
Governmental Finances, *various years.*

Major Events Under Reagan

This article focuses on the history and composition of federal aid under Reagan, first looking at major developments and then at federal aid by functional areas of spending. This closer view of the Reagan period again reveals shifts that are important, and may be surprising to some readers. Seven events dominate the federal aid story under Reagan. One is the Omnibus Budget Act (OBRA) of 1981, which has already been mentioned. Another is the elimination of the Comprehensive Employment and Training Act's public service employment (PSE) program. The Reagan administration's termination of this

program in 1982 along with cuts in spending for job training accounted for $3.4 billion in reductions, more than half of the outlay cuts achieved between 1981 and 1982. The PSE program was large and unpopular, although our own research suggests it was unfairly maligned.[1] The odds are that the CETA-PSE programs would not have survived even under a more liberal Carter administration in the early eighties.

The third major federal-aid event under Reagan, as it turned out, was a nonevent. It was the president's swap and turnback proposals introduced in his "State of the Union" message in January 1982. Under this proposal, the administration recommended

Table 1
Federal grant outlays in nominal and constant (1986) dollars.

Year	Nominal $ in Millions	Constant $ in Billions
1960	$ 7,019.4	$ 26.2
1965	10,910.0	38.2
1970	24,065.2	69.9
1975	49,791.3	105.9
1980	91,461.0	125.4
1981	94,761.9	117.0
1982	86,194.9	101.7
1983	92,495.3	102.6
1984	97,577.3	104.1
1985	105,997.0	108.9
1986	113,746.6	114.3
1987	106,392.0	105.5
1988	116,644.0	109.0

Change:			
	1960–70	17,046.8	43.7
	Percent	242.8%	166.9%
	1970–80	67,386.8	55.5
	Percent	280.0%	79.4%
	1980–87	16,941.0	(19.9)
	Percent	18.8%	−15.9%

Notes: Outlays for 1988 are estimated.

Inflation adjustments based on the Consumer Price Index.
Sources: Office of Management and Budget, *Historical Tables, Budget of the United States Government, Fiscal Year 1988,* tables 1.1 and 12.1; *Special Analysis, Budget of the U.S. Government, Fiscal Year 1989,* table A-4.

that the federal government take over medicaid, and in return states assume responsibility for aid to families with dependent children (AFDC) and food stamps. The federalism initiative also would have had states assume some 40 federal programs and revenue sources in education, transportation, community development, and social services. Transfers would have occurred over a five-year period beginning in 1987 had Congress accepted the proposal.

The fourth major federal-aid event under Reagan was the enactment by Congress of two stimulus measures to combat the 1981–82 recession. The November 1982 elections brought an additional 26 Democrats to the House; many in Congress viewed the elections as a mandate to respond to the nation's rising unemployment, which by December had reached 10.8 percent. The first stimulus measure enacted was the Surface Transportation Assistance Act of 1982, signed by the president on 6 January

1983. The law raised the federal gasoline tax by a nickel-a-gallon and increased transportation outlays over the next five years. Between fiscal years 1983 and 1986, spending in this functional area rose by $5.1 billion. Outlays for federal highway programs accounted for most of this growth. The second stimulus measure, the Emergency Jobs Appropriations Act of 1983, authorized $4.6 billion in supplemental funds for fiscal 1983, over half of which came in the form of restorations of federal aid programs cut by the 1981 budget act.

The fifth major federal-aid event under Reagan was the elimination of the general revenue sharing program. Reagan had never been a fan of this Nixon "new federalism" initiative. Indeed, there are those who view it remarkable that the revenue sharing program avoided the budget guillotine as long as it did. Carter eliminated the state portion of revenue sharing in 1980 (one-third of the program's funds had gone to states). Reagan finally finished the job in 1986, eliminating the local portion of the program, which carried an annual price tag of $4.6 billion.

The sixth major development in grant spending under Reagan involves the medicaid program, by far the largest federal aid program. Provisions included in omnibus budget bills enacted in the mid-1980s—often provisions opposed by the administration—expanded the scope and coverage of medicaid. Outlays went from $18.9 billion in fiscal 1981 (21 percent of total federal outlays that year) to $29.5 billion in fiscal 1987 (27 percent). In constant dollars, federal outlays for medicaid grew by 23 percent between 1981 and 1987.

The seventh major event, the Gramm-Rudman-Hollings anti-deficit act, became law on 12 December 1985, but has yet to have a discernible effect on grant outlays. Many of the larger federal grant programs, including medicaid, aid to families with dependent children, food stamps, child nutrition, and nutritional assistance for women, infants, and children, are exempted from the automatic sequestering process specified by this law.

The history of federal aid under Reagan can be divided into three periods reflecting the events just discussed. They are: (1) the enactment of OBRA 1981; (2) the stimulus measures of 1982 and 1983; and (3) the remaining years of the Reagan period, in which federal aid continued to rise in real terms after the 1982 cuts. This latter increase was fueled in large measure by the growth in medicaid spending.

In this third period, federal spending for operating and capital programs declined in a number of key functional areas as will be discussed below.

Along with colleagues in fourteen states, we studied the effects of Reagan's cuts in federal grants-in-aid to state and local governments.[2] Among the findings from the study, which focused on the first Reagan term, were:

- The 1981 OBRA cuts, reducing spending for federal grants, are the only decline in nominal dollars in the past twenty-five years.
- The initial cuts fell more heavily on people, particularly the so-called working poor, rather than on the operating programs of state and local governments.
- States and local governments responded to federal aid reductions wih "coping" strategies, such as the use of carryover funds, transfers of funds among accounts, and other ways, delaying the effects of the spending cuts, until federal aid restorations came on the scene.
- These coping strategies generally did not occur for welfare (such as aid to families with dependent children and food stamps) and the public service employment programs, where the 1981 cuts tended to be passed directly onto recipients.

Major Functional Areas

Although total grant spending has increased following the historic 1982 cuts, the pattern of the restorations was uneven. Spending increases occurred for entitlement programs, especially medicaid, which mask the significant cuts that were made in operating and capital programs. The discussion that follows examines outlays in six functional areas of the budget. Together, these budget functions accounted for above 95 percent of federal aid spending in fiscal 1987. Three functional areas—natural resources and environment; community and regional development; and education, training, employment, and social services—received the largest cuts based on a comparison of outlays under Reagan versus spending under Carter. Overall grant spending for the remaining budget functions discussed below—transportation; health; and income security—grew in real terms as well as nominally.

The figures presented in this part of the article (Figures 2 through 7) show grant outlays in nominal

dollars, perhaps somewhat understating the size of the federal aid cutbacks under Reagan, but nonetheless reflective of the difference in grant spending under Reagan and grant spending in the last two years of the Carter administration, in which grant spending was level in nominal terms.

National resources and environment. Federal outlays in this functional area declined in nominal as well as in real terms under Reagan. In fiscal 1987, outlays totaled $4.1 billion, 24 percent less than in fiscal 1980, (a 46 percent cut in constant dollars). The biggest grant program in this functional area provides funds to states and localities for the construction of wastewater treatment facilities (see Figure 2). For fiscal 1982, the Reagan administration succeeded in lowering budget authority for this program to $2.4 billion, where it remained until fiscal 1987. The outlays shown for the wastewater treatment program in Figure 2 exceed the $2.4 billion budget authority, as state and local governments continued to spend federal aid from prior year authorizations.

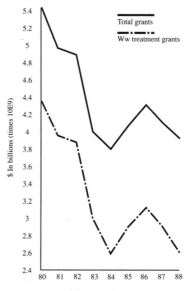

Figure 2

Natural resources and environmental grant outlays in nominal dollars.
Note: Outlays for 1988 are estimated.
Source: Office of Management and Budget, Historical Tables, Budget of the United States Government, Fiscal Year 1988.

In its 1986 budget request, the administration proposed that the federal government end its involvement in the wastewater treatment program by 1990, expressing a desire to have communities finance such facilities with assistance from states if necessary. For fiscal 1989, the administration proposed that the program's budget authority be reduced to $1.5 billion, half of which would capitalize a new revolving fund program that states would administer to help localities meet wastewater treatment needs.

Community and regional development. Fiscal 1987 outlays for grant programs in this functional area were $1.9 billion less than in 1981, a 31 percent reduction (see Figure 3). In real terms, spending declined by 45 percent.

OBRA 1981 significantly changed the community development block grant by creating a new block grant out of the small-cities portion of the program and giving states the option of administering the small-cities program. In 1983 funding for the community development program increased as a result of the emergency jobs act by $1 billion, to $4.456 billion. This increase, however, was temporary, as the program's budget authority dropped in fiscal 1987 to $3 billion, $600 million more than was requested

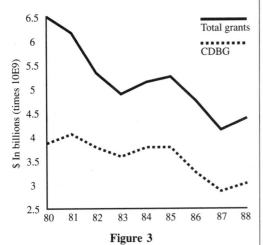

Figure 3
Community and regional development
grant outlays in nominal dollars.
Note: Outlays for 1988 are estimated.
Source: Office of Management and Budget,
Historical Tables, Budget of the United States
Government, Fiscal Year 1988.

by the administration but still nearly $500 million below the funding level for fiscal 1984.

In addition to the cuts in community development funds, several smaller programs in this functional area were cut under Reagan. The administration has proposed elimination of the urban development action grant (UDAG) program created by Carter to help finance commercial and residential development in cities. Since the days of David Stockman, Reagan officials have criticized this program as a subsidy for hotels and other businesses. Although the U.S. Department of Housing and Urban Development still administers UDAGs, the program is much smaller than it was under Carter. Funding in fiscal 1987 amounted to only $225 million, $450 million less than in 1981. For fiscal 1989, the administration has again proposed the program's termination.

Reagan also won nominal cuts in assistance programs administered by the Economic Development Administration. Since the early 1980s, Reagan budgets have annually proposed ending these economic development grants. The assistance programs still remain, though budget authority in 1987 totaled $192 million, nearly half the funding level in 1981.

Education, training, employment, and social services. After sustaining deep cuts in the early 1980s, spending in nominal dollars has returned back to pre-Reagan levels (see Figure 4). In real terms, this functional area was cut by 39 percent between 1980 and 1987. Between 1970 and 1980, grant spending had increased in real terms by 61 percent.

The distribution of cuts within this functional area was uneven. CETA-PSE, as mentioned earlier, accounted for the brunt of the initial big reduction. In October 1982, Congress passed the Job-Training Partnership Act (JTPA), replacing CETA job training programs with grant programs that gave states new administrative authority and increased the influence of the business community in job training programs through private industry councils. Under CETA, most job training grants went directly from the U.S. Department of Labor to local prime sponsors. Under JTPA, states became the intermediaries, responsible for overall planning, coordination, and evaluation of the program and the distribution of most federal job training grants to localities.

The administration's budget for fiscal 1989 proposes a further refinement in job training programs, requesting an additional $945 million for a new

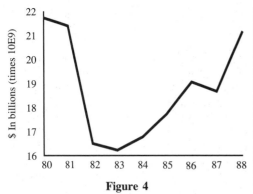

Figure 4
Education, training, employment, and social
service grant outlays in nominal dollars.
Note: Outlays for 1988 are estimated.
Source: Office of Management and Budget,
Historical Tables, Budget of the United States
Government, Fiscal Year 1988.

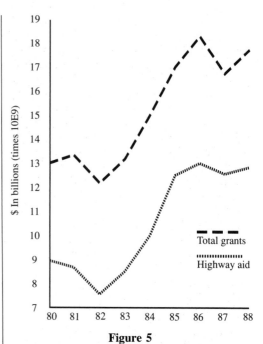

Figure 5
Transportation grant outlays in nominal dollars.
Note: Outlays for 1988 are estimated.
Source: Office of Management and Budget,
Historical Tables, Budget of the United States
Government, Fiscal Year 1988.

worker readjustment program intended to replace
existing job training programs for dislocated workers.

For most of the Reagan presidency, Congress has
regularly appropriated more than the administration
has requested for education grants such as compensatory education for disadvantaged students and the
education block grant created by OBRA 1981.
Budget authority for the compensatory education program is estimated at $4.3 billion for fiscal 1988 and
$940 million for the education block grant, a nominal
increase of $1.3 billion and $400 million, respectively, compared to spending levels in fiscal 1982.
For fiscal 1989, the administration has proposed a
budget authority of $4.6 billion for compensatory
aid programs.

Spending for social services has not fared as well
under Reagan. Budget authority for the social services block grant has remained at about $2.7 billion.
Congress has rejected several proposals by the
administration to eliminate the Work Incentive
(WIN) program and the community services block
grant program. Budget authority for WIN grants,
which ironically support job training services for
welfare recipients (a policy the administration favors)
was cut to less than $100 million in 1988, three-and-
a-half times less than the level in 1981.

Transportation. After early cuts in 1982, spending in this functional area has grown in nominal
dollars (see Figure 5). Still, in constant dollars, fiscal

1987 outlays remain at about their 1981 level. The
high-water mark came in 1986, when outlays reached
$18.4 billion. Most of this, $13.8 billion, consisted
of spending for federal highway grants.

Grant spending for airport construction increased
13 percent in real terms between 1980 and 1987.
Outlays for mass transit, on the other hand, have
declined nominally, as well as in real terms. Although
Congress has consistently rejected proposals from
the administration to eliminate operating subsidies
for urban transit systems, it has capped spending for
this program. For fiscal 1989 the administration has
again requested elimination of the program.

Health grants.   No functional area of federal aid
has grown faster than health. It increased by 87 percent between 1980 and 1987, a 33 percent rise in
constant dollars. The rate of growth has slowed under
Reagan, however. Between fiscal years 1970 and
1980, health grant outlays grew in real terms by

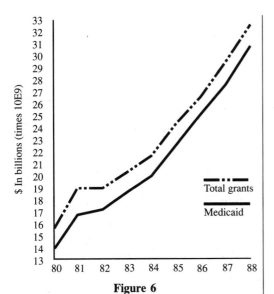

Figure 6
Health grant outlays in nominal dollars.
Note: Outlays for 1988 are estimated.
Source: Office of Management and Budget,
Historical Tables, Budget of the United States
Government, Fiscal Year 1988.

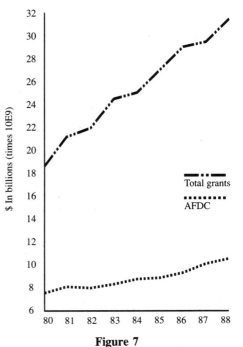

Figure 7
Income security grant outlays in nominal dollars.
Note: Outlays for 1988 are estimated.
Source: Office of Management and Budget,
Historical Tables, Budget of the United States
Government, Fiscal Year 1988.

93 percent. Most of this growth stems from the rapid increase in medicaid (see Figure 6), which makes up over 90 percent of the outlays in this functional area.

In 1981, Reagan succeeded in cutting medicaid outlays below the levels that they otherwise would have been. The administration reduced the amount of federal matching funds to states and tightened eligibility requirements for welfare, thus reducing the number of people qualifying for medicaid; Congress however, rejected efforts by the administration to cap the program's outlays. In fact, omnibus budget bills enacted in the mid-1980s gave states more authority and flexibility over the program, allowing them to extend home- and community-based services to the poor and to expand medical coverage to all pregnant women, infants, the elderly and disabled people with incomes below the federal poverty line.

Income security. Though the administration succeeded in making significant cuts in individual programs in this functional area, overall spending increased by more than $11 billion between fiscal years 1980 and 1987, a 15 percent real growth (see Figure 7). As with health grants, the rate at which

spending has grown under Reagan is less than the rate for the 1970s. Between 1970 and 1980 outlays for income security grants increased by a real rate of 51 percent.

Outlays for aid to families with dependent children, the largest grant program in this functional area, declined by two percent between fiscal years 1981 and 1982; the reduction stands out, however, not because of its size but because it came during a time when the country was in the midst of a recession and spending for the program normally would have increased. OBRA 1981 raised the income standards used by states to determine AFDC eligibility. These standards were later relaxed by Congress. The 1981 budget act also gave states authority to experiment with programs requiring welfare recipients to participate in job training and employment programs, which has spurred extensive state innovations in this field.[3]

Assisted housing grants also withstood fundamental change under Reagan. The administration cut housing assistance funds for the construction of large housing complexes for low-income people and advanced a much smaller program that disperses assistance in the form of vouchers that low-income people can use to purchase housing from the existing housing stock. Budget authority for the subsidized housing program went from $17.8 billion in fiscal 1981 to around $5 billion in fiscal 1987. Housing-aid outlays, however, have remained relatively constant in this period because of the delayed effect that a change in budget authority has on actual spending for construction programs; however, long-term outlays are expected to decline by "over $100 billion compared with the programs of the Carter administration."[4]

OBRA 1981 reduced outlays for the school lunch and other child nutrition programs by tightening income standards. Congress has rejected proposals from the administration for further cuts. Budget authority in fiscal 1984 for child nutrition grants totaled $3.4 billion, $500 million more than was requested by the administration, and in all but one of the budget years thereafter, Congress continued to authorize more than the Reagan administration requested. Outlay estimates for fiscal 1988 show that spending for this program has grown 43 percent in real terms since the 1982 Reagan cuts, but nonetheless remains lower than the level under Carter.

The Rising Role of States Stands Out

Turning now to the federalism impact of the federal aid policies of the Reagan years, we find that the most important developments are twofold—the relative decline in the federal role and the rising role of state governments. In part, the latter trend was a response to Reagan's policies. His theory of federalism, following the Tenth Amendment, has consistently favored the role of state governments. As governor of California and as president, Reagan has often sounded this theme. We find a paradox in these terms in Reagan's policies. As president, his call to action by the states may have undercut his own superordinate commitment to reducing the size and scope of the government in domestic affairs. The states in the Reagan period took his rhetoric seriously. State initiatives in the field of education, new training and job programs for welfare recipients, health policy initiatives (fueled in many cases by medicaid enhancements), and state infrastructure investments in the name of economic development underlie a rise in total state spending, which can be seen in Figure 8. In the late 1970s and early 1980s, direct general expenditures by states grew in constant dollars at a sluggish rate of 1.3 percent. Direct state spending began a sharp rebound in 1983.

Other factors besides Reagan's devolutionary and retrenchment policies underlie the increase in state

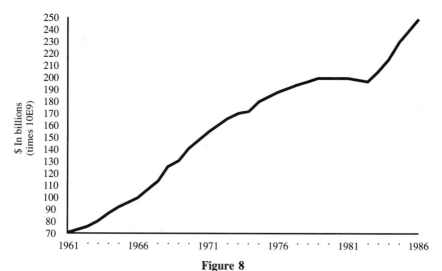

Figure 8
State direct general expenditures in constant (1986) dollars.
Notes: Inflation adjustments based on the Consumer Price Index.
Source: U.S. Census, Governmental Finances, various years.

involvement in domestic affairs. States on the whole benefitted materially from strong recoveries from the 1981–82 recession and had the resources to expand their programs in domestic affairs when the Reagan administration was cutting federal aid spending and signaling its intention to continue to do so.

State governments have also modernized in recent decades in terms of their managerial, technical, and administrative capacity. In a 1985 report on state government capability, the U.S. Advisory Commission on Intergovernmental Relations concluded, "state governments have been transformed in almost every facet of their structure and operations."[5] In addition, Martha Derthick believes that the civil rights revolution of the 1960s and the "end of Southern exceptionalism" has created a situation in which "the case for the states can at least begin to be discussed on its merits."[6] The long-term effects of the Supreme Court's *Baker vs. Carr* ruling, which reduced rural/urban imbalances in state legislatures, have also made states more legitimate contenders in the domestic arena.

We can only speculate about the future of the growing role of the states in domestic affairs. History offers one lesson. States have tended to take the lead in domestic affairs in times when conservative, anti-government ideology has predominated. In the early twentieth century, for example, when the country was "keeping cool with Coolidge," many states, though not all of them, were out front in such areas as workers' compensation, unemployment insurance, and the establishment of public assistance programs. These and other state initiatives planted the seeds for the New Deal. James T. Peterson writes that "states preceded the federal government in regulating large corporations, establishing minimum labor standards, and stimulating economic development." He adds that "the most remarkable development in state government in the 1920s was the increase in spending."[7]

Earlier in our history, over a century ago in the latter part of the 19th century, the states initiated new social policies in a period when the official policy in Washington was to resist the idea that the national government should get involved in the domestic arena.

What about the future? Will a cyclical pattern of alternating state and national government activism recur? Will the national government have a burst of domestic policy initiatives in the 1990s, and will the states in that period become relatively more quiescent?

Our inclination is to think that the nineties are not likely to be a period of dramatic federal government innovation on anything like the scale of the New Deal and the Johnson Great Society and Nixon New Federalism periods. One obvious reason for this is the serious budget pressures in Washington. Another is less obvious. The social agenda, as we see it, involves fewer big-spending issues on which there is a broad consensus for national action similar to those that spurred past periods of substantial domestic program innovation from the national government. We may be wrong, but we do go out on a limb: The 1990s will not in our view see a dramatic fiscal federalism shift involving large relative increases in federal spending for domestic purposes and a relative decline in what is currently the rising role of the states.

Notes

We received helpful comments on this paper from Lawrence Hush of the U.S. Office of Management and Budget.

1. Richard P. Nathan, Robert F. Cook, Richard Long, and Janet Galchick, *Job Creation Through Public Employment*, V. 2 *Monitoring the Public Service Employment Program, An Interim Report to the Congress* (Washington, D.C.: National Commission for Manpower Policy, March 1978); *Monitoring the Public Service Employment Program: The Second Round* (Washington, D.C.: National Commission for Manpower Policy, special report no. 32, March 1979).

2. Richard P. Nathan, Fred C. Doolittle, and Associates, *Reagan and the States* (Princeton, N.J.: Princeton University Press, 1987); Idem, *The Effects of the Reagan Domestic Program on State and Local Governments* (Princeton, N.J.: Princeton Urban and Regional Research Center, 1983); John W. Ellwood, ed., *Reductions in U.S. Domestic Spending: How They Affect State and Local Governments* (New Brunswick, N.J.: Transaction Books, 1982).

3. See, for example, Judith M. Gueron, "Work Initiatives for Welfare Recipients" (New York: Manpower Demonstration Research Corporation, March 1986).

4. John C. Weicher, "The Domestic Budget after Gramm-Rudman—and after Reagan," in Phillip Cagan, ed., *Deficits, Taxes, and Economic Adjustments,* (Washington, D.C.: the American Enterprise Institute, 1987), 263.

5. U.S. Advisory Commission on Intergovernmental Relations, *The Question of State Capability,* commission report, (Washington, D.C.: ACIR, Jan. 1985), 2.
6. Martha Derthick, ''American Federalism: Madison's Middle Ground in the 1980s,'' *Public Administration Review* 1 (Jan.-Feb. 1987): 72.

7. James T. Peterson, *The New Deal and the States, Federalism in Transition* (Princeton, N.J.: Princeton University Press, 1969), 4, 7.

18
The Rise
of Competitive
Federalism

John Shannon
The Urban Institute
James Edwin Kee
George Washington University

From the Stock Market crash of 1929, signalling the Great Depression, to the peak of federal aid flows to state and local governments in 1978, the American federal system appeared to be locked on a course leading to ever-increasing centralization of political and fiscal powers in Washington D.C. Since 1978, however, American federalism has veered sharply away from this centralizing course towards greater governmental competition—a surprising development that may be traced largely to the disappearance of the once formidable fiscal advantage that the national government enjoyed over the state-local sector.

This new era of "Competitive Federalism" may be better understood in an historical context of how the nation has sorted out responsibilities in the federal system. A federal system must have some standards to sort out those functions or responsibilities that are to be discharged by the national government and those to be carried out by the states. In the United States, those standards have been set by law and sustained by fiscal strength and underlying political values.

From 1789 to 1929, shaped by the values of the Founding Fathers, the federal system relied on a constitutional approach to set standards and sort responsibilities. The federal government's role was largely limited to the performance of those relatively few tasks specifically delegated to it by the Constitution—all other responsibilities were reserved to the states and to the people. States were also fiscally stronger than the national government, which relied on customs duties and the sale of western lands to finance the federal budget.

Source: Public Budgeting & Finance (Winter 1989): 5–20. Reprinted by permission.

A series of national crises between 1929 and 1954 shredded the constitutional standards and the national government became legally free to move into areas once considered the preserve of the states. Crises brought a political call for national action and allowed the federal government to expand greatly its taxing authority. From 1954 to 1978, buoyed by its great fiscal advantage, Washington became increasingly involved in the financing and policy direction of virtually all aspects of state-local government.

Since 1978, however, increasing fiscal constraint at the federal level has halted the centralizing forces that once favored Washington. The nation's political jurisdictions are now locked in a competitive struggle for scarce taxpayer resources, essentially battling over the same economic base. Competition is occurring both vertically, between levels of government, and horizontally, among governments at the same level.

We have designated the current era "Competitive Federalism" for two main reasons. First, in sharp contrast to the traditional constitutional era (1789–1929), the national government is now deregulated. It is no longer restricted to a narrowly defined area of government; it is legally free to move into virtually any area of state-local government and compete with those governments for domestic policy leadership.

Second, neither the federal government nor the state-local sector has a clear fiscal advantage. The great fiscal advantage once held by the federal government from 1929–1978 has evaporated. The federal income tax, restricted by tax cuts and reform, is heavily committed to a limited set of national priorities, primarily national defense, payments for individuals (entitlements), and interest payments on the national debt. Now federal officials must compete head to head with the state and local officials for taxpayer support. In this fend-for-yourself fiscal environment, commentators have noted the resurgence of the states as domestic program initiators.[1]

In the judgment of the authors, there is growing evidence to support the view that our intergovernmental system has decidedly veered away from the centralizing federalism period of 1929 to 1978. For the foreseeable future, we are likely to see a continuation of competitive federalism, characterized by multiple governmental policy actors contending for the attention and support of American taxpayers. Underpinning this judgment is an historical interpretation of American federalism that challenges previous conventional projections of an increasingly centralized system of government.[2]

The Three Historical Periods of Federalism

American federal-state-local relations may be divided into several historical phases with distinct characteristics. Deil Wright has suggested seven overlapping phases, beginning with Conflict Federalism from 1789 to the 1930s and concluding with Contractive Federalism of the 1980s and 1990s—with Cooperative, Concentrated, Creative, Competitive, and Calculative in between.[3] Many commentators have suggested other demarcations.

There are probably many ways to divide the last 200 years, but three major time periods stand out: 1789–1929, a period dominated by the limited national government views of our constitutional founders; 1929–1978, a period marked by national crises and easy federal money sources that facilitated the centralization of power at the federal level; and 1978 to the present, when reemerging fiscal constraints and declining federal aid flows created a period of competitive federalism.

Constitutional Federalism, 1789–1929:
A Regulated System of Limited Government

The first 140 years of the Republic were strongly shaped by the views of the Founding Fathers. Madison reflected the prevailing view as he attempted to assuage the fears of those who were concerned about federal encroachment on state authority:

> The State governments will have the advantage of the Federal Government, whether we compare them in respect to the immediate dependence of the one on the other; to the weight of personal influence which each side will possess; to the powers respectively vested in them; to the predilection and probable support of the people; to the disposition and faculty of resisting and frustrating the measures of each other.[4]

The 10th Amendment, a concession to concerned state conventions, was added to the Constitution to stipulate that all powers not delegated to the federal government were reserved to the states and the people. The powers delegated by the Constitution are few and defined, said Madison, while "Those

which are to remain in the State governments are numerous and indefinite.''[5]

The Constitutional Federalism period was characterized by a limited national government, tightly controlled by court decisions and public opinion. The Supreme Court strictly interpreted the 10th Amendment, and the public voiced and voted its preference for small government in general and a very small federal domestic presence in particular.

While the federal and state-local sectors never operated in separate, air-tight compartments, there were fairly clear lines of responsibility.[6] The federal government provided for the national defense, postal services, customs, and foreign affairs. State and local governments supplied most of the domestic governmental needs of a society marked by a very modest taste for public goods and services. By 1929 total government spending equaled only 10 percent of GNP, with federal spending amounting to just 2.5 percent of GNP.

The federal government's domestic role was seen primarily as the cheerleader for the common market interests of a steadily growing free enterprise economy. President Calvin Coolidge captured the spirit of this 140-year era of limited national government with his remark that "the business of America is business."

Centralizing Federalism, 1929–1978:
The Deregulation of the Constitutional System and Collapse of Fiscal Constraints

The Stock Market crash of 1929 set in motion economic forces and a federal government reaction that led to the demise of the neatly ordered, regulated, constitutional federalism period. While the Supreme Court was initially hostile to the unprecedented federal legislation of the Roosevelt Administration's New Deal, in 1937 it began to take a far broader view of the role of the national government.[7] By 1942, the nation witnessed the virtual disappearance of the once powerful judicial and political constraints on federal regulation of the economy.

Three war crises—World War II, the emergence of the Cold War, and the Korean War—enormously strengthened the fiscal power of the federal government. The federal income tax was the fiscal engine of federal government growth. By increasing tax rates and introducing income tax withholding in 1943, Congress converted a "rich man's tax" into an "everyman's tax," creating a powerful revenue

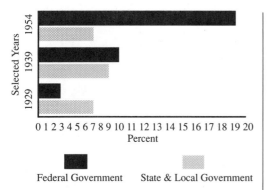

Figure 1
Explosive growth of federal government
(expenditures as a percent of gross national product)
1929–1988.
*Source: Advisory Commission on
Intergovernmental Relations, updated by authors.*

raiser. At the beginning of this period, federal spending amounted to 2.5 percent of GNP. During the first half of this period, federal spending grew 8 times as fast as the economy, and equalled nearly 19 percent of GNP by 1954. State and local spending remained relatively constant at between 6 and 8 percent of GNP. (See Figure 1).

During the second half of this 50-year period, the centralization of government activity continued, fueled not by crisis, but by "easy" federal money sources generated during the great crises. During this 25-year period there was an explosive growth in federal domestic activity. Federal aid programs to state and local government soared from 38 in 1954 to almost 500 by 1978 and the federal flow grew faster than state and local own-source revenues. As a result, states and localities became increasingly dependent upon federal aid, which by 1978 represented over 26 percent of state and local expenditures. (See Figure 2).

State and local governments were not idle during this period, enacting new and increasing old taxes to fund new state/local initiatives. In fact, since 1946, the state-local sector has increased its revenue, as a share of Gross National Product, at a faster rate than the federal sector. (See Table 1.) However, in sharp contrast to the relatively tranquil federal growth, the path to stronger state and local revenue systems was paved with the political bones of many state and local officials.[8]

Federal policymakers were able to move much further and faster, and more safely, than state and local officials into the domestic public sector, because they came out of the crises/war period

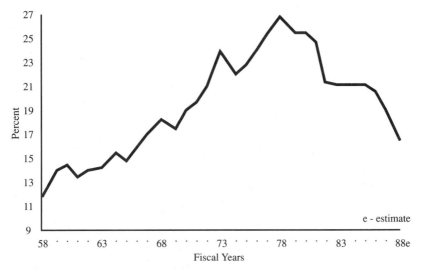

Figure 2
The rise and decline of federal aid, 1958–88
(as a percentage of state-local outlays).
Source: Advisory Commission on Intergovernmental Relations, updated by authors.

Table 1

Revenue by sector as a share of gross national product

(Own-source general and trust fund revenue as a percent of gnp)

	Federal		State-Local	
Year	Total: General and Trust Fund	General Revenue (only)	Total: General and Trust Fund	General Revenue (only)
1936	6.2	6.1	10.2	8.9
1946	21.8	20.5	6.1	5.4
1956	18.9	17.1	8.9	7.3
1966	18.3	15.4	10.9	9.1
1976	18.7	13.8	14.4	11.6
1986	20.1	13.7	15.9	12.5

Source: Bureau of the Census.

holding several fiscal trump cards—easy money sources—which enabled them to expand rapidly on the domestic front at little political risk.

The first trump card was the federal income tax. The interaction of economic growth, inflation and progressive rates produced sufficient tax revenue to finance repeated tax cuts and, at the same time, allow the expansion of federal domestic programs.

The United States also came out of the Korean War with a massive military commitment—12 percent of GNP—almost twice as many dollars earmarked for defense related programs as the combined revenue of all states and localities. As defense spending declined as a percent of GNP, to a low of 4.9 percent in 1978, Congress was able to shift funds to nondefense, domestic programs—its second fiscal trump card. No governor or mayor had such a fiscal fountain of youth—an easy money source that permitted both increased domestic federal spending and tax reductions.

Finally, the U.S. fell into the habit of deficit financing during this period, not just during bad economic times, but during good times as well—its third easy money trump card. In 22 of the 25 fiscal years from 1953 to 1978, federal policymakers covered revenue shortfalls through increased Treasury borrowing, thereby avoiding the political pain associated with program cuts or tax hikes.

In summary, in the 50-year period, from 1929 to 1978, a crisis driven federal government had sprung up in jack-in-the-beanstalk fashion to tower over the state-local landscape. Empowered by the easy money sources generated by the earlier national crises, Washington policymakers were able to pump new

money into the state-local sector during the second half of the period at a fast clip. During this affluent/Great Society era, state and local officials increasingly looked to Washington for policy guidance and funds. Many commentators feared that states and localities were becoming "federal aid junkies" and viewed this erosion of state and local power and responsibility with alarm.[9]

Competitive Federalism 1978–Present: The Reemergence of Fiscal Constraints

By the late 1970s, the federal government no longer possessed the easy new money sources that for over two decades had given it a towering fiscal advantage over the state-local sector. The essence of Competitive Federalism is that now Washington policymakers as well as state and local officials must go back, hat-in-hand, to a common source—the nation's taxpayers—when additional tax revenue is needed. While to some extent this has always been true, crises and later affluence, during the centralizing era, anesthetized the pain of increasing federal activity and tax burdens. The anesthesia has worn off and there is growing evidence to suggest that absent a national crisis, Washington does not have the inside track in the emerging intergovernmental race for taxpayer support.

Since 1978 we have seen a reemergence of fiscal constraint, brought about by increasing taxpayer resistance to larger government, especially at the national level. Proposition 13 in California and similar initiatives in other states, and the 1980 campaign and election of Ronald Reagan were two indicators of the growing resistance of citizens to the rising tax burden.

Marked by tight federal budgets, and increasing federal commitments to defense and transfer payments for individuals, federal aid has become a progressively smaller fraction of state and local budgets, as federal programs have been terminated, consolidated, or "frozen." While federal influence on state and local policymaking has tended to decline, it has not dropped as rapidly as the fall-off in federal aid. Federal expenditure strings are often "stickier" than the federal dollars that accompany them.

In this period of Competitive Federalism, the ability of each level to expand its influence depends upon the willingness of the taxpayers to support that expansion. Using the adjective "competitive" to describe the general condition of our intergovernmental system since 1978 signals a major shift in thinking about the dynamics of federalism. The Competitive Federalism designated challenges the old view that continued centralization of power was inevitable, if not desirable—a natural progression to a more unified "one Nation."[10] It also reinforces the emerging consensus that the state-local sector will continue to play a strong policy role in domestic affairs over the foreseeable future.

The use of the term Competitive Federalism does not mean that the various actors in the intergovernmental system are constantly at each others' throats. There is a remarkable degree of cooperation both vertically (between levels of government) and horizontally (among governments at the same level). But the great fiscal advantage once held by the federal government—facilitating centralization at the national level—has now ended. This far-reaching development has led to a more balanced intergovernmental playing field.

Factors that Have Shaped the Competitive Federalism Era

We believe that there are several important reasons why the centralizing tendencies have ended and why the United States has entered a Competitive Federalism era.

The Disappearance of the Federal Government's Fiscal Advantage

By the 1980s the fiscal trump cards of the federal government had disappeared as an easy money source for new initiatives. The great revenue engine of the federal government, the individual income tax, was running out of steam. While it remains the major national tax source, indexation (for inflation) and "tax reform" have greatly reduced the automatic growth of federal revenue. And during the 1980s the federal budget became increasingly committed to national defense, payments for individuals and interest on the federal debt.[11] Taxes will have to be raised explicitly to produce new federal revenue, and major increases in federal individual income taxes have occurred only in times of crisis. While the federal budget deficit is viewed by some as such a crisis, it is not so perceived by the president, the Congress or most of the public. The pledge to avoid tax increases at the federal level appears to have become the litmus test for successful presidential candidates.

The Russian invasion of Afghanistan in 1979 put an end to the defense trump card, as defense outlays started on their upward course during the second half of the Carter Administration. The Reagan Administration quickly strengthened this defense build-up with outlays for the Pentagon reaching 6.5 percent of GNP by the middle 1980s.

Finally, during the Reagan Administration, budget deficits became so massive that the public and politicians could no longer ignore them. Where once deficits provided an "easy" source of additional funding for federal spenders, the perceived need to reduce budget deficits has strengthened the hands of fiscal conservatives—the Gramm-Rudman-Hollings Act serves as a dramatic manifestation of the current mood.

The Legacy of Ronald Reagan

While we believe that the Competitive Federalism trend was set by 1978, it was accelerated by the election in 1980 of Ronald Reagan. In his campaign and his administration, Reagan captured the tide of popular sentiment when he proposed a limit on the expanding role of the federal government and a turning over of responsibilities to the states.

Although federal domestic activity had enormously increased during the Centralizing Federalism period, people remained skeptical of the federal government's ability to solve public problems. Outright failures in the war in Vietnam, continued poverty after 25 years of affluence and expanded programs to the poor, scandals such as Watergate, and the stagflation of the 1970s fueled the skepticism. By 1980, public opinion polls of the U.S. Advisory

Commission on Intergovernmental Relations began to indicate declining confidence in the federal government's ability to spend their tax dollars wisely.

Ronald Reagan certainly did not create the national feeling but he sensed its historical impact and took full advantage of it. While his eight-year administration fell short of a "revolution," Reagan's series of initiatives (the 1981 tax cut, the block grants, the proposed swap of program responsibilities, 1986 tax reform, and the constant pressure on domestic spending) accelerated the swing of the pendulum away from federal power towards increased state responsibility.[12]

The ultimate Reagan legacy may be the large federal deficit, created in large part by the simultaneous build-up of national defense expenditures and the 1981 tax cut. The tripling of the national debt during the Reagan Administration has constrained those policymakers who would like to see a more activist federal government in domestic policy. This deficit constraint is likely to continue well into the 1990s. While the fiscal trump cards were disappearing even as Ronald Reagan took office, his deficit legacy may have actually created a fiscal disadvantage for the federal government compared to the state-local sector.

The Resiliency of the State-Local System

Perhaps the most underrated feature of the Competitive Federalism era is the demonstrated ability of the 50 states and thousands of localities to absorb and then rebound from regional and national shocks. Since 1978, the state-local systems have absorbed the following shocks:

Revolt of the taxpayers. Despite Proposition 13 in California and its progeny in other states, state and local governments have been able to increase funding for such critical areas as education and economic development.

Recession. The 1981–82 economic downturn was the most serious since the Great Depression. States survived even though the federal government provided no countercyclical aid as it had in past recessions.

Reduction in federal aid. Federal aid has declined when adjusted for inflation, and it now represents a declining share of state and local revenue.[13] Yet with the exception of the most seriously depressed states and localities, the state-local system appears remarkably resilient.

More recently, many of the states have been hit hard by regional downturns. The farm states have been pinched severely by the agricultural recession and the energy states hit hard by the drop in oil prices. Yet, despite all these shocks, the states as a whole are doing far better than most students of state and local finance would have predicted a few years ago because they have developed very strong and diversified revenue systems.

The Emergence of Relatively Strong State-Local Revenue Systems

State and local governments are widely believed to rely on regressive tax sources, the property and sales tax, which are often thought to have a disproportionate impact on low and moderate income families. Highly progressive taxes are difficult to enact in state and local jurisdictions because of competition among governments for business and upper-income investors.

While tax systems vary widely among state and local governments, those governments have been able and willing to raise their taxes during the 1980s to meet domestic needs. For example, nearly 20 percent of all new revenue generated at the state level from 1981 to 1986 was a result of legislative actions.[14] State-local tax structures have also become more balanced and equitable, with state income taxes playing an increasingly important financial role. In addition, modification of state sales and property taxes have provided most states with a broad-based, proportional tax structure.[15]

Over the last three decades, the trend toward more balanced state-local use of property, income, and sales taxes has caused one of the most dramatic turnarounds in the annals of American public finance. In 1957, the dominant local property tax produced more revenue than did all of the state and local income and sales taxes combined. By 1986, the income and sales taxes combined produced more than twice as much revenue as the property tax.[16]

Another powerful advantage of the state-local governments is to be found in the fact that citizens can see a more direct relationship between the benefits received and taxes paid than is the case with federal income tax payments. Because state and local governments provide those services that are of most direct benefit to their citizens, mayors and governors are more easily able to argue for a specific tax increase to satisfy local demand. Even during the Centralizing Federalism period states and localities never lost control of those functions that are closest to the people—maintenance of law and order, education of the youth, regulation of domestic relations, protection of public health, control of land-use decisions, promotion of state and local economic development policy, and provision of regional and local public amenities (libraries, parks, and museums).

Interstate competition, often thought to preclude states from increasing taxes, provides a natural equilibrium. The 50 state-local systems behave much like ships in a naval convoy in wartime. Because they are spread out over a great area, there is considerable room for each state to maneuver within the convoy. But they dare not move too far ahead or lag too far behind the convoy.

If a state or locality moves too far out ahead of the convoy on the tax side, it becomes increasingly vulnerable to tax evasion, taxpayer revolts, and tax competition for jobs and investments. If it lags too far behind on the public service side, it becomes increasingly vulnerable to quality of life and economic development concerns—poor schools, poor roads and inadequate support for high-tech operations. Interjurisdictional competition on the public service side often *forces* states and localities to raise taxes.

Table 1 provides a comparison of revenue trends in the federal and state-local sectors since 1936. Even after seven years of the Great Depression, state-local revenue, as a percent of Gross National Product, exceeded that of the federal government. But by the end of World War II, the federal government had a lead in revenue generation which it has not relinquished. However, if trust fund revenues are excluded (mainly social security at the federal level and pension income at the state level), the state-local sector collects almost as much in general revenues as does the federal government. As a percent of GNP, state-local revenues increased from 5.4 percent in 1946 to 12.5 percent in 1986, while federal general revenues actually declined from 20.5 to 13.7 percent. A remarkable turnaround over the last forty years!

State and Local Government Institutional Reform

Since the major domestic policy initiators from 1929 to 1978 were to be found at the federal level, it was repeatedly argued that the federal government

attracted the "best and the brightest." State and local government personnel were portrayed as patronage ridden, their agencies controlled by politically appointed boards or separately elected officials, and their management and professional skills and techniques virtually nonexistent. In 1967 former Governor Terry Sanford (D-NC), in *Storm Over the States,* chronicled the failure of state government in leadership, management, responsiveness and accountability.[17]

Today's state and local governments, however, are led by more qualified elected officials, with streamlined executive branches, modern financial management systems, and more representative and effective legislative bodies. The innovators of domestic policy of the 1990s are most likely to be found at the state and local level, not in the federal government.

It is important to note that many of the institutional reforms that occurred in state and local governments during the 1960s and 1970s were stimulated in large part by federal action—either congressional or judicial. For example, in *Baker* v. *Carr,* 369 U.S. 186 (1962) and *Reynolds* v. *Sims,* 377 U.S. 533 (1964) the Supreme Court required the states to reapportion their legislatures on the basis of "one person, one vote." The end of domination by rural interests led to reforms of state legislatures, increased staff resources, and greater attention to the urban needs in states that had long ignored them.

Many of the Great Society programs of Lyndon Johnson required the increased professionalism of state agencies, improved financial management and accountability, and the modernization of state laws, in return for new federal money. While some of these changes may have occurred in any case, the federal "carrot" and "stick" accelerated institutional reform at the state and local level.

Finally, and painfully, the federal government through Supreme Court actions (*Brown* v. *Board of Education,* 347 U.S. 483, 1954) and civil rights acts forced the states to abandon racial segregation. Segregation had become synonymous with "States Rights"; the image of Governor Wallace barring black students from the University of Alabama was etched in people's minds. Segregation is no longer synonymous with states rights, freeing the states from the politics of racial segregation and enabling them to assert a stronger role in the federal system.

Political Values Underpin a Competitive System

The Founding Fathers and millions of immigrants fled nations with strong central governments and often onerous tax levels. The first 140 years of our nation reflected their beliefs in a limited government, with most service delivery at the local level. Crises and wars created the climate for stronger national actions and the "easy" money from 1953 to 1978 greased the way for increasingly greater federal involvement in the state-local sector. Yet, fundamentally, there was no immutable groundswell for a highly centralized national state.

In a recent article, Daniel Bell argues that the reason why there is no American "State," no unified, rational will expressed in a political order, is because of individual self-interest and a passion for liberty. In European nations the state ruled *over* society, whereas the United States government is a political marketplace, an arena in which interests contend and in which deals are made. The underlying philosophical theme of the Declaration of Independence is one of unalienable rights, vested in individuals, not groups. Government was designated to embody and protect individual rights and economic liberty.[18]

Behind the Constitution, according to Bell, stood a distinct political culture, a civic concern for republican virtue that attempted to avoid both "the centrifugal dangers of faction and the centripetal hazards of centralized powers. . . . "[19] Bell claims that the rise of the central state in America was unplanned and not consistent ideologically. "It was a response, framed during crises, to three things: increases in the scale of society, shifting political alignments, and the logic of mobilization for war."[20]

Bell argues that what has been occurring in the last decade, the growing resentment of taxes and government intrusion, has been an attempt to restore the balance between factionalism and centralization. It is a demand for a return to "civil society" characterized by a manageable scale of social life. It emphasizes voluntary associations, churches and communities and decision making at the local level. George Bush's "Thousand Points of Light," derided by the liberal establishment and cartoonists, perhaps comes closer to capturing the enduring American mood than his critics would want to admit.

Criticism of Competitive Federalism

The current state of federalism is not without its sharp critics. Those critics with a liberal point of view emphasize the equity problem—that Competitive Federalism does poorly by those individuals and jurisdictions least able to fend for themselves. Critics on the right (joined by many state and local officials) point to a menacing constitutional or power imbalance. They paint a grim scenario of things to come—a constitutionally unconstrained but financially strapped Congress is likely to be pushed by special interests to make ever-increasing use of unfunded mandates and push costs and responsibilities back on states and localities. The Supreme Court has flashed Congress a green light.

In *Garcia* v. *San Antonio Mass Transit District* 469 U.S. 528 (1985) and *Baker* v. *South Carolina* (1988), the Supreme Court took itself out of its traditional role of umpire of disputes between the states and the Congress—arguing that the states are protected through the political process. So far, the Court's assessment seems to be correct. Although the Court in *Garcia* placed state and local employees under the provisions of the Fair Labor Standards Act, Congress did adjust the act to accommodate state and local concerns. And while *South Carolina* appears to open the door to general taxation of the interest on public purpose municipal bonds, Congress has not yet yielded to the temptation.

Perhaps what will ultimately hold Congress in check on unfunded mandates is the fear that the states will call for a Constitutional Convention to require reimbursement of unfunded mandates. No one knows for sure what would happen in such a convention; the threat of a "runaway" convention is one that Congress cannot afford to take lightly.

Admittedly, however, there are serious problems associated with Competitive Federalism operating in a deregulated, fend-for-yourself environment. Hopefully the national government soon will provide special financial assistance to the poorest states and localities, thus enabling them to compete on more equal terms with the wealthier jurisdictions. In addition, interjurisdictional competition for economic development can work against any jurisdiction that provides a relatively high level of assistance to the poor or enforces a strict code to protect the environment. In these "spillover" areas a countervailing federal presence is needed to smooth over the rough edges of interjurisdictional competition.

While we believe that the decentralizing trend since 1978 is not an aberration, a significant national crisis could trigger a major new source of federal revenue that might swing the pendulum back towards centralization. Clearly the current federal budget deficit is not seen as that crisis. The public is even less excited about paying off the accumulated federal debt than it is about paying off last year's credit card balance. A major environmental crisis might prompt increased federal taxes and funding for that purpose. Whether that development would result in the creation of a powerful new source of revenue for the federal government is highly problematic.

Conclusion: Striking a New Balance

A federal system, such as that in the United States, has to have some kind of a constraint system—a balancing force—to prevent either complete disintegration or complete centralization of the system. The Constitution itself was written to prevent the disintegration feared under the Article of Confederation and it was sorely tested during the Civil War, but the Union prevailed.

During our first 140 years the balancing force was essentially the vision and values of the Founding Fathers—individual liberty and a national government limited to its delegated powers. This sorting out of functions ensured a fairly distinct separation of intergovernmental responsibilities. The most significant feature of this Constitutional (regulated) Federalism period was that the centralizing tendency of the national government was legally held in check, keeping the federal government on a short, limited-government leash.

Crises, wars, and new sources of "easy money" severed that restraining leash and led to enormous growth of government, ushering in Centralizing Federalism, 1929 to 1978. Now a "deregulated" Washington was largely free to become involved in virtually any phase of state-local activity. Thanks to its new found sources of easy money, it now had the fiscal wherewithal to become an important player on the state-local front. The intergovernmental world became a mishmash of responsibilities and accountability as state-local officials increasingly looked to Washington for both policy guidance and new money sources, which usually came with strings attached.

With the disappearance of the federal government's commanding fiscal advantage, American federalism entered its third stage—Competitive Federalism—in the late 1970s. While still legally free to move about in the state-local sector, Washington had played out its fiscal trump cards, its easy money sources. Fiscal stringency—the new balancing force—emerged to check the federal government's centralizing tendencies. As is the case of their state-local counterparts, federal policymakers must now face the voters/taxpayers when additional funds are needed to finance expansion.

The almost $2 trillion run-up in federal debt during the last decade provides emphatic evidence of Washington's aversion either to imposing a major tax increase on the electorate or to making deep cuts in programs strongly supported by powerful constituencies. However, a sorting out of responsibilities is occurring—not under any grand scheme—but mainly through the grinding attrition of these programs with the weakest claim for national support. Federal aid for individuals (largely social security, welfare, and medical care) is increasing, while other federal domestic programs are declining in real terms and as a percent of GNP.[21]

As long as three critical ingredients remain in place, Competitive Federalism—the new balancing force—will govern the sorting-out process between Washington and the fifty state-local systems for the foreseeable future:

1. *Functional Ingredient*—continued state/local control of those governmental programs that most directly impact voters/taxpayers where they live and work, e.g., education and police protection;
2. *Competitive Resource Ingredient*—a continued tight fiscal situation in which neither Washington nor the state/local sector enjoys a decisive fiscal advantage, i.e., access to easy money sources;
3. *Anti-Centralist Political Value Ingredient*—a continuation of the national mind set that strongly resists centralization of political power except during periods marked by grave national crisis.

Only in the unlikely event of an explosive growth in costly, unfunded federal mandates or a very major strengthening of the federal government's revenue system, triggered by a grave national crisis, could American federalism swing back to its 1929–78 centralizing course.

Notes

In labeling the post-1978 era "Competitive Federalism," the authors acknowledge that the term has been used before by other commentators. However, its general use has been restricted to a discussion of horizontal competition for investment and jobs—interstate and intercity—not competition among layers of governments. Some recent works on competitive federalism in the narrower context include: Daphne A. Kenyon and John Kincaid, "Rethinking Interjurisdictional Competition," *Multistate Tax Commission* (Oct. 1988): 12–14; Daphne A. Kenyon, "Interjurisdictional Tax and Policy Competition; Good or Bad for the Federal System?" (Washington D.C.: ACIR paper, 7 Jan. 1988, reprinted by the Urban Institute, Feb. 1988); U.S. Advisory Commission on Intergovernmental Relations, *Interjurisdictional Competition in the Federal System: A Roundtable Discussion,* M-157 (Washington, D.C.: ACIR, Aug. 1988); Albert Breton, "Towards a Theory of Competitive Federalism," *European Journal of Political Economy* 3 (No. 1, 2, 1987): 263–329; and John Shannon, "Competition: Federalism's 'Invisible Regulator,' " *Intergovernmental Perspectives,* 15 (Winter 1989).

1. See, e.g., Ann O'M. Bowman and Richard C. Kearney, *The Resurgence of the States,* (Englewood Cliffs, N.J.: Prentice-Hall, 1986); and Advisory Commission on Intergovernmental Relations, *The Question of State Capability* (Washington, D.C.: ACIR, 1985). The term *fend-for-yourself federalism* was first coined by author Shannon in "The Return to Fend-for-Yourself Federalism: The Reagan Mark," *Intergovernmental Perspectives* 13 (Summer/Fall, 1987).

2. A. T. Peacock and J. Wiseman, *The Growth of Public Expenditure in the United Kingdom* (Princeton, N.J.: Princeton University Press, 1961). Also see, Robert Higgs, *Crisis and Leviathan* (New York City: Oxford University Press, 1987). After examining various hypotheses for the sources of government growth, Higgs argues that it occurred during relatively brief episodes of great social crises, either war or depression, but created a permanent ratchetting-up of increasing government revenue, employment and central control. There have been challengers to the centralization thesis. Richard P. Nathan has argued that the flow of power and responsibilities, to the states or the federal government, shifts with changing political ideologies, which now favor the states, "America's Changing Federalism," in Anthony King, ed., *The American Political System* (Washington, D.C.: The American Enterprise Institute, 1990 forthcoming).

3. Deil S. Wright, *Understanding Intergovernmental Relations,* 3rd ed. (Pacific Grove, CA: Brooks/Cole, 1988), 66.

4. James Madison, *The Federalist,* No. 45.

5. *Ibid.*

6. In the debate between Elazar and Grodzins versus Scheiber on the degree of cooperation between the levels of government, we concur with Scheiber that demarcations of authority were fairly well defined. See, Daniel J. Elazar, *The American Partnership: Intergovernmental Co-operation in the Nineteenth-Century United States* (Chicago: University of Chicago Press, 1962); Morton Grodzins, from The Report of the President's Commission on National Goals, The American Assembly, *Goals for Americans* (Englewood Cliffs, N.J.: Prentice-Hall, 1960); Harry N. Scheiber, Report of U.S. Senate Subcommittee on Intergovernmental Relations, Committee on Government Operations, S.Res. 205, 89th Congress (Washington, D.C.: GPO, 15 Oct. 1966). Excerpts of the debate are reprinted in Laurence J. O'Toole, Jr., *American Intergovernmental Relations* (Washington, D.C.: CQ Press, 1985).

7. The Supreme Court gave a broad reading of the federal commerce power in the cases upholding the National Labor Relations Act, *NLRB v. Jones and Laughlin Steel Co., 301 U.S. 1 (1937) and *NLRB v. Friedman-Harry Marks Clothing Co.,* 301 U.S. 58 (1937).

8. By the early 1970s the conventional wisdom among state policymakers was that support for state income taxes was the political death warrant for sitting governors. Defeated governors included Norbert Tieman of Nebraska, Richard Olgilvie of Illinois, and John J. Gilligan of Ohio.

9. In an oft-quoted phrase, the U.S. Advisory Committee on Intergovernmental Relations said that American Federalism was in trouble, that "the federal government's influence has become more pervasive, more intrusive, more unmanageable, more ineffective, more costly and, above all, more unaccountable." *The Federal Role in the Federal System: The Dynamics of Growth, An Agenda for American Federalism: Restoring Confidence and Competence* (Washington, D.C.: ACIR, 1981).

10. Samuel H. Beer, "The Idea of the Nation," *The New Republic* (19 and 26 July 1982).

11. James Edwin Kee, "The Presidents FY 1990 Budget: The Last Act in a Decade of Change" *Public Budgeting & Finance* 9 (Summer 1989), Figure 1: 14.

12. For one governor's view of that period, see Scott M. Matheson with James Edwin Kee, *Out of Balance,* (Salt Lake City: Peregrine Smith, 1986). Also see the excellent series of books published by The Urban Institute, edited by John L. Palmer and Isabel V. Sawhill, including *The Reagan Record* (1982) and Charles R. Hulten and Sawhill, ed., *The Legacy of Reaganomics* (Washington, D.C.: The Urban Institute, 1984).

13. Kee, "The President's FY 1990 Budget," Table 5: 25.

14. Marcia A. Howard, *Fiscal Survey of the States,* (Washington, D.C.: National Governors' Association

and National Association of State Budget Officers, March 1989), Table 6: 11.

15. See, e.g., Bowman and Kearney, *The Resurgence of the States,* 23–25; and Steven Gold, ed., *Reforming State Tax Systems* (Denver: National Council of State Legislatures, 1986).

16. Advisory Commission on Intergovernmental Relations, *Significant Features of Fiscal Federalism* (Washington, D.C.: ACIR, 1989).

17. Terry Sanford, *Storm Over the States* (New York City: McGraw Hill, 1967).

18. Daniel Bell, " 'American exceptionalism' revisited: the role of civil society," *The Public Interest* 95 (Spring 1989): 38–56.

19. *Ibid.,* 51.

20. *Ibid.,* 55.

21. See, e.g., Kee, "The President's FY 1990 Budget," 25; and David G. Mathiasen, "The Evolution of the Office of Management and Budget Under President Reagan," *Public Budgeting & Finance* 8 (Autumn 1988): 3–14.

III

Budgeting, Economics, and Popular Control: An Instrument of Democracy

The objectives of the budget should be to implement democracy and provide a tool which will be helpful in the efficient execution of the functions and services of government. Admitting that budgeting is only a process and in no sense an end in itself, it nevertheless plays a vital role in the achievement of orderly management of government affairs. The budget is a device for consolidating the various interests, objectives, desires, and needs of our citizens into a program whereby they may jointly provide for their safety, convenience, and comfort. It has a tremendous impact upon our entire national economy. It is the most important single current document relating to the social and economic affairs of the people.

Harold D. Smith, 1939
Director, U.S. Bureau of the Budget

Budgeting's New Political–Economic Environment

When William F. Willoughby described the various movements or threads of budgetary reform at the beginning of the twentieth century, his first concern for budgeting was that it ensure that "the affairs of government shall be conducted in conformity with the popular will." Half a century later, public budgeting is still wrestling with how to accomplish this prescription. Certainly, everything has been made harder by the change in economic fortunes of the United States. But that is only part of the problem. Basically what has occurred is that the size of government budgets is now so significantly large that changes in tax policy, expenditure aggregates, and deficit and debt levels are a critical, if not the major, part of national, regional, and local economic equations.

In addition, the revenue and expenditure decisions of various levels of government have become so interdependent that decisions at one level have profound effects on other levels. When the federal government eliminated revenue sharing, this exacerbated state and local budget problems. The interdependency effects can be seen at regional levels also. For example, cuts in federal aid to the District of Columbia drove its budget even further into the red. The District, in turn, has already defaulted on its quarterly payment to the Metropolitan Transit Authority (operator of the Metro subway), which must "delay" payments to their creditors.

The articles in this section address a number of the facets of the new political-economics of the public sector budgeting, ranging from balanced budget amendments, deficit control, revenue and expenditure limitations (such as California's infamous Proposition 13), to the issues of intergovernmental finances and relations. The web has become so intricate that even private sector

213

and nonprofit sector organizations are involved. But the major premise is democratic control embodied by the question, To what extent does the public budget represent conscious choices by the public?

The section's first two articles present two important critiques of the issue. The first is Anthony Downs' classic 1957 article, "Why the Government Budget Is Too Small in a Democracy." He argues that "ignorance causes governments to enact budgets smaller than the ones they would enact if the electorate possessed complete information." He sharply criticizes the budget process for creating ignorance or encouraging voter apathy because of information costs.

James M. Buchanan, a Nobel laureate in economics and generally regarded as the leading proponent of what is called "public choice theory," is even more critical of government budgeting decisions. In an excerpt from the 1977 book, *Budgets and Bureaucrats: The Sources of Government Growth* entitled "Why Does Government Grow?", he finds that budgeting is self-serving, invoking the old Chinese proverb: "The appetite grows with eating." There is no rational, compatible method of decision making in budgeting that provides the public with true choice, much less realistic knowledge about the state of the revenue and expenditure implications within an annual budget. To Buchanan's view, it is all fiscal illusion.

A word about the "public choice" school of thought is perhaps appropriate. At its heart, public choice theory challenges two fundamental and influential theories that have dominated thinking about government and the economy. First, it disputes "welfare economics," which has argued that when private markets fail, the government must take over; which presupposes that government can effectively carry out the public interest. Second, public choice theory challenges "pluralist political science," which argues that competition among interest groups forces governments to adopt policy solutions that are best for the public good. Public choice advocates argue that governments are inefficient and have few incentives other than expanding their own programs by increasing the size of their budgets. Instead, public choice theory is dedicated to analyzing what works better by quantifying both the decision strategies and policy outcomes: passion for quantification is its primary driving (and legitimizing) force.

The prescriptions of public choice are many and could easily fill this entire section with solutions to varied economic and political policy problems. (Interested readers will find the journal published by the choice theorists, *Public Choice,* very informative.) Much of the central thrust of the approach is to place as much governmental action (and its expenditures) at the lowest possible levels: local governments. This, it is argued, would encourage a higher degree of experimentation, competition, and innovation. Also, placing more tax and budgeting decisions on the ballot through referenda would make the process more democratic, or at least more responsive to popular control.

Of course, there are many states and localities that have already experienced one form of "democratic budgeting"; specifically, the movement in the late 1970s (beginning in California) that put initiatives on the ballot calling for major fiscal restrictions on government finances. Proposition 13 heralded a number of such voter referendums, generally referred to as revenue or expenditure limitations. Under these types of voter legislated initiatives, governments are limited in the amount of taxes they can raise each year or on the expenditures they can make. In some cases, actual property tax assessed values are required to be rolled back to previous levels. Jerry McCaffery and John H. Bowman provided one of the first evaluations of fiscal limitation initiatives in their 1978 article, "Participatory Democracy and Budgeting: The Effects of Proposition 13," published the year Proposition 13 was passed.

But understanding state and local fiscal limitation initiatives requires an understanding of the complexities and implications of fiscal federalism and finances. Major research was conducted in the 1980s on fiscal stress and fiscal conditions in state and local governments, where so many of the tax revolts started. Up until the 1980s, budgeting had sadly neglected the economic dimensions of state and local budgets. An important framework in this area is provided in "The Growing Fiscal and Economic Importance of State and Local Governments," a chapter from Roy Bahl's major 1984 research work on the revenue and economic aspects, *Financing State and Local Government.*

A major part of the pressure inherent in fiscal limitations is economic performance. From a budgetary perspective, this is best represented in the 1980s by the inability of the federal government to reduce its deficit. No matter that the deficit was clearly "self-imposed" by the series of major tax cuts enacted during the first years of the Reagan administration: critics continued to call for some form of constitutional amendment requiring the federal government to end its budget deficit. Ultimately, the failure to produce such an amendment, coupled with the federal government's reaching the $200 billion deficit high-water mark in the mid 1980s, resulted in Gramm-Rudman-Hollings (Section II). But what of the question of a balanced budget amendment? Among the many perspectives available, both pro and con, William R. Keech provides one of the most "balanced" evaluations in his 1985 article "A Theoretical Analysis of the Case for a Balanced Budget Amendment."

Another argument often made is that the line-item veto stands at the heart of the argument over how to control the budget process. Interestingly, this veto over specific appropriations is generally considered to be an innovation pioneered by the Confederacy during the Civil War. Despite numerous attempts to incorporate it into the federal budget process, it was never passed by the Congress. In contrast, forty-nine out of the fifty states (only North Carolina has no veto authority for its governor) have some form of line-item veto. A 1986 study by the U.S. House of Representatives Committee on Rules revealed the following uses of line-item veto among the states: six states give an "all-or-nothing veto"; ten give an "item-reduction veto," in which the governor may reduce the item down to the level of the original recommendation; and 33 states allow governors a "simple item-veto," through which a separate item in an appropriations bill may be deleted.

Although line-item vetoes theoretically can make a great impact on the outcome of budget decisions, whether they actually do is another question. The general conclusion is that line-item vetoes are not terribly effective mechanisms in terms of fiscal restraint. Included in this section is Glen Abney and Thomas P. Lauth's survey of line-item veto practices of the states, which nicely explains the concept and interprets the arguments.

Gramm-Rudman-Hollings notwithstanding, the federal budget deficit problem remains. Events in 1990 have played around budget summit conferences between an administration that has broken its "read my lips: no-new-taxes" pledge and its "don't touch defense" promises, and a Congress that is actually willing to reduce spending for social programs. The final compromise reached raised taxes, cut social spending levels, and legislated a $500 billion five-year reduction plan (with the vast majority of the cuts slated for later years). Much depends upon the "peace dividend": the hoped-for reduction in defense spending as a result of the end of the cold war and major arms reduction agreements. Fear of a recession looms, which, if realized, would postpone sequestration or the automatic spending cuts of Gramm-Rudman-Hollings.

Still, the country has lived with this impending deficit disaster for nearly a decade—so long that some even argue that it is a nonproblem. Budgeting, however, takes the deficit problem very seriously. This section closes with three articles by economists who examine some of the major themes of deficits and budgets. Alice Rivlin, former head of the Congressional Budget Office, looks at some of the tax issues first in her article, ''The Continuing Search for a Popular Tax.'' The most extensive treatment of the deficit issue is provided by Charles L. Schultze, who provides a comprehensive examination of the economic issues integrally tied to budgets in ''The Federal Budget and the Nation's Economic Health.'' For a counterargument, prominent political economist Robert Eisner rejects some of the basic statistics and policy arguments generally tied to budgetary economics in his article, ''Debunking the Conventional Wisdom in Economic Policy.'' Together they illustrate the richness of the economic dimensions of budgeting that in so many ways have radically changed our understanding of budgetary environments, if not the very fabric of budgeting itself.

19

Why the Government Budget Is Too Small in a Democracy

Anthony Downs

In a democratic society, the division of resources between the public and private sectors is roughly determined by the desires of the electorate. But because it is such a complex and time-consuming task to acquire adequate political information, the electorate is chronically ignorant of the costs and benefits of many actual and potential government policies. It is my belief that this ignorance causes governments to enact budgets smaller than the ones they would enact if the electorate possessed complete information. Yet these undersized budgets stem from rational behavior by both the government and the electorate; hence they are extremely difficult to remedy. Furthermore, the resulting misallocation of resources becomes more and more serious as the economy grows more complex.

As proof of these assertions, I shall present a model of a democratic society based upon the principles set forth in *An Economic Theory of Democracy*.[1] The basic rules for government and voter decision-making in this model are hypotheses, but the environment in which they are set resembles the real world as closely as possible. Furthermore, I believe the hypotheses themselves are accurate representations of what happens in the real world most of the time. My belief is based upon a comparison of the deductions made from these hypotheses in *An Economic Theory of Democracy* with the actual behavior of political parties in various democracies. However, the deductions made from the same hypotheses in this article are harder to compare directly with reality. Nevertheless, if the reader agrees with me that the basic hypotheses are realistic, it should follow that he will find the conclusions of this model meaningful in real-world politics as well as in the theoretical world of my argument.

Source: World Politics 12 (1959–60): 541–563. Reprinted by permission of The Johns Hopkins University Press.

This argument consists of the following topics: (1) how the budget is determined in a democracy, (2) the nature of rational political ignorance, (3) the definition of "correct" and "incorrect" budgets, (4) how an "incorrect" budget might arise, (5) significant differences between transactions in the public and private sectors, (6) distortions in budget evaluation arising from these differences, (7) a countertendency toward overexpenditure, (8) the net results, and (9) the increasing importance of the problem.

How the Budget is Determined in a Democracy

According to the economic theory of democracy, each government sets both expenditures and revenue collection so as to maximize its chances of winning the next election.[2] This follows from the axiom that political parties are primarily motivated by the desire to enjoy the income, prestige, and power of being in office. Each party regards government policies as means to these ends; hence it pursues whatever policies it believes will gain it the political support necessary to defeat its opponents. Since expenditures and taxes are two of the principal policies of government, they are set so as to maximize political support. Out of this rational calculation by the governing party comes the budget.

Rationality likewise prevails among voters. They vote for the party whose policies they believe will benefit them more than those of any other party.[3] These "benefits" need not be conceived in a narrowly selfish sense, but consist of any utility they derive from government acts, including acts which penalize them economically in order to help others.

The budget itself is not arrived at by considering over-all spending versus over-all taxation, but is the sum of a series of separate policy decisions. The governing party looks at every possible expenditure and tries to decide whether making it would gain more votes than financing it would lose. This does not mean that each spending bill is tied to a particular revenue bill. Instead all proposed expenditures are arranged in descending order of their vote-gain potential, and all proposed revenue collections arranged in ascending order of their vote-loss potential. Wherever these two marginal vote curves cross, a line is drawn that determines the over-all budget. Expenditures with a higher vote-gain potential than the marginal one are included in the budget, which is financed by revenue collection methods with lower vote-loss potentials that the marginal one.[4]

Because of the myriad expenditures made by modern governments, this rule may seem impractical. In the real world, it is true, the governing party does not weigh the vote impact of every single expenditure, but groups them into large categories like national defense. It then balances the marginal vote-gain of spending for each such category against its marginal vote-cost and against the marginal vote-gains of spending for other large categories, such as farm subsidies, education, and social security. Thus, in the real world, the aggregate budget for each category is decided in a manner similar to that described above, even though details of spending within the category may be left to nonpolitical administrators.[5]

It should be noted that the government in our model never asks itself whether the over-all budget is "too large" or "too small" in relation to the views of the electorate. In fact, it never makes any explicit decision about what the over-all budget size should be, but determines that size merely by adding up all the items that more than pay for themselves in votes. Similarly, the voters do not evaluate a budget on the basis of its total size but by the particular benefits and costs it passes on to them.

The absence of any specific evaluation of over-all budget size appears to make our original assertion meaningless. How can we say the government budgets are too small when no one ever considers their size in judging them? The answer is that ignorance produces biases in the electorate that cause the government to exclude certain acts from the budget, thus reducing its size from what it "should be." Our original thesis can be more accurately stated as follows: rational ignorance among the citizenry leads governments to omit certain specific types of expenditures from their budgets which would be there if citizens were not ignorant. The fact that this results in budgets that are too small is simply a dramatic way of stressing the outcome.

Rational Political Ignorance

In this model, information is a crucial factor. In order to form policies, each party must know what the citizenry wants; and in order to vote rationally, each voter must know what policies the government and its opponents espouse. But in the real world, information is costly—if not in money, at least in time. It takes time to inform yourself about government policy. Furthermore, the number of policies that a modern government has to carry out is vast and their nature astoundingly complex. Even if the world's most brilliant man spent twenty-four hours a day reading newspapers and journals, he would be unable to keep himself well-informed about all aspects of these policies.

In addition to facing this problem, the average voter knows that no matter how he votes, there are so many other voters that his decision is unlikely to affect the outcome. This does not always prevent him from voting, because he realizes voting is essential to democracy and because it costs so little. But it usually does prevent him from becoming well-informed. Beyond the free information he picks up just by being alive in our media-saturated world, he does not see how acquiring detailed political data will make him better off. Thus a rationally calculating attitude about the use of time leads him to political ignorance. This conclusion is borne out by countless polls that show just how ignorant the average citizen is about major political questions of the day.

In this article we discuss three specific states of rational ignorance. The first is *zero ignorance*—i.e., perfect knowledge. In this state, citizens know (1) all actual or potential items in the budget of each party and (2) the full benefits and costs of each item. The second state is *partial ignorance,* in which voters know all the actual or potential items in the budget, but not all the benefits and costs attached to each item. Their political perception threshold has been raised so that remote or extremely complex events do not cross it, though the budget itself still does. The third state is *preponderant ignorance,* in which citizens are ignorant of both the items in the budget and their benefits and costs. In this state, citizens' perception thresholds are so high that they are aware of only the individual policies or items in the budget that vitally affect them.

"Correct" and "Incorrect" Budgets

My contention is that rational ignorance acts so as to produce an "incorrect" government budget. But what is meant by the term "incorrect" when the government does not seek to maximize welfare? Since I posit no social utility function, how can I say that one budget is "better" or "worse" than another except in terms of its vote-getting power? My answer is that the "correct" budget is the one which would emerge from the democratic process if both citizens and parties had perfect information about both actual and potential government policies. Insofar as an actual budget deviates from the "correct" budget, it is "incorrect." Admittedly, no one has perfect information; hence no one can say what budget would exist if there were no rational ignorance in politics. This fact prohibits use of the "correct" budget for detailed criticism of actual budgets, but it does not prevent generalizations about the tendency of actual budgets to deviate from "correct" budgets because of broad social factors like rational ignorance.

There is no point in denying that the terms "correct" and "incorrect" are ethical judgments. They presuppose that it is good for the citizens in a democracy to get what they want, and to base their wants on as much knowledge as possible. It is not good for them to get something they would not want if they knew more about it. That is the extent of my ethical foundation, and I think it is compatible with almost every normative theory of democracy.

How an "Incorrect" Budget Might Occur

In a two-party democracy like ours, each national election can be considered a contest between two prospective government budgets. These budgets differ from each other in both quality and quantity, but each contains any spending and taxing measures about which there is strong majority consensus. In reality, many factors besides budgets influence people's political choices. However, most of these factors are in some way reflected in the budget, and in the rational world of economic theory we can assume that proposed budgets have a decisive role in determining how people vote. Knowing this, each party carefully plans its budget so as to maximize the support it gets, following the procedures described in Section I.

A key feature of this procedure is that the government gives voters what they want, not necessarily what benefits them. As long as citizens know what benefits them, there should be no difference between the actual budget and the "correct" budget. But if there are benefits which government spending would produce that people are not aware of, the government will not spend money to produce them unless it believes it can make them well-known before the next election. For the government is primarily interested

in people's votes, not their welfare, and will not increase their welfare if doing so would cost it votes. And it would lose votes if it increased taxes or inflation—which people are aware of—in order to produce benefits which people are not aware of. Many citizens would shift their votes to some other party that produced only more tangible benefits at less total cost—even if they would in fact be worse off under this party.

Thus if voters are unaware of the potential benefits of certain types of government spending, party competition may force the actual budget to become smaller than the "correct" budget. This outcome may result even if voters merely discount certain classes of government benefits more heavily than comparable private benefits when in reality they are equal. Thus complete ignorance of benefits is not necessary to cause a "too small" budget—only relative unawareness of certain government benefits in relation to their cost, which under full employment consists of sacrificed private benefits.

Conversely, if citizens are less aware of certain private benefits than they are of government benefits, or if they see benefits more clearly than costs, the actual budget may tend to exceed the "correct" budget. In either case, ignorance causes a distorted evaluation of the relative benefits of public and private spending. This distortion is carried over into the budget by interparty competition, which forces each party to give voters what they want—not necessarily what the parties think would benefit them. Thus the ignorance of the voters may cause the actual budget to deviate from the "correct" budget.

Whether the actual budget is too large or too small depends upon the specific forms of ignorance present in the electorate. Since ignorance influences voters' thinking by distorting their evaluation of public vs. private spending, we must study the way citizens view these two types of spending before analyzing the net impact of ignorance upon the budget.

Significant Differences Between Transactions in the Public and Private Sectors

There are two significant differences between transactions in the private sector and in the public sector that are relevant to our analysis. First, in the private sector nearly all transactions are made on a *quid pro quo* basis, whereas in the public sector benefits are usually divorced from the revenues that make them possible. Whenever a citizen receives a private benefit, he pays for it directly and individually. Conversely, whenever he pays someone in the private sector, he receives a corresponding benefit which he has freely chosen because he wants it. No such direct link between costs and benefits exists in the public sector. Taxes are not allocated to individuals on the basis of government benefits received but on some other basis, usually ability to pay. Thus receipt of a given benefit may have no connection whatever with payment for it. And when a man pays his income tax or the sales tax on his new car, he cannot link these acts of sacrifice to specific benefits received. This divorce of benefits from payment for them makes it difficult to weigh the costs and benefits of a given act and decide whether or not it is worthwhile, as can be done regarding almost every private transaction.

There are two reasons why governments do not operate on a *quid pro quo* basis. First, the collective nature of many government benefits makes it technically impossible. For example, take national defense, which is the largest single item of government spending in most democracies.[6] But the benefits of national defense are collective in nature; that is, if they exist for one man, all men enjoy them. This fact makes *quid pro quo* transactions impossible, because once the benefit exists, enjoyment of it cannot be denied to those citizens who have not paid for it. For this reason, voluntary payment cannot be used to finance collective benefits. Since each citizen benefits whether or not he has paid, he maximizes his income by dodging his share of the cost. But *everyone* has this cost-minimizing attitude; so if voluntary payment is relied upon, no one pays. Consequently the resources necessary to provide the collective good are not provided, and no one receives any benefits. To avoid this outcome, individuals agree to coerce each other into payment through a collective agency like the government.

A second reason why governments do not use *quid pro quo* transactions is their desire to redistribute income. In the private sector, benefits are furnished only to those who can pay for them, or through voluntary charitable activities. But most modern democracies have elected to provide their poorest citizens with more benefits than those citizens can afford individually. This goal requires a deliberate violation of the *quid pro quo* relationship; poor citizens get more benefits than they pay for, and their

richer brethren are forced to give up more in taxes than is spent on benefits for them. One way to accomplish such redistribution and at the same time allocate the costs of collective goods is to tax on the basis of ability to pay. Thus for both technical and ethical reasons, the benefit principle that prevails in the private sector is largely abandoned in the public sector.

The second major difference between transactions in the private and public sectors is the coercive nature of dealings in the latter. Whereas all private transactions are voluntary, most payments to governments —other than direct sales of services—are enforced by law. Even the receipt of collective benefits is involuntary, since they exist whether a given citizen wants them or not. As noted, coercion is necessary because there is no intrinsic link between benefits and payments as in the private sector. Instead, force supplies this link.

But the use of force makes doing business with the government an all-or-nothing proposition. In the private sector, a citizen can enter into those transactions he desires and refrain from those he does not desire. No such selectivity is possible in his dealings with government. He must pay taxes that are used to pay for many projects he does not want. True, he can avoid taxes to some extent by directing his activities into untaxed areas; e.g., by refusing to buy luxury goods or cutting down the time he works. He can also exercise similar limited selectivity in receiving government benefits. But by and large, since his payments to the government are not related to the benefits he receives from it, he finds himself contributing to things that do not benefit him. The result is that no one ever attains marginal equilibrium in his dealings with the government.

For a citizen, such equilibrium exists when the utility produced by that act of government which is least attractive to him (i.e., the "last" government act on his preference scale) is equal to the utility of the least attractive act he undertakes in the private sector (i.e., the "last" completed private act on his preference scale). Furthermore, there must be no additional government acts that would give him more utility than those now being carried out. Under these circumstances, the individual cannot be made better off by shifting resources from the private to the public sector or vice versa, or by any reallocation of resources within the public sector. (We assume he has already allocated his resources within the private sector to his maximum benefit.) This situation corresponds to equilibrium within the private sector as portrayed by classical economists—a state attained by utility-maximizers in a world of perfect competition.

However, even if perfect competition exists, the requirements for attaining perfect equilibrium with a democratic government are highly restrictive. If a majority of citizens have identical preference rankings of both public and private acts, then the government's actual policies will be just what those citizens want (assuming the government knows what their preference rankings are). The division of resources between public and private sectors will be precisely that necessary to assure the majority a state of equilibrium between the sectors.

But, in the real world, people's preference rankings are not identical, so we shall not assume them identical in our model. While almost every man agrees with a majority of his fellows in regard to some policies, he also finds himself in a minority regarding others. It is the presence of these "revolving majorities" that prevents men from attaining equilibrium with governments. The government must carry out a complex mixture of many policies, some pleasing to one majority, some pleasing to another majority, and some pleasing only to a minority with intensive feelings concerning them. It can afford to undertake policies favored only by a minority because it does not stand or fall on any one issue but on the mixture as a whole.[7] If society is at all complex, the government's gigantic policy mix is bound to contain at least one act which any given voter opposes. It is either positively repugnant to him (i.e., it produces negative utility apart from its resource-cost), or else he knows of better uses to which the resources it absorbs could be put. As long as only one such act exists for him, he is out of equilibrium with government. Even if we assume declining marginal utility of income in both private and public sectors, there is always some additional private use of resources (including charity) which would yield him positive utility. There may also be other government acts, not now being performed, which would yield him even more utility than the best private act he can think of. Hence his disequilibrium does not necessarily imply a desire to shift resources from the public to the private sector. It may also imply desire for reallocation within the public sector or even for moving more resources into

that sector. But, in any case, there is always some change in government policy that would benefit him. Furthermore, the government is always spending money on projects he dislikes; hence his welfare would be improved if those projects were eliminated and his taxes reduced. *Therefore every citizen believes that the actual government budget is too large in relation to the benefits he himself is deriving from it.* Even if he feels the optimum budget would be much larger than the actual one, he believes the actual one could be profitably reduced "through greater economy"—i.e., elimination of projects from which he does not benefit.[8]

But if everyone feels the government is spending too much money for the benefits produced, why don't political parties propose smaller budgets? How can budgets which everyone regards as too large keep winning elections? The answer lies in the nature of the "revolving majorities" discussed previously. According to the economic theory of democracy, governments never undertake any policies unless they expect to win votes (or at least not lose votes) by doing so. Hence for every citizen opposed to a given act, there are other citizens in favor of it. Elimination of that act would please the former but alienate the latter. Looking at the whole complex of its acts between elections, the governing party feels that including this act gains more votes than excluding it. The party can afford to offend some voters with this act because they are in the minority regarding it, their feelings against it are not as intensive as the feelings of those for it, some other acts will placate them, or for some combination of these reasons. Since citizens' preferences are diverse, every man finds himself thus ignored by the government on some policy or other. Hence everyone believes the government is carrying out some unnecessary acts. But the government is still maximizing political support for itself, for what one man believes unnecessary is to someone else necessary enough to cause him to thank the government with his vote.

However, the resulting disequilibrium puts tremendous pressure on the government to reduce the budget wherever it can. This means it will make only those expenditures which produce benefits that voters are aware of, for hidden benefits cannot influence votes. Thus the threat of competing parties prevents the government from giving citizens what is good for them unless they can be made aware of the benefits involved before the next election. Only if a party has immense confidence in its ability to win the next election anyway is it free to produce such hidden benefits, no matter how important they are in the lives of the voters. The more "perfect" the competition between parties, the more closely must the government follow popular opinion, and the more likely it is to include in its policies any errors in that opinion caused by ignorance.

Distortions in Budget Evaluation Arising from These Differences

Having analyzed the relevant differences between transactions in the public and private sectors, we now turn to the distortions they produce in benefit-appraisal. Such distortions are of two main types: underevaluation of government benefits in comparison with private benefits, and underevaluation of government cost in comparison with private cost. In both cases, the distortion occurs in estimating the government's contribution or cost rather than that of the private sector. This is true because the *quid pro quo* relationship in the private sector makes accurate estimation of both costs and benefits almost universal. Of course, some private spending is speculative in nature; e.g., people may attend a play not knowing beforehand whether it will be worth the price of admission. But because each private transaction is voluntary, purely individual in nature, and based on *quid pro quo* relations, the persons making it usually know its benefits and costs in advance (except in cases of financial speculation). The absence of these qualities in public transactions gives rise to two major sources of error.

Remoteness

Benefits from many government actions are remote from those who receive them, either in time, space, or comprehensibility. Economic aid to a distant nation may prevent a hostile revolution there and save millions of dollars and even the lives of American troops, but because the situation is so remote, the average citizen—living in rational political ignorance—will not realize he is benefiting at all. Almost every type of preventive action, by its nature, produces such hidden benefits. People are not impressed with their gains from water purification, regulation of food and drugs, safety control of airways, or the regulation of utility and transport

prices, unless these actions fail to accomplish their ends. Then, perhaps for the first time, the absence of effective protection makes them aware of the benefits they were receiving when it was present.

In contrast, the immediate benefits of almost all private goods are heavily emphasized. In order to sell these goods on a voluntary basis, their producers must convince the public of their virtues. Thus consumers are subject to a continuous advertising barrage stressing the joys of private goods, whereas no comparable effort dramatizes the benefits they receive from government action. Even private goods with benefits of a remote nature, such as cemetery lots, are advertised in such a way as to make awareness of these benefits immediate.

Furthermore, much of the cost of remote government benefits is not equally remote. In the private sector, the *quid pro quo* balancing of costs and benefits is often attenuated by time-payment plans which magnify benefits in relation to costs. But in the public sector the opposite is true. The major source of federal government revenue—personal and corporate income taxes—must be computed by taxpayers on an annual basis. Even if these taxes are paid by installments, the fact that each taxpayer must sit down and figure out exactly how much he has to pay each year makes this cost very real to him. His rational political ignorance does not insulate him equally from knowledge of government benefits and their costs, but it tends to emphasize the latter.

In some cases, this asymmetry is reversed. Sales taxes which are passed on to consumers are not strongly felt by them because they are spread over time in a series of relatively small payments, and each consumer does not annually add up his total payments. But the intermediate agent—e.g., the retailer who collects the sales tax—does compute the total amount paid. True, he realizes that this cost is borne by his customers in the long run.[9] Nevertheless, both his short-run interests and his ignorance tend to emphasize the government's acquisition of these resources rather than the benefits they eventually provide; hence this acquisition takes on the elements of confiscation.

The confiscatory cast of taxation is an inevitable result of the divorce of costs from benefits and the remoteness of the latter. Whereas in *quid pro quo* transactions each yielding of resources is justified by immediate receipt of benefits, taxation appears to be outright seizure of privately produced resources.

It thus seems parasitic, rather than self-supporting like other costs of production or consumption. True, a rational taxpayer knows that he receives benefits in return for his taxes, but the remoteness of many such benefits removes the appearance of tit-for-tat balance that is present in private transactions.

In summary, a major portion of government benefits is remote in character compared with either taxes or private benefits. Since citizens are rationally ignorant of remote political events, they fail to realize all the government benefits they are receiving. However, they are well aware of a greater percentage of the taxes they pay and of the private benefits they are sacrificing to pay them. Because of this imbalance, the governing party cannot spend as much money on producing remote benefits as their real value to the citizenry warrants. Every dollar raised by taxation (or inflation) costs votes which must be compensated for by votes won through spending. But when the spending produces benefits that are not appreciated by voters, no compensating votes are forthcoming. Hence such spending must be restricted, or else the competing party will gain an advantage by cutting its own (proposed) spending and charging the incumbents with "waste." True, if the incumbents can demonstrate to the voters that this spending actually produces valid benefits, such charges will be harmless. But such demonstrations absorb resources themselves, especially since the nature of remote benefits makes them hard to document. And since the government is under constant pressure to cut expenditures, it cannot afford to use resources advertising the benefits of its policies. In this respect, it differs from private concerns, which must advertise in order to encourage voluntary purchase of their products. A striking example of this advertising asymmetry is in the field of electric power. Whereas private power corporations advertise both the virtues of their own product and the evils of public power, government utilities cannot even advertise their existence for fear of being accused of wasting public funds.

The outcome is a tendency toward elimination from the budget of all expenditures that produce hidden benefits. Only if the benefits involved are necessary for the survival of democracy itself will the governing party risk losing votes by producing them and spending resources to justify its actions. Even in this case, it tends to get by with the minimum possible amount because it fears charges of "waste"

from its opponents.[10] Clearly, this situation causes government budgets to be smaller than they would be if voters were perfectly informed about all benefits and costs, however remote.

Uncertain Nature of Government Benefits

Closely akin to remoteness is the uncertain nature of many government benefits compared with private ones. Since government must deal with factors affecting society as a whole, the problems it faces are much more complex than the problems facing individuals in their private lives. Many policies undertaken by governments are launched without either control or knowledge of exactly what their outcomes will be. This is particularly true in international relations or fields of rapid obsolescence, such as national defense. Here the future is so beset by unknowns that whether a given policy will produce benefits or penalties is often problematical, and appraisal of the expected value of benefits forthcoming is extremely difficult. In contrast, each citizen in his private life knows of many ways to invest resources which will give him immediate benefits. True, life is full of risks, and the future is unknown to individuals as well as governments. Nevertheless, each person faces a much simpler set of choices in his own life, with many fewer parameters, than does even a local government. Hence the returns from inventing resources privately must be discounted much less than those from investing resources publicly.

This situation is not a result of rational political ignorance, but of the uncertainty inherent in any complex situation involving human action. Even the best-informed government experts cannot predict the outcome of many of their policies. They have plenty of current information, but do not understand all the basic forces at work, and cannot predict the free choices of the men involved. This kind of ignorance cannot be removed by greater personal investment in political information.

Again, the outcome is a budget smaller than the "correct" one. Because voters are led by rational ignorance to undervalue benefits from policies with uncertain outcomes, the government cannot count on gaining political support by spending money on these policies. But since it can count on losing support by raising the money, it tends to eschew such policies altogether.

Throughout the preceding argument, it is assumed that citizens' ignorance conceals benefits lost through failure to spend, but does not conceal losses of utility through excessive spending. Perhaps if citizens became better informed about government policy, they would discover that present policies produce fewer benefits than they had supposed. In that case, increased information might increase their reluctance to transfer resources into the public sector. In other words, they would discover that the actual budget was larger than the "correct" budget instead of smaller.

This objection to our previous conclusion ignores the motivation of the government in regard to expending resources. Essentially, the argument implies that government conceals a great deal of "waste" spending under the cloak of citizens' ignorance; therefore if citizens had perfect information, they would want the government to eliminate this waste. Naturally, in a world of imperfect knowledge, every government makes mistakes, and undoubtedly perfect information would reveal such errors and cause the electorate to desire corrective reallocations. But, aside from this failing, the government has no motive to spend resources without producing tangible benefits. As we have seen, government policies are designed to gain votes by producing definite benefits known to voters. Furthermore, because voters are aware of the costs imposed upon them by government action, government is always under pressure to eliminate policies that do not justify their costs by producing tangible benefits. Hence it is irrational for government to "waste" resources on non-benefit-producing policies, since they lose votes through adding to taxation but do not gain votes by adding to benefits. Such "waste" expenditures would be rational only if (1) the government had a secondary motive of maximizing expenditures *per se* in addition to maximizing its chances for election, or (2) in the process of winning votes, the government spent money to benefit minorities in hidden ways which the majority would repudiate if they had perfect knowledge. The first case posits a government markedly different from the one in our model. Exploration of the behavior of such a government might be very interesting, but it cannot be undertaken in this article.[11] The second case will be dealt with in the next section.

The Tendency Toward Excessive Spending

Up to this point we have discussed two states of information in the electorate: perfect knowledge and partial ignorance. We have shown that when the latter prevails, costs of government action will appear more significant than benefits; so the actual budget will be smaller than the "correct" budget. However, there is also a third state of information: preponderant ignorance. In this state, citizens are ignorant of both the items in the budget and their benefits and costs. The budget that results when such ignorance predominates differs radically from those discussed previously: it tends to be *larger* than the correct size because of voters' ignorance of what items are in the budget.[12]

Government action affects each citizen in many ways, touching nearly all the functional "roles" he plays in society. Two important such roles are those of income-earner and consumer. As an income-earner, each citizen benefits when government spending increases the demand for the service he produces and when his taxes are reduced. He suffers when such spending is diminished or when his taxes increase. As a consumer, he suffers whenever government action increases the prices of the goods and services he buys, and he gains when it causes them to fall relative to his income.

Thus government action influences his welfare in both roles, but the two influences are not equally significant to him. Since almost every citizen receives nearly all his income from one source, any government act pertinent to that source is extremely important to him. In contrast, he spends his income on many products, each one of which absorbs a relatively small part of his total budget. Thus a government act which influences one of the products he consumes is nowhere near as vital to him as an act which influences the product he sells.[13] Under conditions of preponderant ignorance, this asymmetry means he is much more aware of government policies that affect him as an income-earner than he is of policies that affect him as a consumer.[14]

In order to maximize its political support, the government takes account of this situation in planning its budget. It realizes that two excellent ways to gain a citizen's support are to raise his income by giving him something for nothing or to buy what he produces. In some cases, both can be combined in a single act, such as hiring workers to build a public swimming pool which they subsequently use free of charge. But in a society with a complex division of labor, each specific income-earning group is usually a small minority of the population. Therefore government acts designed to please such a group usually distribute benefits to a minority, whereas their costs are added to the general tax burden and spread over the majority. Each recipient of such a boon thus feels he is making a net gain, since his share of the taxes added to pay for this project is much smaller than the benefit he receives. But the government also provides similar projects benefiting other minorities to which he does not belong. The costs of these projects are likewise spread over all citizens—including him—so he winds up paying for other people's special benefits, just as they pay for his. Whether or not he makes a net gain from this process is a moot point.

However, he cannot expect the government to undertake only those special projects which benefit him. Since a majority of citizens would be net losers under such an arrangement, they would vote against it. In order to get them to help pay for acts which benefit him, the government must provide them with benefits for which he helps to pay. Thus the government placates the majority who are exploited by a minority in one field by allowing them to be part of exploiting minorities in other fields.

In this process of "log-rolling," the citizens affected do not enter into direct bargains with each other. The only decision they face is which of the two competing budgets to vote for at each election. All the intervening trading of political support is done within the governing party, which knows that it must present the end result to the voters as a single package in competition with a similar package offered by its opponents. Each voter must then decide which budget provides him with the greatest difference between benefits received and costs imposed. If he receives many benefits from "special-interest" projects, he can expect his taxes to be swelled by the costs of similar projects benefiting other minorities, which the government must undertake to "buy off" the people who paid for his gains. Thus he might be better off if all minority benefits were eliminated and taxes lowered for everyone.

However, the question facing us is not whether budgets will include many or few minority-benefiting projects. It is whether the voters' ignorance of what is in the budget will cause governments to increase or decrease the number of such projects, thereby increasing or decreasing the budget as a whole.

As we have shown, when preponderant ignorance prevails, voters are most likely to be aware of those government policies which directly affect their sources of income. Hence they encourage government policies which raise the relative prices of the products they sell. But since any particular type of producer is in a minority in a complex society, these policies will be minority-benefiting policies. This is also true because such policies injure all buyers of the product, and buyers usually outnumber producers. Thus each citizen's perception threshold is most likely to be crossed by minority-benefiting policies involving government spending that raise (or could raise) his income.

On the other hand, government policies that affect the prices of individual goods he consumes will not be as apparent or as significant to him as policies which affect the price of what he produces. But policies that raise his costs as a consumer also benefit the citizens who produce what he consumes. It therefore appears that government can engage in specialized spending that benefits each type of producer without arousing the antagonism of consumers, especially since each consumer receives such benefits himself in his role as a producer. This situation tends to make the actual budget larger than the "correct" one.

However, this appearance is deceptive, for it ignores the cost side of the budget. When voters are preponderantly ignorant about the budget, they do not realize that special benefits are being provided to minorities to which they do not belong. But these benefits raise the general level of taxation, and voters are quite aware of their taxes, since taxes affect them directly. Thus their knowledge of the budget is narrowed down to two major items: government policies directly affecting their sources of income, and those types of taxes which inherently call themselves to every citizen's attention (e.g., income taxes).

As noted, when any minority gets special benefits from government spending, the minority's taxes are likely to go up much more than just its share of the cost of the benefits it receives. If the taxes that rise cannot be concealed from the citizenry, each minority may prefer to eschew its special benefits and vote for a budget which cuts out such benefits and reduces everyone's taxes. But if the taxes that rise are the type that are less likely to cross the citizens' perception threshold (e.g., sales taxes), then each minority may vote for a budget which provides it with special benefits because its taxes do not appear to go up significantly.

Thus, insofar as taxation can be concealed from the electorate, the government budget will tend to be larger than the "correct" one. Voters will underestimate the costs they are paying for special benefits received, and parties will build this bias into their budgets. However, this tendency does not eliminate the previously discussed tendency toward a too-small budget. Under preponderant ignorance, both forces act simultaneously; so the net outcome in terms of total budget size is ambiguous.

The Net Results

Nevertheless, I believe the actual budget will still be smaller than the "correct" budget because even indirect taxation is much more apparent than many remote government benefits. As noted previously, whoever collects indirect taxes is aware of their existence even if in the long run he does not bear them himself. He tends to look at them as expropriation by the government of resources he could collect himself, since by raising the price of his product, they reduce his sales and cause him short-run hardships. Furthermore, he attempts to placate his customers for his higher price by identifying that element of it caused by the tax—thus making them aware of it. And if this tax is significant enough to support substantial increases over the "correct" budget, it must irritate many such persons. For these reasons, it is difficult to increase taxation to support "hidden" special projects without arousing opposition. True, policies like tariffs, which raise prices but do not increase taxes, can be used to provide minorities with hidden benefits, especially if the persons whose income-earning suffers are foreign citizens. But when a domestic appropriation of revenues is necessary to support a hidden subsidy, some voters are bound to complain. This fact necessarily limits the tendency for budgets to exceed the "correct" amount.

No such inherent brake limits the tendency for remote government benefits to be ignored. Since most remote benefits stem from preventive action, no one feels any immediate loss when they are not forthcoming. Perhaps particular producers might increase their incomes if government adopted policies that produced remote benefits, but their voices are not as loud as those of the taxpayers injured by indirect taxes. In the first place, they are

not suffering "expropriation" of actual private earnings but only loss of potential income, which is rationally less significant because it must be discounted for uncertainty. Second, they are usually few compared with the large number of voters who must be taxed if the budget is to be made larger than the "correct" size. Furthermore, the benefits of preventive action in any field are usually known only to experts in that field, since such knowledge implies the ability to predict future events, which in turn demands familiarity with causal relations in the field. Whenever these experts are members of the government, they are primarily motivated to produce votes rather than benefits. But remote benefits cannot produce votes unless resources are spent to inform people about them—and voters are notoriously hard to inform about anything remote. Thus the experts who usually know most about such remote benefits are not strongly motivated to produce them—nor is anyone else.

For these reasons, the two opposite tendencies acting on the budget are not of equal strength. The forces which tend to enlarge budgets beyond the "correct" level are inherently limited, whereas those which tend to shrink it are not. Therefore I believe the budget will emerge smaller than its "correct" size.

Even if the net size of the actual budget in relation to its "correct" size is ambiguous, certain specific distortions in it (i.e., variations from the "correct" budget) can be expected to result from the two tendencies described. They are as follows:

1. Indirect taxes will be too large in relation to direct taxes.
   Corollary A: Governments which depend on direct taxation for the bulk of their financing will find it more difficult to balance their budgets than similar governments which depend upon indirect financing.
   Corollary B: Since the costs of inflationary finance are not as apparent as those of taxation, this method will be too frequently used to avoid increasing direct taxation.
2. Projects which benefit minorities will be awarded too large a share of the resources allocated to government.[15]
   Corollary A: Costs of projects benefiting all citizens will be distributed with too many loopholes allowing specific minorities to evade their "normal" share.

Corollary B: Producers as a group will receive a disproportionate share of government spending and policy-protection in comparison with consumers.

3. In comparison with policies producing immediate and tangible benefits, government policies which produce remote or problematical benefits will not be allocated as many resources as are warranted by their true importance.

All of these tendencies distort the budget that would prevail if people were perfectly informed. Yet being perfectly informed is impossible, and even being well-informed is irrational; hence ignorance is likely to prevail. Therefore these distortions will probably occur even though a majority would be better off if they were eliminated.

The Increasing Importance of the Problem

As society grows more complex, the role of governmental action becomes relatively more significant. This conclusion applies to all levels of government—local, county, state, national, and international. It results from government's function as a preventer and settler of conflicts among men.[16] Increased social complexity means increased interdependence, which in turn creates more conflicts of interest. Hence the need for more and more regulation, control, and intervention by government in all spheres of action, especially economic.

Social complexity is usually the result of an increasingly specialized division of labor, which also causes higher productivity. Thus societies tend to become richer as they grow more complex. In democracies, this increased wealth is usually distributed to all citizens—by no means equally, but in a generally rising living standard. As men become wealthier, their marginal economic desires shift from material necessities to luxuries and services. Freed from the need to direct all resources to private necessities, they can afford many collective benefits heretofore beyond their means. Thus the need for greater government action coincides with greater ability to pay for it.

However, ability to pay and desire to pay are not identical. We have shown that, in our model economic world, the citizens of a democracy are reluctant to yield their private resources to the government if the benefits to be gained thereby are at all remote from their everyday knowledge. This reluctance is not based on stupidity or irrationality, but on the ignorance in which the average citizen of a complex society is forced to live. He simply cannot afford to be well-informed about all the remote benefits of government action that are or might be important to him. And this ignorance influences the government to refrain from providing him with such benefits. The party in power fears losing to its opponent if it invests tangible resources in less tangible projects, even when it realizes that those projects would benefit the citizenry.

Furthermore, as society grows more complex, the remoteness of possible government action increases. This tendency is most obvious in international affairs, where economic and technical progress have spread a web of interdependency over the whole world. It becomes harder and harder for even experts to keep well-informed on possible benefits to be gained from government policies, including those on the local scene. In short, society's complexity demands more government action, but it also makes each field of action more remote from the ken of the average man. Faced with a gigantic maze of government agencies, each grappling with incredibly intricate problems, a normal citizen soon concludes that keeping himself well-informed is hopeless. Therefore he wraps himself in a mantle of rational ignorance, insulated from knowledge of increasingly important remote benefits by the increasingly high cost of finding out about them.

Thus, as remote benefits become more important, they become less likely to be attained. Their greater importance is accompanied by still greater remoteness, and this makes governments more wary of devoting resources to them for fear of competition from opponents who advocate more immediate gains.[17] The actual government budget shrinks to an ever-smaller percentage of the "correct" budget, even if it increases in size absolutely. Yet most people do not realize this increasing distortion because they are blanketed by an ignorance of political realities which becomes deeper and deeper as the realities become more significant. This ignorance is abetted by every citizen's belief that the government budget is too large in relation to the benefits he is getting from it, because so much of it benefits others at his expense.

Conclusion

In a democracy, information costs tend to make governments enact budgets that are smaller than they would be if such costs were absent. This conclusion is true even if both parties and citizens are rational in their political behavior. It is based on the economic theory of democracy, which treats political parties as part of the division of labor, motivated primarily by self-interest like all other agents in the economy.

Furthermore, if economic growth is injected into the analysis, the tendency for actual budgets to be smaller than "correct" budgets becomes more and more pronounced. As society becomes more complex because of increasing specialization, the governing party is less able to allocate resources to those remote benefits which are of increasing importance to the welfare of the citizenry. It is even conceivable that the growing gap between the actual and the "correct" budgets might precipitate a crisis for democratic government. If the society were suddenly confronted by an external threat heretofore latent, its chronic tendency to underinvest in remote benefits might prove extremely deleterious, if not fatal.

However, such projection goes beyond the limits of my model. I have merely tried to use the economic theory of democracy to draw significant conclusions about democratic governments. This theory has been criticized because it cannot predict the actions of individual men, who play a central role in political events but do not always act selfishly. Therefore, it is said, the theory is useless for political analysis. But if it can reveal underlying tendencies in democracy which operate independently of individuals, then I believe it is a useful theory. In my opinion, it can be used to reach significant, non-obvious conclusions applicable to the real world—especially to the American government. I hope the analysis presented in this article provides an example of such application.

Notes

1. Anthony Downs, *An Economic Theory of Democracy*, New York, 1957.
2. For a complete explanation of this theory, see *ibid.* The government budget is discussed in chap. 4.
3. The remainder of this article assumes a two-party system. Its conclusions are also applicable to multi-party systems, but the corresponding proofs are too complicated to be presented in an article of this length.
4. This explanation of the budget process ignores the effect of government administrative bureaus upon the budget's final size. If self-aggrandizing bureaus were included in the model, each would try to maximize its own income, power, and prestige within the government. Hence it would submit a maximum estimate of its needs to the central budgeting agency (i.e., the directors of the governing party). The bureau might even enlarge this estimate beyond its real needs in anticipation of the budgeting agency's desire to minimize expenditures. Its inflated requests would be bolstered by assertions that all of its spending would pay off well in votes. Since this process would distort the budgeting agency's information about what expenditures would in fact gain votes, the actual budget would tend to be larger than if bureaus were not self-aggrandizing. However, the central budgeting agency would be aware of the bureaus' inflationary tendencies and would develop outside checks against each bureau's vote-gain estimates. If the governing party failed to make such direct checks with the voters, it would be vulnerable to defeat by more alert opponents. Therefore, the information distortion caused by government bureaus could not be expected to offset the basic tendency for government budgets to be too small.

   Another possible impact of administrative bureaus upon the model is their tendency to create situations in which their services are needed; e.g., by building missiles, the defense establishment of country A causes country B to counter with better missiles, thereby increasing the need for country A to spend even more money on missiles, etc. Robert K. Merton describes this process in "The Self-Fulfilling Prophecy" (chap. 7 of *Social Theory and Social Structure*, Glencoe, Ill., 1949). Since this characteristic of bureaus raises a whole set of fundamental problems beyond the scope of my model, I have made no attempt to account for it in this study. However, a model is under development which contains government administrative bureaus as a set of actors in addition to parties and voters. It is hoped that this model will shed further light on the effects of governmental bureaucracy.
5. Some readers of this argument may object that spending for such categories as national defense cannot be evaluated in terms of votes but must be decided largely on technical grounds. I do not agree. For example, the United States government chose to abandon maintenance of strong conventional forces and stake the nation's entire defense upon the use of nuclear weapons. This decision was made against the technical advice of Army planners. From statements made by leading government officials at the time, it is clear that the decision was designed primarily to avoid asking

the electorate to pay for both nuclear and conventional forces. In spite of the fact that every subsequent Army Chief of Staff has bitterly opposed this policy, the governing party has maintained it because the cost of its alternative is politically unpalatable. Thus in the real world, even regarding national defense, major budgetary questions are usually decided by vote possibilities.

6. In the United States, defense expenditures by the federal government constitute over 40 percent of the total spending by all federal, state, county, local, and other government units. This figure applies to 1954 and is taken from U.S. Department of Commerce, *Statistical Abstract of the United States: 1956*, p. 401.

7. Where the government does stand or fall on every issue, as in the French Fourth Republic, it can function successfully only if strong consensus exists among the majority. Otherwise it is continually defeated by "Arrow problems." See Downs, *op. cit.*, chap. 4.

8. This sentence appears to contradict the one preceding it, but in reality they are perfectly consistent. To illustrate, assume that an urban citizen pays $500 per year in taxes toward a government budget which is spent entirely for farm subsidies. Because he has no interest in farm subsidies, he thinks the budget is too large in relation to what he is getting out of it. However, he strongly desires urban renewal, and would be happy to pay $1,000 per year in taxes if the government budget were spent entirely on urban renewal. Thus, in his eyes, the actual budget is simultaneously too large and too small, depending on what alternative it is compared with. It is too large compared with a budget in which those expenditures he dislikes have been eliminated and all others remain the same. Yet it is too small in comparison with a budget in which the expenditure pattern has been changed to what he regards as optimum.

9. If competition is not perfect, he bears some of the cost himself. This fact strengthens the argument that citizens are relatively aware of the sacrifices imposed upon them by taxes, even indirect ones.

10. This is not to deny that there is a great deal of actual waste in government which justly deserves censure. However, many political charges of "waste" are really attacks on production of genuine—but remote—benefits. These attacks are designed to capitalize on rational ignorance for political gain at the expense of the actual benefit of the citizenry.

11. In my opinion, the elected officials of a democratic government are not significantly motivated to maximize expenditures. Their primary rewards are the perquisites of holding an elective office, and their attention and energies are focused upon overcoming the difficulty of remaining in that office in spite of challenges in every election. However, permanent bureaucratic functionaries in large governments do not have their energies absorbed by the problem of retaining their jobs. Hence they can concentrate on increasing their significance through expanding the size and influence of the departments under them, which usually involves increasing the amount of resources they control. Thus whether the expenditure-maximizing assumption enters a model of democratic government depends upon whether government in the model is simply a team of elected officials, or is a team of elected officals *plus* a set of permanent bureaucrats. The impact of the latter assumption has already been discussed in [note] 4.

12. However, this is not the only distortion caused by preponderant ignorance. It also encompasses the previously described tendency to create budgets that are too small because voters are ignorant of remote government benefits. The net effect of these two opposing forces is discussed in Section VIII.

13. Many citizens sell their time and labor rather than an objective product. They are therefore interested in policies which affect both (1) the sale of their labor and (2) the sale of the particular products their labor is used to create.

14. The classic example of this asymmetry is the tariff. A few producers manage to get government to set protective tariffs at the expense of millions of consumers, even though politicians seek to maximize votes. This is possible because producers are much more intensely interested in their income than consumers are in the individual prices that face them. See Downs, *op. cit.*, pp. 253–57.

15. This conclusion and many of the ideas in Section VII [The Tendency Toward Excessive Spending] were developed in discussion with Gordon Tullock, to whom I am much indebted.

16. This is not the sole function of government, but is one of the most central.

17. During periods of rising national income, government receipts will increase without any change in tax rates. Assuming that such increases are not accompanied by an inflation which destroys their real value, the government will have greater purchasing power available to it. It might therefore appear that government could increase its spending beyond the "correct" amount without the voters knowing about it. However, this argument ignores two facts. First, the opposition party serves as a "watchdog" ready to call voters' attention to such tendencies. If the governing party tried to increase spending covertly with these funds, the opposition might defeat it by uncovering the added receipts and promising to return them to voters via tax cuts. Second, voters will realize that their absolute taxes are rising, even if their incomes are also rising. For both reasons, voters will be aware of rising government receipts. Since the governing party has no vested interest in maximizing its spending anyway, it cannot

afford to risk antagonizing voters by trying to hide such increments. Hence it will evaluate them by weighing votes, as with any other receipts, and either return them to voters via tax cuts or spend them so as to gain further support. Thus whether the model is conceived of as static or dynamic is irrelevant to its major conclusions.

20
Why Does Government Grow?

James M. Buchanan

The explosive growth of government at all levels today is alarming. Even people who do not examine the simple statistics should be increasingly concerned about higher and higher taxes levied in support of governmental programs that become less and less efficient in providing benefits of real value. If a forward look is attempted, the picture seems horrendous. In a decade governments will be using up more than one-half of each dollar of national income generated, and well over a third of gross national product will be expended through governmental channels. The propensity of government to seize upon and to spend additional dollars of the income growth that the national economy generates cannot be questioned. But as the share of government in the economy grows, can the private and nongovernmental sector continue to provide the means of satisfying government's voracious appetite?

The need to understand why government grows so rapidly seems urgent. If alarm about the current spending explosion is to lead to effective political countermeasures, if the explosion is to be stopped or even slowed down, we must have some understanding, some explanation, of why it is occurring. We must explain the institutional and political processes that produce the results that we see, results that seem fully desirable only to the bureaucrats on the expanding public payrolls.

The research project undertaken by members of the staff of the Center for the Study of Public Choice, Virginia Polytechnic Institute and State University, and under the sponsorship of the Foundation for Research in Economics and Education, has such explanation as its primary objective. Preliminary results of this research are reported in detail in the following papers; this paper provides a summary overview.

Source: Thomas E. Borcherding (ed.), *Budgets and Bureaucrats: The Sources of Government Growth*, pp. 3–18. Copyright © 1977 by Duke University Press. Reprinted by permission.

Government growth clearly has a momentum all its own, quite independent of general growth in the national economy. Economists have devoted much attention to isolating the sources of economic growth, but, surprisingly, they have paid almost no attention to the problem of determining why governments' share in the national economy continues to increase.

Because of this relative neglect, the research here must be treated as exploratory and provisional. There are no widely accepted paradigms or models upon which specific hypotheses might be constructed and tested. Features of several models will appear in the papers attached, and no single and inclusive explanatory theory emerges full-blown from our efforts. Further research is clearly needed here, and if our preliminary results can stimulate this, one subsidiary purpose will have been accomplished. More importantly, if political leaders and their advisers can be informed of the significance as well as the difficulty of getting answers to the basic question posed, the first step toward corrective countermeasures may be closer than current observation suggests.

What Government Spending, When, and How?

Before we discuss explanations of why government grows, however, some disaggregation is in order. We must look, even if briefly, at the historical record. Growth in total government spending and taxation may exert differing effects with differing mixes among levels of government. Furthermore, growth rates that might be currently observed may be viewed quite differently if they are believed to be temporary phenomena than if they represent long-term patterns. Finally, growth in aggregate governmental activity, even at one level, may depend for its effects on just how this activity is organized, on just what functions are expanding within the public sector.

Borcherding's paper on the record of a century of public spending provides a historical perspective. Significant results emerge from the data presented for the period 1870 through 1970. In the nineteenth century the public sector, overall, was expanding, but it was growing less rapidly than national income. And equally, if not more, important, within the public sector itself decentralization was occurring, with local government spending expanding relative to that of the states, and with state-local spending combined expanding relative to that by the federal government. Both of these results turned around in this century. The twentieth century is characterized by both an increasing governmental share in the national economy and an increasing portion of this public-sector share occupied by the federal government. Centralization *and* growth have occurred, a much more fearsome pair than the converse, growth with decentralization.

Somewhat surprisingly perhaps, within the governmental budget itself, there has been no dramatic shift in spending patterns over the century. Transfers have increased slightly relative to resource-using expenditures, and notably during the 1960s. Furthermore, this element of spending seems most likely to rise during ensuing decades. And, notably, the United States pattern differs from that in other Western nations largely in the relatively smaller share of transfer expenditures undertaken.

The nineteenth century record suggests clearly that an increasing governmental share is not a necessary and inevitable accompaniment to national economic development. The explosion in taxation and public spending that we live with is a twentieth century phenomenon, and the pattern that was changed before can be reversed. Government need not grow more rapidly than the national economy; there is no such relationship written in our stars.

This is not to suggest that a reversal of the trend established over many decades will be easy to accomplish, even if the institutional means are discovered, the political leadership emerges, and the public support is mobilized. Simple and straightforward projections of current trends yield fearful results, as Jacobe's paper demonstrates for the federal government alone. This remains true regardless of the time period used for the basis of projection. As a supplemental note of pessimism, the record suggests that almost every projection of government growth made during the years since World War 2 has been woefully inaccurate, and always on the side of under- rather than overestimation. It is time to become concerned.

Government "By the People"? or Government "Against the People"?

Do governments expand in direct response to the demands of ordinary people for more and better public-service programs? Or do governments operate independently of the people, producing results that may not be related to the wishes of the citizens and which, on balance, do the people more harm than good? These questions get at the very heart of democracy, and they may not seem directly connected to problems of taxation and spending. But until they are answered, no progress at all can be made toward explaining government growth. In a democratic decision model, any explanation for observed high rates of growth in taxation and spending must be grounded on the demands of the citizens. Why do people want governmental agencies to do so much for them, things which they might do better privately?

Why are the people willing to pay onerous taxes for governmental programs? Are those goods and services normally offered by governments characteristically those that become relatively more important as income rises through time? Does the shift from a production to a service economy necessarily embody an expanded role for government? Does increasing population in general, and increasing concentration of this population in particular, generate pressures on governments to supply relatively more services and the private sector relatively less? Does the relatively lower productivity of resources used by governments generate the paradoxical pattern of relatively expanding governmental spending? These subsidiary questions, and more, will be discussed directly or indirectly in the research papers. These questions emerge from a "government by the people" or democratic model of politics. As the questions might indicate, and as the research results support, some part of the overall expansion in the public sector of the national economy can be satisfactorily explained in this way.

But not all. Resort to a quite different and nondemocratic model of the political structure leads to quite different subsidiary questions, the answers to which yield further explanatory potential. Are the people misled into thinking that their taxes are low and that public spending benefits are high? Do they operate under a set of fiscal illusions? If they do, what are the institutions and instruments that foster these illusions, and what individuals and groups find it advantageous to maintain these institutions? Where does the political party, the aspiring politician, the working bureaucrat fit into the picture? What motivates the men who must provide the human bridge between "the people"—those who pay the taxes—and "the people"—those who may secure benefits from governmental programs? Are these two sets of people necessarily equivalent? Or is government increasingly becoming a means of making transfers among groups? What is the role of the political entrepreneur in all this? What are the effects of allowing bureaucrats to vote? Is not this a direct conflict of interest?

Once again, each of these subsidiary questions will be discussed, directly or indirectly, in the research papers here. Note, however, that such questions as these emerge only in a model that is nondemocratic in its essentials, a model that offers an explanation of observed results in terms of a perversion of the true demands of the people.

Neither of these two contrasting models of politics will be proved appropriate or inappropriate here. Any plausibly adequate explanation of the expansion of the governmental sector in the modern American economy requires both models, or some mixture of the two. Without doubt, some considerable part of the observed growth in the public sector, at all levels, is directly traceable to the demands of the citizenry, genuine demands for more services accompanied by an increased willingness to shoulder the tax burdens required for financing. But, once this is acknowledged, there can also be little doubt but that a significant and remaining part of the observed growth in the public sector can be explained only by looking at the motivations of those who secure direct personal gains from government expansion, gains that are unrelated to the benefits filtered down to the ordinary citizens.

The two contrasting models of politics provide a helpful means of presenting the research results in summary form. But they do more than that. The means toward checking the expansion of taxation and spending may depend critically on our ability to separate the two forces at work. Blunderbuss attempts to cut back on public spending programs, willy-nilly, and without recognition that such attempts may be subverted by the bureaucracy, may backfire. If the bureaucracy retains power to allocate general spending cuts among functions, it will, of course, direct the cuts to those areas that are most sensitive, those most in demand by the people. If we adopt the norm that government programs should be directly responsive to the demands of the citizenry, whether we might personally agree with the citizenry or not, but that government should not

offer an instrument of enrichment for self-serving bureaucrats, the prospect for checking the expansion in the public sector may lie not so much in direct spending or taxing limitations but, instead, in structural-procedural reforms within the governmental structure itself. Rules that allow for more contracting out and for less direct provision by governments may do more toward reducing tax burdens than budgetary limits. Changes in pay schedules for teachers may produce more education at less cost more effectively than changes in the size of the educational budget at any governmental level.

Responsive Government

Inflation, Population, and Public Spending

The most obvious explanatory elements in the growth of gross public spending can be covered briefly and without detail. Defined in current dollar magnitudes, total spending, both for the private and the public sectors of the economy, increases as inflation occurs. Even when the gross figures are reduced to real terms, to dollars of constant purchasing power, however, we still are faced with the task of explaining more than 4300 percent increase in aggregate government spending over the years of this century.

One of the first explanations suggested is population growth. To what extent can we "explain" the growth of government as a direct consequence of the population increase over the period? Borcherding's computations suggest that some 25 percent of the increase in real spending by governments might be explained by population, on the presumption that the goods and services supplied by political units are demanded in the same fashion as those supplied in the private sector. That is to say, if there are really no net efficiency gains to be secured through providing the goods and services jointly through governments, we can then "explain" up to 25 percent of the increase in this way. But, somewhat paradoxically, if such efficiencies do not exist, there is no argument for having the goods provided by governments at all. Goods and services had as well be provided and supplied through ordinary markets. On the other hand, if there are clear net efficiency gains to be made through the joint-supply properties of governments, the explanatory potential for population increase falls below the 25 percent figure noted.

The Services Economy and Income
Elasticity of Demand

In either case, our major explanatory task remains before us. What causes the growth in real government spending per capita?

As the general development in the national economy has taken place, there has been a pronounced shift in employment away from production and trade and into the services sector. Since government output is heavily weighted by services, this underlying shift in the structure of the economy would, in itself, explain some of the relative increase in the size of the public sector. When Borcherding examines the data, however, he finds that, even within the services sector, government has increased its relative share in employment. As with population increase, there remains much more to explain.

The growth in income itself will, of course, explain a large share of spending growth in absolute terms. But income will explain some of the relative increase in the government's share only if it can be demonstrated that the goods and services supplied publicly are those for which individuals' demands are highly responsive to income shifts, more responsive than for nongovernmental goods, considered as a package. If the income elasticity of demand is high, to slip into economists' jargon here, there will be a more than proportionate increase in demand consequent on an increase in incomes. Borcherding's estimates suggest that governmentally supplied goods and services possess no such characteristic features, and that the responsiveness in demand to income change is, if anything, somewhat less than that which characterizes private spending. We must look elsewhere for our explanation.

The Public Productivity Paradox

Most of us who use governmental services do not need to be informed that productivity is low relative to that in the nongovernmental sector. Anyone who doubts this statement need only call on his personal experience with the mails during the last Christmas holiday season. And Spann examines the data and he finds that for the five-year period 1962–67 there was no net increase in productivity in the state-local services covered in his study. If anything, productivity may have slightly declined over that period. Earlier work by Professor William Baumol of Princeton University suggested that extremely low rates of productivity growth are characteristic features of the goods and services that governments have traditionally supplied. We need not argue here about whether the relatively low productivity in government employment is inherent in the technology of the goods and services supplied or stems from the motivation system for employees in government. The facts are that, for whatever reason, we witness the phenomenon of increasing productivity in the private sector of the economy alongside stationary or even declining productivity in the public sector.

This unbalanced relationship between rates of productivity increase for the two sectors insures that, in real terms, the relative costs of goods and services supplied governmentally increase. In order to maintain a labor force, wages and salaries in the public sector employments will have to be roughly equivalent to wages and salaries obtainable in the private sector. But the latter, wages and salaries in the market sector, will tend to increase as productivity increases, without necessarily causing an increase in the prices of private-sector output. When governmental employers find it necessary to offer matching wages and salaries, but without the accompanying increase in productivity, the unit costs of goods and services supplied governmentally must rise relative to the costs of market-produced goods and services. To the individual demanders, and consumers, of governmental goods and services the "prices" of these, measured in units of privately produced goods that are given up, must increase.

With an increase in relative price, quantity demanded normally is expected to go down, other things remaining the same. This first principle of economic theory remains valid here. But even though price increases and quantity demanded decreases (if all other determinants of demand should remain unchanged), the buyer or demander may still *spend more* on the good than before. And since we measure the size of the public or governmental sector by total spending, there is nothing really inconsistent about the low productivity in this sector being one of the important causal factors in the growth of spending for goods and services supplied by this sector. The importance of this factor might be more accurately estimated if we did, in fact, have good measures for governmental output in physical terms. Lacking this, we must make do with what we have, and the evidence suggests that this effect, stemming from the combination of low productivity growth and a relatively low price elasticity of demand for publicly supplied goods and services, does add significantly to our explanation of government growth.

Urbanization and Congestion

As population has increased, and as the structure of the national economy has changed, urbanization has taken place. This increases the economic interdependence among persons, and with this the potential for conflict, because of common use of resources that have not historically been assigned as private property. With urbanization comes congestion in all its forms, and this opens up a role for governments in mitigating the evils if not eliminating them. One part of the hypothesis here can scarcely be questioned. More governmental action is required as congestion increases, and congestion is directly related to the concentration of people in space. But the type of governmental action suggested may not, and need not, give rise to large increases in government budgets. To reduce congestion, corrective regulatory measures may be in order (e.g., zoning, traffic controls, emission and effluent standards, etc.). These may require only nominal budgetary outlays.

On the other hand, increases in incomes that accompany urbanization should reduce economic interdependencies of the positive sort and thus should reduce the need for governmental action. In very poor communities, citizens may find it essential to join forces through governmental units to provide common facilities (e.g., swimming pools). As communities, and individuals, become richer, however, each family can afford to provide its own facilities. This should be a force working toward a reduction rather than an increase in the relative share of government in the economy.

Borcherding examines the evidence empirically. He finds that there is little or no explanatory value in urbanization as a cause for government growth.

Growth of Responsive Government

Any or all of the reasons discussed above might explain why governments would grow, even in an "ideal democracy," where the demands of the people are transmitted directly into observed budgetary outcomes. As we have indicated, a large part of any total explanation must take these demand-increasing influences into proper account. Borcherding attempts to make quantitative estimates, and he concludes that perhaps as much as one-half to two-thirds of the real growth in per capita government spending can be

explained satisfactorily by combining all of the elements discussed to this point. As he puts it in his paper, all of these factors combined explain why we might observe an aggregate governmental sector spending about one-fifth of gross national product (GNP), but they do not help us in going beyond this and in explaining why we observe government spending more than one-third of GNP.

The gap that remains after we have exhausted all of the economic elements that might reflect genuine demands of the people for expanded governmental services is a large one. More importantly, this gap is the margin for potential correction, the margin for reduction that might be accomplished with net benefits to most of the citizenry. We need not, in fact, be greatly concerned if governmental growth could somehow be limited to the rates required to allow responsible and responsive adjustment to the demand-increasing factors. We become properly concerned when observed rates of increase clearly exceed these limits, in the current instance by as much as one-third. It is this margin that must be tackled with corrective measures, and, therefore it is essential that our analysis extend beyond those factors treated in part 1.

Excessive Government

Tax Consciousness and Fiscal Illusions

We need to introduce elements of a nondemocratic model of politics. We must search for reasons why budgetary results are not those desired by the citizens for whom spending programs are alleged to be undertaken, why these results are uniformly in the direction of excessively large outlays. Our research must examine possibilities of breakdowns in the transmission of individuals' demands through the political-fiscal process, including the possibility that the transmission institutions may be deliberately perverted by self-seeking politicians and bureaucrats who succeed in isolating themselves from the discipline imposed by the electoral process.

Perhaps the most significant finding in the unpublished 1972 survey of California citizens' attitudes conducted under the supervision of Professor W. C. Stubblebine for the Foundation for Research in Economics and Education concerns the failure of citizens to estimate properly the true tax costs of various state-local spending programs. These costs are underestimated, sometimes by a factor of two-thirds. The people who pay taxes do not realize how much they pay, and they think that they secure government goods and services at bargain prices. Suppose that we know the cost of an automobile to be $3000 and that we ask a buyer how much he paid. If he tells us $10,000, we should indeed be amazed at his ignorance, and we should predict that he would foolishly spend too much on cars. Yet this is roughly what the situation is with respect to individuals' indirect "purchases" of governmental goods and services through the whole political budgetary process.

This prompts our research into the sources for such illusions. Why does the average citizen underestimate the costs of public services? In his paper Goetz suggests several parts of an answer, and details need not be elaborated here. Relatively large amounts of state-local taxes are at least partially concealed in the final market prices of goods and services. The consumer looks at the retail price of a good, and he rarely breaks this down into the "true price" and "tax" components. Income taxes, which have become increasingly important at the state level, and which (along with payroll taxes) dominate the federal revenue structure, are largely withheld at the income source. Withholding has the effect of making the individual unaware that he is paying for a slice of government before he has the opportunity to pay for anything else. He concerns himself with his net or take-home paycheck, and his consciousness of a tax obligation comes home to him only on tax accounting day in March or April of each year. With the property tax, traditionally the mainstay of local governmental revenue systems, the relatively high awareness of the taxpayer is reduced by the inclusion of tax obligations in monthly mortgage payments. And, for renters, property taxes are equivalent to excise taxes; they show up imbedded in rents.

Economists always return to a central principal, TANSTAAFL, "there ain't no such thing as a free lunch," by which they mean that someone must pay, even if a good seems to be costless to those who consume it. Many fiscal institutions have "free lunch" features built into them and foster the notion that some monies are free. The federal government's program of grants to states and localities increased dramatically in the 1960s. Recipient governments, as represented by their politicians, treat federal grants as if these are, in fact, free monies. The elementary fact that individuals who live in California are also federal taxpayers is lost in the shuffle between Washington and Sacramento.

Fortunately, the national economy continues to grow. National income goes up year by year. This growth insures that the base of taxation increases. From this it follows that, even without changes in tax rates revenues collected will rise through time. Legislators, whether in the Congress or in the state assemblies, again treat this automatic revenue increase as free money, to be used for new spending programs if desired. Goetz estimates that only a third of the increase in state-local revenues is generated by new taxes and by increased tax rates. Two-thirds of the increase stems from the automatic increase in collections consequent on income growth in the economy.

Although we have included this brief treatment of fiscal illusions under nondemocratic models of politics, we should note that fiscal instruments that generate illusions may be chosen by the people. Taxpayers may, in fact, prefer to fool themselves (as witness Governor Reagan's unsuccessful fight to keep the California income tax on a nonwithholding basis). Even in a tolerably working democracy, individuals may be reluctant to accept tax instruments that will produce rational budgetary choices. This is a democratic dilemma; rational behavior in selecting among taxes may guarantee irrational budgetary results. All of this may be acknowledged, yet the primary explanation for the persistence of illusions may lie in the behavior of those who find it in their private interests to insure irrational budgetary outcomes.

Politics for Profit

Politicians are politicians because they want to be. They are no more robots than other men. Yet the politician who would do nothing other than reflect the preferences of his constituents would in fact, be robotlike in his behavior. Few, if any, politicians are so restricted. They seek office because they seek "profit," in the form of "political income," which will normally be obtained only if their behavior is not fully in accord with the desires of electoral majorities. Those men who are attracted to politics as a profession are likely to be precisely those who have considerable interest in promoting their own version of good government, along with those who see the potential opportunities for direct and indirect bribes, and those who evaluate political office as means toward other ends.

The electoral process offers, at best, a crude disciplinary check on those who depart too much from constituency preferences. Elections are held only at periodic intervals. Information is poor, and citizens have relatively little private interest in securing more. As a result, almost any politician can, within rather wide limits, behave contrary to the interests of his constituents without suffering predictable harm. If he departs far from these preferences, he may fail to be reelected. But if the stakes are high, if the potential gains to him in "political income" are sufficiently large, reelection may be willingly sacrificed. Bush et al. explore several of these possibilities in one of his papers.

If the behavior of politicians in seeking and securing "political income" while holding elective office does nothing but create some slack between the working of practical government and an idealized drawing-board model, there would be no cause for concern here. But if this behavior of politicians biases results consistently in the direction of larger governments, it becomes relevant for our purpose. The presence of such biases seems clearly established. Even such a straightforward item as the legislative salary level is directly related to budgetary size. It is much easier to justify a legislative salary increase item in a ten- than in a six-billion-dollar budget. It is much easier to increase legislative salaries for an assembly that meets for six months each year than for an assembly that meets for two months each biennium.

If we introduce the opportunities for potential bribes, whether these be illegal or sub rosa, it is equally clear that these opportunities increase, perhaps exponentially, with growth in governmental size. If, however, governments are excessively large for satisfying constituency demands, or at least for satisfying the preferences of the required majority of constituents, why do not political entrepreneurs find it profitable to appeal to those who would benefit, in the net, from budgetary reductions? Why should platforms based on tax reduction, and spending reduction, not be observed? Why should those legislators, and coalitions of legislators, who seek indirect bribes not seek out those who might benefit from reductions in governmental size? The basic reason is that taxes are more general than spending programs. Spending projects tend to be concentrated so as to provide benefits to particular groups whereas taxes tend to be levied generally on all those who qualify in terms of a defined base. Furthermore,

incumbent politicians, elected on a tax-and-spend program are becoming increasingly difficult to displace. The increasing costs of entry into politics serve to maintain incumbents in elected office. The analysis does not suggest that new political entrepreneurs appealing to those who seek limits on governmental growth must fail in their efforts. It suggests only that the task of this type of political entrepreneur is much more difficult than that faced by the aspiring, and especially incumbent, politicians who can appeal to specific constituency demands for new and expanded projects.

Conflict of Interest

When he became Deputy Secretary of Defense in 1969, David Packard was required to dispose of holdings in a company that maintained an interest in defense contracts. Conflict-of-interest rules have been rigorously applied to high-level governmental appointees during the last decade. Given this, it is perhaps somewhat surprising that the obvious conflict of interest presented by the extension of the voting franchise to members of the vast governmental bureaucracy, at all levels, has scarcely been noted. As Bush and Denzau, and Borcherding, Bush, and Spann remark in their papers, almost no one has analyzed this particular problem. And, unfortunately for our purposes, it seems that the initial disenfranchisement of bureaucrats located in the District of Columbia was not related to the conflict of interest discussed here. Even the Hatch Act, which did seek to reduce overt political activity of bureaucrats, is now under fire in the courts, and it may well be jettisoned if some federal judge decides that he likes his bureaucrat neighbor.

We must be specific. Why is there an obvious conflict of interest present when bureaucrats are allowed to vote in elections organized by the jurisdiction that employs them? Bureaucrats are no different from other persons, and, like others, they will rationally vote to further their own interests as producers when given the opportunity. Clearly their interests lie in an expanding governmental sector, and especially in one that expands the number of its employees. Salaries can be increased much more readily in an expanding agency than in a declining or stagnant one. Promotions are much more rapid in an organization that is increasing in size than in one that is remaining stable or declining in size. From this it follows directly that bureaucrats will vote for those politicians and parties that call for overall governmental expansion rather than for their opposites. This introduces yet another bias in voting outcomes, a bias that grows increasingly important as the sheer size of the bureaucracy grows.

Perhaps this conflict of interest need not be of major concern, even now, if all eligible voters chose to exercise their options. The nonbureaucrat, however, has relatively little private, personal interest in voting, per se, unless the alternatives involve issues that directly influence his well-being. He votes largely out of some sense of duty or obligation to democratic forms, and when voting is costly he may not vote at all. Often he does not; only fifty-five percent of eligible voters participated in the 1972 presidential election.

Things are quite different with the bureaucrat. He will have a much greater interest in exercising his franchise, because his own well-being is directly related to electoral outcomes. And, to the extent that a relatively larger proportion of bureaucrats vote, their individual votes have more value in determining outcomes than might be indicated from a simple head count. Bush et al. examine the data on voting behavior and find that the conflict-of-interest hypothesis is corroborated. From the data they compute a power index for bureaucrats which allows us to place effective weights on their votes, and indirectly to measure the bias that their exercise of the franchise introduces.

Education for the People or Education for the Educators?

We bring our discussion down to concrete terms if we look at one part of the bureaucracy. Educational outlays make up more than 40 percent of combined state and local budgetary expenditures. In his two research papers, Staaf carefully examines the data on recent changes in educational organization and asks: Have the changes been implemented for the benefit of the taxpaying public or for the benefit of those educators who make the organizational decisions? The evidence suggests that the changes have been designed to benefit the members of the educational bureaucracy. The taxpaying public has found itself burdened with significantly higher costs without getting demonstrable improvements in the quality of educational services.

The consolidation of school districts is a case in point. Major consolidation reduced the number of districts from 117,000 in 1940 to 18,000 in 1970. This change took place despite the absence of data suggesting that consolidation facilitates superior educational quality. Why, then, did it occur? How can we explain the institutional change? Once we look at the motivational structure within the educational bureaucracy the answer emerges. Consolidation is desired by educators because salary levels and promotion prospects, and notably those for educational administrators, depend directly on district size.

A by-product of consolidation is a reduction in the competitiveness among local school systems, and an increase in monopoly control of local education. One objective of the educational bureaucracy is to shield itself from competitive pressures, pressures that must work for efficiency in terms of results desired by the final consumers of education, even if not by those educators who supply it.

The absence of effective competition, the difficulty in defining output, and the absence of cost-reducing motivation in the governmental sector—these allow cost-increasing institutions to become imbedded in the bureaucratic structure. Staaf looks in one paper at data on teacher salary levels. He finds that salaries depend largely on educational attainment (higher degrees or work toward higher degrees) and on years of teaching experience. Salaries are unrelated to student achievement, and the data indicate that there is little or no relationship between these salary-making variables and achievement of students. Apparently, students do equally well under teachers who have attained only minimal levels of training and who are not experienced as they do under highly educated teachers with long years of experience. These results suggest that education, as a public service, is being purchased inefficiently in almost all jurisdictions. But what person or group in the education bureaucracy has any motive for changing the pattern? Quite the opposite. School system administrators find their own salaries to be related directly to the number of teachers with experience and with higher degrees. The cost-increasing features feed on themselves.

But why don't experience and training matter? Surely experience in teaching should lead to better teaching and surely education has some positive value. Staaf explains the paradox by examining the behavioral situation in which teachers find themselves. Since their rewards are not related in any way to the final output that they produce, which should be measurable in student achievement, teachers have no personal incentive to perform well. They are not so much bad teachers, as they are teachers who have no reason to be good.

Private Provision of Public Goods and Services: Reducing Spending (and Taxes) Without Reducing Benefits

Aspiring politicians who seek to dislodge incumbents from elective office often refer to major cost-savings that might be introduced by greater efficiencies in spending, cost-savings that may be utilized to provide additional goods without the necessity of imposing new taxes. The public accepts most of these arguments for what they are, and it does not expect the pattern of governmental growth to be changed much regardless of which politician or political party gains power. When we look carefully at the institutional structure of government, however, at the internal motivational system at work in the bureaucracy, the prospect of securing dramatic efficiency gains becomes exciting. If major institutional changes could be made, government budgets could be slashed (along with taxes) without reducing either the quantity or the quality of goods and services enjoyed by the final consumer, the taxpaying citizen.

But a shift in approach would be required to accomplish this. *Governmental financing of goods and services must be divorced from direct governmental provision or production of these goods and services.* There may be fully legitimate arguments for governmental financing but little or no argument for governmental provision. Through the simple device of introducing private provision under governmental financing, the growth in public spending may, figuratively speaking, be stopped in its tracks.

Why should this make so much difference? Why should private contractors be able to supply the same quality of goods and services at substantially lower costs? The motivational differences between the private firm, whose managers can secure direct monetary rewards from cost-savings, and the bureaucratic agency are clear enough, even without supporting empirical evidence. But the facts themselves are dramatic. Spann examines the results of the various studies that have compared the costs of private and public provision of similar services. Scottsdale, Arizona, gets its fire protection from a private firm at one-half the cost of the same quality protection under governmental provision. Monmouth County, New Jersey has its garbage collected by private contractors at two-thirds of the cost of doing

it publicly. These are examples of what might be achieved by widespread introduction of private provision under governmental financing. The introduction of educational vouchers, with the education being supplied to families by private firms, might produce higher quality education at substantially lower costs. Even if parental choices through full voucher schemes should not be accepted, the willingness of local governments to purchase education through performance contracting with private firms offers substantial potential for cost reduction.

Such institutional changes may do much toward checking excessive government growth. But even the widespread introduction of the private provision of goods and services that are governmentally financed may not remove the basic bureaucratic influences in democratic decisions. Persons employed by private firms which supply goods on contract to governments may behave similarly to persons who work directly for governments.

Conclusions

We started out to explain why governments grow so rapidly. We end by zeroing in on the motivational structure of the governmental bureaucracy as the primary source for that part of governmental growth that does not represent response to the demands of citizens for goods and services. The policy implication is that attempts to reduce excessive governmental spending might be aimed at the motivational structure of bureaucracy rather than at aggregate budgetary or tax levels. On the other hand, if the bureaucracy is considered to be so firmly entrenched and its institutions so rigid that direct attack would be futile, alternative means may be required. It may prove possible to force through the internal structural changes that might be suggested by the analysis only if aggregate budget and tax limits are imposed on legislative bodies, at the constitutional level. Legislators respond to many constituencies, including that of the bureaucracy. And until the legislator is forced by constitutional restrictions to face up to the inherent conflict between the interests of the citizenry and those of the bureaucracy, he may continue to take the route which, to him, seems that of least resistance. This route has been, until now, that of allowing government budgets (and taxes) to grow.

21
Participatory Democracy and Budgeting: The Effects of Proposition 13

Jerry McCaffery
Indiana University
John H. Bowman
Indiana University

Perhaps the most spectacular attempt at budget control through tax limitations is represented by the passage of Proposition 13,[1] the Jarvis-Gann Initiative, in California on June 6, 1978. Limitations on taxes are not new.[2] However, Proposition 13 has some unique features and special impacts which make it all the more interesting since it quickly became the prototype for limitation attempts in other states. This article explores the complexities of Proposition 13 in the context of fiscal policymaking. One of the major issues to be kept in mind in what follows is that the initiative as an electoral device is generally classified as one of the package of reforms growing out of the Progressive movement of the early 1900's; it permits direct democratic participation. Yet the study of Proposition 13 raises serious questions about the feasibility of participatory democracy in a policy area which commonly has been dominated by experts.

Even the smallest governmental unit exists in an intergovernmental context with diverse revenue structures at its own level and multiple sources of monies and controls stemming from other levels of government. Proposition 13's "meat-axe" approach to taxing—and budgeting—disrupted many of these relationships. What was headlined in petitions as a "property tax limitation"[3] evolved into a complicated and extensive set of consequences. These include a property tax reduction of major proportions (spread unevenly over California's governmental structure), and property tax relief captured only partially by Californians, serious problems of taxpayer equity, and

Source: Reprinted with permission from *Public Administration Review* (November–December 1978): 530–538. © 1978 by the American Society for Public Administration (ASPA), 1120 G Street NW, Suite 500, Washington, D.C. 20005. All rights reserved.

a restructuring of intergovernmental relationships in California. Furthermore, the stringency of that "simple" property tax limit raises the prospect of defaults on certain non-voted debts and may greatly limit the use of general obligation debt instruments. Moreover, the stringency of the limit also will have a direct impact on many of California's cities which have traditionally underfunded pension plans, since these past obligations now must compete with current services for significantly reduced revenues. Ironically, this simple tax limit jeopardizes California's solution to the *Serrano* vs. *Priest*[4] school finance case. Finally, given the initiative's two-thirds voting requirement for passage of new and/or increased taxes at both state and local levels, what has been done electorally will be even harder to undo. Each of these points will be discussed in more detail below.

Initial Local Responses and State Bail-Out

In February, 1978, the staff of the California Assembly Revenue and Taxation Committee estimated that passage of Proposition 13 would cost local governments $7 billion out of an anticipated $33.9 billion in total local revenues—a drop of 20.8 percent.[5] The $33.9 billion figure represented the controller's estimate of a 17.7 percent increase over the actual 1976–77 total of $28.8 billion for local revenues; the $7 billion reduction threatened to cut local revenues almost $2 billion below the 1976–77 dollar base. Consequently, in the middle of the 1977–78 fiscal year, local government budgeters knew that passage of Proposition 13 would not only cut property taxes nearly 60 percent and total revenues 20.8 percent below the levels otherwise expected to be available for the next (1978–79) budget year, but that it would put them 6.6 percent below the base of the *previous* (1976–77) year.

Thus, direct democratic participation limiting the property tax would impose a severe revenue cut on local governments, and a 7 percent inflation rate for government goods and services made the bite even deeper.[6] Not only would there be 20.8 percent fewer dollars than expected, but last year's dollars would buy only 93 percent of what they purchased in 1977–78 and about 86 percent of what they had purchased in 1976–77. For the 1978–79 budget year, therefore, the total decrease approximated a cut of 26 percent. On June 6, 1978, the handwriting on the wall was no longer something that could be wished away. Proposition 13 was passed by about as large a majority as those which had squelched two previous tax limitation attempts.[7]

Andrew Glassberg[8] argues that there is a difference between small or incremental declines in available resources and substantial or "quantum" decreases. If there is an expectation that the cut can be restored by resorting to proper strategies, then the cut may be treated as incremental. Quantum cuts are defined by size and a low leadership expectation of revenue restoration; consequently, says Glassberg, " . . . post-crisis managers are operating in a fundamentally different environment . . . " and their familiar strategies for dealing with incremental changes " . . . are unlikely to be applicable . . . ," although many of their initial reactions " . . . will be of the traditional sort developed to deal with incremental budget declines. . . . "[9] Clearly, California local governments faced a quantum revenue decrease, although with a well-publicized state surplus of some $5–6 billion and a legislature in session, an obvious strategy was to replace local revenues with state revenues.

The size of the potential revenue reduction forced local governments to respond immediately. Changes were made to both sides of the revenue expenditure equation. New budget estimates were called for; increased fees, lay-offs, and service cuts were threatened and often implemented. The largest immediate service reduction occurred in education;[10] in 70 southern California school districts surveyed by the *Los Angeles Times,* about two-thirds eliminated or sharply curtailed summer school.[11] Los Angeles, the biggest school district in the state, not only eliminated summer school, but also closed down its regional occupational training centers and slashed summer recreation by about 60 percent. Additionally, 10,000 clerical employees, who normally worked on an annual basis, were laid-off for two months. Since schools were major users of the property tax, most had prepared a budget in anticipation of the passage of Proposition 13. In its "doomsday" budget, the Long Beach school board had slashed all interscholastic sports, eliminated adult education, drastically cut the length of the school day and sent lay-off notices to nearly half of its 2,916 teachers.[12] Nor did schools eschew raising or creating new fees and charges of various kinds aimed at community use of school facilities, including swimming pools, racquet ball courts, playing fields,

and classrooms for night meetings, adult education, driver education, public lectures, and student health services. At El Camino College, the school catalog now costs $1.00. The San Diego school board decided to charge community groups $70 for use of the school auditorium and the Los Angeles Community College system set a fee of $1.00 an hour for the use of tennis courts and $2.00 if the lights were on.

Cities, counties, and special districts were not idle during this period. Proposition 13 would become law on July 1. After that date local governments would need a two-thirds popular vote to raise taxes, fees and charges. Consequently, for the remainder of June most local governments concentrated on raising various fees, charges, and other non-property taxes. Some also made cuts in services, but service reductions could always be made later in the summer. After July 1, the tax structure would be very difficult to change. The League of California Cities estimated that over a quarter of the state's 417 cities had raised or were considering raising fees and charges during June.[13] The most popular increase seemed to be business licenses, followed by increases in various utilities, e.g., water, gas, electricity, telephone, cable television, but no source of income was too small to be overlooked.

Seal Beach, which has a long and pleasant beach front, increased beach parking fees from $2 to $3; it also increased business license taxes by 100 percent. San Francisco raised its zoo admission from $1 to $2 for adults and from 50¢ to 75¢ for children and eliminated free days.[14] Moreover, museum admissions also were increased. The large cities, although they talked about disastrous cuts, tended to wait for state action. Los Angeles froze salaries for 18 elected officials and 44,000 municipal employees. In June, Los Angeles County had laid off only 67 flood control workers. San Diego rescinded its four percent pay raise and San Diego County established user fees for the flood control district, raised transit district fares by five cents, and eliminated most night service. Some of the communities raised fees and charges dramatically. Beverly Hills' commercial rental tax jumped from $1.25 to $23.50 per $1,000 of gross receipts. Baldwin Park boosted license fees by 40 percent and raised fees for issuing and processing various city permits by 50 percent. Buena Park established a $40 paramedic fee for residents and $50 for out-of-towners. Inglewood enacted a fire service fee which included a levy against any structure requiring more fire protection capability than a home. Laguna Beach increased animal and business license fees by almost 100 percent. Lynwood, in a series of moves that was not atypical, established a fee for almost everything: sewers, fire clearance, fire service, water turn-on and turn-off, the city dump, tree trimming, and sidewalks. Business license fees were increased, as were water rates. Recreation, park maintenance, tree trimming, and sidewalk repair services were reduced. Finally, twenty-six employees were laid off.

Rancho Palos Verdes took out an insurance policy by adding an inflation clause to the existing fee structure. Arcadia provided for street sweeping charges based on front footage of properties. Oakland adopted several new taxes, including a five percent admission tax on entertainment events; it also increased the real estate transfer tax by 50 percent and raised the annual business license tax from 90 cents to $14 per $1,000 of gross revenues. The business tax rate on auto dealers was increased from 30¢ to 60¢ per $1,000 of gross receipts. On the service side, the transit district reduced schedules and personnel by 40 percent. Downey doubled its dog license charge from $5 to $10. Sacramento increased the 18 hole golf fee from $3.50 to $4.50 and raised parking meter fees from 10¢ to 25¢ an hour. Inglewood instituted a "tipplers tax," a 10 percent surcharge on drinks served at bars. Localities with harbor or marina facilities either created or increased fees and charges. Orange County more than doubled charges for guest slips, moorings, and boat storage at Dana Point and Newport Beach,[15] as well as for the county's 14 regional parks, beaches, and campgrounds. Newport Beach also froze salaries of all public employees and cut trash collections from twice to once a week.

Actions taken by communities during the month of June, also included cuts in services. For example, Camarillo extinguished 1,000 street lights; Cerritos eliminated school crossing guards; Compton eliminated its public information and centralized purchasing offices, reduced its senior citizens and recreation activities by 80 percent, cut its public works crews by 30 percent, and closed 25 percent of its fire stations. Covina cut its library staff in half and reduced hours, eliminated crossing guards, and reduced street sweeping from a weekly to monthly basis. Monrovia eliminated most free recreation programs, cut library hours from 56 to 30 a week, and reduced counter time for the public at the planning, building, and safety counters from nine to six hours. Needles closed its city park and recreation department, and transferred the workers to other jobs. Pasadena reduced library hours and maintenance of streets and recreation buildings. Petaluma cut its swimming pool season from eleven months to six. Piedmont eliminated its summer playground program. Riverside imposed fees on swimming pool use and reduced community center hours.

For special districts primarily financed through the property tax (non-enterprise), Proposition 13 was a disaster. About 80 percent of the expenditures of California's 3,407 non-enterprise districts were made by fire (23.0 percent), flood (17.7 percent), planning (29.3 percent), and parks (9.9 percent) districts.[16] The property tax accounted, on average, for funding of 89 percent of the expenditures of fire protection districts, 77 percent of flood control districts, and 71 percent of the funding of recreation and parks districts, while planning districts relied on property taxes for less than 1 percent of their revenues. With the passage of Proposition 13 the total revenues available to the fire, flood, and parks districts would be reduced 51 percent, 44 percent, and 41 percent respectively. These districts now would either have to be supported by other units or get legislative authorization to use a new fee, charge, or tax to replace the property tax revenue loss. Those districts which were able to impose special charges for their services (enterprise districts) tended not to rely heavily on the property tax for revenue. Although the average reliance (14 percent) for these districts was low, some used it as a major revenue source. Moreover, all would suffer some reduction. Consequently, while some waited to see if the state would make up for the property tax loss, others began to shift more of the burden to their fee structure. For example, the Los Angeles Metropolitan Water District took steps, only a day or two after Proposition 13 passed, to shift its revenues to sales and away from the taxing power. This involved a hearing and rate-setting procedure. It was estimated that the District's 12 percent fee increase would represent a 75 percent to 100 percent increase by the time it reached consumers.[17]

In sum, immediately after its passage Proposition 13 was producing visible fee increases and service cutbacks, many of which affected leisure time activities in the season when leisure is most valued, as local governments, large and small, attempted to cope with the prospect of drastically reduced revenues and uncertainty about what the state would do to help them. As Glassberg suggests, even in time of a perceived quantum decrease, they relied mainly on familiar mechanisms, which by and large have some theoretical underpinning, be it an ability-to-pay test (rate based on gross receipts) or economic efficiency (user charges). Meanwhile, threatened cuts in vital services and estimates of Proposition 13 lay-offs continued to appear. On July 1, the Employment Development Division estimated that as of June 28, 3,252 lay-offs had occurred as a result of Proposition 13, with 1,104 occurring in the week of June 21–28. Future lay-offs were estimated to be as high as 165,000.[18]

The State's response came near the end of June. Senate Bill 154 drew upon the large state surplus to provide California local governments with about 90 percent of what they had expected before the tax limitation (Table 1). However, restrictions accompanied the money. Cities were required to use the state aid " . . . first to ensure continuation of the same level of police and fire protection as was provided in 1977–78."[19] However, cities were authorized to effect cost savings so long as they did not impair the protection provided. The same stipulation was applied to counties. Additionally, counties which accepted any bailout money were barred from

disproportionately reducing health services, and their budgets were to be reviewed by the state director of health services. The largest part of the county aid went for a variety of health and welfare related programs ($1 billion), not including a one-year waiver of the state's 10 percent matching requirement for the mental health, alcohol, and drug abuse programs. Money for special districts was distributed to the county boards of supervisors for allocation to the special districts within each county.[20] Most of the money went to fire protection districts, while those districts with authority to levy fees and charges were encouraged to do so. Again, fire and police protection levels were given the highest priority. A $2 billion block grant was extended to school districts to guarantee an average of 90 percent of estimated 1978–79 budgets, but it incorporated a sliding scale so that high spending districts would be guaranteed 85 percent of their 1978–79 budgets and low spending districts 91 percent of theirs. The county office of education also was given a 90 percent budget guarantee, primarily for special education and vocational education service provision, and community colleges were guaranteed 85 percent of their 1978–79 budgets. A $900 million state emergency loan fund was created as a loan of last resort, and finally, a very strict local pay raise control was written in which allowed local discretion only in merit increases and legitimate promotions, but lock-stepped state and local cost-of-living raises (if state employees received no

Table 1

Effects of Proposition 13 and S.B. 154 aid on California local government finances, 1978–79

(dollars in millions)

Government Type	Total Revenues— All Sources	Property Tax				Net Loss	
		Before Prop. 13	After Prop. 13	Prop. 13 Revenue Loss	S.B. 154 Aid	Amount	As % of Total Revenues
Cities[a]	$ 5,292	$ 1,348	$ 542	$ 806	$ 250	$ 556	10.5%
Counties[a]	7,740[b]	3,801	1,565	2,236	1,480	756	9.8%
Schools	12,125	6,468	2,929	3,539	2,267	1,272	10.5%
Sp. Districts (Non-Enterprise)	961	388	172	216	125	91	9.5%
(Enterprise)	4,407	443	196	247	0	247	5.6%
TOTALS:	$30,165	$12,448	$5,404	$7,044	$4,122	$2,922	9.7%

[a]The independent city of San Francisco is included with the counties.
[b]Excludes $1.911 billion in federal aid attached to AFDC received at the state level and subsequently sent to the counties for disbursement to recipients.
Source: California, State Legislature, *Summary of the Conference Reports on S.B. 154 Relative to Implementation of Proposition 13 State Assistance to Local Governments* (Sacramento; June 23, 1978; processed), p. 1.

cost-of-living raise, neither would anyone else). Those who had voted for Proposition 13 in an effort to trade-off property tax increases for part of the state surplus had succeeded, but their victory set in motion a chain of events which would have serious repercussions among taxpayers and for the state and its subunits.

Effects of Proposition 13

Property tax controls typically affect other aspects of government finance (e.g., grants, revenue diversification),[21] and California's Proposition 13 is no exception. Indeed, a bewildering array of consequences is traceable to the deceptively simple 400-odd word initiative. The following discussion illustrates the pervasiveness of the effects in California.[22]

Proposition 13 drops 1978–79 California property taxes some $7 billion (nearly 60 percent below what they otherwise would have been (see Table 1). This sharp reduction is perhaps the most unique—and newsworthy—feature of Proposition 13,[23] although the feature may soon spread to other states. The severity of the property tax cut is quite uneven, both among counties and among types of governments. Intercounty variation occurs because pre-Proposition 13 county-average tax rates per $100 of assessed value ranged from $4.75 to $13.15 (average of $11.19) compared to the new limit of $4.00 (net of bond-service levies).[24] Variation among types of governments occurs because local governments have relied on property taxes to differing degrees (Table 1) and because Proposition 13 stipulates that constituent units within a county share in the new, lower, county-collected property tax "according to law," a phrase defined by the legislature to mean previous years' (one year for schools, 3-year average for others) relative property tax shares.[25] The first-year legislative response to Proposition 13 matches increased state assistance closely to lost property taxes, however, so that the overall loss of revenues averages about 10 percent for each of the major types of local governments (Table 1).

Because the increased state aid for 1978–79 comes from accumulated state surpluses, local governments' property tax losses should translate into tax savings (ignoring for now local revenue adjustments). Not all of the property tax cuts, however, will be captured by Californians. The portion of the $7 billion reduction most likely to remain largely within the state is

that on owner-occupied residences, which accounts for about 35 percent of the total (or roughly $2.5 billion).[26] A significant part of this will rebound to the federal government in the form of higher income taxes resulting from reduced property tax deductions.[27] The remaining 65 percent will go in the first instance to business, including owners of residential rental units, agriculture, and public utilities. How much of this will remain in California is difficult to estimate. Depending upon a variety of circumstances (e.g., extent of market competition, mobility of resources), the property tax—and property tax cuts—may rest with the owners of taxed property (shareholders, in the case of corporations), be passed forward to consumers through prices, and/or be passed backward to labor (and other resource suppliers) through wages. The combination of these three tax treatments practiced by California businesses and the representation of Californians in the three groups which ultimately bear taxes jointly will determine the extent to which Californians will share in the business tax reduction, and solid data on these points do not exist. Additionally, the property tax cut will lower California's tax effort and, thereby, its share of federal revenue sharing (with a lag of a couple of years);[28] matching monies for attracting other federal grants also will be harder to come by. In short, Californians may find that a major part of the property tax cut will leak out of the California economy.

Tax savings also will be less to the extent that replacement revenues are raised at either the local or the state levels. It will be difficult, however, to raise taxes for two reasons. One is that the post-Proposition 13 mood at the state level favors tax *cuts*—the legislature enacted a $1 billion state income tax cut in late August, featuring increased personal credits and inflation-index brackets.[29] Indexing will slow the growth of the income tax (and the state surplus). Moreover, Proposition 13 imposes a two-thirds vote requirement for new and increased state and local taxes. For local units, however, it provides that "special taxes" may be imposed with the approval of two-thirds of a jurisdiction's "qualified electors." Neither of these terms is used in California law, so the meaning is not clear.[30] With regard to "special taxes," possible interpretations range from opening to localities revenue sources not previously authorized by the state (e.g., income taxes) if the voters will approve them to removing from local officials the right to adopt or increase the rates of taxes previously authorized by the state.[31] In either case, though, the two-thirds vote requirement may be insuperable. The hurdle would be most easily cleared if "qualified electors" is interpreted to mean those actually voting,[32] but a case can be made for interpreting this to mean those registered to vote, or even those *eligible* to vote—whether registered or not.[33] Interestingly enough, although Proposition 13 is generally said to have received "overwhelming" public support, it would not have passed under any of the above possibilities: those voting yes on Proposition 13 amounted to only 64.7 percent of those voting (the yes vote exceeded 66 percent in only 26 of the 58 counties), 42.3 percent of the registered voters,[34] and perhaps only one-fourth of all potentially eligible voters.

As noted above, many local governments already have turned to new and increased fees and charges to make up part of their revenue losses. It is both appropriate and possible to exact from users the revenues necessary to support some types of publicly provided services, and in these cases greater reliance on user charges should be considered a positive result of Proposition 13, producing improvements in both allocative efficiency (either under- or over-supply can result from divorcing payments from benefits) and equity (non-beneficiaries do not have to subsidize beneficiaries).[35] For other types of services, however, it is either not technically feasible or not desirable (on distributional grounds) to link payments and benefits.[36] These services must be funded from general tax revenues, such as the property tax. Unfortunately, Proposition 13 will present some serious equity problems. One of these results from the large cut in the level of property taxes: there is some evidence that higher levels of taxation are associated with greater assessment uniformity (equity).[37] This source of diminished equity, however, is certain to be dwarfed by inequities resulting from shifting of tax shares among classes of property owners. Proposition 13 requires that new or transferred properties be valued for tax purposes according to their market values at the time of construction or transfer (sale or otherwise), while properties not exchanged since 1975 are valued at 1975 prices, adjusted upward by the lesser of the rate of the state consumer price index increase or 2 percent per year. (These values constitute "full cash value," on which the tax cannot exceed 1 percent). This guarantees inequities—on the standard presumption that current market value is the best

measure of value for tax purposes—because only recently-sold properties can be valued at market value. In some assessment systems, reassessments between mass reappraisals in fact are triggered by sales, but California has the dubious distinction of being first to require this method, while precluding ever putting all properties on the same footing through mass reappraisal—and by constitutional provision! The effect is to make the "property tax" more dependent upon mobility and property turnover than on property value, and to cause newcomers to a community to bear a disproportionate share of the cost of local services. Because business properties sell less frequently than residential properties, this same provision will cause residential properties to bear an increasing share of the property tax over time—probably not a result contemplated by the typical supporter of Proposition 13. Some offset to this business-to residential tax share shift is provided by the fact that Proposition 13's valuation provisions (although not its rate limitations) apply only to real property, for in California the only tangible personal property that is taxable is that of business, and it is revalued annually.[38] The offset is unlikely to be complete, however, since tangible personal property accounted for less than 15 percent of taxable property values before Proposition 13.[39]

Relationships among governmental units, as well as among taxpayers, are affected by Proposition 13 and the state legislation implementing it. In general, the changes are toward greater centralization and decreased local control.[40] At the root of the changes, of course, is the nearly 60 percent reduction of the property tax which dropped this tax's share of total 1978–79 revenues for California local governments from 40 percent to 18 percent.[41] The argument has been made by some that, because of the historically high reliance of local governments on property taxation and the notion that this tax is better suited than other major taxes to local use, anything that weakens the property tax weakens local government (and conversely for strengthening the tax).[42] In California, this tendency of the property tax reduction itself has been reinforced by several provisions of S.B. 154, the statute clarifying Proposition 13 and providing for state assistance to make up much of the revenue loss. State-local and inter-local relationships both are affected. Whereas nearly 6,300 units of local government had imposed property taxes,[43] now only the 58 counties (including the independent city of

San Francisco) can levy a property tax because Section 1 of Proposition 13 provides that the property tax is ". . . to be collected by the counties and apportioned according to law to the districts within the counties" and S.B. 154 gives meaning to this by stipulating that the counties also *levy* the tax and then divide the proceeds on the basis of historic shares of property tax collections.[44] This greatly reduces the ability of local units to effect their own fiscal policies; the county and state roles have increased at the expense of all other units formerly having authority to levy property taxes. This is particularly true for special districts, whose tax-replacement aid goes first to county governments. Each county will receive an allocation of money for special districts (based on the counties' shares of special district property tax losses), but "the county will have complete discretion in allocating the assistance [within state-prescribed] guidelines."[45] While many government "reformers" will applaud this apparent victory of the elected generalists over the special-purpose units,[46] the change will not necessarily be for the better in all cases; special-purpose units with boundaries differing from those of the multi-purpose units often will permit clear equity and efficiency gains—e.g., better correspondence between actual and desired service levels and between benefit and financing areas.[47] Moreover, if "fiscal pressures" are a poor basis for determining the assignment of functional responsibilities,[48] it is not clear that the pressure produced by Proposition 13 will produce the optimal functional realignment.

The advent of uniform county-wide property taxes[49] will have other effects, as well. For example, intra-county tax rate differentials which may distort locational decisions[50] will be eliminated. Another *potentially* beneficial effect would be the reduction of fiscal capacity disparities and the consequent removal of one source of expenditure variation,[51] but as long as the proceeds from these levies are distributed on the basis of prior years' property tax collections, this gain cannot occur (except to the extent that *future* decisions that would have worsened matters are averted). The current combination of uniform tax rates within a county and allocation among units based on historic tax patterns means that rural areas (where taxes generally have been relatively low) will tend to subsidize urban areas (where tax rates generally have been higher), a result that may be either desirable or undesirable depending

upon the circumstances of a particular situation (and, of course, the criteria used to evaluate such a shift). Other results more obviously tend to be undesirable. For example, rapidly growing areas will have no control over their property tax revenues and may be unable to serve expanded populations and/or new properties (e.g., factories, shopping malls) without lowering the overall level of service; growth in a *single* small unit will translate into increased revenues for the entire county area and for *all* units within the county (other than special districts) in proportion to pre-FY 1979 tax shares. This is Twin Cities-style tax-base sharing carried to the extreme.[52] This may affect special districts with no revenue source other than property taxes (and property tax replacement aid) the hardest—e.g., many fire protection districts —but cities and school corporations could fare worse, however, due to the inflexibility of current (S.B. 154) aid distribution provisions; special districts at least have the opportunity to press their cases for increased revenues with the county, which determines intra-county special district tax-replacement shares.

In addition to the largely inter-local effects discussed above, the post-Proposition 13 situation also changes previous state-local relationships. As already noted, the major property tax replacement funds to date have come from an accumulated state surplus, and increased state funding has brought increased state control. Thus, for example, no local unit can receive state tax-replacement aid or loan funds under S.B. 154 if it grants cost-of-living pay increases for 1978–79 to its employees, welfare recipients, or others, in excess of those granted to state employees; the state's police powers are invoked to render "null and void" any contractual provisions to the contrary, and these provisions also ". . . supersede any inconsistent provisions in the charter of any county or city."[53] Other "strings" attached to increased state aid, already noted, include the requirement that counties, cities, and appropriate special districts give first priority to police and fire service so that local units will not drop below 1977–78 levels of *service* in these functional areas; provisions concerning health service reductions; provisions which make special districts dependent upon overlying general-unit discretion for tax-replacement distributions (which could provide leverage for other county- or city-initiated controls); and various provisions pertaining to education finance.

Proposition 13, as noted, threatened to undo the legislature's response to the California Supreme Court's demands in *Serrano* vs. *Priest* for school finance restructuring, a further intergovernmental problem. The Assembly Education Committee argued that the tax limits would preclude high-wealth district tax increases which were to transfer money to the state starting in 1978–79 as part of the equalization provisions, make it impossible for districts to raise the local share of foundation-program funding, and render revenue limits meaningless.[54] S.B.154's education provisions, described earlier, represent the initial reworking of the *Serrano* solution, and it appears that the state's guarantee of a higher percentage of estimated 1978–79 budgets for low-spending districts than for high-spending districts (91 percent vs. 85 percent)—combined with the Proposition 13 tax limits—will cause per pupil expenditure disparities to be reduced more quickly than otherwise.[55]

In short, Proposition 13 has served as the vehicle for some extensive changes in California intergovernmental relations, including structural and functional adjustments as well as increased centralization of both decision-making authority and financing.

Other effects of Proposition 13 are numerous (and some no doubt have not yet been identified), but only a few more can be noted here. The Assembly Revenue and Taxation Committee notes that, "Many cities have seriously underfunded employee pension and retirement systems. . . ."[56] This situation may mean even deeper cuts in current services than otherwise would be necessary, for current services must compete for strictly limited (and reduced) revenues with unliquidated obligations from prior years. The competition between current services and debt service also is intensified. Outstanding debt issued without voter approval (unlike voted debt approved before July 1, 1978) does not entitle the issuing jurisdiction to property taxes in excess of those available under the new general limits. For units with such debt, an already tight fiscal situation is made even tighter. Possible outcomes include one or more of the following: further cuts in current services, default, and New York-style state and/or federal rescue. Future debt issues, whether voted or not, must be serviced within the Proposition 13 tax limitation. This means general obligation borrowing may be infeasible in many—perhaps most—instances in the future,[57] especially if tax-replacement aid is reduced and/or continues to be tied to historic property tax shares. In any event, the fact of property tax reduction and limitation is likely to result in higher bond interest rates.

Conclusion

The complexities associated with Proposition 13 provide a lesson in the hazards of fiscal policymaking through direct voter participation. While the full effects of Proposition 13 are not yet known, it is clear that it has reshaped California local government finance overnight. The financing role of property taxes has been cut from 40 percent to 18 percent for local governments on average. Furthermore, the tax now can be levied by only 58 counties at a countywide uniform rate (excluding levies for old debt) rather than by some 6,300 local units, although these other units still share in property tax revenues on the basis of prior years' levies. Even if a community within a county were to agree unanimously to increase property taxes, it now has no authority to do so. Moreover, within any county this new system will fail to target increased revenue to units with rapidly increasing needs, and the tax-base incentive for cultivating new business development is diminished. Ironically, it appears that much of the property tax savings from this reduction will flow outside California. Homeowners clearly will enjoy some relief from recent high property taxes, but the extent of relief going to renters remains uncertain. In addition, mass reappraisals are now barred and all reassessments (other than an across-the-board increase of up to 2 percent) are triggered by transfer of property or new construction. Over time, this will shift an increasing share of property taxes toward homeowners (and within this group, those who change residences) and guarantee inequities because only recently sold properties can be valued according to current market value; thus, the tax increasingly will become a tax on mobility.

The diminished role of this traditional local tax workhorse dramatically increases the importance of state aids. At least in the first year, increased state aids have meant increased state control over local government finances and structures—a development that is not likely to be reversed.

A huge state surplus played a role that cannot be overestimated. On the one hand, the surplus may have contributed strongly to the passage of Proposition 13. On the other hand, it was essential to an orderly transition. The essential question is whether a surplus of such magnitude will continue to be available for future rescue operations.

Notes

1. Briefly, Proposition 13 sets the maximum property tax rate at 4 percent of assessed value, limits to no more than 2 percent per year the assessed value increase for any real property with unchanged ownership, and requires that both state and local tax increases receive two-thirds approval. These provisions are developed more fully below.
2. Advisory Commission on Intergovernmental Relations (ACIR), *State Limitations on Local Taxes and Expenditures*, A-64 (Washington: Government Printing Office, 1977).
3. As presented on the sheet covering the Jarvis-Gann initiative petitions [California, Assembly Revenue and Taxation Committee, *Facts About Proposition 13: The Jarvis/Gann Initiative*, revised edition (Sacramento; February 21, 1978; processed), Appendix I, p. 56] (hereafter cited as *Facts*).
4. 487 P. 2d 1241, 96 *California Reporter* 601 (1971).
5. *Facts*, p. 41.
6. Increases in the state-local government purchases deflator were 9.1 percent, 6.2 percent, and 6.8 percent for 1975, 1976, and 1977, respectively [U.S., Department of Commerce, *Survey of Current Business*, 57 (January, 1977), Table 27, p. 17; 58 (June, 1978), Table 27, p. 14].
7. The 1968 and 1972 Watson Initiatives were defeated by percentages of 69 percent and 65.9 percent (*Facts*; p. 1). Proposition 13 passed with a 64.7 percent majority according to voting statistics from the California Office of the Secretary of State (Sacramento; June 9, 1978; processed).
8. Andrew Glassberg, "Organizational Responses to Municipal Budget Decreases," *Public Administration Review*, 38 (July/August, 1978), pp. 325–332.
9. *Ibid.*, see discussion pp. 327–328.
10. "Many School Districts Cancelling Summer Classes," *Los Angeles Times*, June 9, 1978, Part I, pp. 1, 16.
11. "Schools Scramble to Make Up Lost Funds," *Los Angeles Times*, Part I, p. 3, July 3, 1978. Unless otherwise cited, the information on schools is drawn from this source, pp. 3 and 16.
12. The state bail-out money made many such actions unnecessary. On average, it was expected that most school districts would be provided with more money

than they had the previous year, but less than what they had expected to have in 1978–79 [*ibid*, p. 16].
13. Ronald Soble, "Local Fees and Taxes Grow Under Prop. 13," *Los Angeles Times*, July 3, 1978, Part I, p. 1.
14. "Prop. 13 Impact This Year Still Uncertain," *Los Angeles Times*, July 3, 1978, Part I, pp. 3, 12–14, is the source for information on cities and counties, unless otherwise cited.
15. Soble, *loc. cit.*
16. California, Legislative Analyst, *An Analysis of Proposition 13: The Jarvis-Gann Initiative* (Sacramento; May 1978; processed), Tables V-34 and V-35, pp. 155–156. (hereafter cited as Legislative Analyst report).
17. "Legislature Passes Prop. 13 Rescue Bill," *Los Angeles Times*, June 24, 1978, Part I, pp. 1, 24–25.
18. *Los Angeles Times*, July 3, 1978, Part I, p. 3. June was a month of sabre rattling. There were some scarce headlines concerning actions which never materialized and other actions were taken and rescinded. Finally, the count of persons who actually lost jobs varied. On June 8, Los Angeles said it would have to fire 8300 workers; by July 8, no one had been laid-off [*Los Angeles Times*, June 8, 1978, Part I, pp. 1, 20, and July 8, 1978, Part II, p. 1]. School districts started cancelling summer classes on June 9, with some expressing doubt about their ability to open on schedule in the fall, without aid, [*Los Angeles Times*, June 9, 1978, Part I, pp. 1 and 17] or to stay open beyond December [*Los Angeles Times*, June 10, 1978, Part I, p. 28]. The state first claimed that as many as 450,000 Proposition 13 lay-offs would occur. On June 11, it cut this figure in half [*Los Angeles Times*, June 11, 1978, Part I, pp. 3 and 22]. The Congressional Budget Office estimated a total of 60,000 jobs would be lost as a result of Proposition 13 [*Los Angeles Times*, July 7, 1978, Part I, p. 1]. On July 13, the Governor's office estimated that 8327 Proposition 13 lay-offs had occurred. The number is and will be hard to determine, due to such factors as early retirements and higher attrition rates caused by diminished pay increases.
19. California, State Legislature, *Summary of the Conference Report on SB 154 Relative to Implementation of Proposition 13 and State Assistance to Local Governments* (Sacramento; June 23, 1978; processed), p. 4. This report is the source of information on the state response to Proposition 13 in the balance of this section.
20. Conversations with legislative staff disclosed that giving the money directly to counties for apportionment to special districts was an attempt at regaining administrative integrity within counties, by making special districts compete with other units for resources.
21. See, for example, the description of Indiana's program in Donald W. Kiefer, "The 1973 Tax Package,"

Indiana Business Review, 49 (October, 1974), Special Tax Issue, pp. 3–31; ACIR, *Limitations,* for a more general treatment of several states' programs; and Helen F. Ladd, "An Economic Evaluation of State Limitations on Local Taxing and Spending Powers," *National Tax Journal,* 31 (March, 1978), pp. 1–18.

22. For excellent analyses of the wide range of effects, see *Facts* and Legislative Analyst report, cited above.

23. Limits typically seek to control future tax growth. Where cuts have been made, however, the state—as an integral part of the program—generally has replaced local revenue losses. For example, see Kiefer, op. cit., p. 3; and Robert J. Kosydar and John H. Bowman, "Modernization of State Tax Systems: The Ohio Experience," *National Tax Journal,* 25 (September, 1972), p. 379.

24. The rates are for 1976–77 [California, State Board of Equalization, *Annual Report 1976–77* (Sacramento: State of California, December, 1977), Table 14, p. A-19.].

25. *SB 154 Conference Report,* p. 2.

26. Figures of the Legislative Analyst as cited in George Skelton, "Major Loss of Property Tax Saving Seen," *Los Angeles Times,* June 13, 1978, Part I, pp. 1, 27.

27. *Facts,* p. 72.

28. *Ibid.,* p. 48, and Legislative Analyst report, pp. 55–56.

29. George Skelton, "State's Biggest Tax Slash Becomes Law," *Los Angeles Times,* August 31, 1978, Part I, pp. 1, 24.

30. *Facts,* p. 27.

31. *Ibid.,* pp. 27–29, presents a discussion.

32. Legislative Counsel advises this interpretation is likely because the literal requirements probably could not be met [Legislative Analyst report, p. 42].

33. *Facts,* p. 27.

34. Voting statistics from the California Secretary of State.

35. Selma Mushkin, ed., *Public Prices for Public Products* (Washington: The Urban Institute, 1972), is an excellent source of information on user charges.

36. See Mikesell, this symposium.

37. John H. Bowman and John L. Mikesell, "Uniform Assessment of Property: Returns from Institutional Remedies," *National Tax Journal,* 31 (June, 1978).

38. *Facts,* p. 17, and California, State Board of Equalization, Assessment Standards Division, *Proposition 13, Jarvis-Gann Initiative* (Sacramento; June 8, 1978; processed), pp. 3, 20. The latter suggests implementation procedures to county assessors.

39. Based on assessed values for 1977–78 [State Board of Equalization, *Annual Report 1976–77,* Table 4, p. A-4].

40. Major intergovernmental effects are summarized well by David B. Walker, "Proposition 13 and California's System of Governance," *Intergovernmental Perspective,* 4 (Summer, 1978), pp. 13–15.

41. The figures, respectively, are from the Legislative Analyst report, p. 13, and *SB 154 Conference Report,* p. 1. Reliance on the property tax varies considerably among governmental units; based on pre-Proposition 13 data (the 40 percent average), counties got from 32–40 percent of their revenues from the property tax; cities, from 0–6 percent; school districts, from 20–90 percent and special districts, 0–100 percent [*Facts,* p 8]. The variation will continue, given the historically-based allocation of property taxes under S.B. 154, although at lower overall percentages.

42. See Richard P. Nathan, "Is Local Control the Loser in Jarvis Vote?", *Wall Street Journal,* June 8, 1978, p. 18; and Glenn W. Fisher, "Property Taxation and the Political System," in Arthur D. Lynn, Jr., ed., *Property Taxation and Public Policy,* TRED 8 (Madison, University of Wisconsin Press, 1976), pp. 5–22.

43. Legislative Analyst report, p. 11.

44. *SB 154 Conference Report,* p. 2. Other possible approaches are discussed in *Facts,* pp. 13–16.

45. *SB 154 Conference Report,* p. 7. Exceptions are multicounty districts (which will receive aid directly from the state) and city subsidiary districts (which will be subject to city council funding decisions).

46. Walker, *op. cit.,* p. 14.

47. For discussions of pertinent considerations, see: Wallace E. Oates, *Fiscal Federalism* (New York: Harcourt Brace Jovanovich, 1972), ch. 2, pp. 31–53; Robert L. Bish, *The Public Economy of Metropolitan Areas* (Chicago: Markham, 1971), ch. 3, pp. 35–62; and Gordon Tulluck, "Federalism: Problems of Scale," *Public Choice,* 6 (Spring, 1969), pp. 19–29.

48. ACIR, *Governmental Functions and Processes: Local and Areawide,* A-45 (Washington: Government Printing Office, 1974), pp. 19, 122–125.

49. In addition to the basic rate ceiling of 1 percent of full cash value (4 percent of assessed value, given the state's 25 percent assessment standard), property taxes to service debt authorized by voters before July 1, 1978, also can be imposed at rates differing among areas as debt loads vary relative to the tax base. As a result, the statewide average property tax rate for 1978–79 is expected to be 5 percent although this will approach 4 percent over time as these earlier debt issues are retired [*Facts,* p. 13]. Richard O'Reilly, "Tax Cut Will Be Less Than Many Expect," *Los Angeles Times,* August 24, 1978, Part I, pp. 3, 22, discusses Los Angeles County effects.

50. Roger W. Schmenner, "City Taxes and Industry Location," in *Proceedings of the Sixty-Sixth (1973) Annual Conference on Taxation* (Columbus, Ohio: National Tax Association-Tax Institute of America, 1974), pp. 528–532.

51. John H. Bowman, "Tax Exportability, Intergovernmental Aid, and School Reform," *National Tax Journal,* 27 (June, 1974), pp. 163–173.

52. Under 1971 state legislation, communities in the seven-counties of the Minneapolis-St. Paul SMSA share 40 percent of commercial and industrial assessed value increases [see Gene Knaff, *Tax Base Sharing: The Minnesota Program After Two Years* (St Paul: Metropolitan Council of the Twin Cities Area; December, 1977; processed); and Walter H. Plosila, "Metropolitan Tax-Base Sharing: Its Potential and Limitations," *Public Finance Quarterly,* 4 (April, 1976), pp. 205–224]. In California 100 percent of the assessed value increase from *all* assessed value increases in a county is shared throughout the county in proportion to pre-FY 1979 tax levies.

53. *SB 154 Conference Report,* p. 12.

54. *Facts,* pp. 50, 53, and Legislative Analyst report, pp. 140–141.

55. Equal spending and equal educational opportunity, of course, are not synonymous; sometimes higher spending is necessary to give some pupils needed services. A nationally syndicated column focused late in July on effects of Proposition 13 budgetary pressures (15 percent cut below previously planned level) in San Francisco schools ". . . where school children speak 17 different tongues as their first language, . . .": special programs are being cut (e.g., 200 nontenured bilingual education program teachers are being terminated) to preserve most programs affecting larger numbers of students [Jack W. Germond and Jules Witcover, "Politics Today: Prop. 13 Squeeze Already Felt in Frisco's Schools," Bloomington, Indiana, *Herald-Telephone,* July 27, 1978, p. 8].

56. *Facts,* p. 43.

57. *Ibid.,* pp. 16, 29–30, and 45–47, discusses these and other debt-related matters. Bonds threatened with default include "assessment" bonds (issued for street lighting and similar localized improvements), "tax increment" bonds (e.g., those issued by redevelopment agencies to be repaid from higher tax revenues resulting from redevelopment), and "lease-purchase" bonds (for facilities financed by government and then leased). This last type is in increased danger of default only if the lessee is another government dependent upon property taxes for lease payment funds.

22
The Growing Fiscal and Economic Importance of State and Local Governments

Roy Bahl
Syracuse University

One might begin a study of state and local government finances by asking about the role of the state and local government sector in the national economy. How important is this sector as a contributor to economic growth, and what part has it played in carrying out the traditional allocation, distribution, and stabilization functions of government? In fact, the state and local government sector constitutes a significant share of GNP—13 percent in 1981—and about half of total government spending. This means that state and local government fiscal actions are an important force to be reckoned with in the formulation of national economic policy.

Policy analysts have long puzzled about the "proper" distribution, stabilization, and allocation objectives of state and local governments and the "proper" federal policy toward the state and local sector. Three important issues have caught the attention of scholars and policymakers:

The distribution question: are subnational governments large enough to significantly influence the interpersonal distribution of income?

The stabilization question: could counter-cyclical behavior by state and local governments influence the pattern of national income growth, and compromise the effectiveness of federal macroeconomic policy?

The allocation question: has the state and local government sector become too large in the sense of discouraging private investment and

Source: From *Financing State and Local Government in the 1980s*, pp. 7–32. Copyright © 1984 by Oxford University Press. Reprinted by permission.

retarding economic growth while vastly overpaying public employees relative to their productivity? Or is it too small in the sense of not providing an adequate level of public services?

This chapter focuses on these three questions, beginning with a description of the changing size and composition of state and local sector activities. Attention is then turned to a questioning of the conventional wisdom about what is and should be the economic role of state and local governments in the system of federal-state-local finances. Finally, we summarize the arguments that government—including state and local government—has somehow become too large and ought to be limited in its size and growth. Some perspective on these issues is an essential prerequisite to evaluating the fiscal health of subnational governments, a task taken up in Chapter 3.

Growth in the State and Local Government Sector

The development of the United States public sector between 1942 and 1976 can be characterized by three major trends: a growing importance of the state and local sector in the United States economy; a shift in public spending toward health, education, and welfare services; and a long-term trend of increase in state and local government dependence on federal intergovernmental transfers.[1] Since 1976, each of these three trends has been reversed. This abrupt change in the pattern of American fiscal federalism, if it continues, suggests a changing role for state and local governments.

A brief digression on how one goes about identifying such trends and turning points would seem in order. Although the quality of the data available is relatively good, measurement of the size of this sector is not at all straightforward. Indeed, whether the state and local government sector has increased in size depends on whether we measure its growth against that of the federal sector or against GNP, whether we measure government activity in terms of employment or expenditures, whether intergovernment aids are counted as federal or state and local government expenditures, how transfer payments to individuals are treated, and what time period is chosen for study.

The two most commonly used indicators of government activity are employment and expenditures. If public employment is taken as the proper measure of activity, state and local governments have clearly dominated the growth in the public sector in the past twenty years. Between 1954 and 1980, state and local government employment increased by 174 percent while growth in the federal sector was only 22 percent.[2] Public employment may not be an appropriate comparative, however, because the functions of the state and local government sector make it quite labor intensive whereas transfers, debt repayment, capital outlays, and other nonlabor expenditures are much more important at the federal level. Total expenditure is probably a better indicator of the relative growth of the state and local sector.[3]

Growth of the Sector

The use of expenditures to measure the growth in government activity raises the question of whether federal grants should be counted as federal or state and local government expenditures. The former would imply measurement of size according to where the funds are raised, the latter according to where they are spent. If grants are counted as part of the federal sector, federal government domestic expenditures[4] are equivalent to a larger and increasing share of total public sector activity (Table 1). If federal grants are included in state and local rather than federal expenditures, then the state and local sector and the federal sector are about the same size but, surprisingly, the federal domestic sector is growing at a faster rate (Table 2). During the past quarter century, the federal government share of local public spending has increased from about 40 percent of total public spending to over 50 percent, *even if defense expenditures are excluded and intergovernmental transfers are counted as state and local government expenditures.* This very important and long-term trend of centralization in the United States fiscal system has not been widely recognized.

A break in this pattern occurred after 1976. The state and local government sector began to decline relative to GNP, and its share of total public spending fell off rapidly. This decline was due in part to a reduced flow of federal assistance and in part to a resistance to tax increases by state and local governments. The latter would seem to be the more important cause, at least until the 1982 round of state and local government tax increases. The Advisory Commission on Intergovernmental Relations (ACIR) estimated that none of the $30 billion in real estate

tax increase during 1976-80 was due to "political actions,"[5] and the ratio of state and local government taxes to personal income fell from 12.8 percent in 1977 to 11.6 percent in 1980. The increased federal role in the United States fiscal system, then, is as much due to a slowdown in state willingness to tax as it is to federal grant retrenchment.

Increased Social Welfare Expenditures

A second dominant trend in the United States fiscal system has been the continuing increase in the budget claim of health, education, and welfare expenditures. The postwar increase in public expenditures at all levels of government, as well as the shift toward an increasing federal share, has been largely due to increased social welfare expenditures.[6]

At the federal level, the expenditure increases of the past two decades have been dominated by increased Social Security expenditures and by increased grants to state and local governments (Table 2). The Social Security share of federal domestic expenditures has more than doubled since 1954, and federal aid to state and local governments doubled between 1954 and 1978. Moreover, there was a marked shift toward social welfare services in the composition of this federal aid. Again, there would appear to be a structural break in the past five years. Assistance to state and local governments as a share of the total federal budget has been declining since it peaked at 24 percent in 1978, and the Social Security share of expenditures has slowed its increase in recent years.

The reversal has been much more dramatic at the state and local government level, where about 60 percent of the expenditure increase during the 1960–76 period was for health, education, and welfare purposes. This share fell to 56 percent between 1976 and 1981. Put another way, the average 1 percent increase in GNP between 1960 and 1976 generated a 1.56 percent increase in social welfare expenditures. Between 1976 and 1981, this income elasticity of social welfare expenditures was only 0.84. The implication seems clear enough. Federal assistance to state and local governments, largely for health, education, and welfare purposes, has been cut. State and local governments have responded relatively more by passing these cuts along than by raising taxes or redirecting expenditures from other areas. On the one hand, this response had undesirable distributional effects, but on the other it came at a

Table 1
Government domestic expenditure

Calendar Year	Percent of Total Domestic Public Sector			Percent of GNP		
	Federal[a]	State[b]	Local[b]	Federal[a]	State[b]	Local[b]
From Own Funds						
1954	45.6	25.4	29.0	6.2	3.5	4.0
1964	48.4	24.2	27.4	8.5	4.3	4.8
1969	48.7	26.2	25.1	9.9	5.3	5.1
1970	50.5	25.7	23.8	11.2	5.7	5.3
1971	51.9	24.9	23.2	12.1	5.8	5.4
1972	54.2	23.7	22.1	12.7	5.6	5.2
1973	54.3	24.3	21.4	12.8	5.7	5.0
1974	54.8	24.2	21.0	13.6	6.0	5.2
1975	57.8	23.0	19.2	15.7	6.2	5.2
1976	58.4	22.8	18.8	15.5	6.1	5.0
1977	59.2	22.2	18.6	15.3	5.7	4.8
1978	59.2	22.2	18.5	14.9	5.6	4.7
1979	59.1	22.5	18.4	14.6	5.6	4.6
1980[c]	61.0	21.6	17.3	15.9	5.6	4.5
1981	61.1	21.5	17.4	15.9	5.6	4.5
1982 (est.)	61.3	21.1	17.6	16.6	5.7	4.8
After Intergovernment Transfers[d]						
1954	39.9	21.4	38.7	5.5	2.9	5.3
1964	39.7	22.4	37.8	7.0	4.0	6.8
1969	38.2	23.4	38.4	7.8	4.8	7.8
1970	39.3	22.9	37.8	8.7	5.1	8.4
1971	40.2	22.9	36.9	9.4	5.4	8.6
1972	40.6	22.8	36.6	9.5	5.4	8.6
1973	41.1	22.4	36.5	9.7	5.3	8.6
1974	42.5	21.9	35.6	10.6	5.4	8.8
1975	44.9	21.4	33.7	12.2	5.8	9.2
1976	45.0	22.2	32.7	12.0	5.9	8.7
1977	45.7	21.7	32.6	11.8	5.6	8.5
1978	45.1	21.7	33.2	11.4	5.5	8.4
1979	45.7	21.6	32.7	11.4	5.3	8.1
1980[c]	48.3	20.8	30.9	12.6	5.3	8.1
1981	50.0	20.5	29.5	13.0	5.3	7.7
1982 (est.)	51.3	20.0	20.0	14.0	5.4	7.8

[a] Excludes federal expenditure for national defense, international affairs, and finance, and space research and technology and the estimated portion of net interest attributable to these functions. Includes Social Security (OASDHI) and all federal aid to state and local governments, including general revenue sharing payments.

[b] The National Income and Product Accounts do not report state and local government data separately. The state and local expenditure totals (National Income Accounts) were allocated between levels of government on the basis of ratios (by year) reported by the United States Bureau of the Census in the government finance series.

[c] Preliminary.

[d] All federal aid to state and local governments, including general revenue sharing payments, is included as state and local expenditure and excluded from federal domestic expenditure.

Source: Summarized from Advisory Committee on Intergovernmental Relation, *Significant Features of Fiscal Federalism,* 1981-82 edition, Tables 1 and 2. Washington: USGPO.

Table 2
Sources of growth in federal domestic expenditures

Calendar Year	Percent Distribution			Percent of GNP		
	Social Security (OASDHI)[a]	Federal Aid[b]	All Other[c]	Social Security (OASDHI)[a]	Federal Aid[b]	All Other[c]
1954	16.2	12.7	71.1	1.0	0.8	4.4
1964	30.3	19.1	50.6	2.6	1.6	4.3
1969	36.4	21.7	41.9	3.6	2.2	4.1
1970	35.8	22.2	42.1	4.0	2.5	4.7
1971	35.2	22.4	42.3	4.3	2.7	5.1
1972	34.9	25.1	40.8	4.3	3.2	5.2
1973	36.9	24.3	38.7	4.7	3.1	5.0
1974	37.0	22.5	40.5	5.0	3.1	5.5
1975	34.3	22.4	43.2	5.4	3.5	6.8
1976	35.7	22.9	41.4	5.5	3.6	6.4
1977	36.6	23.0	40.4	5.6	3.5	6.2
1978	37.0	24.0	38.9	5.5	3.6	5.8
1979	38.2	22.8	39.0	5.6	3.3	5.7
1980	37.7	21.3	41.0	6.0	3.4	6.5
1981	39.7	18.8	41.5	6.3	3.0	6.6
1982 (est.)	41.3	16.4	42.3	6.9	2.7	7.0

[a] National Income and Product Account.
[b] Federal aid as reported in the National Income Accounts (used here) differs slightly from the federal payments (Census) series (used in Table 3). The major difference is the inclusion of federal payments for low-rent public housing (estimated at $3.5 billion in 1980) in the Census series but excluded by definition from the NIA series. Federal general revenue sharing is included in both series.
[c] Includes direct federal expenditure for education, public assistance and relief, veterans benefits and services, commerce, transportation, and housing, and others.
Source: Summarized from ACIR, Significant Features, 1981-82, Table 3.

time when the numbers of school-aged children and welfare recipients were on the decline.

Federal Aid Dependence

The third major trend of the past two decades has been the growing importance of federal aid flows in the public sector. For every 1 percent increase in GNP between 1954 and 1976, federal general revenues (including Social Security) grew by about 1 percent, state and local government revenues from own sources by about 2 percent, and federal aid by about 5 percent. With this trend came a growing reliance by state and local governments on federal aid. By 1978, federal aid accounted for 22 percent of total state and local government revenue and was a more important financing source than any of the property, sales, or income taxes (Table 3).

Between 1976 and 1980, federal revenue grew about 20 percent faster and state and local government revenues, both own source and federal aid,

about 20 percent slower than did GNP.[7] The result is that federal grants have declined in importance as a financing source for state and local governments, reversing a two-decade trend of increase. The National Income Accounts (NIA) at the end of 1981 show that the federal financing share has fallen to 21.3 percent of state and local government revenues.[8]

Increasing Centralization

Accompanying these three important trends has been a growing dominance of state government within the state and local sector. The state government share of total taxes collected rose from 56 to 64 percent between 1965 and 1981, and the states' share of direct expenditures increased from 43 to 46 percent (Table 4).[9] This trend is explainable by two considerations: state government income and sales taxes are more bouyant than local property taxes and there has been a move toward heavier state government financing of locally provided services.

Table 3

Reliance of state and local government on federal aid and major tax revenue sources

	Percent of Total General Revenue			
Year	Federal Aid	Property Taxes	Income Taxes	Sales Taxes
1954	10.3	34.4	6.6	25.1
1964	14.7	31.0	8.0	23.1
1974	20.1	23.0	12.3	22.2
1976	21.7	22.3	12.3	21.3
1977	21.9	21.9	13.4	21.2
1978	22.0	21.0	13.9	21.4
1979	21.8	18.9	14.3	21.6
1980	21.7	17.9	14.5	20.9
1981	21.3	17.7	14.3	20.3

Source: U.S. Bureau of the Census, *Governmental Finance,* Series GF No. 5. Washington, D.C.: GPO, various years.

Table 4

Interstate variations in selected indicators of fiscal importance

	Total Expenditures as Percent of State Personal Income			Federal Aid as Percent of Personal Income			Federal Aid as Percent of General Revenues		
	1965	1976	1981	1965	1976	1981	1965	1976	1981
Mean	17.0	18.9	21.3	3.4	4.5	4.2	18.9	23.5	22.2
coefficient of variation	0.21	0.15	0.27	0.66	0.26	0.26	0.56	0.15	0.17

	Revenues from Own Source as Percent of Personal Income			State Government Percent of Direct Expenditures			State Government Percent of Tax Revenues		
	1965	1976	1981	1965	1976	1981	1965	1976	1981
Mean	13.4	14.5	15.6	43.1	44.4	46.3	56.0	62.2	64.1
coefficient of variation	0.13	0.15	0.70	0.25	0.21	0.21	0.22	0.17	0.16

Source: Governmental Finances, 1980–81, 1975–76, 1964–65.

This centralization of fiscal activity toward the state level is a relatively uniform trend that was not interrupted by the turnaround in 1976. As may be seen from the coefficients of variation reported in Table 4, states have become more alike in their division of fiscal responsibility between the state and local levels.[10] In fact, only fifteen of the fifty states had reductions in the state direct expenditure share between 1976 and 1980 (twelve of these were the less populous and more rural states). The increased state share of tax revenues is also a relatively uniform

trend, that is, states have become much more alike in terms of state government dominance of the tax system. Only thirteen states moved against this trend.

Other fiscal trends are not so uniform among the states. On average between 1965 and 1976, state and local governments increased their expenditure share of personal income, raised tax effort, and received federal grants that constituted an increasing share of state personal income. Whereas states became more homogeneous in terms of the share of personal income spent by state and local governments, there was no such narrowing of the interstate diversity in revenue effort, i.e., the gap between high- and low-taxing states widened. After 1976 the picture began to change. There was much more diversity in the average expenditure share of personal income in 1981 than in 1976, and dependence on federal assistance was down. The average revenue share of personal income (revenue effort) rose slightly, but there was an increase in interstate differences in tax burdens.[11]

The Economic Role of Subnational Governments

What is the place of state and local governments in the formulation and implementation of national economic and social policy? Conventional thought holds that of the three functions of public budgets —stabilization, distribution, and allocation—only the last can be properly addressed by lower-level governments.[12]

State and local government stabilization programs may be quickly ruled out. Fiscal policies affecting the rate of increase of national income and prices require a coordinated effort that is beyond the reach of state and local governments. Certainly control of the size of the money supply could never be decentralized: the temptation to any one government to print enough to cover its deficit and then spread the inflationary effects over the nation would be too great. (Imagine the consequences if the New York City government had been permitted to print money in 1975!) Subnational government fiscal policy is equally improper. If state or local governments borrowed to stabilize national income growth, a heavy burden would be placed on future generations of local residents since most state debt is held by outsiders. Neither would increases or reductions in state spending be an effective stabilization measure because of "leakages" from the state economy, i.e., the typical state resident spends a significant share of his or her income on goods produced in other states, hence the employment-generating effects of such programs would spread to other areas and states. In short, the open-economy problem precludes the use of fiscal and monetary policy by state and local governments to alter national income and price level growth.

The conventional wisdom views income distribution policies in a similar light. This is because mobility may allow residents to offset the distributional intentions of governmental tax and expenditure policies, i.e., high-income taxpayers may migrate to other jurisdictions to avoid paying for redistributive programs while low-income families may migrate in to benefit from them. Some cursory evidence of this effect may be seen in the cases of New York City and New York State, i.e., in the extent to which their fiscal problems may be attributed to attempts to engage in redistribution through the provision of relatively large amounts of public service benefits and transfers to the poor.[13]

It is the allocation decision that is usually identified as the proper budgetary function of individual state and local governments, i.e., the decisions about which and how much local services will be provided and about how budgets will be financed. By leaving these decisions to our fragmented system of 80,000 local governments, the efficiency of the process is improved because the diverse preferences of local voters may be taken into account.

One might argue with this conventional thinking and take the position that the economic role of state and local governments is not so limited. With own-source revenues equivalent to about 40 percent of total federal, state, and local government revenues and with expenditures equivalent to about 13 percent of GNP, the fiscal activities of state and local governments can have an important influence on national income growth and the distribution of real income. Moreover, the additional allocative function of state and local governments has been bent by any number of federal actions, e.g., reducing state and local autonomy through conditional grant programs, expenditure mandates, school finance issues, civil rights legislation, and so forth.

These considerations would seem to call for some rethinking of the traditional views about the proper economic role of state and local governments.[14] Accordingly, the sections below consider the potential role of the state and local government sector in the formulation and implementation of national economic policy and in the redistribution of income. We then turn to the broader allocation issue and particularly to the question of whether the state and local government sector has become, somehow, too large.

Macroeconomic Policy and State and Local Government Finances

One cannot question the traditional view that state and local governments are ill-equipped to formulate independent growth and stabilization policies. Yet events of the past decade have made it clear that the impact of federal macroeconomic policy on state and local governments, and the reaction of state and local governments to such policies, must be carefully considered. In this respect, two issues are of particular importance: (a) whether the budgetary decisions of state and local governments compromise or accentuate federal stabilization programs and (b) whether federal stabilization or economic growth programs which involved stimulating the state and local sector result in unintended changes in the system of fiscal federalism.

Effects on the business cycle. Two issues are important in determining whether state and local governments will reinforce or offset federal stabilization policies. The first is whether their fiscal actions are naturally countercyclical or procyclical and the second is whether federal grants stimulate spending in the state and local government sector.

With respect to the first, it has long been debated whether the discretionary fiscal actions of state and local governments tend to reinforce economic contractions and expansions or are countercyclical. Hansen and Perloff argued that there is a perversity in the fiscal behavior of state and local governments, that they increase spending in times of national expansion and curtail spending and raise taxes in times of national economic contraction.[15] Hence these authors see the fiscal actions of state and local governments as following the cycle and intensifying economic fluctuations. In a careful study of the post-war-to-early-60s period, Rafuse was unable to find evidence of the perversity hypothesis.[16] His results show that state and local government revenues had a stabilizing effect during every expansion and a perverse effect during every contraction and that expenditures had the opposite effects. "To note these conclusions is, of course, simply to spell out the stability implications of receipts and expenditures that continued to rise whatever the phase of the business cycle."[17]

More recent analyses show mixed results, partly because of ambiguities in the measurement of the impact of the state and local fisc. The consensus of studies by the ACIR,[18] Gramlich,[19] Vogel and Trost,[20] Reischauer,[21] and Jones and Weisler[22] is that the state and local government fiscal response is mildly countercyclical but probably differs markedly from state to state and from recession to recession. DeBoer makes the point that the deeper the recession

is and the longer it lasts, the more likely is the state and local government sector to act in a counter-cyclical fashion, i.e., to raise taxes and cut expenditures.[23] This may explain why the destabilizing behavior observed by Hansen and Perloff during the depression has not been repeated in most of the post-World War II period.

The second question is whether federal grants can stimulate state and local government spending. The question is important: if a cornerstone of macro-economic policy is to stimulate aggregate demand by increasing grants to state and local governments, one would want to be sure that state and local governments do not respond by substituting the new grant for what they had intended to spend from their own resources. Much depends on grant design. To the extent that grants are general purpose and lump sum one might expect such a substitutive result, and to the extent that they are matching one might expect a stimulative outcome.[24]

In fact, the federal government attempted to use the state and local government sector as kind of administrative agent for stabilization policy in the aftermath of the 1974-75 recession. A major element of the recovery program was the Economic Stimulus Package, i.e., the CETA, Local Public Works, and Antirecession Fiscal Assistance grants. The idea was to stimulate the economy by pushing new grant moneys through the state and local government sector. However, the performance of the state and local sector during the 1975–78 recovery probably did not add significantly to the expansion. During this period, the federal government's budget deficits were in the $30 to $70 billion range while federal grants to state and local governments increased by $23 billion (42 percent). During this same period, state and local government construction expenditures increased only from $34.6 to $37.6 billion and the general account surplus of state and local governments grew from $6.2 to $27.4 billion.[25] The fact that the state and local sector had accumulated a surplus equivalent to about one third the size of the federal deficit by 1978 (and the fact that much of this accumulation was due to increased federal grants) suggests that the expansionary grant policies of the federal government were to some extent offset by the contractionary actions of state and local governments.

Another example of the need to consider state and local government response can be drawn from economic policy during the 1981–83 period of contraction. The success of the Reagan administration's economic program is affected by the state and local government sector fiscal response. The current version of the supply-side approach is to balance federal tax cuts with reductions in federal aid while assuming that competitive forces will restrain state and local governments from increasing taxes. If, instead, state and local governments attempt to make up for the losses with their own tax increases, some of the federal tax reduction advantages will be offset. This could be a particularly important problem in light of the investment disincentives thought to be associated with high state and local income and property taxes. By 1982 such tax increases had begun to take place.

The point in this discussion is that the fiscal actions of state and local governments have to be reckoned with in the formulation of national economic policy. The sector is simply too large a share of GNP to be ignored.

Effects on government structure. Federal policies instituted or expanded in the name of stabilization objectives may have important long-term effects on the structure of United States federalism. Because such effects can be unintended by-products rather than the result of reasoned policy, they may be inconsistent with the goals of other federal, state, and local government policies. A good example of such an effect is the aforementioned Economic Stimulus Package, which vastly increased the share of federal grants going directly to local governments. This in turn had two important consequences. First, it reduced the role of state governments in the federal-state-local fiscal system at a time when the state government share of total taxing and spending was on the increase. This policy ran counter to the trend of increased centralization and reduced the leverage of state governments in the state and local fiscal system. The second important consequence was a dramatic increase in the dependence of some large cities on direct federal assistance. Such dependence is not easily backed away from, particularly for cities whose economic base is growing slowly or actually declining. The important point here is that neither of these structural changes was an explicit objective of the stimulus package. Indeed, the phasing out of the stimulus package and the general reduction of federal grants created especially

acute problems for those large cities that had become most dependent.

The Reagan administration's federalism program, which is designed to stimulate national economic growth, also introduced structural changes. The proposals for a restructuring of the grant system and the "swap" and "turnback" proposals would considerably strengthen the position of state governments.[26]

Federal macroeconomic policy, then, has introduced or proposed fundamental changes of direction in the federal system—twice in five years. In both cases the changes were consequences of broader economic policies rather than objectives of some thought-out national urban policy.

Distribution Policy and State and Local Government Finance

With state and local governments accounting for 40 percent of nondefense government spending and 13 percent of GNP, it stands to reason that this sector can have potentially important effects on the distribution of income.

State and local governments influence the distribution of income through the extraction of taxes and the provision of public services and assistance. Probably the more significant and certainly the most visible form of distributive influence is through participation in direct income transfers, e.g., public assistance payments. Though the federal government provides about half the funding for public welfare services, there are substantial interstate and even intercity variations in benefit payments. The consensus of research seems to be that low-income families have not migrated to high-payment areas in order to benefit from such programs;[27] hence individual government programs may well be effective in redistributing income. Is is also worth noting that 60 percent of total state and local government spending is for health, education, and welfare—functions with a substantial redistributive potential. Whether these funds are spent to primarily benefit lower-income individuals is not known because of data limitations and because of problems with the estimation of expenditure benefits across income classes.[28]

There may be less potential for redistributive effects on the tax than on the expenditure side, in part because the federal government finances about one fifth of state and local government expenditures through grants. The burden distribution of state and local government taxes is probably not progressive, although there is more than a little debate over the incidence of the property tax.[29] Even if property taxes are less regressive than has been traditionally assumed, however, the tax system is overall probably no better than proportional. Sales taxes are proportional to slightly regressive, depending on the treatment of food, and the federal tax deduction provision tends to make the whole system more aggressive. The net result, according to Okner and Pechman, is a heavy tax burden on the very low income and an approximately proportional distribution of tax burdens over most of the rest of the income distribution.[30]

What one would like from research in this area is an estimate of "net fiscal incidence," i.e., an estimate that takes both expenditure benefits and revenue burdens into account. Is the postbudget distribution of income more equal than the prebudget distribution? Hard research may not give a clear answer to this distribution question, but one might offer the hypothesis that the very poor do not fare so well. State and local governments tax housing, utilities, and sometimes food, imposing a heavy tax burden on low-income families. A potentially offsetting effect is that health, education, and welfare expenditures may make an inordinately heavy contribution to the real income of low-income families. Yet are these expenditures made in a way to primarily benefit the lowest-income? It is not just the amounts spent for these functions but the composition and spatial distribution of such expenditures —e.g., in poor or rich neighborhoods, in central cities or suburbs, for clinics or hospitals—that significantly affect the real-income position of low-income residents. At least the concerns of state courts in school finance cases suggest that the actual distribution of these expenditures is not pro-poor.

Whether or not state and local government budgetary actions actually have a significant effect on income distribution, it does seem clear that state and local governments consciously pursue distributional objectives. The concern with distribution effects in virtually every tax reform proposal must be taken as evidence that distribution is seen as a valid role. It is not important that the motives behind this concern are political, only that changes in the distribution of real income are sometimes a stated policy objective of state and local governments. Tangible evidence of this concern is the enactment of property tax relief measures, such as "circuit breakers" and sales tax exclusions for food and other

necessities. There is parallel evidence on the expenditure side. State grants, particularly for education, are sometimes allocated among jurisdictions on an equalizing basis, and some states have moved toward programs of "overburden aid" for hard-pressed central cities. State courts have shown a concern with the distributional role of state and local government in the celebrated school finance cases, where the property tax has come under attack as a financing mechanism that discriminates unfairly in favor of wealthier jurisdictions.[31]

It is also significant to note that the federal government has recognized the possibility for using state and local governments in national redistribution policies through public service employment programs. On balance, this evidence suggests that income redistribution cannot be thought of as exclusively or even primarily a federal government function. State and local government budgets, whether by design or not, have come to play an important distributional role.

Is the State and Local Government Sector Too Large?

The economic function left to state and local governments in the United States system is the allocation function, i.e., the determination of the amount and the mix of local public services to be offered. This determination cannot be separated totally from the growth question; it is possible that the fiscal choices made by state and local governments have contributed to a stunting of national economic growth. The issue is really that some analysts, politicians, and voters have come to believe that government is too big. Nondefense expenditures increased from 13.7 percent of GNP in 1954 to 26 percent in 1981. One question for the 1980s is whether the size of government—federal, state, and local—should be reduced and, if so, how and at what level?

Neither economic nor political theory provides guidelines for judging the optimal size of government. Because public goods cannot be bought for individual use as private goods can, consumers do not reveal their relative preferences for government services. Hence, they are unable to signal government decision makers that public goods are being oversupplied at their current prices.[32] Without a normative basis to establish whether government has become too large or is not large enough, the debate has become popularized, politicized, and more impressionistic than objective. Illustrative of the confusion are the postmortems on Proposition 13. By now it is not at all clear what revolted California's voters—low public sector productivity, high property taxes, or large state surpluses.

If one were looking for more objective guidelines to suggest whether the public sector is somehow too large, three possibilities might be raised: government is too small by comparison with other industrialized countries; government is too large because it interferes unduly with the market, lowers the return to investors, and retards economic growth; and government is too small because it has not succeeded in markedly correcting the unequal distribution of income.

Intercountry comparisons. Intercountry comparisons of the size of government implicitly assume that average practice somehow constitutes a norm. Whether or not such criterion is telling of anything,

it is true that the size of government in the United States is small by comparison with that in other advanced economies (Table 5).

Even if intercountry comparison is a reasonable way to establish a norm for the size of the public sector, there are two important problems with this kind of comparison. First, it does not compare the same package of public services, e.g., some countries have national health plans and more extensive welfare programs. It follows that it is not possible to use these data to show greater or lesser efficiency in government operations. Rather, the comparison shows differences in the scope, quality, cost, and efficiency of public service provision. To use the low government share in the United States to show that the public sector is too small implies a belief that services such as welfare, health, and higher education should be financed relatively more by general taxation, rather than partly through the private sector.

Table 5
Intercountry comparison of government size

	Ratio of Taxes to GDP	Per Capita GDP ($U.S.)
	1980	1979
Australia	27.7	8,836
Austria	41.2	9,107
Belgium	42.9	11.260
Canada	30.6	10,660
Denmark	45.5	12,925
Finland	34.2	8,701
France	41.0	10,720
West Germany	37.9	12,419
Italy	32.4	5,686
Japan	24.7[a]	8,627
Netherlands	44.8	10,624
Norway	46.4	11.486
Sweden	46.8	12,831
Switzerland	30.2	15,006
United Kingdom	34.9	7,192
United States	25.2	10,777
		Per Capita Personal Income
United States	26.7[b]	8,655
New York	42.5[b]	9,214

[a] 1979.
[b] Ratio of taxes to personal income.
Source: *United Nations Yearbook of National Accounts Statistics,* 1977, 1981, Tables 1 and 14a, International Monetary Fund, *Government Finance Statistics Yearbook,* Vol. 6, 1982; and *International Financial Statistics,* Vol. 35, 1982.

A potentially more serious problem with such a comparison is that it does not consider variations in the size of government within countries. Certainly the variation within the United States is great enough to where the overall federal, state, and local tax burden in some areas might compare favorably with those of some more highly centralized European countries. For example, if we add the federal, state, and local government tax share of personal income in New York State, the tax ratio rises to well above the United States average and the comparison with European countries is much more favorable.[33]

Investment disincentives. An argument that has attracted much attention of late is that government has become too large and discourages economic growth through excessive taxes and unduly restrictive regulation. The most popular version of this argument is Arthur Laffer's "curve" (Figure 1) which shows that the tax rate may get so high that government revenues actually fall. Though Laffer saw tax rates as being within the "prohibitive range" in the late 1970s,[34] the little systematic testing that has been given his hypothesis does not support the claim that there is an inverse relationship between United States tax rates and government revenues.[35]

A stronger argument is that government taxes have gotten so high that they act as a disincentive to capital formation. The main culprits are said to be taxes on income and property, which have risen to 70 percent of total federal, state, and local

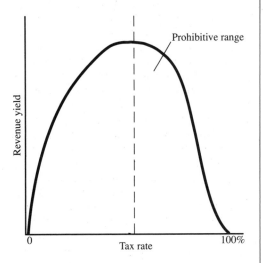

government taxes and to approximately 15 percent of GNP. Income taxes distort the choice between labor and leisure, particularly for the very young members of the labor force and for lower-earning spouses, and may significantly reduce the overall level of work effort in the economy. Income taxes also bias the choices between savings and consumption since income saved is taxed as current income and the returns from savings are taxed again as current income. Corporate income taxes, property taxes, and personal income taxes all lower the rate of return to capitalists. Boskin, among others, has argued that savings do respond to changes in the after-tax rate of return to capital and hence higher taxes on capital reduce the future size of the capital stock, labor productivity, wages, and income.[36]

If one accepts the argument that the current level of taxation of capital income does significantly retard capital formation, then two avenues of reform are open. The first calls for structural changes in the tax system that would reduce the tax burden on capital, such as integrating personal and corporate income taxes, replacing the current income tax with an expenditure tax, or indexing the income tax for inflation.[37] The other reform possibility follows the line of argument that government has gotten too large and that a growing taxation of capital income has accompanied this government growth. A reduction in the size of government, if accompanied by a reduced rate of taxation on capital income, would result in increased investment and eventually increased real wages, income, and government revenue.

Though the capital formation argument is usually brought up in connection with federal tax reform, there are important state and local government fiscal implications. There are three good reasons why a realistic reform of the taxation of capital would also require reductions at the state and local government level. First, about one third of taxes on capital are levied by state and local governments, as compared to about one fifth as recently as ten years ago. Second, because of the deductibility provisions under the federal income tax, a tax rate reduction at the federal level would generate an automatic increase in effective tax rates paid at the state and local level, thereby off-setting a part of the federal reduction. Finally, reduced federal taxes would probably lead to reduced intergovernment transfers. This would require state and local governments to either cut expenditures or raise tax rates, and if they increased taxes in accordance with present tax structures, about half of the increase would come in the form of income and property taxes.

Income redistribution. It has long been argued that there is a direct relationship between the size of the public sector and the distribution of income.[38] From this argument one might make the point that the size of government in the United States is too small to generate an acceptable distribution of income.

The exact relationship between the growth in government size and changes in the income distribution is not known, but there is evidence to give an impression. Gillespie's work on the United States shows that the net fiscal impact of government taxing and spending is progressive,[39] but more recent work has shown little effect.[40] On the other hand, some comparative research against European countries, where the government sector is larger, indicates that (a) there is substantial redistribution through the public sector in most countries and (b) the United States has one of the least-equitable income distributions.[41]

One might weave these piecemeal findings into an argument that the larger governments in European countries reflect a greater government involvement in social insurance and social welfare activities. Such services are of immense importance to the real income position of the poor, and hence their provision through the public sector markedly reduces the degree of income inequality.[42] The implication for policy is that the size of government in the United States ought to be increased in the name of improving the distribution of income.

There are important flaws in this conclusion. Since the United States fiscal system is more decentralized than that in most advanced countries with a larger government sector, the direct relationship between growth in the government sector and reductions in the income inequality may not hold. Growing state and local government taxes would not likely improve the income distribution since sales and property taxes are not progressive and state income taxes tend to be less progressive than the federal income tax. Moreover, it is a question not simply of increased funding but rather of the effectiveness of this funding in providing benefits to the low income. Consider that the United States welfare payment system is badly flawed, the level of Social Security benefits is ever under fire, and federal and state education grants are as likely to land in suburbs as in cities. In light of this track record, can one say with any conviction that increasing the size of government in the United States will improve the income distribution? The track record in recent years would suggest not.

Summary

The growth in the United States public sector during the past three decades was dominated by several important trends: (a) the share of GNP accounted for by state and local governments increased substantially; (b) the federal share of total public sector activity increased; (c) the expenditure increase was dominated by health, education, and welfare functions; (d) the state and local government sector became much more dependent on federal grants; and (e) state government became increasingly dominant in the state and local government financial system. There seems to have been a turnaround, or at least a long pause, in the first four of these trends since 1976.

Nevertheless, the importance of the state and local government sector in the economy has increased in the past three decades, and with this increasing importance has come new economic roles, particularly in the areas of macroeconomic policy and income distribution. The relationship as concerns federal stabilization policy attracted a good bit of attention in the mid and late 1970s when state and local governments were used as administrative agents of federal fiscal policy. The fiscal behavior of the state and local government sector was mildly countercyclical through most of the 1970s as financial assets were accumulated during recoveries and drawn down during recessions. This explains the lack of success of Antirecession Fiscal Assistance, CETA, and Local Public Works grants as a stimulus package during the 1975–78 period. During the 1981–83 recession, however, procyclical actions became increasingly apparent as state and local governments raised taxes and cut spending to meet anticipated deficits.

The potential role of state and local government in income redistribution is becoming more important as their tax and expenditure levels increase, and as their responsibility for social service delivery grows. The net effect of state and local government budgets on the distribution of income has not been adequately measured. However, based on the best available evidence, we might guess that the distribution of tax burdens is proportional and that the distribution of expenditure benefits is mildly progressive.

The future growth of the state and local government sector and changes in its structure are uncertain. Recent trends suggest a slowing of the growth in the state and local government share of GNP. The late 1970s seemed to bring a feeling that government at all levels had gotten too big, that it was producing too little, and in particular that too much government was largely responsible for the weak economic performance of the U.S. economy. This has led to the limitation movement. Though there does not seem to be a clear logic supporting the argument that government has become too big, the mood in the nation seems to be in the direction of slowing the growth in the public sector.

Notes

1. Anyone studying the United States federal system is in the debt of the Advisory Commission on Intergovernmental Relations. In particular, their excellent biennial compilation *Significant Features of Fiscal Federalism* is most useful in tracking the development of state and local government finances.
2. A review of the long-term growth in public employment, by level of government, is in Jesse Burkhead and Shawna Grosskopf, "Trends in Public Employment and Compensation," in *Public Employment and State and Local Government Finances,* edited by Roy Bahl, Jesse Burkhead, and Bernard Jump, Jr. (Cambridge, Mass.: Ballinger, 1980).
3. Current data on government expenditures are regularly reported by the United States Department of Commerce, Bureau of Economic Analysis in the *Survey of Current Business.*
4. We follow the usual definition of federal domestic expenditures as federal expenditures other than for national defense, international affairs and finance, space research and technology, and the estimated portion of net interest attributable to these functions. Social Security is included.
5. ACIR, *Significant Features of Fiscal Federalism 1980–81 Edition,* p. 29.
6. The term "social welfare expenditures" is used here to include all health, education, and welfare expenditures and Social Security.
7. The GNP elasticities between 1976 and 1980 are 1.19 for federal revenues, 0.82 for own-source state and local government revenues, and 0.83 for federal aid.
8. *Survey of Current Business,* April 1982, p. 13.
9. In Table 4, we define "average" as the unweighted mean value of the variable across the fifty states. The average percent of taxes to personal income ($\bar{T}y$) is

$$\bar{T}y = \sum_{i=1}^{50} Ty_i / 50$$

This is different, of course, from

$$\bar{\bar{T}}y = \sum_{i=1}^{50} T_i / \sum_{i=1}^{50} Y_i$$

For our purposes, the former seems the more appropriate way of defining a benchmark against which to compare interstate variations.

10. The standard measure of relative variation used in Table 4 is the coefficient of variation, i.e., the standard deviation as a percent of the mean. The smaller the coefficient, the less dispersed the distribution. For example, the reduction in the coefficient for the ratio of federal aid to personal income means that the states are grouped more closely about the mean in the latter year.
11. As may be seen in Table 4, there was a substantial increase in the diversity of revenue effort by state and local governments; i.e., the coefficient of variation rose from 0.15 in 1976 to 0.46 in 1980. Most of this, however, was due to substantial increases in severance tax collections in Alaska. Indeed, if Alaska is omitted from the interstate distribution of revenue effort, the mean revenue effort remains constant at 14.1 between 1976 and 1980 and the coefficient of variation changes only from 0.13 to 0.17.
12. Many public finance economists have made this point. For a summary of the issues involved, see Wallace Oates, *Fiscal Federalism* (New York: Harcourt Brace Jovanovich, 1972), pp. 4–13.
13. See, for discussions of this issue, Roy Bahl, Alan Campbell and David Greytak, *Taxes, Expenditures and the Economic Base: Case Study of New York City* (New York: Praeger Publishers, 1974), and Edward Gramlich, "The New York City Crisis: What Happened and What Is To Be Done?" *American Economic Review* 66(5):415 (1976).
14. A good questioning of the conventional thinking about the local government role in income redistribution is in Richard Tresch, *Public Finance: A Normative Theory* (Plano: Texas Business Publications, 1981), Chapter 30.
15. Alvin Hansen and Harvey Perloff, *State and Local Finance in the National Economy* (New York: Norton, 1944).
16. Robert Rafuse, "Cyclical Behavior of State-Local Finances," in *Essays in Fiscal Federalism,* edited by Richard Musgrave (Washington, D.C.: Brookings Institution, 1965).
17. Ibid., p. 117.
18. ACIR, *State-Local Finances in Recession and Inflation* (Washington, D.C.: GPO, 1979) and *Countercyclical*

Aid and Economic Stabilization (Washington, D.C.: GPO, 1978).

19. Edward Gramlich, "State and Local Government Budgets the Day After It Rained: Why Is the Surplus so High?" *Brookings Papers on Economic Activity* 1 (Washington, D.C.: Brookings Institution, 1978) and Edward Gramlich, "State and Local Budget Surpluses and the Effect of Federal Macroeconomic Policies," U.S. Congress, Joint Economic Committee (Washington, D.C.: GPO, 1979).

20. Robert Vogel and Robert Trost, "The Response of State Government Receipts to Economic Fluctuations and the Allocation of Countercyclical Revenue Sharing Grants," *Review of Economics and Statistics* LXI(3):389 (1979).

21. Robert Reischauer, "The Economy, the Federal Budget and the Prospects for Urban Aid," in *The Fiscal Outlook for Cities,* edited by Roy Bahl (Syracuse, N.Y.: Syracuse University Press, 1978).

22. Frank Jones and Mark Weisler, "Cyclical Variations in State and Local Government Financial Behavior and Capital Expenditures," in *Proceedings of the Seventieth Annual Conference on Taxation* (Columbus, Ohio: National Tax Association-Tax Institute of America, 1978).

23. Larry DeBoer, "The Response of State and Local Government Finances to Economic Fluctuations," Ph.D. Dissertation, Syracuse University, 1982, chapter 6.

24. These possibilities are discussed in Edward Gramlich, "Intergovernmental Grants: A Review of the Empirical Literature," In *The Political Economy of Fiscal Federalism,* edited by Wallace Oates (Lexington, Mass.: Lexington Books, 1977).

25. *Survey of Current Business,* July 1979.

26. In 1982, President Reagan proposed a swap whereby AFDC and food stamps would be fully funded by the state and local governments and Medicaid would become a federal responsibility. A second element of the program proposed a phased turnback of more than forty federally funded programs to state and local governments. This program was first described in "The President's Federalism Initiative," White House press release, January 26, 1982.

27. For a review of the evidence on this point, see "Domestic Consequences of United States Population Change," report prepared by the House Select Committee on Population (Washington, D.C.: GPO, 1978).

28. For a good discussion of these problems, see Charles McLure, "The Theory of Expenditure Incidence," *Finanzarchiv* 30:432 (1972).

29. The standard reference on this issue is Henry Aaron, *Who Pays the Property Tax?* (Washington, D.C.: Brookings Institution, 1975).

30. Benjamin Okner and Joseph Pechman, *Who Bears the Tax Burden?* (Washington, D.C.: Brookings Institution, 1975).

31. For examples, see Serrano versus Priest, 5 Cal., 3d 584 (1971) and San Antonio Independent School District versus Rodriguez, 411 U.S. 1 (1972).

32. Some would argue that voters can send such signals to elected politicians and hence government decision makers try not to stray too far from the preferences of the median voter. This approach is reviewed in Robert Inman, "The Fiscal Performance of Local Governments: An Interpretative Review," in *Current Issues in Urban Economics,* edited by Peter Mieszkowski and Mahlon Straszheim (Baltimore: Johns Hopkins University Press, 1981). Niskanen rejects even this possibility with the argument that fiscal decisions are primarily influenced by bureaucrats whose ultimate objective is to maximize their power by maximizing the size of their bureau budget. See William Niskanen, *Bureaucracy and Representative Government* (New York: Aldine, 1971).

33. It should be noted, however, that this estimate for New York overstates the tax burden because it takes account of neither exporting nor the federal offset.

34. Arthur B. Laffer, "Statement Prepared for the Joint Economic Committee, May 20, 1977." Reprinted in Arthur B. Laffer and Jan Seymour (editors), *The Economics of the Tax Revolt: A Reader* (New York: Harcourt, Brace, Jovanovich, 1979), pp. 75–79.

35. Don Fullerton, "On the Possibility of an Inverse Relationship Between Tax Rates and Government Revenues," *Journal of Public Economics* 19 (1982):3–22.

36. Michael Boskin, "Taxation, Saving and the Rate of Interest," *Journal of Political Economy* 86(2):S3 (1978).

37. For a discussion of these alternatives, see *Federal Tax Reform: Myths and Realities,* edited by Michael Boskin (San Francisco: Institute for Contemporary Studies, 1978).

38. Simon Kuznets, "Economic Growth and Income Inequality," *American Economic Review* 45(1):1 (1955).

39. W. Irwin Gillespie, "Effects of Public Expenditures on the Distribution of Income," in *Essays in Fiscal Federalism,* edited by Richard Musgrave (Washington, D.C.: Brookings Institution, 1965).

40. Morgan Reynolds and Eugene Smolensky, "The Post-Fisc Distribution: 1961 and 1970 Compared," *National Tax Journal* 27:515 (1974).

41. Malcolm Sawyer, "Income Distribution in OECD Countries," and Mark Wasserman, "Public Sector Budget Balance," *OECD Economic Outlook,* occasional studies, July 1976.

42. It must be admitted that estimates of the distribution of expenditure benefits are based on a primitive methodology. For a careful review of this work, see Luc DeWulf, "Fiscal Incidence Studies in Developing Countries: Survey and Critique," *International Monetary Fund Staff Papers* 22(3):61 (1975).

23

A Theoretical Analysis of the Case for a Balanced Budget Amendment

William R. Keech
The University of North Carolina at Chapel Hill

Introduction

The proposed amendment to the U.S. Constitution to require a balanced federal budget raises several theoretical issues that are independent of and logically prior to problems of practicality and enforcement, which are prominent among the arguments of opponents to the amendment. Questions about the desirability of the principle of annually balanced budgets are sometimes begged, and some important questions about the desirability of putting such provisions into the Constitution are often not raised. (For important exceptions see Ackley, 1982; Aranson, 1983; Noll, 1983; and Shepsle, 1983.) This essay identifies and discusses a series of such issues.

Specifically, many opponents observe that the amendment could not be effectively enforced, for example because expenditures could be shifted to "off budget enterprises," because certain other government goals could be met by regulations instead of direct expenditure, or because the relevant numbers could be manipulated (see Shepsle, 1982). These arguments are telling, but they sometimes beg the question of whether or not the amendment is desirable in principle. Of course, if the proposal were sure to be rejected on grounds of practicality and enforceability, the questions of desirability would be moot. But since there is a risk that the arguments about enforceability may not prevail, and that the amendment may not be

The author would like to acknowledge the support of National Science Foundation Grant #SES-8218421, and the comments of the following persons on an earlier version: Arthur Benavie, J. Budziszewski, Henry Chappell, Richard Froyen, Paul Kress, Peter Lange, Jeffrey Obler, Donald Searing, Kenneth Shepsle and the late Clement Vose. Of course, none of the above bears any responsibility for the content. *Source: Policy Sciences,* (Amsterdam: Elsevier Science Publishers B.V., 1985), pp. 157–168. Reprinted by permission of Kluwer Academic Publishers.

rejected, the theoretical case is important. If the theoretical case is unsound, then the practicality arguments are moot. This essay concentrates on questions of desirability in principle.

The Perspectives of Self-Command and the Authentic Self

To put a policy goal such as a balanced budget requirement into the Constitution implies that the government cannot be depended on to achieve this goal without a rule. Imposing such a rule is similar to what Thomas Schelling (1984a, b) calls "self-command," an effort to "overrule one's own preferences." Schelling develops this concept in the context of theories of rational choice on the individual level, such as consumer behavior. He suggests, for example, that the alternation between the desire to smoke and the desire to quit smoking is a problem of choice between two selves, an issue of interpersonal comparison of utilities, with all of the well-known intellectual difficulties that go with that problem.

Indeed, some of the proponents of a balanced budget amendment explicitly use the analogy that the government is like an alcoholic, drunk on deficits and unable to achieve the sobriety of balanced budgets without a rule such as that proposed (Buchanan and Wagner, 1977, p. 159). What should we infer from this analogy? As Jon Elster (1985) observes, Schelling suggests that there are sometimes genuine dilemmas in identifying the "authentic self." If so, the elements of the political system which seek to balance the budget may not be superior to or more "authentic" than the elements which produce large and repeated deficits. There is no doubt about the hierarchy of authority between the civil society, which amends the Constitution, and the government, which defines the balance between revenues and expenditures. Yet there is reason to doubt that the representatives of the people who may act to pass a balanced budget amendment to the Constitution act on behalf of a more authentic self than the other representatives of the same people, who produce deficits.

Elster suggests that "the authentic self is the one who is capable of acting strategically towards the other self or selves" (1985, p. 92). If some of the critics are correct, this definition implies that the "authentic" governmental self may be the one that would defeat the purpose of a balanced budget amendment with techniques such as off budget enterprises, since these may be stategically chosen ways of avoiding the scrutiny of the budget process.

Of course there is a collective action problem in the present case, i.e., a problem of preference aggregation. Is an expression of collective wishes through constitutional amendment more authentic than an expression through the budget process? The former demands extraordinary majorities regarding a simple sounding proposition. The latter involves only simple majorities in a process which allows a much more elaborate expression of specific interests.[1]

The proposed amendment would involve the representatives of the people acting as amenders of the Constitution, limiting the discretion of other representatives of the people acting as policymakers. The proposed amendment amounts to the argument that the normal political process is insufficient to achieve objectively desired ends, so that the process must be constrained by rules.

Before incorporating the desire for balanced federal budgets into constitutional superiority over a political process that produces deficits, we should know more about why balanced budgets are to be considered superior to deficits, and, if so, why the government cannot be relied on to make this judgment without a rule. We consider first the nature of the case for balanced budgets, and then the possibility that government decisions need to be constrained by rules.

The Case for Balanced Budgets and Its Relation to Other Goals

In my reading of the literature, I find no sustained argument that balanced budgets are first principles or ends in their own right.[2] Budget deficits are opposed for instrumental reasons. Deficits are said to be related to other implicitly higher goals such as price stability, capital formation, and, by extension, long term growth.

Clearly there are circumstances in which this is true. As Martin Feldstein demonstrates (1980, p. 647):

a permanent increase in the government's real deficit in a fully employed economy . . . must raise the rate of inflation or lower the capital intensity of production or both.

But as he also points out, "deficits may have no adverse effect in an economy with sufficient unemployed

resources" (p. 637). Deficits are not necessarily undesirable in all circumstances, at least with respect to the goals of price stability and capital formation.

The balanced budget amendment most commonly discussed (Senate Joint Resolution 58. See Rabushka, 1983) does not explicitly distinguish these situations. War is the only condition which the proposed amendment recognizes as grounds for waiving the balanced budget requirement. Presumably this is because the consequences of losing a war may be even worse than the consequences of deficits. Surely this is so, and since the effort to win wars typically involves deficits, this is a reasonable exception.

The fact that other exceptions are conceivable is recognized in the provision that "Whenever three fifths of the whole number of both Houses shall deem it necessary, Congress may provide for a specific excess of outlays over receipts by a vote directed solely to that subject." One wonders what the exceptions would be that might generate a three fifths vote. I imagine at least two kinds.

One kind of exception would be cases in which deficits would not have the adverse consequences for price stability or capital formation that make them otherwise undesirable, i.e., cases in which the basic rationale for balanced budgets does not apply. The Great Depression is the classic example. Another is presented in a recent *Economic Report of the President* (1984, pp. 38–40), where current deficits are defended as contributing to economic recovery, while persistent deficits are acknowledged to have potentially adverse effects for price stability and capital formation.

The balanced budget amendment is of course proposed because its advocates seem to believe that the President and Congress cannot tell the difference between cases in which a balanced budget is warranted and those in which it is not (when the advocates recognize such a distinction at all). An amendment with a requirement of a three fifths vote for unbalanced budgets merely makes the presumption of a balanced budget explicit and raises a high hurdle for exceptions. In other words, the amendment says that an extraordinary majority must acknowledge exactly what they're doing when they vote for an excess of outlays over receipts. It does not say that they may never do so.

A second kind of exceptional situation would be analogous to war, namely cases in which other goals besides economic management competed with the rationale for a balanced budget. War as a threat to survival of the society clearly deserves to be on the same plane with or higher than a balanced budget. But if winning a war is so high a priority, how much lower is the avoidance of war, or national defense in a nuclear age? A former director of OMB opposes the amendment on grounds that the budget would be balanced at the expense of adequate national defense (*Wall Street Journal,* 25 July 1984, p. 1).

And if defense of the society is allowed to interfere with budget balance, why could not other allocation goals do the same? Peter Aranson, an erstwhile defender of the balanced budget amendment, suggests that "the public sector deficit, like its private sector counterpart, must be justified by the nature of the activities it supports," and he identifies several conditions which "welfare theory" suggests could be grounds for deficit spending (1983, pp. 161–163).

Furthermore, the nominal size of budget deficits, which receives so much attention, may be a misleading measure of the meaningful magnitude of deficits. Robert Eisner and Paul Pieper (1984) identify a series of ways in which the excess of government expenditures over receipts may misstate the nature and size of government deficits or surpluses. They take into account differences between par and market value of government obligations, between capital and current accounts, and between high employment and nominal deficits. The clear implication is that nominal deficits are not a good indicator of economic health. Indeed, in a study of seventeen OECD countries between 1949 and 1981, Guess and Koford (1984) find that "there is *no support* for a *consistent* causal relationship from deficits to inflation, reduced GNP, or reduced investment" (1984, p. 399, emphasis in original).

The above discussion implies that the balanced budget should not be placed at the top of a hierarchy of goals, i.e., of a lexicographical ordering. If it were, and the political process regularly subordinated budget balance to goals that ranked below it, this fact could be grounds for an "external and superior rule" such as the proposed amendment. But since even the proposed amendment itself recognizes circumstances in which other goals may legitimately compete with a balanced budget, the rationale must be more subtle.

Even though a balanced budget may not always be objectively desirable, some deficits may be too large, as Benjamin Friedman (1983) points out. If the political process consistently generates deficits which are too large even after taking other considerations into account, a balanced budget requirement may be a second best solution. Annually balanced budgets are surely not optimal regardless of other conditions, but they may be better than the deficits produced by an unconstrained political process. If the case for a balanced budget actually rests on these second best grounds, it will have to be made more carefully than it has been as yet.

Rules, Discretion and the Theory of Economic Policy

At present, elected officials have the "discretion" to weigh the considerations mentioned above as they see fit. Under the proposed amendment their discretion would be constrained by the "rule" mandating budget balance. If things worked as intended, the budget would normally be balanced, with the consequences for other objectives being subordinated to this concern, for better or worse.

The case for "rules" rather than "discretion" is an old one in economics, going back at least to Henry Simons (1936).[3] It is usually associated with monetary policy and Milton Friedman is its leading contemporary exponent. Yet the case for rules in monetary policy, however sound, is not equivalent to a case for rules in fiscal policy, such as an annually balanced budget. Moreover, the case for a rule is not equivalent to the case for a constitutional amendment.

The rule Friedman advocates is a fixed growth rate for the money stock regardless of cyclical fluctuations. His rationale is that discretion does not give clear enough guides to policy and criteria for performance evaluation. Imperfect knowledge and the unpredictability of the lags in the relation between money and prices make it likely that discretionary stabilization policy may actually *destabilize* the economy. That is, monetary measures designed to be countercyclical may actually turn out to be procyclical because economic conditions may have changed by the time they take effect (Friedman, 1959, pp. 86–90).

On one level the case for rules rather than discretion is approximately as strong for fiscal as for monetary policy. The difficulty of accurately forecasting the economy is the same. And the risk exists in fiscal policy too that policy responses may actually destabilize because of unpredictable lags. However, on another level the case for a balanced budget rule is much weaker. A rule of a constant growth rate in the money supply would avoid the risk that stabilization policy would destabilize by accident. But although a fixed monetary growth rule is not actively destabilizing, a rigidly balanced budget may be. If the economy goes into a recession due to an autonomous reduction in aggregate demand, tax receipts will fall and government transfer payments will rise. Each contributes to a deficit, and an effort to balance the budget would be procyclical rather than countercyclical. Balancing the budget under such circumstances would further reduce aggregate demand and make the recession worse. Unlike a fixed monetary growth rate, the balanced budget amendment is a rule it may be actively destabilizing to follow.

There is theory of economic policymaking which would provide a rationale for full discretion. A balanced budget role would almost certainly obstruct the effectiveness of economic policymaking under such theory, because it would take away a policy instrument. In one formulation, a series of economic goals, such as inflation and unemployment, could be combined in an "objective function" that identifies target values and marginal rates of substitution between them. This objective function can be "optimized" subject to real world limitations by suitable manipulation of policy instruments. For example, Chappell and Keech (1983) show how a president might minimize a weighted combination of inflation and unemployment (the objective function) by suitable choice of government spending (the control variable) subject to the constraint (a multi-equation model of the U.S. economy). It is possible in principle for stabilization policy to achieve a series of specific goals or targets, so long as the number of policy instruments is at least equal to the number of targets.

A balanced budget amendment would in general add to the difficulty of the problem in the theory of economic policy, since it would require that government spending not exceed tax revenues. Taxes and government expenditures are commonly viewed as separate policy instruments for purposes of achieving economic targets. To ask that one be limited to the value of the other at best adds a target or removes an instrument, thus making it more difficult to achieve a full set of goals. A rule such as a balanced budget amendment does not make much sense in a world described by such theory of economic policy

so long as balanced budgets are seen as instrumental and not as a goal in their own right (See Benavie and Froyen, 1984, pp. 9–17).

The case for discretionary macroeconomic policy has been undermined and the case for rules has been revitalized by the rational expectations hypothesis, which has had a deep impact on macroeconomic theory in the last decade. The rational expectations hypothesis is based on the assumptions that economic agents use all information readily available to them and that they do not make systematic errors (see Begg, 1982; Fischer, 1980). In the context of macroeconomic policy, this has been shown to lead to the conclusion that systematic stabilization policy cannot work. The rational expectations hypothesis implies that

> systematic, and therefore anticipatable monetary policy would have no real effects even in the short run; systematic fiscal policy would not affect current real output or employment, and would affect these variables only to the extent that, by manipulating the composition of the given output level, it could affect investment and therefore future aggregate supply (Begg, 1982, pp. 132–133).

There is serious question that the policy ineffectiveness proposition holds in its strongest form, for example in labor markets which do not clear (Begg, 1982, pp. 150–153), and even in its strongest form it permits policy to have an effect through surprises. Still, the rational expectations hypothesis has undermined confidence in the theory that shows how policymakers can use their discretion to achieve macroeconomic targets.

In addition, rational expectations brings us full circle back to the advocacy of rules rather than discretion in macroeconomic policy. Sargent and Wallace (1975) and Kydland and Prescott (1977) argue that rational expectations/assumptions imply that predictable rules lead to more desirable policy than does the use of discretion. Ironically, Friedman's rationale for rules was that we don't know enough to use discretion in fine tuning the economy, whereas rational expectations produces the same recommendation for rules from assumptions that expectations are not systematically in error (see Gapinski, 1982, ch. 8).

But the rejuvenated case for rules is not equivalent to the case for a balanced budget. The case is made in terms of monetary rather than fiscal rules (Sargent and Wallace, 1975). Benavie and Froyen show that even under rational expectations a balanced budget rule would be suboptimal. Automatic stabilizers reduce the variance in real output, and constraining taxes to match expenditures would make prices or output more unstable (1984, pp. 21–24). In general, the case for rules over discretion collapses as we move from monetary to fiscal policy.

The main advantage for the balanced budget as a policy rule derives from its simplicity and its widespread support, but not from the argument that it is a good rule in its own right. Kydland and Prescott suggest that in a democratic society, "it is probably preferable that the rules be simple and easily understood, so it is obvious when a policy-maker deviates from the policy" (1977, p. 487). Henry Simons argued that the rules should be "definite, simple (at least in principle) and expressive of strong, abiding and pervasive popular sentiments" (1936, p. 29). There is no rule that is more intuitive to the public than the rule that budgets shall be balanced. While this may not be the best rule for public officials to follow, it is hard to imagine subtler rules, such as fixed monetary growth or constant full employment surpluses, having the public impact or public support of the balanced budget.[4] If we are to have a rule which reflects "abiding and pervasive popular sentiments," the balanced budget rule is by far the most likely candidate, even if it is not a good rule. Whether it is better than no rule depends in part on our understanding of the political process.

Three Views of the Nature of the Political Process

The balanced budget amendment was proposed by advocates who felt that the normal political process produces outcomes which are objectively undesirable. The above review rejected the view that a balanced budget is more desirable than an unbalanced budget regardless of other conditions, and it considered some rationales for rules over discretion. The next question becomes how adequate the political process is to make appropriate decisions about budget size without being constrained by rules. I consider three basic possibilities.

The possibility that a theory exists which would show when and how the political process can be relied on to produce desirable outcomes. The basic

fact is that there is no widely accepted theory that relates political preferences and institutions to the desirability of policy outcomes. We have an idea of what such theory would look like in microeconomic general equilibrium theory, which relates preferences and procedures to outcomes with explicit standards of evaluation. And John Rawls gives us an intuitive idea of what such a theory might do in his concept of "perfect procedural justice," with the metaphor of the rule that provides an incentive for equal division of a cake (Rawls, p. 85). But efforts to achieve comparable success regarding political activity have achieved negative results.[5]

As Rawls (1971, p. 360) puts it:

> There seems to be no way to characterize a feasible procedure guaranteed to lead to just legislation. . . . So far at least there does not exist a theory of just constitutions as procedures leading to just legislation which corresponds to the theory of competitive markets as procedures resulting in efficiency.

Although our concern here is with desirable outcomes in general, rather than with "just legislation," the point stands nonetheless.

The problem is twofold. On the one hand we do not have the theory to identify what the most desirable outcomes are. On the other, we do not have the theory that would tell us how political institutions might aggregate preferences or guide behavior towards optimal outcomes.

In Herbert Stein's words (1984, p. 352) regarding the first point, the decision as to the optimal size of government surplus or deficit is a decision about rates of economic growth, and

> There is no objective way to determine how much the nation should forego current government services and private consumption in order to make future national income greater.

On the second point, the greatest recent progress in theories about how institutions guide preferences into collective outcomes has had to do less with optimizing than political pathologies, or putatively undesirable consequences of political processes.

The possibility of political pathologies. One of the major developments in political science and economics in recent years has been theory that suggests conditions under which the political process might lead to outcomes that are objectively undesirable, or at least not within a certain range of desirability. If this is the case, a rule such as the balanced budget amendment might be worth a second look as a possible means of keeping outcomes within such a range.

The first of these developments starts from the context implied by the theory of macroeconomic policy, in which this theory would guide the choices of a welfare maximizing planner. The theory of the political business cycle shows how, under certain definitions of economic constraints, a politician/planner who maximized votes instead of welfare could create politically induced business cycles which would lead to suboptimal outcomes (see Nordhaus, 1975; Keech and Simon, 1985; Chappell and Keech, 1983).

Considerable research has been done to investigate whether or not there is substantial evidence of such cycles on electoral periods and empirical support is uneven at best (see Keech, 1985, for a review). While some politicians may from time to time try to manipulate the economy in the fashion suggested by this theory, such manipulation appears to be neither systematic nor regular. Furthermore, rational expectations assumptions discussed above deny that it would be possible for politicians to behave this way on a regular basis. And while most empirical studies of how the public evaluates economic policy suggest that voters would reward such manipulation if it existed, there is more recent evidence that questions whether voters would do so (Chappell and Keech, 1985). Even if there were full empirical support for political business cycles, the case is not yet made that a balanced budget amendment would be an effective antidote.

Another model of political pathologies for which the balanced budget amendment is seen to be relevant is what might be called theory of distributive politics (Fiorina, 1981; Shepsle and Weingast, 1981). This is theory which shows how there are incentives for the organized to seek publicly-provided private benefits, the costs of which are distributed across the population. The benefits may not be justifiable in terms of the normal grounds that justify public expenditures, yet the organization of representative government on a geographic basis provides incentives for public officials to respond positively to these demands.

Because these programs increase the size of the public sector and increase government expenditures without necessarily being accompanied by corresponding revenue increases, a balanced budget amendment is sometimes seen as relevant to their control. Indeed, the proposed amendment includes a provision that would limit the growth of public expenditures. But preferences for a large or even "too large" public sector do not imply a preference for deficits until it is demonstrated that there is a systematic unwillingness to raise enough revenues to pay for these expenditures (Noll, 1983).

Buchanan and Wagner (1977, ch. 7, 8) argue that there is such an unwillingness. They contend that without a balanced budget rule, there is a bias in democratic politics in favor of deficits and against surpluses. If people can avoid direct payment for public expenditures with deficits, they will support more expenditures than they otherwise would because the tax price is lower. The undesirable consequences of deficits, such as inflation or reduced capital formation, are not clearly perceived, especially by persons who anticipate a short term gain, according to Buchanan and Wagner, but no systematic evidence is presented by the authors.

Crain and Ekelund (1978), argue that deficits are likely to be a systematic product of political rivalry in democratic governments, especially when public debt is financed by taxes on human capital, i.e., income taxes. Taxes on physical capital are immediately reflected in reduced value of that capital, Crain and Ekelund contend, whereas the burden of taxes on human capital can be shifted to future generations. They present some modest evidence that deficits are positively associated with dependence for revenues on taxes on human capital.

Roger Noll (1983) addresses the possibility that the theory of distributive politics might lead politicians to pay less attention to the overall level of revenues than to the distribution of tax breaks, but he does not find compelling reason to believe that this is a systematic cause of excessive deficits. If it were, he suggests, we would have to explain why deficits have been so small. As it stands, Noll argues that deficits are well explained by wars and the state of the economy, and without variables reflecting political pathologies.[6]

The liberal interpretation of democracy.   In the absence of convincing theories of political optimization or of political pathologies, we are left in a rather large middle ground. William Riker provides one interpretation of the resulting situation. He argues that "the outcomes of voting are not necessarily fair and true amalgamations of voters' values" (Riker, 1982, p. 233), and suggests that the outcomes of political decision procedures may be arbitrary and without moral content. Democratic institutions are best defended on grounds that there is always another election and another opportunity to reject current policies, including, presumably, excessive deficits. While he argues that voters can always reject incumbents of whom they do not approve, his work undermines the prospect that the electoral process can assure any pattern of outcomes, whether desirable or not. He does not address the possibility of "objective" standards for evaluating outcomes, or of rules designed to assure adherence to such outcomes. Yet he clearly undermines contentions that the electoral process is predictably either optimizing or pathological.[7]

Conclusion: Policy and Procedures in the Constitution

A balanced budget amendment would be an effort to incorporate a policy goal into the Constitution. While the clearest precedent is probably the Prohibition Amendment, a balanced budget amendment seeks to constrain not individual but governmental behavior. It is an exercise in self-command on the part of the political community. Just as it is the case with individuals, the government can command itself to be more disciplined about some activity such as matching revenues with expenditures. It can do so without establishing a rigid rule. A constitutional amendment is an extreme solution that might conceivably be justified under certain conditions.

If balanced budgets were unconditionally superior to deficits, or if the political process were shown systematically to produce objectively inferior results, a balanced budget amendment would make more sense than it can now be shown to make. The case for rules rather than discretion in policymaking has been given new vitality by rational expectations theory, but this case has not been extended to balanced budgets as well as monetary growth rates. Even if it had been, the case for such rules is not equivalent to the case for a constitutional amendment. Rules can be followed without being incorporated into a constitution. And to incorporate a rule into the U.S. Constitution without any more intellectual justification than this one has would be hasty and premature.

Notes

1. Conceivably the regularity with which the budget process produces deficits is similar to the strength of the shortsighted selfishness position in the prisoners' dilemma game.
2. Perhaps the closest approximation is Adam Smith's observation that "What is prudence in the conduct of every private family, can scarce be folly in that of a great kingdom" quoted in Wagner, Tolleson, et al., 1982, p. 7.
3. Simons argued for "a stable framework of definite rules" designed to assure "a minimum of uncertainty for enterprisers and investors" (1936, p. 29).
4. See Blinder and Holtz-Eakin, 1984, for a discussion of sources of public support for a balanced budget amendment.
5. The landmark is of course Arrow, 1963.
6. For a more systematic effort to explain deficits, which is consistent with this view, see Barro, 1984.
7. John Rawls' concept of pure procedural justice is potentially relevant to a situation in which there is neither a theory of optimization nor of pathology (1971, pp. 85–86).

References

ACKLEY, G. (1982). "You can't balance the budget by amendment," *Challenge* 25: 4–13.

ARANSON, P. A. (1983). "Public deficits in normative economic and positive political theory," in L. H. Meyer (ed.), *The Economic Consequences of Government Deficits*. Boston: Kluwer-Nijhoff, pp. 157–182.

ARROW, K. J. (1963). *Social Choice and Individual Values*. New York: John Wiley.

BARRO, R. J. (1984). "The behavior of U.S. deficits." Cambridge, MA: National Bureau of Economic Research Working Paper #309.

BEGG, D. K. H. (1982). *The Rational Expectations Revolution in Macroeconomics: Theories and Evidence*. Baltimore: Johns Hopkins University Press.

BENAVIE, A. and FROYEN, R. (1984). "A balanced budget amendment in modern stochastic macromodels." Processed. University of North Carolina at Chapel Hill.

BLINDER, A. S. and HOLTZ-EAKIN, D. (1984). "Public opinion and the balanced budget," *American Economic Review* 74: 144–149.

BUCHANAN, J. and WAGNER, R. E. (1977). *Democracy in Deficit*. New York: Academic Press.

CHAPPELL, H. W., JR., and KEECH, W. R. (1983). "Welfare consequences of the six year presidential term evaluated in the context of a model of the U.S. economy," *American Political Science Review* 77: 75–91.

CHAPPELL, H. W., JR., and KEECH, W. R. (1985). "A new view of political accountability for economic performance," *American Political Science Review,* 79: 10–27.

CRAIN, W. M. and EKELUND, JR., R. B. (1978). "Deficits and democracy," *Southern Economic Journal* 44: 813–828.

Economic Report of the President (1984). Washington DC: U.S. Government Printing Office.

EISNER, R. and PIEPER, P. J. (1984). "A new view of federal debt and budget deficits," *American Economic Review* 74: 11–29.

ELSTER, J. (1985). "Review of Schelling (1984), *Choice and consequence," Journal of Economic Behavior and Organization* 6: 90–92.

FELDSTEIN, M. (1980). "Fiscal policies, inflation and capital formation," *American Economic Review* 70: 636–650.

FIORINA, M. P. (1981). "Universalism, reciprocity and distributive policymaking in majority rule institutions," *Research in Public Policy Analysis and Management* 1: 197–221.

FISCHER, S. (ed.) (1980). *Rational Expectations and Economic Policy*. Chicago: University of Chicago Press.

FRIEDMAN, B. (1983). "Managing the U.S. government deficit in the 1980s." Cambridge, MA: National Bureau of Economic Research Working Paper #1209.

FRIEDMAN, M. (1959). *A Program for Monetary Stability*. New York: Fordham University Press.

GAPINSKI, J. H. (1982). *Macroeconomic Theory: Statics, Dynamics and Policy*. New York: McGraw-Hill.

GUESS, G. and KOFORD, K. (1984). "Inflation, recession and the federal budget deficit (or, blaming economic problems on a statistical mirage)." *Policy Sciences* 17: 385–402.

KEECH, W. R. (1985). "Elections and macroeconomic policy," in J. P. Pfiffner (ed.), *The President and Macroeconomic Policy*. Philadelphia: Institute for the study of Human Issues.

KEECH, W. R. and SIMON, C. P. (1985). "Electoral and welfare consequences of political manipulation of the

economy," *Journal of Economic Behavior and Organization* 6: in press.

KYDLAND, F. and PRESCOTT, E. (1977). "Rules rather than discretion: the inconsistency of optimal plans," *Journal of Political Economy* 85: 473–491.

MEYER, L. H. (ed.) (1983). *The Economic Consequences of Government Deficits*. Boston: Kluwer-Nijhoff.

NOLL, R. G. (1983). "Discussion," in L. H. Meyer (ed.), *The Economic Consequences of Government Deficits,* Boston: Kluwer-Nijhoff, pp. 201–210.

NORDHAUS, W. D. (1975). "The political business cycle," *Review of Economic Studies* 42: 169–190.

RABUSHKA, A. (1983). "A constitutional cure for deficits," in L. H. Meyer (ed.), *The Economic Consequences of Government Deficits*. Boston: Kluwer-Nijhoff, pp. 183–200.

RAWLS, J. (1971). *A Theory of Justice*. Cambridge: Harvard University Press.

RIKER, W. H. (1982). *Liberalism Against Populism*. San Francisco: W. H. Freeman.

SARGENT, T. J. and WALLACE, N. (1975). "Rational expectations, the optimal monetary instrument and the optimal money supply rule," *Journal of Political Economy* 83: 241–254.

SARGENT, T. J. and WALLACE, N. (1976). "Rational expectations and the theory of economic policy," *Journal of Monetary Economics* 2: 169–183.

SCHELLING, T.C. (1984a). "Self-command in practice, in policy and in a theory of rational choice," *American Economic Review* 74: 1–11.

SCHELLING, T. C. (1984b). *Choice and Consequence*. Cambridge, MA: Harvard University Press.

SHEPSLE, K. A. (1982). "Constitutional regulation of the U.S. budget." St. Louis: Washington University Center for the Study of American Business.

SHEPSLE, K. A. (1983). "Discussion," in L. H. Meyer (ed.), *The Economic Consequences of Government Deficits*. Boston: Kluwer-Nijhoff, pp. 211–219.

SHEPSLE, K. A. and WEINGAST, B. R. (1981). "Political preferences for the pork barrel: a generalization," *American Journal of Political Science* 25: 96–111.

SIMONS, H. C. (1936). "Rules versus authorities in monetary policy," *Journal of Political Economy* 44: 1–30.

STEIN, H. (1984). *Presidential Economics*. New York: Simon and Schuster.

WAGNER, R. E., TOLLESON, R. D. et al. (1982). *Balanced Budgets, Fiscal Responsibility and the Constitution*. Washington, DC: The Cato Institute.

24

The Line-Item Veto in the States: An Instrument for Fiscal Restraint or an Instrument for Partisanship?

Glenn Abney
Georgia State University
Thomas P. Lauth
University of Georgia

Introduction

Ronald Reagan has proposed that the president be given the power to line-item veto appropriation bills in order to reduce the deficit and to discourage wasteful spending.[1] Throughout his administration, President Reagan has been thwarted by Congress in his attempt to eliminate certain established programs from the federal budget. He has also had to accept appropriation bills containing both items he desired and pork barrel items desired by members of Congress.[2] If President Reagan possessed the item veto, then his power vis-à-vis Congress would have been enhanced in these cases.[3]

Although this reform is discussed in the literature,[4] little empirical or comparative evidence is available as to whether the line-item veto actually works to curtail spending and promote efficiency in government. It is usually argued that the line-item veto, through its use or the threat of its use, mitigates logrolling and pork barrel appropriations and makes government more fiscally responsible. However, a chief executive could also use the line-item veto as an instrument to promote partisan and/or executive interests. Such usage would be most likely to occur where the chief executive confronts a legislature wholly or partially under the control of an opposition party. Although such use of the veto would reduce expenditures, fiscal restraint would be only a symbolic goal.

Source: Reprinted with permission from *Public Administration Review* (May–June 1985): 372–377. © 1985 by the American Society for Public Administration (ASPA), 1120 G Street NW, Suite 500, Washington, D.C. 20005. All rights reserved.

This article examines the line-item veto in state governments to determine whether it is used as an instrument for fiscal restraint or an instrument of partisanship. The line-item veto is available to 42 (or 43 depending upon interpretation[5]) of the 50 state governors. Although an investigation of the veto power in state government is a legitimate and valuable end in itself, research findings from the state level may also inform discussions about incorporating this power into the national Constitution. State budgeting is, of course, different from national budgeting in that state budgets are often required by constitutional provision to be balanced. Nevertheless, similarities between the two levels of government regarding budgeting are more common than differences. Both levels of government are subjected to conflicting pressures for the expansion of services and the alleviation of tax burdens. Further, proponents of the item veto for the president frequently cite as evidence in support of their cause the fact that the item veto is possessed by governors.

The virtues and limitations of the line-item veto have been debated for over half a century in the literature.[6] A principal virtue of the item veto is its reputation as a tool for legislative efficiency. It is said to provide the chief executive with the opportunity to discourage pork barrel activities, logrolling, and extravagance in appropriation bills because it protects the integrity of the gubernatorial veto. In appropriation bills, legislatures may include expenditures which are unacceptable to the governor along with those desired by the executive. The value of the governor's veto power is weakened unless he or she is able to eliminate objectionable items without having to veto the entire appropriation measure.

The limitations of the item veto, however, are not insignificant. First, it is said to reduce the responsibility of legislative bodies.[7] Legislatures may include a host of "pork barrel" provisions expecting the governor to veto many of them. Thus, the veto power, and the line-item veto in particular, may be an invitation to legislative irresponsibility. In this way the item veto might actually promote inefficiency by discouraging legislative discipline. As one governor is reported to have commented: "Avoid threatening to veto a bill. You just relieve the legislature of responsibility for sound legislation."[8]

A second set of limitations focuses on the impact of the executive on the legislative process.[9] The item veto may enhance the influence of the executive over the legislature so as to violate the principle of separation

273

of powers. This concern was expressed by President William H. Taft when he wrote: "While for some purposes, it would be useful for the Executive to have the power of partial veto, if we could always be sure of its wise and conscientious exercise, I am not entirely sure that it would be a safe provision. It would greatly enlarge the influence of the President, already large enough from patronage and party loyalty and other causes."[10] For Taft the concern was not just the increased influence of the executive, but also how the executive might use that power. If it were used to reward loyal legislators and to promote partisan causes, then the item veto would threaten the separation of powers principle. Even if the executive should not use it to reward and punish individual legislators, the item veto would enhance the legislative powers of the governor and thereby provide the executive with a dominant role in the appropriations process.[11]

Despite the extensive discussions in the literature on the pros and cons of the line-item veto, little empirical evidence exists upon which to base an assessment of how this instrument of executive power has actually been used. We have attempted to inform the item veto debate by asking participants in the state budgetary process about their perceptions of how the item veto is actually used in state budgeting. Our data come from a 1982 mail survey of state legislative budget officers. In those states which do not have a legislative budget office, the chief staff member of the house appropriations committee served as the respondent. Responses were received from 45 of the 50 states. Although our respondent population of 45 state officials is relatively small, it does represent 90 percent of the relevant experts.

Use of the Item Veto

The use of the line-item veto varies greatly among the states. Respondents were asked to indicate how many times in the three years prior to the survey their respective governors had used it. Thirteen of the respondents indicated that the governor had not used the item veto during that period; however, eight of those respondents were from states where the governor does not have item veto power. Another seven respondents reported that the veto had been used only once. At the other extreme, seven respondents reported use of the veto 100 or more times during

the three years prior to the survey. Fourteen respondents reported frequencies which were scattered between these extremes. Four respondents failed to provide information about the frequency of item vetoing in their states. Of those respondents from states with the line-item veto who reported frequency (n = 33), 20 indicated that the veto was used less than three times per year and 13 reported use of three or more times per year.

When governors use the veto, their actions are not usually overridden by votes of the legislatures. Of the respondents (n = 28) who reported the veto having been used in their states in the past three years, 20 reported no overrides. However, in one state (Alaska) with a Republican governor and an assembly with a Democratic majority in both houses, 75 of 100 vetoes were reported to have been overridden in the past three years. This state is a very unique case.

The lack of successful overrides of line-item vetoes can be explained in part by requirements of extraordinary majorities. Furthermore, the ability of legislatures to write appropriation bills so as to make even line-item vetoes difficult for the governor may reduce the need for overrides. Sixteen of the 37 respondents from states having the item veto reported that legislatures write appropriation acts so as to limit the item veto opportunities of the governor.

Just as the effectiveness of the general veto has been thwarted by legislative manipulation, so also has the purpose of the item veto been at least partially undermined. Legislatures can combine items desired by governors with those opposed by them into one item. In most states, governors cannot reduce an item, they must either accept or reject it. Furthermore, in general, governors can veto the item of appropriation but they cannot change the legislative intent as expressed through substantive language.[12] The Virginia Supreme Court has held: " 'An item in an appropriation bill is an indivisible sum of money dedicated to a stated purpose. It is something different from a provision or condition, and where conditions are attached, they must be observed. . . . ' "[13] In a Missouri case the state supreme court held that the governor's veto power does not include authority to eliminate words indicating the purpose of the appropriation.[14] Unable to veto the legislature's intent or conditions, governors may find vetoing particular items difficult.

Fiscal Restraint and the Item Veto

Do governors use the item veto against legislative bodies engaged in fiscal irresponsibility?[15] If governors use the item veto to promote fiscal restraint, then governors theoretically should use it against spendthrift legislative bodies. Opponents of the item veto suggest that such use discourages fiscal restraint by legislatures and thereby encourages irresponsibility.[16] The opposition to the item veto suggests that it may shift final responsibility for legislation from the legislature to the chief executive, causing lack of discipline by legislatures and increasing the powers of governors.[17] Whether the use of the item veto actually encourages fiscal restraint or causes fiscal responsibility may be in dispute, but the conclusion that the use of the veto and fiscal irresponsibility are found together does not appear to be in dispute. However, our data do not support this conclusion. Legislatures against which the item veto is used are not more fiscally irresponsible than are other legislatures.

We have used three measures of fiscal restraint or responsibility to determine the linkage between use of the item veto and degree of legislative discipline. The first measure was the propensity of the legislature to make decisions on the basis of benefits for the districts of legislators. Such behavior is often referred to as pork barrel and is generally considered wasteful and inefficient. To measure such propensity, we asked the respondents to indicate if "addition of items benefitting constituents or districts of individual legislators tends to characterize legislative changes in the executive budget each year." Fifty-six percent of all respondents indicated agreement with this statement. Where legislatures have this characteristic, governors might be expected to use their veto power to restrain the legislature. Our data do not necessarily support this proposition. Nine of the 17 respondents (53 percent) with governors who used the item veto less than three times per year characterized their state legislatures as adding pork barrel benefits to the executive budget compared to eight of 13 respondents (62 percent) from states where the veto was used three or more times. While governors are slightly more likely to use the veto in states with a pork barrel legislature, this tendency is too slight to attach importance to it. A similar result is obtained when examining a second measure of pork barrel. Respondents were

asked to identify what kinds of information the legislature is most interested in during its consideration of the budget. The significance of an "agency's program for the districts of legislators" was cited by 10 of the 20 respondents from states where governors cast less than three vetoes per year and by seven of the 12 respondents from states where governors cast three or more vetoes per year. While we have chosen three vetoes as a cutting line for discussion purposes, other divisions of the data provide a similar conclusion; vetoes tend not to be cast more often in states having legislatures with a tendency to use pork barrel.

A second measure of legislative restraint used to assess the linkage between veto use and legislative responsibility was the propensity of the legislature to increase the budget recommendations of the governor. Nineteen of 41 respondents characterized the legislature as tending to add to the governor's proposed expenditure levels compared to 14 of 41 who said that the legislature tends to decrease the overall expenditure amounts. If the veto is used to promote restraint by governors, presumably it would be used against legislatures tending to increase executive recommendations.

Just as the line-item veto is not used as an instrument to block pork barrel, it is similarly not used to maintain the expenditure levels of the executive budget. Forty-two percent of the respondents (15 of 36) from states having the line-item veto characterized legislative changes in the executive budget each year as being an "overall increase in proposed expenditures." Seven of the 17 respondents (41 percent) from states where less than three vetoes per year were cast characterized legislative behavior in this manner compared to six of the 13 (46 percent) from states with three or more vetoes per year. Again, different divisions of the respondents by number of vetoes cast does not affect the conclusion.

A third measure of legislative restraint used to assess the linkage between use of the item veto and legislative responsibility was the respondents' perception of the consideration of an agency's efficiency in legislative decisions about the agency's budget. Presumably, governors who use the item veto to promote efficiency would use it more frequently against the less "efficiency minded" legislatures. Thirteen of 20 (65 percent) respondents from states where governors have the item veto and where the chief executive has used the veto less than three times each year indicated that such information was important to the legislature, compared to 9 of the 12 respondents from states where the veto was used at least three times annually in the three years prior to the survey. Although the difference between the two groups is in the predicted direction of supporting a linkage between concern for efficiency and use of the veto, it is too small to conclude that the use of the veto is strongly related to executive concern for fiscal restraint.

Perhaps the absence of a linkage between the use of the veto and fiscal restraint results from the ability of some legislatures to avoid the veto by writing appropriation bills so as to make such gubernatorial action difficult. As noted earlier, 16 of the 37 respondents from states where the governor possesses the item veto reported that their legislatures write the appropriation act so as to limit the veto opportunities of the governor. If legislatures in these states are successful, the item veto would tend not to be used even though the legislatures might be fiscally irresponsible. Thus, the failure of our data to establish a linkage between the use of the veto and fiscal irresponsibility on the part of the legislature may result from successful legislative undermining of the veto. In fact, where legislatures are perceived by respondents as writing appropriation acts so as to limit veto opportunities of governors, governors are less likely to use the line-item veto. Ten of 15 respondents from states where the governor has used the item veto no more than one time in the last three years reported such a legislative strategy compared to 6 of 17 respondents from states where governors have used the veto more often.

Even though this legislative activity is linked to reduced use of the item veto, it does not appear related to fiscal irresponsibility on the part of legislatures. Indeed, legislatures engaged in so writing appropriation bills are apparently more fiscally disciplined than other legislatures. Fifteen of the 16 respondents from states where the legislatures are perceived to write restrictive appropriation acts reported that their legislatures seek information about the efficiency of an agency in considering its budget compared to 8 of the 20 respondents from other legislatures. Only 6 of the 16 respondents from the former states characterized legislative changes in the executive budget as adding benefits for districts and constituents compared with 13 of the 20 respondents from the latter states. Respondents (8 of 16) from the former states were also more likely to characterize legislatures as acting to reduce executive budgets than were respondents (5 of 20) from the latter. In essence, legislatures which write appropriation acts so as to limit gubernatorial vetoes are fiscally more restrained than other legislatures. The absence of a linkage between the use of the item veto and fiscal irresponsibility does not seem to result from legislatures' taking the veto away from the governors.

While the line-item veto may not be used to encourage fiscal discipline, does evidence show that its presence may encourage fiscal restraint? Specifically, do states with governors who lack this power have less restrained legislatures than do other states? Our data suggest that the two types of states are not necessarily different in regard to fiscal restraints. While legislatures in states where the governor possesses the item veto are more likely to reduce the expenditure requests of governors, they are in fact more prone to use pork barrel and less likely to use information on efficiency. In essence, the presence of the veto does not seem to produce fiscal restraint.

In fact, on the basis of these data it could be argued that the presence of the veto discourages legislative discipline.

Partisanship and the Veto

Previous research on the relationship between partisanship and gubernatorial use of the general veto found that governors of states where the opposition party controls the legislative branch veto a higher proportion of bills than their counterparts from states where the same party controls both branches of government.[18] A linkage between partisanship and use of the item veto also exists. Republican governors might be expected to use the veto more than Democratic governors. In the past, Republicans have decried the spending policies of Democrats. The line-item veto would theoretically offer Republican governors an opportunity to make a symbolic if not tangible point. As can be seen in Table 1, Republican governors are more likely to use the line-item veto than are Democratic governors. According to our respondents, eight of the 17 (47 percent) Democratic governors used it more than one time annually compared to 12 of the 16 (75 percent) Republican governors.

Table 1
Number of item vetoes cast in each state[a] by party of governor

	Number of Item Vetoes in Each State in Three Years Prior to the Survey			
Party of Governor	*None*	*One or Less per Year*	*Between One and Three Times per Year*	*Three or More Times per Year*
Democratic	5	4	2	6
Republican	0	4	5	7

[a] This table excludes respondents from states lacking the item veto power and from states where the party of the governor changed in the three-year period prior to survey.

The line-item veto is also more likely to be used where the governor of one party faces a legislature wholly or partially controlled by the opposition party. This statement appears true for Democrats as well as Republicans. However, the latter are more likely to confront this situation than are Democratic governors in the states. Consider the seven Republican governors in the cell of highest veto use in Table 1. Five of the seven governors confronted legislatures in which the number of Democrats outnumbered Republicans. In fact, five of the seven confronted legislatures with both houses under Democratic control. On the other hand, three of the four Republican governors who cast one or fewer vetoes per year faced legislatures in which Republicans outnumbered Democrats. Only one of the four (a Southern governor) faced a legislature with both houses controlled by Democrats.

The same point can be made about Democratic governors. Of the six governors in Table 1 who cast three or more vetoes annually, two faced legislatures where both houses were controlled by Republicans, and one faced a legislature with divided control. Two of the other three governors faced legislatures where Republicans were within six votes (three seats) of the Democrats in one house. The sixth Democratic governor of this group was from a Southern state with a legislature known for its professionalism, independence and a relatively large (for a Southern state) Republican contingent (33 percent of the legislature). The five Democratic governors in the table who had not cast a veto were from states where Democrats solidly controlled both houses. For the five states combined, Democrats held 594 seats to 120 seats for the Republicans. Three of the states in this group are Southern.

The relationship between the party of the governor, the partisan nature of the legislature, and the use of the veto is further demonstrated in Table 2. Where control of both executive and legislative

Table 2
Number of item vetoes cast in each state[a] by division between governor and legislature in party identification

	Number of Item Vetoes Cast in the States in the Three Years Prior to the Survey			
Party Affiliations of Governor and Legislature	*None*	*One or Less per Year*	*Between One and Three Times per Year*	*Three or More Times per Year*
Governor of same party as majority in both houses of legislature	5	4	2	3
Governor of different party as majority in one or both houses of legislature	0	6	3	10

[a] This table excludes respondents from states lacking the item veto power and from states where the party of the governor changed in the three-year period prior to survey.

Table 3
Legislatures characterized as using pork[a] by partisan nature

Partisan Nature of Legislature	Legislature Does Not Tend to Use Pork[a]	Legislature Does Tend to Use Pork[a]
Both houses have Democratic majorities	10 (7)[b]	15 (7)[b]
One house has Democratic majority and one house has Republican majority	3	1
Both houses have Republican majorities	8	5

[a] The respondents characterized legislative changes in the executive budget each year as benefitting constituents or districts of individual legislators.

[b] Numbers in parentheses exclude the Southern states which were members of the Confederacy.

branches is in the province of the same party, the veto is used much less frequently than in states with divided control. At least, two (California and Florida) of the three states in the cell (three or more vetoes with control of both branches by one party) that contradicts this point have legislatures known for their professionalism and independence.[19] Partisanship and the use of the veto are intricately related. This finding is consistent with research on use of gubernatorial vetoes in the states.[20] Furthermore, it is neither a Republican nor Democratic instrument, it is used by both. In that Republican governors tend to face legislatures under the influence of the other party more often than Democratic governors face Republican legislatures, the line-item veto does tend to take on a Republican flavor.

When Republican governors use the veto, they may be more concerned about fiscal restraint than Democratic governors. At least, the characterizations of legislative behavior offered by respondents suggest such a difference between Democratic and Republican legislatures. The latter appear to be more concerned about fiscal conservatism. Consider the matter of pork barrel legislation. The data in Table 3 suggest that states with Democratic legislatures are more prone to use pork. However, many of the states where pork is present are Southern. Controlling for the Southern states results in a great deal of similarity between states with Democratic and Republican legislatures. The propensity of Southern state legislatures for pork may result from the absence of party discipline in these legislatures and/or the close linkage between state and local governments in the South. In any event, controlling for Southern states, the difference between Republican and Democratic legislatures diminishes in regard to pork. Yet, there

is evidence of a greater sense of fiscal restraint on the part of Republican legislatures.

Republican legislatures are more likely to place greater value on information regarding efficiency when they consider the budget requests of agencies. Ten of 12 legislatures (83 percent) with Republican majorities in both houses value such information according to our respondents, compared to 17 of 26 (65 percent) legislatures with both houses controlled by the Democrats. Also, Democratic legislatures tend to increase executive budgets while Republican legislatures are more likely to decrease executive budgets. The respondents characterized only two of 10 Republican legislatures as tending to increase executive budgets compared to a similar description by 13 of 23 (57 percent) respondents of Democratic legislatures. In regard to decreasing executive budgets seven of 12 respondents from states with Republican legislatures so characterized the behavior of their assemblies compared to only five of 23 (22 percent) respondents from states with both houses of the legislature controlled by Democrats. This information suggests that Republican legislatures and presumably Republican governors are fiscally more conservative. When Republican governors use the item veto, it is more likely to serve as an instrument of fiscal restraint.

Conclusion

Is the line-item veto used as an instrument for fiscal restraint or an instrument for partisanship? Often, it is a partisan instrument that may have the result of promoting fiscal restraint. Of course, any time the item veto is used, a state's budget is reduced.

However, reductions are not the same as efficiency. Indeed, reductions can be inefficient. Furthermore, efficiency is a relative term. What may seem an extravagance for one person may be seen as a necessity by another. It is easier to portray the item veto as an instrument of the executive increasing his or her legislative powers rather than as an instrument for efficiency.

Does the item veto encourage fiscal responsibility? The line-item veto has been around in most states for a considerable time. Legislatures in states with it do not seem more fiscally responsible than legislatures in other states. Of course, our data are not longitudinal, and we cannot measure change following the introduction of the veto. However, given its partisan use, the item veto probably has had minimal effect on making legislatures or state government fiscally more restrained.

Because the president does not have the line-item veto, we can only speculate about how it might be used if established in the future. However, based upon state experiences with the item veto we anticipate it would enhance the president's ability to deal with the Congress on matters of a partisan nature, but it is not likely to have much impact on such fiscal matters as the size of the deficit.

Notes

1. Richard E. Cohen, "Congress Plays Election-Year Politics with Line-Item Veto Proposal," *National Journal*, vol. 16 (February 11, 1984), pp. 274–276.
2. "Reagan's Deficit-Cutting Bid May Spotlight Line-Item Veto," *Congressional Quarterly*, vol. 42 (January 21, 1984), pp. 114–115.
3. Though the item veto may have enhanced the president's power in these cases, figures from the Congressional Budget Office suggest that the utility of the item veto as an instrument to reduce the federal deficit is limited. The CBO has noted that a large percentage (54 percent) of the federal budget would be exempt from the item veto. Included in this exemption would be such non-discretionary items as entitlements and interest on the federal debt. If defense expenditures are added to these non-discretionary items, only 18 percent of the budget contains domestic items that would be subject to the item veto. *Ibid.*
4. Russell M. Ross and Fred Schwengel, "An Item Veto for the President," *Presidential Studies Quarterly*, vol. 12 (Winter 1982), pp. 66–79.
5. In Maryland the governor may only item veto supplemental appropriation bills and capital construction bills.

In several other states, limitations are placed on the use of the item veto. Council of State Governments, *The Book of the States 1982-1983* (Lexington, Ky.: Council of State Governments, 1982), pp. 212–213.
6. V. L. Wilkinson, "The Item Veto in the American Constitutional System," *Georgetown Law Journal*, vol. 15 (November 1980), pp. 106–133; Roger H. Wells, "The Item Veto and State Budget Reform," *American Political Science Review*, vol. 18 (November 1924), pp. 782–791.
7. For an example of such behavior in Pennsylvania, see Wells, *op. cit.*, p. 784.
8. Thad L. Beyle and Robert Hueffner, "Quips and Quotes from Old Governors to New," *Public Administration Review*, vol. 43 (May/June 1983), pp. 268–269.
9. Wells, *op. cit.*, pp. 784–786; Timothy P. Burke, "The Partial Veto Power: Legislation by the Governor," *Washington Law Review*, vol. 49 (1974), pp. 603–615.
10. William H. Taft, *Our Chief Magistrate and His Powers* (New York: Columbia University Press, 1916), p. 27.
11. Wilkinson, *loc. cit.*
12. For a discussion of the state of Washington as an exception to this point, see Burke, *loc. cit.* For a discussion of Wisconsin as another exception to the point, see "The Use of the Partial Veto in Wisconsin," *Information Bulletin 75-lb-6* (Madison: Legislative Reference Bureau, State of Wisconsin, September 1975), pp. 1–6.
13. Ada E. Beckman, "The Item Veto Power of the Executive," *Temple Law Quarterly*, vol. 31 (Fall 1957), pp. 27–34.
14. J. M. Vaughn, "Constitutional Law—The Governor's Item Veto Power," *Missouri Law Review*, vol. 39 (Winter 1974), pp. 105–110.
15. Previous studies have raised questions about the efficiency of the item veto as a means of fiscal restraint. In 1950 Frank Prescott, referring to his study and that of Wells in 1924, said, "The doubts pertaining to its efficacy as an instrument of budgetary control which were cast upon this device by Professor Wells some twenty-five years ago appear to have been well founded in light of the new evidence." Frank W. Prescott, "The Executive Veto in American States," *Western Political Quarterly*, vol. 3 (March 1950), pp. 112; Wells, *loc. cit.*
16. Wilkinson, *op. cit.*, p. 122; Beyle and Hueffner, *loc. cit.*
17. Wilkinson, *op. cit.*, pp. 122–123; "Item Veto," *State Policy Reports* (November 1983), pp. 22–23.
18. Charles W. Wiggins, "Executive Vetoes and Legislative Overrides in the American States," *The Journal of Politics*, vol. 42 (November 1980), pp. 1110–1117.
19. Alan Rosenthal, *Legislative Life: People, Process and Performance in the States* (New York: Harper and Row, 1981); Citizens Conference on State Legislatures, *The Sometimes Governments* (Kansas City, Mo.: Citizens Conference on State Legislatures, 1971).
20. Wiggins, *op. cit.*, p. 115.

25
The Continuing Search for a Popular Tax

Alice M. Rivlin
The Brookings Institution

For the next few years, perhaps for a longer time, federal tax policy will be inseparably intertwined with deficit-reduction policy. As a result, tax decisions will be more closely related to spending decisions and attention will shift to new kinds of taxes.

For decades, federal tax policy debates have been quite separate from debates over what these taxes are supposed to finance. Federal tax controversy has focused heavily on the major general revenue sources, the individual and corporate income taxes. Economists have analyzed the effects of these levies on economic behavior and on the distribution of income, and this analysis has played a considerable role in policy formulation. The substantial reduction in marginal tax rates, as well as base broadening, indexing, and changes in the treatment of depreciation and consumer interest, were greatly influenced by the views of economists.

The frequency of recent changes in the income tax rules, capped by the surprisingly comprehensive tax reform legislation of 1986, have left both politicians and tax reformers with little appetite for further tinkering with the income taxes. Moreover, the continuing large deficits in the federal budget, only partially offset by growing surpluses in the Social Security trust fund, have forced policymakers to focus on a new aspect of an old problem: how to get citizens to want less from their federal government or be willing to pay more for it.

As a consequence, the tax debates of the next few years are likely to be less concerned with the equity and efficiency of taxes than with their political

The Brookings Institution, 1775 Massachusetts Avenue, NW, Washington, D.C. 20036. The views set forth here are solely my own and do not necessarily represent the opinions of the trustees, officers, or other staff members of the Brookings Institution.
Source: AEA Papers and Proceedings 79, no. 2 (May 1989): 113–117. Reprinted by permission of the American Economic Association.

acceptability. Economists may find themselves borrowing the tools of sociologists and psychologists to find out how people think about taxes and what kinds are least objectionable. In the process, attention seems likely to shift from general revenues to taxes earmarked for particular purposes, from broad-based taxes to user fees, premiums, and narrowly based revenues, and from income taxes to consumption taxes.

The New Conventional Wisdom

In the late 1980s, candidates for federal office and their advisers appear to find two propositions self-evident. First, voters have strong negative feelings about federal taxes. Tax cutting is popular and proposing a tax increase is political suicide. Second, voters have positive feelings about government services, although not necessarily about "government" in the abstract. Successful candidates need to make at least modest claims that they will do more and avoid specifying any program they will cut.

There is one apparent exception to the tax rule: taxes held in trust funds and earmarked for specific purposes can be raised. There was no perceptible backlash when the gasoline tax was raised in 1983, presumably because the increase was thought necessary to fix the roads. While no one would claim payroll taxes are popular, voters have tolerated repeated increases in the taxes that fund Social Security, including the substantial increases in contributions required to shift the Social Security system from a pay-as-you-go mode to the accumulation of surpluses designed to prefund the retirement claims of the baby-boom generation. Payroll tax increases are apparently regarded by voters as necessary to pay for Social Security benefits. General revenue levies, however, appear not to be seen as necessary to fund any particular level of general services. Social Security trust fund revenues have risen from 3.4 percent of GNP in 1970 to 5.1 percent in 1988; while other tax revenue has fallen from 16.1 to 14.2 percent.

This set of political attitudes—or at least the politicians' belief that they exist—has perpetuated the new fiscal phenomenon of the 1980s: a deficit in the federal government's general fund of about $200 billion. This general fund deficit is projected to increase gradually over the next few years if policies are not changed, even if moderate growth in the economy continues. Only because the general fund deficit is partially offset by the rising surplus in the Social Security trust funds, is the unified deficit projected to decline absent tax or spending changes. Unless policies are altered, the Congressional Budget Office projects that federal revenues outside the Social Security trust fund will still cover only about 80 percent of spending in fiscal year 1993.

Many economists have pointed out that the current general fund deficit comes at a singularly inappropriate moment in U.S. economic history (Robert Litan, Robert Lawrence, and Charles Schultze, 1988). The relatively small labor force of the first half of the next century will have to be substantially more productive to achieve a rising standard of living for itself and for the relatively large retired population simultaneously. With private saving rates at low levels, reducing public dissaving by reducing the general fund deficit is crucial to generating the increased saving needed to finance productivity-increasing investment. This reasoning implies the desirability of running a surplus in the unified budget, thus using at least part of the growing Social Security surplus to reduce federal debt held by the public, and the rest to fund increases in public investment designed to increase future growth.

The notion that the reserves accumulating in the Social Security trust fund ought to be invested for the benefit of future Social Security recipients has common sense appeal, especially to the baby-boom generation, but it implies actions that collide with the new conventional wisdom that voters want more government services and lower general purpose taxes. Politicians and public policy analysts may be called on for some creative thinking to resolve the impasse.

Exploring the Conventional Wisdom

Strongly held convictions about political acceptability of public actions often rest on flimsy evidence. For example, it was widely believed in Washington that taxing Social Security benefits would set off a firestorm of protest, but, in fact, the inclusion of part of Social Security benefits in taxable income for the first time (part of the 1983 reforms) proved uneventful. The withholding of interest and dividends,

which involved no new tax liability, unexpectedly provoked far more outrage. It would be useful to know a lot more about how people feel about paying for federal services than can be gleaned from repeatedly citing the fact that Walter F. Mondale advocated a tax increase and lost the presidential election in 1984.

The public would also like to pay less for privately produced goods and services and to have more of them. Nevertheless, paying for goods and services received from private producers is regarded as normal and rarely arouses protest, while paying for the general services of the federal government is now perceived by politicians as widely resented. One step toward finding a politically acceptable way to reduce the general fund deficit would be to find out more about the nature of this resentment and the reasons for it.

Taxes may be more resented than prices simply because they are compulsory. Price increases also arouse resistance when the increase involves a service, such as rent or medical care, which the buyer does not regard as optional. The greater willingness of taxpayers to pay earmarked taxes, however, suggests that resistance relates less to the compulsory nature of federal general purpose taxes than to the services they finance. Taxpayers may have no clear idea of what the money is spent for, they may believe that the money is spent wastefully or even fraudulently, or that a substantial part of it goes for services of which they disapprove. Private firms spend a great deal on marketing and advertising to convince the buying public that they give value for the customers' money. Public agencies, barred from activities that could be regarded as propaganda or lobbying, have few ways of informing the public what services are being provided. Federal grants for domestic programs, moreover, are often commingled with state and local funds and not identified as federal spending, even to immediate beneficiaries.

Other reasons for resentment of federal taxes may relate to the perceived unfairness of taxes themselves, rather than to the services they finance. Part of the impetus for reform of the federal income tax was taxpayer perception that the tax was unfair, that loopholes enabled rich people with ingenious tax lawyers to escape paying their fair share. The 1986 tax reform probably did not reduce these perceptions much, and the publicity accorded the high profits of drug dealers and Wall Street financiers may feed the general suspicion that a few high rollers make a lot of money that probably is not taxed.

In sum, if taxpayers perceive that they pay an unfair share of general federal taxes that support vaguely understood and inefficiently produced services, the deficit in the federal general fund may prove hard to reduce. Moving beyond this kind of speculation to more solid information on how the public views federal taxes and the spending they finance would help policymakers a lot.

Deficit Neutrality

Tax policy in the deficit era is likely to bear the impact of a recent legislative innovation, the deficit-neutral bill. The tax reform legislation of 1986 was greatly influenced by the announced intention of all parties to avoid adding to the deficit by making the bill "revenue neutral." Since each revenue-losing amendment had to be accompanied by a revenue gainer or an equivalent increase in tax rates, the result was fewer loopholes.

The deficit-neutral principle also strongly influenced the Medicare "catastrophic" legislation of 1988. New benefits for long stays in hospitals and large prescription drug costs were financed by increases in the premium for Supplementary Medical Insurance with part of the premium dependent on income for the first time. This approach insured that the cost of the program would be borne by the beneficiaries themselves, especially those best able to afford it. Another example is the superfund program to clean up toxic wastes, which is financed by a special package of business taxes.

Growing concern about the burden of nursing home and home care costs for the disabled elderly has generated strong political support for federal long-term care benefits. Discussions of alternative approaches are proceeding on the general assumption that whatever long-term care program is enacted will have to be self-financing.

User Fees, Benefit-Taxes, and Earmarking

As long as a general fund deficit persists, which could be a long time, the use of specially tailored revenues to fund new programs seems likely to continue. Reliance on user fees to finance federal expenditures and on trust funds to segregate revenues for special purposes will doubtless increase.

Greater reliance on user fees could have significant efficiency benefits. Increasing fees for waterways and harbors could lead to more cost-effective decisions and fewer white elephant projects. Increasing fees for irrigation water and grazing on public lands, as well as moving toward unsubsidized timber sales from national forests, would lead to more economic use of public resources and reduce environmental degradation. Recent analysis has indicated substantial benefits from shifting the basis of highway-user taxes to better reflect pavement wear and congestion costs (Kenneth Small, Clifford Winston, and Carol Evans, forthcoming). There is also potential for increased financing of regulatory activities out of fees on the industries regulated, and for reducing subsidies to train passengers, general aviation, boat owners, national park users, and other direct beneficiaries of federal services.

User fees have always appealed more to economists than to politicians. Applying them retrospectively causes genuine and often drastic hardship for those who have relied on the subsidized service. Transition benefits for those directly injured—workers and sawmill owners dependent on subsidized timber, for example—might make some of these changes more politically attractive.

If it is true that taxes are more acceptable when the taxpayer knows exactly what they are to be used for, then the search for politically feasible ways of funding federal activities is likely to involve new types of dedicated taxes. Possibilities include estate tax increases to finance long-term care expenses of the elderly, tobacco and alcohol taxes to finance health programs, energy-use fees to finance conservation and pollution control, and perhaps even an income tax surcharge to fund national defense.

In general, dedicated taxes seem most likely to find political favor as a means of financing new services and to be of little help in reducing the existing deficit. There is some interest in Congress and elsewhere, however, in designing a dedicated deficit-reduction tax that could be used only to close the deficit gap without financing any new spending. The tax might be triggered by achievement of a specified reduction in spending—the opposite of a "last resort" tax enacted after spending reduction has failed.

Getting the Deficit Down—Phase One

The big challenge to the new administration and Congress in the fiscal arena is to get the general fund deficit on a sustained downward track toward balance, so that surplus in the unified budget is a realistic possibility at high employment by the mid- to late 1990s. Given the new administration's strong campaign stance against tax increases, congressional weariness with continued spending cuts, and perceived pent-up pressure for new federal social spending, the task seems daunting indeed. Only strong presidential leadership and a willingness to negotiate a genuine compromise with Congress will avoid continuation of the Reagan era deadlock.

Assuming that some revenues must be part of the compromise, what should they be? The argument for moving toward a broad-based federal consumption tax, such as a value-added tax, to reduce private consumption while raising public saving, is strong, but, in the near term, irrelevant. The newly elected president could not conceivably retreat from his election promise and agree to a major new tax, Congress and the country are unfamiliar with value-added taxes and understandably wary of them, and, in any case, the Treasury could hardly be expected to be ready to collect a complicated new tax without several years of lead time. Revenues to be raised quickly must come from taxes already on the books. Leading candidates are taxes for which a substantial rationale for the increase exists independent of the need for revenue. Alcohol and tobacco taxes are low by historical standards and serve to discourage unhealthy consumption. Gasoline taxes are extremely low by world standards and raising them would encourage oil conservation and provide incentives for producing more fuel-efficient cars. A gas tax increase might be combined with a moderate oil import fee to reduce the opposition of the domestic oil industry. The income tax offers some prime candidates as well, especially in combination with regressive increases in consumption taxes. The anomaly of a top-bracket marginal income tax rate rising to 33 percent and then falling back to 28 percent could be corrected by keeping the top rate at 33 percent, and more base broadening could clearly be defended on grounds of fairness and better use of resources, as well as revenue. Modest movement toward taxation of fringe benefits and limiting large mortgage interest deductions ought to be considered.

A Bolder Program: Devolution and Tax-Sharing

It is possible, although not easy, to imagine the administration and the Congress making substantial progress on deficit reduction by whittling down spending and raising revenues in ways that could be thought of as user fees or conservation measures rather than "new taxes." For the next couple of years this is probably the most that can be hoped.

It is not realistic, however, to expect that this painstaking piecemeal process will both move the budget to surplus and allow the kind of public investments that will give us rapid technological progress and a substantially more productive labor force. For this there must be more revenue—at some level of government.

One solution is to find a new source of revenue for the federal government, such as a value-added tax (VAT). The advantages of a VAT are that it would bring in substantial revenue and also serve to discourage consumption. The disadvantages, however, include likely opposition from state and local governments, who think broad consumer taxation is their prerogative, and, more important, that it makes increases in federal spending all too easy.

The only alternative, however—besides abandoning the goal of unified budget surplus—is to rethink what the federal government ought to be doing and turn over major federal functions to the states, a process sometimes known as "devolution." The federal government could concentrate on defense, social insurance, and a few obviously national functions like air traffic control and funding basic scientific research. Other functions—housing subsidies, education, health services, highways (except interstates) and economic development—would then be clearly the responsibilities of state and local governments. Rough calculations indicate possible devolution of federal programs costing about $70 billion (in 1988 dollars).

But, even assuming less taxpayer resistance to funding more visible services at the state level, where would the states get the resources to improve education, child development, health services, job training, and the other prerequisites of a high-growth economy? It would be harder for states to raise taxes than for the federal government, because they have to compete with each other to attract new industry.

Hence, an attractive possibility is to combine the two ideas: devolve major functions to the states, but have the federal government collect a VAT or a national sales tax and pass it on automatically (on a formula basis) to the states. This would capitalize on (and accelerate) the new vigor and responsiveness of state and local government, leave the federal government doing what it clearly does best, and resolve the budget deficit problem at the same time.

References

LITAN, ROBERT E., LAWRENCE, ROBERT Z. and SCHULTZE, CHARLES L., *American Living Standards: Threats and Challenges,* Washington: Brookings Institution, 1988.

SMALL, KENNETH, WINSTON, CLIFFORD and EVANS, CAROL, *Road Work: A New Highway Policy,* forthcoming.

26
The Federal Budget and the Nation's Economic Health

Charles L. Schultze

In fiscal 1990 the federal government will run its eleventh large budget deficit. Not since 1979 has the deficit been less than 2 percent of gross national product, and not since 1974 below 1 percent. In the early years of large deficits—1980 through 1983—they did little or no harm because the U.S. economy was in a recession or just recovering from one. Excess capacity was available to meet the demands of both the private economy and the federal government. Borrowing to finance the federal deficit neither crowded out domestic investment nor required large amounts of overseas borrowing. But since 1984 the nation has been running a string of substantial deficits in a fully employed economy.

A reversal of the buildup in defense spending in 1986 allowed the budget deficit to fall from 5.4 to 3.2 percent in 1988, but progress has been slow since then, and the 1990 deficit will still be 2.5 percent. This string of large deficits has dominated budget making for a number of years, sharply limiting new initiatives and the growth of most existing civilian programs—which some view as a major evil and others as a blessing in disguise.

Until recently all possible sources of maneuver to relieve the budget squeeze were apparently blocked. Presidents Reagan and Bush were able to prevent any significant increase in taxes except payroll taxes. The defense buildup was halted in 1986, but the subsequent debate about the defense budget took place within fairly narrow limits, producing neither sharp reductions nor large further increases. Congress avoided major increases in program spending but, with a few exceptions early in

The author wishes to thank Bruce K. MacLaury, George L. Perry, and Alice M. Rivlin for their comments and Allen L. Sebrell for his research assistance.
Source: Henry J. Aaron (ed.), *Setting National Priorities: Policies for the Nineties* (Washington, D.C.: The Brookings Institution, 1990), pp. 19–63. Reprinted by permission.

Reagan's first term, proved unwilling to enact the deep program cuts he repeatedly proposed. Meanwhile, the mounting federal debt and the high interest rates (caused mainly by the large budget deficits) kept pushing up federal expenditures for interest on the debt. Just the *increase* in interest payments on the debt during the 1980s accounted for the entire budget deficit in 1990.

The administration's budget for 1991, like all of its predecessors in recent years, forecasts a substantial reduction in the deficit, from $138 billion in 1990 to $63 billion in 1991. Such a deficit would meet, by a hair, the Gramm-Rudman targets and would amount to only 1.2 percent of GNP, the lowest share since 1974. The actual budget deficit in 1991 will almost surely be much larger than the administration's projections, which are based on a quite optimistic economic forecast and presume Congress will agree to a series of expenditure cuts it has repeatedly refused to enact. A twelfth successive year of substantial budget deficits is a virtual certainty.

In this chapter I argue that large deficits are significantly harming America's future growth prospects because of what they are doing to national saving and investment, and make the case for converting the deficits into surpluses over the next six to seven years. After reviewing recent trends in spending and evaluating costs and benefits of major federal programs, I suggest that a combination of reasonable cuts in defense and entitlement programs and a modest tax increase could finance both some needed spending increases and the conversion of the current budget deficit into the desired surplus.

How Large Are Budget Deficits Likely to Be?

The administration not only projects a rapid fall in the budget deficit in the coming fiscal year to $63 billion, it also foresees a gradual conversion of the deficit into a surplus starting in 1993. Moreover, this conversion from deficit to surplus would occur even as the large annual surplus in the social security trust fund was being removed from the calculation of the budget balance. And the administration projects the achievement of this objective with only modest cuts in the (inflation-adjusted) level of defense spending. These projections, however, are far too optimistic, both for 1991 and for the longer term, given the budget policies the administration is proposing.

The Congressional Budget Office (CBO) estimates that with unchanged budget policies the 1991 deficit is likely to be $134 billion, slightly above last year's $127 billion.[1] The CBO's deficit projection is higher than the administration's partly because its forecasts of economic growth and interest rates for 1990 and 1991 match the average of outside economic fore-casters, while the administration projects higher economic growth and lower interest rates for both years.[2] The administration's estimates also assume Congress will accept some $15 billion in proposed spending cuts, most of which have been repeatedly rejected. The administration further counts on raising some $5 billion in additional revenues from its proposed reduction in capital gains taxes, based on the assumption that stockholders will rush to sell appreciated assets once the tax is reduced. (Whatever this tax change does to revenues in the first year, it will lose money over longer periods of time.)

If recent history is any guide, Congress will cut defense spending modestly below the president's request. Some small cuts will be made in civilian spending, but these are likely to be nearly matched by increases elsewhere. For purposes of trying to meet the Gramm-Rudman deficit target for the year ($64 billion), Congress will probably agree to accept the administration's rosy forecast. But in the end, the actual budget outcome for fiscal 1991 may not be much below the $134 billion CBO projection.

The administration's long-term forecast of a budget surplus by 1993, achieved without counting the surplus in the social security trust fund, is based on economic assumptions equally as optimistic as those used to estimate the 1991 budget. The CBO projection of the current services budget—that is, a budget with no changes in laws governing taxes or entitlement programs and with discretionary spend-ing increasing only enough to offset inflation—shows much higher deficits (see Table 1). By definition the CBO budget estimates do not include the civilian and military spending cuts that are incorporated in the administration's projections, which build up to more than $70 billion by 1995. But even apart from these conceptual differences, the CBO projects higher deficits. The major reason lies in the economic assumptions underlying the estimates. The admin-istration assumes economic growth at an average of 3.1 percent a year between 1990 and 1995, despite the widely held view among economists that the capacity or potential growth of the U.S. economy at the present time lies in the neighborhood of 2.5 percent a year. The CBO accepts that view and assumes a 2.4 percent long-term growth rate. This seemingly small difference between growth assump-tions produces a difference in national output and income that by 1995 yields some $63 billion in additional revenues.

Along with higher economic growth, the admin-istration projects a large fall in interest rates: it foresees ninety-day Treasury bill rates at 4.4 per-cent in 1995, compared with a CBO projection of 5.8 percent (itself quite optimistic relative to the 8.1 percent level in 1989). Each percentage point of lower interest rates has a major budget impact, given the $2 $\frac{1}{2}$ trillion federal debt.

Since taxable income and federal revenues will continue to rise in line with real economic growth and inflation combined, why, in a growing economy, does the CBO budget projection, allowing for neither new nor expanded programs, continue to show such a large deficit? Table 2 provides the answer. In addi-tion to increases needed simply to cover inflation—

Table 1
Congressional Budget Office projections of current services deficit, fiscal years 1990–95[a]
billions of dollars

Item	1990	1991	1992	1993	1994	1995
Outlays	1,194	1,271	1,345	1,425	1,488	1,557
Revenues	1,067	1,137	1,204	1,277	1,355	1,438
Deficit	127	134	141	148	133	119

Source: Congressional Budget Office, *An Analysis of the President's Budgetary Proposals for Fiscal Year 1991,* March 1990.
[a] Excludes noninterest outlays of the Resolution Trust Corporation. See [note] 1.

Table 2
Components of increased outlays, fiscal years 1990–95
billions of dollars

Component	Increase
Inflation	199
Increased use of medical care in federal programs	61
Work load, number of beneficiaries[a]	60
Interest on the debt	29
Other	14
TOTAL	363

Source: Congressional Budget Office: Testimony of Robert D. Reischauer before the Committee on the Budget, U.S. House of Representatives, January 31, 1990, table 6, p. 18.
[a] Includes the rise in real benefits for new social security beneficiaries.

which affects revenues and expenditures about equally—the federal government has many entitlement programs under which the number of beneficiaries grows each year. It has two large programs for medical care—medicare for the elderly and disabled and medicaid for the poor—in which prices are rising faster than general inflation and the utilization of medical services per beneficiary is also growing. And, of course, so long as the budget runs huge deficits, servicing that debt costs more each year. Indeed, had the CBO not been somewhat optimistic in its projections, the current services deficit would be projected at an even higher level.

In the absence of major changes in budget policy, the deficit is likely to remain near current dollar levels for the first half of the decade. This would imply some decline in the deficit relative to GNP, from 2.3 percent in 1990 to 1.6 percent in 1995. But this improvement is made possible only by the large and growing surplus in the social security and other retirement trust funds, and the budget, exclusive of these funds, should be moving toward balance.

Why Worry About the Budget Deficit?

Had a representative group of economists or other budget experts been told in 1980 that the federal budget would average over 4 percent of GNP for six years—as it did from 1983 to 1989—almost all of them would have predicted an inflationary boom, followed by a severe cyclical contraction as the Federal Reserve slammed on the monetary policy brakes. In fact, the U.S. economy experienced not boom and bust, but seven years of relatively steady growth, with falling unemployment and moderate inflation. And this stability was achieved in the face of unprecedented budget and trade deficits, huge swings in the exchange rate of the dollar, and a stock market crash second only to that of the Great Depression.

Why the Deficit Produced No Economic Crisis

The principal reason for the economic stability of recent years has been the monetary policy of the Federal Reserve. In 1981 and 1982 the Federal Reserve broke the back of the double-digit inflation of the late 1970s with a severe bout of tight money accompanied by a deep recession. But since 1982 the Fed has consistently followed two major policy guidelines. First, it will do whatever it has to do by way of tight money and high interest rates to offset the potential economic overheating generated by the huge federal budget deficits. Thus, beginning in May 1983, only five months into the fledgling economic recovery, the Federal Reserve encouraged and engineered a rise in interest rates of more than 3 percentage points as a means of keeping the growth of aggregate demand within reasonable bounds. Again, in early 1987, as the falling dollar set off an export boom, the Fed boosted interest rates sharply to prevent inflationary pressures from getting out of hand.

Second, the Federal Reserve will not pursue monetary restriction to the point of bringing on another recession in order to push inflation lower. Despite the stern rhetoric when they testify before Congress, the chairman and the members of the Board of Governors seem quite prepared to live with

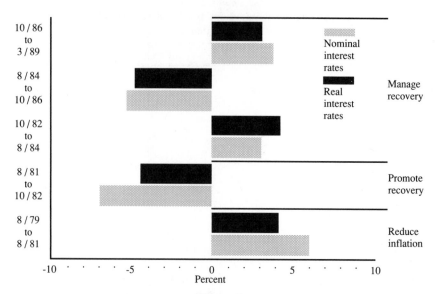

Figure 1

Change in short-term interest rates, selected periods, 1979–89[a]

the 4–5 percent inflation that has characterized the economy for most of the recent past. And so, in 1985 and 1986, when the budget deficit was being reduced and the growth of aggregate demand was easing, the Fed engineered a sharp decrease in interest rates. It did the same after the stock market crash of October 1987. Figure 1 shows how truly large the fluctuations in interest rates have been in recent years as the necessary accompaniment to a monetary stabilization policy operating in an environment of large expansionary budget deficits and essentially deregulated financial markets.[3]

The result of the Fed's monetary policy has not been complete economic stability; both GNP growth and inflation have fluctuated over the past seven years. But recession and even temporary stagnation have been avoided while major inflationary pressures have been kept in check. The political freedom that the public and the politicians have given the Fed to raise interest rates sharply when necessary is a prerequisite for this success.

It is, of course, impossible to rule out another large oil shock. Barring that, the odds are high that the Federal Reserve can continue to manage the economy without a major cyclical crisis even if the federal budget deficit remains large, so long as it

is free to raise interest rates when necessary. In the postwar period economic recoveries have not usually died from internal causes, but were killed either by outside shocks or by the severe monetary restrictions needed to reverse inflations that had been allowed to get under way. Only two of the seven postwar recessions were self-induced and those were quite mild. More important for the point at hand, however, even if a recession should occur, it will not be because the federal deficit remains at current levels.

Many of those who do worry that continuation of large budget deficits will lead to a cyclical crisis see that crisis coming in the form of a "dollar strike." Foreigners, observing that budget and current account deficits remain high, would suddenly lose confidence in the U.S. economy and desert the dollar in droves. The dollar's exchange value would plummet, import prices soar, and the U.S. price level rise sharply. To prevent the one-shot rise in the price level from turning into a persistent and possibly accelerating wage-price spiral, the Fed would have to tighten monetary policy severely, raise interest rates sharply, and put the economy through a recession.

This chain of events is possible, but unlikely. In the years ahead the dollar may well decline. But it is likely to do so precipitously only if international

Table 3
Net national saving, selected periods, 1951–89
Percent of national income[a]

Item	1951–80	1984–86	1989
Private saving[b]	9.3	8.1	6.8
Minus government dissaving (budget deficit)	–1.3	–5.0	–3.6
Equals national saving	8.0	3.1	3.2

Source: Author's calculations based on U.S. Department of Commerce, *The National Income and Product Accounts of the United States* (selected issues).

[a] Net national product is used as the measure of national income.

[b] Surplus in state and local insurance funds (mainly pension funds of state and local employees) classified as private saving.

investors come to believe that the Federal Reserve would lose its political freedom or its willingness to raise interest rates to neutralize inflationary effects of the budget deficit.

All in all, the wolf is not likely to appear at the door so long as the Federal Reserve continues to pursue a credible set of noninflationary policies—a quite reasonable assumption given recent history.

The Effect of High Deficits on National Saving and Interest Rates

That the nation can muddle through, sustaining large budget deficits without a cyclical crisis, does not mean that deficits do no harm and can be ignored. A successful economy ought not only to avoid recession and inflation, but also to provide for future growth. To that end it should save a reasonable fraction of its income to invest in increasing its stock of capital, which contributes to the growth of national living standards. In the past decade the national saving rate in the United States has fallen to an abysmally low level by comparison either with its own past (see Table 3) or with the saving rate of other modern economies. The rise in the federal budget has been a major contributor to that fall in national saving. Its elimination, and indeed conversion into a surplus, may be the only sure way to restore a healthy level of national saving.

National saving is that portion of national income *not* consumed by governments or households. A corresponding portion of national output is therefore available to invest in the nation's future growth, through the construction of new housing or business plant and equipment or through investment in profitable assets abroad. National saving is equal to private saving *plus* the government surplus, or (more commonly) *less* the government budget deficit, whose financing absorbs some of private saving, leaving that much less available for private investment.

National saving in the United States fell from an average of 8 percent of national income in the thirty years before 1980 to 3.2 percent in 1989. Both elements of national saving contributed to the decline: private saving fell and the federal budget deficit increased.[4] The current U.S. saving rate is also quite low compared with those in virtually all other industrial countries. Except for the United Kingdom, other large industrial countries save more than the United States by a wide margin.

When a country's saving rate collapses, it can free up the resources needed to satisfy the rise in public and private consumption demand in one of two ways: by curtailing domestic investment or by importing more than it exports, borrowing from abroad to finance the excess of imports. The United States adjusted to lower saving partly by decreasing investment and partly by supplementing its shrunken national saving through borrowing from abroad (see Figure 2). Although the trade deficit and the associated foreign borrowing forestalled an even larger drop in domestic investment, that approach has not been costless. The United States has abandoned its position as a net creditor abroad, is now a large and growing net debtor, and each year pays an increasing fraction of national income in debt service to foreigners.[5] The inflow of foreign saving into this country could conceivably continue for some time, but eventually it will taper off. Then domestic investment will have to be cut to fit within the limits of the shrunken national saving—unless in the meantime the problem of low saving has been solved.

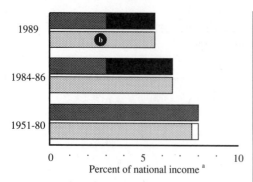

1989

1984-86

1951-80

0 · · · · 5 · · · · 10
Percent of national income ᵃ

a. National income = net national product.
b. Includes 0.5 percent statistical discrepancy.

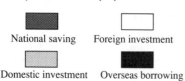

National saving   Foreign investment

Domestic investment   Overseas borrowing

Figure 2
Financing U.S. domestic investment,
selected periods, 1951–89

Low national saving has led to high real interest rates. (Real interest rates, which represent the true cost of borrowing, are the difference between quoted or "nominal" interest rates and the inflation rate.) The rise in interest rates was the mechanism by which investment was reduced and foreign funds attracted into the United States to finance the spending binge. From 1983 through 1988 real short-term and long-term interest rates averaged, respectively, $3\frac{1}{2}$ and $5\frac{1}{2}$ percentage points higher than their earlier postwar averages (see Table 4), a huge increase by any historical standard. Recently interest rates have fallen somewhat as the economy softened and some progress was made in 1986 and 1987 in cutting the budget deficit. But they remain well above their earlier postwar levels. Should the dollar decline and the U.S. trade deficit narrow further, the inflow of foreign savings into the United States would shrink and interest rates would rise again—unless, of course, steps are taken to raise national saving.

Lower national saving and higher interest rates had another more subtle but highly damaging effect on the U.S. economy. High interest rates particularly penalize *long-term* investments. When interest rates are 4 percent, for example, a one-year investment of $100 has to return $104 dollars to make it worthwhile; an increase in interest rates to 6 percent raises

Table 4
Average real interest rates, selected periods, 1951–89
Percent

Period	90-day Treasury Bills ᵃ	AAA Corporate Bonds ᵇ
1951–73	0.3	1.6
1974–82	0.5	2.2
1983–88	4.1	7.4
1989	4.0	5.0

Source: Data from Federal Reserve Board; U.S. Department of Commerce; and author's calculations.
ᵃ The nominal interest rate in one quarter minus the prior quarter's inflation rate in the GNP deflator.
ᵇ The nominal interest rate in one quarter minus an "expected" inflation rate based on a weighted moving average of the prior twelve quarters' inflation.

the required one-year return to only $106. But the return needed to make a fifteen-year investment worthwhile goes from $180 to $240, a rise of one-third, when interest rates go up from 4 to 6 percent. Any potential investments that paid off in the $180–$240 range would be ruled out after the interest rate increase.

A common explanation for America's loss of competitiveness and the slow growth of U.S. productivity is that this country's businesses are too interested in short-term payoffs and hence are reluctant to undertake many long-term investments to improve productivity. If the charge is true—and there is surely some truth in it—the explanation may not be simple shortsightedness, but a rational response to the extraordinarily high real interest rates brought on by the budget policies of the 1980s.

National Saving and the Social Security Surplus
As a result of legislation in 1978 and 1983 that boosted payroll taxes and restricted benefits, the nation's social security system of old age survivors and disability insurance (OASDI) is now collecting revenues far greater than future benefits. Moreover, these annual surpluses will rise from $66 billion in 1990 to $128 billion in 1995. This accumulation of reserves was intended to reduce the burden on future workers of supporting the social security benefits that will be collected by the large baby boom population, which will begin retiring in the early decades of the next century. The annual surplus in all the federal

government's retirement funds will reach $2\frac{1}{2}$ percent of GNP by 1995.[6]

The mere accumulation of paper claims in a trust fund does not, of course, enable one generation to finance its own retirement and relieve the next generation of the burden. When today's workers retire, their consumption must come out of the production of future workers. To finance this generation's retirement, the nation as a whole must now add to its aggregate saving, accumulate productive wealth, and raise the income and productivity of the next generation so that real resources can be devoted to the consumption of retirees without placing an added burden on the generation that is then at work.[7]

But if the annual surplus in the social security funds is used to justify dissaving (a larger deficit) elsewhere in the budget, national saving and wealth accumulation will not have been increased. And that is exactly the posture of current federal budget policy. In fiscal 1990 the overall federal budget deficit is estimated at $127 billion. But that figure is the result of a huge $245 billion deficit in the general operating budget of the federal government, partially offset by a $119 billion annual surplus in the retirement trust funds. Even if the overall deficit of almost $120 billion in 1995 were eliminated, the operating budget would still show a deficit of some $182 billion (offset by a surplus of the same amount in the retirement trust funds).[8]

What Is a Reasonable Target for the National Saving Rate?

Because of the accumulating obligations to provide for retirement of the baby boomers early in the next century, the United States, now and for the foreseeable future, should raise its national saving rate, which includes both public and private saving.[9] The $2\frac{1}{2}$ percent of GNP that will soon be accumulating each year as surpluses in the federal government's various retirement funds is a pretty good measure of how much that extra saving ought to be. But what is the base level to which the extra saving should be added? Table 5 represents an effort to provide a rough answer.

Output per worker in the United States is now rising at about 1 percent a year. To maintain that relatively sluggish growth of productivity, the nation must invest enough to replace the capital that depreciates each year, equip new additions to the labor force with today's average amount of capital

Table 5
Projected saving requirements and availability, 1989–2000
Percent of national income

Net National Saving	1989–2000
Targets	
To maintain a base level of saving	5.3
Additional saving needed for future retirement needs	2.5
TOTAL	7.8
Availability	
Private saving	7.0
Required federal budget surplus[a]	0.8
TOTAL	7.8

Source: Charles L. Schultze, "Of Wolves, Termites, and Pussycats, or, Why We Should Worry about the Budget Deficit," *Brookings Review,* vol. 7 (Summer 1989), p. 32.
[a] The unified budget, which includes retirement trust funds such as social security, medicare, and federal employee retirement.

per worker, and increase that stock of capital per worker by about 1 percent a year for all workers. Providing that much new investment—over and above depreciation—without continuing to rely on an inflow of borrowed funds from abroad would require a net saving of 5.3 percent of national income. Adding to that base saving the extra 2.5 percent saving needed to deal with the accumulating obligations for retirement benefits, as roughly measured by the surpluses in the retirement trust funds, yields a target for national saving in the 1990s of almost 8 percent of national income. If the private saving rate continues at roughly its current 7 percent of national income, achieving an 8 percent national saving rate would require an overall *surplus* in the federal budget of 1 percent of national income.[10]

It will take time to convert the present large budget deficit into a surplus. Occasional recessions or economic slowdowns will sometimes cause the budget balance to fall below target. And so, to achieve a reasonable accumulation of national saving in the 1990s as a whole, budget policy should probably aim for a gradual transition to an overall surplus of about $1\frac{1}{2}$ percent of national income for the last half of the 1990s. It would probably make political sense to move to this target in two stages: first balance the overall budget by fiscal 1993 and then move to the $1\frac{1}{2}$ percent surplus over the next three to four years. Given continued moderate economic growth and the current inflation rate, that would imply a surplus of almost $110 billion in the *overall* budget by fiscal year 1996: a $200 billion surplus in the retirement trust funds and a deficit of $90 billion in the general operating budget.

How Deficit Reduction Would Improve the U.S. Economy

Reducing the budget deficit will require some combination of tax increase and expenditure reduction. The tax increase would reduce private income. Precisely where the cuts occurred in private spending would depend upon the nature of the tax increase, but most of the cut in income would be translated into reduced comsumption. Cutting federal outlays would, of course, directly lower public spending. The accompanying reduction in the budget deficit and the decline in federal borrowing would reduce interest rates, but those interest rate cuts would not be large enough to produce a fully offsetting increase in other forms of spending. Taken by themselves, the fiscal actions needed to cut the budget deficit would reduce aggregate demand for goods and services in the economy and produce lower output and employment, at least for a substantial period. And so, when the budget deficit was being slashed, the Federal Reserve would have to ease monetary policy, providing additional bank reserves and driving interest rates down still further, in order to stimulate enough additional private spending to take up the slack. (This would be exactly the opposite of what the Fed did to avoid excessive aggregate demand when the budget deficit was ballooning in the 1980s.)

The record of the Federal Reserve in recent years gives no reason to doubt that it would pursue the appropriately accommodating policy. Thus a deficit reduction would leave the U.S. economy with output, employment, and inflation roughly unchanged but interest rates substantially lower. And the composition of national output would be altered. Public and private consumption would fall, while spending of the kind favored by low interest rates— business investment, housing construction, consumer durables, and exports—would rise. A slightly greater fraction of the country's demands would be met from domestic production and a little less from imports. In short, the nation would consume less and save more, and the higher saving would lead to some combination of more domestic investment and less borrowing from abroad.

The direction of the change in interest rates can be projected with a good deal of confidence, but estimating its magnitude involves a great deal of uncertainty. In one attempt to analyze this question, a number of prominent economic models were used to estimate the effects of a cut in federal spending phased in over four years and amounting to 1 percent of GNP ($70 billion) by fiscal year 1994, offset by a Federal Reserve easing of monetary policy sufficient to keep GNP from falling.[11] While the estimates varied across the different models, on average the results suggest that interest rates would fall by some $1\frac{1}{2}$ to 2 percentage points. Other estimates of the effects on interest rates of across-the-board tax increases gave about the same results. The interest rate effects of deficit reduction are not significantly determined by whether the reduction is accomplished by spending cuts or tax increases.

A substantial reduction in interest rates would be a major tonic for the U.S. economy. It would generate a substantial saving in interest payments on the debt.[12] Further interest savings would arise from the fact that the deficit reduction would lower the projected federal debt itself. According to the average result from the model simulations, a phased-in reduction of federal spending or an increase in taxes amounting to 1 percent of GNP (approximately $75 billion by fiscal 1995) would save an additional $45 billion through lower interest payments on the debt, for a total deficit reduction of $120 billion. A cut of this size would eliminate the overall budget deficit, although the federal operating budget would still show a deficit of $180 billion and national saving would remain well below the target level of 8 percent of national income.

Reducing the overall budget deficit would change the composition of GNP. If deficit reduction came from tax increases or a cut in federal transfer payments to individuals, private consumption would tend to fall; reduced spending by the Defense Department or other government agencies would lower public consumption. But the accompanying fall in interest rates would tend to increase housing construction, business investment in plant and equipment, and exports. The effect on home construction and business investment is obvious. Lower interest rates encourage exports by reducing foreign demand for dollars, and when the dollar falls, U.S. exports rise.

As a general proposition, the fall in interest rates would spread its benefits widely. Workers laid off in defense or consumer goods production would have opportunities for good jobs elsewhere, principally in construction, machine building, and exports. The decline in the budget deficit would raise national saving by roughly an equivalent amount. Living standards would begin to grow faster because the country would be investing more at home in productivity-improving projects, management's attention would more likely be focused on longer-term payoffs, and the United States, borrowing less from abroad, would face a reduced burden of foreign debt service.

Where Does Federal Spending Go?

Converting the current budget deficit to a surplus, as a way to lift the national saving rate to a reasonable level, would substantially improve the long-run prospects for U.S. economic growth and competitiveness. But wishing will not make it so. As noted earlier, a "standstill" budget policy—with tax laws unchanged and spending keeping pace with increases in prices and work loads under existing legislation—would leave the country with a $140 billion deficit in each of the next three years. The deficit would then drop slightly, to about $120 billion, by 1995. To convert that deficit into a $120 billion surplus by 1995 or 1996, a $240 billion swing, would require very large tax increases, spending cuts, or both.

The inherently difficult problem of getting political consensus on what painful deficit reduction steps to take has been exacerbated by the prevalence of inconsistent views about the social worth of government programs. There is a widely held view that federal spending in general had been "getting out of hand" before 1980, and that Ronald Reagan succeeded in halting but not reversing the upward trend. Particular programs, however, command substantial support, some from small groups of powerful beneficiaries but others among the broad public. Indeed, in the last few years there has been a growing perception, even among some conservatives, that budget austerity has shortchanged several important areas of public spending, especially on human and physical investment, sometimes called "public infrastructure." And both liberals and conservatives have often banded together to protect

a number of ongoing programs from the deep slashes proposed by the Reagan and Bush administrations.

The general belief that the government is overspending has made it impossible to raise taxes, but both substantive and political pressures have limited expenditure cutting. The result is a political impasse. To assess the merits and feasibility of alternative deficit reduction proposals, it is necessary first to put government spending in perspective and to look more closely at specific categories.

Defense Spending

There is virtually unanimous agreement across the spectrum of politicians and defense analysts that the recent political developments in the Soviet Union and Eastern Europe enable the United States safely to reduce its armed forces and its military procurement programs. But how much and how fast remains controversial. In chapters 3 and 4, John Steinbruner and Lawrence Korb argue the case for a sizable restructuring and reduction in U.S. military forces and a substantially larger cutback in defense spending than the administration has so far requested. In one scenario, defense spending could fall over the next ten years by 4 percent a year, from the current level of almost $300 billion to about $200 billion (in dollars of today's purchasing power). An alternative and more ambitious cutback in military spending could be achieved if the downsizing of the forces was accompanied by a reduced rate of weapons modernization and a lower level of readiness. In that case, military spending could fall to $150 billion at the end of the decade. By 1995 the constant-dollar value of defense spending could be some $45 billion to $65 billion below the CBO's "standstill" projections, depending on which alternative is chosen.

The administration's current plans for reducing the military budget are somewhat less ambitious, calling for cuts in the real value of military spending of some $30 billion by fiscal 1995.[13] To the extent the budgetary saving from these cuts are not offset by increased spending on other federal programs or through tax reductions, the resultant fall in interest rates and lower federal debt would, as explained above, generate additional deficit reduction.

Federal Spending for Civilian Programs

Table 6 traces the development of the federal budget (as a share of GNP) over the past thirty-five years in two major parts: the social security trust

Table 6
Budget outlays and revenues as a share of GNP, fiscal years 1955–90
Percent unless otherwise specified

Budget Components	1955	1960	1965	1970	1975	1980	1985	1990	Value in 1990 (Billions of Dollars)
Total budget[a]									
Outlays	17.7	18.2	17.6	19.8	21.8	22.1	23.9	21.9	1,194
Revenues	16.9	18.3	17.4	19.5	18.3	19.4	18.6	19.6	1,067
Social security[b]									
Outlays	1.1	2.2	2.5	3.5	4.7	5.3	5.9	5.7	310
Revenues	1.4	2.1	2.6	4.2	5.1	5.3	6.2	7.2	391
General operating									
Outlays	16.7	16.2	15.2	16.5	17.4	17.0	18.2	16.8	915
Revenues	15.6	16.3	14.9	15.6	13.5	14.2	12.7	12.9	706

Sources: All data for 1955–85 from *Historical Tables of the Budget of the United States Government for Fiscal Year 1990.* For fiscal 1990, here, and throughout this chapter, the Congressional Budget Office (CBO) estimates and projections of outlays and revenues are used as control totals for fiscal 1990 and later years. (Congressional Budget Office, *The Economic and Budget Outlook: Fiscal Years 1991 and 1995,* January 1990). The various budget components for fiscal 1990 in Tables 6 through 15 are also CBO estimates where those are available in sufficient detail. Where CBO does not provide sufficient detail, the current service estimates of the Office of Management and Budget for fiscal 1990 are substituted. (*Budget of the United States Government for the Fiscal Year 1991,* various tables.) Since the OMB current service estimates of expenditures for fiscal 1990 are quite close to those of the CBO, the data in the tables should be consistent.
a Total outlays and revenues are smaller than the sum of the two components because intrafund transactions such as interest payments from the general fund to the social security fund are netted out in the total.
b Includes outlays and revenues of the old age and survivors, disability, and hospital insurance trust funds.

funds and all other federal programs, called the general operating budget. Three basic facts stand out. First, both the outlays and revenues of the social security funds have increased steadily relative to GNP throughout the postwar period.[14] The rise mainly reflects growth in the number of beneficiaries, but also a rise in the level of benefits relative to average per capita income and an associated rise in dedicated payroll tax revenues. The American people, rightly or wrongly, have repeatedly displayed their willingness to pay steadily higher payroll tax rates for the higher benefits.

Second, federal outlays for all purposes other than social security—the general operating budget—have been virtually flat as a share of GNP over the past thirty-five years. There was a temporary peak in 1985 at the height of the Reagan defense buildup and a low in the mid-1960s before spending on the Vietnam War or Lyndon Johnson's Great Society programs had gotten under way. Otherwise their share of GNP fluctuated between 16 and 17 percent. Social security apart, the historical pattern of

spending in the federal operating budget does not support the notion that U.S. political institutions caused federal spending to grow relentlessly or to absorb an increasing share of the national economy.

There are indeed biases in the budget process. Pork barrel politics do influence congressional budget making. But, contrary to widely held opinion, the amounts of money involved in such practices do not bulk large in the aggregate and they explain neither the evolution of total federal spending nor the large budget deficits of recent years. Congressional budget politics produces inefficiency in the small rather than in the large.

The third basic fact is that general operating revenues—all federal taxes except the payroll taxes dedicated to social security—have fallen as a share of GNP, most notably in the early 1980s following enactment of the Economic Recovery Tax Act of 1981. Table 6 also displays starkly how the budget deficits developed in the 1980s. In the first half of the decade, the defense buildup raised the GNP share of federal operating outlays (the nondefense outlay share actually fell), while large tax cuts sharply reduced the flow of general revenues relative to GNP. By 1990 defense spending and total outlays in the general operating budget had fallen back to their 1980 share of GNP, while general revenues remained depressed. While federal operating spending relative to GNP is only slightly above the average of the quarter century before 1980, general revenues are some 3 percentage points of GNP below their historical level. Except for payroll taxes supporting the social security program, Americans now pay a lower federal tax rate than at any time in the past four decades.

Government Spending in Other Countries

The relative size and role played by central, provincial, or state, and local governments differ widely among countries. France, for example, concentrates much responsibility for spending in the central government. The German federal system more closely resembles ours, but uses the taxing power of the central government to collect and redistribute large amounts of revenues to its states (Länder). Because of this variety, meaningful comparisons of spending can be made only by combining data from all levels of government, as is done in Table 7. The United States and Japan stand out with government spending at least 10 percent of GNP below that of other countries. If defense spending is excluded, governments in the United States spent a smaller share of GNP than any other country including Japan. Finally, the government spending share rose in all countries, but less in the United States than elsewhere.

Table 7
Six countries' government spending as a share of GNP, selected years, 1965–86[a]
Percent

Country	1965	1970	1980	1986
United States				
TOTAL	27.83	32.20	34.07	37.16
Excluding defense	20.72	24.86	28.79	30.54
Excluding defense and social security	17.45	20.26	22.09	23.37
France				
TOTAL	n.a.	44.45	46.99	52.85
Excluding defense	n.a.	41.24	43.69	49.71
Excluding defense and social security	n.a.	27.41	28.03	32.29
Germany				
TOTAL	36.94	38.99	48.77	47.18
Excluding defense	n.a.	36.06	46.04	44.52
Excluding defense and social security	n.a.	27.18	34.25	33.08
Sweden				
TOTAL	n.a.	43.72	61.95	64.90
Excluding defense	n.a.	40.41	58.90	62.29
Excluding defense and social security	n.a.	37.74	51.82	53.86
United Kingdom				
TOTAL	35.86	39.54	45.23	46.02
Excluding defense	n.a.	n.a.	40.28	41.21
Excluding defense and social security	n.a.	n.a.	33.85	34.45
Japan				
TOTAL	19.05	19.10	32.09	33.03
Excluding defense	n.a.	18.34	31.23	32.09
Excluding defense and social security	n.a.	14.81	23.08	22.20

Source: Author's classification of data from Organization for European Economic Cooperation and Development (OECD), *National Income Accounts,* pt. 2 (available on computer disc from OECD).
n.a. Not available.
[a] All levels of government.

Table 8
Federal general operating outlays as a share of GNP, selected fiscal years, 1955–90
Percent unless otherwise indicated

Category	1955	1960	1965	1970	1975	1980	1985	1990	Value in 1990 (Billions of Dollars)
TOTAL	16.7	16.2	15.2	16.5	17.4	17.0	18.2	16.8	915
Defense	11.1	9.5	7.5	8.3	5.7	5.0	6.4	5.4	297
Net interest	1.4	1.5	1.4	1.6	1.8	2.1	3.4	3.7	202
Civilian programs	4.2	5.2	6.3	6.6	9.9	9.9	8.4	7.6	416

Source: See Table 6. Figures are rounded.

The Major Components of General Operating Outlays

Table 8 divides the federal government's general operating outlays into three major components: defense, net interest, and civilian programs. The share of GNP devoted to defense spending has been declining since the mid-1950s, except for an increase during the Vietnam War and a lesser one during the defense buildup of the early 1980s. An increase in other spending, initially for civilian programs and more recently for interest payments, roughly offset the decline in the defense share. The growth of civilian spending on the operating functions of the federal government slowed in the late 1970s and was reversed after 1980.

The pattern of federal spending before 1980 hints at a set of underlying forces governing budget outcomes. Although Congress raised payroll taxes to pay for social security, it never raised the general tax burden except for gasoline taxes to support highway construction.[15] The fear of large budget deficits kept general operating spending from getting seriously out of line with general revenues. Before the introduction of inflation indexing in the personal tax, which took effect in 1985, periodic tax cuts kept the ratio of income taxes to personal income from rising despite the tendency of inflation and economic growth to push people into higher tax brackets. With the total general operating budget kept in line by a combination of unwillingness to raise taxes in peacetime and a fear of large budget deficits, the civilian spending share expanded only as the defense share came down.

These implicit budgetary rules were broken in the 1980s. Taxes were cut and defense spending was increased without a commensurate cut in spending elsewhere. Although federal spending on civilian programs was pared significantly—from 9.9 percent of GNP in 1980 to 7.6 percent in 1990—this was not enough to offset the fall in the share of GNP going to general operating revenues. As a result, the operating deficit rose sharply, causing the federal debt to rise and generating an increase in interest rates. Interest payments on the debt consequently rose as a fraction of GNP by almost as much as civilian spending fell. And so, in the end, the budget policies of the 1980s, heralded as an all-out assault against excessive or wasteful federal programs, ended up by replacing spending whose benefits may have been smaller than its costs with spending that provided no benefits at all.

Where Does the Civilian Operating Budget Go?

The largest, and until 1975 by far the fastest growing, component of the civilian budget is the category "payments to individuals" (see Table 9).[16] These are often called entitlement programs, since in most of them the eligibility to receive benefits is specified by law; the amount of annual spending is not controlled by the appropriation process. Total payments to individuals in the form of cash, food stamps, medical care, and other "in-kind" benefits grew much more rapidly than GNP until the late 1970s, when their share stabilized. Federal payments for medical care continued to grow rapidly; the rise in spending under most other benefit programs slowed. Table 10 shows how the major components of payments to individuals, measured in dollars of 1990 purchasing power, have changed since 1980.

Table 9
Federal civilian programs as a share of GNP, selected fiscal years, 1965–90[a]
Percent unless otherwise indicated

Category	1965	1970	1975	1980	1985	1990	Value in 1990 (Billions of Dollars)
TOTAL	6.29	6.64	9.95	9.90	8.43	7.62	416
Payments to individuals[b]	2.47	2.96	4.89	4.89	4.68	4.80	262
Discretionary programs	4.70	4.55	5.95	5.76	4.25	3.35	183
Investment	1.69	1.76	1.85	2.07	1.68	1.43	78
Work load	0.62	0.62	0.73	0.69	0.62	0.68	37
Other	2.39	2.17	3.37	3.00	1.95	1.25	68
Undistributed receipts and special items	−0.88	−0.87	−0.89	−0.75	−0.50	−0.53	−29

Source: See Table 6.
[a] Federal general operating budget excluding defense and net interest; see Table 8.
[b] Excludes hospital insurance (included in social security) and assistance to college students (included in investment outlays).

Table 10
Federal programs of payments to individuals, fiscal years 1980 and 1990[a]
Billions of 1990 dollars

Category	1980	1990
TOTAL	208	262
Medical care[b]	52	97
Welfare-like programs[c]	66	76
Federal employees' retirement[d]	63	72
Unemployment insurance	27	17

Source: See Table 6.
[a] Excludes hospital insurance (included in social security) and assistance to college students (included in investment outlays).
[b] Deflated with the same price index as the other components (the personal consumption deflator).
[c] Principal components are aid to families with dependent children, food stamps, supplemental security income, earned income tax credit, and veterans' non-service-connected pensions.
[d] Includes railroad retirement ($7 billion in 1990) and veterans' service-connected compensation.

Medical care. Two major medical care programs are financed out of general revenues. Medicaid provides acute and long-term care for the poor. Part B of medicare provides physician care for the elderly and disabled and is included here because, unlike the rest of social security, it is paid for not by the payroll tax but by a combination of premium payments from the beneficiaries and appropriations from general revenues. The continued growth of the medical care programs after 1980 occurred despite increasingly strenuous efforts to hold down medicare costs and restrictions on eligibility for aid to families with dependent children, through which many people gain access to medicaid. Spending grew because the price of medical care rose more rapidly than the general inflation rate and because of the increasing use of ever more expensive types of medical procedures.

Rapidly rising health care prices and steadily increasing use of expensive medical technology are common in all the developed industrial countries. But the share of GNP now going to health care (public and private) is larger in the United States than elsewhere. The United States is also distinctive in another respect. A much smaller fraction of the nation's medical bills is paid for by the government than is true anywhere else in the industrial world (see chapter 8 for a discussion of U.S. health care).

Other payments to individuals. Real growth in the other types of payments to individuals has slowed sharply, and payments for unemployment insurance have declined. Unemployment compensation payments fell in the 1980s both because unemployment dropped sharply after the 1982 recession and because many states tightened up on eligibility and other standards. More generally, the fraction of the unemployed receiving unemployment compensation has fallen since 1980; less than one-third of the unemployed drew unemployment compensation in 1989.

Spending for the means-tested programs for the poor and near-poor—cash assistance, food stamps, and housing subsidies—has grown quite slowly since 1980, except for housing assistance, which has risen sharply. Although budget authorization for new subsidized housing units dropped sharply, housing payment subsidies rose as housing units that had been authorized earlier were built and added to the stock of subsidized housing. Other assistance payments changed little. Both average benefit levels and numbers of recipients remained roughly constant.

Discretionary Federal Spending

In contrast to the entitlement programs, spending under the discretionary programs can be varied from year to year by congressional appropriations actions. Table 9 distinguishes three major categories: investment spending, the costs of supporting the federal government's many services (labeled "work load items"), and a residual category of miscellaneous spending programs. Real federal spending for investment purposes stopped growing during the 1980s, and as a share of GNP it fell. Three major forms of civilian investment spending—physical investment, education, and research and development—declined as a share of GNP; one of them fell in absolute value (see Table 11).

Physical investment. The federal government supports physical infrastructure investment in two ways. It directly invests in physical assets, such as in the large water resource projects of the Corps of Engineers and the Bureau of Reclamation, as well as in office buildings, computers, autos, and trucks for its own use. It also provides grants-in-aid to state and local government for infrastructure investment such as highways, airports, waste treatment control facilities, and urban rehabilitation projects. Directly and indirectly, the federal government finances about 40 percent of the nation's total public investment in physical infrastructure, the rest being provided by state and local governments.

Infrastructure investment by all levels of government in the United States reached a peak in the 1960s as state and local governments spent heavily on highways, school buildings, and sewer and water systems. Starting in the early 1970s, investment declined, reaching a trough in 1982. It then began to recover, climbing back to the levels of the late 1960s by the end of the 1980s. As a result of this investment pattern, the stock of public capital grew faster than GNP in the 1950s and 1960s; the ratio of public capital to GNP reached a peak in the early 1970s and then began a decline that has continued until now. One recent study has argued that the declining stock of public infrastructure relative to GNP bears much of the responsibility for the fall in national productivity growth that began in the early years of the 1970s.[17] In a similar vein, others have called for a substantial expansion of federal investment expenditures, even at the cost of a higher federal budget deficit. These arguments are examined below in an analysis of future spending priorities.

Table 11
Federal investment spending, selected fiscal years, 1965–90

Category	1965	1970	1975	1980	1985	1990
As a percentage of GNP						
TOTAL	1.69	1.76	1.85	2.07	1.68	1.43
Physical investment	1.19	0.97	1.03	1.14	0.91	0.75
Nondefense R&D (excluding space)	0.34	0.36	0.39	0.42	0.37	0.31
Education	0.16	0.43	0.43	0.51	0.40	0.37
In 1990 dollars						
TOTAL	48.4	60.6	59.8	78.1	76.3	78.1
Physical investment	31.2	30.5	31.7	39.4	41.1	40.7
Nondefense R&D (excluding space)	11.7	14.2	13.7	18.0	17.1	17.1
Education	5.5	15.9	14.4	20.7	18.1	20.3

Source: See Table 6.

Investment in education and R&D. Federal investment in civilian research and development outside the space program has always been small relative to GNP and the importance of technological advance to national productivity growth. And even that modest amount was hard hit during the 1980s, when real R&D spending fell slightly and its share in GNP was significantly reduced (see Table 11).[18]

The federal government has never provided more than a modest fraction of the nation's public spending on education—a little less than 10 percent in 1988. About half the federal government's $20 billion in educational assistance went to state and local governments, providing only 6 percent of what those governments spent for that purpose. Most of the remaining federal funds were spent for aid to college students in the form of loans and grants. The federal share of educational spending declined during the 1980s as federal budgets were squeezed and critics questioned the efficacy of some earlier federal educational programs in support of elementary and secondary education.

In recent years evidence has accumulated that the quality of U.S. education at the elementary and secondary level has slipped well behind that in other advanced countries. There is also growing evidence that the deficiencies in the education of those entering the work force are harming U.S. productivity and competitiveness. Just as in the case of infrastructure investment, a number of groups are now arguing for a substantial additional infusion of federal money into the educational process (see chapter 7 for a discussion of how to improve the quality of U.S. education).

Work load items. The federal government provides many services that are essential to the operation of a modern society. They include operation of the air traffic and air safety system; the federal prison system; maintenance and operation of the national parks, national forests, and federal resource projects; the services of the Coast Guard and the Internal Revenue Service; and a number of other similar items. Only the operating budgets of the relevant agencies are included here; investment and R&D spending is classified in the previous category. Total spending on such activities is not large, $37 billion in 1990. In the first five years of the 1980s, real spending for these work load activities was roughly constant despite a growing economy. But in the next five years budgets expanded, and these activities'

share of GNP returned almost to their earlier level (see Table 9). However, the work loads facing many of these programs are growing faster than the economy as a whole. Air traffic is increasing more rapidly than GNP; the war on drugs has severely burdened the Coast Guard; sharp growth in the prison population has crowded federal prisons well beyond capacity. And the demands on the government's environmental control operations continue to mount as more stringent environmental laws are enacted. Looking to the future, many of these work load activities will have to expand faster than the rate of general economic growth.

Other federal spending. The final category is a miscellany of federal expenditure programs that do not fit any of the earlier categories. Spending on this group of programs (virtually constant in nominal dollars) has been cut in half as a fraction of GNP over the past ten years (Table 12). There has been a wide diversity of experience within the group. However, the Reagan administration was successful in dramatically scaling back real spending on one group of programs (labeled, in lieu of a better term, the "losers"), which fell by 80 percent, accounting for half of the decline in federal civilian spending as a fraction of GNP over the past ten years. Two of these programs were abolished: the public service employment programs and general revenue sharing with the states.

The two other large programs in this category developed in a different way during the 1980s. Spending on farm price supports, responding mainly to developments in world agricultural markets, rose sharply in the middle of the decade but by 1990 fell back to about its 1980 share of GNP. The space program (included in remainder) followed the opposite pattern, languishing during most of the 1980s and then expanding sharply in the last few years as shuttle activity expanded and the development of a manned space station began.

How Can the Deficit Be Turned into a Surplus?

Under the CBO current service projections of federal spending that I have been using, current laws specifying various payments to individuals are assumed to remain unchanged, and in the other

Table 12
Federal spending on miscellaneous programs, selected fiscal years, 1980–90
Billions of 1990 dollars

Category	1980	1985	1990[a]
TOTAL	126.2	92.6	68.2
Major "losers"	63.4	23.5	13.8
Energy excluding R&D	10.9	1.8	0.1
Community and regional development	17.8	9.2	6.4
Training and employment	16.2	6.0	5.3
Revenue-sharing general-purpose fiscal assistance	13.6	7.7	1.8
International financial programs	3.8	−1.8	−0.3
Education and training of health care workers	1.1	0.6	0.5
Farm income stabilization	11.7	28.5	13.8
Remainder[b]	51.1	40.6	40.6

Source: See Table 6.

[a] Amounts in baseline budget.

[b] Important components include: mortgage and housing credit, energy (excluding R&D), international security and economic assistance, community and regional development (except physical investment), veterans' housing assistance, and space programs (except physical investment).

programs, where spending can be changed from year to year through the appropriations process (such as the investment, R&D, and work load budgets), spending is assumed to be held constant in real terms. Since real GNP will be expanding over the period, the projected federal spending share for discretionary programs will fall, continuing the trend begun in 1980. Table 13 sets forth the pattern of spending that would occur by 1995 if civilian outlays followed the rules set forth above.

The civilian spending share would be lower than at any time since the early 1970s (compare with Table 8). Payments to individuals would remain at slightly under 5 percent of GNP, but the discretionary spending programs would fall by 1995 to levels well below anything in the postwar period: 3.1 percent of GNP, compared with an average of about 4.5 percent in the thirty years before 1980. The proposals for expenditure increases and decreases discussed below represent changes from these current service levels.

In formulating budget policy for the 1990s, a number of often competing goals have to be weighed against each other: deficit reductions that will bring large economic benefits; expansion of federal spending in a limited number of areas where significant benefits could be demonstrated; further cuts in low-priority spending; and keeping the tax burden low, both to avoid unwarranted reductions in

disposable income and to minimize the supply-side consequences of high taxes (often overstated but nevertheless real).

Differences in value judgments, ideologies, self-interest, and the way the evidence is read strongly influence the relative importance people give to each of these goals. But analysis of the evidence, although itself sometimes in conflict, can make an important contribution to the debate.

Candidates for Increased Spending

Four major components of federal spending are most frequently cited as areas for significantly enlarged spending: investment in physical infrastructure, education, civilian R&D, and health insurance for more than 30 million uninsured Americans. A fifth candidate for additional spending encompasses many of the routine "work load" elements of federal programs.

Investment in physical infrastructure. As noted earlier, the stock of public physical infrastructure in place has steadily declined as a share of GNP since the late 1960s. Moreover, projection of current budget policy to 1995 implies that investment in federal infrastructure would continue to fall relative to the size of the economy. Modest increases in public outlays for highways, bridges, and airports may well be desirable. But recent claims that

Table 13

Federal general operating outlays for civilian programs, fiscal years 1990 and 1995

| | 1990 | | 1995 | |
| | Billions of Current Dollars | Percent of GNP | Billions of Current Dollars | Percent of GNP |
Category				
TOTAL	416	7.6	562	7.5
Payments to individuals	262	4.8	366	4.9
Discretionary programs	183	3.4	231	3.1
Offsetting receipts	−29	−0.5	−35	−0.5

Source: See Table 6. Figures are rounded.

additional public investment on physical infrastructure would strongly boost national productivity and output are substantially overstated. In any event, few are calling for a major expansion of the traditional federal water resource projects or a surge in the construction of public buildings or sewer and water pipelines. Rather, attention has been focused on the transportation infrastructure: roads, bridges, and airports.

A recent task force report of the National Governors' Conference calls for outlays of $1 trillion to $3 trillion over the next twenty years to build and make major repairs to roads and airports. But recent studies cast serious doubt on the need for such massive sums.[19] In fact, they argue that if the nation simply spends more on highways and airports without altering the current planning of highway investment and doing something to discourage congestion, it will end up spending more money on highways, bridges, and airports that will soon clog up again with congestion, and, in the case of highways, deteriorate too rapidly.

The authors of these studies propose, therefore, that the government change the way it charges for the use of highways and airports. Currently gasoline and diesel taxes pay for highway construction and maintenance. In the proposed system, drivers would pay charges scaled to the degree of congestion on the highways over which they travel. Inexpensive devices are now feasible that could register and identify the passage of vehicles, and monthly bills could then be sent.[20] With this approach, congestion could be quickly reduced and revenues raised to finance the necessary transportation investment. Over the longer run, such charges would reduce congestion further by providing improved incentives

for firms about where to locate and for individuals about where to live. Congestion fees on airplane landings and takeoffs would similarly reduce congestion at airports. Unlike highways, however, there is a national need for additional airport runways, or conceivably whole airports, even after the imposition of congestion-reducing fees. The imposition of congestion-related charges to pay for airports and highways would generate benefits worth $12 billion a year (in 1990 dollars), principally by reducing the time wasted in traffic jams and airport delays.

Another important recommendation of these studies is a change in the way taxes are levied on trucks in an attempt to remedy road deterioration. Road wear is closely related to truck loading per axle. The incentive of the present gasoline tax is perverse because the use of additional axles on a truck requires larger engines and more fuel per ton carried. Thus truck taxes should be based on axle loading. In addition, if highways were significantly thickened as they underwent major repairs and reconstruction, the resultant reduction in future highway maintenance and wear and tear on trucks would generate handsome returns on the initial investment. An optimal program of investment in highway thickening and in airports (principally in more runways), coupled with the recommended change in truck taxes, could generate about $18 billion a year in national benefits.

Highways can only be reconstructed gradually, or inordinate delays would be imposed on travelers. The estimated gains could be achieved by a fifteen-year program of highway reconstruction and a ten-year program of airport building that would add about $4 billion a year to what is now being spent for those purposes. If highway responsibilities continue to be split as they now are among federal, state, and local governments, the federal budget would have to absorb perhaps 50 percent of the added outlays. Most airports are owned by state or local authorities or by airlines. While the federal government might provide some up-front (but repayable) investment to induce changes in airport pricing policies, the federal budget share of an airport investment program should be small.

Education.   A national awareness has formed that the quality of U.S. elementary and secondary education has deteriorated, especially in comparison with other countries. Similarly, evidence has been accumulating that there is a noticeable connection between the poor school achievements of workers with a high school education or less and their per-formance on the job. Many observers now blame low educational quality at the elementary and secon-dary level for an important share of America's sluggish productivity performance.[21]

Unfortunately, diagnosis is not cure. And finding a proper role for the federal government in improv-ing elementary and secondary education is harder still. The federal government for several decades has provided financial assistance to college students. But it has never been a big player in elementary and secondary education, either as standard setter, policymaker, or financial supporter. The federal government has provided relatively modest finan-cial support to schools dealing with high concentra-tions of disadvantaged children and to state and local school authorities to promote various educational reforms. Evaluations of these federal programs have not been able to identify major results in terms of better educational performance (see chapter 7).

The evidence that low-quality education is a barrier to high national productivity and the fact that Americans work far from the state or local jurisdic-tion that paid their public school bills might be reasons to enlarge the role for the national govern-ment in financing and influencing policy at the elementary and secondary education level. *If* there were wide consensus on how to improve educational quality, and *if* those improvements required increased spending, there might be a rationale for the federal government to provide a large share of the additional funds, perhaps through a special educational tax.

Unfortunately, consensus does not exist on what to do. And as John Chubb and Eric Hanushek argue in chapter 7, evidence is lacking that more money

for education spent in traditional ways would help much. Research has been unable to demonstrate educational payoffs from reducing the number of students per teacher, from longer school years, or from higher teacher pay that is unaccompanied by other reforms. One reform, though not guaranteed, has promise: more policy independence for indi-vidual schools and reduction in central control and bureaucracy. While this reform does not require extra money, modest extra funds for the newly enfranchised local school authorities might help gain acceptance for difficult changes in various school policies and practices.

In sum, given the present state of knowledge, increased federal spending on education, other than modest financial inducements for those school districts that decentralize control over educational policy, has low priority compared with other spend-ing needs and deficit reduction.

Civilian research and development.   The case for substantially increased federal support for civilian research and development is overwhelming. The highly specialized space program aside, federal support for civilian research and development is pitifully small. At $17 billion, real outlays are less than they were ten years ago. At only one-third of 1 percent of the nation's GNP, they are a smaller share than that provided by governments in other advanced countries. Two-fifths of that amount is for medical research at the National Institutes of Health. This is by far the largest government-sponsored pro-gram of biomedical research in the world and essen-tial, among other things, for the rapidly growing biotechnology industry. But there is precious little left for other purposes. Moreover, the defense research budget will be shrinking over the coming years, and although military research is not an effi-cient way of supporting civilian science and tech-nology objectives, lower spending on defense R&D will erode the nation's scientific base.

Successive economic studies have confirmed that, on average, research yields business firms a return well above that on conventional investments. The payoff to society as a whole is even higher. Because new knowledge cannot be hoarded or fully protected with patents, many of the gains from successful R&D spill over into the public domain.

While federal spending on R&D has begun to edge up in the last several years, much of the increase is for the space flight program and for the expensive supercollider, and the magnitude of the remaining effort is still paltry for a nation with a GNP of $5 trillion. A long-term program to boost the federal research support merits high priority.

Such a program should observe three basic principles. First, it should speed up the output of scientists and researchers from the nation's universities and colleges, which means increasing assistance to graduate students and research teams. Second, it should push but not outpace the scientific establishment's ability to absorb the increases, to avoid unneeded wage and price increases. And third, federal expenditures for research and development should be concentrated toward the research end of the R&D spectrum. Carefully selected assistance for commercial R&D ventures may sometimes be warranted, but organizational support and seed money should be the main instruments of policy. The government should resist becoming the principal financial backer of commercial projects; it has a bad history with such investments.[22]

Medical care.   More than 30 million Americans lack health insurance. The cost of health care is rising sharply. In chapter 8, Henry Aaron examines how the nation might deal with these problems. He notes that the United States relies heavily on employer-sponsored health insurance. Whether the system is optimal or not, it is too late to unravel it and begin again. And so he proposes the federal government mandate the extension of this approach to cover all workers employed more than a minimum number of hours, with backup public coverage for everyone else. This system would require increased national expenditure for health services for people now lacking access to care. Part of the increased expenditure would show up on the federal budget, roughly $40 billion a year for acute care (and as much as an additional $25 billion if long-term care benefits are increased). Aaron proposes that these health care activities and current federal health programs be brought together under a single trust fund that would receive payroll taxes currently dedicated to the hospital insurance trust fund, a dedicated 6 percent value-added tax (VAT), and certain other revenues. By 1995 this 6 percent VAT would raise some $75 billion more revenues than needed to offset the additional health care spending that Aaron proposes; it would also help pay for some existing

health spending.[23] The tax would thus contribute to deficit reductions and is discussed further in that context below.

Other national priorities.   In addition to increasing its investment in human, physical, and technological resources and extending health insurance to those who are not now covered, the United States faces other social challenges. While drug use appears to have been declining generally, drugs and drug-related crimes are an increasing scourge in the central cities. Quite apart from drugs, the crime rate remains tragically high. And the growing number of the homeless in the city streets are a visible reminder of major social distress.

To make progress against these problems will require, in varying degrees, some form of collective action and undoubtedly some provision of public expenditures. At the moment, however, there is no consensus on exactly what government should do, what level of government should take principal responsibility, and how much money might be required.

There is, however, a link between the recommendation for deficit cutting presented below and the social problems outlined above. So long as the federal government continues to run large budget deficits, it is almost certain that nothing but token actions will be seriously considered to attack such problems. In an era of "normal" budgets, when real military spending is not increasing and large deficits are not driving up interest payments on the debt each year, the annual growth in revenues tends to be a little larger than the growth in spending on existing programs. In such an environment it would be possible to have a serious debate about the merits of particular proposals to deal with social problems, either in terms of their relative priority or compared with a tax reduction. But until the problem of large and persistent deficits is dealt with, this sensible approach to deciding how the nation's resources should be allocated at the margin is foreclosed. In that sense, dealing with budget deficits will make an indirect, but nevertheless important, contribution to a rational debate about how to attack some of the country's social problems.

Candidates for Budget Cutting

After the early years of the Reagan administration, when Congress accepted a number of deep cuts in several federal programs (see the "losers" category in Table 12), it has remained penurious about increasing spending but has repeatedly rejected other large program reductions repeatedly proposed by Presidents Reagan and Bush. The prospect of significant further deficit reductions through such budget cutting is quite small. And even if Congress enacted all the spending cuts proposed in the administration's 1990 budget, there would still be deficits over the next five years, instead of a transition to the surpluses advocated earlier in this chapter. Finally, as the history of the 1980s makes clear, the continuation of high budget deficits inexorably raises interest payments on the federal debt, making the job of deficit reduction increasingly hard as time goes by. Continued refusal to consider a tax increase, on grounds that the existence of large deficits and the pressure of the Gramm-Rudman deficit reduction targets will eventually force Congress to make deep expenditure cuts, simply guarantees that the deficits will continue.

While the budget cannot be balanced by spending cuts, it is equally clear that it cannot be balanced by tax increases alone. Budget balance, and eventually budget surplus, will never come about without some "grand compromise" between liberals and conservatives that includes more spending cuts than Congress now seems willing to accept. Some variant of across-the-board spending restraints could be used. But, as the experience of the 1980s amply demonstrates, this practice eventually undermines the capacity of the federal government to provide needed services and restricts the public investment outlays needed to foster growth. Far better, but much more difficult politically, would be an agreement on priorities that would concentrate cuts where they would not have such unwanted effects. Four approaches (which are not exclusive) can be identified.

Approach 1. Continue the recent practice—which administrations have proposed and Congresses have partially accepted—of putting caps and limits on reimbursement to hospitals and physicians under the medicare and medicaid programs. The administration's 1991 budget proposes another 5\frac{1}{2}$ billion of such cuts. However desirable fundamental reforms in the medical delivery system might be, the practice of putting the regulatory hand on the spigot by capping medical reimbursements in federal programs simply causes upward cost pressures to "squirt out"

in the private sector, as hospitals and physicians make up there what they cannot get from the federal government. Making significant deficit reductions by this route would be politically unfeasible and substantively harmful.

Approach 2. Cut "middle-class" subsidies. Presidents and OMB directors of both parties have tried for years to get Congress to cut a long list of benefits for particular industries and middle-class individuals. The following is a list of examples of such cuts, with estimated savings for 1991 and 1995 shown in parentheses.[24]

• Eliminate school lunch and related subsidies to middle-class children ($360 million, $520 million).
• Eliminate disability compensation to veterans with low disability ratings, using half the saving to raise compensation to severely handicapped veterans and saving the rest ($1,350 million, $1,700 million).
• Eliminate annual operating subsidies to U.S. merchant vessels, including the requirement that all military cargo and a high percentage of other government cargo be carried on U.S. flag vessels ($390 million, $370 million).
• Charge fees closer to commercial levels for grazing and other commercial activities on federal lands ($65 million, $160 million).
• Liberalize, without eliminating, the Davis-Bacon Act, which in effect requires the federal government to pay union wage rates at journeyman levels or higher on federal construction projects ($190 million, $680 million).
• Tighten up the rules relating to the maximum price support payment one farmer can receive; by dividing ownership of one farm among relatives, farmers now can substantially stretch the maximum payment limits (0, $500 million).
• Raise the interest rate for rural electrification loans to the rate on Treasury securities (which would still be lower than that paid by other utilities) and put lower limits on the annual loan amounts ($70 million, $500 million).

These reforms, or something like them, have been blocked by opposition from the lobbies of the affected groups for over thirty years. Not even a grand budget compromise is likely to change things. In any event, when fully in effect the cuts would save only $4 billion a year. Although other such cuts might be included in this group, the total would still not be sizable.

Approach 3. Eliminate programs with low or questionable benefits. Value judgments differ on which federal programs belong in the list. My favorite candidates are given here, with estimated savings for 1991 and 1995 shown in parentheses.[25]

• Eliminate NASA's planned space station; it is a very expensive way to get modest scientific benefits and squeezes out more scientifically important unmanned space launches ($900 million, $2.05 billion).

• Cut the capital grants for mass transit to a 50 percent federal cost share and eliminate the operating subsidy. The program has done little to relieve congestion and much of the subsidy goes for the benefit of middle-class suburban commuters. If local jurisdictions wish to provide such subsidized transit, let them do so with their own funds; there are few benefits for the nation as a whole, and it is surely not an effective way to aid the poor ($610 million, $1.55 billion).

• Eliminate the loan and loan guarantee program of the Small Business administration except for assistance to minorities and disaster victims. Financial markets are now more efficient and less susceptible to market failures than they were when the loan program was begun many decades ago. The sums provided are a drop in the bucket compared with the annual flow of private credit to small business firms and have no effect on the health of the small business segment of the economy ($40 million, $310 million).

Except for the NASA space station, these programs—and those that others might choose as favorite candidates—have withstood repeated assaults for years. The potential savings again are not large. Moreover, hinging deficit reduction on getting agreement to eliminate whole programs usually means that the deficit is not reduced.

Approach 4. Cut social security benefits or tax social security benefits like other retirement income. If a comprehensive program to convert the budget deficit into a surplus includes a broad-based tax increase, a powerful case can be made that all nonpoor segments of the population should make some contribution, including those who receive non–means-tested federal benefits. And in fact, when in March 1990 Representative Dan Rostenkowski advanced such a deficit reduction proposal, a spokesperson for the elderly stated that they would be "willing to make sacrifices" as long as "everyone is making sacrifices on the same basis."[26]

The social security trust fund, however, is already accumulating reserves. Reducing benefits without changing payroll taxes would add to reserve accumulations, increase the degree to which the payroll tax is being used to support the general operations of government and draw strong opposition. But if social security benefits and payroll taxes were cut equally, and income taxes raised, the deficit could be reduced without having increased the overall tax burden on the country. A reduction of benefits by withholding 1 percentage point of the cost-of-living allowances in all non–means-tested programs for each of the next five years would lower the budget deficit by about $9 billion in fiscal 1993 and $16 billion in 1995.

While a benefit reduction is harder on the poor than on the rich, taxing social security benefits more nearly like other retirement income would raise substantial revenues for deficit reduction while making the tax system fairer and sparing those with low incomes. Currently, social security benefits are taxed only to the extent that they raise income above $32,000 for couples ($25,000 for single persons), and then only half of those benefits are subject to income tax. There is no logic to the threshold; the income tax itself provides a threshold for low-income households through exemptions and a standard deduction. And the apparent logic of the 50 percent assumption is also spurious, since the workers' payroll taxes paid during their working life typically cover no more than 15 percent of the value of the benefits.

Removing the special threshold and, conservatively, taxing 60 percent of social security benefits would bring in some $13 billion a year by 1995. If social security benefits were treated the same as similar benefits from private pension funds, taxes would be levied on 85 percent of their value, and the 1995 revenue yield would be $24 billion. (Accompanying the higher taxes on social security benefits with a 1 percent reduction in non–means-tested entitlement programs outside social security would add another $6 billion in 1995 spending cuts.)

Planning for a Budget Surplus: A Summary

The target for national saving set out earlier in this chapter implied the need for an overall surplus in the federal budget of about $1\frac{1}{2}$ percent of national income by the latter half of this decade. As noted, that surplus target for the overall (or unified) budget is less than the surplus in the social security and other retirement funds. There would still be a modest deficit in the federal government's operating budget.

Movement to the target should be expeditious, but gradual enough to avoid transition problems. Cutting the deficit by something like 0.6 percent of GNP each year would reduce the deficit to $25 billion by fiscal 1993 and produce a budget surplus of $70 billion in 1995 (on the way to attaining the full surplus target of nearly $110 billion by 1996). As noted earlier, the CBO projects deficits of $148 billion in 1993 and $119 billion in 1995 under current budgetary policies. To meet the 1995 target, a large package of expenditure reductions and tax increases will obviously be necessary. But the opportunities opened up by the winding down of the cold war and the magic of the interest "bonus" that accompanies large deficit reductions both reduce the size of the job.

Decisions of three major kinds will be involved in achieving the budget target. First, the defense budget can and should be reduced. The alternative programs for defense cutbacks developed by Korb and Steinbruner would produce gradually increasing spending cuts below the CBO projections of $55 billion and $80 billion in fiscal 1995, in dollars of then current purchasing power. For purposes of developing a long-range deficit reduction package, I have assumed a defense spending cut of $65 billion, roughly halfway between the two alternatives (see Table 14). Taking into account the interest bonus, the budget deficit would be reduced to $15 billion in 1995, a major improvement but still short of the target by $85 billion in 1995.

The second aspect of planning for an eventual budget surplus involves consideration of civilian

Table 14
Deficit reduction, stage 1:
Defense cuts, fiscal year 1995
Billions of dollars

Item	1995
Budget deficit with no policy change	−119
Defense spending cuts	+65
Interest bonus	+39
Resulting deficit	−15
Budget target	+70
Remaining to be cut	+85

spending priorities: where should spending be increased and where decreased? The analysis above identified a limited number of areas where federal spending should be increased and some where it should be cut. With reforms in investment and pricing policies for highway and airport investment, the nation's infrastructure needs can be met for additional federal outlays of only $2 billion or $3 billion a year. Federal spending for civilian R&D should be increased very sharply, but almost doubling that support could be done with an addition of only $15 billion a year to federal spending in 1995.

A case can be made that the nation should extend health insurance to all citizens. Aaron argues that the costs should be financed independently of the general budget with a special earmarked tax. A large increase in federal spending on elementary and secondary education is unwarranted at the present time, although educational grants, costing perhaps $6 billion a year (about $150 per elementary and secondary public school student), might be used to encourage the kind of reforms that Chubb and Hanushek propose. Finally, some modest increases in federal spending on certain "work load" items are called for to make up for the penny pinching of recent years. But the sums involved would not be large; $7 billion a year would provide a 20 percent increase across the entire category.

In total, all these outlay increases, converted to prices prevailing in 1995 (assuming a 4 percent annual inflation rate), would add $37 billion a year to the 1995 budget. If agreement could be reached either to tax social security benefits more fully or to make a modest reduction in cost-of-living adjustments (in all non–means-tested programs), the savings by 1995 should amount to about $17 billion a year. And if, in the rest of the civilian budget, a "grand compromise" could produce modest expenditure cuts growing to $10 billion a year by 1995, then $27 billion, or almost three-quarters of the additional $37 billion in outlays on high-priority programs, could be offset with outlay reductions elsewhere. The net addition to spending would be only $10 billion.[27]

The final step in the decisionmaking is the tax increase needed to close the remaining gap. If the spending reductions discussed above were enacted (including cuts in social security benefits or the equivalent amount of additional taxes on social security benefits), the required tax increase would be relatively modest—$67 billion in 1995, 1 percent

Table 15
Deficit reduction, stage 2: Tax increase, fiscal year 1995
Billions of dollars

Item	1995
Alternative A[a]	
Deficit reduction needed after defense cuts	85
Additional civilian spending (net)	10
Deficit reduction required	95
Tax increase	67
(Percent of national income)	(1.0)
Interest bonus[b]	28
Alternative B[c]	
Deficit reduction needed after defense cuts	85
Additional civilian spending (net)	27
Deficit reduction required	112
Tax increase	84
(Percent of national income)	(1.3)
Interest bonus[b]	28

[a] Assumes reduction in means-tested payments.

[b] The interest "bonus" is smaller, relative to the size of the deficit reduction, than the one shown in earlier tables. The econometric models on which the calculations of interest rate reductions were based imply that the second $50 billion of deficit reduction would yield the same fall in interest rates as the first $50 billion, and that the third $50 billion would yield an additional reduction as large as the second, and so on. But this is clearly unrealistic. It implies that after time interest rates could become negative, which clearly cannot happen. And so the 1995 estimate of the interest bonus for the second slice of deficit reductions (after the defense cuts have already been taken) was scaled down to equal 50 percent of the initial budgetary action, in comparison with the 60 percent bonus that comes in the first tranche of deficit reduction.

[c] Assumes no reduction in means-tested payments.

of national income (see alternative A in Table 15). Almost three-quarters of that amount could be raised, for example, by changing the 15 and 28 percent personal tax brackets to 16 and 30 percent and raising the corporate rate to 35 percent. All of it could be raised by an $8\frac{1}{2}$ percent surcharge on all personal and corporate taxes; or by a gasoline tax of sixty-five cents a gallon; or by some combination of both. It could also be reached by a package that eliminated the bubble in the personal income tax,[28] taxed capital gains by constructive realization at death, and added fifty cents to the gasoline tax. Aaron's proposal to create a new trust fund for the government's health care expenditures financed, in part, by a new 6 percent value-added tax would, as explained earlier, generate extra revenues for deficit reduction that would generate more than sufficient revenue to produce the target surplus ($75 billion versus $67 billion).

Alternative B in Table 15 repeats the calculations under the assumption that the cuts in social security benefits, or their equivalent, are impossible. The necessary tax increase by 1995 would be some $17 billion larger, amounting to 1.3 percent of national income by 1995.

From both an economic and a political standpoint, achieving the budget targets should not be done piece-meal, year by year, with no overall strategies or broad budget compromise. Enactment of a phased multiyear budget plan would be highly desirable. Both the tax increase and the changes in the social security COLAs could be enacted at the beginning of the period but come into effect gradually. And while one Congress cannot bind its successor, multiyear appropriations—at least for the next two years—could launch both the additional spending and the expenditure reductions on track toward the five-year target.

A Final Thought

For the past seven years a political impasse has prevented the country from dealing with its budget deficit and its low national saving rate. But as Western Europe reinvigorates itself by ▶rming a true common market and opening economic ties with

Eastern Europe, and as Japan continues to grow in productivity, technological capability, and market power, one has to hope that the United States will finally take the painful steps to end its own decade-long consumption binge and restore its national saving, investment, and productivity growth to levels worthy of a modern industrial power. The one sure way of doing this is to convert the current federal budget deficit into a significant surplus by the middle of the decade. For both substantive and political reasons, a program to do so will have to include large cuts in defense spending, reductions in middle-class subsidy and benefit programs, and a tax increase.

Appendix A: Do the Official Accounts Overstate the Size of the Federal Budget Deficit?

Robert Eisner of Northwestern University and some others argue that the official accounting measures normally used exaggerate the size of the federal deficit and substantially overstate its contribution to the decline in national saving.[29]

First, Eisner holds that the budget deficit should be adjusted downward to recognize the fact that inflation reduces the real value of the federal debt. Some part of the interest payments received by government bondholders—equal to the inflation rate times the public debt—has to be considered not as income to be consumed, but as an asset transfer needed to restore the real value of the bondholders' principal and consequently to be saved. This part of the deficit does not lower the national saving rate and should be excluded from the deficit calculation. If it were, the 1990 deficit would equal about 0.8 percent of GNP, not the 2.3 percent commonly cited. By the mid-1990s the inflation-adjusted deficit would disappear.

In assessing the effect of the budget deficit on private spending and saving, it may make sense to subtract the inflation adjustment as Eisner suggests. But the whole question is irrelevant to the measurement of national saving. If the inflation adjustment is subtracted from the budget deficit because part of government interest payments are not truly income to bondholders, then current statistics overstate not only the budget deficit but also the income and the saving of those same bondholders. The Eisner adjustment simply reallocates national saving among its

components: less private saving, less government dissaving, with no net effect on national saving itself. Moreover, the inflation adjustment as a share of national income has recently been about the same as its average during the 1970s. Hence the increase in the budget deficit, and its contribution to the decline in national saving, is just about the same whether the inflation adjustment is made or not.

Second, Eisner argues that some of the federal deficit finances net investment in public capital, which adds to the nation's productive wealth. Hence government spending, and the deficit, should exclude that investment. In fact, however, making such an adjustment at the present time would not significantly modify the size of the deficit. Net investment equals gross outlays on capital goods less depreciation. In recent years federal outlays on capital goods (excluding military weapons) have been only slightly higher than depreciation: federal net investment in recent years has been running at only about $4 billion a year.

Third, Eisner and others say that the budget deficit for total government is much smaller than the deficit for the federal government alone because state and local governments are running a large surplus. In fact, the operating budgets of state and local governments are now in deficit. Their overall budgets are in surplus according to the national income accounts because that accounting system includes in state and local budgets the large annual accumulation of reserves in their employee pension funds. Were these same employees in the private sector, those pension fund surpluses would be considered as part of personal saving. The data in Table 3 have been reclassified to shift this pension fund accumulation from public to private (personal) saving. In any event, wherever these pension fund accumulations are classified does not change the measure of national saving one whit and in no way diminishes its recent collapse.

Appendix B: The Productivity Payoff from Public Infrastructure Investment

In a widely cited work, David Aschauer argues that the rate at which public physical infrastructure increases can explain an important part of changes in the rate of growth of business productivity, including the fall in productivity growth since 1973.[30]

The Aschauer study regresses the rate of growth in human output, relative to a weighted index of labor and private capital inputs, against the rate of growth in the stock of public infrastructure, relative to the same weighted input index. His regression results imply, for example, that a $1 increase in the stock of public infrastructure adds about as much to productivity as a $4 increase in the stock of private business capital.[31] Those same results also imply that a one-time increase of $10 billion in the net stock of public infrastructure would yield a permanent increase of $7 billion in the annual level of GNP. While not a free lunch, this would be a very cheap banquet.

What the study actually demonstrates is simply that the time pattern of national productivity growth and the time pattern of the growth in public investment are similar. The growth rate of public capital peaked and began to decline at about the same time as productivity growth began to sag. This correlation tends to generate grossly inflated estimates of the returns to infrastructure investment. To be sure, carefully selected public investment in infrastructure can improve national productivity and output—the building of the interstate highway system, for example, was undoubtedly a major contributor to the rise in national productivity during the 1960s and early 1970s. But the kinds of payoffs promised by this study are not to be had.

Notes

1. All the expenditure estimates for 1990 and later years cited in this chapter *exclude* the net outlays (except interest) of the Resolution Trust Corporation, which is financing the bailout of the thrift institutions. As the Congressional Budget Office points out, "A clear economic case exists for excluding . . . all of RTC's net expenditures except payment of interest. . . . Such spending does not change the government's balance sheet and does not affect national saving in the way that most federal spending does." CBO, *An Analysis of the President's Proposals for Fiscal Year 1991,* March 1990, p. 199.

2. An average of private forecasts is given by *Blue Chip Economic Indicators,* Eggert Economic Enterprises, February 10, 1990.

3. Measured as deviations from a long-term (eight-year) moving average, fluctuations in long- and short-term interest rates were 3 1/2 to 4 times as large in the 1980s as they had been in the prior twenty-five years.

4. Robert Eisner of Northwestern University has argued that the official statistics overstate the size of the federal

deficit and its role in reducing the national saving rate. Appendix A examines his arguments and concludes that they do not warrant any change in the conclusions reached here or elsewhere in this chapter.

5. The current situation is not like the nineteenth century, when the United States also borrowed heavily abroad. In that case the proceeds were used to increase national investment in productive assets and to generate a stream of additional national income, out of which the debt service was paid. The country still ended up better off.

6. The other retirement funds in the federal budget include medicare, civil service retirement, and military retirement. The $2\frac{1}{2}$ percent estimate allows for some increase above the current schedule in payroll taxes to support medicare part A, which is actuarially underfunded.

7. One should be very careful about stating exactly how an appropriate current increase in national saving will ease or eliminate the burden of a large retired population on the then working generation. No matter what is done now through a surplus in the social security fund to put away additional saving, the next working generation will have to devote a larger fraction of its national income to paying retirement benefits than is now the case. What a current increase in saving and productive investment can do is to raise the future level of productivity and income. The higher proportion of income going to the retired will then be taken from a higher level of national income. But by, say, the third decade of the twenty-first century, no one except a few economic historians will realize that the level of national income is higher then because in the three preceding decades the country saved more. From a social and political standpoint, an increase in the "burden" of social security will appear to be occurring. (I am indebted to George Perry for this point.)

8. The problem is *not* that the social security surplus is being invested in Treasury bonds. Even if the rest of the budget were in balance, the trust funds would still be buying Treasury bonds. But in that case, since no new bonds would be issued to finance the operating budget, the social security reserves would be used to buy back government bonds now held by the private sector, making an equivalent amount of funds available for private investment. But now, when the social security funds buy government bonds, the proceeds simply go to finance the deficit in the remainder of the budget.

9. Even if there were no public social security system, the demographic projections imply the need for the nation to increase its national saving rate and raise its future national output and income. The consumption of retirees, whether publicly or privately financed, must come from future production.

10. This assumes aggregate balance for the operating budgets of state and local governments. As noted in

appendix A, the operating budgets of those governments do not on average run a surplus—indeed they are now in deficit. And the large surpluses of state and local governments in pension funds for their own employees have been reclassified as private saving, matching the treatment of the pension funds of private employers. As indicated earlier, net national product is used as the measure of national income.

11. These calculations were performed by Ralph Bryant at the Brookings Institution as part of a project devoted to comparing the performance and characteristics of a large number of econometric models. The spending cuts were assumed to take the form of a reduction in federal purchases of goods and services. The simulation proceeded in two steps: first Bryant calculated, model by model, how large an expansion of the money supply would be needed to offset the demand-depressing effects of the deficit reduction, and he averaged those results. He then estimated, model by model, the interest rate (and other) consequences of the stipulated 1 percent of GNP fiscal action combined with this particular monetary expansion.

12. With the federal debt currently at $2.3 trillion, a 1 percentage point decline in interest rates would ultimately lower interest payments on the debt by $23 billion. But since some of the debt is in long-term issues, these savings would not be realized all at once. This 1 percentage point lower interest rate would produce $10 billion in savings at the end of three years and $22 billion after six years.

13. Translated into the higher prices that are expected to prevail in 1995 (which are incorporated in the CBO deficit projection), the Korb-Steinbruner cuts would amount to $55 billion to $80 billion a year and the administration's reductions to $35 billion a year.

14. I include in "social security funds" only those financed by payroll taxes, that is, the old age and survivors, disability, and hospital insurance (OASDHI) trust funds.

15. Taxes were raised to pay for the Korean and Vietnam wars, but were quickly reduced when hostilities ended.

16. The high fraction of GNP going to individuals in 1975 is somewhat misleading. It was a year of deep recession. In recessions GNP falls more than federal spending. Payments to individuals actually rise above their long-run trend, since this category includes unemployment compensation. Had it not been for the recession, "payments to individuals" would have been about 4.3 percent of GNP in that year.

17. See appendix B for an analysis of why this study by David A. Aschauer overstates the productivity-raising effect of public investment.

18. These numbers exclude R&D outlays on the federal government's space program. While some spillovers for national productivity do stem from this activity, on balance outlays for the space program do not seem

to belong in a measure designed to gauge how the federal government is investing in technological advance that contributes to productivity growth. And including the outlays on the space program ($6.8 billion in 1990) would not change the basic pattern of small federal support for civilian R&D relative to GNP.

19. See Kenneth A. Small, Clifford Winston, and Carol A. Evans, *Roadwork: A New Highway Pricing and Investment Policy* (Brookings, 1989); and Clifford Winston, "Efficient Transportation Infrastructure Policy and Deregulation," *Journal of Economic Perspectives*, forthcoming.

20. See William S. Vickrey, "Pricing in Urban and Suburban Transport," *American Economic Review*, vol. 53 (May 1963, *Papers and Proceedings, 1962*), pp. 452–465, for an early discussion of possibilities.

21. John S. Bishop, "Incentives for Learning: Why American High School Students Compare So Poorly to Their Counterparts Overseas," in Commission on Workforce Quality and Labor Market Efficiency, *Investing in People: A Strategy to Address America's Workforce Crisis,* Background Papers, vol. 1 (Washington: U.S. Department of Labor, 1989), pp. 1–85.

22. Linda R. Cohen and Roger G. Noll, *The Technology Pork Barrel* (Brookings, forthcoming).

23. A VAT of $1\frac{1}{2}$ percent would provide the extra revenue required simply to pay for the Aaron proposal without deficit reduction.

24. The estimates of savings are from Congressional Budget Office, *Reducing the Deficit: Spending and Revenue, A Report to the Senate and House Committees on the Budget,* pt. 2 (February 1989 and February 1990).

25. CBO, *Reducing the Deficit.*

26. Steven Mufson, "Rostenkowski's Proposal Gets Surprising Response," *Washington Post,* March 21, 1990, p. D1.

27. If the reduction in non–means-tested benefits cannot be achieved, the net addition to spending would be $27 billion, not $10 billion.

28. When tax rates were cut in 1986, the top bracket rate was set at 28 percent. However, taxpayers with incomes between $82,000 and $218,000 (for a family of four) pay 33 percent. On higher incomes the rate drops back to 28 percent. The proposal above would keep the 33 percent bracket rate in effect for those higher incomes.

29. Robert Eisner, "Budget Deficits: Rhetoric and Reality," *Journal of Economic Perspectives,* vol. 3 (Spring 1989), pp. 73–93; and Robert Eisner and Paul J. Pieper, "A New View of the Federal Debt and Budget Deficits," *American Economic Review,* vol. 74 (March 1984), pp. 11–29.

30. David A. Aschauer, "Is Public Expenditure Productive," *Journal of Monetary Economics,* vol. 23 (March 1989), pp. 177–200.

31. According to Aschauer's regression, a 1 percent increase in the stock of public infrastructure raised the level of output—everything else held constant—by 0.39 percent during the period from 1949 to 1985. By virtually all estimates that increase was larger than the gain in output from a 1 percent increase in the stock of private business capital. Yet the stock of business capital (in 1987) was 3.3 times the size of the stock of public capital.

27
Debunking the Conventional Wisdom in Economic Policy

Robert Eisner
Northwestern University

Is the budget deficit a swarm of termites, starving national saving while eating away at the foundations of future prosperity? Is our trade deficit its inseparable and insupportable twin, and has it made us "the world's greatest debtor nation?" And are we forever trapped by a prospect of accelerating inflation that constrains monetary policy to slow the economy?

Is the old and minimal goal of 4 percent unemployment unattainable, and not an unwonted casualty of changes in conventional wisdom? Should we be building surpluses in the Social Security trust funds to provide for retirees of thirty years from now? Should we be forcing or seducing more private saving for that purpose—or paying off the federal debt?

The answers to all of these questions should be a clear and unequivocal "No!"

That this hasn't been the message from most prominent spokesmen for the economics profession—let alone the pundits of the press and body politic—merits some pondering, and keen analysis.

The 1970s saw the apparent collapse of the Keynesian neoclassical synthesis under the weight of growing inflation and unemployment. This seemed a clear contradiction of the Phillips curve—unless, in worshipping at the newly enshrined NAIRU (nonaccelerating inflation rate of unemployment), one associated it with an exorbitant "natural" rate of unemployment.

The petroleum supply shock and its reversal in the 1980s, along with persistently tight monetary and fiscal policy and sharp increases in unemployment, brought a sharp deceleration to the inflation. The curious notion that abrupt increases in joblessness might be best explained by worker preferences—

Source: Reprinted with permission of the publisher, M. E. Sharpe, Inc., 80 Business Park Drive, Armonk, New York 10504 USA. From the May/June 1990 issue of *Challenge*.

"waves of contagious laziness," in Modigliani's pungent phrase—should always have been hard to accept. It was certainly all the less plausible after the surge in unemployment to 10.7 percent at the end of 1982 in our greatest recession since the Great Depression. And then, how explain the extended recovery in the last seven years, cutting that unemployment percentage in half? Was it really unrelated to the initiation of huge deficits and the swing back to ease by the Fed in 1982?

I have often argued that economists and policymakers alike are confused by a failure to match the critical variables of economic theory and analysis with relevant empirical measures. In fact, fiscal policy was not stimulatory at the end of the 1970s. Appropriate accounting for the inflation tax—the reduction in the real value of outstanding government debt held by the public—meant that the much maligned Carter nominal deficits ($60 billion in 1980) were substantial real structural surpluses! Along with Paul Volcker's suffocating monetary policy, they slowed the economy and, initially prolonged in the Reagan Administration, drove it eventually to collapse in 1982.

Appropriate measures tell us that there was a huge real swing to real deficit at the end of 1982. This stemmed not only from the effectuation of statutory tax cuts and increased military spending, but also from the major reduction in the inflation tax as double-digit increases in prices receded into the past. All this should reconfirm that fiscal and monetary policy do matter, and matter very much in the ways that we used to agree they did when Richard Nixon and Milton Friedman defined us all as Keynesians.

Wisdom Through a Prism

The *1990 Economic Report of the President* is a good starting point for looking at the interface between economic science and economic policy. The first such document submitted by President Bush's new Council of Economic Advisers, it reflects much of the good sense and frequently counterintuitive insights that economics has to offer. It also contains much of the conventional wisdom that, for one reason or another, seems to have dominated both public discussion and the thoughts of many in the profession. And, perhaps as must be expected, it comes through a prism, moderated to be true, of the conservative coloration that has emanated from the White House for the last decade.

The premier macroeconomic issues, as ever, are achieving maximum current output and providing appropriately, with economic growth, for the future. These get entwined with questions of trade and current account deficits and net foreign investment in the United States.

Increasing current output, the *Economic Report* would have us believe, is essentially a matter of reducing the role of government and leaving everything possible to the market. Little space is left for discretionary macroeconomic intervention, in accordance with "The Administration's principle of systematic and credible fiscal and monetary policies . . . designed to minimize policy mistakes by not changing policy frequently on the basis of the economic conditions of the moment or any short-run forecast."

An often-repeated word here is "credible." One may be excused for wondering if the firm commitments to Gramm-Rudman targets—without smoke and mirrors or sealing presidential lips—and subsequent paying off the federal debt are very credible, let alone desirable fiscal policy. And is monetary policy supposed to eschew the kind of Federal Reserve response "of the moment" we witnessed with regard to the stock market crash of October 1987?

"The most direct and important step that can be taken to increase U.S. national saving," we are told, "is to reduce the federal budget deficit." But then, "The most pressing need . . . is not to invest more in education, but to invest more effectively." This latter stricture is not repeated with regard to private business investment where permanent reductions in the business cost of capital are advocated to encourage the acquisition of more hardware and bricks and mortar.

We are told (correctly) "that studies find that growth in current output serves as a good proxy for expected growth in demand and . . . has the strongest effect on investment." But then the *Economic Report* repeatedly recommends cuts in the capital gains tax and favors policies presumed to induce more (attempted) private saving, along with those budget cuts which—it is acknowledged—may reduce output "in the short run."

The report embodies some of the remarkable confusion—or at least consequences of the confusion—between identities and economic behavior and causation that has repeatedly bedeviled economic analysis. To invest more we are urged to save more. Has a whole political generation forgotten that while gross saving is identically equal to gross investment, the attempts to save more—or government tax gimmicks to induce more saving—by reducing consumption and aggregate demand may actually reduce investment and saving? Of course, if output is always determined by an unchanging "natural" rate of employment, less consumption and less government spending must imply more investment. Is this conditional statement now taken properly as the foundation of appropriate national policy?

An associated identity, that net national saving equals net private domestic investment plus net foreign investment, also looms large in the *Economic Report*. And it leads us down the slippery slope of the other side of the net foreign investment coin: "Current account surpluses primarily reflect the gap between domestic saving and domestic investment" and "efforts to reduce the U.S. current account deficit will need to focus primarily on measures to raise public and private saving."

It is curious that the *Economic Report* did not suggest reducing domestic investment as a way of reducing the current account deficit. That too, if one can assume saving is given, must reduce the gap between saving and domestic investment and thus raise net foreign investment. Of course, again, there is no assurance that measures to encourage saving, public or private, will not either actually reduce total saving or, if you believe some of their advocates, increase domestic investment by as much, thus leaving no room for "improvement" in net foreign investment or the current account balance.

I must confess that reducing fiscal stimulus by reducing government dissaving may well reduce the current account deficit. My own regressions indicate such a relation in the past. And it should work beautifully if our deficit-cutting gets us into a sufficient recession so that, along with the collapse of sales in Detroit, Americans' purchases of Hondas and Toyotas shrink as well.

Fundamental Questions

Economic analysis and policy decisions, once more, are confused by a widespread failure to match concepts and relevant real-world variables. We want to maximize current output but fail to recognize that major components of the product of government and households are not included in official or conventional measures of GNP, raising fundamental questions about our measures of productivity as well as aggregate income and product.

We exude concern over presumably inadequate rates of saving and investment. We are told that we are on a mindless consumption binge which is depriving future generations of their birth rights. But our measures of saving and investment exclude perhaps 80 percent of the accumulation of capital, intangible as well as tangible, on which future output depends.

We worry about a reported current account deficit that is adding to our obligations to the rest of the world, making us that "world's greatest debtor nation." But few bother to point out that the measures on which the statement is based warrant no such conclusion.

Let me put it bluntly. If we don't know what we are talking about, how can we tell what to do about it?

Thus, we boast appropriately of the large increases in market employment of the last decade. This has added to GNP, if at a reduced rate. But should we not note the loss in nonmarket output as millions of women forsake household activity, and McDonalds and TV dinners replace home cooking? And shouldn't we be prepared to act on the need for additional child care to replace that lost in the home?

In what sense, we may add, is productivity declining if women leave low-productivity nonmarket work at home for more productive market work? (It may be argued *a priori* that market output must be more productive; otherwise, aside from the pressure to escape home tedium and the drive for independence and self-identity, women would not leave the home to take market jobs.) The aggregate rate of growth of productivity, as conventionally defined, may be declining as women move into less well-paying and hence less productive jobs, thus driving down average market productivity. But the average total productivity, market and nonmarket, may be rising because the less productive, nonmarket share is declining.

Effective policies to increase labor force participation may then increase total productivity, even if they bring about a decline in market productivity (or its rate of growth). What about cutting payroll taxes, instead of capital gains taxes, to raise productivity?

The big policy issue these days, in the *Economic Report* and in general discussion, is "saving." Net national saving, we are told, is too low. A prime cause, we are further told, is the large budget deficit. Again, careless application of an identity appears to justify the conclusion. Gross saving is the sum of personal saving, corporate saving, and government saving, the last being the sum of federal and state and local government surpluses. Clearly, if one component is lower, and all other components remain the same, the total must be lower. But surely, it cannot be simply assumed that these other components remain the same.

The federal government, for example, currently gives some $100 billion a year to states and localities in grants in aid. If these were to be eliminated, the deficit would presumably decline. But if taxpayers apply their reading of President Bush's lips to state and local governments, *their* surpluses would have to decline (or deficits grow).

Further, suppose the deficit was reduced by either tax increases (or higher user-cost fees) or expenditure reductions. Disposable personal income would be decreased (or consumption increased to pay those user fees) and personal saving would have to decline. Whether the decline in personal saving might be as great as the decrease in government dissaving would depend on the further repercussions on investment and income. If the latter are negative, part of the initial decrease in government dissaving may indeed be canceled as tax revenues decline. But can we properly assume, in any event, that more public saving will mean more total saving?

The results of my own quantitative analysis indicate a relationship between the conventional measure of national saving (for the years 1957 to 1988) and the previous year's cyclically adjusted and inflation-adjusted or real budget deficit, both measured as percents of GNP (see Table 1). Each percentage point of deficit was associated on the average with half a percentage point more of national saving. Introduction of a monetary instrument, in the form of the similarly lagged change of monetary base, over the years 1962 to 1988, left the positive relation between saving and the budget deficit intact, although the coefficient of the deficit variable was reduced from about a half to a third.

Table 1

Adjusted budget deficits, changes in monetary base, and conventional national saving, NSO

Variable or Parameter	Regression Coefficients and Standard Errors		
	1957–88	1962–88	
	w/o DMB	w/o DMB	with DMB
C	5.407	4.825	3.500
	(2.178)	(3.326)	(4.970)
PAHED(–1)	0.508	0.568	0.324
	(0.317)	(0.341)	(0.319)
DMB(–1)	—	—	4.575*
			(1.814)
AR(1)	0.854	0.897	0.917
	(0.105)	(0.105)	(0.098)
$\hat{R}^2$	0.633	0.687	0.755
D-W	1.843	1.777	1.953
n	32	27	27

Notes: *Significant at 0.05 probability level.
The dependent variable NSO equals conventional national saving in 1982 dollars (net private domestic investment plus statistical discrepancy in 1982 dollars plus current dollar net foreign investment divided by GNP implicit price deflator) as percent of GNP in 1982 dollars.

C	Constant term
PAHED(–1)	Lagged price-adjusted, high-employment budget deficit as percent of GNP
DMB(–1)	Lagged real change in monetary base as percent of GNP
AR(1)	First order autoregressive coefficient
D-W	Durbin-Watson coefficient
$\hat{R}^2$	Adjusted coefficient of determination
n	Number of observations

Source: Author's calculations.

These results should not be surprising. Others may have noted, as have I, that increased structural deficits have been associated with increases in the rate of growth of GNP and the rate of growth of gross private domestic investment. They were also associated, as I have already noted, with decreases in net foreign investment, but these decreases did not fully offset the domestic investment increases.

All of this tells only a small part of the saving story though. If we are concerned with saving as a measure of what the economy is providing for the future, we should be concerned with a measure of saving that is equal to the total of all investment in the economy, in households and government as well as in business and nonprofit institutions, and in human and intangible capital as well as in machinery and bricks and mortar.

The U.S. National Income and Product Accounts, however, do not even include public tangible investment. We thus have the anomaly that govern-ment construction of roads and airports is not investment, but private acquisition of trucks and planes is investment. The cars bought by Hertz and Avis are gross private domestic investment, but the ones bought by private individuals are "personal consumption expenditures" and the police vehicles bought by the city of Chicago are "government expenditures for goods and services," essentially treated as government consumption.

A comprehensive measure of net national saving, corresponding to the change of total fixed reproducible capital plus net foreign investment (minus the statistical discrepancy), averaged 5.56 percent of GNP over the years 1982-88 as compared to 2.30 percent for the official BEA NIPA measure, which had come to 6.87 percent over the years 1971-81. The broader measure also showed a decline from its 1971-81 average (of 9.35 percent). The relevant point, though, is that the structural, inflation-adjusted real budget deficit was all the more sharply, and

Table 2
Adjusted budget deficits, changes in monetary base and real national saving, NS1
(including saving in public and household reproducible capital)

Variable or Parameter	Regression Coefficients and Standard Errors		
	1957–88	*1962–88*	
	w/o DMB	*w/o DMB*	*with DMB*
C	8.113	7.514	6.211
	(2.284)	(3.526)	(4.327)
PAHED(–1)	0.770*	0.876*	0.588
	(0.332)	(0.367)	(0.339)
DMB(–1)	—	—	5.280*
			(1.932)
AR(1)	0.861	0.897	0.911
	(0.096)	(0.099)	(0.092)
$\hat{R}^2$	0.668	0.711	0.782
D-W	1.677	1.689	1.916
n	32	27	27

Notes: *Significant at 0.05 probability level.
The dependent variable NS1 equals change in total fixed reproducible capital plus net foreign investment minus statistical discrepancy, in 1982 dollars as percent of GNP.
Source: Author's calculations.

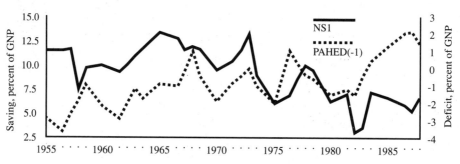

Figure 1
Real national saving (1) and previous adjusted deficit.
Source: Author's calculations.

statistically significantly, associated with more saving by the broader measure, as may be seen in the regression results reported in Table 2 and, graphically, in Figure 1.

But why restrict our saving to an identity with investment in reproducible, tangible capital? Are business, government, and nonprofit R&D expenditures not properly counted as investment in the future? Can we not save for our children by investing in their education as well as by leaving them an inheritance? Can we not invest in developing our land and its resources as well as in constructing structures on its surface?

My most comprehensive measure of saving, including all intangible and tangible capital and a measure of foreign investment that reflects changes in market values of claims, is all the more positively related to those adjusted budget deficits, as shown in Table 3. And again the reason may not be hard to find. "Deficits" created by increased public

Table 3

Adjusted budget deficits, changes in monetary base and comprehensive measure of national saving, NS2 (including all tangible and intangible capital and adjusted net foreign investment, 1972–81)

Variable or Parameter	Regression Coefficients and Standard Errors	
	w/o DMB	with DMB
C	41.117	39.537
	(3.659)	(2.565)
PAHED(-1)	9.819*	9.261*
	(3.817)	(2.576)
DMB(-1)	—	32.518*
		(13.555)
AR(1)	0.248	0.118
	(0.521)	(0.466)
$\hat{R}^2$	0.644	0.817
D-W	1.369	1.808
n	10	10

Notes: *Significant at 0.05 probability level.

The dependent variable NS2 equals change in total fixed reproducible capital plus adjusted net foreign investment minus statistical discrepancy plus change in real value of land plus investment in intangible capital and in government and household inventories and semidurables plus net revaluations exclusive of net revaluations on land.

Source: Author's calculations.

expenditures for infrastructure and education and research should certainly be expected to increase measures of saving defined to include such investment.

Ignoring the Implications

The *Economic Report* (and the Council of Economic Advisers) are to be commended for recommending that we move toward the United Nations System of National Accounts (SNA) that includes government capital expenditures as investment and saving. But they would appear to ignore the implications of this in their repeated admonitions to reduce the federal deficit by reducing government "spending." Implementation of programs to balance the budget and then pay off the federal debt, coupled with literal application of the "no new taxes" pledge would make it virtually impossible to maintain public investment, let alone increase it.

The notion that budget deficits must crowd out domestic investment, belied by regressions over several decades, is particularly rejected in recent data. Gross private domestic investment in real terms has averaged 17.6 percent of GNP over the past two

years, equal to or above the ratio a decade ago. The real ratios, it is true, are higher than those in current dollars, as there has been a substantial decline in the relative price of investment goods. But if our nominal saving is now buying us more real investment, that is hardly to be ignored.

It is also true that net saving and investment have not fared as well. This reflects in part a shift to shorter-lived capital. But capital consumption allowances will rise relative to gross investment as the rates of growth of output and hence investment decline. Those rates of growth may well be declining because of stagnation in public and intangible investment. Ultimately, in a stationary economy, with constant capital-output ratios, the rate of net saving must be zero.

The most substantial argument that our high rate of domestic investment should not dissipate our alarm over low saving rates is the negative foreign investment that this implies. Each year that it continues, we are told, adds to foreign claims on our capital and income and hence to the burden on those future generations. The deficit is again presumed to be the culprit, and this time it may well be. On closer examination, however, the disease may not be all that bad. The complaint may even reflect a bit of hypochondria. And the recommended cure of budget deficit reduction is likely to be far worse.

Our negative net foreign investment—the foreign capital pouring into the United States to finance that alleged consumption binge—is supposed to be adding to our "debt" to the rest of the world, and to have made us "the world's greatest debtor nation." In fact, however, the value of U.S. assets abroad has until recently exceeded the value of foreign holdings in the United States. The major problem is that our official data carry direct investment at original cost. The CEA is wisely asking the BEA to attempt to add market valuations. Since our investment abroad is generally older than foreign investment here it has appreciated considerably more. Correction of all assets to market values would wipe out all but $100 billion of the alleged $532 billion of reported net foreign claims at the end of 1988.

Continued current account deficits will in themselves add to net foreign claims, but even here there is an often neglected built-in corrective. If foreign investment in the United States gets to the point where foreigners want to "get out," they can not do so any more than we can collectively "pull out" of the stock market. As they try to convert to their own currency they can only sell their dollars to other foreigners (except for the limited amount of foreign currency held in the United States.). In the effort, though, they drive down the value of the dollar, and thus increase the dollar value of the trillion or so dollars of foreign claims that we have in foreign currencies.

What this suggests is that a monetary policy that permits the dollar to decline, even before it corrects the conventionally measured current account deficit, will increase a measure of net foreign investment that reflects the dollar market value of claims, here and abroad. An adjustment of investment income in the current account to reflect these capital gains would then entail a corresponding adjustment to gross saving.

Back to the Central Issues!

How do we improve the quality of life for today and tomorrow? The *Economic Report* and most economists properly urge a maximum feasible use of free markets, domestically and internationally. But most economists recognize as well the need for government intervention, preferably by taxes, to discourage negative externalities, and expenditures or subsidies to provide adequate quantities of public goods. And critical, so far intractable, problems face us in large proportions of the population at or below minimum living standards, many locked in endless cycles of poverty.

A rising tide does not raise all boats. Some sink! But maximum employment remains the single greatest source of current improvement for our poor. Its achievement offers the greatest potential for improving the future. This relates in part to the fact that movement to and maintenance of high levels of output offer the greatest stimulus to business investment. Most important, the achievement of maximum employment will require vast investment in human capital, so that all of our population is equipped for productive labor in a fast-moving, technologically advanced world.

Much of the current conventional wisdom fades in the light of these realities and these needs. Raise taxes, many tell us. But how can we reconcile this with the need to maintain aggregate demand for maximum employment and output? Along with higher taxes and a reduced deficit can come sufficiently easier monetary policy and lower interest rates to maintain aggregate demand with a higher rate of investment. I am repeatedly amazed that so many who should know better can have such supreme confidence in this outcome. Do we rely on the pre-Keynesian assurance that full employment is the normal state of affairs and that automatic movements in the rate of interest and/or the general level of prices will guarantee equality of investment demand and saving at full employment? Or are we sure that Alan Greenspan and his cohorts will do everything necessary to bring about that result. Are we even sure that they could if they tried?

The administration presumably sees unspeakable evil in raising taxes—at least unless they can be given another name, or be raised at a different level of government. It counsels reductions in federal expenditures, to reduce the deficit and then to balance the budget. And now the CEA would even have us pay off the federal debt. In addition to having the same deleterious effect on aggregate demand as raising taxes, this policy also blocks efforts for critical public investment.

Articles in the March-April 1990 issue of *Challenge* sharpen the debate. Charles Schultze, in *Use the*

Peace Dividend to Increase Saving, "would have most of the peace dividend absorbed into the sinkhole of budget deficit reduction."

"Given what a reduced budget deficit and lower interest rates would do for the long-term vigor of the American economy," he concludes, "I can't think of a better sinkhole." Well, I can.

Charlie sees declines in currently high real interest rates as stimulating private investment if there is increased fiscal constraint. He explains currently high investment—if not high enough for his taste—as the consequence of foreign financing. But this raises some troublesome questions he does not address. If investment can remain as high as it has with those high real interest rates—and Charlie acknowledges that most of the (presumed) hit of budget deficits has been on foreign, not domestic investment—how sensitive to these rates can investment be?

Many of us who have studied investment have found it not all that sensitive. It depends much more, as the *Economic Report* suggests, on the general state of demand and growth in demand. But then if fiscal constraints curb our "consumption binge" and the economy slows, how much of a compensating effect can we expect from lower interest rates, even if Alan Greenspan does cooperate to the best of his ability? To the extent that lower interest rates will help, why not pressure Alan to ease up on money and credit and stimulate investment (and exports by thus letting the dollar fall) without insisting on the fiscal constraint that might kill off investment, along with the economy in general?

And as for Charlie's rough use of models to show that interest rates would fall if the budget deficit were reduced, he might enlighten us as to what they show about the effects on GNP and employment. I would bet that all of them, certainly the ones in which Charlie would have the most confidence, would also show at least initial declines in both, as may be inferred from my Figures 2 and 3. And with those declines, one would be foolhardy to expect a pickup in investment.

In another *Challenge* article, *Why We Must Raise Taxes,* Francis Bator, demanding an increase in taxes, argues that "since 1983 the federal budget has been much too stimulative" and has "caused public plus private expenditure for consumption to grow much faster than inflation-safe GNP" and has forced the Fed to raise real interest rates. This, I fear, may have become conventional wisdom along the Cambridge-Brookings axis, but is again hard to credit.

Unemployment at the end of 1983 was still over 8 percent. Is that a rate at which we should complain about an overly stimulative fiscal policy? The inflation rate, as measured by the change in the GNP implicit price deflator, had fallen from 9.7 percent to 6.4 percent to 3.9 percent from 1981 to 1983. Did that suggest a need for either fiscal or monetary constraints? Or was it that unemployment had fallen from its December 1982 peak of 10.7 percent and was still falling. Does Professor Bator object to a falling rate of unemployment?

And is a falling or low rate of unemployment reason to demand fiscal restraint or to condone a monetary policy that was a major culprit in rising real interest rates? A markedly easier monetary policy has long been in order to drive down nominal

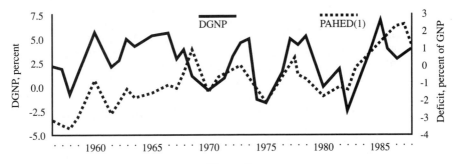

Figure 2
Change in GNP and the previous adjusted deficit.
Source: Economic Report of the President and author's calculations.

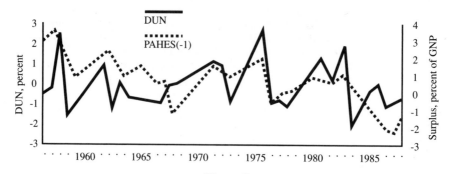

Figure 3
Change in unemployment and previous adjusted surplus.
Source: Economic Report of the President and author's calculations.

interest rates and thus permit real interest rates to decline in the face of lesser inflation.

It is time to face the real hang-up in this whole debate: the anachronistic fear of inflation and the associated abandonment of our commitment to truly full employment. In the years 1984 to 1989, since Bator feels fiscal policy turned too stimulatory, inflation has run successively at percentage rates of 3.7, 3.0, 2.6, 3.2, 3.3 and finally 4.1. Where is that accelerating inflation that so many NAIRU and "natural rate of unemployment" faddists were writing about? The nonaccelerating-inflation-rate-of-unemployment was some 6.5 percent according to some, 6.0 percent for "liberal" proponents of the concept. Unemployment has now been below 6 percent for almost three years—since August 1987.

Was it really Paul Volcker's and then Alan Greenspan's fingers in the dike that held back the inflation? Or did some economists cave in awfully fast to the notions, ever popular in financial and generally conservative circles, that the menaces of the modern world are inflation and budget deficits, and that there is little or nothing to be done to combat unemployment?

Indeed, why must our current 5.3 percent unemployment rate raise fears of an "overheated" economy? Is GNP really too high? What happened to the 4 percent unemployment target that was the goal for many years? Unemployment was down to the 3 percent range during the Viet Nam War and inflation never reached 6 percent until the oil supply shocks of 1973 and 1974. Must it take a war to generate the aggregate demand to bring us to relatively full employment?

Historians of economic thought may well—I hope soon—see the whole concept of a NAIRU, let alone one at the high levels some have found it convenient

to accept, as one of the odder perversities that swept up some economic theorists and policymakers with no direct empirical support. Supply shocks and a host of self-inflicted wounds that kept up costs and prices were mistaken for excess-demand inflation, something that I would insist has never occurred in modern American history except during or in the immediate aftermath of wars.

And oh, the damage that these notions cause! Because of the exaggerated fear of inflation, monetary policy must be tight, keeping interest rates too high and the dollar too costly. This generates trade deficits that bring undue hardship to various industries and protectionism that threatens economies the world over. And the related pressure to reduce the budget deficit, swollen in part by high interest payments, blocks attention to the vital needs of our society.

Make no mistake about it. Monetary and fiscal policies aimed at "zero inflation" and balancing the budget, and then running a surplus and paying off the federal debt, are fraught with the danger of disaster. In the first instance, they threaten to bring us into a major recession. They are likely to raise rather than lower real interest rates and this, in combination with a slowed economy, is more likely to devastate private investment than to raise it.

Repeating Past Mistakes

But most important of all, these misconceived policies are inhibiting the actions most essential for our future. The needs of our retirees of the 21st century will not be met by piling up surpluses in the Social Security trust funds, whether they are used to buy government notes or private stocks and bonds (in the latter case, socializing the economy?).

They will be met by accumulating productive capital—of all kinds. These include homes and durable goods for consumers. They include investment by government in roads and bridges and airports and all the rest of our crumbling infrastructure. They include investment in preserving our environment of land and water and air. And they include all of the vital investment in the intangible capital of research and knowledge, of education and health on which productivity and prosperity depend.

All this is not easy to accomplish in any event. It is all the harder if we continue to fight the demons of the past, demons that we thought were exorcised in the Keynesian Revolution of a half a century ago. Must every—or every other—generation of policy-makers and economists repeat the mistakes of the past before it can move on?

IV

Budgeting Systems and Management: An Instrument for Securing Administrative Efficiency and Economy

It has been said that the hand is subdued to the dye in which it works. This is true. So budget reform bears the imprint of the age in which it originated. Wearied of the continued story of public expenditure for corrupt purposes designed to serve the ends of political machines, citizens demanded an accounting. This is literally what they got. . . . How far it hampers the upright official and leads to innocent waste of funds is another matter. But new economies in management are to come not from a return to old practices but from advances made from points now gained.

C. A. Beard, 1917
New York Bureau of Municipal Research

Budgeting Systems Revisited

Any discussion of the management dimension of budgeting properly begins with the budget systems developed through budget reform. In this sense, it is important to remember that the line-item budget itself was a budget reform of tremendous significance. While performance budgeting had been on the scene at the same time as the line-item budget, a certain amount of development or education under the mantle of the line-item budget was necessary first. Line-item budgets codified spending rules, allowed comparisons by expenditure category across organizations, and, most importantly, permanently injected the accounting dimension into public expenditures. Behind every object of expenditure category, there was a body of rules and regulations that were enforced by the line-item budget. This section examines current management dimensions of public sector budgeting, but it begins with several historical articles that explain the objectives and mechanics behind three primary budgeting systems. These were developed and utilized in one form or another by the federal government and most state and local governments: Performance Budgeting, Planning-Programming-Budget-Systems (PPBS), and Zero-Based Budgeting (ZBB).

Performance Budgeting and Efficiency

Although the first line-item executive budgets marked a significant advancement in budgetary technology, many public managers had become increasingly dissatisfied with the deficiencies of this process by the end of World War II. Perhaps the major criticism of line-item budgeting, with its extensive emphasis on classification by objects of expenditure, was the consequent lack of information about the total programs and functions of government. As government programs were expanding, public sector administrators were demanding more information about management, the service and delivery processes, and the efficiency of programs than line-item budgets were capable of providing.

Budgeting systems concerned with performance work data and efficiency concepts were first developed just before World War I in New York City at the New York Bureau of Municipal Research. The first federal efforts at performance budgeting were in the Department of Agriculture and the Tennessee Valley Authority during the 1930s. Then, under the auspices of the Hoover Commission of 1949, the designation *performance budgeting* was officially sanctioned as the preferred budgeting method. The Hoover Commission stated its recommendation bluntly: ''A program or performance budget should be substituted for the present budget, thus presenting in a document of much briefer compass the Government's expenditure requirements in terms of services, activities, and work projects rather than in terms of the things bought.''

A specific definition of performance budgeting has long been elusive. Jesse Burkhead, in his benchmark textbook, *Government Budgeting* (New York: Wiley, 1956), maintained there could be no precise definition of performance budgeting because performance budgeting systems tend to be so varied in their operations. Nevertheless, a general definition of performance budgeting is both possible and useful. Performance budgeting presents purposes and objectives for which funds are being allocated, examines the costs of programs and activities established to meet these objectives, and identifies and analyzes quantitative data measuring work performed and accomplishments.

One problem of no small significance must be clarified. The terms *performance budgeting* and *program budgeting* tend to be used interchangeably, but they are not synonymous. In performance budgeting, programs are generally linked to the various higher levels of an organization and serve as labels that encompass and structure the subordinate performance units. These units—the central element of performance budgeting—are geared to an organization's operational levels, and information about them is concrete and meaningful to managers at all levels. Program budgeting, on the other hand, might or might not incorporate performance measurement, yet may still be useful for delineating broad functional categories of expenditure for review at higher levels. Overall, performance budgeting tends to be retrospective, focusing on previous performance and work accomplishments, while program budgeting tends to be forward looking, involving policy planning and cost and spending forecasts.

While the predominant orientation of performance budgeting was for the purpose of better management and enhanced efficiency, most of its early advocates expressed hope that its associated processes would further executive–legislative budgeting relationships. Indeed, the generally recognized success of performance budgeting was instrumental in obtaining congressional approval of the Budgeting and Accounting Procedures Act of 1950, which gave the president greater discretion over the format and content of executive budget submissions. Certainly systematic performance measurement data were more useful to appropriations committees than traditional line-item submissions, and better served the purpose of legislative oversight.

Catheryn Seckler-Hudson's overview article, ''Performance Budgeting in Government,'' written in 1953 (four years after the Hoover Commission's recommendation), provides one of the best introductions to the objectives and mechanics of performance budgeting. One additional note is appropriate. Over the last decade, a considerable body of literature has emerged on productivity analysis and measurement. Ironically, the contentions of this ''new'' productivity field and now the even ''newer'' total quality management field are remarkably reminiscent of earlier claims for performance budgeting. Performance budgeting sought to establish management's right and responsibility to ascertain how much work was being accomplished, at what cost, and for what results, as measured against specified performance standards. In the 1990s, the same questions are being asked. An interesting illustration of this is A. Premchand's article exploring the historical relationship between public sector productivity management and budgeting systems, "Government Budgeting and Productivity," which is included near the end of this section. But don't relegate performance budgeting completely to budgeting's historical experience: many cities (San Diego and Phoenix, for example) still use performance budgeting. In 1990, Senator Roth of Delaware introduced legislation in the Senate that would require federal agencies to adopt such a format, and the OMB began reviewing how applicable performance based budgeting could be to the federal government.

PPBS: Planning and Effectiveness

The 1960s witnessed the departure of performance budgeting from preeminence and the emergence of a major new development in budgeting technology. Some contend that performance budgeting simply faded away, in part because its requirements for immense amounts of data from lower levels of management generated a considerable lack of enthusiasm. Furthermore, as government programs continued to expand, budget officials—already faced with a considerable burden of calculation in making resource allocation decisions—were less and less interested in a micro-oriented budgeting system and more inclined to some form of macro-oriented system that would facilitate budgeting in aggregate terms. Others contend that the demise of performance budgeting was a slight exaggeration. Conceding that it had been replaced in some jurisdictions, it was, for the most part, still functioning. Nevertheless, performance budgeting and its concern for data bases paved the way for the next major innovation in budgeting systems.

In the 1960s, Planning Programming Budgeting Systems (PPBS) took the budgeting world by storm. Widely hailed as an exciting, new approach to rational decision making, PPBS in fact did promise much. It began by insisting that it could interrelate and coordinate the three management processes constituting its title: planning would be related to programs that would be keyed to budgeting. To emphasize further the planning dimension, PPBS pushed the time horizon out to half a decade by requiring five-year forecasts for program plans and cost estimates. PPBS placed a whole new emphasis on program objectives, outputs, and alternatives and stressed the new watch word of evaluation: the "effectiveness" criterion. Finally, PPBS required the use of new analytical techniques from strategic planning, systems analysis, and cost–benefit analysis to make governmental decision making more systematic and rational.

David Novick, an economist with the Rand Corporation, is generally considered the developer of PPBS. His article, "What Program Budgeting Is and Is Not," is still the best description of the origins, objectives, and operation of PPBS from its development in the U.S. Department of Defense (DOD) during the late 1950s to its apex in the late 1960s. PPBS remained essentially a strategic planning and analysis tool until Robert McNamara's tenure as secretary of defense. McNamara was not pleased with what he found at DOD when he arrived in 1961. Plans were being formulated without considering costs, alternatives were not being considered, and each of the four services was submitting separate budgets delineating their own priorities. McNamara's response was an integrated planning program budget (one budget for all four services) that allowed him to make some budgetary decisions of real consequence.

PPBS succeeded admirably in DOD, both in producing quality budgetary analysis and establishing a new modicum of control for the Secretary of Defense. What remained unclear was the degree of uniqueness of DOD's example. Aaron Wildavsky ("Rescuing Policy Analysis from PPBS," *Public Administration Review,* 1969) observed that numerous requisites existed in DOD that were nonexistent in the domestic sector. Among them were: lengthy staff experience with defense strategy and logistics; the prior establishment of common terminology and analytical techniques; an experienced planning staff and established planning systems (not to mention having the Rand Corporation available as developer and ongoing consultant); and finally, with the advent of McNamara, top leadership that actually comprehended policy analysis and was willing to make a commitment to it. Perhaps Wildavsky's most telling point for why DOD was a bad model for PPBS was the relative size of the budgets involved: cost figures for most domestic programs do not even approximate the magnitude of small defense programs. Consequently, the cost and applicability of the type of analysis employed at the Department of Defense in PPBS was neither transferable nor affordable.

Undaunted, Lyndon Johnson made PPBS mandatory for all federal agencies in 1965, embracing it as the method and system that would ensure the success of his Great Society programs. But opposition to PPBS came from various quarters, especially from bedeviled agency administrators and staff who experienced one difficulty after another in complying with PPBS's submission requirements. PPBS was formally abandoned in the federal government by the Nixon administration in 1971. State and local governments, on the other hand, were rapidly modifying their PPBS programs and installing hybrid versions. And, perhaps most ironic of all, PPBS continues to be used (in modified format) at the Defense Department: a run of more than thirty years.

PPBS was, above all, a planning system for budgets. If it did nothing else, it recognized the primacy of the planning process within budgeting. This was harder to grapple with at state and local levels, where managers were less certain about how planning and budgeting interacted. One of the most insightful books written during the early 1970s, after the fall of PPBS, was the late S. Kenneth Howard's *Changing State Budgeting.* An excerpt from that work entitled "Planning and Budgeting: Who's on First?" superbly illustrates the management and political problems involved here.

Zero-Base Budgeting and Political Relevance

It may well be that the last of the major systems of budgeting is really the oldest. Zero-Base Budgeting (ZBB) refers to a budgeting process that is first and foremost a rejection of the incremental decision-making model of budgeting. A comprehensive system, it demands a rejustification of the entire budget submission (from ground zero), whereas incremental budgeting essentially respects the outcomes of previous budgetary decisions (collectively referred to as the budget base) and focuses examination on the margin of change from year to year. Two points of significance should be noted in the contrast between incremental and comprehensive (zero-base) budgeting: (1) incremental budgeting was accepted up until the late 1970s as the reality of our budgeting experience, and (2) would-be, more rational decision makers over the past thirty years have been adamant in their criticism of incrementalism.

Some of the origins of this debate (almost feud) stem from the legislative–executive dichotomy in budgetary decision making. One expects an incremental approach out of a legislature because it so appropriately fits their decision-making process. It is argued that decision making in the executive branch, via the budgetary process, need not be so constricted. The executive branch can, after all, order and reorder budgeting processes and systems in order to counter incrementalism. One cannot help but suspect that the growing rapidity with which new budgeting systems are adopted and abandoned is in part a reflection of the old adage that the rules should be changed occasionally just to keep the players honest. Certainly the adoption of ZBB by a newly elected president in 1977 had certain connotations of this. It should be clear from the outset, however, that ZBB was first and foremost a refutation of the incremental nature of budgeting processes.

ZBB also focused on the concept of priorities, which was much more than the elaboration of the consideration of alternatives proposed by Verne Lewis (Section I). It reflects a concern that among its options, governments should choose only the most important to act upon. Also, in part, it continues the progressive concern with the criteria for management evaluation. In examining public programs, administration first stressed accountability, then efficiency, then effectiveness and impact, and now relevance: the most significant and critical problems are those that should be addressed.

The roots of ZBB are further complicated by the historical variations of ZBB systems. Three such ZBB versions are generally acknowledged. One first generation version was part of PPBS called "zero-based review," and was implemented for one year by the Department of Agriculture in 1962. The USDA's experiment had a simple objective: each agency and major organizational unit within USDA was required to examine its budget submission from scratch and justify each item. Subsequent evaluations showed that this zero-based review failed to change budget outcomes very much and was not especially valued by program managers. The reviews were to be conducted periodically and were deemed most useful when a new administrator had taken over and wanted a complete review of department expenditures.

A second variation of ZBB was tied to legislative review and oversight. Early experiments were conducted in the 1970s in several states, most notably New Jersey and New Mexico. New Mexico's state legislature developed a budgeting submission system that resembled a simplified zero-base review approach, except that it was used by a legislative body that coupled it with a sunset effect. (Sunset legislation attaches fixed expiration dates to specific programs with continuation of the program contingent upon evaluation, review, and reapproval by the legislature.) As with zero-based review, legislatures felt no need or had no wish to conduct such reviews continually or even systematically.

The ZBB that became so popular in the mid-1970s was a true comprehensive budgeting system. First designed in the late 1960s by Peter Pyhrr for Texas Instruments, Inc., his landmark description of ZBB appeared in the *Harvard Business Review* in 1970. Two years later, then Governor Jimmy Carter hired Pyhrr as a consultant to develop and implement a ZBB system for the state of Georgia. In 1976, presidential candidate Carter promised a new budgeting system to make good his contentions that government expenditures could be reduced 10 to 15 percent by more efficient and effective management. A year later, President Carter ordered the installation of ZBB for the entire federal government. Graeme M. Taylor's "Introduction to Zero-Base Budgeting" provides an excellent overview of basic ZBB concepts and mechanics.

Even before its implementation, criticism of ZBB was substantial, and it was soon clear that two primary obstacles stood in the way of its successful implementation. First, the ranking process stands as a penultimate variable. Ranking priorities is essentially a political process, and the extent to which it can be ordered, structured, and mechanized by ZBB processes will always be unclear. Certainly there was little interest in the U.S. Congress and other legislatures that they would be swayed one way or the other by ranking mechanisms and outcomes. In most cases, they simply ignored ZBB submissions and insisted that the executive branch cross-walk their budget submissions into the "usual formats." (*Cross-walking* is an old PPBS term in which the program descriptions and formats of the executive budget are translated or "cross-walked" back to the appropriate line-item budget formats normally provided to the legislature for their review.)

The second obstacle involved political strategies. There is every indication that political strategies should work just as well with ZBB as with any other system, but they have little chance of real success in systematic ZBB. In fact, Allen Schick ("The Road from ZBB," *Public Administration,* 1978) told of "budgeteers" who reportedly were able to synthesize any variation of information into a ZBB format without appreciably altering any major aspect of their ongoing budgeting decision-making process. In the case of federal zero-based budgeting in the late 1970s, it produced (in Schick's words) the biggest case of "decremental budgeting" since Wildavsky and others coined the concept.

ZBB was discontinued in the first quarter of the Reagan administration with very few tears shed in either executive or legislative quarters. As a comprehensive budgeting system, it seemed too big and too time-consuming to go through every year. As one critic noted, it would be like going through an identity crisis every year: once in a great while it might prove useful, but once every year would be too destructive.

Cutback Management and Resource Scarcity

No major budgeting system dominated the 1980s public sector landscape. American politics was changing and a critical aspect was the withering away of liberal public support for continued government growth and increased public programs. Even more significant was the changing economic situation, addressed in depth in Section III. The vulnerability of public budgets to expenditure and revenue limitation initiatives (following the advent of Proposition 13 in California) was inescapable. Reflecting on the new political–economic environment, the late Charles H. Levine described how organizations must adapt and alter budget strategies in his 1978 article, "Organizational Decline and Cutback Management." The article notes that more than half a century of "positive budgeting" was over and that a new period of "negative budgeting" had arrived.

But cutback management was to become more than a management reaction to adverse economic conditions. In *Managing Fiscal Stress* (Chatham, N.J.: Chatham House Publishers, 1980), Levine laid out the guidelines for cutback management. Briefly, public sector managers would respond to revenue shortfalls based on the degree of political uncertainty (i.e., the probability of the cuts being restored) and the magnitude of the budget shortfall. Responses could range from simply "stretching the budget" to get through the fiscal year; "rationing demands" by limiting service or charging fees; and "selective withdrawal" by redrawing geographic divisions of the organization or terminating specific programs; to "retrenchment" by permanently altering the structure, programs, and staffing of the organizations.

Cutback management was not intended to be a budget system; it was a process. Its objective was to fuse political–economic realities with management strategies that would reestablish in the public's mind the value of public sector programs and services. In its most basic sense, this was a return to V. O. Key Jr.'s and Verne Lewis's questions about the basis of value in resource allocation decisions. In positive budgeting (strong growth) environments, the public needed little reassurance of the value of public spending. In negative budgeting (weak or slow growth, sometimes called ''slowth'') environments, the nexus between tax payments for public revenues and budget benefits for public expenditures must be reestablished.

Other Management Dimensions

While students of public administration have traditionally shown greater interest in the political, economic, and managerial aspects of government budgeting, the accounting dimension has also reemerged in importance. The literature of public budgeting gives the impression that the politics of budgeting ends with the legislature's approval of the final budget document. Of course, nothing could be further from the truth. There is great managerial discretion in the actual encumbrance and spending of allocated funds. Chief executives can advance or delay grant payments or bills; enlarge or depress revenue and expenditure estimates; allocate funds liberally or conservatively; and in many other ways manipulate surpluses, deficits, and corresponding budgetary behavior.

Of course, such manipulative tactics are reflective of the highly charged political environment in which budgeting takes place. In a future world of scarcer fiscal resources, one might reasonably expect that the auditing of public accounts will flourish in order to ensure that each governmental dollar is wisely spent. Given a tight fiscal environment, the management focus of a modern budgeteer becomes increasingly financial: the essential concern is to manage programs for the maximum benefit and least cost.

This became a major concern of financial management in the public sector in the 1980s. Accounting, budget reform's first major focus in the line-item budget, had long taken a backseat. But accounting is now a critical prerequisite for true budgeting knowledge. In part, this is because the public manager's private sector and nonprofit sector counterparts rely on general accounting, and there is much more interaction among the sectors than in the 1980s. The increasing importance of accounting to the managerial focus in public budgeting also relates to major definitional and informational changes in accounting. James L. Chan reviews this development and provides an analysis of the renewed and improved relationship of budgeting to accounting in ''Standards and Issues in Government Accounting and Financial Reporting.'' Five years later, Comptroller General Charles A. Bowsher provided a ''state of the field'' review in a 1985 symposium in *Public Budgeting & Finance,* ''Governmental Financial Management at the Crossroads.'' As the title implies, financial management has much further to go before it realizes the potential impact it should have on both government spending and management decision making.

In summary, budgeting reform's management thread has changed dramatically. Lacking any one dominant budgeting system (a Performance Budget, PPBS, or even a ZBB) to lead the way, public sector organizations in the 1980s resorted to developing their own eclectic budget systems. The emergence of a loose body of strategies and tactics under the general rubric of cutback management has captured much of the management attention in public budgeting. Major developments in financial management and accounting standards have had great impacts. Another development—the use of computers and information technology—may have the greatest impact of all. Estimates are that the financial management and budgeting functions are the most heavily automated functions in all governments. The drives to automate reporting; the use of spreadsheet software and graphics to improve analysis and examine alternatives; the development of information systems for integrating tax and revenues, user charges and fees, expenditures, cash management, and even investments is nothing less than extraordinary. The 1980s may ultimately be best known as the decade of budget computerization in terms of management improvement.

But the central management question remains: Has budgeting improved and has it had a real impact on government decision making? Donald Axelrod, in an excerpt from his 1988 book *Budgeting for Modern Government*, provides a final assessment of this question to conclude this section of readings about the management thread of budget reform and budget theory.

28
Performance Budgeting In Government

Catheryn Seckler-Hudson

The Concept

The performance budget concept, revived in 1949 by the Commission on Organization of the Executive Branch of the Government (popularly known as the "Hoover Commission") *basically means a focus of attention on the ends to be served by the government rather than on the dollars to be spent.* In the formulation of a performance budget the most important single task, then, is the precise definition of the work to be done and a careful estimate of what that work will cost. In the United States where the annual national budget approaches the 100-billion dollar mark, where annual federal spending amounts to more than 25 percent of the national income, and where more than 50 million individuals contribute to the public purse of the nation, the concept of *ends to be served* by the government takes on practical meaning for everyone.

The Presentation

The performance budget document is prepared on the basis of functions and objectives of the several agencies and departments of government rather than exclusively on the basis of objects of expenditure and organizational units. This presentation is especially important for those who give attention to the budget *after* it leaves the unit which originally prepares it. Thus, the format and presentation are vitally important to the legislative bodies that pass judgment on the merits of what is presented, and that authorize funds for the administration of the substance. Also, the form of presentation is important for responsible citizens or groups of citizens who actively participate in the

budget process, and who ultimately finance the programs authorized by the legislatures.

In the total sequence of performance budgeting, where an executive budget system is used, there are *two documents. The first document contains the executive proposal of a governmental work program, stated in financial terms, and with proposed costs and revenues shown in relation to each other.* The second document contains the appropriation acts as passed by the legislative body (in one or more parts) authorizing the use of public funds for the programs as modified by the legislature. *The second document represents legislative decision on executive proposals and it is the official budget of the governmental unit it represents.* The format of the legislative document should follow in pattern and style that of the executive budget proposal, for it becomes the controlling instrument in the administration of the governmental functions and activities as authorized in public law. The presentation of the executive budget proposal is especially significant in that it establishes the basic pattern for appropriation structure.

The Hoover Commission maintained that if the executive preparation of the federal budget were on a performance basis,—centering the attention on volume of work to be done, accomplishments achieved, and the cost of the services needed, it would concentrate " . . . congressional action and executive direction on the scope and magnitude of the different Federal activities." Furthermore, it would place " . . . both accomplishment and cost in a clear light before the Congress and the public."[1]

The Practical Meaning

When the Hoover Commission made its recommendation that the federal government adopt a budget based upon functions, activities and projects, there were grave misgivings on the part of many federal officials. Specifically, what would the practical meaning of "performance budgeting" come to be and with what implications? How would it be defined by the Bureau of the Budget? By the Congress and its committees? Within each individual agency?

Four years after the Commission's recommendations, these questions have not been answered fully. *Because of multiple participation in the federal budgetary process* it is possible that there will never be complete and final answers to these questions (See

Source: From *Advanced Management* (March 1953), pp. 5–9, 30–32. Copyright © 1953 by the Society for Advanced Management. Reprinted by permission.

MULTIPLE PARTICIPATION
in the Federal budgetary process

WHO ARE THE PERSONS OR INSTITUTIONS WITHIN THE FORMAL FRAMEWORK OF THE GOVERNMENT WHO INFLUENCE OR SHAPE THE BUDGET OF THE UNITED STATES?	1. The President of the United States 2. The Council of Economic Advisers 3. The Bureau of the Budget 4. The Department of the Treasury 5. The Individual Agencies and their subdivisions 6. The Federal Reserve Board 7. States and Municipalities having Grants-in-aid programs 8. The Congress of the United States and its Committees 9. The General Accounting Office 10. The Federal Courts ——— The multitude of interrelationships and frictions growing out of this multiple participation in the budgetary process often conditions action and decision beyond the letter of the law. The most delicate problems of public budgeting arise from the quality of interactions and working relationships of those who participate in the process. Although official titles and methods of operation may differ, there are comparable participants in the budgetary process at the state and local levels of government.

Figure 1

Figure 1). It is now rather generally accepted that as a minimum the performance budget process involves:

1. *the formulation and adoption of a plan of activities and programs for a stated time period;*
2. *the relating of program costs to resources; and*
3. *the achievement of the authorized plan, according to a time schedule and at a cost within available resources.*

This work plan to be meaningful must lie within the framework of a central public policy. It should include such substance as will provide reasonably accurate answers to the following questions concerning each program in the budget:

WHAT are we proposing to do and WHY?
HOW MUCH do we propose to do and WHEN?
WHAT resources will be needed and at what cost?
WHEN will we be through?

The process of forecasting the answers to these questions is one that never ends. On the contrary it is a continuous, on-going activity of arranging, authorizing and administering the work plan of the nation.

At the federal level of government the development of a unified and comprehensive work plan is made especially difficult because of the distinguishing features of the governmental environment. Among these features are:

1. *The gigantic size of the budget.*
2. *The multifarious activities and programs of government* ranging from research on atomic energy to the combating of white lice on roses, and from the waging of war in the Far East to the effective delivery of Christmas cards before December 25th of each year.
3. *The number of persons and institutions participating* in one way or another in the budget process (See Figure 1).
4. *The range and delicacy of human and group relationships involved,* not only between agencies and branches of the federal government, but among the subdivisions within any given agency.
5. *The political setting of the budget* including the influence of such matters as political elections, campaign promises, changes in executive and administrative leadership, competing social and economic interest groups, international tensions, and national security.

6. *The high degree of accountability of the Congress in the budgetary process.*

7. *The significant role of the budget in conditioning the total national economy.*

These and other complicating conditions have made many individuals seriously question the possibility of developing a comprehensive, meaningful, or coordinated performance budget for the federal government.

Decision-Making

Performance budgeting involves decision-making by all those who participate in the budgetary process. These decisions are often so complex in nature that they seem to present no orderly pattern. However, it seems possible to isolate at least six areas wherein decisions are made by one or more of those responsible for public budgeting. These areas may be stated as follows:

1. Somehow and somewhere there is, or should be, an analysis and comparative evaluation of all the needs of the people who live within the jurisdiction to be served by the budget. **Question requiring decision:**—*What are the needs of the people and what are their relative merits?*

2. There is at some point or points a selection, from among these needs, of those to be administered by the government and which will therefore be included in the government's plan of activities. **Question requiring decision:**—*What choices are made from among the many needs for inclusion in the public budget, and on what basis are these decisions made?*

3. There must be at some point the establishment of fiscal resources to meet the costs of the planned activities. **Question requiring decision:**—*What fiscal policy shall be authorized to meet the costs of the work plan?*

4. There must be appropriations, apportionments, and allocations of resources and funds among the many authorized activities and programs. **Question requiring decision:**—*How much money and other resources shall be allocated to each program and at what rate of expenditure?*

5. Responsibility for the direction and administration of the budget must be located. **Question requiring decision:**—*What persons or organizations shall direct and administer the program and how shall this be done?*

6. There shall be an accounting for performance and a justification of the administration of the budget. **Question requiring decision:**—*Who shall be held accountable for results and to whom shall the account be made?*

Readily it can be seen that these areas of decision-making reach into every aspect of public budgeting. They embrace both long-range decisions, and manifold short-range decisions. Furthermore, between and during the stages of formulation, adoption, and administration of the budget, revision and change inevitably occur. New needs arise and old ones disappear. Hence, the budget must provide for such flexibility as will permit consideration of all contingencies. At the time when the budget is presented to the legislative body, it represents executive decisions upon how limited resources shall be distributed among numerous programs. *The budget, as finally enacted into public law, represents executive and legislative compromises as they are translated into legal decisions concerning specific programs.*

Old Idea—New Emphasis

While credit for formally introducing a performance type budget into the federal government of the United States should be given to the Hoover Commission, the idea is by no means new. At various times and in different places it has been called "functional," or "activity," or "program" budgeting. Progressive cities in many parts of the United States have used one form or another of this type of budgeting for many years.

Since departmentalization at the city level is generally on a functional basis, and appropriations are usually made for departments, the elementary aspects of performance budgeting have existed in city budgets for half a century or more. Among the cities which have made progress in performance budgeting are Richmond, Va.; the City and County of Denver, Colo.; Oxnard, Calif.; Kissimmee, Fla.; San Diego, Calif.; Kansas City, Mo.; Detroit, Mich.; Rochester, N.Y.; Los Angeles and Berkeley, Calif.; Slater and Lebanon, Mo.; Wichita, Kan.; and Phoenix, Ariz.[2] It should be emphasized that a study of these and other budgets reveals that no one pattern of presentation has been used exclusively. Rather, there are a number of patterns emerging, differing according to the particular unit to which each applies.

More complex in function than the city, but less complex than the federal government is the state jurisdiction. However, with the strengthening of the position of the governors as one state constitution after another has been rewritten or amended, it is a natural development that the progressive states have tended toward performance budget systems. Oklahoma has done significant work in developing a functional budget. California is outstanding for the progress made in building appropriations in terms of programs, and Maryland voted to adopt a performance state budget system in November, 1952. Other states are converting to program budgeting in some degree.

Many of the individual agencies and departments of the federal government have justified their activities on a program basis for years. The Department of Agriculture has a score of clearly identifiable programs which have long been presented as such. The Department of the Interior has clearly developed activity schedules. Many of the so-called government corporations have presented well developed program budgets since the passage of the Government Corporations Control Act of 1945.[3]

With the passage of the National Security Act Amendments of 1949[4] the Congress of the United States made mandatory the presentation of performance budgets by the Department of Defense and the three military establishments—the Department of the Army, the Department of the Navy, and the Department of the Air Force. Although the military establishments had made considerable progress in developing performance budgets before the passage of the 1949 act, additional strides have been made since. Especially important is the work of each in implementing the concept of comptrollership in government.[5]

Government—Today

In 1950 the Congress of the United States provided for government-wide presentation of the budget on a performance basis. The Budget and Accounting Procedures Act of 1950,[6] while not using the words "performance budget," provides that:

The Budget shall set forth in such form and detail as the President may determine—(a) functions and activities of the Government; (b) any other desirable classification of data; (c) a reconciliation of the summary on expenditures with proposed appropriations.[7]

This provision has been interpreted as providing for a performance budget on a government-wide basis particularly in view of the Conference Report on the bill which states that the words "performance budget" had been eliminated from the Senate amendment as being superfluous and possibly, at a later date, restrictive.[8] Even before the final passage of the act, the director of the United States Bureau of the Budget had announced that the Budget of the United States government for the fiscal year 1951 would be presented on a "performance" basis with a breakdown of over 90 percent of the proposed expenditures into activity schedules showing programs and costs.[9] Indeed, as early as January 1947, the budget document was sent to the Congress containing a functional system of classification of government programs and expenditures.[10] Since then there has been a noticeable attempt to present the federal budget on a performance basis. Especially there has been an effort to locate costs of a major program within a single appropriation act.

Supplementing the Budget of the United States for the past four fiscal years is the simplified version known as *The Federal Budget in Brief.* Each year this graphic booklet has clearly presented the budget expenditures in the form of broad government programs, classified according to the purposes and functions they are designed to serve.[11] Almost three-fourths of all federal expenditures for the fiscal year 1954 (according to the President's January 1953 estimate) will be for six major national security programs—military services, international security and foreign relations, the development of atomic energy, the promotion of defense production and economic stabilization, civil defense, and merchant marine activities. It is estimated that these six programs will cost the United States over 57 billion dollars. These and other government programs are shown together with their estimated costs in Figure 2. The government's estimated receipts under present laws are shown in Figure 3.

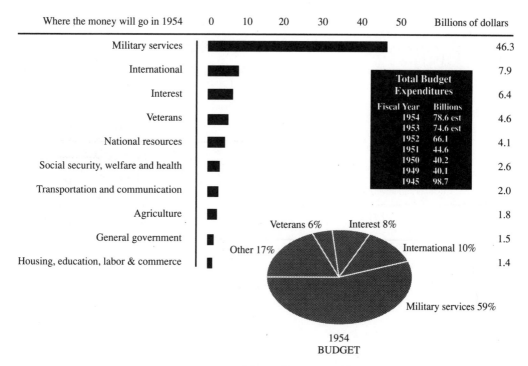

Figure 2
The federal budget—fiscal 1954 budget expenditures by program
Source: The Federal Budget in Brief, page 9

Principal Elements

Performance budgeting especially at the national level poses a challenge not only for executive leadership but for the Congress of the United States as well. It invites a change in approach to the problems of legislation and administration. It requires vigilant study, a receptiveness to new ideas and techniques, and painstaking thoroughness in research which heretofore have been reserved too often for the scholar. In the fullest sense, performance budgeting embraces a theory of management which is to be found partially in the best experience of the past combined with on-going study and research in the future. If a more restricted interpretation is given the concept, it is doubtful whether "performance budgeting" will endure at the federal level of government. A narrower definition could readily result in oversimplification which would not be applicable or adequate in a

system of government as complex as that of the United States.

In studying a given governmental unit is it possible to identify the existence and application of the theory required for fully implemented performance budgeting? Are there tangible evidences of such a theory and if so, what are they (See Figure 4)? This writer believes that there *are* certain necessary elements in a system which maintains a fully developed performance budget operation. Time, experience, and further research may add to or subtract from those which seem clear today. However, at the present time features which should be identifiable in such a system would of necessity include, at least, the following:

1. The use of work programs and activities.
2. The installation of work measurement and the application of performance standards.

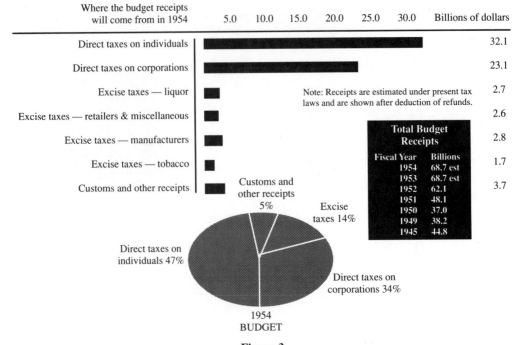

Figure 3
The federal budget—fiscal 1954 budget receipts
Source: The Federal Budget in Brief, page 7

3. The improvement of administrative reporting to include reporting on a performance basis, and the establishment of a progressive system of record keeping along functional lines.
4. The installation and maintenance of an accrual basis of accounting and improved cost accounting methods where applicable or desirable.
5. The provision for a comprehensive and continuous system of management analysis, evaluation, and improvement, including a system of internal auditing.
6. The presentation, justification, and authorization of public expenditures by appropriate primary categories—usually current operating expenditures and capital expenditures.
7. The revision of appropriation structure in terms of programs and activities to be administered.
8. The consistency of all the above elements with a central public policy.

Each of the above does not stand alone—each is valuable principally to the extent it interacts upon

or operates in relation to each of the others and to the whole. It is in the total complex of these interactions that one finds the full meaning of program or performance budgeting (See Figure 4). It is only for purposes of discussion that these several elements are treated separately in the following paragraphs.

1. Work programs and activities. The use of work programs and activities is one of the principles of budget management formulated by the late Harold D. Smith while he was director of the United States Bureau of the Budget.[12] He referred to it as the principle of "executive budget programming." It requires that individual agency programs should be formulated and considered in terms of the government program as a whole and should be in accordance with the policies established by the President. A sound work program for a specified time period, should include for each activity a clear definition of objectives, the choice of basic methods for achieving the objectives, a forecasting of how much and what kind of work is to be done, at what cost and when.

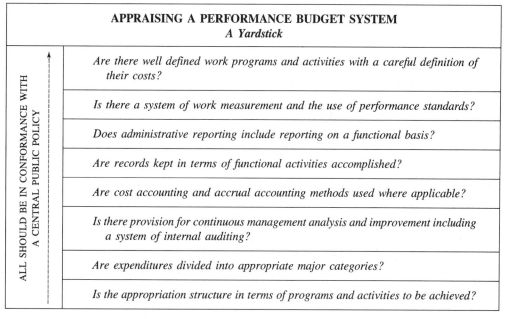

APPRAISING A PERFORMANCE BUDGET SYSTEM
A Yardstick

ALL SHOULD BE IN CONFORMANCE WITH A CENTRAL PUBLIC POLICY

Are there well defined work programs and activities with a careful definition of their costs?

Is there a system of work measurement and the use of performance standards?

Does administrative reporting include reporting on a functional basis?

Are records kept in terms of functional activities accomplished?

Are cost accounting and accrual accounting methods used where applicable?

Is there provision for continuous management analysis and improvement including a system of internal auditing?

Are expenditures divided into appropriate major categories?

Is the appropriation structure in terms of programs and activities to be achieved?

Figure 4

It is generally agreed that the first step toward performance budgeting is the improving and extending of activity schedules. In expressing activity schedules these steps are minimal:

a. Consideration of the major purposes to be served.
b. Specification of the programs to carry out the purposes.
c. Indication of the program activities under each appropriation or fund.
d. Volume of work, with data on past, current, and anticipated work load.

These matters should be set forth in terms of objectives or functions rather than in terms of organizational structures, unless the organizational structure is a functional one. Obviously, if the organizational structure corresponds to the functional framework of an agency or department, it will facilitate the decentralization of budgeting, program, and financial responsibility at every level within the organization. The basic data underlying these points will be, or should be, needed at every level of budget review if intelligent consideration is given to budget requests. Interim and final decisions on program requests can be no better than the information on which these decisions are made.

2. The installation of work measurement and the application of performance standards. After the agency programs are budgeted their execution is largely in the hands of the administrator. Operations should have been planned in advance according to established performance standards including both the quantity and quality of work expected. This is the basis for later performance estimates and a basis for supervision of and accounting for program achievement. The quantitative plans provide a yardstick of administrative intentions against which actual progress can be measured, and subsequent budgetary requests determined. Without a reliable system of work measurement and performance standards, program budgeting could be defeated within the administrative agency.

The installation of work measurement and performance standards will vary in nature from agency to agency. There is no one correct pattern for measuring of activity or for determining performance standards. In general it is preferable to decentralize the responsibility for discovering and using the method most suitable for a given program. The variety of government programs, both in nature and volume is so great that to insist on a particular method of measuring performance is naive. The principle is that there be a method of measuring performance rather than that there be a general prescription. Some agencies can use workload and unit cost data; others can use workload data but not unit cost data; still others can use only explanatory or descriptive material. Furthermore, in the improvement of performance measurement, it should be kept in mind that different agencies are in different stages of development, and may move progressively from one stage to another over a period of time. Also, it should be kept in mind that in federal budgeting Congressional attitude toward program budgeting is sharply conditioned by the evidence which is presented concerning the quantity and quality of work in a given program which has been accomplished with the funds appropriated. In establishing suitable performance standards for a given agency these guides seem minimal:

a. Those who decide upon the standards must have a complete understanding of the nature of the work.
b. The standards should be arrived at only after an examination of past records and of similar work done by other organizations.
c. Standards should be considered tentative until tested by experience and application.
d. Deviations from the established standards should be allowed, but only when warranted.

3. The improvement of administrative reporting and the establishment of record keeping along functional lines.

The success of performance or program budgeting will rest in no small measure on the improvement of administrative reporting with special reference to reporting on a functional or performance basis. Frequent and regular reports are necessary if management is to check on work done, objectives achieved or not achieved, and utilization of funds and personnel in terms of programs. Such reports become essential as a part of an agency's justification to the legislature both with respect to past performance and future budgetary requests. Harold D. Smith maintained that budgetary administration without full financial and operating reports flowing periodically from the administrative units of the government was blind and arbitrary. Indeed, he elevated this concept to the level of "the principle of budget reporting."[13]

The performance reporting systems currently in use in the several federal agencies fall into these major categories:

a. Those reporting only volume of workload for each activity.
b. Those reporting both volume and quality of workload.
c. Those reporting volume and quality of workload and time expended.
d. Those reporting volume, quality, time expended, and costs of each program or activity.

Within these performance reports the content may be as simple or detailed as appropriate. As a minimum the performance budget must be supported by reports on the total costs of each activity which in turn can be summarized by object of expenditure and by organizational unit.[14]

Closely related to both proper accounting and adequate reporting is the necessity for a progressive system of record keeping along functional lines. Reports are for the purpose of providing information needed in order to make proper decisions and to take appropriate action. These reports must receive prompt attention if they are to serve their purposes. Careful supervision and direction calls for continuous analysis of the reports, appropriate follow-up, and regular inspection to ascertain results. In fact, record keeping along functional lines must become the basis for any enduring system of program budgeting.

4. The installation and maintenance of an accrual basis of accounting and improved cost accounting methods.

The purpose of this element is to provide financial information and financial controls needed in the formulation, presentation, and execution of a budget on a cost of performance basis. If performance budgeting is to be considered the end product of financial planning, then financial planning, as expressed in the budgets of the public agencies, requires adequate and proper accounting support. Indeed, performance budgeting cannot become a reality without such accounting support.

Basically there must be an integration of budgeting and accounting classification in order to provide adequate and reliable accounting support for budgets. Where appropriate, accrual accounting (e.g., that which involves determining costs and expenses in relation to changes in assets and liabilities) should be utilized and integrated with appropriation accounting. Further developments must be made in the field of cost accounting, where appropriate, and its integration with appropriation accounting. In turn these developments should lead to the establishment of quantitative and financial control of inventories and other property. Accounting should be decentralized within the agencies to the degree practicable in terms of delegated operating responsibilities and central controls required.

In short, performance budgeting calls for a vastly improved public accounting system which will enable all responsible persons to appraise the value of programmed activities in the light of program costs and accomplishments. These accounts must present full, accurate and timely facts concerning financial results of operations. They must provide for control not only of funds, but of property and other assets for which any given agency might be responsible.[15]

5. The provision for a comprehensive and continuous system of management analysis, evaluation, and improvement. It is generally agreed that performance budgeting along functional lines, calling in turn for improved methods of accounting, reporting, record keeping, etc., must necessarily be implemented by a program to improve the organization and management of each agency concerned. Such a program should provide an organized and systematic attempt to find more effective ways of organizing in terms of ends to be served; more efficient procedures to be used in the achievement of the ends; for economical methods and techniques of operation; and for a reliable system of internal auditing.

Concrete recognition of this need was evidenced by the establishment of the President's government-wide management program aimed at improving operations within the individual Federal agencies. This program was authorized by Executive Order 10072, dated July 29, 1949.[16] The Congress of the United States supported this program by the enactment of Title X of the Classification Act of 1949.[17]

Both the executive order and the public law direct the heads of federal agencies to make systematic reviews of their activities and to increase effectiveness and economy in operations. Responsibility for leadership of the government-wide program is placed on the Bureau of the Budget. Significant progress has been made in improved management within government agencies although the program has been in operation less than four years.[18]

6. The division of budget estimates and appropriations into two categories—current operating expenditures and capital expenditures. An important element in performance budgeting is that types of expenditures, essentially different in character should be presented, justified, and authorized separately under each major program in the budget. Two primary categories are capital outlays and current operating costs. A *capital cost* is an expenditure for the acquisition, construction, or improvement of property or equipment (fixed assets) such as land, buildings, plant, or machinery. An *operating cost* is an expenditure other than a capital cost incurred in carrying out a specific program or activity. These two types of costs are different in character and in a program budget should appear separately under each major activity.

Too often one finds these two classifications intermingled in the federal budget. Other fixed charges, such as grants-in-aid, often appear as though they were operating costs. This makes it practically impossible to find the ultimate costs of either a given program or a large capital project. Furthermore, many of the annual appropriations on given capital projects are made without an understanding of total previous appropriations or of what may be requested in the future. It would seem therefore, that costs of capital projects should be set forth in the budget in terms of programs to which they relate and that current operating expenditures for these programs be grouped separately. The Hoover Commission noted that:

> While capital projects may be carefully analyzed for usefulness, timeliness, and total probable costs at the time of original authorization, the total remaining costs of all capital projects should be set forth in the budget each year, together with costs incurred to date. These costs should be revised in succeeding years to keep them current with later developments.[19]

7. The revision of the appropriation structure along functional lines. Performance budgeting, if it is to be fully effective and carried to its logical conclusion, must extend into the appropriation structure. The final responsibility for authorizing the work programs of the federal government rests with the legislative branch of that government. The structure of the appropriations which provide the life blood for these activities should be in accordance wih the underlying purposes of program budgeting.

If the separate departments and agencies are expected to present program budgets to the President with expenditure estimates related to program costs; and if the President is expected to propose to the legislative body a comprehensive work plan for the government in terms of programs and their measured costs; it follows that the legislative body should enact appropriate legislation on a functional basis—that is, grouping together all appropriations relating to a single program or project. If this were done the President would be strengthened by having his proposed work plan returned to him, meaningfully intact, except for such modifications as the Congress had seen fit to make. In turn, the President could return the individually authorized programs to the appropriate and responsible department heads for execution. This would not only help clarify the location of responsibility by *purpose* but sharpen accountability as measured by *achievement* of that purpose. Furthermore, there would then have been established not only an executive performance budget, but a *legislative performance budget* which is the only official budget of the United States government.

In the federal government, the long, tedious process of agency preparation of budgetary estimates for program needs, followed by the numerous levels of critical review within the agency, at the Bureau of the Budget, and by the President, reaches its climax when the budget document reaches the Congress for final legislative action. It is in the Congress, and more particularly in the spotlight of Congressional committee hearings, that the agency renders an acceptable or unacceptable amount of performance. It is here that the agency presents its justification of each of its major programs by content, by cost, by necessary or contemplated changes, and by rate of progress achieved. And finally, it is according to the judgment of the Congress, formalized in the appropriation acts, that the agency programs continue to exist or not.

Congressional appropriation acts should in form and structure indicate that the Congress concentrated its attention on spending public funds according to some general policy and plan, which provided for the most equitable allocation of resources among alternative programs, and the determination of policies and priorities according to the most pressing social needs. If the appropriation acts were enacted on a program basis, they would no longer emphasize organizational rigidities which do not necessarily reflect program operations. Instead, appropriation legislation would tend to encourage the responsible administrators to arrange their operating organizations in such a way as to most effectively achieve the program ends for which they are responsible.

In working toward a fully developed performance budget system for the federal government for what goals should the Congress strive? If the legislature wishes to continue to carry its full share of responsibility and high accountability in determining national public policy it seems essential that the following improvements be made:

a. The appropriation structure should be revised to correspond to the functional lines of the performance budget.
b. The *number* of "separate" appropriation bills should be sharply reduced.
c. The *variety* of appropriations should be reduced to the lowest number of kinds necessary for long-range planning and program control.
d. The budget calendar should be modified, both in terms of the most acceptable length of the regular fiscal period and a possible longer period for capital budget items and long-range programs.
e. Such accounting records and financial reports as are necessary for intelligent Congressional action should be made mandatory.

Conclusion

Performance budgeting in the government of the United States is well under way. Significant improvements have been made within many of the agencies and departments as well as on a government-wide basis. States and cities have added substantially to the progress made to date. The major elements of performance budgeting have been generally agreed upon. However, these elements have not been fully implemented.

Ideally, in the establishment of a performance budget system *all* elements of improvement or change should move forward simultaneously. This is especially desirable since no one of these elements stands alone. However, no one aspect of performance budgeting should remain static merely because some other part is imperfect. For improvement in one area stimulates and encourages other improvements and the interactions of all will finally determine the level of accomplishment.

While performance budgeting should never be regarded as a magic formula for the cure of all governmental weaknesses, it can provide a meaningful basis for administrative planning, executive coordination, legislative decisions, and administrative accountability at all levels of government. It could, if properly implemented, go a long way toward achieving program coordination within the far-flung executive branch of the federal government, and vastly improve the relationships between the legislative and executive branches, and between the legislature and the agencies and departments. More important, it could provide a basis for rational public appraisal of responsible government. In conclusion:

The performance budget process in government is a continuous, on-going activity on the part of all who participate in it. It is not a destination but a pilgrimage—never perfect, but being perfected—as the light of experience and careful research point the way to greater improvement in the management of public affairs.

Notes

1. U.S. Commission on Organization of the Executive Branch of the Government, *Budgeting and Accounting*, Report to the Congress, (Washington: Government Printing Office, 1949), pp. 8–9.
2. For the development of city budgets—much credit is due the outstanding efforts of professional organizations such as the Municipal Finance Officers' Association and the International City Managers' Association in the establishment of departmental work programs, and in the development of helpful documents and manuals.
3. 59 Stat. 597.
4. 63 Stat. 578.
5. See especially *Comptrollers in the Navy*, Office of the Comptroller of the Navy, Department of the Navy, June 1951.

6. 64 Stat. 832.
7. Title I, Section 102, amending Section 201 of the Budget and Accounting Act of 1921.
8. See U.S. Congress, House. Committee on Conference. Budget and Accounting Procedures Act of 1950, Conference Report No. 3030 to accompany H.R. 9038, 81st Congress, 2d Session, (Washington: Government Printing Office, 1950), pp. 16–17.
9. U.S. Bureau of the Budget Release, August 4, 1949. See also "Federal Budget on Performance Basis," *National Tax Journal*, Vol. II, No. 3 (September 1949).
10. U.S. Bureau of the Budget, *The Budget of the United States Government for the Fiscal Year Ending June 30, 1948*, (Washington: Government Printing Office, 1947), p. 1353.
11. See entire booklets *The Federal Budget in Brief*, Fiscal Year 1953 and Fiscal Year 1954, Executive Office of the President, Bureau of the Budget, Washington, D.C., for an excellent summary of the national program budget for the current and next fiscal years.
12. See Harold D. Smith, *The Management of Your Government*, (New York: McGraw-Hill, 1945), p. 90.
13. *Ibid.*, p. 91.
14. See the graphic booklet on *Performance Reporting* issued by the United States Treasury Department, May, 1950.
15. See the First, Second, Third, and Fourth Annual Joint Reports by the Comptroller General of the U.S., the Secretary of the Treasury, and the Director, U.S. Bureau of the Budget, *Progress Under the Joint Program to Improve Accounting in the Federal Government*, Processed. Dated respectively January 12, 1950; January 12, 1951; January 25, 1952; and December 4, 1952. The Third and Fourth Joint Reports give an excellent account of progress made in the several agencies of the Federal Government.
16. 14 Fed. Reg. 4797.
17. 63 Stat. 954.
18. The nature and coverage of the program is described in detail in a document issued by the Bureau of the Budget, Executive Office of the President, December 1, 1950, titled *Progress in Improving Federal Administration*.
19. Report on *Budgeting and Accounting, supra*, pp. 15–16. There is some disagreement as to the relationship of capital budgeting and performance budgeting. See especially "Symposium on Budget Theory." *Public Administration Review*, Vol. X, No. 1 (Winter 1950), pp. 26–27.

29
What Program Budgeting Is and Is Not

David Novick

During the 1960s the concept of program budgeting generated substantial interest, speculation, experimentation and literature in business and at all levels of government throughout the western world. With the widespread introduction of this new management idea that started in the middle of the decade, many and varied activities have been undertaken in its name. Most of them have included some or all of the major features of this new management system. However, some of the new proposals bear little resemblance to it other than the use of the words Program Budgeting as part of an argument for management changes that really are not at all program budgeting or the Planning-Programming-Budgeting System (PB, PPB or PPBS).

What Program Budgeting Is

Program Budgeting is a management system that has ten distinctive major features. These are:

1. Definition of the organization's objectives in as specific terms as is possible.
2. Determination of programs, including possible alternatives, to achieve the stated objectives.
3. Identification of major issues to be resolved in the formulation of objectives and/or the development of programs.
4. An annual cycle with appropriate subdivisions for the planning, programming and budgeting steps to ensure an ordered approach and to make appropriate amounts of time available

Source: Reprinted by permission of the Rand Corporation and David Novick from *Program Budgeting 1970* by David Novick, pp. 1 to 19, a Rand Corporation-sponsored research study published in 1972. Mr. Novick is a member of the Research Council of the Rand Corporation and is generally credited as the originator of program budgeting as applied to government.

for analysis and decision-making at all levels of management.

5. Continuous re-examination of program results in relationship to costs and anticipated outcomes to determine need for changes in stated programs and objectives as originally established.
6. Recognition of issues and other problems that require more time than is available in the annual cycle so that they can be explicitly identified and set apart from the current period for completion in two or more years as the subject matter and availability of personnel require.
7. Analysis of programs and their alternatives in terms of probable outcomes and both direct and indirect costs.
8. Development of analytical tools necessary for measuring costs and benefits.
9. Development each year of a multi-year program and financial plan with full recognition of the fact that in many areas resource allocations in the early years (e.g., years one through five) require projections of plans and programs and their resource demands for ten or more years into the future.
10. Adaptation of existing accounting and statistical reporting systems to provide inputs into planning and programming as well as continuing information on resources used in and actions taken to implement programs.

The General Approach

To carry out the major objectives of program budgeting, three general areas of administrative and operational activities are involved. These are:

1. The Program Format which identifies the organization's objectives, programs established to meet them, and the program elements through which the operations are carried out. This identification of the overall activity in program terms is sometimes referred to as the "format or structural phase" to distinguish it from the analytical and informational parts of the total which are described below.

Program budgeting for an organization begins with an effort to identify and define objectives and to group the organization's activities into programs that can be related to each objective. This is the revolutionary aspect of this new management system since it requires groupings by end product or output rather than as in traditional budget practice by line items of input arranged in terms of administrative organizations or activities. The new method allows us to look at *what* we produce—output—in addition to *how* we produce or what inputs we consume.

The program budgeting summary document presents resources and costs categorized according to the program or end product to which they apply. This contrasts with traditional budgets that assemble costs by type of input—line item—and by organizational or activity categories. The point of this restructuring of budget information is that it aids the planning by focusing attention on competition for resources among programs and on the effectiveness of resource use within programs. The entire process by which objectives are identified, programs are defined and quantitatively described, and the budget is recast into a program budget format, is called the format or structural phase of Program Budgeting (PB) which also is frequently termed the Planning-Programming-Budgeting System (PPBS).[1]

One of the strengths of the program budgeting process is that it cuts across organizational boundaries, drawing together the information needed by decisionmakers without regard to divisions in operating authority among jurisdictions. Bringing everything together has its obvious advantages because a program can be examined as a whole, contradictions are more likely to be recognized, and a context is supplied for consideration of changes only made possible by cutting across existing agency line barriers.

An outstanding feature of program budgeting is the emphasis on analysis at all stages of activity. Although it is sometimes not recognized, the development of the appropriate format or structure in and of itself requires analysis. In fact, just examining an organization's objectives and identifying its programs and program elements in and of itself can constitute a major contribution to improvement of management in the organization even when the more complete analytical capability contemplated in the program budget is not fully developed.

One product of the structural phase is a conversion matrix or crosswalk from the budget in program terms to the traditional line-item, organization and activity budget. In program budgeting, organization gives way to program, and line-item detail is aggregated into summary figures more appropriate to decisionmaking.

For example, the wages and salaries figure for Environment Program in Figure 1 is not only the sum of personnel service payments in the program

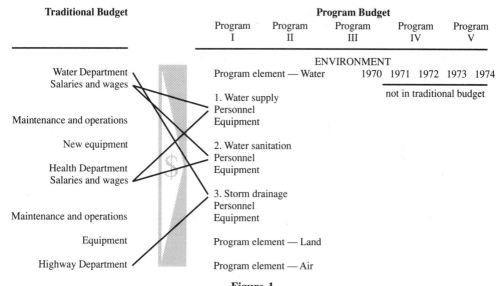

Figure 1
Crosswalk: Traditional line-item budget to new program budget

elements which constitute environment-oriented activities in water, air, land, pollution, etc., but also an aggregation of pieces of the wages and salaries data in each operating department whose activities contribute to environmental control. If Figure 1 were not space limited, the illustration would extend to include the contributions from other departments and supporting services like central electronic data processing. Detail is not the objective, however, and such activities are instead grouped into a general support program.

To aggregate the multitude of line items in the traditional budget or even its operating department summaries into their program element contributions or costs, allocations must be made and some of them may be rather arbitrary ones. The important features of the crosswalk are (1) to have the two documents balance no matter what the dimensions of the classifications, and (2) to ensure that decisionmakers and reviewing entities can identify next year's traditional budget in program terms and vice versa.

Through the crosswalk we also are able to translate existing methods of record keeping and reporting into data for program planning. It permits program decisions to be translated into methods already in use for directing, authorizing, controlling, recording and reporting operations. If the management methods now being used in any of these areas are inadequate or unsatisfactory, they should be upgraded and improved, whether or not the organization has a program budgeting system. In any case, the program budget must derive its information and relationships from existing management records and practices and must rely on them for the implementation of the programs.

2. The second area of the general approach is Analysis. The program budgeting method of decisionmaking subsumes a systems analysis capability with which the resource and cost implications of program alternatives and their expected "outputs" or accomplishments may be estimated, examined and compared. When a systems analysis capability does not exist or is inadequate, it should be created or upgraded since analysis is the most important part of this approach to management. A wide range of techniques is employed in these program analyses, including statistical analysis, modeling, gaming and simulation, operations analysis and econometric techniques. The analysis examines both the resource/cost side and the benefit/effectiveness side of program consequences.

Quantification is sought wherever possible but many of the effects or outcomes involved do not readily lend themselves to quantitative measurement. In these instances, qualitative analysis is required. In every case, whether the analysis is quantitative, qualitative, or an appropriate mixture of the two, there is explicit identification of the problem, the alternative ways of resolving it and an attempt to measure the cost and effectiveness of each possibility.

Program analysis is not confined to predetermined alternatives; development of new and better alternatives is part of the process. It is likely that analysis of possibilities A, B, and C will lead to the invention of alternatives D and E, which may be preferable (more cost/effective) to the original candidates. Therefore, the analytical part of program budgeting cannot be viewed merely as the application of a collection of well-defined analytical techniques to a problem. The process is much more flexible and subtle, and calls for creativity by the managers and the analysts and interaction between analysts and decisionmakers during the process.

3. The third part of the program budgeting system deals with Information and Reporting. This covers identification through the accounting and related statistical reporting systems of information on all of the activities of the organization. This does not call for the creation of either new accounting or new statistical reporting systems. Instead, it means re-identification or structuring in the existing systems so that their product can be utilized in the planning and programming parts of the activity. When program determinations are made, the reporting requirement imposes on existing systems the need to provide continuing information (usually monthly and/or quarterly) on the use of resources and the operational steps taken in the implementation of the programs.[2]

Although the accounting and statistical reports of necessity are carried on in terms of actions in the current calendar, the reporting provision must require and provide specific identification of current activities in terms of impact in both the balance of the current year and the future years of the multi-year plan.

A brief summary that relates the areas of operation to the major features of program budgeting and to the kinds of documents the system produces may be useful at this point. This is sketched in Figure 2.

Major Features	Operation Areas	Representative Documents
Define objectives Determine programs Assign activities to programs Establish plan-program-budget cycle	Structural Aspect	Multi-year program and financial plan
Develop cost/benefit measurement methods Identify and evaluate alternatives Develop and apply criteria	Analytical Aspect	Program memoranda including alternatives Issue Analysis Special Studies
Use existing reporting system Update programs	Data and Information Aspect	Accounting and statistical reports Program change proposals

Figure 2

Sketch of program budgeting

Reasons for Program Budgeting

The primary reason for program budgeting is that it provides a formal, systematic method to improve decisions concerning the allocation of resources. Obviously, these allocation problems arise because available resources usually are scarce in relation to demand. This leads to a need for making choices amongst demands in terms of: what to do, how much to do, and when to do it.

Program budgeting is designed to open up debate and put discussion on a new basis. It does this by requiring explicit identification of all actions— ongoing or new proposals—in terms of programs related to stated objectives. This enables the top decisionmakers to act in terms of the total organization rather than on the basis of ideas limited by individuals or operating units. The orientation of this new method is planning the future in both near-term and long-range aspects, and making decisions on what is to be done.

A second reason for program budgeting is that planning should be carried on with adequate recognition of both what is to be done and what it will cost. When an organization's plans call for more resources than it has or is likely to have available to it, then planning becomes a game not played for "keeps." When an organization is unable to carry the costs of its objectives, then it should revise its objectives or otherwise it will be wasting some of its substance. Resource considerations introduce realism into planning.

Since we should examine as many alternative plans as we have imagination to construct at the planning level, resource considerations should be in highly aggregated terms. We should use "in the ball park" estimates of costs to facilitate examining a large number of possibilities in a reasonably short period of time. In program budgeting the name of the game is "alternatives" and we seek the longest possible menu.

When we have selected the most promising plans from that menu, we analyze them in a less aggregative but still not completely detailed form. This is programming. Here activities are identified and feasibility is established in terms of capability, resource requirements, and timing of each one of the alternatives. The selection is linked to a budget-like process because the final budget decisions determine the allocation of resources not only for next year but also in many cases make commitments for many years into the future.

To formulate a single program requires that we make decisions on feasibility, resource demands and timing. Even so, data used for programming are still not in the complete detail of next year's budget. The budget is an operating and financial plan and as such must be in great detail for inputs like personnel, supplies, equipment, etc., and assignment of such resources to administrative units. That kind of detail overwhelms and makes unmanageable a process designed for choosing between alternatives—even a limited number of them.

The third basic reason for program budgeting is to choose between available and feasible alternatives, which choice takes place at the conclusion of the programming. At that point we have illuminated the issues involved and the decisionmakers can exercise their judgment and experience in an appropriate and informed context. They can make the important decisions on "what to do" in the multi-year program and financial plan on the basis of program information that is not in the massive detail of next year's budget.

Given these decisions, the detail of operations and expenditures can then be laid out so that the final and less important budget decisions are on "how to do it." This is the point at which performance budgeting, management by objective, work measurement, and other methods of improving efficiency take over. In program budgeting the objective is annual allotments of funds that allow the next step to be taken along a path the general direction of which has been thoughtfully set by policymakers at all levels. Probably more important, the direction of the path and the distance to be covered in the next year will have been established after considering a number of possible futures for the entire government or business organization.

Program budgeting was not designed to increase efficiency in the performance of day-to-day tasks, nor was it designed to improve control over the expenditure of funds. It is instead a recognition of the fact that more money is wasted by doing the wrong thing efficiently than can be wasted by doing the right thing inefficiently. In short, the focus of the program budget is the decisionmaking process; that is, the determination of what to do, how much to do, and when to do, rather than deciding on how to carry on day-to-day operations, decisions which are best made by those who are closest to the activity.

What Program Budgeting Is Not

In both government and business, responsibility for the work required to accomplish a coherent set of objectives is divided among a number of organizations. In government, for example, programs with objectives for health and education are each fragmented among a dozen bureaus and independent agencies and levels of government—in the United States; e.g., federal, state and local units. The activities of each one are sometimes complementary, sometimes contradictory, or in conflict with those of the others. As a result, there is no overall coordination of the resource allocations relevant to program objectives in, for example, health and education.

Since program budgeting cuts across organization and administrative lines, there are cases where this has been translated to mean that the activity is limited to the structural phase and resultant reorganization to fit the new identification of programs. This is not only an incomplete view of what is involved but also a most undesirable one.

It should be recognized, as indicated above, that this management concept calls for continuous re-examination of program results and for re-identifying and restructuring programs and objectives. Normally, this would be done on an annual basis. One can readily visualize the chaos that could result in administration and operations if organization changes were required for every change in program format.

The program budgeting system is not a reorganization plan nor does it seek or require changes in organization to fit the program structure.

In the same way, the information and reporting requirement of program budgeting, with its emphasis on accounting and recurring statistics, has sometimes been translated into the need for the development of a new accounting system or a major change in the existing one. As indicated in the just-preceding discussion of organization, programs can be expected to change or, at a minimum, be modified on a recurring basis. This makes it not only unnecessary but undesirable to change the accounting or the reporting systems to the currently identified program structure.[3]

The emphasis on maintaining existing accounting and reporting systems derives from the recognition of two major factors. First, temporary change is always undesirable and since programs and objectives are both continuously subject to change, molding them to fit the format developed at any one point in time provides only limited advantage and has all the disadvantages that will be encountered when they must be changed to fit the next development of the format. The second reason is that both the operators and decisionmakers are knowledgeable about the existing system and therefore will find it more comfortable to operate in a situation in which changes have been kept to a minimum and are of a kind that will be made essentially once and for all time.

Another reason for not making changes is that in providing information for the inputs into the planning and programming process, and in reporting on actions taken in the execution of programs, the emphasis on detail changes from that in traditional line-item budgets. As we move through the process from the lowest level of operation and decision up through the higher levels of executive decision-making, there is a steadily increasing need to present aggregated instead of detailed information. The important new development for accounting and statistical reporting is to ensure that, as we move up the ladder and aggregate the data, the units of record do not lose integrity through the continuing introduction of judgment or "fudge factors."

What is needed is an examination of both the accounting records and the basic records from which statistical reports are drawn to ensure that these can in fact be translated into the required inputs in planning, programming, and budgeting activities as well as in recording and reporting. This means an emphasis on units of account that are "pure"; that is, ones that can be carried upward in the accounting or statistical reporting system "as is" and do not require the introduction of adjustments when accumulated into more aggregative units of information.

Program budgeting is not a new accounting system nor does it require changes in the existing accounting and statistical reporting systems to fit the program structure.

Management Information Systems have also come into fashion. As a result, in many cases the development of program budgeting has been regarded as synonymous with the installation of a new computer system and the related techniques for making management data more readily available and nothing more. Although a good MIS is always desirable and can be used to very good advantage in the working of a program budgeting system, it should be obvious that the MIS may lack the planning emphasis on structure, and surely does not include the appropriate recognition of the development of programs, the analysis of alternatives, and the development of all of the related analytical activities and tools that are so important to the total concept of program budgeting.

Program budgeting is not a Management Information System even though a good MIS is very useful to its operations.

Although program budgeting, because of its emphasis on analysis, frequently calls for individuals with an analytical approach and/or training, the requirement for analysts does not mean that program budgeting requirements are met just by introducing elaborate new personnel recruiting, education or training efforts. For the most part, what is required is some redirection of existing personnel and the kind of education and training essential for this purpose. On the other hand, the program requirements will not be met just by the introduction of sweeping new personnel policies and activities.

The word "budget" in program budgeting—or the planning, programming, budgeting system—sometimes leads to the assumption that, if the title Program is introduced into the existing budget documents, the result is in fact a program budget. Obviously, the word "program" is available for anyone to use in any manner that he sees fit.

The emphasis on program in this new system is on output, or end-product measurement rather than on the inputs as they are emphasized in traditional budgetmaking. Therefore, whether the existing budget is the straight line-item type, performance oriented, or based on organization and function, adding the word program in selected places or in the title does not make them program budgets. Introducing the words "program" or "major program" into the groupings used in traditional budgets in no way accomplishes the purpose of program budgeting.

It is especially worth noting that program budgeting is not performance budgeting. Performance budgeting developed mainly in the 1930s and has had a major impact, particularly at the state and local government levels. It has also been used extensively in business. The performance budget is a way of choosing between a series of alternative ways of "how to do" a specific task. It does not provide for evaluation of the importance of the task in terms of either the total program or individual programs designed to meet a set of goals. In short, it is a way of choosing among alternative means available for doing a task rather than a way of determining whether the task should be performed at all or, if it is to be included, the amount of it that is required for a program.

Program budgeting recognizes the need for administrative and organizational budgets as well as performance budgeting and does not contemplate that these should be abandoned or relabelled. Instead, it requires that through the crosswalk they be used in conjunction with it.

The program budget has a time element that extends beyond the typical next-year's budget. The multi-year program and financial plan lays out not only next year's budget but also the budgets that would be required for future years on the basis of decisions already made when the final action is taken. In this sense, next-year's budget is an important first step in the operation of the multi-year program.

This does not mean making fundamental changes in existing budget practice. In the traditional line item, performance, or organization and function budget, there is a need for detailed identification by object or activity classes which requires more detail than is either necessary or possible to use as the program budget moves upward in the decision process. For this reason, the primary change is the addition of program budgeting to the ongoing annual budget process. This permits the development of the multi-year financial plan at a high level of aggregation from which a "crosswalk" can be made to the traditional line-item budget by object class.

Summing Up "What It Is" and "What It Is Not"

In short, program budgeting is characterized by an emphasis on objectives, programs, and program elements, all stated in output terms. Cost, or the line items of the traditional budget, is treated at an appropriate level of aggregation which ensures that plans and programs are developed with adequate recognition of their resource implications.

Analysis and the use of a large variety of analytical techniques are the backbone of this new system of management. It requires explicit identification of assumptions, the development and as complete treatment as time and personnel availability permit of all relevant options and alternative outcomes. It is in the process of analysis that we are forced to recognize the organization and operation line-cutting features of programs. In the same way, the analytic process forces translation of broad goals like better

education, into operational terms like courses, students, teachers, libraries, etc. that identify both the purposes of the education process and the resources that can reasonably be made available for it. Analysis takes many forms and places substantial emphasis on the use of tools like computers and mathematical models. However, the computer and the model are simply part of the kit of tools for analysis rather than either the analytical process or the decision-making process.

Program budgeting also places a new emphasis on continuous reporting of both the accounting and statistical type, including ad hoc data collection methods when appropriate. This is for the purpose of providing inputs into the next planning and programming cycle as well as providing a measure of how the determinations on resources and programs are being carried out.

New organization charts, accounting systems, personnel recruitment and training systems, management information systems, or the generous use of the word program in traditional budgets are not program budgeting. Although all of these kinds of activities have been undertaken in the current vogue for program budgeting, from the foregoing they can easily be identified as not fitting into the context described above or promising the improvement in decisionmaking that is the primary goal of the program budgeting process.

Notes

1. PPBS is the more common usage in the United States. In England, Australia, Canada and New Zealand and most other countries Programme Budgeting is favored. In France, it is "Rationalization des Choix Budgetaires" (RCB). Program Budgeting (PB) will be the preferred usage herein.
2. Complete enumeration on a periodic basis is not always required. For example, sample surveys might be used.
3. This is especially true if sample surveys can be used.

30
Planning and Budgeting: Who's on First?

S. Kenneth Howard

A budget is a plan, but not all plans are budgets. All administrators should plan—that is, use a planning process, but some professional staff personnel specifically identify themselves as "planners" and specified organizational units are established to do "planning." Professional planners have established a wariness about "politics," but they increasingly recognize that public policy decisions lie at the heart of politics and that the effectiveness of professional staff work is demonstrated by the impact of that work on policy decisions.

These statements circumscribe a series of dilemmas and ambiguities that currently confound people engaged in planning and budgeting activities at the state level. The advent of planning-programming-budgeting systems has re-emphasized certain underlying truths about both planning and budgeting and the necessary relationships between these two activities in policy-making, but it has also exacerbated the ambiguities, insecurities, and not totally compatible movements and changes that have been taking place among career public officials who specialize in the planning and finance fields.

So far this book has focused almost totally on the budgeting process. Planning-programming-budgeting systems and other rationalistic budgeting approaches are typically couched in terms of linking planning and budgeting activities in a single integrated process for policy-making. Much of this chapter will discuss the planning process and state planning activities as it explores the concepts that underlie the proposed linkages.

To talk about linking planning and budgeting makes little sense conceptually because budgeting is an example of the more generalized planning process at work; it is a type of planning. Program planning—which covers substantive program

Source: S. Kenneth Howard, *Changing State Budgeting*, pp. 196–213. Copyright © 1973 The Council of State Governments. Reprinted with permission.

activities, personnel requirements, legislative changes and a number of other matters besides financial requirements—is another illustration of the planning process at work.

However, it is possible to distinguish between planning as a process and the practice of planning as carried out by state planning departments or agencies. Much of the current confusion stems from the inability of both operating officials and writers in this field to recognize consistently that the planning process as such entails a good deal more than the activities of planning agencies or units. Once a particular central agency is charged with doing planning, and once that agency tries to establish itself in the state political milieu, a host of issues are raised. It is in this organizational context that planners and budgeters can be spoken of as individual officials who occupy positions or hold specific titles and whose activities need to be linked.

The Planning Process

Planning is a key responsibility of all executives, and not inappropriately does the first letter in the acronym POSDCORB stand for planning.[1] Since planning is an activity expected of all administrators, there are inevitably many kinds of planning. Even a cursory examination of the literature of this field reveals references to long-range, short-range, futuristic, policy, advocacy, fiscal, strategic, tactical, regional, comprehensive, and contingency planning. This listing scarcely exhausts the possibilities, but it does highlight the degree of semantic confusion that abounds under the general rubric "planning." Few words are less sharply defined or more widely used today in the field of public administration.

Not all planning processes are alike. Planning activities can represent dreaming, can project future conditions and determine program priorities, can be parochial or comprehensive, and can be either integrated with budgeting or an independent process outside the main decision flow.[2]

Different types of planning are required in state governments. The most apparent is that done by line agencies as they determine how to proceed in meeting particular responsibilities. Becoming more commonplace is the planning that covers a functional or problem area like health or transportation.

Normally this type entails participation by a number of different agencies. Central planning services have also become widespread. Usually these services are statistical in nature, providing standardized information for all agencies about such matters as population projections, economic forecasts, and other types of uniform data useful to the entire spectrum of state agencies.

Line agency, functional area, and central services planning activities need to be coordinated, and the thrust of a state's total planning effort needs to be more innovative. Coordination and innovation responsibilities are usually laid upon an agency that is near the governor. Budgeting has been a major coordinative process for a long time; its possibilities for innovation are now getting more thorough appraisal.

All these forms of planning have been encouraged in recent years. Line agencies have been urged to do planning in connection with federal grants, the preparation of plans frequently being a prerequisite to receiving any aid. Of course, the federal grant requirements do not always sufficiently encourage coordination with other agencies in the same functional area; they sometimes promote unwarranted agency independence from gubernatorial direction. Special efforts at functional planning, again stimulated in part by federal grants, have taken place in many fields, but especially in health, higher education, and criminal justice. Central services have been improved as techniques of projection, data collection, and presentation have been refined. Gubernatorial interest in innovation has been apparent most recently in urban affairs, environmental control, and consumer protection.

Underneath the multitude of state expenditures lie program necessities and needs for services that cannot be adequately provided without manpower, financial, operational, and other kinds of planning.

Dimensions of Planning

Plans can be described in terms of the scope or diversity of the programs they consider, by the amount of detail they encompass about those programs, and by the time period they span.

Figure 1 depicts the typical shape of state budgeting, using the dimensions of scope, detail, and time. State budgets cover virtually all state activities, do not provide a great deal of detail about programs, and are usually limited to an annual or biennial

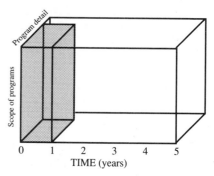

Figure 1
How current budgeting fits the
dimensions of planning

perspective. Determining the amount of program detail to include in budgeting is always a problem. PPB approaches do not solve this issue; instead, they strive to change the *nature* of that detail to include outputs and effectiveness measures.

Rationalistic conceptions urge expansion of the time horizon considered in state budgeting, but with less and less detail the longer the time perspective becomes. The PPB approach is diagrammed in Figure 2.

An effort must also be made to improve agency planning—the basic but currently weakest link in the chain. The greatest detail in planning will be needed at this level, but the time perspectives must be broadened. Also, agencies need to appreciate more fully the interrelationship of their activities with those of others. The scope of their planning needs to be more encompassing—a perspective fostered by functional planning. Figure 3 presents these ideas.

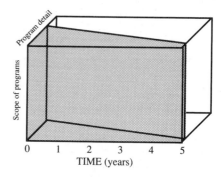

Figure 2
How PPB fits the
dimensions of planning

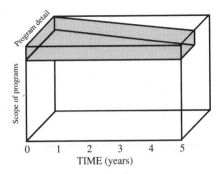

Figure 3
Ideal agency planning
on the dimensions of planning

Judged on the same criteria, comprehensive long-range state planning tends to be more two-dimensional, as Figure 4 shows. It covers the whole scope of state programs, but with a much longer time perspective than PPB or agency planning, and includes virtually no program detail.

The planning that states do should recognize that the decisions they face often depend heavily upon actions of others who are only tangentially under their control. Federal grant programs, population shifts, and economic movements are ready examples of the problem. The states must be adaptive, and they have less autonomy in their selection of both means and ends than may be thought.

What, Then, Is State Planning?

As a continuing and continuous process, planning has no end; this characteristic adds to the frustration of trying to say what planning is: " . . . planning

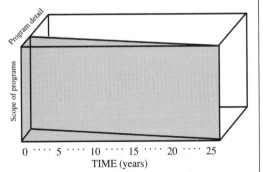

Figure 4
Comprehensive long-range planning
on the dimensions of planning

is a continual process in which there is no last word, there is only the latest word."[3]

In its simplest form, planning may be defined as rational forethought, as an attempt at rationally determining the best actions to achieve a desired goal.[4] Like the flag and motherhood, planning can hardly be opposed. But if generalizations are to be helpful, they must certainly get beyond this level. Since planning comes in such varied forms, it is necessarily the underlying process rather than specific plans that is common to this wide spectrum of purposes and planners. This, then, is a cardinal point: planning is a process used by all kinds of officials for varying purposes; it is not the unique province of a few who call themselves "planners."

Our central theme is that the state planning agencies constitute only a part of the planning activities in each state, not the entirety. Rather than speaking as if they were the proprietors of all planning, the agencies must define for themselves an individual strategy relating their planning activities to planning and policy-making throughout state government.[5]

A clear definition of state planning does not emerge from analyzing the work being done by men titled "state planners." The current activities of state planners hardly reflect a consistent discipline. Residual to their past, many central state planning agencies still give great emphasis to matters related to economic development.[6] Others focus on developing state goals and on providing a single information base about population growth and shifts, land use, and other general matters. Some agencies stress the acquisition of federal grants and information-clearinghouse activities. Others actually administer some of the programs thus obtained. Some planners advocate and play highly political roles as gubernatorial advisers over a rather wide range of issues. They recognize the need for political support if plans are to be implemented and they expect planners to turn over rather frequently and to be politically vulnerable. (In one instance, a state planner has made political speeches on behalf of a nonincumbent in a *primary* election campaign!)

At first glance, the only common denominator of all these activities is that they take place within the states that make up the United States of America. But they have one other similarity: they reflect the struggles that these planners and their agencies are going through to survive in their particular environments.

Clearly, in implementing state planning, notions of the process give way to the necessities of organizational realities, and the reason for some of the existing confusion about the nature of state planning becomes apparent. In its totality, state planning can be seen as dealing with the entire range of state governments' concerns and taking many different forms. In large and complex organizations, the organizational challenge lies in integrating all of these different parts of the total planning process in such a way that the effectiveness of state governments is enhanced.[7]

If state planning is defined too broadly, it seems to encompass everything, as illustrated by the following exchange between the planning director of one state and the former finance director of another:[8]

Planner: I view state planning as a process in which the whole social, economic and physical system of the state is analyzed and the options are developed as to the optimum development of the state as people (with development occurring) through the state's and executive's intervention into those social, physical and economic systems. This occurs and is implemented by virtue of the budget in resource allocations, through legislative programs, through changing the rules of the game—the basic law and structure of charters—through executive leadership in leading the private sector, through local government—both mandating local governments to do certain things and through other instruments of getting incentives—through channeling of federal money. What I am trying to say is that there are many ways state plans are implemented and budgets are only one of them.

Finance Director: I cannot distinguish between your description of planning and what I would regard as a description of administrative government. As far as I'm concerned, you have described what government is.

Perhaps some other definitions of the planning process will shed some light on this matter.

State comprehensive planning is most effectively employed as an element of the executive function of State government. The Governor, therefore, is the official primarily responsible for its conduct and execution. The State comprehensive planning program should be conceived as a continuing process to provide central policy formulation for the inter-related social, economic and physical aspects of State development, to give direction to the various governmental programs involved, and to effect coordination of departmental or functional agency activities and programs.

The primary tasks of State comprehensive planning are:

(1) to articulate goals and objectives for the development of the State; (2) to identify and analyze significant development problems and opportunities facing the State; and (3) to propose alternate courses of action to be taken by the State to solve the problems or realize the opportunities. The consequences of each alternate course of action should be presented in terms of its relation to the goals and objectives for State development, to the efficient allocation of resources for State development, and to specific program activities and proposals.[9]

This concept of state planning promulgated by the Department of Housing and Urban Development stresses the process and program nature of state planning. It does not mention preparing a single comprehensive state plan comparable with the master plans found at the local level. These statements were modified in 1969 to note that state planning should strengthen the capacity of governors, legislators, and other officials " . . . to plan an effective role in the process of resource allocation."[10]

Slightly less sure of its footing than HUD and admitting that "there presently is no single universal definition of state planning on any but the most general level," the Committee on State Planning of the American Institute of Planners said:

The state planning process is often seen as either all, or any combination of: the identification and formulation of state objectives; the provision of information to facilitate decision-making, coordination and the production of a comprehensive framework for social, economic and physical development efforts in local government, state government, federal assistance programs, and the private sector. It also is frequently viewed as providing the policy basis for gubernatorial action in the development of a legislative program, and as an aid for the legislature in policy determination. . . . Assuming that a basic purpose of state planning is to introduce more systematic thought into the decision-making process of state government, then state objectives become a primary framework in providing direction for the state planning process.[11]

Clearly there is no single generally accepted definition of state planning. Obviously there are many different types of plans and planners, particularly in terms of their time perspective and their degree of substantive specialization. Indeed, budgeters may well have been the first planners at the state level. But the planning capabilities of budgeting were submerged by the need to make the budget process work as an institutionalized procedure and to meet certain nonplanning objectives, especially financial control. Today, the concept of planning has even been broadened to the point of suggesting that a planner is an agent of change and any agent of change is a planner.[12]

With this wide spectrum of possible planning activities, comprehensiveness can be a function only of the total planning process, not of an individual planning agency, no matter how well staffed or located. The required breadth can be obtained only if the line agencies, those responsible for plan implementation, are actively involved in the planning process. Comprehensiveness relates to the issues or total concerns of state government, not to traditional activities of planning agencies. In this sense, comprehensive functional planning is a contradiction in terms. Such plans can be coordinated, but comprehensive planning would encompass the entire warp and woof of state government, and comprehensive coverage of the entire scope of programs can be achieved only at the top—in the governor's office.

All planning should be comprehensive. Every level of government and each section, bureau, division, commission or department should plan. The central planning office should have the capacity to require that all agencies use the same information base, relate all planning activities to the governor's program, and insure that broad goals result in specific action in the shortest possible time.[13]

Linking What to What?

This chapter began by stating that "a budget is a plan, but not all plans are budgets." More precisely, the budget document presents for a given future period the financial implications of a whole range of decisions to be made currently. This document can be viewed as one item in the series of products that should be produced by a variety of planning activities taking place simultaneously within a government. Too ofen, however, the preparation phase of the budget process is the only effective systematic means used for looking to the future.

Budgeting and the planning process are both government-wide in scope, but budgeting appears to be more derivative, hopefully being distilled from a more general and inclusive planning process that recognizes events and actions well beyond the usual jurisdictional bounds of governments. This idea is not alien to budgeters. As one state budget director noted:

We have come to this view that planning is the more important of the aspects and that budgeting should be one of the tools of planning and not relate solely to money. I think that both functions should be under a planning department.[14]

If planning is conceived to be a comprehensive process in these terms, and if analysis and budgeting are elements or components of a more comprehensive and generalized planning process, how can planning and budgeting be "linked" in the manner postulated in planning-programming-budgeting? The problem lies in the way that slippery word planning is defined in PPB. PPB assumes that *strategic* planning will be done and will provide the basis for subsequent detailed budgeting.

Strategic planning is reviewing objectives and the results of past policies at the highest level for the purpose of recommending objectives, policies, and resource allocations to the governor so that he in turn can set strategies or issue strategic plans with which all other state actions should accord.[15] It often depends heavily upon information that is external to the state government and upon projections and approximations. Strategic planning derives stimulus from ideas and research and strives to devise alternatives from which choices can be made. It differs from management control and programming, which occur within the major policies and constraints already determined as a result of strategic planning and are largely concerned with the efficient use of resources in accomplishing defined objectives.

Some of the common underlying ideas of strategic planning and budgeting are frequently weighted differently when the two activities are actually undertaken. State budgeting reflects the need to be adaptive, and it tends to be allocative—to focus on the rational and efficient distribution of the available pie while striving to maximize the general welfare. Strategic planning tends to be more innovative than budgeting, to show more concern for mobilizing resources and finding new ones than for their maximal and efficient use.[16] Despite its talk, PPB better fits an allocative process than one that seeks to establish *new* objectives or values, to alter priorities, or to create *new* institutions. In general, states find it difficult to improve the allocative planning of their budgeting in the way PPB visualizes because they lack sufficiently clear over-all objectives. They also fail to provide adequate innovative strategic planning that could indicate new directions in which they might go.[17]

If strategic planning activities become linked to budgeting activities in the manner postulated by PPB, the resultant process may become dominated by budgeting and allocative considerations rather than by more innovative considerations because the character of an administrative process is usually defined by where it ends rather than by where it begins.[18] The innovative thrust may be seriously inhibited, for example, if the budget calendar is retained as the device that sets the time sequence for events. Budgeting is a *now* process that tends to limit planning activities to producing only such information as is needed to make present decisions cognizant of the future. Multi-year program and financial plans fulfill a planning role in PPB, but they may be projections of present trends rather than comprehensive estimates about the future.

According to PPB precepts, strategic planning, to have an impact, must precede budgeting. It is during the strategic planning stage that goals and objectives are defined, priorities established and alternatives uncovered. Systematic consideration of purposes, future implications, and program alternatives is virtually impossible once the rush of budgeting has begun. Ideally, budget proposals should be based upon comprehensive program plans that encompass all facets of the programs, not just financial considerations.

Although the rush of the budget season does tend to drive out contemplative work, and strategic planning is desirable, PPB proposes too narrow a definition of budgeting.

Budgeting takes the alternatives selected and the resources defined and prepares the detailed steps for accomplishing the alternatives. There is little evaluation of alternatives involved in the budget process. It is more of a detailed blueprint for accomplishing a specific task or set of tasks.[19]

Few state budget officials, unless perhaps they are the "planners" postulated in PPB, can readily accept this conception of budgeting. They see the budget process as being much broader and having far more policy impact than PPB contemplates, even though budget preparation is scarcely the only locus in which policy issues arise.[20] The "costing-out" perception of budgeting limits it to a strictly allocative and more or less mechanical process. This limited definition is unacceptable to state budgeting officials, not just because its adoption would severely restrict their power within state government but also because it seems highly unrealistic in the state environment as they know it. They know, for example, that the needs of budgeting will affect plan disclosures when budget allocations and other politically sensitive matters are still unsettled.

It might prove embarrassing to the administration to have plans laid out in advance which might reveal or seem to reveal a hidden strategy or cause unwarranted criticism of tentative plans on which decisions had not yet been made. These risks are real, but I suspect that as planners become more sophisticated and better able to specify the connections between goals and expenditures, the obvious advantages of planning ahead begin to outweigh the disadvantages.[21]

Besides assigning different weights to allocation and innovation, budgeting and strategic planning have other important differences that should be recognized.[22] First, strategic planning is concerned with a wide variety of activities, including both public and private actions, whereas budgeting is predominantly focused upon public actions, particularly spending programs. Second, budgets retain their traditional legal, political, and managerial control functions, along with their usefulness in program formulation and appraisal. The budget process can be extremely important in fostering the general planning process within a given government, but the budget system still must fulfill operational requirements that do not similarly constrain strategic planning. It is therefore not surprising that the classifications and measurements needed for strategic planning are frequently different from those needed for the control function of budgeting. The same accounting system may be able to produce figures that are useful for both strategic planning and fiscal control purposes, but it is apparent already that the informational demands of the two activities are not totally compatible. Furthermore, the time spans of budgeting and strategic planning are usually different, and the kinds of filters through which men experienced in each of these fields view problems also vary.

Planning must start with a broad vision, and only secondarily are the immediate steps considered which lead in the direction of the plan. In contrast, the emphasis in budget making has been on the ensuing year for operations reasons, and only as a supplement have longer-term budget outlooks been adopted or recommended.[23]

Some Other Differences

Budgeters and planners are eclectics, drawing insights, techniques, and help from wherever they can. But each group has its traditional specialized concerns: public expenditures for the one, and space and physical elements for the other.

Even though both processes require feedback about past accomplishments, budgeting tends to be more retrospective and control-dominated, while planning is more prospective and analytic. They stress different phases of the budget cycle—execution in budgeting, and preparation in planning—and consequently have different views of the amount and nature of detail that is desirable in preparation. Planners tend to think of spending to meet needs, while budget staffs tend to think of cutting expenditures to meet available resources. Budgeting seems to be dominated by a sense of scarcity, planning by a sense of opportunity. Budgeting stresses the cost of doing all that government agencies want to do, while planning stresses the benefits that will accrue from doing it. Budget staffs sense that explicit regard for future objectives may intensify spending and political pressures, while planners favor explicit rationality. Planning tries to be comprehensive while

budgetary decisions tend to be incremental and marginal. Budgeters traditionally view themselves as managers of a governmental organization, while planners see themselves as appraisers of the state of the polity.

Besides their differences in perspectives and emphases, planning and budget agencies have also assumed or acquired rather different kinds of operating responsibilities. Budget agencies tend to respond to initiatives originating from others rather than within themselves. Budget staffs look to others—planners of all sorts—to make physical, economic, and social studies and to formulate alternative plans, projects, or programs. Budgeters obviously do some initiating, but in most governments, planners have more administrative responsibility for initiation. Planners also have many central coordinative responsibilities, especially in a wide variety of intergovernmental programs and grants, but they do not have the effective coordinating power that comes with control over the purse strings.

The discipline of an annual budget can be very sobering and beneficial for planning, and budgets will continue to be important management tools. Budgeting may be the ingredient that disciplines the entire planning process.[24] Nonetheless, there needs to be a more comprehensive planning process into which budgeting fits, a process that considers long-range goals and raises choices about how best to use resources to achieve those goals. Goals and strategies should provide the framework within which more specific budgetary choices are made; the compilation of budgetary matters should not be allowed to determine effectively what the goals and strategies are. It is probably easier but not wiser to decide to cross a bridge when it is reached than to decide in advance what bridge to reach and what new bridges to build and how.[25]

The ideas presented here are neither new nor unique, as the following summarizing quotation indicates.

The problem of giving intelligent direction to the administration of public programs through adequate planning cannot be divorced from the budgeting function. The linking of the two in practice has proved the sterility of the theory, widely held among the professional planners, that planning must be divorced from administration and "political" influence in order to preserve its purity. Fortunately, a substantial and growing number of planners have recognized the futility of attempting to detach planning from administration. To them, it will come as no great shock to think of budgeting as a form of planning and of planning as the basis of progressive budgeting. If the planners will accept the accomplished fact that planning, as a function of government, is as broad in scope as governmental activity itself—and hence is coextensive with the budgeting function—the organized planning movement will have taken an important step toward restoring its lost vitality. Otherwise, budget agencies may be expected to assume an even greater responsibility for encouraging and coordinating program planning, for good planning is the base upon which good budgeting must stand.[26]

Conclusion

Planning needs to underlie the entire policy-making process, including budgeting. It encompasses not a single activity or precise methodology but rather a broad range of activities that strive to bring greater rationality to policy-making and are performed by different individuals throughout the organization. Planning as a process must be built into the structure of state government at many points. Interest must be directed to spreading planning capability broadly rather than to specific planning activities.[27] The planner must be an educator who seeks to spread sensitivity to the planning process among all the people who must be involved in it.[28] Planners must give more attention to teaching and proselytizing functions in which they help others learn the planning process and its advantages.

The most acceptable approach is for state planning agencies to assist other state agencies develop better departmental or functional plans by insuring that overall state goals which have been formulated by the chief executive are infused into such plans, and by providing basic information, technical assistance, and other necessary coordinative activities.[29]

State government has room for several planning enterprises, all of which can and should be future-oriented. The planning that goes into developing programs and proposals for changes in legislation needs substantial improvement. But the development of improvements need not be coupled directly with the budget process in the manner that PPB suggests—

it can be undertaken independently. This separation has the advantage of freeing innovative planning efforts from the formidable and perhaps inherent constraints of the budget process—a particularly desirable consequence if budgeting becomes simply "costing out" decisions already made rather than a process for making policy choices.[30]

To say that others should also plan is scarcely news to planners. But they may have failed to propagate this gospel adequately because of their own needs to identify a purpose for their existence, obtain staff and other resources, meet federal requirements, develop grass-roots support through technical assistance, define the boundaries of their administrative jurisdictions, and protect themselves against the sallies of other empire builders and the antiplanning forces that seem to exist on all sides. Planning has many potential uses: It can serve as a control mechanism and as a weapon in intraorganizational struggles; it can be used in interorganizational struggles between groups with different priorities and perspectives that represent different groups and alliances; it can serve as a rational method for allocating resources or for *acquiring* resources. In state governments where planning traditions are not firmly entrenched and a multiplicity of new planning enterprises have been seeded by federal grants and state initiatives,

state planning is pluralistic, with centers of planning forming within departments, in programs that crosscut department jurisdictions, and at the top of the executive structure. In this multi-centered environment, the task of central planners is more to coordinate the work of others and to relate it to financial and program policies than to design some comprehensive blueprint for the whole state.[31]

Notes

1. It was Luther Gulick who suggested that management consists of planning, organizing, staffing, directing, coordinating, reporting, and budgeting. See Luther Gulick and Lyndall Urwick, eds., *Papers on the Science of Administration* (New York: Institute of Public Administration, 1937).
2. Allen Schick, "Budgets, Plans and Scarcity" (unpublished paper prepared for 1969 National Conference of the American Society for Public Administration, Miami, Florida, May 1969).

3. L. E. Burney, "Background of the Current Idea of Comprehensive Health Service Planning," *State Budgeting for Comprehensive Health Service Planning*, National Association of State Budget Officers' Institute on Comprehensive Health Planning (Chicago: Council of State Governments, 1968), p. 2.

4. For a more systematic definition of planning and its components, see Yehezkel Dror, "The Planning Process: A Facet Design," *International Review of Administrative Sciences* 29, no. 1 (1963), 44–58.

5. Francis H. Parker, "Strategy and Effectiveness of Planning in State Government" (Ph.D. diss., University of North Carolina at Chapel Hill, 1970), p. 209.

6. Thad L. Beyle and Deil S. Wright, "The Governor, Planning and Governmental Activity," in Thad L. Beyle and Deil S. Wright, eds., *The American Governor in Behavioral Perspective* (New York: Harper and Row, 1972), pp. 193–205.

7. Parker, "Strategy and Effectiveness of Planning in State Government," p. 2.

8. Taken from a tape-recording made at "Symposium on the Link Between Budgeting and Planning," Institute on State Programming for the 70's, Chapel Hill, North Carolina, April 25, 1968.

9. "State Comprehensive Planning," In *Urban Planning Program Guide*, Policies and Procedures for Federal Assistance Under the Urban Planning Program, Department of Housing and Urban Development (Washington, D.C., September 1966), p. 5-1.

10. The 1969 changes are taken from Parker, "Strategy and Effectiveness of Planning in State Government," p. 125.

11. *State Planning in the Sixties*, The Committee on State Planning, American Institute of Planners, December 1968 (Washington, D.C.), p. II-1.

12. Leonard J. Duhl, "Planning and Predicting: Or What To Do When You Don't Know The Names of the Variables," *Daedalus* 96, no. 3 (Summer 1967), 780. See also Alfred J. Kahn, *Theory and Practice of Social Planning* (New York: Russell Sage Foundation, 1969), p. 129.

13. *A Strategy for Planning*, Report of the Committee on State Planning, The National Governors' Conference, October 18, 1967 (Lexington, Ky.), p. 9.

14. See footnote 8.

15. These ideas are derived from Robert N. Anthony, *Planning and Control Systems, A Framework for Analysis* (Cambridge, Mass.: Harvard University Press, 1965). For an excellent but brief application of Anthony's ideas to budgeting, see K. E. Rose,

"Management Processes and Systems Development," *Local Government Finance* 74, no. 10 (October 1970), 338–342.

16. Dichotomizing planning along development-adaptive and allocative-innovative criteria has been suggested by John Friedmann, "A Conceptual Model for the Analysis of Planning Behavior," *Administrative Science Quarterly* 12, no. 2 (September, 1967), 225–252.

17. Parker, "Strategy and Effectiveness of Planning in State Government," p. 45.

18. Allen Schick, *Budget Innovation in the States* (Washington: The Brookings Institution, 1971), p. 214.

19. Irwin T. David, *Challenge of the 70's: Effective Systematic Financial Management* (Chicago: Municipal Finance Officers Association of the United States and Canada, Special Bulletin 1970 C, May 16, 1970), p. 2.

20. This finding also appears true at the local level. See Deil S. Wright "The Dynamics of Budgeting—Large Council Manager Cities" (unpublished paper, Institute for Research in Social Science, University of North Carolina at Chapel Hill, July 1969).

21. Alice M. Rivlin, "The Planning, Programming and Budgeting System in the Department of Health, Education and Welfare: Some Lessons from Experience," in Robert H. Haveman and Julius Margolis, eds., *Public Expenditures and Policy Analysis* (Chicago: Markham Publishing Co., 1970), p. 513.

22. These suggestions are taken from Gerhard Colm, *Integration of National Planning and Budgeting*, National Planning Association, Center for Development Planning, Planning Methods Series No. 5, March 1958 (Washington, D.C.), pp. 18–25.

23. *Ibid.*, p. 23.

24. Frederick C. Mosher, *Program Budgeting: Theory and Practice* (Chicago: Public Administration Service, 1954), p. 49.

25. This language and idea are paraphrased from Yehezkel Dror, *Public Policymaking Reexamined* (San Francisco: Chandler Publishing Company, 1968), p. 136.

26. Robert A. Walker, "The Relation of Budgeting to Program Planning," *Public Administration Review* 4, no. 2 (Spring 1944), 107.

27. This conception underlies Parker, "Strategy and Effectiveness of Planning in State Government."

28. Duhl, "Planning and Predicting," 784.

29. *State Planning in the Sixties*, p. III-4.

30. Schick, *Budget Innovation*, p. 213.

31. *Ibid.*, p. 40.

31

Introduction to Zero-Base Budgeting

Graeme M. Taylor

The term *zero-base budgeting* is not new. In the most literal sense, ZBB implies constructing a budget without any reference to what has gone before, based on a fundamental reappraisal of purposes, methods, and resources. This interpretation of ZBB has been roundly condemned as naive and impractical, if not downright mischievous. The U.S. Department of Agriculture's attempt at this sort of ZBB for FY 1964 was widely regarded as a failure. As Allen Schick has remarked, even a teenager doesn't have an identity crisis every year. Or, as Dean Acheson pointed out in another context, we can't have a foreign policy if we pull it up every year to examine its roots.

But there is another version of ZBB. Developed originally at Texas Instruments by Peter A. Pyhrr as a method of controlling overhead costs, and subsequently implemented by Jimmy Carter in the state of Georgia, this latter-day ZBB is simply the systematic application of marginal analysis techniques to budget formulation. It is this version of ZBB which is the subject of this article.

Although the basic concepts of ZBB as used at Texas Instruments and Georgia are indeed simple, putting them into practice is difficult, complex, and demanding. Many organizations, however, apparently believe the results are worth the effort. Within the past three years, at least one hundred major corporations have applied ZBB to portions of their operating budgets. A handful of states and several local governments have adopted ZBB. A few federal agencies have introduced ZBB on a limited basis within the past year.

Some of the growing popularity of ZBB must no doubt be attributed to presidential campaign publicity. But it would be a mistake to think that the bandwagon syndrome is the main reason for ZBB's adoption. The real explanation lies in certain intrinsic features of the process itself coupled, fortuitously, with the needs of the times.

Industry views ZBB as a more rational approach to the perennial problem of controlling overhead. The recent recession forced most companies to reappraise their discretionary costs, and many found ZBB an instrument ideally suited to the task.

In the public sector, the example of New York City looms like a severed head placed on a spike as an awful warning. Today, virtually everyone is a fiscal conservative. There is a growing realization that program initiatives to meet public needs must go hand-in-hand with sound financial management. As President Carter pointed out in *Nation's Business* (January 1977):

There is no inherent conflict between careful planning, tight budgeting, and constant management reassessment on the one hand, and compassionate concern for the deprived and afflicted on the other. Waste and inefficiency never fed a hungry child, provided a job for a willing worker, or educated a deserving student.

Zero-base budgeting has come a long way since its origins at Texas Instruments and Georgia. These early models have been substantially improved upon and refined in later, less publicized applications while still retaining the original fundamental principles. Experience indicates that there are almost limitless ways to adapt the basic ZBB concepts to the varying decisional needs of different organizations. This should come as no surprise. ZBB is, after all, a management-oriented approach to budgeting. It follows, then, that its basic principles must be adapted to fit each organization's unique management structure and culture.

This article will attempt, somewhat boldly, to summarize the state of a complex and rapidly evolving art. The writer's viewpoint is not that of a scholar, but rather a practitioner, one who has been actively involved in helping organizations design and implement ZBB. The reader will therefore not find much in the way of public administration theory, nor any glittering generalities to serve as a conceptual framework. If any apology is needed, it would be this: It is too early to predict the ultimate fate of ZBB in the public sector. It could evolve in many different ways to serve different needs in different government organizations. Many versions of ZBB could comfortably coexist in Washington, in the states, and

Source: From *The Bureaucrat* (Spring 1977), Vol. 6, No. 1, pp. 33–55. Copyright © 1977 The Bureaucrat, Inc. Reprinted by permission.

in city halls. Different approaches may be quite appropriate even within the same government, at different levels and for different kinds of programs. No unified theory is likely to emerge; certainly none can be discerned at this time.

The basic principles and elements of ZBB, common to virtually all applications, are first summarized. Each of the elements of ZBB is then treated in more detail. Certain considerations affecting the design and implementation of ZBB are then reviewed, emphasizing the variety of possible approaches and the importance of tailoring the approach to the unique circumstances of each organization. Some differences between ZBB in the public and private sectors are then discussed, and results of a survey of corporate ZBB users are presented. The concluding section attempts to examine certain options for the application of ZBB to the federal government.

Principles and Elements of ZBB

The distinctive and essential hallmark of ZBB is its focus on the total budget request. The current spending level is not regarded as an inviolate base, immune from detailed scrutiny. Existing activities are examined along with proposed new activities.

In traditional incremental budgeting sytems, all participants behave as if the relevant question were: At the margin, is an increment in Program A more important than an increment in Program B? Decision makers are forced to accept or reject a program increment, or to reduce its amount. Incremental budgeting effectively denies decision makers the option of trading off a requested increase in one activity against a reduction in another.

ZBB places a premium on offering decision makers a range of choices among alternate funding levels. The relevant budgetary question is: At the margin, is an increment in Program A more important than an increment in Program B or a previously funded item in Programs A, B, C . . . ? It is explicitly *not* assumed that present activities must necessarily be continued. Given revenue constraints, an existing activity may be reduced or eliminated entirely to make way for new activities, or one program may be cut back to permit another to expand.

Basic Elements of ZBB

The three basic elements of ZBB are: (1) identification of "decision units"; (2) analysis of decision units and the formulation of "decision packages"; and (3) ranking. The decision units are the lowest-level entities for which budgets are prepared. One important requirement is that each decision unit have an identifiable manager with the necessary authority to establish priorities and prepare budgets for all activities within the decision unit.

ZBB calls for two kinds of analysis. First is the analysis which most truly deserves the name "zero base"—a reexamination of the purposes, activities, and operations of the decision unit. In this analytic phase questions such as the following are addressed: What would be the consequences if the decision unit were entirely eliminated? How can the decision unit's purposes be achieved in a more cost-effective manner? How can the efficiency of the decision unit's operations be improved? Following the zero-base review of purposes, activities, and operations, the decision unit manager then segments the decision unit's activities into a series of "decision packages." The first package contains those activities, or portions of activities, deemed highest in priority. The second package contains the next most important items, and so on. The costs and consequences of each package are documented for higher-level review.

The third basic element of ZBB is "ranking," the process whereby higher level managers establish priorities for all decision packages from all subordinate decision units. The priority-ordered set of all decision packages for the entire organization is then reviewed in light of the probable level of funding available to the organization. Packages which can be funded within the available total are included in the organization's formal budget request; those which fall "below the line" are dropped from the budget request—unless the organization chooses to seek an increase in the total funding level.

Decision Units, Decision Packages, and the Ranking Process

Identifying and Defining Decision Units

Decision units are the basic entities for which budgets are prepared. Decision units must be identified and defined as a necessary first step in implementing ZBB. This step is part of the initial design of the ZBB approach and need not be repeated in subsequent budget cycles, except to accommodate new activities or to improve the decisional usefulness of the budget structure. Decision units may be programs, functions, cost centers, organizational units or, in certain cases, line items or appropriation items.

A key consideration in selecting decision units is the organization's "responsibility structure." Decision units should generally be selected to parallel the flow of responsibility for budgetary decision making within the organization. To illustrate this point, consider an organization which operates a number of neighborhood health centers, each of which offers a variety of health services such as tuberculosis control, venereal disease control, lead poisoning control, maternal and child health clinics, and so forth. The decision units may variously be (1) each center, encompassing all health services provided within the center; (2) each separate health service provided in each center; or (3) each health service aggregated across all centers.

If each center has a manager responsible for resource allocation within the center, then the individual centers may be logically selected as decision units. If each health service within a center has an identifiable manager responsible for resource allocation within that service, each service within a center could be viewed as a separate decision unit. On the other hand, if resource allocation decisions within health services are made system-wide by identifiable managers at the organization's headquarters, then the individual health services, aggregated across all centers, would be logical decision units. The key criterion is how responsibility for resource allocation decisions is distributed.

There is a fourth option: the entire organization may be considered a single decision unit. This option would make sense if all resource allocation decisions are made by the organization's chief executive, or if other considerations become important—such as the relative size of the organization with respect to the government of which it forms a part. For example, if an entire city is engaged in ZBB, then, from the standpoint of the mayor, the entire neighborhood health center program might be logically one single decision unit. Relative size, therefore, is a second important consideration in identifying decision units.

Availability of data often constrains the choice of decision units. The organization's accounting system may not provide reliable cost data for the "ideal" decision unit structure. Compromises may have to be made, or the accounting system may be modified so that something approaching the ideal structure may become feasible at a later time.

Analytic Emphasis

Some organizations emphasize a fundamental reexamination of each decision unit before its manager is permitted to proceed with the formulation of decision packages. In other instances, only perfunctory attention is paid to the questioning of objectives, activities, and operating methods, and decision packages simply reflect the status quo. The relative emphasis on each type of analysis is a matter to be decided by the architects and users of the ZBB system. Both types of analysis are useful, but considerations of time, practicality, and available analytic skills sometimes dictate that the former be sacrificed and attention concentrated on the latter.

Formulation of Decision Packages

The decision unit manager formulates, in priority order, a series of decision packages which together equal the sum total of his budget request for the decision unit. Each decision package consists of a discrete set of services, activities, or expenditure items. The first, or highest priority package addresses the most important activities performed by the decision unit, *i.e.,* those which produce the highest priority services or which meet the most critical needs of the decision unit's target population. The cost of this first package is usually well below the current level of funding for the decision unit. The first, highest priority package is often thought of as the *minimum level* or *survival level* for the decision unit, the level of service and funding below which the decision unit might as well be eliminated.

In some cases decision unit managers are allowed complete freedom in determining the appropriate magnitude of the first package, subject only to the constraint that it costs less than the current funding level. In other cases, guidelines are provided in the form of a percentage of the current level, for example: "the first package should be less than 75 percent of current"; or "the first package should be between 40 to 60 percent of current." In most cases no firm rule is established for the total number of packages for each decision unit. In practice, the number can usually be expected to vary between a minimum of three and a maximum of around 10. Typically, packages are smaller and more discrete as their cumulative total cost approaches and exceeds the decision unit's current funding level. This offers decision makers a more practical range of flexibility in the subsequent ranking process.

The decision unit manager's analysis of decision packages is communicated on a series of forms, using a separate form for each decision package. Each form documents: (1) precisely what services are to be provided or activities performed, if this package is funded; (2) the resource requirements of the package and their cost; and (3) a quantitative expression of workload, output, or results anticipated if the package is funded. Usually, each form displays, in addition to the cost of the package, the cumulative cost of this plus all preceding (higher priority) packages in the series for the decision unit. Often the cumulative cost is also expressed as a percentage of the prior year's total for the decision unit. Similarly, the quantitative program measures are also usually cumulated and expressed as a percentage of the prior year's figure. In some cases, the decision unit manager is asked to identify additional information on each decision package form, such as "benefits of funding this package"; "consequences of not funding this package"; "present services which would not be provided if only this package and those which precede it are funded"; "support required from other decision units if this package is funded"; and the like.

The amount of cost and object class detail required on the decision package form can vary considerably depending on the requirements of the ZBB system's users. One approach is simply to record the package's total dollar cost and the number of positions involved. Or the dollar cost may be broken down into considerable object detail. A breakdown by source of funds can also be shown, if appropriate. In many cases it is helpful for the next level of management to conduct a preliminary review of proposed decision packages before the decision unit managers prepare the detailed forms. This review can help ensure that each decision unit manager and his superior agree on the priorities governing the formulation of decision packages before detailed cost estimates are prepared and forms filled out.

Ranking

Ranking is the process in which a manager reviews all decision packages (from all decision units reporting to him) and establishes their relative priority. A "ranking table" is prepared, listing all decision packages in descending order of priority. A running cumulative total is kept to indicate the total budget request for the sum of each package plus all preceding (higher priority) packages. Ranking may be performed in a variety of ways, for example, unilaterally by a single manager, or in a committee fashion where the manager meets with his decision unit managers. Depending on the size and complexity of the organization, a series of rankings by successively higher levels of management may be required to produce a single, consolidated ranking table for the entire organization. To avoid overwhelming higher levels of management with excessive detail, the ranked decision packages are often consolidated into a smaller number of "superpackages" for review and ranking by the next managerial level.

In the ranking process, attention is usually concentrated on those packages which lie within a reasonable range around the probable cutoff line, *i.e.*, the expected funding level for the collection of decision units whose packages are being ranked. For example, if 40 packages are being ranked, it is usually not necessary to determine precisely the relative priorities among numbers one, two, and three, nor numbers 38, 39, and 40. It is more important to ensure that those packages which fall just above and just below the probable cutoff line are indeed in the order which properly reflects management's priorities.

Designing and Implementing ZBB

Before embarking on ZBB, an organization must carefully weigh several factors:

- What are the strengths and weaknesses of the existing budget process?
- What are the organization's objectives and expectations for ZBB?
- Who is the principal intended "consumer" of the information generated by the ZBB process?
- What implementation strategies shall be followed?
- What degree of linkage to existing management systems is appropriate?

- What particular ZBB "technology" shall be employed?

Any decision to launch ZBB should normally be preceded by a systematic appraisal of the strengths and weaknesses of the existing budget process. This review may be thought of as a "budget audit" during which managers assess the degree to which the current budget process serves or fails to serve the organization's planning, management, and control needs. Design of the approach to ZBB can then attempt to build on existing strengths and correct deficiencies in the current process.

The organization should next explicitly address the question of what it hopes to achieve by implementing ZBB. Different organizations may have quite different objectives and expectations for ZBB. Some of the more common are:

- Cut budgets rationally.
- Reallocate resources from lower to higher priority areas.
- Yield better information or more credible justifications to support budget requests.
- Forge a better link between budgeting and operation planning and control.
- Provide top management with better insights into the detailed workings of the organization.
- Create more substantive involvement by line managers in budget formulation.
- Achieve various "organization development" objectives (such as improved communication between managerial levels, greater sense of participation, more identification with the organization's mission).
- Enable top management to evaluate the managerial capabilities of subordinate managers.

The design of the ZBB process may vary depending on who is to be the principal consumer of the information produced. The consumer may be the legislative body, the chief executive, the department head, or line managers—or all of the above.

Implementation strategies must be carefully considered. For example, should ZBB be applied to the entire budget or should certain activities or expenditure items be excluded? Should full-scale implementation be attempted immediately, or should a pilot test be first conducted? Should ZBB replace or supplement the existing formal budget process?

The organization must also determine the appropriate form and degree of linkage to management systems already in place. What should be the relationship of ZBB to current planning, control, and information systems? Can ZBB be appropriately meshed with an existing MBO system?

Finally, the organization must design the technical and procedural aspects of the ZBB process. Particular attention must be paid to the following:

- The logic by which decision units are identified and defined.
- The type of analysis to be emphasized.
- The particular forms, procedures, timetable, guidelines, and instructions to be used in implementing the process.
- The type and amount of training and technical assistance to be provided.

ZBB can take many forms and be used for many purposes. Existing public sector applications illustrate this variety. For example, the U.S. Navy, in response to a congressional mandate, is using a partial version of ZBB to provide more detailed justification of its FY 1978 Operations and Maintenance appropriation request. The Environmental Protection Agency has used ZBB principles to develop a FY 1977 operational plan for one of its programs. HEW's Date Management Center uses ZBB as part of a total management system, for manpower planning and project planning and control, as well as budget formulation.

ZBB need not rely on a "bottom-up" approach. In some cases a bottom-up approach may be entirely inappropriate. A structured "top-down" approach to ZBB is illustrated in the following example, drawn from a large municipal hospital.

A framework of very specific and detailed planning guidelines, developed by the hospital administrator in conjunction with teams of doctors and other professional staff, was provided to all departments in the hospital. The guidelines consisted of, first, a series of "capacity" figures (*e.g.,* varying numbers of in-patient beds), and second, a number of "service levels." Each service level was defined in terms of the medical and surgical specialties to be offered by the hospital at that level, and also in terms of the standards set for a number of "quality" proxies (*e.g.,* nursing hours per patient-day). Each department head then developed estimates of resource requirements for every combination of capacity and service level. The departmental estimates were reviewed and then aggregated, producing a capacity/service level cost matrix for the hospital. This permitted the administrator to develop a budget which, in his judgment, reflected the appropriate balance between size, range of medical services offered, and standards of service. An alternative to the approach described above would have been the more traditional bottom-up ZBB process. Individual units, such as pathology and food service, would have independently formulated decision packages for subsequent ranking by division chiefs and then by the administrator. But this approach would have ignored critical interdependencies between units in providing service.

By linking dollar figures explicitly to service variables, at various possible funding levels, the administrator's budget presentation clearly demonstrated the service impact of increases or decreases in his recommended budget. This was useful in the case of this particular hospital, since it had undergone successive budget reductions but was still expected by the city government to continue providing the same level of patient care (what the "same level" meant was never precisely defined by the city fathers). The budget presentation made clear the consequences of further budget reductions—either wards would be closed, or the level of service would deteriorate, or both. Budget reductions could no longer be divorced from their service impacts.

In concluding this section on considerations affecting the design and implementation of ZBB, a number of issues will be listed. It is not possible, in the scope of this article, to give them the detailed discussion they deserve.

The users of ZBB must decide how to modify the process in the second and subsequent cycles following the initial year of implementation. Priorities may be reviewed to ensure that they are still relevant, decision units may be added or deleted as appropriate, new decision packages may be formulated to meet newly identified needs, and cost and output data may be refined and updated. But it is usually not necessary to repeat the considerable development effort normally required in the first year. Illustratively, the focus can shift to areas of the budget not included in the first year, or the process can be driven deeper in the organization, or the reliability of data can be improved, or the process

can be more selective in concentrating analytic efforts on particular issues.

Other design and implementation issues might include the appropriate role of the computer, for example in reducing paperwork, aggregating data in various ways, helping decision makers ask "what if" questions, or aiding the formulation of decision packages by providing analytical modeling capabilities to predict cost/output relationships. The treatment of administrative support units deserves special attention; it is necessary to ensure that packages formulated for support units are consistent with packages formulated for the primary "mission" units. Another important design issue is the degree to which top management wishes to drive budgetary accountability deeper into the organization. Although the existing responsibility structure may be the starting point for identifying decision units, management may elect to delegate budgetary responsibility to lower levels—not merely for the purposes of ZBB, but as a means to increase management commitment throughout the organization.

Private Versus Public Sector Use of ZBB

The annual operating budget plays a less central role in the private sector than it does in government. Corporations employ a variety of management systems in addition to budgeting, to help set goals, acquire and allocate resources, and measure performance. Strategic decisions, such as decisions to enter new markets or launch new products, are usually completely divorced from the annual routines of budgeting. Formal business plans are prepared to set short-term goals for sales and profits and to monitor progress. The marketplace sends a variety of signals to the decision maker on the need to change direction or to shift resources from one venture to another.

In government, on the other hand, the budget process must generally serve many purposes. Certainly, many strategic policy decisions are initially made outside the budget, for example, through legislation or regulation. But the budget is the only conduit for funds to implement legislation or to enforce a regulation. It is only through the budget process, by appropriation or ordinance, that a president, governor, or mayor may legally draw from the public purse.

The budget process, in addition to its legal function in conferring authority to expend public funds, also serves, explicitly or implicitly, as the mechanism for establishing public priorities. Through the budget process, competing claims are resolved and expenditures brought into balance with revenues. Choices are made about which programs will expand and by how much and, less often, which programs will be cut back.

The public budget process also serves in lieu of a management control system. Unlike a private corporation which can point to growth, market share, and earnings, and despite a mounting clamor for "accountability," governments are rarely able to demonstrate the link between funding and results. For a government, simply living within its means is an achievement. The budget therefore carries with it strong sanctions to discourage deviations from its totals and subtotals; underspending and overspending are equally discouraged. Control is therefore exercised via inputs rather than outputs.

The different role and scope of budgeting in the two sectors partially explains a striking contrast in the application of ZBB in the private and public sectors. Virtually all private corporations using ZBB have confined it to overhead expenses, whereas most government bodies employing ZBB have applied it to program expenditures as well as to support costs.

Another part of the explanation lies in the different determinants of manufacturing and overhead costs. In manufacturing, unit costs are largely determined by technology, the price of raw materials, and union contracts. Strong competitive pressures, reinforced by financial incentives, encourage managers to pursue a continual search for improved manufacturing methods, cheaper raw materials, and more productive ways to use labor inputs. Given unit costs, total production costs are then a function of sales volume.

Overhead costs are quite another matter. With respect to these costs, it is much harder to answer the central budgetary question: How much is enough?

Management generally has much more discretion in funding overhead activities, and there is rarely any direct benefit-cost relationship to serve as a guide to appropriate expenditure levels. However, control of overhead costs is critically important. Excessive overhead undermines profit margins; savings are reflected directly in the "bottom line." Any budget process, such as ZBB, which offers a more systematic approach to control of overhead, is therefore likely to be warmly endorsed by private sector managers.

Corporate managers have found that ZBB has advantages other than overhead cost control, according to a survey of 54 private corporations which had recently implemented the process for the first time. All respondents were on *Fortune's* 1,000 list.[1] Respondents were asked by how much their operating budgets had changed from the prior year. Twelve percent reported a budget decrease of more than 10 percent; 30 percent reported a budget decrease of between 5 and 10 percent; 51 percent said that their budgets had changed (increased or decreased) less than 5 percent; and 7 percent of the respondents reported a budget increase of more than 5 percent.

Respondents were also asked to rate ZBB as (a) a tool to change total expenditure levels, and (b) a tool to reallocate resources from lower to higher priority areas. Results [are shown in Table 1].

Respondents were asked for their overall evaluation of ZBB as a management planning and control system. Twenty-eight percent gave an "excellent" rating, 59 percent rated ZBB as "good," 13 percent gave only a "fair" rating, and none rated ZBB as "poor." In response to a question asking them to compare ZBB with other formal management systems, 67 percent of the respondents described ZBB as "better," and 33 percent said it was "about the same"; none described ZBB as "worse."

The following table [Table 2] shows how the respondents rated ZBB as a process to achieve a number of managerial purposes other than changing budget levels or reallocating resources.

Table 1
Respondents' rating of ZBB (%)

	Excellent	Good	Fair	Poor	N/A
Tool to change total budget level	28	46	20	0	6
Tool to reallocate resources	34	42	20	2	2

Table 2
Respondents' evaluation of ZBB (%)

	Excellent	*Good*	*Fair*	*Poor*	*N/A*
Learn more about the organization	55	42	3		
Manage overhead activities with more flexibility	20	54	23	3	
Improve efficiency/effectiveness	18	58	18	3	3
Improve communications	16	47	29	3	5
Develop alternative methods of operation	15	46	36	3	
Plan organizational changes	13	39	24	16	8
Evaluate staff performance	13	35	35	11	5

The Future of ZBB in the Federal Government

In this concluding section, some options for the application of ZBB to the federal government are discussed, employing the design and implementation framework described in a previous section. At best, this section can only present a partial and preliminary list of some issues and options. It was written before the inauguration, without the benefit of any inside knowledge of the plans of the new administration. The discussion may therefore be overtaken by events.

Strengths and Weaknesses of the Existing Federal Budget Process

The federal budget process works. It comprehensively reconciles the competing claims of a myriad of programs into a unified whole. Each party understands the rules of the game, and open conflict is kept to a minimum. The budget, quite properly, is a central and well-understood fact of life in both executive and legislative branches of government.

Some weaknesses are apparent. Budget justifications focus almost exclusively on increments—the additional positions and dollars requested above the "adjusted base." Neither the president nor Congress are routinely provided the opportunity of examining whether objectives should be changed, or whether the same objectives could be attained more economically, or what would be the consequences of funding a given program at varying levels. Interagency trade-off opportunities, within the same general program area, are difficult to examine without special analyses. The link between costs and services provided is hard to discern. Often, cuts are imposed without any explicit recognition of which services will be reduced by what amounts. Agencies are frequently expected to absorb cuts and still somehow maintain the current level of operations.

Objectives for ZBB in the Federal Government

Objectives for ZBB should be formulated realistically, with due regard for the limitations of the process. Macro policy changes or changes in legislation might better emerge from the type of process envisioned in the so-called sunset bills discussed during the last session of Congress. Or within the executive branch, the kind of long-term policy, program, and organizational review that produced Elliot Richardson's "mega-proposal" for the restructuring of HEW might be more applicable to the design of fundamental changes in how public needs are to be addressed.

A tentative set of primary objectives for ZBB in the executive branch of the federal government might be as follows:

• Provide the president a range of choices within a given program area so that he can ensure that the total resources committed correspond to his policy preferences for that program area.

• Yield more credible budget justifications, at all levels within the executive branch, in support of total budget requests, and not merely with respect to proposed changes from the prior year. The information should be structured so as to illuminate the consequences of various levels of funding, both above and below current levels.

• Encourage agency operating managers to surface recommendations for improved methods of operation as part of the formal budget process.

Consumers

There are many potential consumers of the results of ZBB in the federal government: the Congress (its substantive, budget, and appropriations committees, as well as the Congressional Budget Office and the GAO), the president and his Office of Management and Budget, agency heads and their policy, planning, and budget staffs, and the several levels of operating "line" managers within each agency.

Implementation Strategies

The central question is to identify the most productive targets of opportunity for ZBB and then determine how best to implement the process in the selected areas.

Although the president's budget embraces virtually all federal expenditures, ZBB may not be equally appropriate for all types of expenditure. The interest on the national debt is hardly susceptible to annual zero-base review. A variety of income and other transfers such as social security payments, veterans' benefits, welfare payments, and general revenue sharing are controllable only in the long run and can be changed only if there is a significant shift in the political consensus. Other major expenditures have powerful constituencies; it would take more than a new budget process to significantly affect expenditures from the Highway Trust Fund or the various agricultural price support programs. Stability and credibility in national security and foreign affairs require a degree of continuity in the scale and distribution of resource commitment. Significant or abrupt changes in long-range procurement or construction programs, both civilian and military, could cause severe economic dislocations even if decision makers are persuaded to ignore such costs.

In the long run nothing is fixed. In the short run, much is, at least within the realm of practical politics. This is not to say that programs such as those cited in the previous paragraphs should not be thoroughly reappraised from time to time. But the annual budget process may not be the proper forum for the debate. There are, however, several classes of federal expenditures ideally suited to the type of ZBB described in this article:

• The overhead agencies of government, *i.e.,* those agencies providing services not to the public but to government itself (*e.g.,* GSA, the Civil Service Commission, parts of Treasury and Justice, etc.).
• The overhead (administrative and support) activities of agencies, in Washington and in countless field offices. This is a very diverse category including a multitude of functions such as legal, ADP, personnel,

training, accounting, research, planning, procurement, printing, communications, transportation, etc.
• Virtually all formula and project grant programs.
• Many operating programs of government, where the government itself acts directly as the provider of service without any intermediaries. This group would include organizations such as the National Park Service, the Forest Service, the VA Hospitals, the Customs Bureau, the FAA, the FDA, and so forth.

A fundamental implementation issue to be resolved is the relationship of ZBB to the overall federal budget process. ZBB could be implemented as a supplement to the existing budget process, as a substitute for the existing budget process, or elements of ZBB could be incorporated into the existing budget process.

The first option would leave undisturbed the normal routines of budgeting, and therein lies both its advantages and disadvantages. Treating ZBB as supplementary to the existing budget process would cause the least disruption for both OMB and the agencies. True, it would generate an additional workload but this could be accommodated. OMB and the agencies would in all likelihood set up special staffs to handle ZBB, effectively insulating it from the "real" budget process. This, of course, is precisely what happened to PPB.

The second option is only superficially a real option. The concept of "replacing" the existing budget process with ZBB is wrongheaded. In the first place, the budget process serves many purposes other than those for which ZBB is suited. Besides, a budget process is not an integrated circuit module which can be unplugged or reconnected at will.

The third option is real—the only one which makes sense. The basic principles of ZBB could be made an integral part of the agency budget formulation process and could form the basis for both the Spring Preview and Director's Review. The formats of detailed supporting budget schedules need not necessarily be altered, but the schedules would probably be completed only after basic program allocations are made by OMB.

It is probable that at least three overlapping ZBB cycles would operate, each with a different focus. The first cycle would operate at the most detailed level within the agency. At this stage, operating managers would formulate zero-based budget requests which, through a successive ranking process, would flow upwards to the various line assistant secretaries. During the second cycle, the agency head would formulate the agency-wide budget and review it with OMB. The third cycle would involve OMB's own zero-base analysis and preparation of priority-ranked budget proposals for consideration by the president. In practice, the process would not be as simple and sequential as suggested above. Several iterations might be required, each cycle would operate within a framework of planning and policy guidelines, much as in the present process.

Remembering the bitter lessons of PPB, it is to be hoped that OMB will not simply issue a general "ZBB Circular," leaving it up to each agency to interpret the instructions as best they can. At the other extreme, OMB should not attempt to design and prescribe for all agencies a single, uniform set of forms and procedures. A more workable, middle-ground scenario might be as follows:

• OMB determines the most useful format for its analysis and presentation to the president of budget options, probably built around interagency program groupings.
• OMB negotiates, individually with each agency, the format for presentation of the agency's budget so that it is compatible with both agency top management needs and the requirements of presidential decision making.
• Each agency head is held responsible for development of an internal ZBB structure and process which most appropriately meets the agency's own management needs, subject to the condition that it is compatible with the joint agreement on format for presentation of the total agency budget to OMB. The internal agency structure and process may well vary between bureaus to take account of differing kinds of programs and varying decisional needs of lower-level management.

A major implementation issue concerns the form in which the budget will be presented to Congress. ZBB could be viewed solely as an aid to preparation of the president's budget, with the zero-base backup excluded from the justification material submitted to Congress. This would certainly conform to the stance adopted by previous presidents in dealing with Congress. It also agrees with the commonly accepted, some would say constitutionally mandated, view that the president must present and defend a single budget total for each appropriation requested from Congress.

It is difficult to imagine any president, even one who believes strongly in the value of ZBB, presenting to Congress a rank-ordered list of decision packages and saying, "this is my recommended budget figure, but if you want to increase or decrease it, here's my priority list of possible increases or decreases." On the other hand, it is difficult to imagine a Congress refraining from demanding such material when it is known to exist, or from asking witnesses to explain those items which fell just above or below the president's cutoff line.

Linkage to Existing Management Systems

The budget, whether zero-based or not, will have to be capable of reconciliation with the Treasury's accounts. Various OMB reporting requirements, if maintained, will also have to be accommodated. However, unlike state and local governments, most of the federal government's management systems are not government-wide but are developed by each agency for its internal use. Since the most probable approach to ZBB in the federal government would be on a selective, agency by agency basis, the question of linkage to existing management systems arises primarily at the agency level. To the extent possible, the design of the ZBB approach in each agency should take account of and build upon management systems already in place, such as planning systems, manpower management systems, specialized information systems unique to each program, performance measurement systems, and cost-accounting and other financial management systems.

ZBB Technology

As this article has attempted to emphasize, ZBB may be variously implemented for different reasons, in different ways, and to serve the needs of different users. The federal government is so diverse that no one ZBB "technology" can suffice. What constitutes a decision unit in one part of one agency will not apply in other parts of the same agency nor at different levels in the same agency, still less in other agencies. The decision variables governing the formulation of decision packages will vary within and among programs and agencies.

It would be possible, however, to develop models, standards, or guidelines to deal with similar classes of programs or activities commonly found throughout the federal government. Several agencies operate hospitals, for example; similar approaches to ZBB would probably be applicable regardless of the agency. Again, at a more detailed level, similar approaches could be used in different agencies to deal with functions such as maintenance, ADP operations, and the like. Within OMB, it would be desirable to develop a consistent framework to analyze programs from different agencies within the same general program area.

Conclusion

ZBB has proven, in diverse settings, that it can make a useful contribution to the art and practice of management. Whether it can be equally helpful if applied extensively in the federal government is an open question. Its success will depend on how it is conceived and presented, and on the political will to make it work. If, as seems probable, ZBB is launched on a broad scale, it is to be hoped that it will be viewed as an *approach* to resource allocation rather than a uniform set of procedures to be applied by rote regardless of the nature of the program, organization level, or management's needs.

The ZBB approach will most likely be applied selectively, its purposes and technology geared to management's unique decisional needs, and building to the extent possible on systems already in place. The federal ZBB structure will probably not be a monolith, a gigantic pyramid with the president at the apex and agency branches, sections, and field offices at the base. Rather, the structure for ZBB will most likely be integrated and unified, if at all, only at the level of OMB for presidential decision-making purposes, and rather loosely coupled to the structures designed by individual agencies for their internal needs.

Tantalizing questions remain. How will responsibility for design and implementation of ZBB be distributed between OMB and the agencies? Who will conduct the necessary development and training? For what purposes will it be used? What parts of the federal budget will be included? Will it be applied to "tax expenditures"? To the entire revenue side of the budget? How will its results be communicated to Congress? What will be the administration's timing? How much will be attempted for the FY 1979 cycle?

Finally, what will be the lasting impact of ZBB? PPB is no longer a formal, government-wide system, but its effects are very much with us. The legacy of PPB has been a demonstrable improvement in the amount and quality of policy, program and budgetary analysis, in the federal government and in state and local governments throughout the nation. Regardless of the ultimale fate of ZBB, the chances are that, after the next few years, budgeting will never be quite the same.

Note

1. The survey was conducted in 1976 by Paul J. Stonich of MAC, Inc. The results presented here are taken from his forthcoming book, *Zero-Base Planning and Budgeting: The State of The Art.*

32

Organizational Decline and Cutback Management

Charles H. Levine
University of Maryland

Government organizations are neither immortal nor unshrinkable.[1] Like growth, organizational decline and death, by erosion or plan, is a form of organizational change; but all the problems of managing organizational change are compounded by a scarcity of slack resources.[2] This feature of declining organizations—the diminution of the cushion of spare resources necessary for coping with uncertainty, risking innovation, and rewarding loyalty and cooperation—presents for government a problem that simultaneously challenges the underlying premises and feasibility of both contemporary management systems and the institutions of pluralist liberal democracy.[3]

Growth and decline are issues of a grand scale usually tackled by only the most brave or foolhardy of macro social theorists. The division of scholarly labor between social theorists and students of management is now so complete that the link between the great questions of political economy and the more earthly problems of managing public organizations is rarely forged. This bifurcation is more understandable when one acknowledges that managers and organization analysts have for decades (at least since the Roosevelt Administration and the wide acceptance

Source: Reprinted with permission from *Public Administration Review* (July–August 1978): 316–325. Copyright © 1978 by the American Society for Public Administration (ASPA), 1120 G Street NW, Suite 500, Washington D.C. 20005. All rights reserved.
An earlier version of this paper was presented at the 1978 Annual Meeting of the American Society for Public Administration, Phoenix, Arizona, April 12, 1978. I wish to thank the following people for providing valuable comments about that draft: Pierre Clavel, Pat Conklin, Richard Cyert, Paul Gallagher, Eugene Lewis, Laurence O'Toole, Nancy Petrovic, Sam Postbrief, Allen Schick, Frank Sherwood, Fred Thayer, Richard Schramm, and Dwight Waldo.

of Keynesian economics) been able to subsume their concern for societal level instability under broad assumptions of abundance and continuous and unlimited economic growth.[4] Indeed, almost all of our public management strategies are predicated on assumptions of the continuing enlargement of public revenues and expenditures. These expansionist assumptions are particularly prevalent in public financial management systems that anticipate budgeting by incremental additions to a secure base.[5] Recent events and gloomy forecasts, however, have called into question the validity and generality of these assumptions, and have created a need to reopen inquiry into the effects of resource scarcity on public organizations and their management systems. These events and forecasts, ranging from taxpayer revolts like California's successful Proposition 13 campaign and financial crises like the near collapse into bankruptcy of New York City's government and the agonizing retrenchment of its bureaucracy, to the foreboding predictions of the "limits of growth" modelers, also relink issues of political economy of the most monumental significance to practices of public management.[6]

We know very little about the decline of public organizations and the management of cutbacks. This may be because even though some federal agencies like the Works Progress Administration, Economic Recovery Administration, Department of Defense, National Aeronautics and Space Administration, the Office of Economic Opportunity, and many state and local agencies have expanded and then contracted,[7] or even died, the public sector as a whole has expanded enormously over the last four decades. In this period of expansion and optimism among proponents of an active government, isolated incidents of zero growth and decline have been considered anomalous; and the difficulties faced by the management of declining agencies coping with retrenchment have been regarded as outside the mainstream of public management concerns. It is a sign of our times—labeled by Kenneth Boulding as the "Era of Slowdown"—that we are now reappraising cases of public organization decline and death as exemplars and forerunners in order to provide strategies for the design and management of *mainstream* public administration in a future dominated by resource scarcity.[8]

The decline and death of government organizations is a symptom, a problem, and a contingency. It is a symptom of resource scarcity at a societal, even global, level that is creating the necessity for governments to terminate some programs, lower the activity level of others, and confront tradeoffs between new demands and old programs rather than to expand whenever a new public problem arises. It is a problem for managers who must maintain organizational capacity by devising new managerial arrangements within prevailing structures that were designed under assumptions of growth. It is a contingency for public employees and clients; employees who must sustain their morale and productivity in the face of increasing control from above and shrinking opportunities for creativity and promotion while clients must find alternative sources for the services governments may no longer be able to provide.

Organizational Decline and Administrative Theory

Growth is a common denominator that links contemporary management theory to its historical antecedents and management practices with public policy choices. William Scott has observed that "... organization growth creates organizational abundance, or surplus, which is used by management to buy off internal consensus from the potentially conflicting interest group segments that compete for resources in organizations."[9] As a common denominator, growth has provided a criterion to gauge the acceptability of government policies and has defined many of the problems to be solved by management action and organizational research. So great is our enthusiasm for growth that even when an organizational decline seems inevitable and irreversible, it is nearly impossible to get elected officials, public managers, citizens, or management theorists to confront cutback and decremental planning situations as anything more than temporary slowdowns. Nevertheless, the reality of zero growth and absolute decline, at least in some sectors, regions, communities, and organizations, means that management and public policy theory must be expanded to incorporate non-growth as an initial condition that applies in some cases. If Scott's assertions about the pervasiveness of a growth ideology in management are correct, our management and policy paradigms will have to be replaced or augmented by new frameworks to help to identify critical questions and strategies for action. Put squarely, without growth, how do we manage public organizations?

We have no ready or comprehensive answers to this question, only hunches and shards of evidence to serve as points of departure. Under conditions and assumptions of decline, the ponderables, puzzles, and paradoxes of organizational management take on new complexities. For example, organizations cannot be cut back by merely reversing the sequence of activity and resource allocation by which their parts were originally assembled. Organizations are organic social wholes with emergent qualities which allow their parts to recombine into intricately interwoven semi-lattices when they are brought together. In his study of NASA's growth and drawdown, Paul Schulman has observed that viable public programs must attain "capture points" of public goal and resource commitments, and these organizational thresholds or "critical masses" are characterized by their indivisibility.[10] Therefore, to attempt to disaggregate and cutback on one element of such an intricate and delicate political and organization arrangement may jeopardize the functioning and equilibrium of an entire organization.

Moreover, retrenchment compounds the choice of management strategies with paradoxes. When slack resources abound, money for the development of management planning, control, information systems, and the conduct of policy analysis is plentiful even though these systems are relatively irrelevant to decision making.[11] Under conditions of abundance, habit, intuition, snap judgments, and other forms of informal analysis will suffice for most decisions because the costs of making mistakes can be easily absorbed without threatening the organization's survival.[12] However, in times of austerity, when these control and analytic tools are needed to help to minimize the risk of making mistakes, the money for their development and implementation is unavailable.

Similarly, without slack resources to produce "win-win" consensus-building solutions and to provide side payments to overcome resistance to change, organizations will have difficulty innovating and maintaining flexibility. Yet, these are precisely the activities needed to maintain capacity while contracting, especially when the overriding imperative is to minimize the perturbations of adjusting to new organizational equilibriums at successively lower levels of funding and activity.[13]

Lack of growth also creates a number of serious personnel problems. For example, the need to reward managers for directing organizational contraction and termination is a problem because without growth there are few promotions and rewards available to motivate and retain successful and loyal managers—particularly when compared to job opportunities for talented managers outside the declining organization.[14] Also, without expansion, public organizations that are constrained by merit and career tenure systems are unable to attract and accommodate new young talent. Without an inflow of younger employees, the average age of employees is forced up, and the organization's skill pool becomes frozen at the very time younger, more flexible, more mobile, less expensive and (some would argue) more creative employees are needed.[15]

Decline forces us to set some of our logic for rationally structuring organizations on end and upside down. For instance, under conditions of growth and abundance, one problem for managers and organizational designers is how to set up *exclusionary* mechanisms to prevent *"free riders"* (employees and clients who share in the consumption of the organization's collective benefits without sharing the burden that produced the benefit) from taking advantage of the enriched common pool of resources. In contrast, under conditions of decline and austerity, the problem for managers and organizational designers is how to set up *inclusionary* mechanisms to prevent organizational participants from avoiding the sharing of the *"public bads"* (increased burdens) that result from the depletion of the common pool of resources.[16] In other words, to maintain order and capacity when undergoing decline, organizations need mechanisms like long-term contracts with clauses that make pensions non-portable if broken at the employee's discretion. These mechanisms need to be carefully designed to penalize and constrain *"free exiters"* and cheap exits at the convenience of the employees while still allowing managers to cut and induce into retirement marginally performing and unneeded employees.

As a final example, inflation erodes steady states so that staying even actually requires extracting more resources from the organization's environment and effectuating greater internal economies. The irony of managing decline in the public sector is particularly compelling under conditions of recession or so called "stagflation." During these periods of economic hardship and uncertainty, pressure is put on the federal government to follow Keynesian dictates and spend more through deficit financing; at the same time, critical public opinion and legal mandates require some individual agencies (and many state and local governments) to balance their budgets, and in some instances to spend less.

These characteristics of declining public organizations are like pieces of a subtle jigsaw puzzle whose parameters can only be guessed at and whose abstruseness deepens with each new attempt to fit its edges together. To overcome our tendency to regard decline in public organizations as anomalous, we need to develop a catalogue of what we already know about declining public organizations. A typology of *causes* of public organizational decline and corresponding sets of *tactics* and *decision rules* available for managing cutbacks will serve as a beginning.

The Causes of Public Organization Decline

Cutting back any kind of organization is difficult, but a good deal of the problem of cutting back public organizations is compounded by their special status as authoritative, non-market extensions of the state.[17] Public organizations are used to deliver services that usually have no direct or easily measurable monetary value or when market arrangements fail to provide the necessary level of revenues to support the desired level or distribution of services. Since budgets depend on appropriations and not sales, the diminution or termination of public organizations and programs, or conversely their maintenance and survival, are political matters usually calling for the application of the most sophisticated attack or survival tactics in the arsenal of the skilled bureaucrat-politician.[18] These strategies are not universally propitious; they are conditioned by the causes for decline and the hoped-for results.

The causes of public organization decline can be categorized into a four-cell typology as shown in Figure 1. The causes are divided along two dimensions: (a) whether they are primarily the result of conditions located either internal or external to the organization, or (b) whether they are principally a product of political or economic/technical conditions.[19] This is admittedly a crude scheme for lumping instances of decline, but it does cover most cases and allows for some abstraction.

	Internal	External
Political	Political Vulnerability	Problem Depletion
Economic/ Technical	Organizational Atrophy	Environmental Entropy

Figure 1

The causes of public organization decline

Of the four types, *problem depletion* is the most familiar. It covers government involvement in short-term crises like natural disasters such as floods and earthquakes, medium length governmental interventions like war mobilization and countercyclical employment programs, and longer-term public programs like polio research and treatment and space exploration—all of which involve development cycles. These cycles are characterized by a political definition of a problem followed by the extensive commitment of resources to attain critical masses and then contractions after the problem has been solved, alleviated, or has evolved into a less troublesome stage or politically popular issue.[20]

Problem depletion is largely a product of forces beyond the control of the affected organization. Three special forms of problem depletion involve demographic shifts, problem redefinition, and policy termination. The impact of demographic shifts has been vividly demonstrated in the closing of schools in neighborhoods where the school age population has shrunk. While the cause for most school closings is usually neighborhood aging—a factor outside the control of the school system—the decision to close a school is largely political. The effect of problem redefinition on public organizations is most easily illustrated by movements to *de*institutionalize the mentally ill. In these cases, the core bureaucracies responsible for treating these populations in institutions has shrunk as the rising per patient cost of hospitalization has combined with pharmaceutical advances in anti-depressants and tranquilizers to cause public attitudes and professional doctrine to shift.[21]

Policy termination has both theoretical import and policy significance. Theoretically, it is the final phase of a public policy intervention cycle and can be defined as " . . . the deliberate conclusion or cessation of specific government functions, programs, policies, or organizations."[22] Its policy relevance is underscored by recent experiments and proposals for sunset legislation which would require some programs to undergo extensive evaluations after a period of usually five years and be reauthorized or be terminated rather than be continued indefinitely.[23]

Environmental entropy occurs when the capacity of the environment to support the public organization at prevailing levels of activity erodes.[24] This type of decline covers the now familiar phenomena of financially troubled cities and regions with declining economic bases. Included in this category are: market and technological shifts like the decline in demand for domestic textiles and steel and its effect on the economies and quality of life in places like New England textile towns and steel cities like Gary, Indiana, Bethlehem, Pennsylvania, and Youngstown, Ohio;[25] transportation changes that have turned major railroad hubs and riverports of earlier decades into stagnating and declining economies; mineral depletion which has crippled mining communities; and intrametropolitan shifts of economic activity from central cities to their suburbs.[26] In these cases, population declines often have paralleled general economic declines which erode tax bases and force cities to cut services. One of the tragic side effects of environmental entropy is that it most severely affects those who cannot move.[27] Caught in the declining city and region are the immobile and dependent: the old, the poor, and the unemployable. For these communities, the forced choice of cutting services to an ever more dependent and needy population is the cruel outcome of decline.[28]

Environmental entropy also has a political dimension. Proposition 13 makes clear, the capacity of a government is as much a function of the willingness of taxpayers to be taxed as it is of the economic base of the taxing region. Since the demand for services and the supply of funds to support them are usually relatively independent in the public sector, taxpayer resistance can produce diminished revenues which force service reductions even though the demand and *need* for services remains high.

The *political vulnerability* of public organizations is an internal property indicating a high level of fragility and precariousness which limits their capacity to resist budget decrements and demands to contract from their environment. Of the factors which contribute to vulnerability, some seem to be more responsible for decline and death than others. Small size, internal conflict, and changes in leadership, for example, seem less telling than the lack of a base of expertise or the absence of a positive self-image and history of excellence. However, an organization's age may be the most accurate predictor of bureaucratic vulnerability. Contrary to biological reasoning, aged organizations are more flexible than young organizations and therefore rarely die or even shrink very much. Herbert Kaufman argues that one of the advantages of organizations over solitary individuals is that they do provide longer institutional memories than a human lifetime, and this means that older organizations ought to have a broader range of adaptive skills, more capacity for learning, more friends and allies, and be more innovative because they have less to fear from making a wrong decision than a younger organization.[29]

Organizational atrophy is a common phenomenon in all organizations but government organizations are particularly vulnerable because they usually lack market generated revenues to signal a malfunction and to pinpoint responsibility. Internal atrophy and declining performance which can lead to resource cutbacks or to a weakening of organizational capacity come from a host of system and management failures almost too numerous to identify. A partial list would include: inconsistent and perverse incentives, differentiation without integration, role confusion, decentralized authority with vague responsibility, too many inappropriate rules, weak oversight, stifled dissent and upward communication, rationalization of performance failure by "blaming the victim," lack of self-evaluating and self-correcting capacity, high turnover, continuous politicking for promotions and not for program resources, continuous reorganization, suspicion of outsiders, and obsolescence caused by routine adherence to past methods and technologies in the face of changing problems. No organization is immune from these problems and no organization is likely to be afflicted by them all at once, but a heavy dose of some of these breakdowns in combination can contribute to an organization's decline and even death.

Identifying and differentiating among these four types of decline situations provides a start toward cataloging and estimating the appropriateness of strategies for managing decline and cutbacks. This activity is useful because when undergoing decline, organizations face three decision tasks: first, management must decide whether it will adopt a strategy to resist decline or smooth it (i.e, reduce the impact of fluctuations in the environment that cause interruptions in the flow of work and poor performance); second, given this choice of maneuvering strategies it will have to decide what tactics are most appropriate;[30] and third, if necessary, it will have to make decisions about how and where cuts will occur. Of course, the cause of a decline will greatly affect these choices.

Strategic Choices

Public organizations behave in response to a mix of motives—some aimed at serving national (or state or local) purposes, some aimed at goals for the *organization as a whole*, and others directed toward the particularistic goals of organizational subunits. Under conditions of growth, requests for more resources by subunits usually can be easily concerted with the goals of the organization as a whole and its larger social purposes. Under decline, however, subunits usually respond to requests to make cuts in terms of their particular long-term survival needs (usually defended in terms of the injury which cutbacks would inflict on a program with lofty purposes or on a dependent clientele) irrespective of impacts on the performance of government or the organization as a whole.

The presence of powerful survival instincts in organizational subunits helps to explain why the political leadership of public organizations can be trying to respond to legislative or executive directives to cut back while at the same time the career and program leadership of subunits will be taking action to resist cuts.[31] It also helps to explain why growth can have the appearance of a rational administrative process complete with a hierarchy of objectives and broad consensus, while decline takes on the *appearance* of what James G. March has called a "garbage can problem"—arational, polycentric, fragmented, and dynamic.[32] Finally, it allows us to understand why the official rhetoric about cutbacks—whether it be to "cut the fat," "tighten our belts," "preserve future options," or "engage in a process of orderly and programmed termination"—is often at wide variance with the unofficial conduct of bureau chiefs who talk of "minimizing cutbacks to mitigate catastrophe," or "making token sacrifices until the heat's off."

Retrenchment politics dictate that organizations will respond to decrements with a mix of espoused and operative strategies that are not necessarily consistent.[33] When there is a wide divergence between the official pronouncements about the necessity for cuts and the actual occurrence of cuts, skepticism, cynicism, distrust, and noncompliance will dominate the retrenchment process and cutback management will be an adversarial process pitting top and middle management against one another. In most cases, however, conflict will not be rancorous, and strategies for dealing with decline will be a mixed bag of tactics intended either to *resist* or to *smooth* decline. The logic here is that no organization accedes to cuts with enthusiasm and will try to find a way to resist cuts; but resistance is risky. In addition to the possibility of being charged with nonfeasance, no responsible manager wants to be faced with the prospect of being unable to control where cuts will take place or confront quantum cuts with unpredictable consequences. Instead, managers will choose a less risky course and attempt to protect organizational capacity and procedures by smoothing decline and its effects on the organization.

An inventory of some of these cutback management tactics is presented in Figure 2. They are arrayed according to the type of decline problem which they can be employed to solve. This collection of tactics by no means exhausts the possible organizational responses to decline situations, nor are all the tactics exclusively directed toward meeting a single contingency. They are categorized in order to show that many familiar coping tactics correspond, even if only roughly, to an underlying logic. In this way a great deal of information about organizational responses to decline can be aggregated without explicating each tactic in great detail.[34]

The tactics intended to remove or alleviate the external political and economic causes of decline are reasonably straightforward means to revitalize eroded economic bases, reduce environmental uncertainty, protect niches, regain flexibility, or lessen dependence. The tactics for handling the internal causes of decline, however, tend to be more subtle means for strengthening organizations and managerial control. For instance, the management of decline *in the face of resistance* can be smoothed by changes in leadership. When hard unpopular decisions have to be made, new managers can be brought in to make the cuts, take the flak, and move on to another organization. By rotating managers into and out of the declining organization, interpersonal loyalties

built up over the years will not interfere with the cutback process. This is especially useful in implementing a higher level decision to terminate an organization where managers will make the necessary cuts knowing that their next assignments will not depend on their support in the organization to be terminated.

The "exploit the exploitable" tactic also calls for further explanation. Anyone familiar with the personnel practices of universities during the 1970's will recognize this tactic. It has been brought about by the glutted market for academic positions which has made many unlucky recent Ph.D's vulnerable and exploitable. This buyers' market has coincided neatly with the need of universities facing steady states and declining enrollments to avoid long-term tenure commitments to expensive faculties. The result is a marked increase in part-time and non-tenure track positions which are renewed on a semester-to-semester basis. So while retrenchment is smoothed and organization flexibility increased, it is attained at considerable cost to the careers and job security of the exploited teachers.

Cutback management is a two-crucible problem: besides selecting tactics for either resisting or smoothing decline, if necessary, management must also select who will be let go and what programs will be curtailed or terminated. Deciding where to make cuts is a test of managerial intelligence and courage because each choice involves tradeoffs and opportunity costs that cannot be erased through the generation of new resources accrued through growth.

As with most issues of public management involving the distribution of costs, the choice of decision rules to allocate cuts usually involves the tradeoff between equity and efficiency.[35] In this case, "equity" is meant to mean the distribution of cuts across the organization with an equal probability of hurting all units and employees irrespective of impacts on the long term capacity of the organization. "Efficiency" is meant to mean the sorting, sifting, and assignment of cuts to those people and units in the organization so that for a given budget decrement, cuts are allocated to minimize the long-term loss in total benefits to the organization as a whole, irrespective of their distribution.

Making cuts on the basis of equity is easier for managers because it is socially acceptable, easier to justify, and involves few decision making costs. "Sharing the pain" is politically expedient because

	Tactics to Resist Decline	*Tactics to Smooth Decline*
External Political	*(Problem Depletion)* 1. Diversify programs, clients and constituents 2. Improve legislative liaison 3. Educate the public about the agency's mission 4. Mobilize dependent clients 5. Become "captured" by a powerful interest group or legislator 6. Threaten to cut vital or popular programs 7. Cut a visible and widespread service a little to demonstrate client dependence	1. Make peace with competing agencies 2. Cut low prestige programs 3. Cut programs to politically weak clients 4. Sell and lend expertise to other agencies 5. Share problems with other agencies
Economic/ Technical	*(Environmental Entropy)* 1. Find a wider and richer revenue base (e.g., metropolitan reorganization) 2. Develop incentives to prevent disinvestment 3. Seek foundation support 4. Lure new public and private sector investment 5. Adopt user charges for services where possible	1. Improve targeting on problems 2. Plan with preservative objectives 3. Cut losses by distinguishing between capital investments and sunk costs 4. Yield concessions to taxpayers and employers to retain them
Internal Political	*(Political Vulnerability)* 1. Issue symbolic responses like forming study commissions and task forces 2. "Circle the wagons," i.e., develop a seige mentality to retain esprit de corps 3. Strengthen expertise	1. Change leadership at each stage in the decline process 2. Reorganize at each stage 3. Cut programs run by weak subunits 4. Shift programs to another agency 5. Get temporary exemptions from personnel and budgetary regulations which limit discretion
Economic/ Technical	*(Organizational Atrophy)* 1. Increase hierarchical control 2. Improve productivity 3. Experiment with less costly service delivery systems 4. Automate 5. Stockpile and ration resources	1. Renegotiate long term contracts to regain flexibility 2. Install rational choice techniques like zero-base budgeting and evaluation research 3. Mortgage the future by deferring maintenance and downscaling personnel quality 4. Ask employees to make voluntary sacrifices like taking early retirements and deferring raises 5. Improve forecasting capacity to anticipate further cuts 6. Reassign surplus facilities to other users 7. Sell surplus property, lease back when needed 8. Exploit the exploitable

Figure 2

Some cutback management tactics

it appeals to common sense ideals of justice. Further, simple equity decision making avoids costs from sorting, selecting, and negotiating cuts.[36] In contrast, efficiency cuts involve costly triage analysis because the distribution of pain and inconvenience requires that the value of people and subunits to the organization have to be weighed in terms of their expected future contributions. In the public sector, of course, things are never quite this clear cut because a host of constraints like career status, veteran's preference, bumping rights, entitlements, and mandated programs limit managers from selecting optimal rules for making cuts. Nevertheless, the values of equity and efficiency are central to allocative decision making and provide useful criteria for judging the appropriateness of cutback rules. By applying these criteria to five of the most commonly used or proposed cutback methods—seniority, hiring freezes, even-percentage-cuts-across-the-board, productivity criteria, and zero base budgeting—we are able to make assessments of their efficacy as managerial tools.

Seniority is the most prevalent and most maligned of the five decision rules. Seniority guarantees have little to do with either equity or efficiency, *per se*. Instead, they are directed at another value of public administration; that is, the need to provide secure career-long employment to neutrally competent civil servants.[37] Because seniority is likely to be spread about the organization unevenly, using seniority criteria for making cuts forces managers to implicitly surrender control over the impact of cuts on services and the capacity of subunits. Furthermore, since seniority usually dictates a "last-in-first-out" retention system, personnel cuts using this decision rule tend to inflict the greatest harm to minorities and women who are recent entrants in most public agencies.

A *hiring freeze* is a convenient short-run strategy to buy time and preserve options. In the short run it hurts no one already employed by the organization because hiring freezes rely on "natural attrition" through resignations, retirements, and death to diminish the size of an organization's work force. In the long run, however, hiring freezes are hardly the most equitable or efficient way to scale down organizational size. First, even though natural and self selection relieves the stress on managers, it also takes control over the decision of whom and where to cut away from management and thereby reduces the possibility of intelligent long range cutback planning. Second, hiring freezes are more likely to harm minorities and women who are more likely to be the next hired rather than the next retired. Third, attrition will likely occur at different rates among an organization's professional and technical specialties. Since resignations will most likely come from those employees with the most opportunities for employment elsewhere, during a long hiring freeze an organization may find itself short on some critically needed skills yet unable to hire people with these skills even though they may be available.

Even-percentage-cuts-across-the-board are expedient because they transfer decision-making costs lower in the organization, but they tend to be insensitive to the needs, production functions, and contributions of different units. The same percentage cut may call for hardly more than some mild belt tightening in some large unspecialized units but when translated into the elimination of one or two positions in a highly specialized, tightly integrated small unit, it may immobilize that unit.

Criticizing *productivity criteria* is more difficult but nevertheless appropriate, especially when the concept is applied to the practice of cutting low producing units and people based on their *marginal product* per increment of revenue. This method is insensitive to differences in clients served, unit capacity, effort, and need. A more appropriate criterion is one that cuts programs, organization units, and employees so that the *marginal utility* for a decrement of resources is equal across units, individuals, and programs thereby providing for *equal sacrifices* based on the *need* for resources. However, this criterion assumes organizations are fully rational actors, an assumption easily dismissed. More likely, cuts will be distributed by a mix of analysis and political bargaining.

Aggregating incompatible needs and preferences is a political problem and this is why *zero base budgeting* gets such high marks as a method for making decisions about resource allocation under conditions of decline. First, ZBB is future directed; instead of relying on an "inviolate-base-plus-increment" calculus, it allows for the analysis of both existing and proposed new activities. Second, ZBB allows for tradeoffs between programs or units below their present funding levels. Third, ZBB allows a ranking of decision packages by political bargaining and negotiation so that attention is concentrated on those packages or activities most likely to be affected by cuts.[38] As a result, ZBB allows both analysis and politics to enter into cutback decision making and therefore can incorporate an expression of the *intensity of need* for resources by participating managers and clients while also accommodating estimates of how cuts will affect the *activity levels* of their units. Nevertheless, ZBB is not without problems. Its analytic component is likely to be expensive—especially so under conditions of austerity—and to be subject to all the limitations and pitfalls of cost-benefit analysis, while its political component is likely to be costly in political terms as units fight with each other and with central management over rankings, tradeoffs, and the assignment of decrements.[39]

These five decision rules illustrate how strategic choices about cutback management can be made with or without expediency, analysis, courage, consideration of the organization's long-term health, or the effect of cuts on the lives of employees and clients. Unfortunately, for some employees and clients, and the public interest, the choice will usually be made by managers to "go along" quietly with across-the-board cuts and exit as soon as possible. The alternative for those who would prefer more responsible and toughminded decision making *to facilitate long run organizational survival* is to develop in managers and employees strong feelings of organizational loyalty and loyalty to clients, to provide disincentives to easy exit, and to encourage participation so that dissenting views on the location of cuts could emerge from the ranks of middle management, lower level employees, and clients.[40]

Ponderables

The world of the future is uncertain, but scarcity and tradeoffs seem inevitable. Boulding has argued, "in a stationary society roughly half the society will be experiencing decline while the other half will be experiencing growth."[41] If we are entering an era of general slowdown, this means that the balance in the distribution between expanding and contracting sectors, regions, and organizations will be tipped toward decline. It means that we will need a governmental capacity for developing tradeoffs between growing and declining organizations and for intervening in regional and sectorial economies to avoid the potentially harmful effects of radical perturbations from unmanaged decline.

So far we have managed to get along without having to make conscious tradeoffs between sectors and regions. We have met declines on a "crisis-to-crisis" basis through emergency legislation and financial aid. This is a strategy that assumes declines are special cases of temporary disequilibrium, bounded in time and space, that are usually confined to a single organization, community, or region. A broad scale long-run *societal level* decline, however,

is a problem of a different magnitude and to resolve it, patchwork solutions will not suffice.

There seem to be two possible directions in which to seek a way out of immobility. First is the authoritarian possibility; what Robert L. Heilbroner has called the rise of "iron governments" with civil liberties diminished and resources allocated throughout society from the central government without appeal.[42] This is a possibility abhorrent to the democratic tradition, but it comprises a possible future—if not for the United States in the near future, at least for some other less affluent nations. So far we have had little experience with cutting back on rights, entitlements, and privileges; but scarcity may dictate "decoupling" dependent and less powerful clients and overcoming resistance through violent autocratic implementation methods.

The other possible future direction involves new images and assumptions about the nature of man, the state and the ecosystem. It involves changes in values away from material consumption, a gradual withdrawal from our fascination with economic growth, and more efficient use of resources—especially raw materials. For this possibility to occur, we will have to have a confrontation with our propensity for wishful thinking that denies that some declines are permanent. Also required is a widespread acceptance of egalitarian norms and of anti-growth and no growth ideologies which are now only nascent, and the development of a political movement to promote their incorporation into policy making.[43] By backing away from our obsession with growth, we will also be able to diminish the "load" placed on central governments and allow for greater decentralization and the devolution of functions.[44] In this way, we may be able to preserve democratic rights and processes while meeting a future of diminished resources.

However, the preferable future might not be the most probable future. This prospect should trouble us deeply.

Notes

1. The intellectual foundations of this essay are too numerous to list. Three essays in particular sparked my thinking: Herbert Kaufman's *The Limits of Organizational Change* (University, Alabama: The University of Alabama Press, 1971) and *Are Government Organizations Immortal?* (Washington, DC: The Brookings

Institution, 1976) and Herbert J. Gans, "Planning for Declining and Poor Cities," *Journal of the American Institute of Planners* (September, 1975), pp. 305–307. The concept of "cutback planning" is introduced in the Gans article. My initial interest in this subject stemmed from my work with a panel of the National Academy of Public Administration on a NASA-sponsored project that produced *Report of the Ad Hoc Panel on Attracting New Staff and Retaining Capability During a Period of Declining Manpower Ceilings.*

2. For an explication of the concept of "organizational slack" see Richard M. Cyert and James G. March, *A Behavioral Theory of the Firm* (Englewood Cliffs, N.J.: Prentice-Hall, 1963), pp. 36–38. They argue that because of market imperfections between payments and demands "there is ordinarily a disparity between the resources available to the organization and the payments required to maintain the coalition. This difference between total resources and total necessary payments is what we have called *organizational slack.* Slack consists in payments to members of the coalition in excess of what is required to maintain the organization. . . . Many forms of slack typically exist: stockholders are paid dividends in excess of those required to keep stockholders (or banks) within the organization; prices are set lower than necessary to maintain adequate income from buyers; wages in excess of those required to maintain labor are paid; executives are provided with services and personal luxuries in excess of those required to keep them; subunits are permitted to grow without real concern for the relation between additional payments and additional revenue; public services are provided in excess of those required. . . . Slack operates to stabilize the system in two ways: (1) by absorbing excess resources, it retards upward adjustment of aspirations during relatively good times; (2) by providing a pool of emergency resources, it permits aspirations to be maintained (and achieved) during relatively bad times."

3. See William G. Scott, "The Management of Decline," *The Conference Board RECORD* (June, 1976), pp. 56–59 and "Organization Theory: A Reassessment," *Academy of Management Journal* (June, 1974) pp. 242–253; also Rufus E. Miles, Jr., *Awakening from the American Dream: The Social and Political Limits to Growth* (New York: Universal Books, 1976).

4. See Daniel M. Fox, *The Discovery of Abundance: Simon N. Patten and the Transformation of Social Theory* (Ithaca, N.Y.: Cornell University Press, 1967).

5. See Andrew Glassberg's contribution to this symposium, "Organizational Responses to Municipal Budget Decreases," and Edward H. Potthoff, Jr., "Preplanning for Budget Reductions," *Public Management* (March, 1975), pp. 13–14.

6. See Donella H. Meadows, Dennis L. Meadows, Jorgen Randers, and William W. Behrens III, *The Limits to Growth* (New York: Universe Books, 1972); also Robert L. Heilbroner, *An Inquiry into the Human Prospect* (New York: W.W. Norton, 1975) and *Business Civilization in Decline* (New York: W. W. Norton, 1976).

7. See Advisory Commission on Intergovernmental Relations, *City Financial Emergencies: The Intergovernmental Dimension* (Washington, D.C.: U.S. Government Printing Office, 1973).

8. Kenneth E. Boulding. "The Management of Decline," *Change* (June, 1975), pp. 8–9 and 64. For extensive analyses of cutback management in the same field that Boulding addresses, university administration, see: Frank M. Bowen and Lyman A. Glenny, *State Budgeting for Higher Education: State Fiscal Stringency and Public Higher Education* (Berkeley, Calif.: Center for Research and Development in Higher Education, 1976); Adam Yarmolinsky, "Institutional Paralysis," *Special Report on American Higher Education: Toward an Uncertain Future* 2 Vol, *Daedalus* 104 (Winter, 1975), pp. 61–67; Frederick E. Balderston, *Varieties of Financial Crisis*, (Berkeley, Calif.: Ford Foundation, 1972); The Carnegie Foundation for the Advancement of Teaching, *More Than Survival* (San Francisco: Jossey-Bass, 1975); Earl F. Cheit, *The New Depression in Higher Education* (New York: McGraw-Hill, 1975) and *The New Depression in Higher Education—Two Years Later* (Berkeley, Calif.: The Carnegie Commission on Higher Education, 1973): Lyman A. Glenny, "The Illusions of Steady States," *Change* 6 (December/January 1974–75), pp. 24–28; and John D. Millett, "What is Economic Health?" *Change* 8 (September 1976), p. 27.

9. Scott, "Organizational Theory: A Reassessment," p. 245.

10. Paul R. Schulman, "Nonincremental Policy Making: Notes Toward an Alternative Paradigm," *American Political Science Review* (December, 1975), pp. 1354–1370.

11. See Naomi Caiden and Aaron Wildavsky, *Planning Budgeting in Poor Countries* (New York: John Wiley & Sons, 1974).

12. See James W. Vaupel, "Muddling Through Analytically," in Willis D. Hawley and David Rogers (eds.) *Improving Urban Management* (Newbury Park, Calif.: Sage Publications, 1976), pp. 124–146.

13. See Richard M. Cyert's contribution to this symposium, "The Management of Universities of Constant or Decreasing Size."

14. See National Academy of Public Administration *Report* and Glassberg, "Organizational Response to Municipal Budget Decreases."

15. See NAPA *Report* and *Cancelled Careers: The Impact of Reduction-In-Force Policies on Middle-Aged Federal*

Employees, A Report to the Special Committee on Aging, United States Senate (Washington, D.C.: U.S. Government Printing Office, 1972).

16. See Albert O. Hirschman, *Exit, Voice and Loyalty: Responses to Decline in Firms, Organizations and States* (Cambridge, Mass.: Harvard University Press, 1970); also Mancur Olson, *The Logic of Collective Action* (Cambridge, Mass.: Harvard University Press, 1965).

17. The distinctive features of public organizations are discussed at greater length in Hal G. Rainey, Robert W. Backoff, and Charles H. Levine, "Comparing Public and Private Organization," *Public Administration Review* (March/April, 1976), pp. 223–244.

18. See Robert Behn's contribution to this symposium, "Closing a Government Facility," Barry Mitnick's "Deregulation as a Process of Organizational Reduction," and Herbert A. Simon, Donald W. Smithburg, and Victor A. Thompson, *Public Administration* (New York: Knopf, 1950) for discussions of the survival tactics of threatened bureaucrats.

19. This scheme is similar to those presented in Daniel Katz and Robert L. Kahn, *The Social Psychology of Organizations* (John Wiley & Sons, 1966), p. 166, and Gary L. Wamsley and Mayer N. Zald. *The Political Economy of Public Organizations: A Critique and Approach to the Study of Public Administration* (Lexington, Mass.: D.C. Heath, 1973), p. 20.

20. See Schulman, "Nonincremental Policy Making," and Charles O. Jones, "Speculative Augmentation in Federal Air Pollution Policy-Making," *Journal of Politics* (May, 1974), pp. 438–464.

21. See Robert Behn, "Closing the Massachusetts Public Training Schools," *Policy Sciences* (June, 1976), pp.151–172; Valarie J. Bradley, "Policy Termination in Mental Health: The Hidden Agenda," *Policy Sciences* (June, 1976), pp. 215–224; and David J. Rothman, "Prisons, Asylums and Other Decaying Institutions," *The Public Interest* (Winter, 1972), pp. 3–17. A similar phenomena is occuring in some of the fields of regulation policy where deregulation is being made more politically feasible by a combination of technical and economic changes. See Mitnick, "Deregulation as a Process of Organizational Reduction."

22. Peter deLeon, "Public Policy Termination: An End and a Beginning," an essay at the request of the Congressional Research Service as background for the Sunset Act of 1977.

23. There are many variations on the theme of Sunset. Gary Brewer's contribution to this symposium, "Termination: Hard Choices-Harder Questions" identifies a number of problems central to most sunset proposals.

24. For two treatments of this phenomena in the literature of organization theory see Barry M. Staw and Eugene Szwajkowski, "The Scarcity-Munificence Component of Organizational Environments and the Commission

of Illegal Acts," *Administrative Science Quarterly* (September, 1975), pp. 345–354, and Barry Bozeman and E. Allen Slusher, "The Future of Public Organizations Under Assumptions of Environmental Stress," paper presented at the Annual Meeting of the American Society for Public Administration, Phoenix, Arizona, April 9–12, 1978.

25. See Thomas Muller, *Growing and Declining Urban Areas: A Fiscal Comparison* (Washington, D.C.: Urban Institute, 1975).

26. See Richard P. Nathan and Charles Adams, "Understanding Central City Hardship," *Political Science Quarterly* (Spring, 1976), pp. 47–62; Terry Nichols Clark, Irene Sharp Rubin, Lynne C. Pettler, and Erwin Zimmerman, "How Many New Yorks? The New York Fiscal Crisis in Comparative Perspective." (Report No. 72 of Comparative Study of Community Decision-Making, University of Chicago, April, 1976); and David T. Stanley, "The Most Troubled Cities," a discussion draft prepared for a meeting of the National Urban Policy Roundtable, Academy for Contemporary Problems, Summer, 1976.

27. See Richard Child Hill, "Fiscal Collapse and Political Struggle in Decaying Central Cities in the United States," in William K. Tabb and Larry Sawers (eds.) *Marxism and The Metropolis* (New York: Oxford University Press, 1978); and H. Paul Friesema, "Black Control of Central Cities: The Hollow Prize," *Journal of the American Institute of Planners* (March, 1969), pp. 75–79.

28. See David T. Stanley, "The Most Troubled Cities" and "The Survival of Troubled Cities," a paper prepared for delivery at the 1977 Annual Meeting of the American Political Science Association, The Washington Hilton Hotel, Washington, D.C., September 1–4, 1977; and Martin Shefter, "New York City's Fiscal Crisis: The Politics of Inflation and Retrenchment," *The Public Interest* (Summer, 1977), pp. 98–127.

29. See Kaufman, *Are Government Organizations Immortal?* and "The Natural History of Human Organizations," *Administration and Society* (August, 1975), pp. 131–148; I have been working on this question for some time in collaboration with Ross Clayton. Our partially completed manuscript is entitled, "Organizational Aging: Progression or Degeneration." See also Edith Tilton Penrose, "Biological Analogies in the Theory of the Firm," *American Economic Review* (December, 1952), pp. 804–819 and Mason Haire, "Biological Models and Empirical Histories of the Growth of Organizations" in Mason Haire (ed.) *Modern Organization Theory* (New York: John Wiley & Sons, 1959), pp. 272–306.

30. For a fuller explanation of "smoothing" or "leveling," see James D. Thompson, *Organizations in Action* (New York: McGraw-Hill, 1967), pp. 19–24.

31. For recent analyses of related phenomena see Joel D. Aberbach and Bert A. Rockman, "Clashing Beliefs Within the Executive Branch: The Nixon Administration Bureaucracy," *American Political Science Review* (June, 1976), pp. 456–468 and Hugh Heclo, *A Government of Strangers: Executive Politics in Washington* (Washington, D.C. The Brookings Institution, 1977).

32. See James G. March and Johan P. Olsen, *Ambiguity and Choice in Organizations* (Bergen, Norway: Universitetsforlaget, 1976); and Michael D. Cohen, James G. March, and Johan P. Olsen, "A Garbage Can Model of Organizational Choice," *Administrative Science Quarterly* (March, 1972), pp. 1–25.

33. See Charles Perrow, *Organizational Analysis: A Sociological View* (Belmont, Calif.: Wadsworth Publishing Company, 1970) and Chris Argyris and Donald A. Schon, *Theory in Practice: Increasing Professional Effectiveness* (San Francisco, Calif.: Jossey-Bass, 1974) for discussions of the distinction between espoused and operative (i.e., "theory-in-use") strategies.

34. For extensive treatments of the tactics of bureaucrats, some of which are listed here, see Frances E. Rourke, *Bureaucracy, Politics, and Public Policy* (second edition, Boston: Little, Brown and Company, 1976); Aaron Wildavsky, *The Politics of the Budgetary Process* (second edition, Boston: Little, Brown and Company, 1974); Eugene Lewis, *American Politics in a Bureaucratic Age* (Cambridge, Mass.: Winthrop Publishers, 1977); and Simon, Smithburg and Thompson, *Public Administration.*

35. See Arthur M. Oken, *Equity and Efficiency: The Big Tradeoff* (Washington, D.C.: The Brookings Institution, 1975).

36. For a discussion of the costs of interactive decision making see Charles R. Adrian and Charles Press, "Decision Costs in Coalition Formation," *American Political Science Review* (June, 1968), pp. 556–563.

37. See Herbert Kaufman, "Emerging Conflicts in the Doctrine of Public Administration," *American Political Science Review* (December, 1956), pp. 1057–1073 and Frederick C. Mosher, *Democracy and the Public Service* (New York: Oxford University Press, 1968). Seniority criteria also have roots in the widespread belief that organizations ought to recognize people who invest heavily in them by protecting long time employees when layoffs become necessary.

38. See Peter A. Pyhrr, "The Zero-Base Approach to Government Budgeting," *Public Administrative Review* (January/February, 1977), pp. 1–8; Graeme M. Taylor, "Introduction to Zero-Base Budgeting," *The Bureaucrat* (Spring, 1977), pp. 33–55.

39. See Brewer, "Termination: Hard Choices—Harder Questions"; Allen Schick, "Zero-Base Budgeting and Sunset: Redundancy or Symbiosis?" *The Bureaucrat* (Spring, 1977), pp. 12–32 and "The Road From ZBB" *Public Administration Review* (March/April, 1978), pp. 177–180; and Aaron Wildavsky, "The Political Economy of Efficiency," *Public Administration Review* (December, 1966), pp. 292–310.

40. See Hirschman, *Exit, Voice and Loyalty,* especially Ch. 7, "A Theory of Loyalty," pp. 76–105; Despite the attractiveness of "responsible and toughminded decision making" the constraints on managerial discretion in contraction decisions should not be underestimated. At the local level, for example, managers often have little influence on what federally funded programs will be cut back or terminated. They are often informed after funding cuts have been made in Washington and they are expected to make appropriate adjustments in their local work forces. These downward adjustments often are also outside of a manager's control because in many cities with merit systems, veteran's preference, and strong unions, elaborate rules dictate who will be dismissed and the timing of dismissals.

41. Boulding, "The Management of Decline," p. 8.

42. See Heilbroner, *An Inquiry into the Human Prospect;* also Michael Harrington, *The Twilight of Capitalism* (New York: Simon & Schuster, 1976).

43. For a discussion of anti-growth politics see Harvey Molotch, "The City as a Growth Machine," *American Journal of Sociology* (September, 1976), pp. 309–332.

44. Richard Rose has made a penetrating argument about the potential of governments to become "overloaded" in "Comment: What Can Ungovernability Mean?" *Futures* (April 1977), pp. 92–94. For a more detailed presentation, see his "On the Priorities of Government: A Developmental Analysis of Public Policies," *European Journal of Political Research* (September 1976), pp. 247–290. This theme is also developed by Rose in collaboration with B. Guy Peters in *Can Governments Go Bankrupt?* (New York: Basic Books, forthcoming 1978).

33

Standards and Issues in Governmental Accounting and Financial Reporting

James L. Chan
The National Council on Governmental Accounting

It is increasingly desirable and even necessary for practitioners and academicians in public budgeting and financial management to understand the contents of government accounting and financial reporting standards, and to evaluate related institutional issues. Both in theory and practice, these fields are highly interdependent, so much so that problems in one cannot be successfully solved without the assistance of the others. However, the development of specialties and their nomenclatures have tended to inhibit communications across disciplinary and professional boundaries. When budgeting and financial management personnel are familiar with the potentials and limitation of governmental accounting, they will be able to effectively use accounting information. In addition, allegations of deficiencies in accounting and financial reporting standards and practices have been linked with a number of well-publicized local governmental financial crises. Some critics have attempted to generalize these instances into a rather pessimistic picture of the current standards and practice. Since accounting and financial reporting are a responsibility and an integral part of financial management, financial managers need the conceptual tools to oversee, evaluate and assist the accounting and financial reporting function.

The purpose of this article is to discuss some important conceptual and institutional issues associated with current accounting and financial reporting

Source: *Public Budgeting & Finance* (Spring 1981): 55–65. Reprinted by permission.
The views expressed in this article are those of the author and should not be ascribed to the members and others on staff of the NCGA, or its institutional and financial sponsors.

standards for state and local government.[1] Special attention is paid to the interactions between these issues and public budgeting and financial management.

Conceptual Issues in Governmental Accounting and Financial Reporting

The Scope of the Accounting Function

Since accounting is fundamentally a service function, its problems generally result from users' demands or accountants' own increasing competence and desire to expand the scope of their services. About 30 years ago, accounting was defined to be:

the art of recording, classifying, measuring and communicating in a significant manner and in terms of money, transactions and events which are, in part at least, of a financial character, and interpreting the results thereof.[2]

This definition probably is still descriptive of most accounting practices today. But it does not indicate what is meant by the "significant manner" in which financial transactions and events should be measured and communicated. One interpretation enjoying much currency, particularly in the academic community, is that accounting information should facilitate economic decision making. One author has gone so far as to state:

Accounting is a measurement and communication system to provide economic and social information about an identifiable entity to permit users to make informed judgments and decisions *leading to an optimum allocation of resources and the accomplishment of the organization's objectives* (emphasis added).[3]

This normative view of accounting challenges the accounting profession to consider several important problems: (1) the nature of information it provides; (2) to whom the information is provided; and (3) the purposes for which the information is to be used.

Accounting information traditionally is financial information extracted from *past* financial transactions and, to a lesser extent, economic events. This view regards historical cost as at best an approximation of economic value, but justifies it on grounds of objectivity and verifiability. Even though general price level and specific price increases affect both the private and public sectors, governmental accounting standards have not yet systematically dealt with the impact of inflation. The disclosure of future-oriented financial information has also not been mandated or standardized by current reporting standards.

With respect to nonfinancial information, there has been a lengthy debate within the accounting profession and between accountants and non-accountants.[4] Some contend that accountants lack competence in measuring and evaluating nonfinancial performance. Others feel that this could be overcome by changes in educational requirements. This issue affects not only educational policies of the accounting profession, but also the distribution of organizational resources and power within governments. Accountants are competing with other information specialists (e.g., budget analysts, public policy analysts and operations researchers) for decision makers' attention, and therefore come under scrutiny for what they do, or ought to do.

The issue of scope of the accounting function makes it difficult to say exactly what accounting is or should be. For the sake of discussion, it is assumed that there is an identifiable, but evolving, accounting discipline and profession. We may then examine the following issues:

- Generally accepted accounting principles.
- General purpose external financial reporting.
- The appropriate reporting entity.
- The relationship between budgeting and accounting.
- The fairness of presentation of financial position and results of operations.

Generally Accepted Accounting Principles

Generally Accepted Accounting Principles (GAAP) should mean that these rules have won the endorsement of most of those who set them or are affected by them. In the public sector the affected parties would include the preparers of financial reports (government officials), auditors attesting to the fairness of the presentation in accordance with applicable standards, and "users." Acceptance of accounting principles has been deemed necessary because the costs of resolving conflicts and enforcement could be substantial. Because of the diversity of the political and economic interests of those affected by accounting standards, agreement has been difficult to obtain. In addition, the private costs and benefits of participation are such that not all the affected parties are involved to the same extent in the standard-setting process.

While general acceptance is desirable, it has not been universally achieved. It takes a long time for the "survival of the fittest" test to decide which accounting policy is the most accepted. This "social Darwinism" approach has been largely abandoned in favor of creating an "authoritative" body and following "due process." Due process typically requires exposure and public hearings on proposed standards, and inputs from broad-based advisory councils. Formal voting procedures are also adopted to decide on accepted accounting standards.[5]

Professional associations such as the Municipal Finance Officers Association (MFOA) and the American Institute of Certified Public Accountants (AICPA) have assumed leadership by sponsoring standard-setting bodies. The National Council on Governmental Accounting has been sponsored and to a large extent supported by the MFOA. The AICPA's Accounting Principles Board subsequently evolved into the Financial Accounting Standards Board, the standard-setting body for the private sector. These accounting standard-setting bodies derive their authoritativeness from one or more of the following sources: (1) the acceptance, or at least acquiescence, of those subject to their rules; (2) the delegation of authority by government agencies possessing statutory power to set accounting standards with respect to certain entities; (3) the recognition by the independent auditing profession; and (4) the endorsement of the capital market and financial intermediaries such as rating agencies.[6]

"Governmental Accounting and Financial Reporting Principles" enunciated by *Statement 1* of the National Council on Governmental Accounting are currently regarded as Generally Accepted Accounting Principles (GAAP) applicable to state and local government.[7] These principles provide for a fund structure of accounts, budgetary comparisons, fair presentation of financial position and results of operations, and a hierarchy of aggregation levels of disclosure to meet perceived user needs. The disclosures required by *Statement 1* in a comprehensive annual financial report are intended primarily to monitor and enforce public officials' management responsibilities for the resources entrusted to them, and to provide feedback information so that the actual financial performance can be compared with budgets for performance evaluation and for improving subsequent budgetary estimates. However, it is necessary to point out that the term "GAAP" has been used as a basis for recommending the adoption of certain business accounting practices by government, notably consolidated financial statements, depreciation of fixed assets and disclosure of accrued liabilities.[8] Significantly, GAAP has been used by the City of New York to determine the extent of its budget deficit.[9]

In summary, GAAP are developed by designated authoritative policy-making bodies, which follow some form of due process to encourage general acceptance before and after adoption. GAAP are not infallible and need continuing improvements. It is therefore appropriate to examine next some of the key conceptual issues.

General Purpose External Financial Reporting

In the private sector, generally accepted accounting principles govern only "general purpose external financial reporting." The basic rationale is that the managers of individual enterprises have the prerogative of organizing their own management information systems. Also, government regulatory agencies and others having the ability to enforce their information demands can compel firms to prepare "special reports." The role of an accounting standard-setting body, the argument goes, is to assist those members of the society who lack the ability and resources to obtain information needed for their decision making.[10] This concern in business financial reporting has generally been centered on investors and creditors. Current business financial accounting standards are predicated on the theory that the firm is an instrumentality of the owner-investors to earn returns on their investments, and managers are their agents. This view has led to a primary concern for determining the periodic residual income (the "bottom-line") as a predicator of dividend distributions to stockholders. Given the large number of investors and their largely common interest in earning returns on their investments, it appears justifiable and economical to produce general purpose financial reports for this class of users.

As noted earlier, there have been several proposals for the adoption of an investor-oriented financial reporting model in the government sector, particularly for municipalities. Certainly, when state and local governments borrow from the capital market, investor protection is a legitimate concern. Laws and regulations are written, disclosure guidelines are drawn up, and contractual assurances are made for the protection of investors. Their information needs are not being ignored. The existence of debt service funds is an indication of the priority accorded to this class of users of financial information.

However, the automatic application of the investor-oriented reporting model to state and local government is unwarranted on several grounds. There is little evidence that the information needs of investors are shared by other actual or potential users of governmental financial information. Furthermore, the classical theory of the firm is of questionable validity in the private sector.[11] It is even more inappropriate as a normative or descriptive theory of state and local governments in the United States. Besides investors, many other interest groups exchange benefits with state and local governments, including:

Interest Group	*Contribution*	*Inducement*
Voters	Legitimacy of government	Public services to selves and general welfare
Taxpayers	Tax dollars	Same as above
Governing and oversight bodies	Authority, policy guidance and monitoring of performance	Power and discharge of accountability to the electorate
Intergovernmental grantors	Financial resources and policies	Services to target populations, control
Employees	Labor services	Compensation and non-financial benefits
Vendors	Goods and services	Payments

These groups also have incentives to use financial information to assess the balance of the inducements offered and contribution required by government.[12] They are therefore likely to be users of information produced or produceable by government.

Each of the above classes of users is not necessarily homogeneous. If each class of users has similar information needs, a case could be made for general purpose reports for each class of homogeneous user group. At this time, however, there is a lack of empirical evidence or a normative theory that would support the validity of a set of general purpose financial reports for all user groups.

Reporting to discharge public accountability to the parties at interest with government is important. At the same time, the information needs of policy makers, budgeting personnel and financial managers responsible for the day-to-day operations of government should not be overlooked. Individuals in these positions need timely, accurate information to carry out their specific managerial responsibilities. Unless a governmental unit's accounting system carries out this management information function competently, the external feedback process may be too slow and too weak to detect and correct mismanagement. A balance has to be struck among the information demands of management and other user groups.

Appropriate Accounting and Reporting Entities

A major controversy in the government financial reporting literature is the degree of aggregation of funds. Funds or fund types are used as accounting and reporting entities in the public sector because they facilitate budgetary allocations, financial management and control. Recently it has been suggested that investors and the general public should be able to know the financial conditions and operations of the government as a whole, by means of a set of consolidated financial statements.[13] Such statements would overcome, or at least reduce, the information overload resulting from voluminous reporting by fund or fund type. So far the proponents of this approach have relied on the argument that even the largest corporations can, according to GAAP for the business sector, "fairly present" their financial picture in a set of consolidated financial statements. This argument fails to recognize that the FASB and its predecessors have set GAAP in the context of the business sector. The applicability of business GAAP to the government is not a foregone conclusion.[14]

There is no evidence to support the argument for a reporting entity concept generally appropriate for all user groups. To taxpayers, the relevant government entities are all those which have taxing authority over them. To creditors, they are only those whose resources (current and potential) are available to pay specific debts. To voters, they are those jurisdictions whose elected officials are elected by them. All of these governmental entities need not be identical. Consequently, the search for *the* relevant reporting entity is likely to be unproductive, be it a fund, fund group, or whole government. A more sensible approach is to identify a homogeneous user group's scope of interest, as illustrated above.

Proponents of detailed reporting fear that consolidated statements would weaken the monitoring of managerial stewardship. On the other hand, it is also recognized that excessive detail is dysfunctional. Consequently, the NCGA has taken the middle-of-the-road approach. That is, detailed fund-by-fund disclosure is made available in a comprehensive annual financial report. Funds of relatively homogeneous character are aggregated in fund types, and accounts into account groups, and presented as "general purpose financial reports" that are liftable from the more voluminous Comprehensive Annual Financial Report (CAFR).

Relationship Between Accounting and Budgeting

Accounting in the minimal sense of being a score-keeping function derives its utility as the feedback of performance data to facilitate the planning and control functions. A government budget is a resource allocation document, and a planning and control tool. A significant feature of government accounting is the formal incorporation of the legally adopted budget into the government's accounting system. Indeed, an objective of government accounting systems is to facilitate budgetary control and comparisons. This is achieved by using common terminology and a consistent account classification. Estimated revenues and expenditures are recorded in the accounts at the beginning of the fiscal year and periodically compared with actual amounts during the year. This interdependency presents opportunities for cooperation, and also occasions for conflicts between accounting and budgeting.

The common emphasis on short-term financial resources in annual/biennial government budgets is carried over to the accounting for government funds (i.e., the emphasis on expenditures rather than expenses). Clearly, short-term financial resources (including cash) are of critical importance in day-to-day financial operations. But many government financial transactions and events also have major cash consequences beyond the current fiscal year. Indeed, sometimes trade-offs are made to conserve current cash outflows at the expense of future cash outflows, e.g., granting pension benefits in lieu of current salary increases. A dilemma is faced by accounting. On the one hand, the accounting system seeks to be compatible with the budgetary system. On the other hand, accounting standards may call for disclosure of longer-term financial consequences not apparent in a budget prepared on a cash flow basis. Under legal or popular mandates to balance the budget and to limit government spending, government officials are under pressure to employ available devices to achieve a surplus or minimize the deficit. Depending on the definitions of revenues and expenditures/expenses used, the size of the deficit can vary. The issues involve the measurement and disclosure of a government's financial operations and position.

Fair Financial Presentation

Fair presentation is a basic objective of financial reporting by the government. Generally accepted accounting principles provide the operational criteria for judging the extent of fairness. To see what is meant by fair presentation, it is useful to have an overview of the accounting cycle.

The accounting process begins with an analysis of the financial effects of the transactions or other economic events that have already occurred. This historical perspective is regarded by some people as almost an intrinsic characteristic of financial reporting to external parties. However, one should not presume that historical cost information is necessarily useful to decision making in a dynamic environment. The financial position of an entity at a particular time is represented by the costs of the resources acquired and available for future use, and the claims against those resources, as expressed by the accounting equation, assets = liabilities + equities.

The result of financial operations is measured by matching the outflows of resources with the inflows of resources. When the emphasis is on the control of periodic spending, as in the case of government funds, the measurement focus is on expenditures (i.e., the decreases in short-term financial resources), and revenues are recognized on a modified accrual basis (when the financial resources are measurable and available to finance the expenditures in the fiscal period). On the other hand, if the objective is to determine the costs of services, as in the case of enterprise funds, the proper matching of expenses and revenues is essential. Expenses are the costs of all the economic resources utilized in providing the goods and services, and would therefore include depreciation on the fixed assets used. Revenue in this context is the sales proceeds from having provided the goods or rendered the services.

Accounting for the inflows and outflows of current financial resources is important for short-term financial management. The concept of expenditure is designed to meet such needs. However, when some of the costs of services received in the current period are deferred for payments in the future and are not funded with current resources, current expenditures alone do not measure the total costs and do not adequately predict future cash outflows. Unfunded pension and other liabilities are significant because they will require future cash outflows and consequently burden some segments of society. Also, they may be symptoms of deterioration of the fiscal strength of a government. That has led to the underfunding of liabilities. The full disclosure of short-term and long-term liabilities, and the use of the broader concept of expense in addition to expenditure, would serve as integral parts of an early warning system about the fiscal health of government. Early warning is needed to stimulate corrective actions and to force long-term budgeting.

A recurring controversy in governmental accounting is the lack of requirements for computing the depreciation expense of fixed assets financed by governmental funds (as contrasted with proprietary funds). Depreciation, in the accounting sense, is the allocation of the original acquisition costs of fixed assets to each period of their useful lives by means of formulas that are intended to approximate the decline of the service potential of the assets. Such cost allocations are arbitrary, but may still serve some useful purposes.[15] For example, it is financially beneficial for a local government to be reimbursed for the "expired" service potentials of the fixed assets used in mandated or assisted programs. The arbitrariness of depreciation computation is due to the patterns of decline of usefulness assumed in the several acceptable depreciation methods.[16] Perhaps the utility of measuring fixed assets (in monetary and nonmonetary terms) lies in warning public officials and others about the unfavorable consequences of fixed asset deterioration. Unless capital programs are undertaken to maintain or enhance the service capabilities of fixed assets, the original cost figures in the general fixed asset account group are meaningless. Rather, the cash flow requirements of fixed asset acquisition, replacement, repair and maintenance are more likely to be useful than depreciation expense figures unless these figures serve some identifiable purposes such as cost reimbursement.

Institutional Issues in Government Accounting

The standards in *Statement 1* of the National Council on Governmental Accounting are regarded as generally accepted accounting principles for state and local governments. However, general acceptance requires persuasive standards as well as education, encouragement and enforcement. An impediment to general acceptance is the role of other sources of standards. These include requirements or recommendations made by legislatures and oversight bodies, the auditing profession, grantors and other standard-setting bodies.

Statutory provisions on accounting and financial reporting carry the force of law, and compliance is mandatory. To the extent they are inconsistent with GAAP, financial officers are put in an uncomfortable position of choosing allegiance. The NCGA *Statement 1* regards both GAAP reporting and legal compliance reporting as "essential" and recommends the preparation of basic financial statements in conformance with GAAP, and, if necessary, additional schedules and explanations to satisfy legal compliance requirements in the comprehensive annual financial report. This state of affairs reflects the reluctance of many legislative and oversight bodies to delegate their legal authority to prescribe accounting standards, and the relatively slow progress made by the accounting profession in securing legislative endorsement for nationwide uniform standards. Legislative, administrative and judicial endorsements would help accounting standards set by professional bodies gain enforceability.

In 1974 the American Institute of CPAs, in response to its members' need for authoritative guidance in auditing state and local governments, issued an audit guide, which was recently made consistent with NCGA *Statement 1*. The AICPA is regarded as a potent enforcer of accounting standards. Indeed, the governing council of the AICPA designates the body whose standards are Generally Accepted Accounting Principles under Rule 203 of the AICPA Code of Professional Ethics.[17] Since CPAs are called upon to enforce accounting standards, the auditing profession has a stake in ensuring the enforceability of those standards. It therefore participates in the current standard-setting process and in determining the future of the process.

Virtually all state and local government units receive federal financial assistance and are therefore subject to the federal government's accounting, financial reporting and audit requirements. The federal government's grant audit requirements call on grantees to prepare financial statements in conformance with GAAP. However, there remains the need to make grant disclosure requirements compatible with GAAP.

The Financial Accounting Standards Board has recently concerned itself with non-business accounting and financial reporting. The non-business sector is defined broadly to include state and local governments, but not the federal government, in deference to the statutory authority of the Comptroller General of the U.S.

It has recently deferred a final decision on whether the objectives of financial reporting by non-business organizations should apply to state and local governments, pending the resolution of the appropriate structure for setting financial accounting and reporting standards for those governments.[18]

The development of accounting standards in the United States has proceeded through the leadership of professional organizations of specialists in codifying preferred practices. As the tasks have become more burdensome and controversial, alternatives to volunteer part-time operations have been sought. The 21-member National Council on Governmental Accounting has had some notable achievements, but it also has had its share of difficulties. With the impetus provided by proposals to create a federal institute to set accounting standards for state and local governments, interested parties have been searching for a non-federal solution to the institutional problem. A wide range of alternative institutional arrangements has been explored. These range from having the FASB set standards for all entities in the U.S. to the creation of an independent government accounting standards board (GASB) coexisting with the FASB structure.

Each of the proposals has advantages and disadvantages depending on the interested parties' institutional perspectives. The deliberations progressed to the point where the Government Accounting Standards Board Organization Committee was formed in April 1980 to prepare a report for public comment. The report will be released for public comment in early 1981, followed by a public hearing. Regardless of the Committee's recommendations and subsequent decisions, a number of institutional issues will persist:

- An accounting standard-setting framework consistent with the prevailing relations among federal, state and local governments.
- The need for cooperation among the various interested parties.
- The role of the FASB, if any, in setting standards for the public sector.
- Cooperation between the financial specialists (e.g., accountants, finance officers and auditors) and the generalists (the political leadership and top policy makers).
- The exchange of expertise and perspectives among the information professions, such as accounting, budgeting, and financial management.
- The creation of an institutional framework for users to articulate their information needs and allow greater participation in the policy-making process.

These complex institutional issues demand the attention of multiple professions, levels of government and organizations. Objectives and standards of state and local government are likely to be influenced by normative theories as well as by the interactions of the institutional forces that are both conflicting and complementary. Building and maintaining this fragile network of coalitions to promote progress in state and local government accounting and financial reporting will make for an active agenda in the 1980s.

Notes

1. Current authoritative accounting and financial reporting standards are contained in *Statement 1* issued in 1979 by the NCGA as a restatement of the principles of the 1968 *Governmental Accounting, Auditing, and Financial Reporting* (GAAFR). The Municipal Finance Officers Association (MFOA) published a 1980 GAAFR to provide detailed guidance to the application of *Statement 1*. All of these publications are available from the MFOA, 180 N. Michigan Avenue, Chicago, Illinois, 60601.
2. American Institute of Certified Public Accountants, Committee on Terminology, *Accounting Terminology Bulletin, No. 1* (New York: AICPA, 1953), p. 3.
3. Harold Q. Langenderfer, "A Conceptual Framework for Financial Accounting," *The Journal of Accountancy* (July 1973), p. 50.
4. This debate was triggered particularly by M. E. Francis, "Accounting and the Evaluation of Social

Programs: A Critical Comment," in *The Accounting Review* (April 1973), pp. 245–257. For a most recent report on this topic, see Paul K. Brace, et al., *Reporting of Service Efforts and Accomplishments* (Stamford, Conn.: FASB, November 1980).
5. For a provocative analysis, see Harvey Kapnick, "The Concept of 'Generally Accepted' Should Be Abandoned," in *Institutional Issues in Public Accounting*, Robert R. Sterling (ed.) (Lawrence, Kansas: Scholars Book Co., 1974), pp 375–393.
6. Standard & Poor's has recently issued a policy statement endorsing governmental financial reporting in accordance with Generally Accepted Accounting Principles—NCGA *Statement 1*. It would consider failure to comply with GAAP as a negative factor in its rating process. A research study recently undertaken by S & P came to the conclusion that "the market may be penalizing issuers for deficiencies in financial reporting. Poor accounting may be costing taxpayers many millions of dollars in higher interest costs." "Who's Watching the Books?" *Standard & Poor's Perspective* (November 1980).
7. AICPA, "Audit of State and Local Governmental Units" (1974), and "Accounting and Financial Reporting by Governmental Units"—an amendment to the previous audit guide, Statement of Position 80-2 (June 30, 1980), p. 3.
8. Coopers & Lybrand and the University of Michigan, *Financial Disclosure Practices of the American Cities: A Public Report* (New York: Coopers & Lybrand, 1976): Sidney Davidson, et al., *Financial Reporting by State and Local Government Units* (Chicago: University of Chicago Graduate School of Business, 1977).
9. Comptroller of the City of New York, *Annual Report*, Fiscal Year 1979, "Foreword."
10. This idea was expressed by the AICPA Study Group on the Objectives of Financial Statements in its report in 1973, and has been affirmed by the FASB.
11. See Herbert A. Simon, "A Comparison of Organization Theories," in *Review of Economic Studies*, Vol. 20, No. 1 (1952-1953).
12. This application is based on the basic ideas proposed by C.I. Barnard, *The Function of the Executive* (Cambridge: Harvard University Press, 1938), and Herbert A. Simon, *Administrative Behavior*, 3rd ed. (New York: The Free Press, 1976), particularly Chapter VI.
13. In addition to the studies cited in note 8, refer also to William H. Holder, *A Study of Selected Concepts for Governmental Financial Accounting and Reporting* (Chicago: NCGA, 1980); John C. Burton, "Public Reporting by Governmental Units: A Revised Financial Reporting Model for Municipalities," in David Solomons (ed.), *Improving the Financial Discipline*

of States and Cities (Reston, Va.: The Council of Arthur Young Professors, 1980).

14. Allan R. Drebin, "Governmental vs. Commercial Accounting: The Issues," in *Governmental Finance* (November 1979), pp. 3–8. For another interesting contrasting of viewpoints, see Robert N. Anthony, "Making Sense of Nonbusiness Accounting," and Regina E. Herzlinger and H. David Sherman, "Advantages of Fund Accounting in 'Nonprofits'" in *Harvard Business Review* (May-June 1980).

15. Arthur L. Thomas, *The Allocation Problem in Financial Accounting Theory* (Evanston, Ill.: American Accounting Association, 1969).

16. These include straight-line, double declining balance and sum of years' digits, to name just three methods.

17. Rule 203 in essence requires that an AICPA member not express an opinion that financial statements are in conformity with GAAP if such statements contain any departures from the standards promulgated by the body designated by the AICPA Council to establish GAAP, except in unusual circumstances in which a heavy burden of justification and disclosure is imposed. So far only the FASB has been so designated pursuant to the above rule.

18. Financial Accounting Standards Board (FASB), *Statement of Financial Accounting Concepts* No. 4, "Objectives of Financial Reporting by Non-Business Organizations," December 1980.

34

Governmental Financial Management at the Crossroads: The Choice Is Between Reactive and Proactive Financial Management

Charles A. Bowsher
Comptroller General of the United States

It is perhaps to be expected that when we address governmental matters, we tend to focus upon policy and programmatic rather than financial management issues. There is always an air of excitement and immediacy about guns-versus-butter debates, while budgeting, accounting, and related financial management subjects are often perceived as being important mainly to accountants, business and public administration faculties, and agencies' comptroller office personnel.

Every so often, however, there is a realization that effectiveness in the public policy arena depends in large measure upon the quality of financial management information and procedures. Unfortunately, this realization does not always come soon enough, but rather in the aftermath of a crisis that serves to raise our awareness of the need for sound financial management. In short, we often practice *reactive* rather than *proactive* financial management.

One of the better known cases involved New York City and New York State in the mid-1970s. In 1975 the city entered a severe financial crisis when the financial markets declined to purchase securities issued by the city. Financial analysts had been expressing concern about the city's overextended financial position and rapidly growing short-term debt, but seemingly no one in the city government took the warnings very seriously. When the city was unable to acquire refinancing of its debt, it faced the real prospect of bankruptcy, and when New York State tried to help, the threat of bankruptcy spread to it as well.

Source: Public Budgeting & Finance (Summer 1985): 9–22.
Reprinted by permission.

At the heart of the New York problem were the policies that led to excessive spending levels. But underlying those policies was the fact that the governments of New York State and New York City did not have good pictures of their own financial conditions. After the crisis began, it took the state a year to find out how much debt it had, and in the city not even the professional accountants could make sense of all the numbers. For example, city officials could not even reconcile the cash accounts, for which the budget office and the comptroller's office carried different numbers. Since 1975 though, both the city and state have taken important steps to improve their fiscal policies and quality of financial reporting, including steps to assure annual publication and audit of financial statements prepared according to generally accepted accounting principles.

Moreover, the New York crisis precipitated important changes in financial management beyond New York's borders, mainly in other cities and states. It may be said that the 1975 New York fiscal crisis was to the United States governmental sector at the state and local levels what the 1929 New York stock exchange crash was to the private sector. Following the 1929 crash, many observers expressed concern about the unreliability and noncomparability of U.S. corporations' books and financial statements, and the Congress and president established the Securities and Exchange Commission in the early 1930s with the goal of improving private sector financial reporting. The commission required annual audits of publicly held corporations and the development of accounting standards to be set and followed by the private sector. Ultimately, the commission delegated this standard-setting responsibility to the accounting profession and then in the 1970s to the Financial Accounting Standards Board (FASB).

The New York crisis' similar impact upon the governmental sector was first seen in the late 1970s as many state and local governmental entities, drawing upon the lessons learned in New York, adopted more rigorous budgeting and accounting standards and reporting, including independently audited financial statements. The Single Audit Act of 1984 followed, requiring independent audits of state and local entities receiving $100 thousand or more in federal funds. Also, the Government Accounting Standards Board (GASB) was established in 1984 to set accounting standards for state and local governments.

The Need for Improvements
at the Federal Level

Those of us involved in federal government financial management need to ponder these earlier experiences and work to bring about needed improvements before a financial crisis at the federal level forces remedial actions. Hopefully, we can be foresighted enough to practice sound financial management and help forestall the kinds of crises that happened in 1929 and 1975.

Most observers believe that the current financial problem with the most potential for assuming crisis proportions is the growing federal debt. It is sobering to realize that the total federal debt, as a percentage of the Gross National Product, rose from about 35 percent in 1974 to 44 percent in 1984, with budget projections showing the figure rising to over 50 percent in the later years of this decade. Net interest payments on the $1.6 trillion debt in fiscal year 1984 alone were about $111 billion, which compares with $12.6 billion spent on all natural resources and environmental activities, and $7.7 billion spent on all community and regional development programs.

There is no question that the public and fiscal officials alike are beginning to lose patience on the debt issue and are searching for ways to deal with it, including even the approach of a constitutional amendment to limit spending and require the adoption and execution of a balanced budget. Financial management surely must address the debt question and ways to bring the government's spending into line with its receipts base. This should be our number one fiscal priority.

Furthermore, developing solutions to this problem must include bringing about some fundamental changes in the government's underlying financial management systems, processes, and reporting. Weaknesses in these areas have contributed to the current problem. Outlined below are key reforms that are needed.

Expanded Conception of
"Financial Management"

For too long, "financial management" in the federal government has been seen or at least practiced as a rather narrow function involving mainly accountants and budget analysts. Somehow, the idea of bringing management issues and analyses to bear upon budgeting and accounting questions, and vice versa, has not taken firm root throughout the government, in spite of some progress made in this direction over the last two decades. The Department of Defense took a significant step in the 1960s with its adoption of a planning, programming, and budgeting (PPB) system, and at the governmentwide level the old Bureau of the Budget (BOB) was transformed into the Office of Management and Budget (OMB) in 1970. Unfortunately, the government did not adequately build upon these steps, perhaps because the concurrent years of expanding budgets and attenuated conflicts over budget choices lessened the pressures for careful financial management.

This narrow concept of financial management has not served us well, because it has helped perpetuate in agencies fragmented and isolated analyses and reporting that should come together for optimum effect. A broader conception of financial management, particularly one set forth in an explicit model, could help overcome this problem and enhance the quality of governmental decisionmaking. The following model shows the key features of an expanded approach to financial management.

The basic idea is that a modern financial management process encompasses the phases identified in the four arrow segments—planning/programming, budgeting, budget execution/accounting, and audit/evaluation—and is supported by a fully integrated system of data and information. The four phases should be closely linked in a continuous financial management process. In this continuous loop process, the information and decisions in each phase "track through" and influence the subsequent phase and perhaps other phases as well.

If federal agencies fully practiced such an integrated financial management approach, the benefits at all stages would be real and substantial:

- *Planning/programming.* Agency officials would more systematically sift out plans and programs found by audits and evaluations to be ineffective or uneconomical. Today, planning and programming are often unimaginative "boiler plate" exercises, with relevant audit and evaluation results being ignored.
- *Budgeting.* Resource requests, if tied to sound multiyear plans and programs, would be more "disciplined" in the best sense. Too frequently, we find haphazard budget initiatives that have not been carefully analyzed with respect to their long-term

costs or consequences for an agency's overall plans and programs.

• *Budget execution/accounting.* Managers, if given adequate incentives, would be more cost conscious in the execution of their programs. At the present time, many managers take an almost exclusive fund control orientation to their tasks, where "success" means spending up to, but not beyond, the appropriated limits. Such an orientation comes easily under current budget practices that do not adequately compare budgeted objectives with the results and their costs and are not oriented toward holding managers accountable for cost outcomes.

• *Audit/evaluation.* Follow-up studies of agency practices and program results would be more meaningful, because they could focus upon a clearly articulated, integrated set of long-term goals (plans), near-term steps to reach the goals (programs), and applied short-term resources (budget execution). What we find today instead is that the frequent absence of such a "roadmap" makes it most difficult to gauge an agency's progress. Also, poor quality accounting data can lessen the reliability of financial statements and increase the difficulty of auditing those statements.

There are many reasons why the federal government has not made more headway in adopting or implementing this expanded concept of financial management, ranging from parochialism in

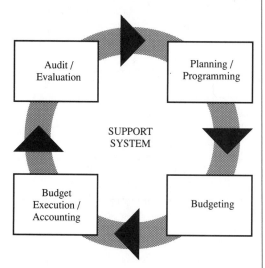

Figure 1
The financial management process

bureaucratic and professional areas to more technical considerations. The latter are touched upon in parts of the following discussion of other needed improvements.

More Comprehensive and Consistent Budget

The history of financial management reform includes periodic attempts to reestablish a comprehensive budget to assure that all federal activities are subject to the same budgetary scrutiny, and that the fiscal consequences of governmental decisions are fully disclosed in the most understandable way— i.e., at one time under one cover. This was, for example, an aim of the 1937 Brownlow Committee Report and the principal objective of the 1967 Report of the President's Commission on Budget Concepts.

In reality, there probably have been only a few times in the nation's history when the budget's boundaries encompassed all federal activities. The development of new kinds of programs and funding procedures outside the budget has not been uncommon—for example, note the rapid growth of trust funds in the 1930s and postwar years. Also, legislation from time to time has removed certain activities from the budget. It is the existence of such legislation today that makes this again a matter of concern.

Since fiscal year 1972, off-budget outlays of the government grew from zero to about $21 billion in fiscal year 1981. The level in fiscal year 1985 could be lower, about $12.5 billion according to Office of Management and Budget estimates. These outlays would mainly represent the off-budget Federal Financing Bank's financing of governmental credit activities.

It is particularly important at this time of heightened concern over governmental spending and deficits to have an accurate and full reporting in the budget on the government's fiscal actions. For fiscal year 1986, OMB took the step of including the off-budget amounts in the budget's totals, reflecting the president's proposal to repeal the provisions of law placing these activities off-budget. Favorable congressional action would restore the budget's comprehensive scope and assure more consistent treatment of like activities.

There is another problem that, while it does not pertain to the budget's boundaries per se, lessens the utility of the budget for comprehensively comparing federal programs. This concerns the varying budget reporting and appropriations practices that make it difficult to compare the budgetary consequences of programs. Budgetary terms, definitions, and usages are not as precise or formalized as those in accounting. As a consequence, and also because of certain statutory provisions, there are numerous cases in the budget where significantly different procedures are employed for like or similar activities. Some examples are:

- Reporting as "budget authority" the authorized level of agency *gross* borrowing from the Treasury in some cases, and the level of *net* borrowings in other cases.
- Treating agency borrowings as "sales of assets" in some instances, which allows an agency to offset the obtained amounts against its outlay total, or treating the transactions as borrowings with no offset.
- Reporting "operating" and "capital" subtotals for some accounts, while failing to make this important distinction in other accounts.
- Using appropriated budget authority in some acquisition programs for making cash purchases of property, while using non-appropriated, "backdoor" means in other programs (e.g., the extension of credits that may later be applied on other transactions to reduce payments to the government).
- Disclosing the full costs of some multiyear commitments, while reporting only "next-year" amounts in other cases.

A major case concerning the disclosure of future costs relates to the government's liability for retirement benefits. A recent report estimated the unfunded portion of retirement benefits to be several hundred billion dollars. But the budget only partially recognizes retirement benefits being earned by today's civilian employees, while those of military personnel were not recognized at all until the Congress recently changed the law. To avoid the risk of inappropriately mortgaging the future, decisionmakers should recognize the long-term consequences of current benefits and any proposed changes to them.

These are only a few of the inconsistencies found among the approximately 1,200 accounts and over 5,000 programs or activities in the budget. More uniform treatment of like or similar activities would greatly simplify the budget and enhance its usefulness to the public and governmental officials. And again, efforts at improvement will have to be continuing ones. The words of President Jefferson, written in 1802, show that problems of budget complexity are by no means new:

> I think it an object of great importance . . . to simplify our system of finance, and to bring it within the comprehension of every member of Congress . . . the whole system [has been] involved in impenetrable fog. [T]here is a point . . . on which I should wish to keep my eye . . . a simplification of the form of accounts . . . so as to bring everything to a single centre[;] we might hope to see the finances of the Union as clear and intelligible as a merchant's books, so that every member of Congress, and every man of any mind in the Union, should be able to comprehend them to investigate abuses, and consequently to control them.[1]

More Timely Budget Process

The last major reform of federal government budgeting occurred with the enactment of the 1974 Congressional Budget and Impoundment Control Act (Public Law 93-344) which, among other actions, established a "top-down" budget process in the Congress. Under provisions of the 1974 act, the Congress each year sets budget resolution target spending totals, and later controlling totals, to guide individual congressional actions. There also are similar totals on revenues, any annual deficit, and on the cumulative public debt. Furthermore, during each session there is a continuous scorekeeping of the individual budget-related amounts that are passed against the budget resolution totals. The underlying rationale is that individual appropriation and revenue actions should flow from, and be consistent with, an overall congressional fiscal policy.

There is no question that the reforms of the 1974 act have been successful in providing needed visibility on the implications for general fiscal policy of individual budget-related actions. This has been a major step forward. The current heightened awareness in the country at large about spending levels, deficits, and other fiscal questions stems at least in part from the greatly improved reporting on such matters that came about because of the 1974 act.

In one area, however, the 1974 reforms did not produce the intended results. The government still finds it practically impossible to complete actions on a budget before the beginning of the applicable fiscal year. Since the 1974 reforms, there has been only one fiscal year, 1976, for which all regular appropriations bills were enacted before the start of the year. Even then, one of the bills was incomplete in coverage, requiring a continuing resolution for some federal activities. Most recently, at the beginning of fiscal year 1985, only four of the regular appropriations bills for the year had been enacted, requiring much of the federal government to operate on continuing resolutions.

A problem with this, particularly when an agency is forced to operate under a succession of two- to four-month continuing resolutions, is that agency efficiency and effectiveness can suffer. Officials have to devote considerable time to simply "crunching" the changing numbers and insuring compliance with legal spending limitations. This leaves less time and incentive for carefully managing costs; doing thorough planning, programming, and budgeting for future periods; and giving adequate attention to a whole range of management questions (long-term data processing requirements, personnel skills and needs, etc.).

These problems are magnified when the continuing resolutions themselves are not passed on time, leading to some funding gaps and the beginning of office closedowns at considerable expense to the taxpayers. This, in turn, weakens the morale of the government's workforce and, just as importantly, the reputation of the government at home and abroad. We saw this in October 1984, when some agencies did not get funded even under continuing resolutions until a week or more into the fiscal year.

The Congress itself has also experienced some difficulties in maintaining its effectiveness while handling its growing budget-related workload. It is worth remembering that the 1974 act layered a new set of procedures on existing ones, adding to the workload a complex set of annual budget process steps concerning authorizing and appropriating actions. At the same time, budget-related workload pressures were increasing because of a trend toward shorter-term authorizations (annual or biennial).

The overall result is a rather cumbersome and time-consuming congressional process. Program funding levels may be debated and acted upon several times during a session—at the time of authorization, the first concurrent resolution on the budget, appropriations, reconciliation actions, and second or third concurrent resolutions on the budget. Many participants and observers feel that such revisiting of decisions crowds out other important business, especially oversight activities.

There probably is no one solution to this problem. Indeed, much of the heavy workload experienced by the Congress on budget-related actions stems from controversies generated in the political arena. Nevertheless, serious thought should be given to streamlining the process. Several possible changes are being considered by various observers and participants:

- Moving to less frequent authorizations for some programs now authorized annually.
- Formally shifting to a single, binding concurrent budget resolution procedure.
- Consolidating budget-related bills, including appropriations and revenue measures, into a single omnibus bill.
- Restricting use of the budget reconciliation procedure.
- Adopting permanent legislation providing for automatic continuing resolutions.
- Moving to some form of biennial budgeting.

Time and space do not permit a discussion of the pros and cons of each of these reforms. However, each should be assessed carefully not only for its feasibility, but also for its possible unintended consequences. For example, could biennial budgeting result in an unacceptable loss of legislative control over spending levels? Might an automatic continuing resolution further weaken congressional resolve and discipline by removing the incentive for completing regular appropriations actions? The answers to such questions will not come easily, and finding a way to streamline the process is one of the most challenging tasks confronting us.

Improved Financial Data

Good financial data, readily available when needed, lie at the heart of sound financial management. This too is an area where improvements are needed. Data that are inconsistent, inaccurate, incomplete, or untimely are often the weak links in an otherwise well designed set of financial management procedures and support systems. Following are several specific areas where these kinds of problems exist.

Better accounting/budgeting integration needed. Concerted efforts are needed to develop more integrated accounting and budgeting systems in agencies.

A key function of accounting systems is to provide managers, including budget officers, full and reliable reporting on how funds are being spent and the financial results of recently completed fiscal periods. If accounting system data are not used in budget analyses and reporting, data gaps occur that can lessen the soundness of budget decisions.

A case in point is the Department of Defense's (DOD's) failure to tie its Selected Acquisition Reports (SARs) directly to its accounting systems. SARs are quarterly reports to the Congress on certain costs of major weapon system acquisitions. Although the concept of SARs is good, they rely on contractor and other data that do not necessarily tie to DOD's accounting systems. Furthermore, they can be reconciled to the budget only once a year. This partially explains inconsistencies found in DOD budget reporting on its acquisition programs. Such data problems confuse the picture and make it difficult for the Congress to hold defense managers accountable for their decisions. Similar problems may be found in civil agencies of the government.

Gaps between accounting and budgeting can easily develop as managers of accounting and budget offices pursue their own needs and priorities. Accounting system categories and data elements must serve internal control needs and, consequently, they capture and report data on, at a minimum, the objects of managerial control such as salaries, supplies, equipment, travel, etc. These are rather stable categories of expenditure, and so accounting system structures tend to show a fair amount of continuity from year to year.

Budget structures tend to be a different matter. The reporting categories and data elements focus more upon the end purposes of the expenditures. In other words, the systems are designed primarily for tracking and estimating expenditures for congressionally funded programs and projects, not the objects of those expenditures (equipment, etc.). Furthermore, because budgets are oriented to programs, which can change with shifts in presidential and congressional policies, budget categories change relatively rapidly.

Given the divergent tendencies between accounting and budget systems, it is not surprising that discontinuities in data between the two are frequently found. An accounting system may track obligations mainly by "object class," forcing the agency's budget officials to rely on ad hoc and less reliable reporting systems for the distribution of amounts by program category. Overcoming this kind of disconnect should be an important aim of financial management reform in the federal government.

More modern systems.   Part of the problem with integrating budgeting and accounting systems stems from the government's reliance on many fragmented and antiquated systems. The capacity, speed, flexibility, and relative ease of use of modern systems equipment and software make it feasible to integrate budget and accounting systems without adversely affecting their data needs and reporting objectives.

There was a time when, because systems were manual or only partially automated in batch-processing facilities, there were some technical impediments to maintaining integrated budget and accounting systems. There should be no significant technical impediments of that type today. What is needed is a long-term commitment by officials at all levels of the government to take advantage of current and emerging capabilities to effect this integration.

Furthermore, to take full advantage of these capabilities, the government's basic structure of financial management could be revised to reduce the number of disbursement and accounting centers. If more agencies shared facilities, productivity in federal financial management operations would be higher and financial information would be more timely, compatible, and reliable. The current, decentralized structure is a result of earlier technological limitations and certain expediencies required during World War II. Those factors are no longer compelling, and the government should effect the improvement in efficiency that can come with consolidation of systems.

Better Planning for Capital Investment Decisonmaking

The federal government participates in a significant way in developing and maintaining a wide variety of public capital facilities, either through its own construction and acquisition programs or through grants-in-aid, direct loans, loan guarantees, and tax expenditures for state and local programs. In recent years, as the deteriorating state of the country's capital infrastructure has become apparent, there has been growing concern over the governments lack of a structured planning, programming, and budgeting approach to capital needs and priorities.

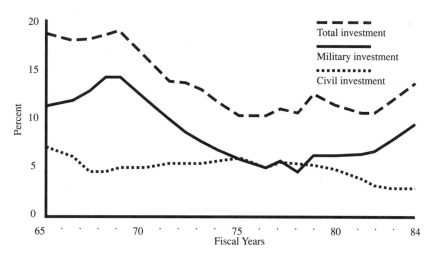

Figure 2
Federal capital investment as a percent of total budget outlays

The government's capital activities are now managed through numerous agencies, programs, and funding sources, with only the beginnings of a structured, governmentwide approach (discussed below) for assessing capital investment needs and making capital investment decisions. The lack of better visibility for investment decisions, coupled with a budget and accounting approach that treats capital spending as if it were the same as spending for current operations, creates what some consider to be a systematic bias against capital investment.

Business organizations and most state and local governments budget separately for operating and capital investment spending. The federal government's budget, however, should be as comprehensive as possible, reflecting the importance of the budget totals for economic policy purposes and the need to consider the full scope of government activities in the budget process. The needed visibility of capital budgeting within the unified budget could be achieved by displaying capital investment activities separately. Thus, each major functional category in the budget (e.g., national defense, energy, agriculture) would include an operating component and a capital investment component.

This separation of capital and operating expenditures within the unified budget would:

• Elevate the visibility of capital investment decisions.
• Facilitate the development of replacement planning.

• Allow a comparison of the long-term costs and benefits of capital investments across budget functions.

A significant step toward better capital budgeting was taken recently with the enactment in 1984 of Public Law 98-501, which includes the Public Works Improvement Act of 1984 and the Federal Capital Investment Program Information Act of 1984. These two acts provide for the establishment of a federal National Council on Public Works Improvement and staff to report annually on the condition of the nation's infrastructure; an advisory group representing federal, state, county, and city entities to assist and advise the council; and expanded presidential budget reporting on capital needs, issues, economic factors, and current service and alternative spending levels.

Implementation of this 1984 law will certainly put federal needs assessments and planning for capital items on a sounder footing, but it may stop short of systematically providing separate visibility on capital and operating amounts within the structure of budget functions and related accounts. Providing that information would make it easier for the Congress to track and understand the president's budget proposals for capital items and would facilitate congressional budget control over that part of the budget.

Increased Accountability for Costs and Results

All of the above improvements would be necessary but not, in themselves, sufficient for assuring that programs are conducted in the most cost-effective way. Sound financial management includes additional procedures for determining how well funds are being utilized.

One area concerns management reporting on performance. Although most federal officials acknowledge the importance of monitoring and evaluating performance, there are cases where their management reporting systems do not adequately address program, organizational, and project reporting. Missing critical elements may include any of the following:

- Agreement on objectives and relevant measures of accomplishment.
- Systematic collection of reliable, consistent, and comparable information on costs and accomplishments.
- Supply of that information routinely for use in management planning, programming, budgeting, and evaluating.

All three of these elements are key building blocks in effective reporting, and managers need to devote constant attention to assuring that each block is in place. The reporting structure's usefulness to decisionmaking breaks down whenever one of the blocks in the hierarchy is missing.

A second area is cost consciousness. As alluded to before, the emphasis in budget execution today is on funds control, wherein management attention is directed at controlling the levels of obligations and outlays. Obligations occur when orders are placed, contracts awarded, or similar kinds of commitments are undertaken that will eventually require cash payments (outlays). The budget itself promotes this orientation by stating requests in terms of the budget authority needed for entering obligations, and by reporting mainly on the levels of obligations and resultant outlays.

Fund control is a necessary ingredient in budget execution. Without it, there would be no way of assuring that spending for federal activities does not exceed the levels provided in appropriation acts. Fund control is also necessary for implementing fiscal policy on deficit levels.

The trouble is that there is a too exclusive emphasis upon fund control, at the expense of paying sufficient attention to costs. A well designed budgeting and budget execution process would provide more equal visibility and treatment to obligations, outlays, and costs. Figure 3 illustrates that the key distinction among these concepts is the timing of a transaction's recognition.

Although a program's obligations, outlays, and costs theoretically will be the same over the life of the program, it is important to have a budget reporting system that discloses the separate amounts at any one time, especially in procurement, construction, and other programs where there can be a significant time lag between incurring obligations and recognizing costs. In such cases, the availability of cost information permits managers to match program outputs or effects with the spending that was required to produce those results—in other words, to start making cost-benefit calculations and comparisons.

For example, in programs of acquiring and providing spare parts to airplanes or ships, a given year's obligation or outlay levels would not necessarily be reliable measures of the spending associated with the spare parts installed and used that particular year in the planes and ships. It would be necessary to have measures of this to make accurate calculations of the costs of spares required to maintain the year's

Figure 3
Financial information for management

airplane "flying hours" programs, or ship "steaming hours" programs. The year's obligation and outlay amounts could indicate levels of support for future flying or steaming hours programs, not the realized costs of that year's programs. Only a "cost" figure would reliably provide that amount.

At this time, there is a statutory requirement that agency budgeting be "cost based," but this is not being carried to the point of providing cost amounts in the budget. As a result, the Congress does not systematically review agency or program costs when it considers and acts upon budget submissions. Steps to incorporate costs into budget documents and deliberations would be a significant step forward and would provide the Congress with information needed to oversee adequately the efficiency and effectiveness of agency activities. This could even be done without eliminating the customary congressional practice of providing budget authority for obligations (by budget schedule "crosswalks" from costs to obligations).

Finally, there is a need for agency and government-wide consolidated financial statements, prepared according to accepted accounting procedures and audited annually. These statements could supplement other budgeting and accounting information by giving an overall picture of the financial health of the government and its agencies. Most importantly, they could disclose the cumulative financial effect of decisions on the nation's resources and provide early warning signals to policymakers. Also, the discipline of preparing auditable financial statements will direct more attention to the quality of agency systems and data and will stimulate upgrading in many areas.

Many organizations, such as publicly owned corporations, are required to present comprehensive financial reports to the public. Just as shareholders expect management to report the financial positions of their companies, so taxpayers should hear about the financial position of their government. Many state and local governments are moving toward this practice, partially influenced by federal reporting requirements for revenue sharing and other grant programs.

The federal government is a unique entity, and its financial statements must adequately reflect that fact. Though requiring further development, the "prototype" consolidated financial reports prepared by the Treasury are a useful first step toward this goal.

With the installation of modern integrated systems and the adoption of comprehensive accounting principles and standards, agencies can effectively provide the information for consolidated federal financial statements that can be annually audited.

Conclusions

Action along the lines laid out above would provide the federal government with the tools needed for practicing proactive financial management. We need to realize, too, that this cannot be a short-term effort. Although policymakers should feel a sense of urgency about this and begin now to plan and take initial steps, they have to realize that a full implementation would span several years.

Unfortunately, several obstacles could easily arise over the years to impede progress. The short tenure of many top management officials always presents a challenge to structural changes requiring a concerted effort over a number of years. Also, there are periodic foreign and domestic policy distractions. It is of the utmost importance that the country's citizens, legislators, administrators, and educators see this as a matter of real significance for our future. All concerned individuals should give serious attention to this and work in their respective spheres to build a consensus for comprehensive reform.

Note

1. *The Writings of Thomas Jefferson* (Washington, D.C., 1903), vol. 10, p. 306.

35
Government Budgeting and Productivity

A. Premchand
International Monetary Fund

Budgeting is essentially concerned with the allocation of resources, while productivity measures aim at revealing the efficiency of the utilization of resources. Seemingly, therefore, these two activities are symbiotic, at least in theory. If they were so in practice, there would be little need for further discussion, but recent experience suggests that these activities have not been harmonized, a factor that contributes to renewed discussion about the role of each and the degree of their interdependence.

The debate about these issues has received substantial impetus recently from several economic and attitudinal factors. To mention a few, the consistent growth in government expenditures across a wide spectrum of countries—both industrial and developing—has raised the issue of whether that growth was necessary. For example, in the United States, federal expenditures, which were 1.4 percent of national income in 1799 and about 3 percent of gross national product (GNP) in 1929, rose sevenfold over the next fifty years. Similar trends are observable in other countries. While growth has been a common characteristic, the share of government sector in GNP differs widely among countries.

The important issue, from the point of view of productivity, is whether the growth in public expenditures has been due to government's having to pay more for its inputs—whether a larger growth in expenditures has been prevented by improved productivity or whether declining productivity has contributed to an otherwise avoidable increase in public expenditures. To be sure, the growth in government expenditures raises several other important issues, such as the factors contributing to growth and those that are helpful in explaining the disparities in levels and rates of growth, but these are outside the focus of this article.

Source: Public Productivity Review, no. 41. (San Francisco: Jossey-Bass, Spring 1987): 9–19. Reprinted by permission. The views expressed in the paper are solely those of the author and should not be interpreted as official Fund views.

A major factor contributing to the debate on productivity is the spread of inflation in several countries, which stimulates emphasis on productivity in public services to mitigate the impact of wage increases in government and of inflation in general. Although productivity is a continuing concern and is not related to a specific phase of a business cycle, it would appear to get most attention in inflationary periods.

Yet another factor, with more important political implications than the preceding ones, is the general perception of the citizen and the taxpayer that the government sector has become a kind of Gulliver tied down by myriad Lilliputian ropes, each rope infinitesmally thin, yet all the ropes together immobilizing the fiscal giant and reducing the efficacy of its functions. While this perception is partly due to ideological factors emphasizing the need for adjusting "the borders" of the public sector, it is also partly based in economic literature.

It is not the intention here, however, to deal with these aspects in any comprehensive manner. This article has a more limited focus. It discusses primarily experiences with government productivity and the problem this implies. It raises and seeks to answer the following questions: What role has been assigned to productivity in the budgetary process? What have been the experiences? How can the budgetary process be strengthened to improve productivity?

Productivity in the Public Sector

The purpose of emphasizing productivity is to produce greater economic benefit or greater beneficial effect on the economics of various operations. Productivity depends on an input-output relation that takes into account all factors of production used in outputs. The efficiency with which the factors of production are utilized, in turn, is generally measured both by a narrow concept of efficiency and by a broader or economic concept. The narrower concept refers to the increased output obtained with the same volume of inputs, or the same volume of output from a reduced level of inputs. Economic efficiency, in contrast, measures allocative efficiency and improvement in consumer satisfaction. For practical purposes, however, the former is referred to as *efficiency* and the latter as *effectiveness* (see Burkhead and Ross, 1974).

Productivity in government is a complex phenomenon and can result, as it can elsewhere, from technical changes or, where these are not feasible, from the acquisition of improved or new skills. Government productivity, however, has the following particular features. Government services—particularly concerning education, health, and such other public goods as defense—tend to be labor-intensive. It is generally recognized however, that productivity increases come largely from technological change embodied in capital equipment; to the extent that such equipment tends to be less important in service sectors, productivity gains could be lower. While the traditional service sectors have been increasingly relying on capital equipment, such reliance may have contributed to better services, rather than to productivity gains. In fact, adherents of national income accounts assume no gains in the productivity of government employees and that increases in the volume of services are achieved only through manpower increases (see Premchand, 1983). Pragmatic policymakers, however, have different views. For example, in Japan and Sweden it is assumed for budgetary purposes that productivity gains in government are about the same as those experienced in the private sector.

Productivity in government is the result of several complex factors—design of organizations, resources, laws, money and people, and programs. Productivity cannot be an abstraction in the context of a highly diversified and heterogeneous organization, such as the government. Potential for increased productivity is likely to be higher with greater specialization, and such specialization in turn implies interdependence, cooperation, and coordination among activities. In the public sector, there can be extensive specialization of roles and functions, as in the way individual cells are specialized in a multicellular biological organism. Of the factors enumerated here, design of organizations, amounts of financial resources allotted and laws are exogenously determined; the only variable element, at least in theory, is the given human resource.

A related aspect is the behavior of people in governments. Proponents of public choice argue that government bureaucrats tend to concentrate on expanding the size of their bureaus—to expand their own power and influence through larger budgets (see Niskanen, 1971). This gives credence to the widely held belief that unit costs of government services tend to be higher than in the private sector. (One reason for the advocacy of privatization is the high cost of government services and the belief that such costs tend to be lower when identical services are provided by the private sector.) Some even suggest that if public goods do not have commercial counterparts, governments may not emphasize the need for economies or productivity. This, however, is not entirely valid; there are adequate criteria to assess the efficiency of an organization, even when there is no commercial counterpart.

In evaluating productivity in government, a parallel is drawn with the experiences of the private sector. However, the parallel is only partly valid. Differences, as well as similarities, have to be recognized. For example, services in the public sector are widely heterogeneous. While the private sector itself has a substantial variety of products, not all the functions of the government are replicable in the private sector; and if they are replicable, the social costs may be sizable. Organizationally, a firm in the private sector has several features that ensure regular monitoring of productivity. These include financial planning on a rolling basis, cost centers, and determination of standard costs and actual costs. Although the relevance of these features for the government is no longer controversial, progress, as will be shown later, has been less in these areas than generally known. For these reasons, there is a perception that productivity gains associated with economic growth are not manifested in public sector activities to the extent that they are manifested in private manufacturing activities.

There are also some organizational dynamics unique to governments. Productivity measurements, to the extent to which they are agreed upon, are more applicable to controlled or relatively closed organizations. As a corollary, it can be argued that such measurements tend to be less achievable in huge, complex, and more open (thus more vulnerable) organizations like governments. A related feature is uncertainty (what Keynes called "the dark forces of time and ignorance") about the economy, which in turn affects the outlook and operations of government. Thus, reduced budget allocations reflecting volatile movements in resource availability may add to unit costs in the presence of rigid personnel management.

Relating Productivity to Budgeting

Given the distinctions between government and commercial organizations, the former had to evolve systems and methodologies suited to their own requirements. The basic inspiration for such systems was, however, drawn from the commercial world. The relevance of productivity measurement to government budgeting was recognized all along. For example, it was clear to budgeters that productivity measures were of considerable help in analyzing the needs of manpower, materials, and money. In particular, such measures helped to answer such questions as these: Are planned outputs being performed? What are their implications for resource requirements? In short, productivity data proved helpful in analyzing the estimates of the spending agencies for the volume of projected output and productivity rates and prices of resources. To that extent, the data were expected to provide objective measures for determining the allocation of funds and, by the same token, an agreed-upon framework within which the central reviewing agency and the spending agencies could assess requirements.

Although the inherent virtues of higher productivity were known, productivity outputs had no major role in budgetary processes until the early 1950s. The preoccupation of the reviewers in central agencies, as well as of the initial compilers of budget estimates, was with budget inputs and not with the efficiency of producing outputs. It is not surprising that productivity did not emerge as a concern in the budgetary process. This changed for the better in 1949, when the Hoover Commission, inspired by the experiences of some local governments, raised two issues that have haunted the consciences of government policymakers since then. The commission asked for specification of the desirable level of expenditures for any major government program and the desirable proportion of total government expenditures to the gross national product. The commission also asked how efficiently and economically an approved program could be executed (or, in other words, how the same amount of work could be performed satisfactorily through other arrangements or through improved procedures at less cost). These two issues spurred more interest in productivity per se, and attempts were (and are being) made to find satisfactory answers and systems. (For a more detailed study of these two issues, particularly the first, see Premchand, 1983.)

The search for efficiency and economy, with productivity as an integral part, continued over the years. Although there were several innovations—each with its own degree of acceptance, partial implementation, and agonizing appraisal and reappraisal of experience as well as assessment of future tasks—few have been free from controversy. For analytical purposes, these innovations will be analyzed here in three groups: performance budgeting, program evaluation, and incrementalism.

Performance budgeting (which was introduced in the federal government in the 1950s, and which has been reappearing since then in one form or another, both in the United States and in other countries) emphasized the need for cost measurement and sought to divert the excessive emphasis on budgetary inputs to budgetary outputs. It stressed the improved classification of government transactions, the measurement of costs, and the evaluation of the efficiency and effectiveness of government programs after their completion. Budgeters recognized that the application of productivity criteria to the implementation of public operations was important; but in view of the diversity of operations and the difficulties in evolving standard productivity measures, budgeters chose to evolve workload measures as a kind of substitute for productivity.

The main virtue of performance budgeting, despite poor implementation in general, was that it required an expanded budgetary process, in which the program of work, its cost, and its effectiveness were considered explicitly. It sought an equation between inputs and outputs, and between financial and physical aspects, and facilitated the identification and measurement of linkages among manpower and materials and other factors of production.

But workload measures are not the same as productivity measures. As Kendrick (1977) noted, the former relate actual output to a norm and seek to reflect changes in efficiency under a given technology. Productivity measures, however, reflect changes in technology and other factors in addition to change in labor efficiency. This should not suggest that work measurements have no utility of their own; although they are incomplete as an index, they do provide an understanding of the broad efficiency of an organization, both in intertemporal and interspatial terms. Since productivity emphasizes the relationship between outputs and all resource inputs, work measures, which primarily deal with human resources, may provide at best a limited relationship between outputs and inputs. Moreover, work measures do not really attempt an assessment of the output; rather, they delineate the contribution of manpower to a given program.

The lack of success with performance budgeting led to experiments with modified versions, such as program budgeting. By the mid-1960s, these in turn had yielded place to more ambitious schemes, such as Planning-Programming-Budgeting-Systems (PPBS), Zero-Base Budgeting Systems (ZBB), and Program Evaluation Systems. PPBS and ZBB aimed at ensuring a more rational allocation of resources through the application of quantitative techniques. As a corollary of this approach, they concentrated on the analytical stage of budget formulation. It was program evaluation that concentrated more on budget implementation; thus, productivity received an indirect stimulus.

Program evaluation had at its core the objective of assessing the effectiveness of a program after implementation. Its lessons were for future application and applied both to resource allocation and to utilization. One of its ingredients was assessment of the use of component resources of a program and measurement of efficiency by use of a ratio of output to input. (See the Treasury Board of Canada, 1981, for a more detailed discussion of program evaluation as applied to government operations.) As a prebudget analytical tool, program evaluation stressed (a feature it had in common with PPBS and ZBB) the analysis of alternatives, and as a tool of accountability, it laid emphasis on cost containment. It was not intended to be an operational tool that would hold program managers to specified responsibilities, except in terms of retrospective assessment. The method assumed that the prevailing budgetary system would somehow specify the efficiency factors and norms against which evaluation would be undertaken after the event.

The third approach—incrementalism—is the antithesis of the preceding two and should essentially be viewed as a strategy to receive political approval for the budget. Insofar as it is viewed as an explanation of budgetary approaches in governments, it implies that budgets generally change only marginally from one year to the next and that budgetary processes are designed to facilitate the minimal-change approach. It also implies that a strategy of minimal change is acceptable to politicians, spending agencies, and central budgetary agencies. Not intended as a system, but only as a polemical treatment of certain administrative traits, incrementalism did not even attempt to consider productivity, let alone its improvement. To that extent, incrementalism can be considered as an oversimplification of budgetary processes.

Why Productivity Concerns Did Not Become Fully Operational

In the light of the preceding brief discussion, a logical question is how, with all the emphasis on productivity and after all the effort, productivity did not become a continuing and operational goal in the management of public bodies. Several factors contributed to this gap between what should have been and what was. On the basis of experience in several countries, and for purposes of brevity, they can be analyzed in terms of environment and management.

As already noted, the economic environment in which governments were operating was changing by the 1960s. While change itself is a natural part of evolution, the rate of change and its associated uncertainty became a problem. Inflation and stagflation came to characterize economies, and the manifold increase in the size of government budgets also became a major problem. The growing share of entitlements and related expenditures resisted efforts toward making government budgets viable instruments of countercyclical policy. Inflationary policies, followed by restrictive, unemployment-creating actions, became dominant features of macroeconomic management in the 1960s and the 1970s but proved to be too ambitious. In several cases, measures were put into effect too late and often were based on faulty economic forecasts (see Premchand, 1981; Premchand and Burkhead, 1984).

To counteract these trends, several institutional improvements were introduced. These included PBB-related systems, manpower ceilings, post-budget evaluation, strengthening of financial management capabilities in spending agencies, and associated measures, but they appear to have had a minimal impact on the growth of expenditures. Consequently, solutions outside the normal budget processes were envisaged. Balanced-budget amendments and constitutional limitations (both these approaches have acquired adherents in large numbers) are a part of the packages so envisaged. Ironically, although productivity was emphasized in all these approaches, it is the kind of emphasis placed that reduced productivity. The truth is that productivity was not the major concern in these efforts and was at best a secondary concern. Even those who stressed productivity appeared to share the perception that improving productivity in government was a complex and formidable task better suited to the talents of a long-distance runner than to those of a sprinter. This hesitant approach, in a way, prevented productivity from receiving the support that it badly needed.

Several management factors, by and large, proved to be obstacles to improving productivity in the public sector. The first factor was the ambiguity of productivity concepts. Finding acceptable ways of measuring the output of governmental activities has continued to be a problem that bedevils all quantitative analysis in the public sector. Benefit-cost analysis has been one of those techniques similarly afflicted. For example, in a study made by the U.S. Bureau of the Budget (1964), it was stated that "meaningful measures of productivity could not be obtained because of the difficulties inherent in defining the end product outputs" (see also Williams, 1967). No single measure could capture the wide variety of tasks, and a system comprising several indicators proved to be too "technical and mysterious" (Civil Service Commission, 1972). Productivity measurement became too complex in its application to organizations whose outputs were nonhomogeneous and were subject to rapid change.

A second factor was the misuse of component productivity measures. The U.S. Civil Service Commission (1972) pointed out that some productivity results were "forced" during the budget process by reducing manpower, notwithstanding an increased workload. This resulted, in the short term, in a superficial improvement in productivity, but in the medium term it adversely affected the quality of work and, more important, it alienated the spending agencies. Instead of contributing to a cooperative process, such cuts injected an avoidable adversarial element into the process.

A third factor undermining improvement in productivity was lack of sufficient commitment by management and lack of the positive and imaginative management action so vital for achieving improvement in each organization. To the extent that such goals were general or did not reflect the details necessary for day-to-day control of agency operations,

the agency managements considered them to be distant, intended more for central agencies than for their own use. Although general measures provide insights into the operations of an activity, managements tend to focus more on issues that are direct and specific and that reflect their own concerns.

Fourth, the emphasis on productivity remained separate from the budget process. Although, starting from performance budgeting, most budget innovations emphasized cost aspects of programs and the need for reducing costs, cost measurement itself did not make much progress, except in areas like defense and health care (U.S. General Accounting Office, 1984). In view of the failure to integrate productivity into the budgetary process, monitoring of productivity goals became a subsidiary exercise. What is more significant, budget constraints adversely affected capital improvements. As a result, outdated equipment became a constant feature of public sector organizations (see Grace, 1984). Finally, there was not adequate follow-up on the measures introduced. In some measure, this lack reflected the preceding factors—an ambiguity in concepts, abetted by apathy of agency managements, and a lack of firm guidance and of adequate implementation for the new systems that were expected to provide improved infrastructure.

Outlook

In view of the importance of productivity and its continuing, if unglamorous, results, efforts need to be made to restore it to its place of primacy. As a first step in this direction, we need to address the factors enumerated in the preceding section as contributors to the relative decline in effective measures of productivity enhancement.

Productivity has to be pursued over a period of years, and assiduous efforts, phased in an appropriate way, need to be made. To be effective, productivity has to be viewed as an integral part of the budgetary process, so that allocation of funds and linkage with productivity can be monitored on a regular basis. Pursuit of productivity as an independent goal is likely to be difficult and ultimately nonremunerative. The advocacy of an integrated budgetary process should not, however, be indiscriminate. As it is, the budgetary process is becoming more complex as it collects additional tasks (in the form of assessment of tax expenditures and impact of credit programs), and these are proving complex enough. Adding productivity as an invariable feature of all programs is likely to impose new burdens which in the short run have the potential of being counterproductive. The goal of productivity should, therefore, be properly focused and pursued.

Budget expenditures of governments can be classified into three broad groups: public goods, quasi-commercial goods, and transfers to individuals and productive sectors (Civil Service Commission, 1972). Of these, outlays for the last category form the highest share in the budgets of industrial countries and, to a lesser extent, in the budgets of developing countries. These operations, while important, are primarily money-intensive, while public goods and quasi-commercial goods are money- and labor-intensive (Rose, 1983). Gains in the application of productivity enhancement schemes can be better realized when they are applied to public goods (hospitals, defense, education, post offices, and so on) and the provision of industrial goods and services. In processing activities, work measures are likely to be more useful, given the absence of identifiable outputs. This type of selective approach needs to form the cornerstone of any policy intended to build productivity in government.

The selective application of productivity to programs should be supplemented by a strategy emphasizing improvement in measurement and information systems, identification of capital and labor mix and its impact, and central direction and decentralized implementation.

Improvement in measurement is a constant need and can never be taken to be a completed task. Government operations are rapidly changing. Along with this change, the "shelf life" of productivity ratios tends to be reduced. Basic improvements are still needed in developing data on work measures, unit costs, evaluation of the impact of government programs, and information systems. These elements, as noted earlier, are essentially the same ones that are associated with performance budgeting systems (which, however, have not become a permanent feature of governmental operations). The need now is not so much for a reiteration of these well-recognized principles, but rather for their selective application to the areas of public goods and quasi-commercial goods.

The choice of the areas where productivity gains can be achieved depends on where improved technology is to be used and on its relationship with labor inputs. During recent years, several governments have resorted to improvement in the infrastructure and in other capital assets to compensate for the fixed manpower ceilings ushered in as part of austerity measures or expenditure-containment programs. The impact of such substitution efforts, both in the short and the medium term, needs to be assessed. Further, a phased program for the introduction of improved technology has to be formulated. The need for such a program can hardly be overemphasized in a period when budget reductions have tended to be made across the board, rather than on a selective and targeted basis. Finally, direction and impetus for improved productivity should be central, but implementation has to be determined by the individual agency. If the flexibility of management is reduced through manpower or other ceilings, escape mechanisms and perverse fiscal behavior are likely to emerge. In addition to efforts aimed at retaining management flexibility, efforts must be made to mitigate any potential negative impacts of productivity goals on personnel. Personnel need to be trained and motivated to do their part (see Executive Office of the President and U.S. Office of Management and Budget, 1986).

The above elements have to be seen as part of an integrated program, rather than as areas that can be pursued in a piecemeal fashion. Indeed, previous experience shows that piecemeal implementation has been more damaging than advantageous. Current fiscal realities are such that nations can ill afford to delay the pursuit of productivity improvements.

References

BURKHEAD, J., and ROSS, J. P. *Productivity in the Local Government Sector.* Lexington, Mass.: D. C. Heath, 1974.

CIVIL SERVICE COMMISSION, U.S. General Accounting Office, and Office of Management and Budget. *Measuring and Enhancing Productivity in the Federal Sector.* Washington, D.C.: U.S. Government Printing Office, 1972.

EXECUTIVE OFFICE OF THE PRESIDENT and Office of Management and Budget. *Management of the United States Governmental Fiscal Year 1987.* Washington, D.C.: U.S. Government Printing Office, 1986.

GRACE, J. P. *War on Waste.* New York: Macmillan, 1984.

KENDRICK, J. W. *Understanding Productivity.* Baltimore: The Johns Hopkins University Press, 1977.

NISKANEN, W. A., Jr. *Bureaucracy and Representative Government*. Chicago: Aldine, 1971.

PREMCHAND, A. "Government Budgetary Reforms." *Public Budgeting and Finance*, 1981, pp. 74–85, 16–24.

PREMCHAND, A. *Government Budgeting and Expenditure Controls*. Washington, D.C.: International Monetary Fund, 1983.

PREMCHAND, A., and BURKHEAD, J. *Comparative International Budgeting and Finance*. New Brunswick, N.J.: Transaction Books, 1984.

ROSE, R. *The Programme Approach to the Growth of Government*. Glasglow, Scotland: University of Strathclyce, 1983.

TREASURY BOARD OF CANADA. *Guide on the Program Evaluation Function*. Toronto: Treasury Board of Canada, 1981.

U.S. BUREAU OF THE BUDGET. *Measuring Productivity of Federal Government Organizations*. Washington, D.C.: U.S. Government Printing Office, 1964.

U.S. GENERAL ACCOUNTING OFFICE. *Managing the Cost of Government*. Vol. I. Washington, D.C.: U.S. Government Printing Office, 1984.

WILLIAMS, A. *Output Budgeting and the Contribution of Microeconomics to Efficiency in Government*. London: HMSO, 1967.

36
Do Budget Reforms Make a Difference? Some Conclusions

Donald Axelrod
State University of New York, Albany

Do the eleven budgetary reforms[1] make a difference? This depends on the yardsticks used to measure the impact of the reforms. Among the measures prized by the reformers are expenditure control; allocative efficiency (targeting funds on justifiable programs and projects); improvements in the efficiency and effectiveness of programs and projects; strengthened accountability; and, above all, the impact of reforms on budget decisions. For Schick the last point is the overriding test:

> Did the innovation alter the basis for making budget decisions? Only if the answer is "yes" can an innovation be considered successful.[2]

Some Critics Blast Budget Reforms

On the basis of this criterion several influential commentators on the budget scene score the reforms as failures since they find little evidence of their utility in decision making. The critique generally takes two tacks. One, on the optimistic side, favors the reforms but finds they will not work unless the following impediments are overcome: limited resources allocated to the implementation of the reforms; difficulty of relating inputs to outputs; uncertainty about available resources in the future; poor data; conflicts between the budget office and operating agencies; the indifferent quality of top management; the lack of a constituency for budgetary improvement; the heterogeneity of government, making adjustments and compromises difficult; and the lack of commitment to budget improvements

Source: Copyright © 1988 from *Budgeting for Modern Government,* by Donald Axelrod, pp. 259, 303–308, 397, 407. Notes have been renumbered. Reprinted with permission of St. Martin's Press, Inc.

for the long pull.[3] If this indeed is the obstacle course, it's enough to dishearten the most ardent advocates of budget reform.

Most serious is the pessimistic outlook, which finds the reforms flawed at the core because they run counter to political and administrative decision-making styles. The leading proponents of this view are Wildavsky in the United States and Tarschys in Sweden who claim that incrementalism rather than comprehensive and rational budgeting is the dominant form of budgeting in nearly all political systems. The focus is on marginal changes in last year's budget with regard to both revenue and expenditures—in short, on increments and, in recent years, on decrements. This results not from political perversity, but necessity.[4]

Wildavsky's eloquent explanation and defense of incrementalism has become almost conventional wisdom, at least to students and academicians if not practitioners. His argument generally runs along these lines: The starting point in budgeting is the base budget, which brings forward all the accumulated political decisions of the past including mandatory and uncontrollable expenditures. To review this budget from scratch annually is to invite large-scale political warfare. It is therefore essential to contain conflict and to reach a consensus by concentrating on relatively few manageable and politically feasible issues, namely the increments. This may be an untidy and fragmentary approach. But it works. It facilitates political calculations by limiting the number of choices. It brings to the surface sequentially and repetitively familiar and controllable issues. It enables participants in budget bargaining to determine whether they are getting their fair share of the gain or the pain. With the rules of the game understood by all players, incrementalism promotes stability in the budget process. In contrast, comprehensive and zero-based budgeting would result in confusion and disarray as an unmanageable number of centers of political influence and interest groups vied for public funds.[5]

Hence, Wildavsky challenges would-be reformers who fail to understand "the political implications of budgetary reform":

> The tradition of reform in America is a noble one not easily to be denied. But in this case it is doomed to failure because it is aimed at the wrong target. If the present budgetary process is rightly or

wrongly deemed unsatisfactory then one must alter in some respects the political system of which the budget is but an expression.[6]

This leads Wildavsky to a defense of the traditional, line-item budget, which has survived because it is a mechanism for incremental choices. In his view no better tools exist to control expenditures and enforce accountability than the line items and the increments and decrements. Despite the add-ons in the budget process such as economic management, program planning and evaluation, and management planning, control remains the dominant feature.[7]

Going further, Schick despairs of budgeting altogether, traditional or reformed. No longer can the budget process perform its most basic functions, especially control of expenditures. In fact, "the budget is out of control" and no amount of innovations can set it right. Control is the very "bedrock of budgeting." Everything else is secondary. As evidence of lack of control, Schick cites uncontrollable expenditures, budgetary decisions made outside of the budget process, expenditures that exceed estimates, unstable budgets that shift with the vagaries of the economy, and the resort to off-budget practices.[8] This crisis:

has brought budgetary innovation to a virtual halt. For the first time in more than a century, no single concept or approach commands widespread support or convincingly promises better results. From the emergence of modern budgeting in nineteenth century Europe until the recent zero-based budgeting debacle in the United States, there was an abiding confidence that the methods by which public funds were spent could be made more rational. Nowadays, however, budgetmakers and scholars alike appear to be paralyzed by the intractability of problems facing government.[9]

Hence, Schick pronounced his epitaph on budgetary reform:

The age of budgetary reform has passed. From executive budgeting early in this century through planning, programming and budgeting (PPB) in the 1960s and zero-based budgeting (ZBB) in the 1970s, the practice and literature of budgeting were repeatedly stirred by efforts to improve the process. Now, however, the cupboard of budgeting innovation appears to be bare; little on the horizon is comparable in

scope and ambition to the major reforms that dominated budgeting in previous decades.[10]

The Practitioners Ignore the Critics of Budget Reform

We now have something of a paradox. Despite the epitaphs on reform, federal, state, and local governments in the United States, at an accelerated rate and in varying degree, have synthesized virtually all the elements of budget reform in their management systems. The same trend is apparent in other countries. Both the practitioners and the Wildavsky-Schick-Tarschys school can't be right. Who is?

Upon close examination much of the critique of budget reforms does not hold up. It either caricatures the reforms, as was done in the case of ZBB and PPBS, or pronounces the reforms unworkable absent instant success, or, simplistically, looks for a cause-and-effect relationship between the reforms and budget decisions, ignoring the complexity of factors that shape decisions. Fundamentally, the critique rests on two crumbling pillars: the theory of incrementalism and the irrelevance of budgetary reform in decision making (the politics v. rationality issue).

Some Doubts About the Usefulness of the Theory of Incrementalism to Explain Budget Decisions

Plausible as is the theory of incrementalism, it has come under increasing attack as but a partial and imperfect explanation of the budget process. What are increments (or decrements)—a combination of increases and decreases, some new programs or projects, selected cutbacks, several policy shifts? If the theory merely holds that decision makers prefer to deal with a limited number of increments at any one time rather than a flash flood of new initiatives, it adds seemingly a note of common sense to our understanding of the dynamics of budgeting. But even this is a shaky generalization when one considers the spate of budgetary changes during the New Deal period, the Great Society era, the early years of the Reagan administration, the Mitterand administration in France, and, at the state level, the Rockefeller years in New York. To call these changes mere increments is to overlook the nature of drastic policy shifts. Or do crises and strong personalities temporarily overcome the incremental bias in budgeting?

Even without crises, the theory of incrementalism fails to explain the changes in the composition of the budget over a five-to-ten-year period. The differences between the beginning and end of the period can be dramatic. Going beyond just marginal adjustments of base budgets, the changes reflect new departures, reordering of priorities, and important shifts of allocations. For example, Gorham noted that, given control over increments growing at the rate of 5 percent a year, the federal Department of Health, Education and Welfare could at the end of eight years change the nature of one-third of its expenditures. If increments accelerated at the rate of 8 percent a year, it could alter the composition of half of its expenditures during the same period. It takes time to turn a big bureaucracy around.[11] Only crises can compress the time schedule. Furthermore, not all decisions are incremental. More selective and useful zero-based reviews take place than the critics suggest.

As the chapter on budget implementation indicates, budgetary changes within the year can be as significant as changes between years. The incrementalists overlook these major developments. The proponents of the theory of incrementalism also fail to spell out what constitutes an increment. Is it a marginal change of 1 percent, 5 percent, 50 percent? A significant percentage change can constitute a major policy shift that can hardly be termed an incremental adjustment.[12]

Finally, the theory of incrementalism turns out to be a creature of its times, the relatively affluent 1960s and 1970s, when fair shares of increments and ploys to protect the base budget appeared to be realistic expectations, at least in the perception of participants. Confident that this relatively stable state of affairs would persist, several analysts, on the basis of some empirical studies, developed theories about determinants of expenditures, which, they claimed, enabled them to forecast expenditures with a negligible margin of error. But, as Premchand reminds us, "after more than three decades of effort, there is as yet no comprehensive theory of public expenditures and their determinants." Too many unpredictable ideological, technical, and economic factors get in the way.[13]

As an explanation of budget decision making, incrementalism, with its emphasis on predictable outcomes, was swamped by an era of austerity, large deficits, expenditure ceilings, cutbacks in base budgets, and changes in fiscal policy.[14] Uncontrollable expenditures narrowed the range of discretion and absorbed most of the funds that might have been used as increments. The hitherto untouchable base budget came under attack.

Are Budget Reforms and Political Decision Making on a Collision Course?

What should we make of the charge that budget reforms are not sufficiently sensitive to the political nature of resource allocations and that they are irrelevant unless they influence budgetary decisions? The impact of budgetary reforms can only be determined on a case-by-case basis. Yet budgetary literature is singularly bereft of such vital data. This serious omission, however, does not inhibit unsupported generalizations. Furthermore, it is difficult to trace the influence of rational analysis on budgetary decisions. Numerous pressures and factors obviously shape the final decisions, including the data generated by reformed budgetary systems. Even if politicians reject recommendations flowing out of such systems, this does not signify a systems breakdown. The important issues and options surface. The significant data are there. Decision makers are aware of the consequences of the road taken or not taken. If they come to the conclusion that political values transcend efficiency values, they still will have utilized meaningfully a system that defines problems, offers a range of choices, and reduces uncertainty. In this sense the process works. Budget reforms in effect today constitute "politically responsive, research oriented, and information-sensitive governmental decision systems." They make possible an interaction of political bargaining and analytic processes and facilitate, but do not guarantee, informed political decisions.[15]

We now come full circle to the issues raised in a classic article by V. O. Key, Jr. in 1940. Key found American budgeting literature "singularly arid" in dealing with "the most significant aspect of public budgeting, i.e. the allocation of expenditures among different purposes so as to achieve the greatest return." No budgetary theory enabled governments to deal with the basic question: "On what basis shall it be decided to allocate X dollars to activity A instead of activity B!'' Ultimately the question comes down to ''value preferences between ends lacking a common denominator.'' In looking for an approach to ''the practical working out of the issue,'' Key suggested ''the canalizing of decisions through the governmental machinery so as to place alternatives in juxtaposition and compel consideration of relative values.''[16] This is precisely what the budgetary reforms seek to achieve.

Notes

1. The reforms are as follows:
   1. The executive budget
   2. Functional budgeting
   3. Program and performance budgeting
   4. Multiyear expenditure projections and budgets
   5. Unified or comprehensive budgets
   6. P.P.B.S. (Planning, Programming, Budgeting System)
   7. Budgeting M.B.O. style (management by objectives)
   8. Productivity budgeting
   9. ZBB (zero-based budgeting)
   10. Budgeting as a tool for economic management (Chapter 8)
   11. Legislative budgeting (Chapter 6) . . .
2. Allen Schick, ''Budgetary Innovations'' in International Monetary Fund, *Budgeting and Expenditure Control,* (Washington, D.C., 1982), p. 91.
3. These are the views of Frederick O'R Hayes, former budget director of New York City, as cited by Schick in ''Budgetary Innovations,'' p. 98.
4. For an excellent summary of the views and writings of Tarschys see Daniel Tarschys, ''Rational Decremental Budgeting: Elements of An Expenditure Policy for the 80's,'' *Political Life in Sweden* (New York: Swedish Information Service, February 1982), pp. 1–8. See also Tarschys, ''From Expansion to Restraint: Recent Developments in Budgeting,'' *Public Budgeting and Finance,* Vol. 6, No. 3 (Autumn 1986), pp. 25–37.

5. Wildavsky, *The Politics of the Budgetary Process,* 3rd edition (Boston: Little, Brown and Co., 1979), pp. 6–62.
6. Aaron Wildavsky, ''Political Implications of Budgetary Reform in Allen Schick, ed., *Perspectives on Budgeting,* (Washington, D.C.: American Society for Public Administration, 1981), p. 72.
7. Aaron Wildavsky, ''A Budget for all Seasons? Why the Traditional Budget Lasts,'' *Public Administration Review,* Vol. 38, No. 6 (November/December 1978), pp. 501-505.
8. Schick, ''Budgetary Innovations,'' pp. 100–106.
9. Ibid, p. 95.
10. Allen Schick, ''Macro-Budgetary Adaptations to Fiscal Stress in Industrialized Democracies,'' *Public Administration Review,* Vol. 46, No. 2 (March/April 1986), p. 124.
11. William Gorham, ''Sharpening the Knife that Cuts the Public Pie,'' *Public Administration Review:* Vol. 28, No. 3 (May/June 1968), p. 207.
12. John J. Bailey and Robert J. O'Connor, ''Operationalizing Incrementalism: Measuring the Muddle,'' *Public Administration Review,* Vol. 31, No. 1 (January/February 1971), pp. 60–66.
13. A. Premchand, ''Government Budget Reforms: Agenda for the 1980's,'' *Public Budgeting and Finance,* Vol. 1, No. 3 (Autumn 1981), p. 20.
14. Barry Bozeman and Jeffrey D. Straussman, ''Shrinking Budgets and the Shrinkage of Budget Theory,'' *Public Administration Review,* Vol. 42, No. 6 (November/December 1982), pp. 509–515; John R. Gist, ''Increment and 'Base' in the Congressional Appropriations Process,'' *American Journal of Political Science,* Vol. 21 (May 1977), pp. 341–352.
15. Robert J. Mowitz, *The Design of Public Decision Systems* (Baltimore: University Park Press, 1980), pp. 56–59; see also John D. Young, ''Reflections on the Executive Budgetary Process'' (Paper presented at Maxwell School, Syracuse University, April 10, 1974).
16. V. O. Key, Jr., ''The Lack of a Budgetary Theory'' in Albert C. Hyde and Jay M. Shafritz, eds., *Government Budgeting: Theory, Process, Politics* (Oak Park, Il.: Moore Publishing Co., Inc., 1978), pp. 18–23.

V

Closing Perspectives on Budgetary Politics

The United States government's program for arriving at a budget is about the most irresponsible, Mickey Mouse arrangement that any governmental body has ever practiced.

Ronald Reagan, 1982

This closing section finishes with two summary perspectives on budgeting theory, process, and politics by the field's most significant theorists: Allen Schick and Aaron Wildavsky. Neither requires any introduction to the serious student of public administration. Their writings have served to define and direct public budgeting as a field of study for more than three decades.

The objective of this last section is to present some comparisons. First, there is Schick's discussion of incrementalism in his 1983 article, "Incremental Budgeting in a Decremental Age." Schick has devoted most of his research in the 1980s to the congressional budgeting process, but his review of the theory of budget behavior in positive and negative fiscal environments provides the most fitting closing for this book's purposes. Schick provides his own warnings about the current political–economic environment: "The budget cannot make order out of chaos, it cannot bring concord where there is unlimited strife."

Aaron Wildavsky provides a perfect contrast in "The Politics in Budget Reform," the conclusion to his 1988 revision of *The New Politics of the Budget Process*. In addition to his thoughts about incrementalism in budgeting, he examines line-item vetoes, balanced budget limitations, and deficit-reduction legislation. As always, he reminds the field of its limitations— politics must lead. As he warns on his last page, "Budgeting is a forum for the exercise of political power, not a substitute for that power."

Following this section is a three-part appendix. Appendix A contains the appropriately titled chapters "The Federal Budget as a Second Language" and "Overview: The Gramm-Rudman-Hollings Budget Process" from Stanley Collender's invaluable annual reference work, *The Guide to the Federal Budget*. Appendix B has excerpts from the now infamous 1991 federal budget: "The Budget Message of the President" and the "Director's Introduction to the New Budget." Appendix C is the CRS (Congressional Research Service) Report for Congress by Edward Davis and Robert Keith, which summarizes the major provisions of "Budget Enforcement Act of 1990."

37
Incremental Budgeting in a Decremental Age

Allen Schick
University of Maryland

For almost two decades (since the publication of Wildavsky's *The Politics of the Budgetary Process*), incrementalism has been the preeminent theory of budgeting. It is the leading explanation of how the budget process works, and for many scholars and participants, it is also a prescription for how the process should work. For some, incrementalism is simply a statement of the fact that most programs and expenditures—the "base"—escape serious review:

> Budgeting is incremental, not comprehensive. The beginning of wisdom about an agency budget is that it is almost never reviewed as a whole each year. . . . Instead it is based on last year's budget with special attention given to a narrow range of increases or decreases.[1]

But incrementalism's hold on budgeting stems more from its normative claims than from its factual basis. Wildavsky has forcefully argued that a process which concentrates on the increment is preferable to one that attempts to review the whole budget because it moderates conflict, reduces search costs, stabilizes budgetary roles and expectations, reduces the amount of time that busy officials must invest in budgeting, and increases the likelihood that important political values will be taken into account.

Incrementalism depends on increments, that is, on an increase in the resources available for distribution through the budget process. These increments can come from economic growth or from an enlargement in the relative size of the public sector; they cannot come from the redistribution of resources among government programs. Redistribution means that some budgets must shrink so that others may grow. A process that leads to this outcome must concentrate at least as much on the base as it does on the increment.

Source: Policy Sciences (Amsterdam: Elsevier Science Publishers B.V., 1983), pp. 1–25. Reprinted by permission of Kluwer Academic Publishers.

Incrementalism came of age during an era of economic growth and governmental expansion that extended (with some interruptions) from the late 1940s until the late 1970s. But because the U.S. economy has been stagnant in recent years and the Reagan Administration has sought to curtail the relative size of the federal government, federal budgeting has become decremental. There have been cutbacks (some of them severe) in many domestic programs and, with the exception of defense and some favored programs, budgetary attention during the early 1980s has been focused on the base rather than on increments. Arguably, therefore, the theory of incrementalism has to be discarded, or at the very least modified to suit the new realities.

This article considers how budgeting might be altered if it lacks increments. Does decrementalism require a new politics of budgeting that is not anchored in incremental norms? What happens to the base when budgeting is redistributive rather than distributive? Has budgeting become so dependent upon growth that it cannot adapt to cutbacks? Can there be budgeting if it is not incremental budgeting?

One possible conclusion is that nothing needs to be changed, that the key to incrementalism is that only a small portion of the budget is examined and that it does not matter whether this portion is from the base or from an increment. In this view, it would be just as incremental to make small cuts in the base as it is to budget for marginal increases. But this approach turns incrementalism into marginal analysis, which is a rather different form of behavior than budgeting for expansion. The term "incrementalism" itself promises budgetary growth and most of the literature on this subject is oriented to program and expenditure increases. Statistical analyses of incremental outcomes typically measure the amounts and rates of increase; descriptive studies concentrate on the tactics used to augment the base.

What happens if growth is not possible? Answers are not easy to come by because incrementalism is an extraordinarily elastic and elusive concept. It can be made to fit just about every budgetary circumstance. When expenditure trends for particular activities and projects were shown to include budgetary decreases, the concept was reformulated into one that deals with total spending by agencies, so that incrementalism could coexist with declines in particular programs.[2] When big dollar shifts were shown to occur in some agency budgets, incrementalism was redefined in terms of "the regularity or irregularity of the change in size, not the absolute amount of the changes themselves."[3]

If the size of change is not an appropriate yardstick, then incrementalism can be stretched to cover most budgetary outcomes. A two percent annual growth rate would be deemed incremental; so, too, might a fifteen percent annual increase. Fundamental shifts in the relative size of programs can be defined as incremental. If two programs were of equal size in 1970, a decade later the one with fifteen percent annual increments would be almost four times larger than the program that had two percent growth rates.

Incrementalism says more about what budgeting is not—and cannot be—than about what budgeting is. It asserts that budget makers cannot reexamine every item in the budget every year. They cannot pit all programs against one another in a competition for scarce funds. They cannot canvass all the options that might merit consideration. They cannot look much beyond the next budget to gauge the effects of current decisions on future programs.

To do these things would overload the budget process, require more data and calculations than can be handled in the time available for preparing the budget, and would open intractable conflicts over money. So rather than being "rational" and comprehensive, budget makers are incremental. But within the broad expanse of the increment, incrementalism offers little explanation as to how decisions are made. It does not deal with how the increment is divided, with "who gets what" which Wildavsky pinpointed as the all-important issue in budgeting.[4] It does not explain why some programs grow more than others, and why shares in the budget change over time. It does not explain why spending increases are big in some years but small in others. It says very little about budget outcomes, other than that they are incremental. It cannot explain, for example, why defense spending slipped from approximately 50 percent of the national budget in 1960 to only about 25 percent in 1980, why real spending on defense declined for eight consecutive years in the 1970s, but now seems likely to grow for eight or more consecutive years. It cannot explain why some programs have gained protection as entitlements while others have remained vulnerable to discretionary budget reductions.

Incrementalism is an appealing but puzzling concept. It has more to say about the base than about the increment. Incrementalism is a label for an idea that has not been adequately developed into a theory. An incremental theory of budgeting would have to be much more than a trendline of government spending or a repertoire of the games budget makers play. It would have to be a theory about budget growth, and it would apply therefore only to those periods when expenditures increase.

The Politics of Budgetary Growth

If one is unsure of what incrementalism is, how can one consider the changes that might emerge during a period of cutbacks? The approach proposed here is to conceive of incrementalism as a pattern of behavior associated with budget growth, and then to consider how the pattern might be affected by the lack of increments.

Incrementalism is a pattern of budgetary behavior in which continued growth is taken for granted. It is not just a mechanistic process in which spending agencies ask for and get more money. In an incremental environment, budgeting becomes an engine of expansion, a means of providing larger allocations in the next budget than there are in the current one. When incrementalism flourishes, growth is seen as legitimate, not as something that occurs because spending agencies outmaneuver budget officials. Indeed, the whole process of budgeting is oriented to produce expansionary outcomes. Everybody behaves in a growth-oriented manner, even those whose job it is to constrain agency spending appetites.

This incremental mood was effectively captured by Maurice Wright in an introduction to a collection of essays on government spending in the United Kingdom. "Over the period of more than a generation," he observed,

> the assumption of growth has become written into the structure and processes of local and central government. . . . Uniformity of provision becomes the organizing principle, and consensus rather than conflict prevails. The building of that consensus is helped by the increased scope for bargaining which the expectation of annual increments provides. With time, it is assumed that resources will be available; the principle task of allocation is one of ordering developments over time. Choice is less concerned with the alternative use of resources than with timing.[5]

The expectation of growth prevailed until recently in the United States and in most industrialized countries, at the national level, as well as in most states and localities. But this was not always the dominant expectation in budgeting. Modern budgeting began in a pre-incremental era; its overriding objective was to constrain public spending. This was the purpose of the national budget system installed in 1921 and effectively implemented during the 1920s, a decade during which federal expenditures, taxes, and the public debt were reduced. The job of the new Budget Bureau was to monitor agency finances and to intervene as it deemed necessary to prevent excessive or improper expenditure. Centralized control reached to the particulars of agency expenditures; just about everything that cost money required advance approval from the budget office.

The successful implementation of budget control was not solely the result of a tough anti-spending attitude in the Bureau of the Budget. Equally important was acceptance in Congress and other political quarters of the view that federal expenditures should be curbed. The Budget Bureau, supported by the President, promoted this attitude by sponsoring economy drives and other activities that emphasized the virtues of saving public money.

The most important feature of pre-incremental budgeting was the perceived legitimacy of spending control. Congress understood that it had to be denied budgetary information to facilitate budget control and it did not complain when appropriated funds were not spent. Agencies generally requested annual budget increases, but they did not mount aggressive campaigns to circumvent the new controls.

There were some exceptions to the prevailing parsimony, notably in expenditures for roads, post offices, and other public works, where pressure for more money was intense and where Congress was an active and effective advocate for higher spending. Generally, however, budgeting was the routine business of estimating next year's costs of ongoing activities. The base was protected, but there was not much of an increment.

Pre-incremental budgeting was ended by two "revolutions" in American politics: the New Deal before World War II and the "new economics" after the war. Both enlarged the scope of the federal government, the first by giving it new tasks, the second by giving it new resources. The New Deal did more than enlarge the federal government; it changed public attitudes toward public expenditure and paved the way for the development of active and expansionist policies. What started as a response to economic crisis came over time to be perceived as a legitimate role of government in enhancing the quality of life by providing tangible benefits and services to the American people. Through public expenditure, homes could be built, land reclaimed, health care improved.

In an era of positive government, budgeting could not persist as the process that held the spenders at bay. Budgeting was transformed into an annual opportunity for buying public goods with public funds. Agency budgets were permitted to grow, not because of bureaucratic avarice or waste but because benefits were deemed to accrue from public expenditure. Spending money became legitimate, and the budget process encouraged agencies to ask for more.

Inevitably, the techniques of budgeting were adjusted to promote incremental outcomes, but changes in budgetary expectations were much more significant. The budget came to be seen as an opportunity for agencies to ask for more money and for central officials to give them more. When incrementalism reached its peak in the postwar era, it became customary for chief executives at all levels of American government to point to increased spending as a measure of the benefits they were providing through the budget. More money in the budget for education was offered as prima facie evidence that more education was to be provided. More for roads, more for parks, more for hospitals, these were the fruits of budgetary incrementalism.

If chief executives changed their attitudes, so, too, did the budget officials who worked for them. The central budget agency loosened its financial controls and embraced a positive role in the development and management of public programs. The U.S. Bureau of the Budget became less concerned with inputs and more with outputs; its job during an expansionary period was to improve programs, not to starve them. The Bureau continued to trim budget requests (after all, agencies became even more ambitious in their budget demands) but it also granted big increases. Although they did not get all that they asked for, agencies were confident that their budgets would grow from year to year.

The Budget Bureau's adaptation to incremental expectations has been perceptively described by

Philip S. Hughes who rose up the ranks to become its highest career official:

> It's very hard for me to say that, you know, on ''x'' date we had a philosophical change. I'm sure the historians will describe it that way at some point, but I'm too much in the trees to see the forest in that kind of perspective. Over the years, and I think it started in the middle of the later part of the Eisenhower Administration, the role of the Bureau has changed somewhat; as government grew, as it did in the Eisenhower Administration and subsequently, the Bureau has acquired a programming role that it did not have, at least to the same extent, before. The problem of choice among the programs has become increasingly important. And perhaps, to some extent the negative role of the Bureau has become less important, at least in relative terms. . . . In the old days, speaking in very oversimplified terms, our initial answer was supposed to be no and everybody would have been surprised if we said yes the first time around. As time has passed, we're supposed to do something a little different than that. We can say no, perhaps in a fairly high percentage of cases, but in some of the more crucial ones we're supposed to give pretty serious consideration to alternative and better ways of accomplishing an objective which the President or an agency head or a member of the majority party in the Congress thinks is a desirable objective.[6]

In the decade before World War II, there was no systematic change in budget procedure, but some innovations were harbingers of the more fundamental reforms attempted in the 1950s and 1960s. In the 1920s, the budget was a ''book of estimates'' with column after column of line item detail; in the 1930s, the Budget Bureau clothed the numbers in words that explained what the funds were to be used for. By the analytic standards of the 1960s, the narrative descriptions were of little value, but they were among the earliest efforts to reorient the federal budget from inputs to outputs. A related development was the measurement of the outputs to be produced by public expenditure. These workload and (in some agencies) unit cost measurements were forerunners of postwar performance budgets.

As federal expenditures soared, line items receded in importance and were consolidated into broad expense categories. The line item details were useful for cutting budgets, but now that growth was the order of the day emphasis shifted to functional classifications. These were used mostly for display, not for making budget decisions. After the war, program budgeting tried to convert these into decisional categories.

The language of budgeting adapted to incremental aspirations. What once were called ''estimates'' now were termed ''requests,'' signaling a more active and ambitious search for funds by government agencies. The term ''deficiency appropriation'' faded from use; additional funds were provided in ''supplemental appropriations,'' a term that suggests growth rather than failure. Over time, supplementals came to be regular features of the annual budget cycle, as expected as the regular appropriation bills.

A revealing indication of changed attitudes toward public expenditure was the emergence of impoundment disputes between Congress and the President. Although impoundment dates back to the early years of American nationhood, the word was hardly used before the 1940s and it was not until the postwar heyday of incrementalism that impoundment became a persistent issue in legislative–executive relations. Impoundment was not a new practice, but a new attitude toward an old practice. The difference was that while appropriations were once understood to be limitations on expenditure, in an incremental age they also were seen as mandates to spend.

The second ''revolution'' was the use of the budget as an instrument of fiscal policy. Economic growth and government growth went hand in hand; the public economy could grow because the private one also would grow. Indeed, during slack times, public expansion would sustain economic growth, bringing high employment without inflation. Active fiscal policy would make everybody into winners. Government could provide more programs without raising taxes and without shifting productive resources from the private to the public sector.

Economic growth would resolve a chronic contradiction in American public opinion. Over several decades, public opinion polls have shown most Americans to be of two minds about the size and services of government. Since the New Deal, a majority has wanted the federal government to continue (and in some cases) to increase its services; yet most Americans favor balanced budgets, lower taxes, and smaller government.[7]

Economic growth offered a convenient way out of this attitudinal quandary. Government would expand, not by taking from the disposable incomes of Americans but from the growth dividends of a buoyant economy. As a consequence, economic growth was seen as a costless pro bono policy which would benefit everybody.

In the postwar era, budgeting became incremental because the economy was incremental. Real GNP grew an average of four percent a year in the 1950s and 4.2 percent a year in the 1960s. Disposable personal income doubled during these postwar decades. Unemployment averaged about 4.5 percent, only slightly above the four percent "full employment" target, while inflation (as measured by the GNP deflator) was at a 2.5 percent annual rate.

Table 1 shows the growth of GNP and budget outlays in five-year averages since 1950. During the first fifteen years covered by the Table, outlay increases were virtually matched by economic expansion. As the economy expanded, federal receipts grew (though Congress periodically lowered the income tax rates) and provided incremental resources for program and spending increases. Yet budget outlays were about the same percentage of GNP in 1965 as they were ten or fifteen years earlier (see Table 4). Moreover, federal income taxes were fairly stable as a percentage of personal income. In sum, budget incrementalism was financed by an expanding economy, not by transfers from the private to the federal sector.

With the economy providing abundant resources for enlarging the public sector, budgeting could be a distributive process in which the federal government allocated increments to claimants. Since the increments were ample, agencies did not have to compete against one another for scarce resources;

each had its turn at the public trough. Agencies did not get all that they wanted, but virtually all got more than they had the year before. Because it was assumed that all claimants benefitted from the process, there was little inclination to examine the outcomes to determine who got what. As long as the process was incremental, incrementalists were certain that the outcomes were the right ones.

Adapting to Incrementalism

Incrementalism brought much more than bigger budgets; it changed budgeting. For government expenditures to grow, it was necessary that the behavior and expectations of participants be altered, that techniques adapt to the new opportunities, and that budgeting be more open to political influence. As it adapted to incrementalism, budgeting became more dependent on the availability of increments.

Role of the Budget Bureau

As discussed above, the Bureau of the Budget (and budget offices in many states and localities) adopted a more positive attitude toward public expenditure. It deemphasized the control of expenditure details and concentrated instead on the "big" issues—the performance of the economy and development of the President's program. As custodian of the increment, it had a major role in determining which programs would grow and by how much.

But it now had powerful rivals in the budgetary arena. As long as its mission was to control spending, the Bureau had a role that no other participant could fill. No other central unit had the skill, determination, and perspective to guard the treasury. However, once its role shifted to economic and program planning, the Bureau faced stiff competition from economic experts and program advocates. The President's economic and policy staffs devoted their full energies to the increment, the former urging active fiscal policy to generate it, the latter generating good ideas for spending it. These good ideas were not constrained by the size of the increment, and it was difficult for the Bureau to resist proposals that spent future increments before they became available. Economic growth became essential for financing past commitments, not just for making new ones.

The Bureau's attitudinal change was an adjustment to competition for presidential attention. It could not

Table 1
Growth in GNP and budget outlays
(% change over preceding 5-year period)

Period	GNP (%)	Outlays (%)
1955–1959	29.6	28.7
1960–1964	28.5	35.1
1965–1969	43.6	47.1
1970–1974	48.1	49.3
1975–1979	61.8	76.3
1980–1983 (est.)	58.3	77.2

The GNP data are for calendar years; the outlay data are for fiscal years. The 1982 GNP data are preliminary; the 1983 and 1984 GNP and outlay data are estimates.

rebuff White House task forces merely by saying "No" to their plans for a better tomorrow; after all, these plans were the stuff that presidential dreams were made of. The Bureau wanted to show the President that it, too, could think positively, but it could not compete merely by outpromising the program advocates. It knew that although resources were expanding, they were not unlimited and that if all the new ideas were implemented, their cost would exceed available resources. Its solution was the abortive planning-programming-budgeting system (PPB). Through PPB, it was hoped, the federal government would plan new programs but still live within its budget.

The relationship between the Budget Bureau and spending agencies also was affected by incrementalism. Agencies became more vigorous (and successful) in pressing their claims for larger budget shares. The relationship became more a matter of bargaining, and less one in which higher authority dictated the outcome. The agencies brought two material advantages to the bargaining table: they had programs which the President wanted, and they could call on interest groups and program beneficiaries for support.

Opening Up the Budget Process

In budgeting, the most effective expenditure control is the inhibition, not the rejection, of demands. What agencies do not ask for, they usually do not get; if they persistently demand increases, they are likely to get them, perhaps not right away or all at once, but over time the more demanding the spenders are, the more they get to spend.

Demand is the seedbed of budgetary growth and is, in turn, a function of expectations about the prospect for growth. Agencies request more when they expect incremental resources to be available. But their assertiveness also is a function of the pressures they face from program beneficiaries. The greater the pressure, the more they ask for. In pre-incremental budgeting, demand was inhibited by closing the budget process to outsiders. Little was known about the next budget until it was released, at which time it was too late to influence the recommendations in it. Section 206 of the Budget and Accounting Act barred agencies from going directly to Congress with their budget requests and the Budget Bureau backed this up with tough restrictions on the release of agency requests. When they appeared before congressional committees, agencies had to

defend the President's recommendations, not their own demands, and though there were occasional breaches, this rule usually was adhered to. Agencies had permanent authorizations; hence, congressional budget activity usually was limited to the appropriations committees which acted on the budget behind closed doors. Floor amendments were discouraged, and most appropriations were below the President's request.

Outside pressure also was inhibited by a lack of understanding about the numbers in the budget. The line item details obscured the program implications of the budget and made it easier to cut spending without stirring up opposition. There were few outside analyses of the budget, and few outside budget watchers.

Incrementalism opened up the budget process by encouraging the demand for increases. With resources available and spending considered a welcome stimulus to the economy, it no longer was deemed essential to veil knowledge of the budget and to limit participation on decisions about it to a small circle of executive and legislative leaders. Agencies became more adept at disclosing their real preferences without violating the rules, and congressmen became more vigorous in prying the information from them. Program information in the budget made it easier for interest groups to know what was in it for them, and independent analyses increased though it was not until the 1970s that these became widely available.

Budgeting also became more open in Congress, as many authorizing committees gained budgetary influence by providing temporary (rather than permanent) authorizations and by specifying dollar amounts in legislation. Some muscled their way into the budget process by resorting to "backdoor spending" schemes that evaded the regular appropriation controls. Pressure on appropriations also came from an increase in the number of floor amendments and by the spread of budgetary competence and information on Capitol Hill. Committees expanded their staffs and began to take a more active interest in budgetary matters.

The appropriations committees responded to the pressures by relaxing their spending controls. This entailed little adjustment in the Senate where the appropriations committee functioned as a "court of appeals," but the House Appropriations Committee was induced to significantly adjust its role, though it continued to claim success in cutting the President's budget.[8]

Transforming the Budget

The interest and involvement of outsiders in the budget process was stimulated by the transformation of the federal budget from a mechanism for financing the operations of government agencies into a source of funds for various outsiders.

During the pre-incremental era, the federal government operated a simple two stage expenditure process. First, Congress voted appropriations for agencies; then the agencies spent these funds on their own operations—paying the salaries of employees, purchasing supplies and equipment, and paying for the many other goods and services consumed in everyday activities. The budget was essentially an accounting for what happened inside government and, understandably therefore, the demand for information by outsiders was limited.

This simple budget structure no longer prevails. Nowadays, the budget is dominated by transfers from government to "third" parties. Most of the federal budget goes to contractors, state and local governments, and recipients of transfer payments. In place of the two-stage budget process, there now is a third state in which appropriations nominally made to public agencies are disbursed to parties on the margins of government. More than three quarters of the federal budget is spent in this manner.

Table 2 shows how the composition of the federal budget (in the national income and products account) has changed during the past quarter of a century. More than 60 percent of the budget was spent on goods and services in 1958; these purchases now account for only one third of total expenditures. The share of the budget spent on transfer payments doubled during these years, from approximately one-fifth to two-fifths. Grants in aid have had a more volatile record, tripling in relative size between 1958 and 1978, but declining as a share of the budget during the most recent five-year period shown in Table 2.

But more has been changed than the locus of expenditure; the process of demanding government funds has also been altered. The outsiders who receive federal checks are parties to the budget as are federal agencies which submit formal budget requests. The outsiders cannot settle for ignorance in which only privileged insiders know what is happening. Because they have a direct stake in budget outcomes, they make it their business to be involved in the process.

Why did the composition of the federal budget change in the incremental era? Was it because the growth in federal spending made it possible to transfer resources to outsiders without taking them away from government agencies or did pressure for transfers impel the budget to grow? Was incrementalism, in other words, cause or effect in the transformation of the federal budget? It probably was both: the budget would have been much smaller if most of it had continued to be spent by agencies on their own operations; the transfers would have been much smaller if increments were not available to pay for them.

Budgeting for Entitlements

The federal budget was little more than $100 billion when *The Politics of the Budgetary Process* was published in 1956; it is now approaching one

Table 2
Composition of the federal budget
NIPA basis
5-year intervals, 1958–1983

Fiscal Year	Purchase of Goods and Services (%)	Payments to Individuals (%)	Grants to States and Localities (%)
1958	61.7	21.5	5.7
1963	57.0	23.7	7.4
1968	55.2	24.8	10.3
1973	39.5	34.1	15.8
1978	33.4	39.7	16.6
1983 (est.)	33.7	41.3	10.9

Source: Computed from Table B-76, *Economic Report of the President, February 1983.*

trillion dollars. No one can deny that the overall trend has been incremental, but the manner in which the increments have been distributed is not quite the one depicted by Wildavsky. His incremental process is one in which agencies expand their budgets by skillfully protecting and augmenting the base. But the tactics he described have accounted for much less than half of the ensuing growth in federal expenditures. Entitlements rather than agency behavior have been the principal force in driving federal spending upwards.

Entitlements are legal rights to payments from the federal treasury. At present there are approximately 60 entitlement programs adding up to more than $400 billion in expenditure. Most of the entitlements are open ended; their expenditures are not set by the budget but are determined by exogenous factors, principally the number of persons eligible to receive payments. Many are indexed to the consumer price index and their expenses grow automatically during inflationary periods. Entitlements grow even if agencies do not want them to, and even if they eat into the increments (and sometimes the base) that would otherwise be available to agencies.

Entitlements are a byproduct of incrementalism. In an expanding economy, it was deemed responsible to vest outsiders with assured shares in future budgets, and through indexation to fix these shares in real terms. Because economic growth was expected to continue, it was assumed that even after paying for the entitlements incremental resources would be available for discretionary increases in agency budgets. It has not worked out this way, however, which is the main reason for the current budget crisis.

Offbudget Expenditures

During the heyday of incrementalism, not only did the budget grow; so, too, did offbudget expenditures—transactions that are excluded from the budget totals. Offbudget activities include credit guarantees, tax subsidies, the finances of public corporations, and the shifting of costs to private parties through regulation and to other units of government through mandates.

It is widely assumed that offbudget expenditures are responses to tight financial controls such as legal restrictions on total expenditures or on deficits. There is reason to believe, for example, that some states have authorized public corporations to issue revenue bonds to evade debt restrictions in their constitutions.

Nevertheless, it would be erroneous to regard the growth of offbudget expenditures solely as evasions of budget control. During the incremental era, financial control was not very stringent; governments could do and spend as they wanted in the budget without having to evade controls. Moreover, the growth in offbudget expenditure was concurrent with the growth in direct expenditure. The same factors that impelled governments to spend more in the budget gave them license to engage in offbudget practices. Incremental expectations generated a permissive attitude toward the budget. Why worry about the niceties of control when there were resources aplenty to finance public aspirations? Incrementalism invited "creative financing" in which the means for providing for government programs were not limited by the budget.

Budget Innovation

The changes discussed thus far were "natural" adjustments to the incremental expectations that blossomed during the postwar boom. There was no formal decision to change the composition of the federal budget or to open it to outsiders. These and the other changes occurred because of the opportunities made possible by expectations that expenditures and the resources to finance them would grow.

Several innovations were conscious adaptations to incrementalism. Foremost were the efforts to make budgeting more systematic, analytic, and planning oriented: PPB was the most ambitious of these efforts and in some ways the least successful.

Wildavsky regards program budgeting, PPB, and multiyear budgeting as anti-incremental innovations. This interpretation is based on a conception of incrementalism as "small steps" budgeting. Obviously, an innovation that would enlarge the scope of budget decisions from one year to three or more years and would group expenditures into broad program categories would compel budget makers to take bigger steps and might, from this standpoint, be deemed as anti-incremental.

But if incrementalism is interpreted as growth-oriented budgeting, the postwar innovations, including PPB, were very much in accord with the spirit of the times. If they failed, it was in part because budgeting lost its growth increments before the reforms were fully implemented.

Multiyear budgeting was a device for committing future increments. Once it was placed in the plan, a projected expenditure had a preferred claim on future budgets. Planning was an expansionist process, showing the additional accomplishments that would be achieved with additional resources. Similarly, program budgeting was a means of buying objectives in the budget. With ample resources, the budget process would no longer be confined to paying for current activities. It could venturously be deployed as a search for new opportunities to do public good. PPB was conceived as the overall system for linking plans, objectives, and budget decisions.

It did not work out that way because shortly after PPB was introduced governmentwide in 1965, demands on government began to exceed available resources. By the late 1960s, the budget debate was centered around "guns versus butter" and there was growing recognition of the need to "set national priorities." Although incremental aspirations lingered for a number of years (and still have not been fully extinguished) in the 1970s, budgeting became preoccupied with limitations, not with the opportunities for growth. The market for growth-oriented budget innovation dried up.

From Growth to Limitation

What went wrong? The conventional widsom is that the U.S. economy was stagnant during the 1970s. It was wracked by two oil shocks and three recessions, by stagflation (high inflation and high unemployment), and by low productivity. Table 3 displays the GNP and productivity changes during the postwar era. Note the sustained high levels of

growth during the 1950s and 1960s and the lower growth rate in the 1970s. The same pattern appears in the data for productivity improvement. Productivity grew during the 1970s at only half the rate that it did in the two preceding decades. If the economy had grown as much in the 1970s as it had in the two preceding decades, the relative size of the federal government would have been stable.

But this is not the whole explanation. It is important to recall that the economy did expand during that troubled decade. Per capita real disposable income was 25 percent higher at the end of the decade than at the start. There were twenty million more workers in 1980 than in 1970. Indeed, the U.S. work force increased as much during those ten years as it did in the preceding twenty.

However, the economy did not grow fast enough to accommodate the demands on the budget. While the economy had three percent annual growth, the federal budget was growing at a four percent rate. Although the difference between these growth rates seems small, over the course of the decade it impelled a substantial shift in resources from the private sector as well as big and persistent deficits.

Inevitably, the budget reflected the shortfall in the economy. Receipts and expenditures edged upwards as percentages of national output. Table 4 shows that during the 1955–65 years, expenditures averaged less than nineteen percent of GNP; the average was twenty percent during the next ten years. Since 1980, federal outlays have accounted for approximately 23 percent of the national economy. Although federal receipts increased, they could not keep pace with soaring expenditures and, as a result, the deficit grew to more than three percent of the GNP in the post-1970 period, compared to only one percent in the previous decade.

Table 3
GNP growth and productivity, 1950–1982

Period	Average Annual Change in Real (1972 Dollars) GNP (%)	Average Annual Change in Productivity (%)
1950–1954	4.7	3.7
1955–1959	3.2	2.8
1960–1964	4.0	3.3
1965–1969	4.4	2.5
1970–1974	2.8	1.6
1975–1979	3.3	1.5
1980–1982	–0.1	0.5

Source: Economic Report of the President.

Table 4
Budget outlays as a percent of GNP:
5-year averages

Period	GNP (%)
1955–1959	18.3
1960–1964	19.3
1965–1969	19.7
1970–1974	20.0
1975–1979	21.6
1980–1983	23.6

Source: Budget of the United States Government.

The first waves of economic weakness did not uproot incremental expectations. In accord with Keynesian precepts, it was deemed appropriate to budget according to the potential of the economy. As a result, deficits per se did not mean that the budget was "tight"; quite the opposite, the deficit was the amount added to increments provided by the economy. The bigger the deficit, the more there was to spend.

This attitude was based on the expectation that deficits were cyclical rather than structural, due, that is, to fluctuations in economic performance, not to the failure of government to live within its means. But as deficits became chronic, it became apparent that though their size varied with economic performance, they persisted in good times as in bad. One reason for this was that the bad times were worse than in earlier postwar recessions and the good times were not as robust as they had been in earlier recoveries. Real GNP grew about three percent in the 1970s, not enough to keep down the unemployment rate which averaged more than six percent during the decade. The inflation rate was even higher—about 7.5 percent during the 1970s.

When recovery proved to be weak and short lived and inflation and unemployment climbed concurrently, reexamination of budget policy became an urgent task.

But not an easy one. Incrementalism had its own momentum and could not be slowed down because the economy was sluggish. The budget process was programmed for growth, and it could not easily adapt to the changed circumstances. The adjustments in the process that made so much sense when incremental aspirations were dominant could not be quickly undone when the increments vanished. By the end of the 1970s, the budget was much more open and vulnerable to pressure than it had been a decade or two earlier. Data and analyses were widely available, and recipients of federal dollars were vigilant and aggressive in protecting their shares. They were much better informed than in the past as to the spending increases necessary to protect their programs against inflation; hence, the "fiscal illusion" that once made it possible to cut programs while providing additional funds no longer worked to the advantage of budget makers.

They lost something far more important, however: the capacity to decide how much the budget should grow and what the additional funds should be spent on. Budget increases came to be more the product of past decisions than of new ones; the automatic growth built into the budget during the incremental age continued when the increment was gone. Between 1967 (the first year for which comparable data are available) and 1980, the outlays classified as "uncontrollable under existing law" rose from less than 60 percent to more than 75 percent of total spending. In fiscal 1980, federal spending was $483 billion more than it was in 1970, but approximately 85 percent of this huge increase was in uncontrollable programs, mainly open-ended entitlements. The entitlements and indexation that made sense during good times had even more influence on budgetary outcomes during bad times. The budget was programmed to spend the increments it no longer had.

Adjusting to Economic Adversity

Just as it once adjusted to economic growth, budgeting is now adjusting to economic adversity. It does not suffice that government officials want to spend less, though this is an essential condition; what is also required is that the budget process be deprogrammed of its incremental biases and that it be oriented to providing less rather than more. Demands have to be nipped in the bud before they can blossom into inexorable claims on the budget; advocates must have diminished expectations of what they will get; fiscal controls must be strengthened.

One obvious option is not available to contemporary budget makers: return to pre-incremental control in which budget officials guard the purse and suppress demands for spending increases. The federal government has grown too large and diversified to be unilaterally controlled by a central staff; agencies and beneficiaries have become too resourceful to permit their program ambitions to be crushed by central controllers. If the federal government will not shrink to its pre–New Deal role, neither can its budget process revert to pre-incremental control.

Another possibility would be to compensate for inadequate growth by raising effective tax rates. Taxes rates are much lower in the United States than in most industrialized countries; it should be possible, therefore, to narrow the gap between incremental demands and incremental resources by extracting more from taxpayers. To a certain extent, this has happened in recent years. Social security taxes have been substantially increased, and income tax rates have been pushed upward by "bracket creep." But economic adversity has been accompanied by pressure to cut taxes. In the face of huge deficits, Congress voted a tax cut in 1981 that pared an estimated $750 billion from federal revenues over a three-year period. Although some "supply siders" asserted that, by stimulating the economy, the tax reduction would lead to higher receipts in the future, this was not the winning argument. A more compelling reason was that by curtailing the growth in federal revenues, the tax reductions would inhibit the growth in federal expenditures. The response to the deficit and economic adversity was to deprive the federal government of incremental revenues. The deficit might be larger, but total spending would be less.

This line of reasoning was a byproduct of the decline in economic growth. When the economy was robust, the public sector could grow because the private purse also was enriched; take-home pay and government revenues both rose during the incremental years. But when the economy stagnated, private income declined. According to OECD statistics, per capita aftertax wages in the United States grew about 1.5 percent annually during the 1960–73 period, but declined at a 1.9 percent rate during the 1973–75 years.[9] The first oil shock was the seedbed for the taxpayer revolts that afflicted American governments later in the decade.

It could be argued that the principal reaction to economic problems was bigger budgets and bigger deficits. Federal spending grew at about seventeen percent annually during the 1975–81 years, approximately double the growth rate during the previous quarter of a century. Deficits averaged three percent of GNP during the 1975–81 period, twice the percentage of the preceding decade. By borrowing more and spending more, the government lessened the need for cutbacks. The economy did not supply increments, but the government behaved as if it still had them.

Yet these statistics mask a real adjustment to the economic crisis. Federal budgeting has become decremental with some notable exceptions such as defense spending. In constant dollars, federal grants to state and local governments (excluding those passed through as payments to individuals) declined six percent between 1978 and 1981, spending on the direct operations of the federal government (the costs of running domestic federal agencies) had a real

decline of 3.2 percent.[10] Despite these reductions, federal spending has continued to rise because of higher interest payments (due to big deficits and high interest rates), increased defense spending, and the programmed rise in entitlement programs. Real expenditures for all the rest of the federal budget declined from $63 billion (in 1972 dollars) during fiscal 1978 to an estimated $47 billion in the 1983 fiscal year.

The adjustment to economic circumstances has been incomplete. Some areas of the budget continue to grow while others shrink. As a result, budgeting has become redistributive, taking from some areas and giving to others. The changes in budgetary behavior that have accompanied the shift to decremental, redistributive budgeting are discussed below.

Changing Budgetary Expectations

I have already suggested that expectations drive budgets. To slow down or reverse budgetary growth, it is essential that budget participants come to expect less in the future than they received in the past.

The Reagan Administration's efforts to curtail domestic spending have altered some budgetary expectations. By retrenching social programs, the President has induced advocates for some programs to "think smaller." Their immediate objective has become damage limitation, not program enlargement, and they now count it as a victory if they hold down the amount of reduction, even if they end up with less than they had the previous year. Reagan's campaign has necessarily had a multiyear framework because expectations cannot be effectively changed in a single budget cycle. If they have a bad budget (which can occur in good times) agencies can adopt a "wait till next year" outlook. Reagan made it clear that shrinkage was a long-term prospect, not just a one year dip, and that he would maintain pressure on future budgets.

It is too early to tell whether incremental expectations have been uprooted or merely submerged. There might be a resurgence of growth expectations if the economy improves or if political conditions change. The next president might revert to the incremental ways that prevailed in the postwar era.

Changing Budgetary Relationships

Reorienting the budget process from growth to limitation cannot occur without realignment of the relationships between the President and Congress and between OMB and executive agencies.

It is commonly assumed that the President is parsimonious and that Congress is spendthrift. In the age of incrementalism, all political organs promoted budgetary expansion. Nevertheless, it is easier for the President to adjust to fiscal stringency. The legislative branch is more exposed to budgetary pressures; it is more heterogeneous and ambivalent. It mirrors America's budgetary contradictions: it wants to spend less and to provide more benefits. In coping with this contradiction, Congress has become adept at expanding programs, even as it claims to be cutting expenditures.

If the President want to constrain spending, he cannot prevail by veto alone. The veto is a clumsy, weak weapon which Congress can resist by attaching spending additions to ''must'' veto-proof legislation. What Reagan needed was not a veto to strike down additional spending, but congressional acceptance of less spending. To the extent that he succeeded, it was due to his enormous political skills, Republican capture of the Senate, his willingness to make the budget the primary political issue, and adroit use of congressional budget procedures.[11] The last of these warrants discussion because it portends a change in budgetary relationships.

During the early years of the congressional budget process, Congress adopted a number of ''escapist'' budget resolutions. The spending totals in these resolutions were based on assumptions that Congress would approve legislation curtailing various programs. The assumed savings were listed in the reports of the budget committees but were not voted upon by the House or Senate. After the resolution was adopted, legislation to implement the savings was bottled up in committees which had no intention of cutting back on programs that they had sponsored. Congress accommodated to its inaction by raising the spending levels in later budget resolutions.

The ''legislative savings'' game led Congress to apply a reconciliation procedure by means of which committees are instructed to report legislation implementing the changes assumed in the budget resolution.[12] Reconciliation was first applied in 1980 and was substantially expanded in 1981 when the White House pressured Congress to enact massive spending reductions. Through reconciliation, Reagan won passage of more than $100 billion (over a three-year period) in such reductions. Reconciliation forced Congress to vote on the President's demand in a single package, and it thus enabled him to overcome the delays, fragmentations, and evasions that often hobble the chief executive in dealing with the legislative branch. But it remains to be seen whether reconciliation will be a lasting feature of the budget process and whether it will alter presidential-congressional relationships.

The relationship between the budget office and spending agencies also was affected by the cutback mood. During the growth era, OMB permitted agencies to ask for as much as they wanted and to search for program initiatives. It even generated its own ideas for spending money. In a decremental period, OMB cannot simply react to agency spending demands; it must close off pressures for more money before they become irresistible. It must push for spending reductions, for it cannot expect these to well up from the agencies. Most importantly, it must create an expectation that the budget will lead to lower spending. These tasks were undertaken by David Stockman, OMB's ambitious budget director during the first months of the Reagan Administration. Stockman put OMB's stamp on the budget approved by Congress. Unlike the incremental budgets, this one was made by the budget office, not by the spending agencies or by White House planners.

Decremental Budgeting

If incrementalism is defined simply as "small steps" budgeting, cutting expenditures is not very different from increasing them. Most budget reductions are at the margins—a little less rather than a little more. Budget cutting concentrates on what is cuttable. Some of the methods are quite familiar and include postponement (or elimination) of capital investments and maintenance, control of various line items (salary increases, travel, filling of vacancies) and across the board cuts.

In analyzing the effects of these convenient techniques, a distinction must be drawn between one-time and repeated use. The first time its budget is shaved a couple of percentage points by an across the board reduction, an affected agency probably can continue "business as usual." It can find some economies that allow it to hold on to programs (and personnel) while adhering to the spending ceiling. But if the constraint is applied year after year, it is likely to force changes in budgetary behavior. What is true of incremental budgeting applies to decremental budgeting as well: small steps can over time aggregate to big changes.

Decremental budgeting concentrates on discretionary spending where the cuts are easiest to secure and do not entail changes in law. Although some entitlements have been scaled back, thus far the brunt of reductions has been borne by programs whose funding is provided in annual appropriation bills. By setting the spending level at a few percentage points below the current level, billions of dollars can be saved in discretionary spending without reexamining programs.

Decremental budgeting avoids programmatic issues which tend to stir up conflict. It is far better to cut dollars than programs; in doing the former, the cutters can claim that they are sparing the latter. While the claims might have a hollow ring, they cool the budget debate, and ease the path to budgetary agreement.

Decremental budgeting can be distinguished from "cutback budgeting" in which major program changes are made in recognition of the fact that resources do not permit the government to continue doing all that it did in the past. While some cutback budgeting was practiced during Reagan's first two years, most of the reductions were made in decremental fashion. Some of the biggest cuts, such as in CETA and Food Stamps, probably had more to do with the President's political ideology than with his budget objectives. Reagan might have sought these reductions even if the federal government had a big surplus.

The Politics of Inflation: Cutting Back While Spending More

Decrementalism shifts focus from the increment to the base. Budget makers keep score on the size and distribution of the reductions, that is, on how much and what is being cut from the base. The base is the starting point for decremental choice, much as it is for incremental decisions. In decrementalism, participants want to make sure that the cuts are widely distributed (the notion of "fair shares" is as applicable to decrements as it is to increments), that the reductions do not cut into "muscle," and that they do not have unintended side effects such as the elimination of coveted programs.

In decremental budgeting, the way the base is defined determines how the cuts are computed. When the inflation rate is low, the nominal level of expenditure is likely to be the base use for most programs.

Exceptions will be favored programs (for which the base might be adjusted upward by including add-ons such as mandatory or workload increases) and disliked programs (for which the base might be adjusted downward by removing non-recurring items or supplemental funds). However, when the inflation rate is high, computing the decrement depends on how the base is adjusted for price changes.

While it is possible to ignore price changes and use a nominal base, this approach is not likely to satisfy budget participants. If cuts are made to an unadjusted base, the affected agencies and beneficiaries will complain that the real reduction is much greater than it is claimed to be. The budget cutters also will be dissatisfied because they will not be able to claim sizable reductions. Indeed if inflation is very high, they might have to permit dollar increases in agency budgets, thereby impairing their claim to having cut expenditures.

The happy solution to everybody's problem is to adjust the base for inflation. When this is done, the adjusted "baseline" against which the cuts are measured is higher than the base. It is, therefore, possible to cut the baseline without cutting the nominal base. For example, if the baseline is ten percent above the base (because this is the inflation rate), then a five percent reduction would still provide five percent more funds than in the current budget. The budget cutters can show that they reduced spending (because the budget is below the baseline) while the agency will be able to retain more of its funds than if a comparable cut were made against the base.

Does Decrementalism Differ?

In practice, decremental budgeting can be the mirror image of incremental budgeting. Instead of budgeting for small increases, government budgets for small decreases. In both cases, budgeting is a form of marginal choice in which the bulk of expenditures remains unexamined.

But if incrementalism is defined as growth-oriented budgeting, then the size of change is less important that the direction. Budgeting for less cannot be the same process as budgeting for more. A theory of budgeting predicated on the expectation that the size of government will continue to grow cannot fit a situation in which government is expected to shrink. In terms of the theory set forth by

Wildavsky, decrementalism diverges from incrementalism in at least three significant ways. Decremental budgeting is redistributive rather than distributive; it is less stable than incremental decisions; and it generates more conflict.

Decremental Budgeting Is Redistributive

When resources are plentiful, it is not necessary to transfer funds among recipients. One claimant can be given more without anyone else being given less. But when it cuts the budget, government is likely to redistribute resources. It can make across the board cuts which maintain relative shares in the budget, but this tactic is more suited to nibbling at expenditures than for making deep cuts. Across the board reductions rarely amount to more than a few cents on the dollar and they are not effective with respect to mandatory expenditures. If it wants to make deep cuts the government will have to reduce the budget selectively, cutting some portions more than others. Not only will relative shares be changed, but some recipients might actually get increases while others are getting less.

The selective approach has political advantages. While across the board cuts convey the notion that all spenders are being treated equally, not all are equal politically. Powerful interests might be spared the knife or might protect themselves against cuts by having their expenditures mandated by law.

Decrementalism cannot be silent (or ignorant) about budgetary outcomes. It cannot disregard the question of "who loses what?" When the budget is increasing, it is easy to assume that everyone is benefiting and that, therefore, it suffices to consider each budget decision as a discrete choice without regard for governmental objectives or long-term consequences. This assumption cannot be made when the budget is redistributive. A political theory of decrementalism must explain why some are protected against cutbacks while others are not. It must reckon with the distribution of the losses. The irritating issues crowded out of incremental budgeting are at the forefront of decremental budgeting.

Unstable Budgets

Incremental budgets are stable and predictable. As previously noted, Dempster and Wildavsky define incrementalism in terms of the regularity or irregularity of change, not the absolute amount of change. When the economy is expanding, review can concentrate on the increment and the next budget can be based on the current one.

Not so, however, when economic decline is so severe (or protracted) as to create a shortfall in resources. During a cutback, reconsideration of the base cannot be confined to the shortfall. A five percent gap between the base (or baseline) and available resources might have a "multiplier effect" in generating budgetary uncertainty. To identify possible savings, it might be imperative to reconsider a much higher fraction of the base.

Economic adversity destabilizes not only the making of a budget but its execution as well. In every budget cycle, there is apt to be some discrepancy between predicted and actual performance of the economy. If the variance is due to greater than expected growth, the increment can be expanded without reopening any other issues. But when there is a shortfall, it might be necessary to remake the budget during the course of the year.

Economic growth tends to be accompanied by budgetary slack. If outlays exceed the budget, there might be surprise and consternation but no need to go back to the drawing board. When the economy is weak, the odds are that the budget has already been drained of slack resources and that unexpected problems will compel a review of the budget.[13] Economic decline combined with high inflation can be very destabilizing, for the budget will have to adjust to higher expenditures and lower resources.

The poorer the government, the more budgets it is likely to have. The affluent can ride out the storm or call upon reserves; the less fortunate must adjust to every month's or quarter's economic reports.

Since the first oil shock, the federal budget has been a case study in budgetary turbulence. Shortly after he took office in 1974, Ford called for a tax surcharge; a few months later, he signed a tax cut into law. In 1977, Carter proposed and then withdrew a tax rebate, and in 1980 less than two months after submitting his budget to Congress, he negotiated a substantially revised spending plan with legislative leaders. In August 1981, Reagan signed spending and tax reductions into law and announced the success of his economic program, but in September of the same year, he asked for additional budget changes, including tax increases. In 1982, Reagan disowned his budget barely weeks after submitting it to congress.

Instability begets instability. The more a budget deviates from its projected course, the louder are the demands for a reconsideration of the decisions made in it. The problem is not political inconstancy but economic turbulence. If the economy is not stable, the budget cannot be.

Budgetary Conflict

Incremental budgets are consensual budgets. They command wide support and disagreement is confined to marginal issues such as the distribution of incremental resources. This type of dispute can be quickly resolved by giving each claimant a share of the increment. No interest gets all that it wants, but few go away from the budget process empty handed. Budgeting might be the "uniform distribution of discontent," but the conflict is more a matter of griping than of fighting.

In decremental budgeting, fighting rages over the base which attracts more fire than the increment. Not only is the swath of disagreement wider, but conflict is more intense as claimants fight to hold on to the resources they received in previous budgets.

Redistribution invites conflict. Taking from draws more protest than giving to. When resources are plentiful, some claimants might be upset by the favorable treatment that others are getting but their concern can be assuaged by giving them a little more. When resources are being redistributed, there is a greater likelihood of participants looking over one another's shoulder to calculate whether all are giving their fair shares.

Instability which is associated with decremental budgeting also breeds conflict. In incremental budgeting, once an issue is decided, it is likely to remain settled for the rest of the cycle. But when conditions are turbulent, conflict can be rekindled by efforts to reopen budget issues that were decided earlier.

Strife delays budgetary decisions. In recent years, Congress has been compelled to provide stopgap appropriations because of its failure to enact the regular appropriation bills by the start of the fiscal year. This failure has not been due to legislative irresponsibility but to budgetary conflict. When the budget war heats up, it is harder to obtain agreement on the numbers. Increased conflict also is indicated by impoundment battles between the President and Congress, repeated clashes between authorizing and appropriating committees, and between these older committees and the new budget committees, and frequent roll calls on budget issues. In 1981, for example, the Senate took more than 300 recorded votes on budget related legislation.

Can Budgeting Survive If It Is Not Incremental?

Many signs point to the increased importance of the federal budget. When the President sends his budget to Congress, it commands front page and prime time coverage. The President repeatedly uses the media to carry his budget message to the nation; the media lavish extraordinary attention on budget issues; legislation is frequently defined in terms of its cost and effect on the budget; the budget calendar shapes the legislative session.

Could it be, however, that these are signs of budgetary breakdown, not of budgetary potency? When the budget controls things and is conducted in an orderly manner according to prescribed rules and timetables, it is a routine process, not the stuff out of which good news stories are made. Routine is not an incident of budgeting but an essential element of the way the process has been conducted in the United States since the turn of the century and for a bit longer in European democracies. The routine is repeated year after year; it drains the budget of conflict and stabilizes expectations. Budget makers know what to do (including the roles to play) and they enter the budget fray expecting to reach agreement. The budget is not a life or death struggle for survival; just about every agency expects to get at least as much out of the next budget as out of the past one.

But routine itself depends on a stable and peaceful environment. The budget cannot make order out of chaos, it cannot bring concord where there is unlimited strife. Where there is instability and conflict, budget routines continue (unless there is complete breakdown) but they take on a ritualistic rather than a substantive purpose. Budget issues become symbols of larger, unresolved political conflicts. Perhaps this is what is now happening in American budgeting.

The budget gets attention because of the conflicts and turbulence it stirs up; it gets covered again and again because it is so hard to nail down final agreement. Fights between the President and Congress are a good story, but the issues may be more symbolic than substantive. The budget is the battleground, but it is no longer decisive. An unexpected lurch in the economy can do more to the budget than a full year of presidential or congressional decisions.

Naomi Caiden has recently written of the myth of the annual budget, but it could be that what is disappearing is not the annuality of the cycle but the cycle itself.[14] The twelve months fiscal year is an artifact that cannot survive budgetary instability and conflict. It is too long for short-term economic (and political) fluctuations; too short for long-term budget control.

Budgeting cannot fade away, if only because of the importance of resource allocation to the modern state. But the process need not be of the type that has existed for so long. In trying to envision how budgeting might be altered if decrementalism becomes a permanent state of affairs, one is struck by the paucity of contemporary budget innovations. There is nothing on the horizon in the 1980s comparable to performance budgeting in the 1950s, PPB in the 1960s, and zero-base budgeting in the 1970s.[15] The era of big systems has passed, if only because the design of such systems requires some confidence as to the direction that budgeting ought to take.

But this does not mean that budget practices are frozen in the pattern they have been in for so long. Budgeting must be an adaptive process if it is to retain central importance for governments. Some adaptations are beginning to emerge in other countries. They include the use of "envelopes," "frames" and other means of dividing constrained resources— the conversion of multiyear budgeting from a planning into a control process, the development of "packages" which supplant annual budgets.[16] Decremental budgeting will be more centralized and more insulated from economic gyrations. It will be budgeting at the margins, or it will not be budgeting.

Notes

1. Aaron Wildavsky (1964). *The Politics of the Budgetary Process*. Boston: Little, Brown & Co., p. 15.
2. For evidence that there is much more turbulence within agency budgets than the early incrementalists assumed, see Peter B. Nachez and Irwin C. Bupp (1973), "Policy and priority in the budgetary process," *American Political Science Review* 67: 951–963.
3. M. A. H. Dempster and Aaron Wildavsky (1979). "On change: or, there is no magic size for an increment," *Political Studies* 27: 375.
4. "Proposed reforms inevitably contain important implications for the political system; that is, for the 'who gets what' of governmental decisions." Wildavsky, *op. cit.*, p. 127.
5. Maurice Wright (ed.) (1980). *Public Spending Decisions: Growth and Restraint in the 1970s*. London, George Allen & Unwin, 1980, p. 3.
6. Quoted in Martha Derthick (1975), *Uncontrollable Spending for Social Services Grants*. Washington: The Brookings Institution, p. 85.
7. For a discussion of these conflicting attitudes, see Royce Crocker (1981), "Federal government spending and public opinion," in *Public Budgeting and Finance* 1 (3): 25–35.
8. On the change in the role of the appropriations committees, see Allen Schick (1980). *Congress and Money: Budgeting, Spending, and Taxing*. Washington: The Urban Institute, pp. 415–481.
9. Organization for Economic Cooperation and Development (1978). *Public Expenditure Trends*. (Paris: OECD), p. 53.
10. John Ellwood (1982). *Reductions in U.S. Domestic Spending: How They Affect State and Local Governments*. New Brunswick: Transaction Books.
11. For a discussion of Reagan's budget policies and problems, see Allen Schick "How the budget was won and lost," in Norman Ornstein (ed.) (1982), *President and Congress: Assessing Reagan's Year*. Washington: American Enterprise Institute, pp. 14–43.
12. For an examination of how this process works, see Allen Schick (1981), *Reconciliation and the Congressional Budget Process*. Washington: American Enterprise Institute.
13. For budgeting without slack, see Naomi Caiden and Aaron Wildavsky (1974), *Planning and Budgeting in Poor Countries*. New York: John Wiley & Sons.
14. Naomi Caiden (1982). "The myth of the annual budget," *Public Administration Review* 42: 516–523.
15. Most writers interpret zero-base budgeting as a rational-comprehensive budget system similar in its objective to PPB. In fact, ZBB is a form of marginal analysis. If it had not been so misapplied and misunderstood, ZBB might be useful for decremental budgeting.
16. See Daniel Tarschys, "The scissors crisis in public finance," *Policy Sciences* 15: 205–224.

38
The Politics
in Budget Reform

Aaron Wildavsky

The seeming irrationalities of a political system that does not provide for formal consideration of the budget as a whole (except by the president, who cannot control the final result) have led to many attacks and proposals for reform. But such reforms are aimed at the wrong target. If the present budgetary process rightly or wrongly is deemed unsatisfactory, then one must alter in some respect the political system of which the budget is but an expression. It makes no sense to speak as if one could make drastic changes in budgeting without also altering the distribution of influence. This task, however, is inevitably so formidable that most reformers prefer to speak only of changing the budgetary process (as with the Congressional Budget and Control Act of 1974 or Gramm-Rudman-Hollings), as if by some subtle alchemy the intractable political element also could be transformed into a more malleable substance.

In actuality, it is the other way around. The budget is inextricably linked to the political system; by far the most significant way of influencing the budget, therefore, would be to introduce basic political changes. Give presidents powers enabling them to control the votes of their party in Congress; enable a small group of congressmen to command a majority of votes on all occasions so they can push their program through (now that would be a budget committee!); then you will have exerted a profound influence on the content of the budget.

Further, no significant change can be made in the budgetary process without also affecting the political process. There would be no point in tinkering with the budgetary machinery if, at the end, the pattern of outcomes was precisely the same as before. On the contrary, budget reform has little justification unless it results in different kinds of decisions and, when and if this has been accomplished, the play of political forces has necessarily been altered.

Since the budget represents conflicts over whose preferences shall prevail, moreover, one cannot speak of "better budgeting" without considering who benefits and who loses or by demonstrating that no one loses. Just as the supposedly objective criterion of "efficiency" has been shown to have normative implications,[1] so a "better budget" may well be a cloak for someone's hidden policy preferences. To propose that the president be given an item veto, for example, is an attempt to increase the influence of those particular interests that have superior access to the Chief Executive (rather than, say, to the Congress).

Unit of Measurement: Cash or Volume

Budgeting can be done not only in terms of cash but also in terms of volume. Instead of promising to pay so much over the next year or years, the commitment can be made in terms of operations to be performed or services to be provided. The usual way of guaranteeing a volume of activity is indexing the program against inflation so its purchasing power is kept constant. Why might someone want to budget in terms of volume (or in currency held constant as to purchasing power)? To aid planning: If public agencies know that they can count not on variable currency but rather on what that currency actually can buy, i.e., on a volume of activity, they can plan ahead as far as the budget runs. Indeed, if one wishes to make decisions now instead of at future periods, so as to help assure consistency over time, then estimates based on stability in the unit of effort (so many applications processed or such a level of services provided) are the very way to go about it.

So long as purchasing power remains constant, the distinction between budgeting in cash or by volume makes no difference. But should the value of money fluctuate (and, in our time, this has meant inflation), the public budget must expand available funds so as to provide the designated volume of activity. Budgeters then lose control of money because they have to supply whatever is needed. Given large and unexpected changes in prices, the size of the budget in cash terms obviously would fluctuate wildly. But it is equally obvious that no government could permit itself to be so far out of control. Hence, the very type of stable environment

Source: From *The New Politics of the Budgetary Process,* by Aaron Wildavsky, pp. 411–439. Copyright ©1988 by Aaron Wildavsky. Reprinted by permission of Harper-Collins Publishers.

that budgeting by volume is designed to achieve turns out to be its major unarticulated premise.

Given an irreducible amount of uncertainty in the system, not every element can be stabilized at the same time. Who, then, will enjoy stability? And who will bear the costs of change? The private sector and the central budget office pay the price for budgeting by volume. What budgeting by volume says, in effect, is that the public sector will be protected against inflation by getting its agreed level of services before other needs are met. The real resources necessary to make up the gap between projected and current prices must come from the private sector in the form of taxation or borrowing. In other words, for the public sector, volume budgeting is a form of indexing against inflation.

The sensitivity of budgetary forms to inflation is a crucial consideration. It follows that budgeting by volume is counterproductive in fighting inflation because it accommodates price increases rather than encouraging the struggle against them. Indexing benefits against price increases also is counterproductive because the beneficiaries have less reason to be concerned about inflation.[2]

Time Span: Months, One Year, Many Years

Multiyear budgeting, that is, viewing resource allocation in a long-term perspective, has long been proposed as a reform to enhance rational choice. Considering one year at a time, it has been argued, leads to short-sightedness (only next year's expenditures are reviewed), overspending (because huge future disbursements are hidden), conservatism (incremental changes do not open up larger future vistas), and parochialism (programs tend to be viewed in isolation rather than by comparison to future costs in relation to expected revenue). Extending the budget time-span to two, three, or even five years, it is argued, would enable long-range planning to overtake short-term reaction, and to substitute financial planning for merely muddling through. The old tactic of the camel's nose—beginning with small expenditures while hiding larger ones that will arise later on—is rendered more difficult. Moreover, the practice of stepped-up spending to use up resources before the end of the budgetary year would decline in frequency.

A two-year budget would not change much. There is no reason to believe it would facilitate agreement or encourage better understanding. But it might be approved as a sort of budget officers' humane act. Instead of working 80 hours a week every year, participants in budgeting might get a breather every other year. Being less tired, they just might decide more wisely. In any event, no great harm is likely to be done and a bit of good might be accomplished.

A multiyear budget would work well for certain parts of the budget, like military procurements, which take years to complete. But benefit, salary, and operating expense categories are ill-suited to long-term budgeting. The size of these items is significantly influenced by external factors, such as inflation, that are difficult to predict. The problem of prediction appears more formidable when it is recalled that preparation of the budget begins almost a year before the budget is implemented. A two-year budget cycle, consequently, would have to forecast economic changes almost three years into the future. The result may be that budgeters would "spend more time tinkering with the assumptions over the 33-month period and, even assuming good faith, making some decisions on longer-term assumptions that would have to be altered even more dramatically later on."[3]

Much depends, to be sure, on how long budgetary commitments last. The seemingly arcane question of whether budgeting should be done on a cash or volume basis will assume importance if a nation adopts multiyear budgeting. The longer the term of the budget, the more significant becomes inflation. To the extent that price changes are automatically absorbed into budgets (volume budgeting), a certain amount of activity is guaranteed. But to the extent that agencies thus must absorb inflation, the real scope of activity will decline. Multiyear budgeting in cash terms, without indexing, diminishes the relative size of the public sector and leaves the private sector larger. Not always up front in discussing the time span of the budget, but very important, is the debate over the relative shares of the public and private sectors—which sector will be asked to absorb inflation and which will be allowed to expand into the other.

A similar issue of relative shares is created within government by proposals to budget in some sectors for several years, and in others, for only one year. Entitlements, for example, can be perpetual. To operate in different time spans poses the question of which sectors of policy are to be exposed to the vicissitudes of life in the short term and which are to be protected from them. Like any other device, multiyear budgeting is not neutral but distributes indulgences differently among the affected interests. Although being treated as an entitlement, until basic legislation changes, is no guarantee of future success, it is better for beneficiaries. But entitlements, if they grow large, are not necessarily better for government because they reduce legislative discretion.

Another potential downside to multiyear budgeting is the increased permanence of programs. Just as some programs may have a more difficult time getting into the budget, so "hard in" often implies an even "harder out." Once an expenditure gets included in a multiyear projection, it is likely to remain because it has become part of an interrelated set of proposals that might be expensive to disrupt. Thus control in a single year may have to be sacrificed to the maintenance of limits over the multiyear period. And, should there be a call for cuts, promised reductions in future years (which are always "iffy") are easily traded for maintenance of spending in the all-important present.

Suppose, however, that it were deemed desirable to reduce some expenditures significantly in order to increase others. Due to the built-in pressure of continuing commitments, what could be done in a single year is extremely limited. But, making arrangements over a 2-5 year period would permit larger changes in spending to be effected in a more orderly way. This is true; other things, however—prices, priorities, politics—seldom remain equal. At a time when maintaining the annual budget has become problematical, so that the budget may have to be remade several times a year, lengthening the cycle possibly will just compound uncertainty. As Robert Hartman put it, "There is no absolutely right way to devise a long-run budget strategy."[4]

Calculation: Incremental or Comprehensive

Just as the annual budget on a cash basis is integral to the traditional process, so also is the budgetary base; normally, only small increases or decreases to the existing base are considered in any one period. If such budgetary practices may be described as incremental, the main alternative to the traditional budget is one that emphasizes comprehensive calculation. The main modern forms of the latter are planning, programming, and budgeting (PPB) and zero-base budgeting (ZBB).

Think of PPB as embodying horizontal comprehensiveness—comparing alternative expenditure packages to decide which of them best contributes to large programmatic objectives. ZBB, by contrast, might be thought of as manifesting vertical comprehensiveness: Every year alternative expenditures from base zero are considered, with all governmental activities or objectives being treated as discrete entities. In short, PPB compares programs, while ZBB compares alternative funding levels for the same program.

The strength of PPB lies in its emphasis on policy analysis to increase effectiveness: Programs are evaluated, found wanting, and presumably replaced by alternatives designed to produce superior results. Unfortunately, PPB engenders a conflict between error recognition and error correction. Now there would be little point in designing better policies so as to minimize their prospects of implementation. But why should a process devoted to policy evaluation end up stultifying policy execution? Answer: because PPB's policy rationality is countered by its organizational irrationality.

For an error to be altered, it must be relatively easy to correct; but PPB makes this hard. The "systems" in PPB are characterized by their proponents as highly differentiated and tightly linked. The rationale for program budgeting lies in its connectedness: Like groups are grouped together. Program structures are meant to replace the confused concatenations of line-items with clearly differentiated, nonoverlapping boundaries—that is, only one set of programs to a structure. Hence a change in one element or structure necessarily reverberates throughout every element in the same system. Instead of alerting only neighboring units or central control units, which would make change feasible, all are, so to speak, wired together so that the choice is, in effect, all or none.

Imagine one of us deciding whether to buy a tie or a kerchief. A simple task, one might think. Suppose, however, that organizational rules require us to keep our entire wardrobe as a unit. In those circumstances, if everything must be rearranged when one item is altered, the probability that we will do anything is low. The more tightly linked and the more highly differentiated the elements concerned, the greater the probability of error (because tolerances are very small) and the less the likelihood that error will in fact be corrected (because, with change, every element has to be recalibrated with every other that had been previously adjusted). To be caught between revolution (change in everything) and resignation (change in nothing) has little to recommend it.

Program budgeting increases rather than decreases the cost of correcting error. The great complaint about bureaucracies is their rigidity. Viewed from the standpoint of bureau interests, to some extent programs are negotiable: Some can be increased, others decreased, while keeping the agency on an even keel, or if necessary, adjusting agency programs to less happy times without calling into question the agency's very existence. Line-item budgeting, precisely because its categories (personnel, maintenance, supplies) do not relate directly to programs, is easier to change. Budgeting by programs, precisely because money flows to objectives, makes it difficult to abandon objectives without also abandoning the very organization that gets its money for those activities. It is better, I think, to use nonprogrammatic rubrics as formal budget categories, permitting a diversity of analytical perspectives, than to transform a temporary analytic insight into a permanent perspective through which to funnel money.

The cutting edge of dealing with competition among programs lies in postulating a range of policy objectives small enough to be encompassed and large enough to overlap so that there can be choices (tradeoffs) among them. Instead, PPB tends to generate a tendency either toward only a few generalized objectives (so anything and everything can fit under them), or such a multitude of objectives that each organizational unit has its own home and does not have to compete with any other.[5] Participants learn how to play any game.

Despite the force of these objectives, there is an even greater defect: PPB operates without global spending limits. Now PPB is avowedly based on an analogy to economic markets where competition facilitates choice of the most productive alternative. Competitive markets perform feats of calculation. And they also create incentives for the most productive economic choice to be made. Without a global limit on spending, however—where more for one program leaves less for others—participants in PPB lack this incentive. The principle of opportunity costs—the value of an expenditure is what you have to give up to get it—does not apply. And neither does economic theory, because it is based on exchange, and exchange cannot be used to estimate equivalent values if things are no longer worth whatever is given up for them. Since nothing is lost by trying harder, no participant

has reason to stop lobbying for more. Program budgeting might operate effectively if the people involved had to work within known limits on resources. Yet it is precisely these limits that are under stress as the norm of balance has collapsed without an agreed standard to take its place.

The ideal a-historical information system is zero-base budgeting. The past, as reflected in the budgetary base, is explicitly rejected: There is no yesterday; nothing will be taken for granted; everything at every period is subject to searching scrutiny. As a result, calculations become unmanageable.

To say that a budgetary process is a-historical is to conclude that the sources of error multiply while the chances of correcting mistakes decrease: If history is abolished, nothing is ever settled. Old quarrels resurface as new conflicts. Both calculation and conflict increase exponentially, the former complicating selection and the latter obstructing error correction. As mistrust grows with conflict, willingness to admit (and hence to correct) error diminishes. Doing without history is a little like abolishing memory—momentarily convenient, perhaps, but ultimately embarrassing.

Nowhere does a true zero-base budget practice exist. Everywhere the "zero" is ignored and the base gets larger, amounting, in the end, to 80 to 90 percent of the prior year; this, of course, is a reversion to classical budgeting. What is worse, ZBB cannot give expression to the main reason for most activities, namely, to support some other activity. By building the budget entirely from the bottom up, the justification for expenditures is divorced from their connections to other activities and purposes. This does not make sense.[6] It does explain why ZBB has declined in use. But why do people keep resurrecting it? Because ZBB holds out the hope of liberation from restraints of the past, as if they could be willed away.

ZBB and PPB share an emphasis on the virtue of objectives. Program budgeting seeks to relate larger to smaller objectives among different programs, and zero-base budgeting promises to do the same within a single program. The policy implications of these budgeting methods, which distinguish them from existing approaches, derive from their overwhelming, shared concern with ranking objectives. Thinking about objectives is one thing, however; making budget categories out of them is quite another. Of course, if one wants the objectives of today to be the objectives of tomorrow, if one wants no change, then it is a brilliant idea to build the budget around objectives. Conversely, if one wishes to alter existing objectives radically, it may be appropriate to highlight the struggle over them. But if one desires flexibility (sometimes known as learning from experience), it must be possible to change objectives without simultaneously destroying the organization by withdrawing financial support.

Both PPB and ZBB are expressions of a view in which ranking objectives is rendered tantamount to reason. Alas! An efficient mode of presenting results in research papers—find objectives, order them, choose the highest valued—has been confused with proper processes of social inquiry. For purposes of resource allocation, which is what budgeting is about, it is irrational to rank objectives without considering resources. The question cannot be "What do you want?"—as if there were no limits—but should be "What do you want compared to what you can get?" After all, an agency with a billion would not only do more than it would with a million but might well wish to do something quite different. Resources affect objectives as well as vice versa. Budgeting should not separate what reason tells us belongs together.

There is a critical difference between the financial form in which the budget is voted in the legislature and the different ways of thinking about budgeting. It is possible to analyze expenditures in terms of programs, over long periods of time, and in many other ways, without requiring that the form of analysis be the same as the form of appropriation. All this can be summarized: The more neutral the form of presenting appropriations, the easier to translate other changes—in program, direction, organizational structure—into the desired amount without increasing the rigidity in categories, and thus erecting barriers to future changes.

The forms of budgeting that once occupied center stage (PPB, ZBB, and similar reforms) have lost their allure. Now what matters is the level and distribution of spending. Size replaces efficiency as the criterion of a good budget. In a time of growing budgetary dissensus, a concern with radical changes in process replaces concern with modest alteration in technique.

Appropriations or Treasury Budgeting

A classical budget depends on classical practice —authorization and appropriation followed by expenditure, and postaudited by external auditors. But in many countries, classical budgeting does not in fact control most public spending. Rather than appropriations budgeting, nearly half of public spending takes the form of "treasury budgeting," so-called because it bypasses the appropriations process in favor of automatic disbursement of funds through the treasury.

For present purposes, the two forms of treasury budgeting that constitute alternatives to classical appropriations are tax preferences and entitlements. Concessions granted in the form of tax reductions for home ownership or college tuition or medical expenses are equivalent to budgetary expenditures, except that the money is deflected at the source. In one sense, this is a way of avoiding budgeting before the budget comes into being. Whether one accepts this view or not is a matter of philosophy. It is said, for instance, that our government has a progressive income tax. Is that the real tax system? Or is it a would-be progressive tax as modified by innumerable exceptions? The budgetary process is usually described as resource allocation by governing authorities. Is that the real budgetary process? Or is it that process, plus numerous provisions for tax preferences, low interest loans, and other such devices? From a behavioral or descriptive point of view, actual practices constitute the real system. Exceptions are part of the rule. Indeed, since less than half of the budget now passes through the appropriations process, the exceptions indeed are greater than the rule.

Obviously, treasury budgeting leaves a great deal to be desired in controlling costs of programs, since these depend on such variables as levels of benefits set in prior years, rate of application, demographic changes, and severity of administration. If the guiding principle is that no one who is eligible should be denied, at the cost of including some who are ineligible, expenditures will rise. They will decline if the opposite principle—no ineligibles even if some eligibles suffer—prevails.[7]

Treasury budgeting is popular because of its antibudgetary character—it allows spending to rise without calling attention to it. Conflict is reduced, for the time being at least, because no explicit decisions (giving more to this group and less to another) are necessary. Ultimately, of course, there comes a day of reckoning in the form of a loss of flexibility due to the implicit preprogramming of so large a proportion of available funds.

For the purposes of economic management, treasury budgeting is a mixed bag. It is useful in providing what are called automatic stabilizers. When it is deemed desirable not to make new decisions every time conditions change (unemployment benefits, for example), an entitlement enables funds to flow according to the size of the problem. The difficulty is that not all entitlements are counter-cyclical (child benefits, for example, may rise independently of economic conditions), and the loss in financial flexibility generated by entitlements may hurt when the time comes to do less. Nevertheless, treasury budgeting has one significant advantage over appropriations budgeting—timing. Changes in conditions are manifested quickly in changes in spending.

The recalcitrance of all forms of budgeting to economic management is not surprising; after all, spending programs and economic management cannot both be made more predictable if one must vary in order to serve the other. Every way one turns, it appears, budgetary devices are good for some purposes and bad for others.

Capital Budgeting

An idea that is receiving a great deal of attention lately is separating capital expenditures from the current budget. Two budgets would exist: an operations budget and a capital budget. The capital budget would include investment in assets as balanced against debt acquired through purchase of these assets.

Economically, the idea has a great deal of merit. A separate capital budget would help focus on national investment needs. Under current practices, financing for capital assets (which produce long-term benefits) is lumped with expenses. Since short-term factors weigh heavily in budgeting decisions, capital assets, whose benefits may not be immediately apparent, may be sacrificed to more immediately pressing needs.

Yet the distinction between capital expenses and other expenses is not clear-cut. For example, is education a current expense that is payable immediately (yes), or does it represent an investment in human capital (also yes)? Experience in nations around the world shows that it is not possible to separate the political aspects of budgeting—who wants and gets what—from technical definitions. Since a capital budget appears to be good, i.e., an

investment, expenditures in its budget would surely rise.[8] Besides, capital goods, being considered as assets, are often not included in the deficit.

A good idea can take many bad turns when put into practice. The immediate response of budgeters, once provided with an operating and a capital budget, would in all likelihood be to transfer as many expenditures as possible from the operating to the capital budget. The announced deficit would consequently appear significantly smaller. All participants could claim victory in holding the line on deficits even though spending had actually increased. The danger is that expenditures would escalate as attention is turned from deficit reduction. To add insult to injury, the capital budget

is quite likely to unpredictably disrupt the existing budget process. A dual budget would more than likely require some changes in institutional structure, shifts in responsibility, and modifications of the budget cycle's timing. The need to relate aggregate debt, tax, and spending limits to two separate budgets—capital and operating—would introduce greater complexity into the already complicated budget process.[9]

Far better, I think, to include an appendix in the president's budget proposal attempting a breakdown between capital and recurrent expenditure, subject to criticism and refinement over time, than to make matters worse in the guise of making them better.

Why is it necessary to settle for second or third best? Why not combine the best features of the various forms of budgeting, specifically selected to work under prevailing conditions? Observation reveals that a number of different processes do in fact coexist right now. Some programs are single-year while others are multiyear; some have cash limits while others are open-ended or even indexed; some are analyzed in increments while others (where repetitive operations are involved) receive, in effect, a zero-base review. Thus, beneath the facade of unity there is in fact diversity.

Three Directions for Budgeting: Bottom-Up, Top-Down, and In-Between

The classical method of federal budgeting may justly be called decentralized or "bottom-up." Within Congress where, with two-thirds majorities, the power of the purse still resides, consideration of spending was divided between authorizing and appropriations committees and subcommittees, with important aspects of spending—especially entitlements, as well as tax preferences—under the aegis of the House Ways and Means and the Senate Finance committees. On the executive side, in various combinations, bureaus and departments proposed, under different degrees of constraint, and the president and the OMB disposed of, requests that eventually became the president's budget.

The advantages of this extreme decentralization are well known.[10] By factoring the budget into relatively small components, calculation was simplified; the budget as a whole, as its critics never tired of saying, was not formally considered. There were few disputes over the budget in its entirety because the process was organized (critics would say disorganized) to prevent exactly that sort of confrontation. And since the budget was, in effect, factored out to numerous bureaus, departments, OMB examiners, House and Senate substantive appropriations and finance committees, conflicts were limited not only to these smaller subsets but to the increments of these amounts—the differences between the prior year and what was proposed for the next—that participants felt it worthwhile to consider. Calculations were made, conflict diffused, and yet, wonder of wonders, budgets were passed on time while revenues and expenditures stayed within hailing distance.

A bottom-up decentralized process, as we know, required widespread agreement on the norms of balance and comprehensiveness.[11] A commitment to budget balance meant acceptance of a de facto spending limit: Big-ticket items could rise only so far without taking funds from other programs. Playing the game of balance meant agreeing to anticipatory restraints on spending demands. Adherence to the norm of comprehensiveness meant that almost everything was in the same pot. When restraints had to be exercised in the name of balance, therefore, neither substantial revenues nor expenditures were outside the purview of the political authorities for ratcheting up or down.

Economic growth was a facilitating factor. So long as revenues rose, politically painless increases in spending were possible. If the demand for spending went up while growth failed to keep pace, however, there were other informal devices to maintain balance.

Congresses could vote more spending expecting that, if things got worse, presidents would come to the rescue by impounding funds. And if visible tax increases proved difficult, the same result might be obtained by reducing tax preferences, and by "bracket creep" as inflation moved taxpayers into higher brackets.

If all these protective devices failed, our politicians would be reduced to the most basic assumption of all: agreement on the division of sacrifices, at least among the ma jor programs—defense, social security, and other entitlements. If all these giant programs were regarded as contributing to the national interest, accommodations among them might be arranged. By contrast, if "welfare" and "warfare" were considered to be at odds, this polarization of opinion would make agreement difficult if (or, rather, when) a decline in the rate of economic growth rendered this conflict visible.

What happened to bring bottom-up budgeting into disrepute was that every one of these assumptions, understandings, and agreements was undermined. Government became spending. Whether it was defense to bolster America's position as the leader of the West, or social welfare to make long deferred payments on social justice, positive government became the order of the day. Balance withered away. Republicans grumbled but did little, and Democrats took satisfaction in ignoring another shibboleth from olden times that stood in the way of social progress.

Watergate gravely weakened presidential power over impoundment of funds already appropriated. The growth of entitlements, coupled with automatic cost of living increases, substantially reduced the proportion of the budget controllable through annual appropriations and thus through across-the-board reductions. The Reagan administration applied the coup de grace in 1981 when it cut income taxes across the board by 23 percent, thus negating equivalent but silent tax increases in social security, bracket creep, and energy that had been in place at the end of the Carter administration. Congress also indexed tax brackets beginning in 1985. Consequently, the proportion of national income derived from federal taxation failed to rise enough to cover higher spending. As deficits soared to unprecedented levels, participants in budgeting discovered that they had lost their traditional devices for accommodating disagreement—their piecemeal approach had been overtaken by budget resolutions and reconciliation, and impoundment and bracket creep were mostly gone—while disrespect for the president's budget, which once had at least provided a starting point, symbolized the fact that budgeters no longer agreed on the priorities between welfare and defense.

The opposite end of the budgetary spectrum can be called centralized, top-down budgeting. Global levels are set by limits on revenues or expenditures or deficits—the difference between them. A formula exists, say across-the-board cuts, for bringing spending down or revenues up to these limits. This top-down method depends on certain understandings and assumptions. One of these is that enough be thrown up for grabs to make a difference. If, as in a number of European nations, for instance, social welfare entitlements (preeminently payments to individuals) are left out—these programs comprising a half to two-thirds of total spending, with interest on debt making up another fifth—the remainder is not large enough to do the job. So the United States also discovered in the Gramm-Rudman-Hollings process. The attraction of this across-the-board method, however, is precisely its severity: Agreement on innumerable separate items is rendered unnecessary by a formula. Yet the very lack of analysis about individual programs is bound to lead to foolish actions as less and more important matters receive similar treatment.

If both bottom-up and top-down budgeting are unsatisfactory, what else is there? A combination of the top-down and bottom-up methods may avoid the worst excess of each; alternatively, it may bring out the worst of both. The budgetary process is centralized to the extent that there is a global limit but decentralized to the degree that, within such a prescribed total, participants are allowed to work out disagreements, as before, on a case-by-case basis. Indeed, this combination lay behind the Budget Reform Act of 1974, whose budget resolutions were designed to set totals in a top-down fashion so as to structure the work of the committee system. As things turned out, bottom-up penetrated top-down. Totals were set on top with a view to accommodating demands down below. What resulted was the worst of both worlds— disagreement was exacerbated by the need to decide the largest questions of total expenditures and revenues, thus giving up the advantages of decentralization, while the totals were too flexible to exert the necessary downward pressure

on demands so as to produce lower levels of spending. Is there any way out of this trap?

Limits

The idea of budgeting from above—either by limiting revenue and requiring expenditure to fit within it, or limiting spending and forbidding revenue to exceed that level—would revolutionize resource mobilization and resource allocation. Budgeting by addition would no longer be possible; adding requests together would not work because exceeding a prearranged total would be ruled out. More for one program or agency, consequently, would mean less for another. Budgeting by subtraction—tradeoffs among good things that could not all be funded—would usher in a new budgetary order. Budgeting would become more like the 1981 Reagan-Stockman reconciliation procedure than anything before or since.

The spending-and-revenue limit plus budget balance amendment is designed to do just that. By embodying limits in a more permanent form in the Constitution and specifying their total—last year's outlays times the percentage increase in national income—without predetermining priorities within this total, an effort is made to combine centralization with decentralization.

The amendment's supporters believe the existing budgetary process is biased in favor of higher spending because it focuses attention on individual programs rather than totals. They believe that by placing programs in competition, within a limited total, the public's desire for less total spending can be made compatible with its support for many of the programs that make up public expenditure.

The amendment encapsulates a macro- and micropolitical theory. The macro theory expresses a political preference: The public sector should not expand into the private sector. This philosophy is supported by the provision that spending cannot exceed the percentage growth in national income. The micro theory seeks to create incentives for limiting expenditure by motivating program advocates to restrain their demands. Imposing a global limit means that increases for one program or agency above the percentage increase in national income must be accompanied by equivalent decreases in others. Budgeting by addition, in which program costs are piled on top of each other to be paid for by tax increases or debt, would be replaced by budgeting by subtraction, in which desired increases would have to compete within the limits of economic growth.

The political result of constitutional revenue-and-expenditure limitation, according to its advocates, would be to increase cooperation in society and conflict within government. As things stand, so the amendment's supporters contend, program advocates within government, by increasing their total share of national income, have every incentive to raise their spending while reducing their internal differences. Why fight among their public selves if private persons will pay? Thus conflict is transferred from government to society.

Once limits are enacted, however, the amendment's advocates believe, the direction of incentives would be reversed: There would be increasing cooperation in society and rising conflict in government. Citizens in society would have a common interest whereas the sectors of policy—housing, welfare, environment, defense—would be plunged into conflict. Organizations interested in income redistribution to favor poorer people would come to understand that the greater the increase in real national income, the more there would be for government to spend on their purposes. Instead of acting as if it didn't matter where the money came from, such groups would have to consider how they might contribute to enhanced productivity. Management and labor, majorities and minorities, would be thinking about common objectives, about how to get more out of one another rather than about how to take more from the other.

Make no mistake, the amendment would radically alter the character of contemporary budgeting. For one thing, there would have to be grave concern about exceeding allowed totals. Hence money would have to be kept back in the form of large contingency funds. For another, entitlements could not be guaranteed at full value; if the total were about to be breached, payments might have to be reduced, say from 100 to 97 percent of the guarantee. The amendment, that is, would modify open-ended promises to citizens—you will get yours no matter what—with only the promise (by their collective expression, the government) that beneficiaries would get something close to what they expected.

Since constitutional spending limits have so far failed to gather the necessary support, attention has turned either to legislative remedies—the Gramm-Rudman-Hollings offset procedure—or to narrower constitutional changes—the presidential item veto. None of these proposed reforms, I shall argue, does away with the need for prior agreement on the scope and distribution of taxing and spending. Put plainly, the federal government could control spending if it could only agree on how much for what purpose and who is to pay.

The Line-Item Veto

With the 1988 election coming up, facing the unpleasant task of explaining away historically unprecedented deficits, unwilling to talk of raising taxes, and unable to reduce domestic spending—it is understandable that Republicans speak favorably of the line-item veto. So long as the Democrats resist, blame for continuing deficits may be placed on them. And, focusing entirely on the immediate future, Republicans may well indulge themselves in fantasies of their leader cutting and slashing, slashing and cutting, until big government is vetoed out root and branch. But that is all it is—a fantasy.

Experience of States with the Item Veto

Experience in state governments has been cited to support the efficacy of the item veto. The argument for the item veto rests on a combination of alleged cuts made by states, together with a version of the marginal fallacy. On the surface it does appear that under certain governors in some states, such as Ronald Reagan in California, the item veto eliminated 1 or 2 percent of spending, which, if cumulated over a number of years, adds up to significant reductions. I say "alleged" savings because it is well known that legislators pad their requests in anticipation of vetoes.

Apparently, it is possible to interweave items so that they are not separable, thereby nullifying the intent of the item veto. At least, Roy D. Morey, writing about Arizona, says that "A major reason why the governor has not used the item veto more frequently is that the legislature has deliberately constructed appropriation bills in such a way as to stymie its use. Those items which the legislature feels have questionable gubernatorial support are rearranged or lumped with those items the governor is forced, either by conviction or necessity, to approve.[12] For this reason, Morey concludes that "this device has proved to be of little value to Arizona governors."[13] It appears that the item veto is more powerful in Pennsylvania where governors do use it a good deal. But this conclusion must be modified by interaction effects: "When a legislator, even though opposed in principle to an appropriation, is reasonably certain that the governor will slice it down to more moderate size," M. Nelson McGeary states in his study of Pennsylvania, "he is tempted to bolster himself politically by voting large sums of money to a popular cause."[14] Where there is no item veto, as in North Carolina, Coleman B. Ransome, Jr., reports that "the legislature seems to have developed some sense of responsibility; there can be no buck-passing of undesirable legislation to the governor with the knowledge that he will veto the bill in question and thus take the burden from the legislature."[15]

A fatal impediment to a federal line-item veto shows up in the detailed and separable character of state budgets, which makes it relatively easy for most governors to select out the parts they wish to reject. At the federal level, however, budget items are far larger and more aggregated. Thus there would normally be no way for a president to veto individual public works projects, since the budget lists only general totals, while individual projects are found in committee reports. Hence the president would have to veto all public works spending and not just the projects to which he objected.[16]

A Little Tool for a Big Job

It takes little imagination to realize that presidents far different from Ronald Reagan are going to occupy the White House. Would a Mario Cuomo or an Edward Kennedy (to mention just two well-known liberal Democrats) use the item veto to increase defense and decrease domestic spending, or might not it be just the other way around? Might not a president interested in increasing domestic spending hold defense spending ransom to achieve that very purpose?

Even granting proponents the best of their possible worlds—their president in the White House ready to throttle the expenditure machine, Saint Ronald versus the spending dragons—does not rescue the item veto from the charge of inappropriateness. The president does not wish to cut defense, which amounts to around 28 percent of the budget. Reagan has, without the item veto, helped reduce small, means-tested entitlements; and his inability and/or unwillingness to cut the large universal entitlements, especially social security, in view of the political price, would, in any event, remain unaffected by the item veto. Nor is this all. Together these social welfare programs amount to about 46 percent of the budget. Allowing approximately 14 percent (and rising!) for interest on the debt, this leaves little more than a small number (16 percent) on which to try the item veto.

Even there, in the midst of general government, or what is left of it, there is much that will prove resistant to the item veto. There is misadventure. Rejecting smaller items may increase support for overriding vetos on larger ones. There is politics. Perhaps the president's people think he will use the item veto to eliminate or reduce politically important expenditures on which there has long been a negative professional consensus. I refer to agricultural and maritime subsidies, way-below-market prices for grazing rights on federal land, water for irrigation in the west, all sorts of river and harbor projects, and the like. In any event, though there are, as always, tempting targets for elimination, there is not enough to make a big difference in that 11 percent of the federal budget which in part has already been severely pruned.

There is misconception. The item veto cannot quell the widespread will to spend. What it does is convey an image of presidents valiantly trying to stem the tide of spending but, for want of this one weapon, being overwhelmed by hordes of congressional spenders. There is no truth in this. Presidents have been in the forefront of spending. In this respect, think not only of Democrat Lyndon Johnson but of Republican Richard Nixon, in whose administration, and in service to his vaunted flexibility, huge increases took place in social security, loan guarantees, and other prospending developments too numerous to mention. There also are other misconceptions about political systems in general and American politics in particular that lie behind belief in the efficacy of the item veto.

First the general, then the particular: The general case against the sufficiency of the item veto is overwhelming. Line up the world leaders favoring public expenditure as a proportion of GNP among democracies: In all of these countries, cabinets have the power to determine the entire spending budget, item by item. These governments do not need an item veto because nothing gets into the budget without their approval. Why, then, do the budgets grow? Part of the reason (in some but by no means all of these spending leaders) is that most have coalition governments or corporatist arrangements in which the cost of consent is side payments to partners, thus increasing the size of the budget. To the extent that the United States shares this characteristic of divided government—either because the presidency and all or part of Congress are held by different parties or because, though ostensibly of the same party, their policy preferences differ—there is no reason to believe the item veto will do what total formal control of the budget cannot.

It is not that most of these governments do not have periodic budget cutting drives, but that these campaigns are never (that's right, never) successful.[17] Hence the essential nature of the problem is clarified: governmental self-control. Governments must (1) want to reduce spending and (2) have an effective technology for doing so. The item veto does not qualify as an effective instrument of spending control because it locks the Treasury doors after the spending bids have already been proposed. The trick is to inhibit the presentation of expenditure demands, not to engage in the futile task of rejecting a small proportion after they have been made. Nor is this relationship—prevention is preferable to cure—unique to budgeting. Once participants in the budgetary process assume that it is desirable to ask for more or that end-runs around the process (loans, guarantees, entitlements, regulations) pay off, the game is lost. For no central controller has the time to examine so many programs or the capacity to understand them. Where information is a prerequisite of control, the numerous people on the spot are bound to prevail over the few who are far away. Just as criminals should be deterred before crimes are committed, spending agencies must be persuaded to limit their demands at the source. Where governments spend increasing proportions of GNP because that is what citizens want, they will not fix spending because they believe it isn't broken. Under such conditions, the item veto is irrelevant because the idea is to include expenditures in, not exclude them out.

To consider the United States by itself, there is a good chance that the item veto, instead of merely being limited or ineffective, would be positively counterproductive. Understanding why this might well happen requires a brief excursion into the separation of powers. The legislative function is shared between Congress and the president. Every schoolchild knows that. Presidents may veto proposed legislation and Congress may pass it into law by a two-thirds vote. That is also understood. What is not stated, because it is taken for granted, is that Congress may act irresponsibly, i.e., pass a law and not be accountable for it. For then the branches of government really would not be separated—each one responsible within its sphere, cooperating when possible, conflicting when necessary—but joined together. But not openly.

Voting on the understanding that a bill may become law is not quite the same as expecting part of the proposal to be taken out even though the rest will remain. The responsibility of the president has been clarified and strengthened: He is responsible for every part of an appropriation or a law he does not veto. Whereas before he had to make a judgment about whether to accept or to reject the bill as a whole, now he can pick and choose. Thus the old excuse that the president did not want a particular appropriation but had to accept it as part of a package would no longer be acceptable. Instead of putting the onus on Congress to moderate its expenditure proposals, the item veto, by giving presidents more formal power, also places the onus on them.

How tempting! Weakening the formal powers of Congress would make it more irresponsible. Congress would have less reason to consider the collective consequences of its acts. Why should it? After all, presidents can (soon legislators will think "should") veto every item proposing spending of which they do not approve. Why not just throw in whatever is at hand and leave it to the president to get rid of the worst? Certainly, the efforts of congressmen to convince constituents that a particular item was of low priority (every bit of spending helps somebody, or so they think, or they would not want it) is gravely weakened by the retort: Let the president worry about that. With proposals for spending becoming entirely a sign of good will rather than of collective responsibility, who will refuse? How helping Congress avoid responsibility will reduce the growth of spending is not self-evident.

An argument used in favor of the item veto is that it would interfere with the normal practice of log-rolling in Congress. Here is legislation (in this example, items of appropriation) whose passage depends on spreading benefits broadly. If A gets a project but B does not, then A's project is also in jeopardy. At first blush, it appears that withdrawing a log (or logs) from the roll will mean fewer agreements and hence lower spending. QED: the item veto will reduce spending. Or will it? A linear argument suggests a one-way result; bringing in circular interaction effects can lead to the opposite conclusion. As a perceptive congressman put it, in a confidential interview,

> Where Congress has appropriated for A and for B, Congress means to say that it gives to each, conditioned upon the gift to the other, and that it gives to neither unless it gives to both. . . . The new veto power proposed would give the President the right by the veto of one and the approval of the other, to exercise the function of giving to one an appropriation independent of the other, when Congress has only given it conditioned upon the appropriation to the other.[18]

Congress is a highly interactive and tightly linked system. Alter one element and the others are also likely to change. When Congress is faced with the perpetual problem of overriding vetoes, the structure of incentives will change to favor much larger (and, therefore, aggregatively more expensive) log-rolls. The ultimate size of unrepentent logrolling, the making of bargains that cumulate into ever-larger aggregates, cannot be reduced by cutting the number of small bargains because that only increases the incentive to make bigger bargains. What is necessary is to begin at the end, i.e., to start by fixing the total permissible size of all bargains so that all expenditure logs must fit within a preexisting size. Then logrolls would compete with each other, thereby ending their upward spiral.

According to Lord Bryce, the item veto is one of those practices that "is desired by enlightened opinion."[19] The executive would be strengthened (doubly so in Bryce's day, since at the end of the nineteenth century the executive budget was not yet a reality) and responsibility more clearly identified and located in a centralized place. Indeed, the origin of the item veto in the United States lies in the Constitution of the Confederate States. The rationale there and then was avowedly to bring in some of the advantages of the British way. As we know, this hypothesis was never put to the test because the political system in which it was embedded was overthrown.

Without a global spending limit, the line-item veto would be both weak and perverse. It would be weak because the veto would apply only to a small proportion of the budget that is, like general government, either already under severe attack or, like maritime subsidies, has so far proved politically invulnerable. It would be perverse because pro-expenditure presidents could use the veto (or, more accurately, the threat of veto) to increase total spending, and because legislators would use the existence of a veto to increase spending bids on the grounds that presidents could always veto them if they were deemed unsound. Thus a measure designed to reduce spending and increase responsibility for budgetary totals probably would have exactly the opposite effects—increasing irresponsibility as well as the size of the budget.

But I have not yet considered how a line-item veto might work in the presence rather than the absence of global spending limits. Let us suppose that, by congressional or by constitutional action, budget outlays for any year are forbidden to exceed the prior year's totals times the percentage increase in GNP. Everyone would know that spending could not exceed a given sum for years to come. Let us suppose, further, that the usual incentives operated and spending reached this global limit. No doubt such a situation would reduce the demand for an item veto on the grounds that the end in view, i.e., control over spending, had been achieved by far more stringent and effective means. Nevertheless, I believe it will be instructive to consider how the veto would work under these much-altered circumstances.

Presidents so disposed could not use the threat of vetoing an item desired by many in Congress simply in order to increase an item they preferred. For, if more for one item means less for another (recall that everyone is operating at the margin of the global limit), presidents would have to match substantial increases with proposed cuts or leave it to congressmen to cut where they wanted. Such a strategy would be self-defeating.

Nor would congressional spenders be disposed to pad old items or slip in new ones on the supposition that presidents would be responsible for vetoing them. Under the new rules imposed by global spending limits, Congress could not act so as to exceed the global total. Congress itself would have to cut some items to make up for increases in others. Now this is what I understand about taking responsibility for the consequences of one's own actions. If Congress proposed a budget exceeding the limit (and even if it stayed within the limit), presidents could use their veto to cut at will, a process that would leave Congress in the weakest possible position.

With limits in place, therefore, the item veto would be restricted to two uses: (1) reducing the size of the budget below the global total, or (2) enhancing the bargaining power of presidents, vis-à-vis a congressional majority in regard to which items should be included in the budget at what level. Assuming that presidents, over a range of vetoes, have reasonable prospects of support from a little over one-third of the House or Senate, they can eliminate (or, in prior bargaining, reduce the amount of) spending items in dispute. This would spell enormous power for presidents who, with only minority support, could impose their will. Perhaps that threat would suffice to enhance the prospects of items presidents prefer over those desired by an ordinary majority of Congress. Perhaps Congress, mindful of being at a disadvantage, would word items so as to make them difficult to veto. In any event, we see that under global limits the item veto would actually work in the ways its sponsors desire by sometimes decreasing but never increasing the size of spending and by giving presidents greater power to make marginal adjustments in the budget. But if an item veto would work only in the presence of preexisting limits, we must turn to the question of limits for further instruction.

Responsibility, Maybe

If the item veto won't work, if Gramm-Rudman-Hollings is unworkable, if the balanced budget amendment is unpopular, what hope is there for responsible budgeting—i.e., for paying for what you spend?

There is a glimmer of hope. In the letter from the House Republican leadership quoted in the Preface there was concern expressed about the absence of a point of order in the House against an appropriations bill that breaches the outlay total in the budget resolution. This concern is justified. Recently, the

Committee for a Responsible Budget sounded the alarm. (See their letter on p. [439]).

Wonder of wonders, the House voted to cut the supplemental by $2 billion across-the-board to keep the appropriation within the total allocation. Responsibility lives. Maybe.

Wonders never cease. The beekeepers entitlement has been significantly altered. Now, instead of storing honey and encouraging producers to default on their loans, they keep the honey and receive the difference between the support price and the market price. The difference, aside from much lower administrative costs, is that domestic honey producers can now meet market competition. Consequently, American honey producers are now regaining the domestic market that had gone to foreign suppliers. While Senator Dan Quade (R-Ind) would like Congress "to eliminate the program entirely," marketing orders, as these payments are called, make more sense than storage and default.[20]

Overloading Budgeting

In the period of classical budgeting, there was an effective, albeit informal, ceiling beyond which spending could not go. Nowadays there are basic disagreements about the size and composition of the public sector. Bringing back the good old ways implies something that can no longer be achieved, namely, summoning up agreement on the underlying beliefs that once made them work.

Indeed, budget resolutions, automatic spending reductions to achieve balance, item vetos, balanced budget amendments, and offsets are all formal substitutes for what used to be done informally. If (and when) congressional majorities do wish to control spending, we have seen that spending ceilings safeguarded by requiring that additions be balanced by subtractions (or by new revenues) work powerfully well. There's a way if there's a will. Suppose, however, that not one, but several wills are incompatible? Then perhaps the budgetary stalemate of the early to mid-1980s may be seen not as an aberration but as a sign of continuing dissensus. What, then, can be hoped for from budgeting?

The budgetary process is an arena in which the struggle for power over public policy is worked out. Budgeting is a forum for the exercise of political power, not a substitute for that power. By itself,

RESPONSIBLE BUDGET ACTION GROUP

220 1/2 "E" STREET, N E
WASHINGTON, D.C. 20002

(202) 547-4484

April 9, 1987

Members of the 100th Congress
U.S. House of Representatives
Washington, DC 20515

Dear Congressman:

Do you think the supplemental appropriations bill is just business as usual? If so, maybe you ought to consider what the final results on the Gramm-Rudman-Hollings FY87 deficit target will be. The FY87 Spring Supplemental Appropriations Bill (H.R. 1827) is as clear a vote as you ever will face on fiscal responsibility.

The simple fact is: there is no money to pay for this bill. The CBO current status shows that even if Congress does not pass another spending bill this year, outlays will exceed the FY87 budget total by $13.4 billion.

We recognize there may be high priority items for which you must pass a supplemental appropriations bill. This is not an argument for or against the specific spending items in this bill. Congress, however, should find off-sets to pay for those increases—given the fact that you already are over the budget.

In the House, there is no point of order against an appropriations bill which breaches the outlay total in the budget. The Appropriations Committee will argue they are within the budget authority ceiling, and budget authority is all the Appropriations Committee really can control, so there should be no budget argument about this bill.

But outlays do matter. We determine the deficit by subtracting revenues from outlays. The outlay overages which would result from enactment of H.R. 1827 are not assumed in the baseline for FY87. Enactment of this bill without off-sets would increase the deficit both this year and next.

Early last year, the first and only sequester under G-R-H cut FY86 outlays by $11.4 billion. That action had an added benefit. It reduced this year's deficit by $16.3 billion. This supplemental, by contrast, would make the deficit problem worse next year. H.R. 1827 as reported would eat up nearly half the spending cuts contained in the Budget Resolution the House just adopted for FY88.

If you care about the size of next year's deficit, if you care about trying to live within the budget this year, you cannot ignore the impact of this bill. The amounts involved are not large in the context of total Federal spending: less than 1% of total outlays controllable through appropriations actions; but they are significant as a measure of Congress' commitment to spending restraint. If reducing the deficit remains a high priority on your agenda, surely you can find off-sets for spending you believe to be necessary.

Sincerely,

Robert N. Giaimo   John J. Rhodes

RNG/JJR:mfh

budgeting cannot form majorities and enforce their will. While the rules for voting on spending and taxing may make agreement marginally easier or harder, they cannot close unbridgeable gaps. It is more reasonable to suppose that general political processes shape budgeting than that budgeting determines political alignments.

It is one thing to translate decisions and choices on defense and domestic policy into budgetary categories; it is quite another to use the budgetary process itself to decide who shall pay and who shall receive. Only a political system so polarized that it cannot make these choices through the usual legislative, executive, and party mechanisms, I submit, would arrive at a general formula (e.g., GRH) for maximizing discontent rather than trying to agree, case by case, on reasonable choices. To saddle budgeting with a formula for decision making that is nearly as broad as government itself is to make budgeting equivalent to government. I bring up this truism—budgeting is a subsystem of politics, not vice versa—because of the current tendency to overload budgeting. As much as I respect the importance of budgeting and the talents of budgeters, to substitute budgeting for governing will not work.

Notes

1. Dwight Waldo, *The Administrative State* (New York: Ronald Press, 1948); Herbert A. Simon, "The Criterion of Efficiency," in *Administrative Behavior*, 2nd ed. (New York: Macmillan, 1957), pp. 172–197.
2. See Hugh Heclo and Aaron Wildavsky, *The Private Government of Public Money: Community and Policy inside British Political Administration*, 2nd ed. (London: Macmillan, 1981).
3. Symposium on Budget Balance, p. IV-30.
4. Robert A. Hartman, "Multiyear Budget Planning," in Joseph A. Pechman, ed., *Setting National Priorities: The 1979 Budget* (Washington, D.C.: The Brookings Institution, 1978), p. 312.
5. See Jeanne Nienaber and Aaron Wildavsky, *The Budgeting and Evaluation of Federal Recreation Programs, or Money Doesn't Grow on Trees* (New York: Basic Books, 1973).
6. See Thomas H. Hammond and Jack H. Knott, *A Zero-Based Look at Zero-Base Budgeting* (New Brunswick, N.J.: Transaction, 1979).
7. The importance of these principles is discussed in my *Speaking Truth to Power: The Art and Craft of Policy Analysis* (Boston: Little, Brown, 1979).
8. See Naomi Caiden and Aaron Wildavsky, *Planning and Budgeting in Poor Countries* (New York: Wiley, 1974).
9. Report to the Committee on Environment and Public Works, U.S. Senate by the Comptroller General of the United States, "Pros and Cons of a Separate Capital Budget for the Federal Government," GAO/PAD-83-1, September 22, 1983, p. 8.
10. See Aaron Wildavsky, *The Politics of the Budgetary Process* (Boston: Little, Brown, first published in 1964; revised fourth edition, 1984).
11. Aaron Wildavsky, "The Transformation of Budgetary Norms," *Australian Journal of Public Administration*, Vol. XLII, No. 4 (December 1983), pp. 421–432.
12. Roy D. Morey, "The Executive Veto in Arizona: Its Use and Limitations," *The Western Political Quarterly*, Vol. 19, No. 3 (September 1966), quote on p. 512.
13. *Ibid.*, p. 515.
14. M. Nelson McGeary, "The Governor's Veto in Pennsylvania," *American Political Science Review*, Vol. 41, No. 5 (October 1974), p. 943.
15. Coleman B. Ransome, Jr., *The American Governorship* (Westport, Conn.: Greenwood Press, 1982), p. 159.
16. See Louis Fisher, "The Item Veto: The Risks of Emulating the States." Prepared for delivery at the 1985 Annual Meeting of the American Political Science Association, New Orleans, August 29–31, 1985.
17. See Daniel L. Tarschys, "Curbing Public Expenditures: A Survey of Current Trends." Paper prepared for the Joint Activity on Public Management Improvement of the Organisation for Economic Co-Operation and Development, Paris (Technical Co-Operation Service), April 1982.
18. House Resolution No. 1879, 49th Congress, 1st Session, 3.
19. Quoted in John F. Wolf, "The Item Veto in the American Constitutional System," *Georgetown Law Journal*, Vol. 25 (1936), p. 113.
20. Jonathan Rauch, "Why the Honey Bees Aren't Laughing," *National Journal*, July 4, 1987, p. 1737.

A

The Federal Budget as a Second Language

Stanley Collender

The Federal Budget as a Second Language

Authorization Versus Appropriation

Two steps must usually occur before the federal government can spend money on an activity. First, an authorization must be passed allowing a program to exist. The authorization is the substantive legislation that establishes the purpose and guidelines for a given activity and usually sets the limit on the amount that can be spent. The authorization does not, however, provide the actual dollars for a program or enable an agency or department to spend funds in the future. Second, an appropriation must be passed. The appropriation enables an agency or department to (1) make spending commitments and (2) spend money.

Except in the case of entitlements, an appropriation is the key determinant of how much will be spent on a program. In almost all cases, however, an appropriation for a given activity cannot be made until the authorization is enacted. No money can be spent on a program unless it first has been allowed (authorized) to exist. Conversely, if a program is authorized but no money is provided (appropriated) for its implementation, that activity cannot be carried out. Therefore, both an authorization and an appropriation are necessary for an activity to be included in the budget.[1]

A particularly confusing aspect of these two legislative requirements is that both authorizations and appropriations generally describe an activity in dollar terms. For example, the fiscal 1982 authorization for the administrative expenses of the United States Railway Association stated: "There are authorized to be appropriated to the Association for purposes of carrying out its administrative expenses under this Act not to exceed $13,000,000 . . . ,"[2]

Source: Stanley Collender, *The Guide to the Federal Budget*: *Fiscal 1991*, (Washington, D.C.: The Urban Institute Press, 1990), pp. 1–13, 17–32. Reprinted by permission.

whereas the fiscal 1982 appropriation for the same organization stated: "For necessary administrative expenses to enable the United States Railway Association to carry out its functions . . . $13,000,000."[3]

Despite the fact that both seem to be providing $13 million, only the appropriation is actually doing so. The dollar figures in the authorization serve only as an upper limit on what can be appropriated. An appropriation is not supposed to exceed the authorization for the same program.

An entitlement is a particular type of authorization that requires the federal government to pay benefits to any person or unit of government that meets the eligibility requirements it establishes. An entitlement differs from other authorizations because it constitutes a legally binding commitment on the federal government. Although, like all other programs, an entitlement requires an appropriation, its appropriation is permanent and indefinite so that the amount spent each year is not determined through the annual appropriations process. The amount needed to pay all the eligible beneficiaries is provided automatically.

In fact, eligible potential recipients may sue the federal government if entitlement benefits are denied to them because funds are not appropriated. The authorization, therefore, is the key legislation in deciding how much will be spent on an entitlement and relegates the appropriation to little more than a formality. Examples of entitlement programs are Medicare, Medicaid, and Social Security.

Budget Authority Versus Outlays

The dollar amounts listed in both authorization and appropriation bills are stated in terms of "budget authority." Budget Authority (BA) is the permission granted to an agency or department to make commitments to spend money—such as hiring workers (committing funds for salaries) and signing contracts to procure some item (committing funds for payment upon completion of the contract). In most cases, budget authority is not the level at which a program will function but merely the level of new spending commitments that will be or have been made. It is important to remember that although budget authority will lead to the spending of money, it is not the actual exchange of cash.

Outlays (O) are the actual dollars that either have been or will be spent on a particular activity. Outlays are the direct result of budget authority, that is, the commitments to spend money made either this year or in previous years. The level of outlays is the key number to use in determining how much has been or will be spent on a program. The overall level of outlays compared with the overall level of revenues determines whether the budget is in surplus or deficit.

Figures for both budget authority and outlays are needed because many government activities are not completed within a single fiscal year, and it is important to know both what the total cost will be (budget authority) and what will have to be spent this year (outlays). By looking beyond this year's spending requirements to the overall cost of the activity, the president and Congress can know the future spending commitments they are making as well as the cash required immediately.

Knowing future spending commitments is particularly important for activities that take several years to complete, for example, the procurement of an aircraft carrier. In this case, outlays in the first year will be relatively small because it takes a long time to start construction. The budget authority in the first year, however, will be large because it will reflect the full cost of the ship. In the second year there will be no new budget authority because the full cost was provided in the previous year's budget and permission to commit funds was previously granted. Outlays for this ship, however, will begin to increase in the second year as construction continues and accelerates. This pattern of no new budget authority but outlays occurring will continue each year until the procurement is completed.

A good analogy is the purchase of an automobile with a three-year loan. When the purchase of the car (at a total cost of $10,000, for example) is arranged, a contract is signed for the full amount and the "budget authority" is $10,000. But the actual amount to be spent ("outlays") in the first year is only equal to the down payment ($2,500, for example) plus the monthly payments (another $2,500). In the second year no new budget authority is needed because the loan already has been arranged and the commitment made, but the outlays are equal to the monthly payments ($2,500 in this case). In the third and final year again there would be no new budget authority, but the outlays again would equal $2,500, at which point the loan would be repaid. Table 1 shows how the federal budget typically depicts this situation.[4]

It should be clear from Table 1 that neither budget authority nor outlays alone are sufficient to tell the full budgetary consequences of purchasing this car.

Table 1
Purchase of automobile
(in thousands of dollars)

	Fiscal Year		
	1990	*1991*	*1992*
Budget Authority (BA)	10.0	0.0	0.0
Outlays (O)	5.0	2.5	2.5

By looking only at budget authority in fiscal 1990, the program might seem too expensive to undertake because the full cost of the car appears to be needed in that year. Yet by looking only at the budget authority in fiscal years 1991 and 1992, the car looks too good to pass up because it appears to cost nothing even though substantial spending is, in fact, required. But if you look only at the outlays in a particular year, you would not know the full cost of the car because only the yearly spending requirements are obvious.

Some governmental activities, notably the payment of salaries and entitlements, usually "spend out" within the fiscal year in which the budget authority is provided. In these cases, budget authority and outlays are approximately equal. In some cases, however, the level of outlays appears to be greater than the level of budget authority. This situation generally is the result of budget authority that was provided in the previous years but is only now being spent. The level of outlays for a particular year is, therefore, the combination of budget authority provided that year and in previous years.

It is difficult, however, to determine simply by looking at the tables in the budget whether outlays are the result of budget authority provided this year or in previous years; usually some knowledge of the program is necessary. Take the previous example of an automobile purchased with a three-year loan. Table 2 shows how the federal budget typically

Table 2
Purchase of two automobiles
(in thousands of dollars)

	Fiscal Year		
	1990	*1991*	*1992*
Budget Authority (BA)	10.0	10.0	0.0
Outlays (O)	5.0	7.5	5.0

would depict the situation if a second car is purchased in a similar manner at the same cost in fiscal 1991.

It would be wrong to assume that the $7,500 in outlays in fiscal 1991 is the result of the $10,000 in budget authority provided in fiscal 1991. In fact, only $5,000 comes from this new budget authority. The remaining $2,500 comes from budget authority provided in fiscal 1990 that is now coming due (the monthly payments from the automobile purchased in that year). Even if the decision was made not to buy the car in 1991 and the entire $10,000 in budget authority were cut from the 1990 budget, $2,500 still would be spent in fiscal 1991 as the result of the previous spending decision. Fiscal 1992 spending, however, would drop to $2,500.

Figure 1 depicts the relationship between budget authority and outlays in the Reagan fiscal 1990 budget as a whole. The president proposed a budget with outlays of $1,151.8 billion (upper-right hand corner). Only 63.5 percent of that amount, or $731.0 billion was projected to result from the requested fiscal 1990 budget authority of $1,331.2 billion (upper left-hand corner), however. The remaining 36.5 percent, or $420.9 billion was the result of unspent budget authority granted in previous years (lower left-hand corner). The $600.2 billion in budget authority requested for fiscal 1990 that was not expected to result in fiscal 1990 outlays was to be added to the $973.7 billion in budget authority provided in previous years that was expected to continue to remain unspent. This $1,574.0 billion was the total amount of unspent budget authority that was projected to result in outlays in fiscal 1991 and beyond (bottom right-hand corner).[5]

Controllable Versus Uncontrollable Spending

The $1,574.0 billion in unspent budget authority is a significant part of what is classified as "relatively uncontrollable" spending. Such spending is not out of control in the literal sense. It consists of outlays that result from prior-year commitments of the federal government, including previously granted budget authority, entitlements, open-ended programs (which increase automatically as the economy grows), and permanent appropriations (interest on the national debt, for example) that require no further action by Congress. Of the $1,151.8 billion in outlays in the Reagan fiscal 1990 budget, $902.9 billion—78.4 percent—was classified by the administration as relatively uncontrollable.

RELATION OF BUDGET AUTHORITY TO OUTLAYS - 1990
$ Billions

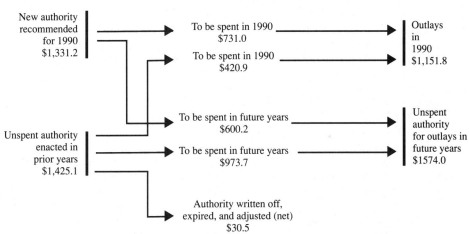

Figure 1
Relation of budget authority to outlays.
Source: Executive Office of the President, Office of Management and Budget (OMB), Budget of the United States Government, Fiscal Year 1990 (Washington, D.C.: U.S. Government Printing Office, 1989) (hereafter referred to as the Budget*), p. 7-5.*

"Controllable" spending will occur only if Congress passes and the president signs an appropriation for it. "Uncontrollable" is, however, a misnomer because if Congress and the president choose to act, they can change many laws to alter the amount expected to be spent or to stop such spending entirely. In other words, controllable spending will occur only if Congress takes some action (such as an appropriation) to cause it. Uncontrollable spending will occur unless Congress takes some action to stop it.

Economic Assumptions

The federal budget is very sensitive to changes in the economy. The spending level of many programs changes as interest rates, inflation, and unemployment increase or decrease. Similarly, the amount of revenues collected by the government changes as the economy, usually measured by the gross national product (GNP), declines or grows because businesses and individuals pay taxes according to their earnings. Whenever the president and Congress formulate the budget, therefore, they must make certain assumptions about how well or how poorly the economy is likely to do in the future.

Economic assumptions have been a source of constant confusion and controversy over the past few years. Because the president, the House and Senate Budget Committees, and the Congressional Budget Office (CBO) often use different economic projections, the budgets are not always comparable. In addition, the same budgets with different economic assumptions produce different results. For example, the Bush fiscal 1990 budget projected a deficit of $92.5 billion using economic assumptions that many believed were optimistic. Using its own forecast that differed substantially from the president's, CBO re-estimated the Bush deficit to be $120 billion, $27.5 billion higher. Both of these estimates were for the same budget and included the same spending and tax proposals.

Table 3 shows the differences that existed between the original Bush Administration and CBO economic assumptions for 1990.

Appendix C [of Collender's text] provides current estimates for the impact of several changes in the economy on revenues, outlays, and the deficit.

Budget Function

The president's budget and the congressional budget resolution present each program according

Table 3

Bush versus CBO 1990 economic assumptions

	Bush	CBO
GNP *(percent change from 1989, in constant 1982 dollars)*	3.4	2.2
Consumer Price Index *(percent change from 1989)*	3.5	4.8
Interest Rate, 91-Day Treasury bills	5.5	7.1

Source: U.S. Congress, Congressional Budget Office, *An Analysis of the President's Budgetary Proposals for Fiscal 1990* (Washington, D.C.: U.S. Government Printing Office, 1989), p. 12.

to the principal national need they are intended to serve. These needs constitute general areas of federal activity (agriculture, health, general government, and so on) and are referred to as "functions." Every program, regardless of the agency or department that administers it, is placed in the one function of the budget that best describes its most important purpose.

A function is not the same as the budget of a particular department. The National Defense function, for example, is different from the Department of Defense budget because the function also includes some nuclear weapons programs administered by the Department of Energy. In addition, a department's budget often is part of a number of different functions. The Treasury Department, for instance, administers programs in a number of different functions, including Commerce and Housing Credit, General Government, and International Affairs. Finally, a function does not correspond precisely to an authorization or appropriation bill, which usually deals with parts of several different functions at the same time.

Each function is separated into subfunctions, which divide the programs according to the "major mission" they fulfill. The first two digits of a subfunction are the same as the digits for the main function; only the last digit is different. For example, function 400, Transportation, contains the following four subfunctions—401, Ground Transportation; 402, Air Transportation; 403, Water Transportation; and 407, Other Transportation.

In the past, one part of the *Budget of the United States Government* described the budget by function. A separate part listed all programs according to the department or agency administering them. Appendix D of this [Collender's] book describes each function

Table 4
Functions of the fiscal 1991 budget

Number	Title
050	National Defense
150	International Affairs
250	General Science, Space, and Technology
270	Energy
300	Natural Resources and Environment
350	Agriculture
370	Commerce and Housing Credit
400	Transportation
450	Community and Regional Development
500	Education, Training, Employment, and Social Services
550	Health
570	Medicare
600	Income Security
650	Social Security
700	Veterans Benefits and Services
750	Administration of Justice
800	General Government
900	Net Interest
920	Allowances
950	Undistributed Offsetting Receipts

and includes a list of the major agencies, departments, and programs each contains.

Sequesters Versus Impoundments[6]

The Balanced Budget and Emergency Deficit Control Act of 1985[7] (commonly known as Gramm-Rudman-Hollings) created a new budget procedure—sequestration.

Under the provisions of this act as it was revised in 1987, the president must issue a sequestration order to cut spending if the director of OMB determines that the GRH maximum deficit amount for the year will be exceeded by $10 billion or more.[8] GRH itself specifies both the amount that must be cut and the formula that must be used to determine how much each program must be reduced.

This is very different from another presidential budgeting decision that can be used to reduce spending—impoundments. An impoundment is when the president proposes not to spend all or part of an enacted appropriation. The president has the total authority to determine whether and when an impoundment will be proposed and which programs will be affected to what extent. However, under the provisions of the Congressional Budget and Impoundment

Control Act of 1974,[9] Congress has the responsibility to review and pass judgment on all proposed impoundments. Without congressional approval, an impoundment cannot become effective and, therefore, spending cannot be cut.

Baselines

A baseline is a projection of what will happen to spending and revenues based on certain assumptions. For example, suppose the federal government spent $100 on a certain program in fiscal 1989, and the assumption was that it would grow every year by 5 percent. This assumption could be based on anything—an automatic cost of living adjustment that is included in the law that created the program; an assumption that Congress will provide enough funds to keep the program even with inflation; an expected increase in the number of people eligible for the program; and so on. Regardless of the reason, as Table 5 shows, a 5 percent annual increase means that the baseline for this program would grow from $100 in 1990 to almost $122 three years later.

A baseline is important because it provides a way to determine the impact of a proposal on what is expected to happen under the current assumptions. In the example shown in Table 5, suppose that in 1990 the president proposes to increase spending in this program to $106. This is an increase over the amount spent in 1989 of $6. However, it is an increase of only $1 over the baseline—the amount that is assumed will be spent anyway.

When Congress or the White House talks about spending or tax reductions, they often calculate the amount of the cut from the baseline, thus making it appear larger than it really is. In the example above, a proposed $5 "cut" in 1991 is actually a proposal to keep spending at about the same level as the previous year. Conversely, talk about spending or tax increases is often based not on the baseline but on the previous year's actual level, thus making the hike seem larger. A proposed spending level of $108 in 1992 is an increase of $3 from 1990. However, it

Table 5
Baseline changes based on 5 percent a year growth

1989	1991	1992	1993	1994
100.0	105.0	110.3	115.8	121.6

is also a $2.30 reduction from what is assumed will otherwise be spent under the baseline assumptions.

Baselines are confusing because most of the organizations involved with the federal budget have their own, and each one uses different assumptions. In previous years, for example, OMB's baseline assumed that military spending would grow by inflation plus 2 percent every year, while CBO assumed that it would only stay even with inflation.

In addition, different baselines are sometimes required to be used at different points in the budget process. For example, Gramm-Rudman-Hollings requires that asset sales, loan prepayments, and certain other one-time revenue windfalls not be counted whenever the deficit is calculated to determine whether sequestration is needed, while they are included in the calculations at all other times. This generally changes the deficit estimate rather significantly. In 1989, for example, CBO's deficit estimate increased by $5.2 billion when the sequestration baseline was used rather than the one CBO uses the rest of the year.

In 1989, baselines became increasingly controversial because of OMB Director Richard Darman's attempt to avoid using the current services baseline and instead to compare everything to what was actually spent the previous year. Current services not only assumes an increase for inflation in most programs, for entitlements it also assumes additional increases to cover such changes as increased numbers of people who are expected to participate in the program. In these programs, the baseline amount can, therefore, be significantly above the amount that was spent the previous year, even though there is no change in policy.

Darman was upset because the Bush proposals to spend more than the previous year looked like cuts in comparison with the current services baseline. When compared with the previous year's actual amount, however, the proposals appeared to be rather generous.

What Darman did not say is that what he really wanted to do was play the same game using a different baseline, one that would show the president's proposals in the best possible light. Those that preferred the current services baseline wanted to be able to claim that the administration was cutting spending even though the amount that would be spent was more than was spent the previous year. Darman wanted to claim that the president was increasing spending even though the amount to be spent under the administration's proposal was less than was needed to maintain the same level of services.

What is most interesting is that, using different baselines, both sides in a dispute such as this can agree completely on what was spent last year and what the president is proposing. In other words, the baselines they use allow them to reach very different conclusions about exactly the same budget figures.

It is important to remember that baselines are not forecasts of what is going to happen. All they do is show how spending or revenues will change if the assumptions hold true.

On-Budget Versus Off-Budget

Not everything the federal government spends money on is reflected in the budget totals. Certain federal entities, programs, and some parts of programs have been specifically excluded from the budget. These are all considered to be "off-budget." Because the spending on these programs is not included in the budget totals, the deficit is not affected by it.

There is no specific list of reasons as to why some program is not included in the budget totals. The decisions are almost always political and can be changed depending on the year and situation. For example, until 1981 the purchase of oil for the strategic petroleum reserve was "on-budget," that is, any spending was included in the budget and the deficit was affected accordingly. In 1981, the Reagan Administration proposed and Congress agreed to take this spending off-budget. There was no specific reason for this other than the fact that the price of oil had increased and the White House did not want the deficit increasing by as much as would have occurred. Rather than propose to spend less or increase revenues or cut other programs to control the deficit, Reagan proposed to take the spending off-budget. In 1985, however, this program was put back into the budget again when Gramm-Rudman-Hollings was enacted.

The whole issue of on-budget versus off-budget spending became a somewhat more popular issue in 1989 because of the savings and loan bailout legislation. The Bush Administration wanted the expected $50 billion in spending between fiscal 1989 and 1991 to be off-budget, while Congress wanted it to be on-budget but to exempt it from the GRH deficit calculations. The compromise was that the first $20 billion would be on-budget and the final $30 billion would be off-budget.

Notes

1. The reasons for this dual requirement are mostly political. For a good discussion of how this process came to be, see Allen Schick, *Congress and Money: Budgeting, Spending, and Taxing* (Washington, D.C.: Urban Institute Press, 1980).
2. Public Law 97-35.
3. Public Law 97-102.
4. This is the typical situation for spending on capital items, such as large weapons, that take more than one year to build. For purchases, such as salaries and benefits, the budget authority and outlays would be approximately the same each year.
5. Theoretically, if the federal government stopped all new spending, budget authority and outlays could be reconciled so that they would equal each other. However, budget authority that was unused for some reason (unspent appropriations, rescissions, and so on) would also have to be taken into account.
6. See chapter 7 for a complete discussion of sequesters and chapter 8 for an explanation of impoundments.
7. Public Law 99-177.
8. The $10 billion cushion does not apply in fiscal 1993.
9. Public Law 93-344.

Overview: The Gramm-Rudman-Hollings Budget Process

The Balanced Budget and Emergency Deficit Control Act (GRH I),[1] which substantially changed the congressional budget process while retaining its existing structure, was signed into law by President Reagan on December 12, 1985, less than three months after it had first been introduced in the Senate by its principal authors, Phil Gramm (R–TX), Warren Rudman (R–NH), and Ernest Hollings (D–SC). Less than two years later, this law was amended substantially by the Balanced Budget and Emergency Deficit Control Reaffirmation Act (GRH II).[2]

This extraordinarily short period between introduction and enactment of the two Gramm-Rudman-Hollings laws is in sharp contrast to the length of time it took for Congress to pass the legislation that created the old process, the Congressional Budget and Impoundment Control Act of 1974. That legislation was adopted almost twenty-one months after a special joint study commission had been formed, and only after five different committees in the House and Senate had had an opportunity to consider the various

problems that had been plaguing the consideration of the budget by Congress.[3]

The different paths that these two laws took to enactment says much about why each was adopted and what each was expected to achieve. The old budget process was not intended to guarantee any particular outcome, but simply to create a framework for congressional budget decisions. Although many of the representatives and senators who voted for the legislation in 1974 thought that the process would reduce the deficit or change federal spending priorities, the only true purposes of the law were to revise congressional procedures so that the budget debate would occur more systematically and to enhance accountability in Congress for budget decisions.

The old process was created in direct response to six problems that had been hampering Congress's consideration of spending and tax legislation:

1. Congress did not have enough time to complete work on all budget bills before the beginning of the fiscal year.
2. Congress had no mechanism to set spending priorities.
3. Congress had no mechanism to set economic policy.
4. Congress could not obtain objective information on budget matters.
5. Congress had no way to impose spending discipline on its committees.
6. Congress had no procedures for overcoming presidential impoundments.

Because the most important considerations were procedural, each of the many participants in the debate on the Congressional Budget Act, including the House and Senate majority and minority leaders, the authorization committees, the appropriations committees, and the tax-writing committees, had to review the proposed law and be convinced that their existing influence would be maintained and their "turf" protected. As a result, the proposal had to be approved in advance by virtually all the key members of both houses, a process that took much time and negotiation.

In addition, the 1974 budget process was debated at a time when the federal budget was not a hot topic, and there was little public clamor for action on the deficit. To be sure, some observers considered the deficit to be very troublesome. However, the deficit was relatively small,[4] and few people, including those in the media and the public at large, paid much attention to it. As a result, there was little pressure on Congress to act quickly.

In contrast, GRH I was enacted in 1985 with almost a single purpose in mind: to reduce the deficit. The process installed in 1974 seemed incapable of forcing Congress and the president to make the hard decisions on spending and taxes that were necessary to reduce the deficit to manageable levels. In fact, both the deficit and the national debt grew substantially while the Congressional Budget Act was in effect, and although the budget process was not the only reason for this situation, it was a highly visible target for much of the blame.[5]

Moreover, Congress considered GRH at a time when the federal budget and its $200 billion deficit were big news. Starting with Ronald Reagan's 1980 campaign for president, when the deficit was one of the leading issues, and continuing through the first Reagan administration, when Office of Management and Budget (OMB) Director David A. Stockman became one of the most powerful and best known members of the president's cabinet, Americans had become increasingly concerned about the budget and its ever-growing deficit. As a result, in late 1985 Congress felt much pressure to develop a solution to the deficit problem and to do so quickly, no matter how radical a change from existing policies and practices the solution might be. Therefore, once the original version of GRH I was passed by the Senate in early October, it rapidly gained supporters and flew through both houses, even though there had been no hearings on it and few people were sure exactly how (or even whether) it would work.

In general the GRH process retains many of the same features that were first created as part of the old budget process. For example, Congress must still pass a budget resolution each year, and reconciliation, one of the most controversial elements of the Congressional Budget Act, continues to be an important enforcement mechanism. But GRH has modified these parts of the process somewhat and has accelerated the timetable. Instead of passing two required budget resolutions each year, Congress must now pass only one, but the deadline is April 15 instead of May 15. And reconciliation, which under the old process was optional, is now mandatory.

The two most significant changes from the old budget process are (1) the setting of specific deficit targets—"maximum deficit amounts"—that the president and Congress must follow, and (2) a new enforcement mechanism—"sequestration"—that is used to cut federal spending by whatever amount is needed to reach the deficit maximum for the coming year when the president and Congress are unable or unwilling to agree on a deficit reduction plan of their own.

The deficit targets originally set by GRH I for each of the following fiscal years were:

FY86	FY87	FY88	FY89	FY90	FY91
171.9	144	108	72	36	0

(in billions of dollars)

The original GRH deficit targets proved to be too optimistic. In fiscal 1986, the first year that the original GRH process was in place, the actual deficit was almost $50 billion above the maximum set for the year.

To a certain extent this situation was expected. For political reasons, the 1986 GRH sequestration reduction was limited to $11.7 billion even though that would probably leave the deficit above the maximum set for the year. It is unclear whether anyone realized just how much above the maximum this figure would be.

The practical effect of missing the first-year deficit maximum by this large amount was that the deficit targets for all the remaining years became almost impossible to reach. The deficit would have had to be cut from approximately $221 billion in fiscal 1986 to $144 billion in fiscal 1987, a $77 billion drop in one year, which would have been unprecedented in U.S. history.[6] Therefore, when the Supreme Court declared that the sequestration process included in GRH I was unconstitutional (see chapter 7), the likelihood of reaching the deficit maximums became even smaller because Congress would have been required to vote in favor of these heretofore unheard of spending cuts or tax increases and the president would have had to sign them before they could take effect. In fact, the one time that Congress was faced with having to approve the fiscal 1987 sequestration cuts using this process, it failed to do so.

The fiscal 1987 deficit was $149.7 billion, apparently in compliance with the GRH I maximum. This is somewhat misleading, however, and needs to be explained. Although the actual deficit was reduced to $149.7 billion, the reduction was basically the result of two events. The first was a windfall in revenues from the 1986 tax act. According to current projections, not only will the windfall not occur again, but federal revenues are expected to *decrease* in the next few years compared with what would have been collected had the tax code not been changed. The second was an increase in revenues from the sale of various federal assets[7] and the prepayment of certain loans.

These one-time savings from the revenue windfall and asset sales totaled about $35 billion. If these savings are added back, a more accurate picture of the deficit for 1987 emerges—$185 billion.

The difference between the 1986 deficit and the 1987 deficit is not insignificant—$36 billion, the largest one-year drop in the deficit in U.S. history. But a $185 billion deficit was also $41 billion above the original GRH maximum for 1987. Despite the large reduction, therefore, there was also widespread dissatisfaction with the budget and GRH I process.

This situation also created substantial apprehension about what was likely to happen in the future. From the $185 billion level in 1987, the deficit was supposed to be reduced under the original GRH process to $108 billion in fiscal 1988, a $75 billion drop that virtually no one thought possible given the many difficult political pressures surrounding the annual budget debate in Washington. So partly in response to this problem of having essentially unattainable annual deficit maximums and partly because of the desire to change the sequestration process so that it would comply with the Supreme Court's ruling, Congress and the Reagan administration agreed in September 1987 to several far-reaching changes in GRH I.

Although the full text of the GRH II budget process is thirty-seven pages long, it really had just two elements. The first major change dealt with sequestration. As will be explained in chapter 7, the process is once again automatic, that is, it no longer requires Congress to approve and the president to sign the legislation for the cuts to be implemented. To meet the Supreme Court's objections, all final decisions are now delegated to the director of the Office of Management and Budget, who as a member of the executive branch meets the guidelines set down by the Court in its ruling.

The second major change is a new set of maximum deficit amounts, as follows:

	FY86	FY87	FY88	FY89	FY90	FY91	FY92	FY93
GRH I	171.9	144	108	72	36	0	NA	NA
GRH II	NA	NA	144	136	100	64	28	0

NA = not applicable.

The most obvious change from GRH I to GRH II is that the year by which the deficit is expected to be eliminated has been stretched from 1991 to 1993. In addition, Congress and the president were given some flexibility in connection with the fiscal 1988 and 1989 maximums. For 1988 the deficit had to be reduced only by a net of $23 billion, regardless of the actual deficit that occurred that year. This is why the deficit negotiations between the Reagan administration and Congress that took place after the October 19, 1987, New York Stock Exchange crash focused so directly on this amount. Had the negotiations not succeeded in reducing the deficit by $23 billion, sequestration would have been triggered.

For 1989, GRH II required either that the deficit be reduced to $136 billion or that the deficit be reduced by $36 billion, whichever was less. There is no flexibility for all years after 1989, with one exception: the deficit targets for 1990, 1991, and 1992 can be exceeded by up to $10 billion before sequestration is triggered. There is no similar cushion for 1993 when the budget is expected to be balanced. Any deficit at all will trigger sequestration.

It is important to remember that neither GRH I nor GRH II guarantees that the deficit will be eliminated forever. In fact, the basic purpose of both GRH laws is to eliminate the federal deficit once—by fiscal 1991 in the original law and by 1993 in the revision. After that, the president and Congress are again free to come up with any mix of spending and taxing laws that they want, and any deficit or surplus.

GRH provides only two ways for these provisions to be changed. If Congress formally declares war, the maximum deficit amounts are suspended automatically. If an economic downturn occurs, a special procedure and at least one vote in each house are required before the maximum deficit amounts can be suspended.[8] The GRH process consists of the following five stages.

Stage One: the President's Budget, January 8 to February 25, 1990

The congressional budget process starts with the submission of the president's budget to Congress.

Under the old process, the budget did not have to be submitted until fifteen days after Congress convened each year. But because Congress sometimes did not convene until late January, this provision often caused a delay in the start of the process until early or mid-February. The new process requires the president's budget to be submitted no later than the first Monday after January 3 every year, regardless of when Congress first meets.

Other than specifying the date that the president's budget must be submitted to Congress, GRH imposes only one other requirement on the administration: the budget must include a deficit no higher than the maximum deficit amount for that year. The president is free to propose any combination of spending cuts and tax increases to reach the target.

The president's budget is only a proposal, albeit a highly significant one. But because of its packaging into several extensive and cohesive documents, the spending and economic policy it embodies, and the media attention it receives, consideration of the president's budget proposal is one of the most important stages of the congressional budget process.

This is generally true even when Congress seems to reject the president's budget early in the process, as has often happened the past few years.[9] But, because most of what is in the president's budget is either uncontrollable[10] or noncontroversial, Congress will eventually accept most of those budget proposals—perhaps as many as 95 percent—with few or only minor changes. Once the president's budget has been submitted, the debate generally will focus on the parts that are controversial, for example, a proposed large increase in a particular function or the elimination of a program.

The president's budget proposal is reviewed by all congressional committees over the next seven weeks. By February 25 each committee must submit to the budget committee in its own house its "views and estimates" on the actions it will probably take on the budget items within its jurisdiction. The old budget process required these reports to be submitted by March 15.

These reports are not binding commitments or final decisions but merely a guide for the budget committees, which are responsible for weighing competing spending requests. During the period, the budget committees hold their own hearings on the president's budget proposal. They also receive guidance from the Joint Economic Committee and the Congressional Budget Office (CBO), which are required to submit special reports during this stage.

Stage Two: The Congressional Budget Resolution, February 25 to April 15, 1990

Under the pre-GRH budget process, Congress was required to pass two concurrent resolutions on the budget each year. The first budget resolution, which was supposed to be passed in final form by both houses by May 15, was intended to provide tentative, nonbinding spending and revenue targets for Congress when it considered all bills later in the year. The second budget resolution, which was supposed to be passed by September 15, was intended to be the final, binding figures for the coming year. If they were needed, reconciliation instructions, which gave Congress the ability to mandate changes in spending and taxes to match the budget policies that it adopted in the second resolution, could have been included.

Under GRH, Congress is required to pass only a single budget resolution each year by April 15. If it wishes, Congress can pass additional budget resolutions later in the year to revise the previously approved totals, but it does not have to do so. In addition, the congressional budget resolution now **must** include reconciliation instructions—orders to one or more committees to change laws within their jurisdiction to comply with the budget resolution just passed—whenever changes in entitlements or taxes are assumed. Although under the old process reconciliation instructions were often included in the first budget resolution, this action was taken without any specific legislative permission. Instead, it was done under the so-called elastic clause, which allowed Congress to adopt whatever procedures were necessary to implement the Congressional Budget Act.

A budget resolution has three main purposes:

First, it is a public statement of the spending priorities and economic policy of Congress—the congressional alternative to what the president proposed several months earlier.

Second, it provides guidance for all other committees when they consider their spending or tax legislation and for Congress when it reviews those bills. In this sense the budget resolution serves as a measuring device—a way for Congress to know whether the spending in a particular bill is too high or too low.

Third, it is the only time all year that total spending will be compared with total revenues in a single piece of legislation that will be voted on by both houses. Therefore, the budget resolution is a way for members of Congress to be held accountable for the deficit.

Like the president's budget, the congressional budget resolution cannot have a deficit greater than the maximum set for that year by GRH II. Congress is free to use any mix of spending cuts and revenue increases it deems appropriate to reach the target.

The budget resolution does not contain spending ceilings for individual line items in the budget. Instead, it contains recommended levels for seven aggregate totals (budget authority, outlays, revenues, direct loan obligations, primary loan guarantee commitments, level of the public debt, and deficit or surplus)[11] and twenty-one functions[12] (National Defense, Agriculture, International Affairs, etc.). The budget committees often make certain assumptions about individual programs when they draft the resolution, but these assumptions are not binding on either the authorizing or appropriations committees.

Despite these nonbinding assumptions, it would be wrong to underestimate the budget resolution's importance. It is the foremost expression of Congress's spending priorities, and except in extreme circumstances, those priorities are seldom changed significantly later in the budget process. In addition, under GRH the resolution's function as a measuring device has taken on added importance. It is, therefore, a significant factor when a committee drafts legislation and when that bill is debated by the full House and Senate.

The congressional budget resolution does not require the president's signature to take effect. It is not, therefore, subject to a veto.

Stage Three: Reconciliation, April 15 to June 15, 1990

GRH specifically requires that the congressional budget resolution include reconciliation instructions to one or more committees to enforce the spending cuts (or increases) and tax increases (or decreases) that are assumed.

Committees ordered to make reconciliation changes must comply with those instructions. If they refuse, amendments that would make the changes required in their area of jurisdiction can be "made in order" during the debate on the reconciliation changes—that is, can be allowed to be offered by members of other committees.

Like the budget resolution, reconciliation instructions do not specify individual program changes, although the budget committees usually make assumptions about which ones should be affected. These assumptions can be altered or ignored by the committees responsible for the areas of the budget in which the changes are to occur as long as the total reduction (or increase) equals the reconciliation instructions.

Any spending and tax changes ordered through reconciliation are supposed to be enacted by June 15. The House is not supposed to be able to adjourn for more than three consecutive days during July until it has completed its work on all reconciliation legislation for the coming year, although it has figured out a way to avoid this prohibition every year that GRH has been in effect.

Stage Four: Authorizations and Appropriations, April 15 to September 30, 1990

Between the passage of the congressional budget resolution and the beginning of the fiscal year on October 1, Congress is expected to complete action on all authorizations and appropriations. In contrast to budget resolutions, these bills include the actual commitments of federal funds to specific programs, and because they require the president's signature to become law, they can be vetoed. Regardless of what is assumed in the congressional budget resolution, no program can be implemented unless it is authorized and money is appropriated to implement it (see chapter 1).

This part of the budget process was not changed substantially by GRH. The major differences are an expedited schedule and new deadlines, both of which were intended to make it more likely that appropriations would be signed into law by the beginning of the fiscal year. The first time this happened was in 1988 when all thirteen appropriations were passed by Congress by October 1. In 1989 only one appropriation was enacted by this date, and a continuing resolution was again needed.

No appropriations are supposed to be considered by the full House of Representatives until the congressional budget resolution has been enacted. As already noted, this is expected to occur by April 15. If, however, the budget resolution has not been approved by May 15, the House can move ahead and consider the appropriations anyway. Under the old process, the House could not consider appropriations until either it had adopted the budget resolution or had voted to "waive" this prohibition, a time-consuming and politically difficult ordeal.

The House Appropriations Committee is supposed to complete its deliberations on the last annual appropriations bill for the coming year and "report" it to the full House by June 10. The House is supposed to pass its version of each appropriation and send it to the Senate by June 30. If the House has not completed its action on all annual appropriations by this date, it is not supposed to be able to adjourn for more than three consecutive days during July.

The Office of Management and Budget is supposed to submit a midsession review of the president's budget proposal to Congress by July 15. The midsession review includes reestimates of the president's proposed budget based on the most recent forecast of the economy. In the past, the review has often been little more than a reaffirmation of the president's original proposal, which has often already been rejected by this point in the process. Therefore, the review often served little or no purpose. However, as a result of GRH II, the midsession review has taken on new importance because the economic assumptions in it must be used by the director of OMB in making all sequestration decisions later in the year.

Stage Five: Sequestration, August 15 to October 15, 1990

Sequestration is the highly controversial mechanism in the budget process created by GRH. Its purpose is easy to understand: if the president and Congress are unable to agree on a plan for the coming year that will reduce the deficit to the maximum deficit amount, spending cuts will be imposed according to the preset formula in GRH itself.

The sequestration procedure established by GRH I was automatic. If Congress and the president were unable to agree on how to reach the deficit maximum for the year, the comptroller general, the head of the General Accounting Office, had the sole authority to determine whether sequestration spending cuts were necessary, and if so, to apply the formula to each program. Once sequestration began, Congress and the president could not stop it unless they reduced the deficit to the maximum amount for that year by October 15.

However, less than seven months after GRH I was enacted, the Supreme Court decided that a sequestration process that delegated the authority to anyone who was not a member of the executive branch of government, such as the comptroller general, was unconstitutional.[13] As a result, a backup sequestration process, which had been included in GRH I in case there was a successful legal challenge to the automatic process, went into effect. It required a bill cutting spending by the appropriate amount to be passed by both houses and signed by the president for sequestration to be implemented. This backup process was obviously open to delays and manipulations.

GRH II reimposed the automatic sequestration process by delegating the final authority to determine whether the spending cuts are necessary, and if so, how large they should be, to the director of OMB. The director is a member of the executive branch of the government and, therefore, met the Supreme Court's requirements.

GRH II Sequestration System

On August 15 every year, OMB and CBO independently take a "snapshot" of the deficit picture for the coming fiscal year on the basis of their separate projections of the economy and estimates of the actions completed so far on spending and revenues. By August 20, CBO sends a preliminary report on the deficit to OMB specifying what it thinks the deficit for the coming year will be. If it estimates that the deficit will exceed the maximum amount allowed for the year plus the $10 billion cushion, CBO will also specify the percentage by which all eligible programs should be cut to reduce the deficit appropriately.

Five days later on August 25, the director of OMB issues to the president and Congress a preliminary report on the deficit and the sequestration cuts that may be needed. In compiling this report, the OMB director is required to review the CBO report, but under GRH II, the CBO estimates are strictly advisory. The report may be completely ignored if the OMB director so chooses. However, any differences between the two reports must be identified and explained.

If the OMB director determines that sequestration is necessary, the president must issue an order to all federal departments and agencies requiring that the funds in all eligible programs be withheld as of the start of the fiscal year on October 1, by the amounts specified in the OMB report. In issuing this initial sequestration order, the "president may not modify or recalculate any of the estimates, determinations, specifications, bases, amounts, or percentages" listed by OMB. In other words, the director of OMB has the authority to impose determinations on the president even though the director serves at the president's pleasure.

Once the president's preliminary sequester order has been signed, Congress and the president can still try to develop and pass an alternative plan to reduce the deficit by the amount required to reach the GRH maximum for the year. In contrast to the sequestration formula, this plan can include any mix of spending cuts and tax increases. However, the legislation implementing the plan must be enacted (that is, passed by Congress and signed into law by the president) by October 15.

Regardless of whether Congress and the president do agree on an alternative deficit reduction plan, the initial sequestration order issued on August 25 becomes effective on October 1, pending the final outcome of sequestration. All agencies and departments must begin to withhold budget authority by the percentages in the August 25 OMB report.

The sequestration process then begins again. By October 10, CBO must send OMB a revised report on the deficit. CBO can only take into account any laws that have been enacted and any regulations that have been promulgated in final form since its first report was issued on August 20. This is the first time, therefore, that an alternative deficit reduction plan enacted between August 25 and October 10 will be formally recognized.

By October 15, OMB must issue its own revised report on the deficit. Once again the director of OMB is not required to use the information supplied by CBO but must identify and explain any differences between the two reports.

Also by October 15, the president must issue a final sequestration order to all agencies and departments instructing them to cancel (as opposed to simply withholding) budget authority by the amount specified in the final OMB report.

Finally, by November 15, the comptroller general must issue a report to Congress that reviews the final OMB report and presidential sequester order. This is the only role left to the comptroller general by GRH II.

Table 6 shows the expected timetable for all congressional and presidential actions on the fiscal 1991 budget.

Impoundments

The impoundment procedures included in the Congressional Budget Act were not changed significantly by either GRH I or GRH II. They continue to be implemented only when the president proposes either not to spend or to delay spending funds that previously were approved by Congress.

A "rescission" is a presidential proposal not to spend an appropriation that has been provided by Congress. The reason for such a proposal can be specific (as when the objectives of the program can be achieved without spending the full amount appropriated) or general (fiscal policy considerations). Regardless of the reason, the president must submit a message to Congress requesting the rescission and explaining the reasons for the request. If both houses of Congress do not pass a bill approving the proposed rescission within forty-five legislative days, the president must spend the money as originally intended.

A "deferral" is a presidential proposal to delay the spending of congressionally approved appropriations. The delay can be for any length of time but cannot last beyond the end of the fiscal year. Regardless of the length of time, the president must submit a deferral message to Congress. Unlike a rescission, which requires specific approval by both houses of Congress, a deferral is automatically assumed to be approved unless, at any time after the president's message has been received, either the House or Senate passes legislation specifically disapproving it.

Deferrals were very controversial during the Reagan administration, which tried to use them to thwart congressional policy. As a result, GRH II codified the circumstances under which a president could propose a deferral. They are: "(1) to provide for contingencies; (2) to achieve savings made possible by or through changes in requirements or greater efficiency of operations; or (3) as specifically provided by law." In addition, the use of deferrals was severely limited by federal courts. At this point, deferrals for policy reasons are no longer permitted.[14]

The budget and appropriations committees in the Senate and the appropriations committee in the House have assumed responsibility for reviewing presidential impoundment messages. But the real monitor of this part of the process is the comptroller general, who[:]

Table 6
Fiscal 1991 Congressional budget process

January 8, 1990	President submits fiscal 1991 budget to Congress.
February 15	Congressional Budget Office (CBO) submits report to budget committees on president's budget.
February 25	All committees submit their "views and estimates" to budget committee in their own house.
April 1	Senate Budget Committee reports congressional budget resolution to full Senate.
April 15	Congress completes action on congressional budget resolution.
May 15	Fiscal 1991 appropriations bills may be considered by the full House even if budget resolution has not yet been passed.
June 10	House Appropriations Committee must report final fiscal 1991 appropriations bill to the full House.
June 15	Congress completes action on reconciliation legislation.
June 30	House completes action on its version of all fiscal 1991 appropriations bills.
July 15	President submits midsession budget review to Congress establishing the economic and technical assumptions to be used in sequestration.
August 15	Office of Management and Budget (OMB) and CBO take separate deficit "snapshots." President must notify Congress if he wants to exempt all or part of military personnel from sequestration.
August 20	CBO sends initial sequestration report to OMB and Congress.
August 25	OMB sends initial sequestration report to president and Congress. President issues initial sequestration order.
August 25–October 14	If desired and possible, Congress and president develop and enact alternative deficit reduction proposal.
October 1	Fiscal year 1991 begins, and initial sequestration order takes effect.
October 10	CBO issues final sequestration report to OMB and Congress.
October 15	OMB issues final sequestration report to president and Congress. President issues final sequestration order.

must review each message and advise the Congress of the facts surrounding the action and its probable effects. . . . The comptroller general is also required to report to the Congress reserve or deferral action which has not been reported by the president; and to report and reclassify any incorrect transmittals by the president. *Such reports by the comptroller general have the same legal effect as rescission . . . messages from the president.*[15] (emphasis added)

The comptroller general also has the power to sue the president if the president refuses to spend an appropriation after Congress has formally disapproved a proposed rescission or deferral.

Notes

1. Public Law 99-177.
2. Public Law 100-119.
3. For a good discussion of the legislative history of P.L. 93-344, see Allen Schick, *Congress and Money: Budgeting, Spending, and Taxing* (Washington. D.C.: The Urban Institute, 1980), pp. 51–81.
4. The federal deficit amounted to $2.8 billion in 1970, $23.0 billion in 1971, $23.4 billion in 1972, $14.9 billion in 1973, and $6.1 billion in 1974.
5. Between 1974 and 1985, the federal deficit grew from $6.1 billion to $222.2 billion, a 3,600 percent increase.
6. Before 1986, the largest one-year reduction in the deficit was $31.7 billion from 1945 to 1946.

7. In fact, the ultimate effect of these policies is to *increase* the deficit in the long term. The reasons are that because the assets have been sold they cannot be sold again. In addition, prepaying loans deprives the government of expected revenues (including interest) that it had anticipated in the future. More importantly, however, a provision of GRH II no longer allows the revenues from asset sales or loan prepayments to be used to avoid sequestration.

8. The CBO director must notify Congress if either CBO or OMB projects the inflation-adjusted growth in GNP to be "less than zero" for the eighteen-month period that begins with the last quarter of the year before the notification is made and continues through the four quarters after the notification. The CBO director is also required to notify Congress if the Department of Commerce reports that, after taking inflation into account, economic growth for the preceding and current quarters is less than 1 percent.

   As soon as Congress receives such a notice, the majority leaders of both houses must introduce joint resolutions suspending the maximum deficit amounts for that year and the next year, as well as several other provisions associated with these limits. This joint resolution must then be passed by the House and Senate. If it is not, all provisions of the Balanced Budget and Emergency Deficit Control act continue to apply.

9. President Reagan's fiscal 1984 budget was informally rejected by Congress less than a month after it was submitted. The 1985 Reagan budget was rejected as soon as it was sent to Capitol Hill. The 1986 Reagan budget was rejected even before it was formally submitted.

10. See chapter 1 for an explanation of uncontrollable spending.

11. The requirement for aggregate levels for direct loan obligations and primary loan guarantees was added by the Balanced Budget and Emergency Deficit Control Act.

12. See chapter 1 for an explanation of budget functions. Appendix D describes each budget function, including a list of the major agencies, departments, and programs they contain.

13. Bowsher v. Synar, 106 S.Ct. 3181 (1986). See chapter 12 for an explanation.

14. GRH II did amend the impoundment control provisions of the Congressional Budget and Impoundment Control Act to prevent the president from proposing two rescissions for the same activity in the same fiscal year. It also codified existing practice with respect to deferrals. See chapter 8 for an explanation.

15. U.S. Congress. House, Committee on the Budget, *The Congressional Budget Process: A General Explanation* (Washington, D.C.: U.S. Government Printing Office, 1981), p. 17.

B

The Budget Message
of the President

To the Congress of the United States:

I have the honor to present the *Budget of the United States Government for Fiscal Year 1991.*

The American economy is now in its eighth consecutive year of expansion and growth. It is essential that the growth of the economy continue and increase in the future. The budget is designed to achieve that goal.

The budget has five broad themes:

• *Investing in Our Future.* With an eye toward future growth, and expansion of the human frontier, the budget's chief emphasis is on investment in the future. It proposes: a capital gains incentive for long-term private investment and new incentives for family savings; record-high amounts for research and development, space, education, and Head Start; a major investment in civil aviation; and a large increase in spending to attack the scourge of drugs. At the same time, the budget maintains a strong national defense while reflecting the dramatic changes in the world political situation that are taking place; and it fulfills responsibilities to protect the environment, and preserve America's cultural heritage.

• *Advancing States as Laboratories.* The budget recognizes the emergence of new ideas and initiatives originating at the State and local level. The Federal Government will foster such innovation and experimentation in numerous fields, from transportation to health, through waivers of certain rules and regulations, and through demonstration grants.

• *Reforming Mandatory Programs.* Entitlement and other mandatory spending now constitutes nearly half the budget, not counting an additional 14 percent for interest. The budget provides for full payment of social security benefits and funds growth in health, low income and other mandatory programs. However, it proposes reforms where warranted to slow the growth in some of these programs and thus leave more room in the budget for priority initiatives.

Source: Office of Management and Budget: *Budget of the United States Government Fiscal Year 1991* (Washington, D.C.: U.S. Government Printing Office, 1990).

• *Acknowledging Inherited Claims.* The budget faces up to such inherited claims as the cleanup of decades old environmental damage at nuclear weapons facilities. It analyzes potential claims from unfunded annuities and Federal insurance programs. It assesses the growing volume of defaults in Federal credit programs and proposes essential credit reforms.

• *Managing for Integrity and Efficiency.* The budget contains suggestions for reforms in the way Congress deals with the budget. It provides more resources and suggests improved methods for managing the vast Federal enterprise better. It identifies low-return domestic discretionary programs where a smaller investment of budgetary resources is warranted.

The budget meets the deficit target of $64 billion for 1991 established by the Gramm-Rudman-Hollings law, without raising taxes. It would balance the budget by 1993 as required by that law, begin reducing debt, and protect the integrity of Social Security.

Each of the themes outlined above is discussed in more detail in Section One of the budget, the Overview. The customary tabular and appendix material is contained in Section Two [in "Director's Introduction," to follow].

I look forward to working with the Congress in the weeks and months ahead to produce a budget that meets the Gramm-Rudman-Hollings target, advances the Nation's essential interests, and keeps the economy on the path of continued growth.

George Bush
January 29, 1990

Director's Introduction
to the New Budget

Green Eyeshades and the Cookie Monster

If anything were meant for viewing through proverbial green eyeshades, it would seem to be the Federal budget. The typeface is small. The text is tedious. Tables are seemingly endless.

The sheer size of the budget makes it seem like a monster. It contains almost 190,000 accounts. At the rate of one per minute, eight hours per day, it would take over a year to reflect upon these! The budget's annual outlays are larger than all countries' economies except those of the United States, Japan, and the Soviet Union. (The Federal budget is roughly the size of the entire West German economy.)

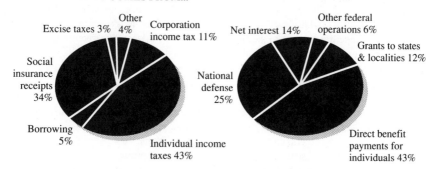

The federal government dollar fiscal year 1991 estimate

Receipts, outlays, deficit/surplus under the president's proposed policy
(in billions of dollars)

	1989	1990	1991	1992	1993	1994	1995
Receipts	990.7	1,073.5	1,170.2	1,246.4	1,327.6	1,408.6	1,486.3
Outlays	1,142.6	1,197.2	1,233.3	1,271.4	1,321.8	1,398.0	1,476.9
Surplus or Deficit (+/−)	−152.0	−123.8	−63.1	−25.1	+5.7	+10.7	+9.4

Clearly, at some point, green eyeshades must be put aside. Detail must be considered; but the capacity to abstract should not be lost.

Of course, with or without green eyeshades, monsters do not naturally invite examination. Still, if a monster is present, one might address certain threshold questions: Is it threatening or potentially helpful, and how is one to tell? The answers are not always as obvious as the questions.

On "Sesame Street," the children's educational television program, there is a wonderful character known as Cookie Monster. As all monsters are, Cookie Monster is initially intimidating. His manner is gruff. His clumsiness occasionally causes damage.

But quickly, Cookie Monster comes to be seen as benign—indeed, downright friendly. He has a few bad habits. He cannot resist gobbling up anything and everything that might be consumed—especially cookies. And he cannot quite control the way in which he spews forth crumbs. He is the quintessential consumer. Yet clearly, he means no harm.

The budget, for all its intimidating detail, might be seen similarly: as the *Ultimate Cookie Monster*. Its excessive tendencies toward consumption are not exactly ennobling. (It does not ordinarily present itself as seriously concerned with investment.) But at the same time, its underlying motivation is clearly not malevolent. What harm it may cause is largely unintended. Its massive presence might be understood as little more than a compilation of cookies received, cookies crumbled, and crumbs spewed forth.

Yet apt though the Cookie Monster perspective may be, it does not suffice. It is not quite fair to either Cookie Monster or the budget. In reality, a budget is not just a monstrous mass of cookies and crumbs. It is more: an implicit statement of values and expectations for the future. Inescapably, it is headed somewhere—or other. To gain a meaningful sense of the whole, and where it may be headed, one must look beyond green eyeshades and the Cookie Monster. One must frame the budget from several broader (and more serious) perspectives. This introduction tries to help do that.

Among the additional perspectives are these: a global historical perspective; a conventional deficit-estimating perspective; a capital budgeting perspective; a perspective that gives greater weight to future liabilities; another that attends to investment in the future; and finally, a congressional perspective. These are discussed (sequentially) below.

And the Wall Came A'Tumblin' Down . . .

Looking a bit beyond Cookie Monster to the television news, one is struck with a rare impression: there may be a compelling pattern to the flow of current events. It is not represented in the budget detail by any quantitative "baseline," nor any conventional statistical measure. It was captured visually by a single dramatic symbol, beamed around the world, and etched in the mind of people everywhere: the fall of the Berlin wall.

To put the symbolic fact more clinically: State-centered, command-and-control systems seem to be decomposing. The Soviet Union has been forced to explore the virtues of restructuring, decentralization, and openness. Communist regimes in Eastern Europe have been falling like dominoes. The Iron Curtain has been opened. And the drama has not been confined to Eastern Europe. Just as liberated celebrants have cheered the opening of the Berlin wall and the decline of communist dictators, so too have liberated Panamanians celebrated the fall of the dictator in near-by Panama.

While it would be naively euphoric to consider this pattern "the end of history" (even in the limited Hegelian sense), clearly the sudden and dramatic shift toward pluralist democracy has far more than the ordinary historical significance. The events of 1989, and what they will have unleashed, may one day rise to a place with those of 1688, 1776, or 1789. This is not small stuff. It is another giant leap of the human spirit yearning to breathe free.

Yet this great historical shift has been almost trivialized in its translation into public debate about the budget. The issue has been framed as: "How big is the 'peace dividend'?"—and, in effect, "How can I get mine?" These are issues that the budget and the political system must treat. They are discussed further in the budget. But they are second-order issues at best.

Ahead of them in line, surely, ought to be these points:

• The favorable pattern of recent events has not been caused exclusively by the political and economic bankruptcy of particular state-centered regimes. It has also resulted from U.S. (and allied) military and economic strength. These, in turn, have resulted from market-oriented economic policies and sound public and private investment policies. It would be a highly unfortunate irony if—just as the

world were affirming more market-oriented and investment-oriented principles—the United States were to do anything other than strengthen its commitment to these very principles.

• As the world moves away (at whatever pace) from an emphasis on the risk of traditional military superpower conflict, the relative importance of U.S. economic strength only increases. Increased economic strength is essential to inspire and to assist evolving lesser powers. And it is fundamental to success in the global competition with rising economic superpowers.

• Thus, there is a first-order issue for the budget (and the economic policy it represents): How can it best preserve and build on America's strengths, while advancing the American economy toward even greater capacities for leadership and growth? If the "dividend" metaphor must be applied to the budget: How can policy best assure that there is a continuing *growth dividend*?

How Big Is the Deficit?—Let Me Count the Ways

In considering this issue, many traditional analysts turn first to the size of the budget deficit. This is not necessarily as relevant a starting point as many argue. But it is relevant.

Unfortunately, a meaningful answer to the question—How big is the deficit?—is not quite as simple as the question. This budget attempts to answer the question from a wide range of relevant perspectives.

The "Gramm-Rudman-Hollings (G-R-H) baseline deficit." This perspective is flawed. It biases analysis toward excessive outlay growth. But it is required by law. It constructs an estimate that uses the Administration's economic and technical assumptions; assumes entitlements grow with the beneficiary population and with prescribed benefit changes; and assumes discretionary programs grow with inflation (in effect, treating them as permanent entitlements). It assumes *no change in current law*. From this perspective, the estimated deficit for the current fiscal year (1990) is $122 billion; and for the coming budget year, 1991, it drops to $84.7 billion. It moves to surplus in fiscal year 1994.

"Adjusted G-R-H baseline deficit." The G-R-H baseline, an artificial construct, is used by some for reference purposes. Even for its advocates, it can

be misleading. This year, for example, the Food Stamp authorization for appropriations expires. It will almost certainly be extended in some form, but G-R-H does not assume that. Conversely, the decennial census of 1990 will not be repeated in 1991. But G-R-H implicitly assumes that it will be. If one adjusts for these anomalies, the adjusted G-R-H baseline deficit for 1991-95 would be as in the chart below.

This suggests that without major legislative action—but *assuming continued economic growth*— the deficit would move toward surplus in 1995. This would mark a steady, although slow, pattern of correction from the deficit high of $221.2 billion reached in 1986.

The "president's policy deficit.'' The President's investment-oriented proposals would help assure that the economic growth assumed in the baseline is actually achieved. Other policy proposals would further improve the rate of deficit reduction by reducing spending on low-return programs, reforming selected mandatory programs, and charging appropriate fees. These additional program savings (relative to the G-R-H baseline) are discussed further in Parts V and VII below. Their total contribution is $36.5 billion for 1991, rising to $95.8 billion for 1995.

As a result, the Administration estimates that implementation of the President's budget would meet (and slightly surpass) the legally required G-R-H deficit targets of $64 billion in 1991 and zero in 1993. The President's Policy deficit would be $63.1 billion in 1991, moving to surplus for 1993-95 (even after adjusting to assure Social Security integrity). (See table.)

Overall spending for 1991 would still *increase*— by about 3.0 percent. Almost every Department of the government would have higher budget outlays than it did the previous year. But the deficit would be reduced because estimated receipts would increase even more—by $96.8 billion or 9.0 percent (without "ducks"). *This reflects the "flexible freeze'' at work:* spending growth is held at a level slightly below the inflation rate; while revenues increase at a higher rate on the strength of economic growth. This is summarized in the table, "President's Policy: Outlays, Receipts, and Deficit Improvement for 1991.''

The treatment of social security. Current law defines Social Security as "off-budget," but requires its inclusion for purposes of G-R-H deficit calculations. Social Security is also included in traditional "consolidated" or "unified" deficit estimates. There are many good and important reasons to continue to include Social Security in these calculations.

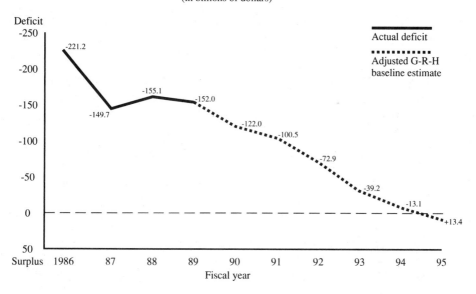

ADJUSTED G-R-H BASELINE ESTIMATE
(in billions of dollars)

President's policy: Outlays, receipts, and deficit improvement for 1991
(in billions of dollars)

	1990	1991	Change Amount	Percent
Outlays:				
Department of Defense	286.8	292.1	+5.4	+1.9%
Non-Department of Defense	910.4	941.2	+30.7	+3.4%
Total Outlays	1,197.2	1,233.3	+36.1	+3.0%
Receipts:				
Current Law	1,072.8	1,156.3	+83.5	+7.8%
New Measures	0.6	13.9	+13.3	+1.2%
Total Receipts	1,073.5	1,170.2	+96.8	+9.0%
Deficit	123.8	63.1	−60.7	−49.0%

But in recent years a problem has arisen. The increasing annual Social Security operating surpluses have masked the true size of the underlying non–Social Security operating deficit. In effect, the surpluses have allowed more non–Social Security spending than might otherwise have been the case. If this were long to continue, it would result in an excessive burden of debt for future generations. It would thus undermine the effect of the build-up of reserves intended for retiring baby-boomers.

To address this problem, without doing violence to the traditional concept of a consolidated budget, the Administration proposes to establish a "Social Security Integrity and Debt Reduction Fund." It would receive each year, as outlays, an amount equivalent to an increasing portion of the projected Social Security operating surplus (reaching 100 percent in 1996). It would be obliged to use these outlays to reduce Federal debt and thus leave a more manageable financing burden for future generations. This Fund would be linked with a continuing obligation to meet a G-R-H deficit target of zero (i.e., a permanent balanced budget) starting in 1993. Thus, the proposal *would effectively prevent the government from spending Social Security receipts on non-Social Security purposes*. The proposal is discussed further in Parts VI-A and VII-A below. Its effects on the deficit are displayed along with the other ways of looking at the deficit in the table: "Deficit/Surplus—Under Selected Definitions."

The effect of alternative economic scenarios. In considering the deficit—by whatever definition—it is important to consider its sensitivity to economic variables. For a discussion of these sensitivities, see Section Two, Part I: "Note on Economic Assumptions and Sensitivities." The single most important variable affecting the size of the deficit is probably the real economic growth rate. As a practical matter, the net deficit-reducing effects of economic growth (or its absence) are likely to be far greater than the effects of a so-called peace dividend.

As a general rule of thumb, a sustained one percent additional increase in real GNP growth—with all else equal—would reduce the deficit by an additional $18 billion in 1991 and an additional $98 billion in 1995. (A sustained one percent lesser increase in real GNP growth—all else equal—would have roughly the equivalent numerical effect, but with the sign changed.) For those seriously interested in either achieving greater deficit reduction or freeing up resources for greater spending, this underlines the importance of pursuing policies likely to maximize the *growth dividend*.

The economic assumptions used by the Administration are toward the optimistic end of the credible range. But the Administration's assumptions are plausible and achievable.

The Administration first presented its own economic assumptions in July 1989—at which point they were also judged to be at the optimistic end of the credible range. Intervening performance has, in fact, been highly consistent with the Administration's forecast. But that does not mean either that macroeconomic science has improved substantially, or

Deficit/surplus—Under Selected Definitions
(in billions of dollars)

	1990	1991	1992	1993	1994	1995
"G-R-H Baseline Deficit/Surplus"	−122.0	−84.7	−55.5	−20.1	7.9	36.3
Adjust for outlay anomalies						
Food Stamps	—	−16.2	−17.0	−17.7	−18.6	−19.5
Census	—	1.0	1.3	1.3	1.5	1.5
Debt service	—	−0.6	−1.7	−2.6	−3.9	−5.0
Total "Adjusted G-R-H Baseline Deficit/Surplus"	−122.0	−100.5	−72.9	−39.2	−13.1	13.4
Adjust for policy recommendations	0.6	36.5	46.9	57.5	75.6	95.8
Adjust for "Social Security Integrity and						
Debt Reduction Fund"	—	—	—	−14.1	−53.6	−101.8
Total "President's Policy Deficit/Surplus"						
excluding "gimmicks" (speed-ups)	−121.4	−64.0	−26.0	4.2	8.9	7.4
Adjust for on-off budget						
Exclude Social Security	−62.0	−80.3	−93.1	−107.4	−124.2	−137.2
Total "On-Budget Policy Deficit/Surplus"	−183.4	−144.3	−119.1	−103.2	−115.3	−129.8
Adjust for G-R-H and speed-ups						
Include Social Security	62.0	80.3	93.1	107.4	124.2	137.2
Include withholding and other speed-ups	—	1.0	—	—	—	—
Total "President's Policy Deficit/Surplus"						
including speed-ups	−121.4	−63.0	−26.0	4.2	8.9	7.4
Adjust for "Consolidated Budget"						
Include asset sales	—	1.6	1.6	1.6	1.6	1.6
Include Postal Service	−2.4	−1.7	−0.7	−0.1	0.1	0.4
Remove nondefense spendout adjustment	—	0.1	—	—	—	—
Total "Consolidated Budget Deficit/Surplus"	−123.8	−63.1	−25.1	5.7	10.7	9.4

that the Administration will always be so fortunate as to be correct.

In developing the budget, the Administration formally considered several alternative economic scenarios. Two of these are discussed in the "Note" in Section Two, Part I. Both of these are also plausible. One is slightly more optimistic, and one more pessimistic, than the scenario actually adopted. These alternative scenarios are specifically described in the Note. If the President's Policy deficit were presented with either the higher growth or the lower growth assumptions, the deficit (or surplus) would appear as follows (after adjusting to assure Social Security integrity).

Deficits as a share of GNP. Meeting the G-R-H deficit target for 1991, as proposed by the President, would reduce the consolidated deficit to about 1 percent of GNP. The deficit would thus fall clearly within the "normal" range for most of America's

Deficit (−)/surplus (+) under alternative assumptions
(in billions of dollars)

	1991	1992	1993	1994	1995
Higher Growth Scenario	−54.6	−16.9	+15.1	+24.7	+31.6
Lower Growth Scenario	−77.5	−48.4	−27.2	−32.9	−42.4

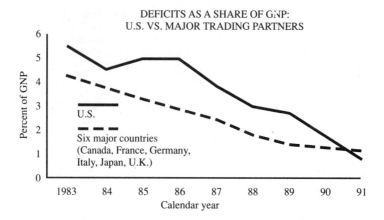

DEFICITS AS A SHARE OF GNP:
U.S. VS. MAJOR TRADING PARTNERS

major trading partners. In any case, it would mark a significant improvement from the 5.2 percent level of 1983 (6.3 percent for the fiscal year). The pattern is suggested by the chart, "Deficits as a Share of GNP: U.S. *vs.* Major Trading Partners." While the trend is favorable, however, it should not be given excessive weight. The United Kingdom and Japan are both running surpluses—but with very different real growth rates. *As with all measures of the deficit, it is necessary to get beyond this somewhat superficial measure, to an examination of the underlying economic policies and their relation to the future.*

Deficit effects of capital budgets. The current budget concept—essentially a "cash" budget—was developed to conform with the President's Commission on Budget Concepts (1967). The "cash" perspective is especially useful for determining needs for financing in the public debt market. Indeed, it is essential. That is why, regardless of whether trust funds are treated as "on" or "off" budget, there must be some consolidated accounting that shows the total governmental cash position. *But if one is seriously interested in the effects of budget policy on the future, one must get beyond the cash budget frame of reference represented by the G-R-H and consolidated deficit calculations.* One needs a better sense of future liabilities and of the extent to which current income and borrowing are financing investment for the future (as opposed to current consumption and transfers).

With this perspective in view, many have criticized the Federal Government's "cash" budget. Some have argued that the Federal Government should adopt one form or another of capital budget and/or

a budget that better distinguishes between trust funds, governmental operating needs, and activities conducted by Government-sponsored enterprises.

In order to begin to address this thoroughly appropriate interest in getting beyond cash budgeting, the President's budget is re-configured as it might appear under the conceptual approach suggested by the General Accounting Office and the approach used by the state of California. These approaches are strictly illustrative—and are presented in Section Two, Part II: "Note on Alternate Approaches to Budget Presentation." They are not intended—now, or in the future—to displace the cash budget; but rather, they are intended to supplement it.

While these additional perspectives are useful, it is clear that they, too, are not fully satisfactory. In going only as far as they do, they tend to do little more than confirm what is now generally accepted wisdom: that the Federal Government invests a relatively small percent of its annual expenditures in capital; and that there is a sharp dichotomy between the operating surpluses in certain trust funds and the operating deficits that characterize the rest of government. They necessarily suggest, but do not satisfactorily settle, many difficult issues of definition as to what is and is not investment. They do not adequately treat "intellectual capital" and "human capital," for example. And they do not provide a dynamic picture of expected future liabilities and future returns.

Stepping back from this surfeit of deficits—all differently conceived and defined—one might summarize where the collection of different deficit pictures suggests things may be, and where they may be headed.

First, by several different deficit measures, *the consolidated Federal deficit seems, at worst, to have stabilized.* If the President's policies were adopted, this pattern of stabilization would obtain, in the near term, even if Social Security were excluded from deficit calculation. *The pattern of continuous erosion that characterized the early- and mid-1980s seems to have been broken.* By many measures, the deficit is headed toward improvement—*assuming that economic growth continues.* Although further progress is not guaranteed, the change in the underlying pattern must be viewed as welcome. See chart: "Alternative Deficit Paths."

The proviso concerning the necessity for continued economic growth is fundamental, however. The economy is in its eighth consecutive year of growth. This is the second-longest period of continuous growth in America's history. (Post-War Japan has enjoyed two longer periods of growth: one of 20 years, 1953-73 and one of 15 years, 1975 to the present.) There is reason to suggest that the traditional notion of the inevitability of a tight business cycle may be overtaken. But, to underline the obvious: Growth is not automatic. It depends on growth-oriented policies being pursued not only by the Administration, but also by Congress and the Federal Reserve.

But second, stabilization of the underlying deficit should not lead to complacency. Complacency would lead to a loss of fiscal discipline. And even with stabilization, deficits mean rising debt. America's recorded Federal debt is already approaching three trillion dollars. (See Parts III-A and VI-A.) That is not necessarily bad per se. It depends on whether or not the debt is being used in conjunction with policies that will increase future productivity, growth, and capacities for debt service—and whether future hidden liabilities are being kept within reasonable bounds. Here, unfortunately, is where conventional Federal deficit accounting and budget presentation have been woefully inadequate. And here is where there is legitimate cause for concern—as is discussed further below.

Hidden PACMEN

The problem with relying solely on the consolidated cash budget—or even on that plus a capital budget—is that it does not give a full picture of the Federal "balance sheet." There is a host of technical reasons why it is not now possible to present a complete and valid Federal balance sheet—not to mention a valid projection of the future balance sheet. But it is possible to do a better job of highlighting potential liabilities, as well as important areas of investment, which have significant future effects. This budget presentation attempts to move in that direction.

One curious thing about future Federal liabilities is that many of them are not yet fully visible. Their particular nature varies. But each is like a hidden

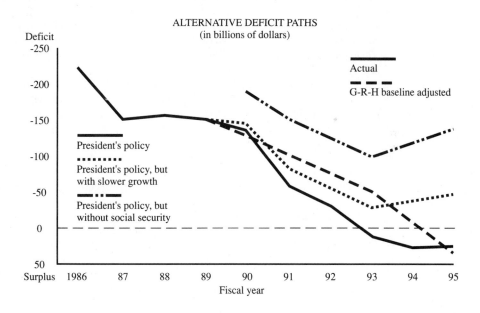

ALTERNATIVE DEFICIT PATHS
(in billions of dollars)

PACMAN, waiting to spring forward and consume another line of resource dots in the budget maze. These hidden PACMEN are discussed in some detail in Parts VI-A and VI-B below. A few introductory points may help outline the problem:

Rising costs of health care. A quarter of a century ago, health care expenditures consumed about 6 percent of America's GNP. Now, that share has almost doubled, to 12 percent. Within the growing Federal budget, the share has risen even more rapidly, from less than 5 percent in 1970 to a projected 15 percent in the early 1990s. Obviously, this is a trend that cannot be sustained forever—or health care costs would drive out all else. There are, nonetheless, increasing demands to assure health insurance coverage for those not now covered, and to provide better financing for long term care. Each of these could entail an additional multi-billion dollar annual bill. Yet the projected health expenditure obligations of current law are not fully covered by projected future receipts. The estimated present value of unfunded liabilities (the actuarial deficiency) for Medicare hospital insurance alone could be over *$250 billion*. (See Parts V and VI-A.)

Rising budgetary claims of mandatory programs. In President Kennedy's Administration, transfer payments to individuals comprised about a quarter of the Federal budget. Now they consume almost half. So-called "mandatory" programs—selected payments to individuals (entitlements) and other automatic spending programs—have grown from 34 percent of the budget in 1970 to roughly half the 1991 budget—and will reach a projected 57 percent for 1995. (Mandatory programs plus net interest expenditures account for almost 62 percent of the budget.) Since these programs generally have broad-based and well-represented beneficiary populations, they tend to have a powerful claim on resources, and grow faster than the economy as a whole. Yet again: It would seem obvious that this pattern of more rapid growth cannot be extended indefinitely. (See Part V.)

Unfunded retirement program liabilities. There is much talk about the projected build-up of Social Security reserves to cover the anticipated obligations to the baby-boom generation when it reaches retirement. The medium term build-up intended by (and projected under) current law is, indeed, enormous.

But even so, over the long term, under some assumptions, the present value of current-law obligations minus projected receipts could be a negative number. This is a speculative matter with a high degree of uncertainty. (See Part VI-A.) Somewhat less speculatively, there are clearly identifiable major shortfalls in unfunded Federal employee retirement programs—although these should be able to be serviced by future contributions. And the Railroad Retirement System, although not fully a Federal responsibility, is substantially underfunded—with a reported actuarial deficiency of *$14 billion*.

Obligations to clean up federal facilities. For a variety of reasons, the Federal Government historically has not been prompt in attending to environmental clean-up at many of its facilities. For reasons of both law and policy, the pattern of the past is now changing. But the bills are yet to be fully paid. The present-value cost of already-identified future clean-up obligations and waste management improvements at Federal facilities over the next 30 years is on the order of *$140–200 billion*. (See Part VI-C.)

Contingent risks of federal credit programs and government-sponsored enterprises (GSEs). The Federal Government's direct and indirect credit subsidies are far more extensive than is commonly appreciated. In housing, over a trillion dollars in outstanding mortgages have been guaranteed by Federal agencies or securitized by GSEs. In agriculture, the Farmers Home Administration has accounted for 15 percent of all farm debt outstanding, and the Farm Credit System has financed another 26 percent—for a combined total of about $55 billion. In education, nearly all student loans are Federally guaranteed. The government helps provide credit for export finance, rural utilities, small businesses, and minority-owned businesses. The purposes of all this credit support are generally worthy. But there can be no denying that there is an enormous and increasing Federal exposure—approaching one trillion dollars in direct and federally guaranteed loans alone. This necessarily involves a risk of substantial future claims against the government. These claims are virtually certain to be in the *tens of billions of dollars*. Without continued economic growth, and the credit reforms proposed by the President, the claims would be substantially higher. (See Part VI-B.)

Contingent risks of federal insurance programs. The Federal Government funds programs that directly insure individuals and firms against many hazards not covered by private insurance. These formal insurance programs cover bank deposits, pensions, veterans life insurance, crops, floods, overseas private investment, nuclear risks, and war risks. The total face value of this insurance coverage (excluding Medicare) exceeds four trillion dollars. Deposit insurance accounts for about 70 percent of this total. But the remainder is still over *one trillion dollars.* Clearly, the Federal Government is not at risk for the entire face value of the insurance. But again: The likely future claims are virtually certain to be in the *tens of billions of dollars.* (See Part VI-B.)

When one adds up all these likely future claims—unfunded health and retirement programs, environmental clean-up obligations, credit risks, and insurance risks—one can produce a rather intimidating total. (See especially Parts VI-A and VI-B.) But it is important to put this, too, in perspective. The claims do not come due all at once. Indeed, they come due over an extended period of time. If one assumed that the likely range of unfunded claims were spread smoothly over the extensive time period in which they are to come due, one would reduce the total to a much less intimidating—indeed, a *manageable*—level.

This is not to say that there is not a built-in shortfall. There is. (See Part VI.) *It is to say, rather, that the "amortized" annual amount of the projected shortfall may be on the order of one-half to one percent of GNP—assuming the problem is managed on an orderly basis.*

Over the long term, there are five ways this shortfall could be handled:

• by reducing the growth of future obligations—through "mandatory" program reforms, credit reforms, and insurance reforms (these are discussed in Parts V, VI-A, and VI-B below);
• by reducing spending on other Federal programs where returns on investment are judged to be of lower relative value (these are discussed in Part VII-B-1 below);
• by increasing the government's managerial integrity and efficiency (this is discussed in Part VII below);
• by pursuing growth-oriented economic and budgetary policies—investing in the future—so that future economic productivity and Federal receipts are higher than otherwise projected (this is the principal area of emphasis in Section One, the Overview, and is discussed especially in Part III below); or
• by increasing the relative burden of debt and/or new taxes (these latter approaches are not a part of the President's program).

Investing in the Future

As noted, "Investing in the Future" is a theme given special emphasis in the Budget Overview. It was first introduced to the presentation of the budget by the President, last year, in *Building a Better America.*

The emphasis is consistent with three fundamental points: First, a budget must be viewed as more than a static snapshot; it necessarily influences the future, and the nature of that influence must be examined. Second, there is a generally accepted moral obligation to try to leave future generations in a better position than their predecessors. Third, the obligations for future expenditures and debt service are more manageable insofar as current expenditures and tax policy contribute to increased growth. Together, these three points argue compellingly for attention to the extent to which a budget (and its associated economic policy) encourage *investment*— investment in the future.

The President's budget encourages investment in a host of ways that are discussed in greater detail in the Overview. These are outlined here—with references to appropriate Parts of the Overview noted parenthetically:

Deficit reduction. By reducing the deficit, meeting the G-R-H targets, and then buying down debt, the President's budget policy would improve the U.S. savings rate and reduce the cost of capital. (This is discussed further in Part III-A below.)

Incentives for private savings and long-term investment. The President's program would improve the incentives for saving and investment through *Individual Retirement Accounts* (IRAs); create a new all-purpose savings incentive through *Family Savings Accounts*; and encourage growth-oriented, job-creating investment through a new long-term *capital gains incentive.* (These are discussed further in Part III-A below.)

Research and development. The President's budget funds initiatives to expand human frontiers in space—NASA would grow 24 percent over 1990 to a record $15.2 billion—and in biotechnology; to advance the development of the superconductive supercollider and to increase investment across the full range of basic research ($12.3 billion—up almost $1 billion); to advance applied research in areas as diverse as defense and health, agriculture and high speed rail transportation, semiconductor development and materials processing. The President also proposes to enact and extend major tax incentives to encourage greater investment in R&D by the private sector. Total proposed governmental expenditures for R&D would exceed $70 billion. (These are discussed in Parts III-B and III-C below.) In the design and implementation of Government programs, the President's budget also recognizes and encourages the innovative role of "States as Laboratories" (discussed in Part IV below).

Investment in human capital. Although Federal money is not the key to solving the nation's serious education problems, the President does propose to increase the discretionary budget authority of the Department of Education by $1.2 billion—bringing the Departmental total to a record $24.6 billion. Program increases are principally in areas of investment that are consistent with the Federal Government's role and responsibilities—reflecting the basic understanding that true solutions must depend heavily on states, localities, parents, and a system that promotes greater innovation, flexibility, and accountability. The budget re-proposes the President's child care initiative—on which the Congress failed to act last year. And the President proposes not only to reauthorize Head Start, but to increase it by half a billion dollars in a single year—bringing Head Start to an unprecedented $1.9 billion. (These and other investments in human capital are discussed in Part III-D below.)

Drug control strategy. Clearly, it makes little sense to invest in human capital only to have drug abuse undermine that investment and, indeed, destroy the very social fabric that makes human growth and investment worthwhile. Drug abuse negates investment. It is fundamentally destructive. It must be stopped. Like education, drug abuse is a problem that cannot be solved by Federal funds alone—or by funds alone whatever their source.

Nonetheless, the 1991 budget proposes $10.6 billion in budget authority and $9.7 billion in outlays to combat drug abuse. These levels represent increases of 12 percent in budget authority and $2.8 billion (41 percent) in outlays relative to 1990. They are necessary to advance the next stage of the comprehensive National Drug Control Strategy (and are discussed further in the Strategy, which is published separately, and in Part III-E below).

HOPE and enterprise zones. The problems of economically distressed areas will be alleviated some by the job-creating effects of continued economic growth. The problems will be mitigated also by the President's anti-drug abuse strategy. But more needs to be done to bring hope and opportunity to severely distressed areas. Thus, the President is re-proposing his initiative to stimulate growth through the creation of special incentives for investment and job creation in *Enterprise Zones*—a proposal on which the Congress has failed to act. And he is introducing legislation to advance project HOPE—Homeownership and Opportunity for People Everywhere. (These proposals are discussed further in Part III-H below.)

Transportation infrastructure. Improving the U.S. transportation system is essential to economic efficiency and growth. It is a shared responsibility involving the private sector, Federal, state, and local government. The Federal contribution is substantial. For example, the President proposes a record $8.6 billion for aviation in 1991 to help keep the U.S. commercial aviation system the best in the world. Of this, $2.5 billion—an increase of 45 percent—is proposed to modernize the FAA's air traffic control system. (These and related transportation issues are discussed in Part III-G below.)

Environmental protection. The emphasis on the importance of economic growth must, of course, be accompanied by a responsible concern for the protection and preservation of the environment. The President proposes over $2 billion in new spending to fund: "America the Beautiful," a new program to improve the stewardship of public lands and natural resources, and to promote reforestation; a major increase in the U.S. Global Change Research Program; an acceleration of hazardous waste cleanup; and a 12 percent increase in the EPA operating budget. (These are discussed in Part III-F below.)

The American heritage. To the extent that investment tends to emphasize rapid technological advance, there is need for a complementary emphasis on aesthetic values, history, and the traditional cultural values that have made America uniquely strong. Although the Federal role in this area must be limited—for important reasons of pluralistic philosophy—it must not be overlooked. America's progress in the future will be the greater for building on its diverse cultural strengths. Thus programs to foster and preserve the American Heritage are treated as themselves an issue of investment. (These are discussed in Part III-J below.)

National security. None of the foregoing would be worth very much if the budget failed to provide for the protection of U.S. national security. Though responsible analysts may differ about the best means of protecting it, national security holds a fundamental claim on governmental investment. Without adequate investment in national security, ultimately, all that America holds dear could be lost. There is, further, an obligation that America has long championed: the advancement of pluralistic, market-oriented democracy throughout the world. These fundamental interests and obligations are dependent upon U.S. economic growth. But they are also, in some respects, preconditional to it. (They are discussed in Part III-I below.)

Management oversight. Federal investments in the future will only achieve their objectives if they are effectively managed. Improved returns on investment require a better budget process and more effective management oversight. Americans are entitled to greater assurance that their tax dollars are being invested wisely and managed with efficiency and integrity. Proposals to manage America's government better are discussed in Part VII below.

Wonderland Revisited—The Current Congressional Path

In the presentation of the first Bush Administration budget, a critique of "Wonderland" budgeting was offered. It focused on the curious Washington habit (indeed, legal requirement) of "current services baseline" budgeting. Under this system, a "cut" may really be an increase; and a deficit said to be going "down" may really be going up. With "current services'" built-in bias toward increasing expenditures,

it should be little wonder that the system has failed to bring the deficit under satisfactory control.

In the Mid-session Review of the Budget, OMB introduced a new budget projection: the "Current Congressional Path." This was done in order to underline what some might think an obvious point. That is, the deficit is not determined, in the end, by either "current services" projections or by mathematical extensions of a "President's Policy." Forecasts based on such projections are almost always bound to be wrong. Budgets are legislated. Congressional action (or inaction) is, therefore, a fundamental determinant of actual deficits. In trying to forecast realistically, it is important to have some sense of the "Current Congressional Path."

Unfortunately, however, the Current Congressional Path is not entirely clear. Indeed, Wonderland seems to be running wild with attractive fantasies, but without yet having established coherent direction. One might consider, for example, the two big games now in play—and a third that is soon to be:

The spend-the-peace-dividend game. This is a new game, premised on the assumption of a substantial, near-term "peace dividend." It starts by over-estimating the dividend. Then each player plans to spend the dividend in his or her preferred way. The sum of all such planned expenditures totals about ten times the over-estimated dividend, which is itself perhaps five times the actual dividend. Thus, Washington entertains the notion of spending fifty times a dividend that has not yet definitively materialized—a true Wonderland phenomenon.

In reality, the *near-term* peace dividend is likely to be smaller than is commonly assumed for three reasons: First, the true cost of the previously planned and Congressionally-approved defense program is substantially higher than the current DoD funding levels (and higher than "current services"). Much of the dividend will have to be used just to adjust the previous program downward toward current levels. Second, this adjustment—while politically popular in the abstract—will not be politically popular in all its particulars. Third, any tendency to cut further would likely focus on reducing U.S. troop strength abroad at a more rapid rate than proposed by the President—a more rapid rate than consistent with preserving a strong alliance and negotiating equitable and enforceable agreements with the Soviet Union. Presumably, these countervailing interests will be better appreciated as the debate about the "peace dividend" unfolds.

The cut-social-security game.   This is ordinarily a very dangerous game politically. But in its most recent form, it has started with a superficially attractive proposal: to cut Social Security taxes. Clearly, that would be desirable if it could be done without significant cost to the people paying the taxes and to the economy as a whole. Unfortunately, the most recent proposal to attract significant attention fails that test.

It is ironic in three respects. First, some of its advocates have argued, until recently, that the government was under-financed (and under-taxed) *not over*-financed. Yet few, in fact, can seriously argue that the government as a whole is over-financed. Second, the emerging conventional wisdom had been that one needed to do more to protect the capacity to pay future Social Security benefits, *not less*. Cutting Social Security taxes now would mean giving up on that objective—giving up on the bipartisan commitment to build up reserves for the future retirement needs of the baby boom generation. Third, and perhaps most telling: Cutting Social Security taxes now would likely hurt the very people it is ostensibly intended to benefit, today's workers. It would either force an increase in their non-Social Security taxes (to compensate for the enormous revenue loss—$55 billion in 1991 alone); or it would force a reduction in their future retirement benefits. (See Part VI-A.)

The President's proposal to establish a "Social Security Integrity and Debt Reduction Fund" is a responsible way to protect the future interests of today's workers. But Social Security is a notoriously volatile subject when it enters the political domain; and whether rationality will prevail remains to be determined.

The beat-the-budget game.   This is the game that begins with the reaction to the President's budget. It has become an annual ritual. At the start, it is predictably partisan. Priorities are judged to be incorrect. Economic assumptions are ridiculed (but later adopted). Gimmicks are scorned (but later outdone). The failure of the budget process is lamented (but ideas for evasion proliferate). The refusal to raise "new taxes" is condemned (as proposals to cut taxes are advanced). Incentives for savings and investment are criticized for their alleged adverse effects on the deficit (as alternative proposals to increase the deficit are advocated). Stalemates are followed by "heroic compromises" that earn the parties self-congratulation, but somehow manage to leave much of the serious job to the future. And the public, understandably, grows more skeptical.

It may be apt to view all this metaphorically as a set of children's games: the Budget as Cookie Monster; its future threatened by hidden PACMEN; its path a journey through Wonderland. But at some point, it is appropriate to put games aside—at least for a while. *At some point, there is an obligation to be serious.* At some point, partisan posturing must yield to the responsibility to govern.

Sooner or later, the American political system will rise to the responsibility to be serious: to complete the job of fiscal policy correction. It may do this in small steps or large. It cannot do it with side-steps.

This year's budget meets the responsibility to be serious. It is seriously presented—giving a more complete and balanced perspective on both the present and the future than has previously been characteristic. Its emphasis on investment and growth-oriented policies and its realistic attention to long-term liabilities should be welcome. Its economic assumptions are not outside the credible range. It meets the Gramm-Rudman-Hollings deficit targets with specific and defensible deficit-reduction measures —and without gimmicks. It seeks to preserve a meaningful consolidated budget, while tightening the budget process. If implemented, it would reach balance in 1993 (as required by law), and would thereafter begin the process of reducing Federal debt.

This, of course, is not to assert that the budget will be treated seriously in the very next round of the Beat-the-Budget game. It is simply to suggest that it should be.

Richard G. Darman
Director,
Office of Management and Budget

C
Budget Enforcement Act of 1990: Brief Summary

Edward Davis
Robert Keith

Summary

The Omnibus Budget Reconciliation Act of 1990, H.R. 5835, was signed into law on November 5, 1990, as Public Law 101-508. Title XIII of the law is referred to as the "Budget Enforcement Act of 1990." The conference report on H.R. 5835 (House Report 101-964, October 26, 1990) is printed in the *Congressional Record* of October 26 (Vol. 136, No. 149, Pt. II).

The Budget Enforcement Act contains five subtitles:

- *Subtitle A*, which provides special five-year procedures for deficit control (affecting fiscal years 1991–1995);
- *Subtitle B*, which makes permanent changes in the congressional budget process;
- *Subtitle C*, which deals with the treatment of Social Security in the budget;
- *Subtitle D*, which cancels the fiscal year 1991 sequester and retroactively authorizes pay for employees furloughed during a three-day funding gap in October 1990; and
- *Subtitle E*, which pertains to the financial safety and soundness of Government-sponsored enterprises.

The Budget Enforcement Act makes numerous and substantial changes in the Federal budget process by amending several laws, principally the Balanced Budget and Emergency Deficit Control Act of 1985 (P.L. 99-177, as amended)—also referred to as the Gramm-Rudman-Hollings Act—and the Congressional Budget Act of 1974 (P.L. 93-344, as amended), and the standing rules of the House. This report briefly discusses the major changes.

Source: Edward Davis and Robert Keith, *Budget Enforcement Act of 1990: Brief Summary*, CRS Report for Congress (Washington, D.C.: Congressional Research Service, the Library of Congress, November 1990): pp. 1–11.

Additional information relating to the Budget Enforcement Act may be obtained from the following CRS Reports to Congress:

Budget Enforcement Act of 1990: Contents Listing, by Edward Davis and Robert Keith. Report no. 90-516 GOV. November 5, 1990, 5 p.;
Budget Enforcement Act of 1990: Cross-References to Laws and Rules Amended, by Edward Davis and Robert Keith. Report no. 90-517 GOV. November 5, 1990, 13 p.; and
Budget Enforcement Act of 1990: Legislative History, by Edward Davis and Robert Keith. Report no. 90-518 GOV. November 5, 1990, 5 p.

Special Five-Year Procedures for Deficit Control

The Budget Enforcement Act establishes special five-year procedures for deficit control (covering fiscal years 1991–1995) by amending the Gramm-Rudman-Hollings Act (principally by amending Sections 251–253) and the Congressional Budget Act (principally by adding a new Title VI, "Budget Agreement Enforcement Provisions").

First, the Act revises the deficit targets in the Gramm-Rudman-Hollings (GRH) Act and extends the sequestration process for two more years—through fiscal year 1995 (although the budget is not expected to be in balance by that time). Second, the Act sets limitations on distinct categories of discretionary spending funded in the annual appropriations process. Third, the Act creates "pay-as-you-go" procedures to require that increases in direct spending (i.e., spending controlled outside of the annual appropriations process) or decreases in revenues due to legislative action are offset so that there is no net effect on the deficit.

In addition to retaining the sequestration process that enforces the deficit targets in the GRH Act, the Budget Enforcement Act also establishes sequestration procedures to enforce the discretionary spending limits and the pay-as-you-go requirements. To the extent that any of the three different types of sequesters must be made, they will occur on the same day (which must be within 15 calendar days after Congress adjourns to end a session); sequestration of this type is referred to informally as "end-of-session sequestration." Further, one or more additional sequesters may occur subsequently in the fiscal year to eliminate any breach in the discretionary spending limits; this type of sequestration is referred to formally as "within-session sequestration."

Sequestration tied to enforcement of the deficit targets would occur only if a deficit excess remained after the other two types of sequestration had been implemented. A number of factors, however, including the operation of the other two types of sequestration, are expected to make sequestration tied to the deficit targets unnecessary, at least through fiscal year 1993.

The deficit targets and discretionary spending limits must be adjusted to take into account a variety of circumstances and developments, as discussed below.

In addition to establishing three separate sequestration procedures, the Budget Enforcement Act requires that budget resolutions considered during this period cover five fiscal years. Further, the procedures for setting aggregate budget amounts in the budget resolution, allocating spending under a budget resolution, and enforcing budget resolution amounts are keyed to the deficit targets and discretionary spending limits (as they may be adjusted).

Revision and Enforcement of Deficit Targets

The deficit targets in the GRH Act are revised for fiscal years 1991–1995, as shown in Table 1. In 1985, the GRH Act set the deficit target for fiscal year 1991 at zero. The fiscal year 1991 target was revised upward to $64 billion in 1987, with the budget expected to be in balance by fiscal year 1993.

Table 1
Original and revised deficit targets
(amounts in billions of dollars)

			H.R. 5835		
Fiscal Year	1985 Law	1987 Law	House Passed	Senate Passed	Public Law 101-508
1986	171.9				
1987	144				
1988	108	144			
1989	72	136			
1990	36	100			
1991	0	64	302.3	242	327
1992		28	276.8	219	317
1993		0	189.7	165	236
1994			58.1	86	102
1995			18.7	62	83

Note: the deficit targets are subject to revision in future years under procedures established by the Budget Enforcement Act of 1990.

The Budget Enforcement Act revises the fiscal year 1991 target upward to $327 billion. Further, the Act does not specify a future deficit target of zero; the deficit target for fiscal year 1995, the last fiscal year covered by the procedures, is $83 billion. The newly revised deficit targets are comparatively greater than the earlier targets because of a change in the treatment of the Social Security trust funds and revised economic and technical assumptions.

The President is required to adjust the deficit targets for fiscal years 1991–1995 (to reflect updated economic and technical assumptions and changes in budgetary concepts and definitions), as applicable, when he submits his annual budget for fiscal years 1992 and 1993. Further, he may adjust the deficit targets for fiscal years 1994 and 1995 (to reflect updated economic and technical assumptions) when he submits his budget for those fiscal years. For any fiscal year, the deficit targets must be adjusted to take into account changes in the discretionary spending limits made under other procedures. Sequestration reports issued by the Office of Management and Budget (OMB) later in the year must reflect these adjustments.

The Budget Enforcement Act retains the sequestration procedures that make across-the-board spending cuts to reduce the deficit down to the target level. As under the earlier procedures, half of the required outlays savings must be made in defense programs and half in nondefense programs. The margin-of-error amount (which is the amount by which the deficit target may be exceeded without triggering sequestration) is set at zero for fiscal years 1992 and 1993 and is set at $15 billion for fiscal years 1994 and 1995. (Formerly, the GRH Act set the margin-of-error amount at $10 billion each year and zero for the last fiscal year covered by the process.)

Enforcement of Discretionary Spending Limits

The Budget Enforcement Act establishes limits on discretionary spending. For fiscal years 1991–1993, separate limits are set for new budget authority and outlays for three different categories—defense, international, and domestic. For fiscal years 1994 and 1995, the limits on new budget authority and outlays are established for a single category—total discretionary spending.

When the President submits his budget for each of fiscal years 1992 through 1995, he must adjust the discretionary spending limits to take into account changes in budgetary concepts and definitions, changes in inflation, and (for fiscal years 1993 and 1994) changes in estimates of credit subsidy costs. Additionally, when OMB submits final sequestration reports for fiscal years 1991–1995, the discretionary spending limits must be adjusted to allow for Internal Revenue Service (IRS) tax compliance funding, debt forgiveness for Egypt and Poland, International Monetary Fund (IMF) quota increases, emergency appropriations (so designated by the President and in statute, and including costs for Operation Desert Shield), and specified special allowances.

On November 9, OMB issued a report, *Final OMB Sequester Report to the President and Congress for Fiscal Year 1991*, revising the discretionary spending limits for fiscal year 1991 following the adjournment *sine die* of the 101st Congress on October 27, 1990. The defense limits were adjusted to reflect emergency appropriations for Operation Desert Shield; the international outlay limit was adjusted to reflect debt forgiveness for Egypt and Poland; and the domestic limits were adjusted to reflect IRS tax compliance funding. For more information on these adjustments, see the following CRS Report to Congress: *Discretionary Spending Limits for Fiscal Year 1991: November 1990 Adjustments and "Mini-Sequester,"* Report no. 90-528 GOV, November 15, 1990, 2 p.

The discretionary spending limits, as adjusted, are shown in Table 2.

Enforcement of the spending limits is accomplished through a special sequestration process and by linking the limits to points of order under the Congressional Budget Act. A sequester under this process would occur only within the category in which a breach occurred. If a sequester under this process is required at the end of a session, it must occur on the same day as any sequestration tied to enforcement of the pay-as-you-go procedures or the deficit targets. During the following session, the enactment of legislation causing a breach in the spending limits would trigger sequestration 15 days later; however, any such enactment occurring during the last quarter of the fiscal year (*i.e.*, between July 1 and September 30) would instead cause the appropriate discretionary spending limits for the next fiscal year to be reduced by the amount of the breach.

Enforcement of "Pay-As-You-Go" Procedures

Under the "pay-as-you-go" process created by the Budget Enforcement Act, legislation proposing new direct spending, or legislation decreasing revenues, must be offset so that the net deficit is not increased. Enforcement of the "pay-as-you-go" process is accomplished through a special sequestration

Table 2
Discretionary spending limits:
Fiscal years 1991–1995
(amounts in billions of dollars)

	FY1991	FY1992	FY1993	FY1994	FY1995
Defense					
Budget Authority	289.918	291.643	291.785	—	—
Outlays	298.825	295.744	292.686	—	—
International					
Budget Authority	20.100	20.500	21.400	—	—
Outlays	18.700	19.100	19.600	—	—
Domestic					
Budget Authority	182.891	191.300	198.300	—	—
Outlays	198.283	210.100	221.700	—	—
All Categories					
Budget Authority	—	—	—	510.800	517.700
Outlays	—	—	—	534.800	540.800

Note: the discretionary spending limits reflect the adjustments made by the Office of Management and Budget on November 9, 1990, and are subject to further revision in future years under procedures established by the Budget Enforcement Act of 1990.

procedure and through links to the Congressional Budget Act.

If a sequester under this process is required, it must occur within 15 calendar days after Congress adjourns at the end of a session and on the same day as any sequestration tied to enforcement of the discretionary spending limits or the deficit targets. The sequester would have to offset the amount of any net deficit increase in that fiscal year and the prior fiscal year caused by the enactment of legislation during the session, and would be applied to non-exempt direct spending programs.

Emergency direct spending and revenue legislation (so designated by the President and in statute) that would cause a deficit increase is not covered by the "pay-as-you-go" sequestration process.

For instances in which legislation causing a net reduction in revenues is enacted, the House provides a special reconciliation procedure under which the committee of jurisdiction over the enacted legislation would have to report new legislation increasing revenues to offset the deficit increase.

Timetable for Sequestration Reports and Orders

The three types of sequestration that may occur—relating to the deficit targets, the discretionary spending limits, and the "pay-as-you-go" procedures—are integrated under a single timetable, as discussed previously. The Congressional Budget Office (CBO) and OMB must each prepare annually three different types of sequestration reports: (1) preview reports, issued in conjunction with submission of the President's budget; (2) update reports, issued in August; and (3) final reports, issued shortly after the end of a session. The CBO reports

(which are advisory only) precede the OMB reports by five calendar days, as was the case under prior sequestration procedures.

The reports must provide estimates regarding all three types of sequestration. In all three types of reports, OMB must explain any differences between its estimates and those of CBO.

If the President must issue a sequestration order in any year, the order is issued on the same day that the final OMB sequestration report is issued and the order must implement without change all of the reductions identified in the OMB report. There is no initial order, unlike under earlier procedures.

Table 3 sets forth the timetable for the issuance of sequestration reports and orders.

Other Budget Process Matters

Deadline for Submission of President's Budget

Under the Budget and Accounting Act of 1921 (31 *U.S.C.* 1105(a)), the President was required to submit his annual budget within 15 days after Congress convened. In 1985, the Gramm-Rudman-Hollings Act changed the deadline for submission to the first Monday after January 3 (the date on which a new Congress convenes). Three of the five budgets submitted since the change in the deadline were submitted between January 29 and February 18, well after the deadline.

The Budget Enforcement Act changes the deadline for submission of the President's budget to the first Monday in February, although he may submit it as early as the first Monday after January 3 (and is urged by the conferees to do so except under pressing circumstances).

Table 3
Timetable for sequestration reports and orders

Date:	Action to be completed:
5 days before the President's budget submission	CBO sequestration preview report
The President's budget submission	OMB sequestration preview report
August 15	CBO sequestration update report
August 20	OMB sequestration update report
10 days after end of session	CBO final sequestration report
15 days after end of session	OMB final sequestration report; Presidential order
30 days later	GAO compliance report

Treatment of Social Security in the Budget

Transactions of the Federal Old-Age and Survivors Insurance Trust Fund and the Federal Disability Insurance Trust Fund (OASDI), commonly referred to as the Social Security trust funds, were excluded from the spending and revenue totals of the Federal Government by the Social Security Amendments Act of 1983 and the GRH Act. Although the trust funds (which reflect a growing surplus) are exempt from sequestration, they were included in the deficit calculations made under the GRH Act.

The Budget Enforcement Act reaffirms the off-budget status of the Social Security trust funds and excludes them from the deficit calculations made under the GRH Act.

The exclusion of the Social Security trust funds from the GRH deficit calculations, in the view of some, may create incentives to "tap into" the growing trust fund balances. Accordingly, the Budget Enforcement Act establishes separate House and Senate procedures to protect these balances.

The House provision creates a point of order (as free-standing law) to prohibit the consideration of legislation what would change the actuarial balance of the Social Security trust funds over a 5-year or 75-year period. In the case of legislation decreasing Social Security revenues, the prohibition would not apply if the legislation also included an equivalent increase in Medicare taxes for the period covered by the legislation.

The Senate provision also creates a procedure (referred to as a "firewall") to protect Social Security financing, but does so by expanding certain enforcement provisions of the Congressional Budget Act. The Senate provision prohibits the consideration of a reported budget resolution calling for a reduction in Social Security surpluses and bars the consideration of legislation causing committee allocations or the aggregate level of Social Security spending to be exceeded.

The Budget Enforcement Act also requires the Board of Trustees of the Social Security trust funds to include in their report to Congress a statement regarding the actuarial balances of the funds.

Federal Credit Reform Act of 1990

The treatment of Federal credit activities in the budget is changed by the Budget Enforcement Act. The Act adds a new title, Title V, to the Congressional Budget Act; the new title is referred to as the "Federal Credit Reform Act of 1990." The purposes of the Federal Credit Reform Act are to provide for more accurate measurement of the costs of direct loans and loan guarantees, to place the costs of credit programs on a budgetary basis equivalent to other spending programs, and to improve the allocation of resources among credit programs and between credit programs and other spending programs.

Beginning with fiscal year 1992, the Federal Credit Reform Act provides that the budget cost of credit programs be the long-term cost to the Federal Government on a net present value basis, excluding administrative costs and certain incidental effects. The remaining cash flows associated with credit programs are treated as a "means of financing" and do not affect spending levels. Federal deposit insurance programs are not covered under the Act.

Under the Act, appropriations must be enacted to cover the cost of direct loan and loan guarantee programs, except for credit programs that are entitlements and credit programs of the Commodity Credit Corporation, before assistance can be provided. Adjustments are made to accounts at a later time if the estimated cost of credit activities proves to be incorrect.

The Director of OMB is responsible for developing guidelines and regulations to be used in carrying out the Act. Both OMB and CBO are charged with developing improved cost estimates for credit programs and reporting, by January 31, 1992, on differences in long-term administrative costs for credit programs versus grant programs.

Government-Sponsored Enterprises

Government-Sponsored Enterprises (GSEs) are entities chartered and established by the Federal Government but privately owned and operated. Because GSEs have public-oriented missions and are closely allied with Federal activities, the Federal Government is seen by many as implicitly backing GSE operations financially. The Budget Enforcement Act defines the following entities as GSEs for purposes of the Act: (1) the Farm Credit System; (2) the Federal Home Loan Bank System; (3) the Federal Home Loan Mortgage Corporation; (4) the Federal National Mortgage Association; and (5) the Student Loan Marketing Associations.

The Budget Enforcement Act requires both CBO and the Treasury Department to report to Congress by April 30, 1991, regarding an assessment of the financial soundness of GSEs, and (in the CBO report only) alternative models for oversight. The Treasury Department report must include legislative recommendations.

The Budget Enforcement Act also provides for the reporting of legislation to ensure the financial soundness of GSEs by the appropriate congressional committees no later than September 15, 1991 and requires that the President's annual budget include an analysis regarding GSEs.

"Byrd Rule" on Extraneous Matter in Reconciliation

The "Byrd Rule" sets forth Senate procedures controlling the consideration of extraneous matter in reconciliation measures. The rule originated as Section 20001 of the Omnibus Budget Reconciliation Act of 1985 (P.L. 99-272), was augmented by two Senate resolutions adopted in the 99th Congress (S.Res. 286 and 509), and has been amended. The rule bars extraneous matter from being included in any reconciliation legislation, defining different categories of extraneous matter and providing exceptions to the prohibition.

The Budget Enforcement Act revises the Byrd rule to clarify what constitutes extraneous matter and to strengthen provisions regarding its enforcement (including the incorporation of the two Senate resolutions adopted in the 99th Congress). Further, the Act transfers the Byrd Rule to the Congressional Budget Act and establishes it as a new section (Section 313, "Extraneous Matter in Reconciliation Legislation").

Cancellation of Fiscal Year 1991 Sequester

Pursuant to the Gramm-Rudman-Hollings Act, President Bush issued an initial sequestration order for fiscal year 1991 on August 25, 1990. On October 15, the President issued a final sequestration order. The implementation of the across-the-board

spending cuts was suspended by a series of five continuing resolutions (Public Laws 101-403, 101-412, 101-444, 101-461, and 101-467), the final one expiring on November 5. Had the sequester gone into effect, budgetary resources would have been cut by an amount sufficient to reduce outlays by more than $80 billion.

The Budget Enforcement Act rescinded the fiscal year 1991 sequestration orders (and provided for the restoration of bugetary resources had they been cancelled).

Federal Operations During Funding Gaps

During the 1980s, there were 8 funding gaps (a funding gap is the period when Federal agencies lack authority to spend funds due to the absence of enacted appropriations). Funding gaps have raised controversy because they sometimes result in the widespread furlough of Federal employees and the shutdown of Federal Government operations. Another concern is that during funding gaps many agencies have been too liberal in classifying employees as "essential" personnel and continuing routine activities under authority that allows only emergency activities involving the safety of human life and protection of property. During the 1980s, following a funding gap, pay for furloughed employees and the conduct of emergency activities was authorized retroactively in continuing appropriations acts enacted after the funding gap.

In 1990, a funding gap occurred during October 6–8. The Budget Enforcement Act retroactively authorized pay for employees furloughed and emergency activities conducted during this period.

In addition, the Budget Enforcement Act amends the Antideficiency Act (31 *U.S.C.* 1341-1342) to make clear that any funds sequestered may not be obligated or expended and that routine activities of the Federal Government should not be continued during funding gaps.